S0-BES-019

BEACON
BIBLE COMMENTARY

Library of Congress
Card Number 64-22906

Printed in the United States of America

BEACON
BIBLE COMMENTARY

In Ten Volumes

Volume X

HEBREWS
Richard S. Taylor, M.A., Th.D.

JAMES
A. F. Harper, M.A., Ph.D., D.D.

I PETER
Roy S. Nicholson, D.D.

II PETER
Eldon R. Fuhrman, B.D., S.T.M., Ph.D., D.D.

I, II, III JOHN
Harvey J. S. Blaney, B.D., S.T.M., Th.D.

JUDE
Delbert R. Rose, M.A., Ph.D.

REVELATION
Ralph Earle, B.D., M.A., Th.D.

BEACON HILL PRESS OF KANSAS CITY
Kansas City, Missouri

BEACON BIBLE COMMENTARY

In Ten Volumes

I. Genesis; Exodus; Leviticus; Numbers; Deuteronomy

II. Joshua; Judges; Ruth; I and II Samuel; I and II Kings; I and II Chronicles; Ezra; Nehemiah; Esther

III. Job; Psalms; Proverbs; Ecclesiastes; Song of Solomon

IV. Isaiah; Jeremiah; Lamentations; Ezekiel; Daniel

V. Hosea; Joel; Amos; Obadiah; Jonah; Micah; Nahum; Habakkuk; Zephaniah; Haggai; Zechariah; Malachi

VI. Matthew; Mark; Luke

VII. John; Acts

VIII. Romans; I and II Corinthians

IX. Galatians; Ephesians; Philippians; Colossians; I and II Thessalonians; I and II Timothy; Titus; Philemon

X. Hebrews; James; I and II Peter; I, II, and III John; Jude; Revelation

Preface

"All scripture is given by inspiration of God, and is profitable for doctrine, for reproof, for correction, for instruction in righteousness: that the man of God may be perfect, throughly furnished unto all good works" (II Tim. 3:16-17).

We believe in the plenary inspiration of the Bible. God speaks to men through His Word. He hath spoken unto us by His Son. But without the inscripted Word how would we know the Word which was made flesh? He does speak to us by His Spirit, but the Spirit uses the written Word as the vehicle of His revelation, for He is the true Author of the Holy Scriptures. What the Spirit reveals is in agreement with the Word.

The Christian faith derives from the Bible. It is the Foundation for faith, for salvation, and sanctification. It is the Guide for Christian character and conduct. "Thy word is a lamp unto my feet, and a light unto my path" (Ps. 119:105).

The revelation of God and His will for men is adequate and complete in the Bible. The great task of the Church, therefore, is to communicate the knowledge of the Word, to enlighten the eyes of the understanding, and to awaken and to illuminate the conscience that men may learn "to live soberly, righteously, and godly, in this present world." This leads to the possession of that "inheritance [that is] incorruptible, and undefiled, and that fadeth not away, reserved in heaven."

When we consider the translation and interpretation of the Bible, we admit we are guided by men who are not inspired. Human limitation, as well as the plain fact that no scripture is of private or single interpretation, allows variation in the exegesis and exposition of the Bible.

Beacon Bible Commentary is offered in 10 volumes with becoming modesty. It does not supplant others. Neither does it purport to be exhaustive or final. The task is colossal. Assignments have been made to 40 of the ablest writers available. They are trained men with serious purpose, deep dedication, and supreme devotion. The sponsors and publishers, as well as the contributors, earnestly pray that this new offering among Bible commentaries will be helpful to preachers, teachers, and laymen in discovering the deeper meaning of God's Word and in unfolding its message to all who hear them.

—G. B. Williamson

Acknowledgments

Permission to quote from copyrighted material is gratefully acknowledged as follows:

University of Chicago Press: W. F. Arndt and F. W. Gingrich, *A Greek-English Lexicon of the New Testament.*

Abingdon Press: *The Interpreter's Bible.*

The Westminster Press: *The Revelation of John,* copyright 1964 (renewal) by Charles R. Erdman.

Scripture quotations have been used from the following sources:

The Amplified New Testament. Copyright 1958 by The Lockman Foundation, La Habra, California.

The Berkeley Version in Modern English. Copyright 1958, 1959 by Zondervan Publishing House.

The Bible: A New Translation, James Moffatt. Copyright 1950, 1952, 1953, 1954 by James A. R. Moffatt. Used by permission of Harper and Row.

The Bible: An American Translation, J. M. Powis Smith and Edgar J. Goodspeed. Copyright 1923, 1927, 1948 by the University of Chicago Press.

New American Standard Bible. Copyright 1960, 1962, 1963 by The Lockman Foundation, La Habra, California.

The New English Bible. © The Delegates of the Oxford University Press and the Syndics of the Cambridge University Press, 1961.

The New Testament in Modern English. © J. B. Phillips, 1958. Used by permission of The Macmillan Company.

Revised Standard Version of the Holy Bible. Copyright 1946, 1952 by the Division of Christian Education of the National Council of Churches.

The Weymouth New Testament in Modern Speech. Copyright by Harper and Row, Publishers.

The New Testament in the Language of the People, Charles B. Williams. Copyright 1937 by Bruce Humphries, Inc., assigned 1949 to Moody Bible Institute, Chicago.

The New Testament, R. A. Knox. © 1951 by Sheed and Ward.

Living Letters, Kenneth N. Taylor. © 1962 by Tyndale House, Publishers, Wheaton, Illinois.

How to Use "Beacon Bible Commentary"

The Bible is a Book to be read, to be understood, to be obeyed, and to be shared with others. *Beacon Bible Commentary* is planned to help at the points of understanding and sharing.

For the most part, the Bible is its own best interpreter. He who reads it with an open mind and receptive spirit will again and again become aware that through its pages God is speaking *to him.* A commentary serves as a valuable resource when the meaning of a passage is not clear even to the thoughtful reader. Also after one has seen his own meaning in a passage from the Bible, it is rewarding to discover what truth others have found in the same place. Sometimes, too, this will correct possible misconceptions the reader may have formed.

Beacon Bible Commentary has been written to be used with your Bible in hand. Most major commentaries print the text of the Bible at the top of the commentary page. The editors decided against this practice, believing that the average user comes to his commentary from his Bible and hence has in mind the passage in which he is interested. He also has his Bible at his elbow for any necessary reference to the text. To have printed the full text of the Bible in a work of this size would have occupied approximately one-third of the space available. The planners decided to give this space to additional resources for the reader. At the same time, writers have woven into their comments sufficient quotations from the passages under discussion that the reader maintains easy and constant thought contact with the words of the Bible. These quoted words are printed in boldface type for quick identification.

Illumination from Related Passages

The Bible is its own best interpreter when a given chapter or a longer section is read to find out what it says. This book is also its own best interpreter when the reader knows what the Bible says in other places about the subject under consideration. The writers and editors of *Beacon Bible Commentary* have constantly striven to give maximum help at this point. Related and carefully chosen cross-references have been included in order that the reader may thus find the Bible interpreted and illustrated by the Bible itself.

Paragraph Treatment

The truth of the Bible is best understood when we grasp the thought of the writer in its sequence and connections. The verse divisions with which we are familiar came into the Bible late (the sixteenth century for the New Testament and the seventeenth century for the Old). They were done hurriedly and sometimes missed the thought pattern of the inspired writers. The same is true of the chapter divisions. Most translations today arrange the words of the sacred writers under our more familiar paragraph structure.

It is under this paragraph arrangement that our commentary writers have approached their task. They have tried always to answer the question, What was the inspired writer saying in this passage? Verse numbers have been retained for easy identification but basic meanings have been outlined and interpreted in the larger and more complete thought forms.

Introduction to Bible Books

The Bible is an open Book to him who reads it thoughtfully. But it opens wider when we gain increased understanding of its human origins. Who wrote this book? Where was it written? When did the writer live? What were the circumstances that caused him to write? Answers to these questions always throw added light on the words of the Scripture.

These answers are given in the Introductions. There also you will find an outline of each book. The Introduction has been written to give an overview of the whole book; to provide you with a dependable road map before you start your trip—and to give you a place of reference when you are uncertain as to which way to turn. Don't ignore the flagman when he waves his warning sign, "See Introduction." At the close of the commentary on each book you will find a bibliography for further study.

Maps and Charts

The Bible was written about people who lived in lands that are foreign and strange to most English-speaking readers. Often better understanding of the Bible depends on better knowledge of Bible geography. When the flagman waves his other sign, "See map," you should turn to the map for a clearer understanding of the locations, distances, and related timing of the experiences of the men with whom God was dealing.

This knowledge of Bible geography will help you to be a better Bible preacher and teacher. Even in the more formal presentation of the sermon it helps the congregation to know that the flight into Egypt was "a journey on foot, some 200 miles to the southwest." In the less formal and smaller groups such as Sunday school classes and prayer meeting Bible study, a large classroom map enables the group to see the locations as well as to hear them mentioned. When you have seen these places on your commentary maps, you are better prepared to share the information with those whom you lead in Bible study.

Charts which list Bible facts in tabular form often make clear historical relationships in the same way that maps help with understanding geography. To see listed in order the kings of Judah or the Resurrection appearances of Jesus often gives clearer understanding of a particular item in the series. These charts are a part of the resources offered in this set.

Beacon Bible Commentary has been written for the new-comer to Bible study and also for those long familiar with the written Word. The writers and editors have probed each chapter, each verse, every clause, phrase, and word in the familiar King James Version. We have probed with the question, What do these words mean? If the answer is not self-evident we have charged ourselves to give the best explanation known to us. How well we have succeeded the reader must judge, but we invite you to explore the explanation of these words or passages that may puzzle you when you are reading God's written Word.

Exegesis and Exposition

Bible commentators often use these words to describe two ways of making clear the meaning of a passage in the Scriptures. *Exegesis* is a study of the original Greek or Hebrew words to understand what meanings those words had when they were used by men and women in Bible times. To know the meaning of the separate words, as well as their grammatical relationship to each other, is one way to understand more clearly what the inspired writer meant to say. You will often find this kind of enriching help in the commentary. But word studies alone do not always give true meaning.

Exposition is a commentator's effort to point out the meaning of a passage as it is affected by any one of several facts known to the writer but perhaps not familiar to the reader. These facts may be (1) the context (the surrounding verses or chapters), (2) the historical background, (3) the related teachings from other parts of the Bible, (4) the significance of these messages from God as they relate to universal facts of human life, (5) the relevance of these truths to unique contemporary human situations. The commentator thus seeks to explain the full meaning of a Bible passage in the light of his own best understanding of God, man, and the world in which we live.

Some commentaries separate the exegesis from this broader basis of explanation. In *Beacon Bible Commentary* writers have combined the exegesis and exposition. Accurate word studies are indispensable to a correct understanding of the Bible. But such careful studies are today so thoroughly reflected in a number of modern English translations that they are often not necessary except to enhance the understanding of the theological meaning of a passage. The writers and editors seek to reflect a true and accurate exegesis at every point, but specific exegetical discussions are introduced chiefly to throw added light on the meaning of a passage, rather than to engage in scholarly discussion.

The Bible is a practical Book. We believe that God inspired holy men of old to declare these truths in order that the readers might better understand and do the will of God. *Beacon Bible Commentary* has been undertaken only for the purpose of helping men to find more effectively God's will for them as revealed in the Scripture—to find that will and to act upon that knowledge.

Helps for Bible Preaching and Teaching

We have said that the Bible is a Book to be shared. Christian preachers and teachers since the first century have sought to convey the gospel message by reading and explaining selected passages of Scripture. *Beacon Bible Commentary* seeks to encourage this kind of expository preaching and teaching. The set contains more than a thousand brief expository outlines that have been used by outstanding Bible teachers and preachers. Both writers and editors have assisted in contributing or selecting these homiletical suggestions. It is hoped that the outlines will suggest ways in which the reader will want to try to open the Word of God to his class or congregation. Some of these analyses of preachable passages have been contributed by our contemporaries. When the outlines have appeared in print, authors and references are given in order that the reader may go to the original source for further help.

In the Bible we find truth of the highest order. Here is given to us, by divine inspiration, the will of God for our lives. Here we have sure guidance in all things necessary to our relationships to God and under Him to our fellowman. Because these eternal truths come to us in human language and through human minds, they need to be put into fresh words as languages change and as thought patterns are modified. In *Beacon Bible Commentary* we have sought to help make the Bible a more effective Lamp to the paths of men who journey in the twentieth century.

A. F. Harper

Abbreviations and Explanations

The Books of the Bible

Gen.	Job	Jonah	I or II Cor.
Exod.	Ps.	Mic.	Gal.
Lev.	Prov.	Nah.	Eph.
Num.	Eccles.	Hab.	Phil.
Deut.	Song of Sol.	Zeph.	Col.
Josh.	Isa.	Hag.	I or II Thess.
Judg.	Jer.	Zech.	I or II Tim.
Ruth	Lam.	Mal.	Titus
I or II Sam.	Ezek.	Matt.	Philem.
I or II Kings	Dan.	Mark	Heb.
I or II Chron.	Hos.	Luke	Jas.
Ezra	Joel	John	I or II Pet.
Neh.	Amos	Acts	I, II, or III John
Esther	Obad.	Rom.	Jude
			Rev.

Vulg.	The Vulgate
LXX	The Septuagint
ASV	American Standard Revised Version
RSV	Revised Standard Version
ERV	English Revised Version
Amp. NT	Amplified New Testament
NASB	New American Standard Bible
NEB	New English Bible
LL	*Living Letters,* by Kenneth N. Taylor
Berk.	The Berkeley Version
Phillips	*The New Testament in Modern English,* by J. B. Phillips
IB	Interpreter's Bible
IDB	The Interpreter's Dictionary of the Bible
ISBE	International Standard Bible Encyclopedia
NBC	The New Bible Commentary
NBD	The New Bible Dictionary
BBC	Beacon Bible Commentary
EGT	Expositor's Greek Testament

c.	chapter	OT	Old Testament
cc.	chapters	NT	New Testament
v.	verse	Heb.	Hebrew
vv.	verses	Gk.	Greek

Quotations and References

Boldface type in the exposition indicates a quotation from the King James Version of the passage under discussion. Readings from other versions are put in quotation marks and the version is indicated.

In scripture references a letter (*a*, *b*, etc.) indicates a clause within a verse. When no book is named, the book under discussion is understood.

Bibliographical data on a work cited by a writer may be found by consulting the first reference to the work by that writer, or by turning to the bibliography.

The bibliographies are not intended to be exhaustive but are included to provide complete publication data for volumes cited in the text.

References to authors in the text, or inclusion of their books in the bibliography, does not constitute an endorsement of their views. All reading in the field of biblical interpretation should be discriminating and thoughtful.

Table of Contents

VOLUME X

The Epistle to the

HEBREWS

Richard S. Taylor

Introduction

A. Authorship

The Epistle to the Hebrews is anonymous. That is the most important single fact for us to note regarding its origin. There is no question here of genuineness. All that we can do is to note the external evidence of the Church and the internal evidence of the Epistle itself, and then draw our conclusions as to who wrote it.

1. *External Evidence*

Clement of Rome (A.D. 95) uses Heb. 3:2; 11:37 in his First Epistle to the Corinthians 17:1, 5. The Shepherd of Hermas (dated by Goodspeed A.D. 95-100) also shows an acquaintance with it. It is not in the Muratorian Canon (late second century).

Westcott writes: "Towards the close of the second century there is evidence of a knowledge of the Epistle in Alexandria, North Africa, Italy and the West of Europe. From the time of Pantaenus it was held at Alexandria to be, at least indirectly, the work of St. Paul and of canonical authority; and this opinion, supported in different forms by Clement and Origen, came to be generally received among the Eastern Greek churches in the third century."[1]

"About the same time a Latin translation of the Epistle found a limited recognition in North Africa, but not as a work of St. Paul."[2]

"In Italy and Western Europe the Epistle was not held to be St. Paul's and by consequence, as it seems, it was not held to be canonical."[3] In the Syriac versions it was evidently treated as an appendix to the Pauline Epistles.

Westcott further states: "To speak summarily, when the book first appears in general circulation three distinct opinions about it had already obtained local currency. At Alexandria the Greek Epistle was held to be not directly but mediately St. Paul's, as either a free translation of his words or a reproduction of his thoughts. In North Africa it was known to some extent as

[1]B. F. Westcott, *The Epistle to the Hebrews* (2nd ed.; London: Macmillan & Co., 1892), pp. lxiii-lxiv.

[2]*Ibid.*, p. lxiv.

[3]*Ibid.*

the work of Barnabas and acknowledged as a secondary authority. At Rome and in Western Europe it was not included in the collection of the Epistles of St. Paul and had no apostolic weight."[4]

We now turn directly to the testimony of the early Church Fathers. Clement of Alexandria (A.D. 195) held that the Epistle to the Hebrews was written by Paul to the Jews in the Hebrew (Aramaic) language, then later translated by Luke and published among the Greeks. As quoted by Eusebius, he wrote: "But it is probable that the title, Paul the Apostle, was not prefixed to it. For as he wrote to the Hebrews, who had imbibed prejudices against him, and suspected him, he wisely guards against diverting them from the perusal, by giving his name."[5] If Paul wrote Hebrews, this is the best suggestion that could be made as to why he omitted his name at the beginning.

The opinion of Origen (A.D. 220), the greatest biblical scholar in the Early Church, is often quoted. He said: "I would say, that the thoughts are the apostle's, but the diction and phraseology belong to some one who has recorded what the apostle said, and as one who noted down at his leisure what his master dictated. . . . But who it was that really wrote the epistle, God only knows."[6]

Westcott concludes: "The Alexandrines emphasized the thought of canonicity and, assured of the canonicity of the Epistle, placed it in connexion with St. Paul. The Western fathers emphasized the thought of authorship and, believing that the Epistle was not properly St. Paul's, denied its canonical authority. . . . We have been enabled to acknowledge that the canonical authority of the Epistle is independent of its Pauline authorship. The spiritual insight of the East can be joined with the historical witness of the West. And if we hold that the judgment of the Spirit makes itself felt through the consciousness of the Christian Society, no Book of the Bible is more completely recognized by universal consent as giving a divine view of the facts of the Gospel, full of lessons for all time, than the Epistle to the Hebrews."[7]

Coming to the general period of the Reformation we note that Erasmus expressed his doubts, not as to the authority, but as to the author, of the Epistle. Luther denied the Pauline authorship and suggested it was written by Apollos. Calvin said

[4]*Ibid.*, pp. lxv-lxvi.

[5]Eusebius, *Ecclesiastical History*, trans. C. F. Cruse (Grand Rapids: Baker Book House, 1955 [reprint]), p. 234 (VI. 14).

[6]*Ibid.*, p. 246 (VI. 25). [7]*Op. cit.*, p. lxxi.

he himself could not be brought to think it was Paul's. He thought that Luke or Clement wrote it.

2. *Internal Evidence*

There are similarities in style and vocabulary between the Epistle to the Hebrews and the writings of Luke and Clement of Rome. The description of Apollos in Acts (18:24-25) fits the author of this Epistle. But the Early Church gives no hint that Apollos wrote it. We must leave the matter unsettled.

Many scholars have pointed out the striking difference in style between Paul's Epistles and the Epistle to the Hebrews. Paul writes in a rather abrupt, broken diction. On the other hand, the style of Hebrews is "carefully polished and rhythmically constructed."[8]

The structure is also different. Paul gives doctrine first, and then practical application. But Hebrews alternates between doctrine and exhortation some half a dozen times.

There is also a theological difference. The Epistle to the Hebrews is built around the high priesthood of Christ. Paul's Christology, which bulks large in his Epistles, never touches on this phase.

All of these facts taken together have led practically all scholars, whether liberal or conservative, to hold that Paul did not write Hebrews. Even the Roman Catholic church has modified its position somewhat. Wikenhauser, a Catholic scholar, writes: "Paul cannot be the immediate author."[9]

B. Date

Kuemmel represents the common liberal position today when he writes: "The Epistle was probably composed between 80 and 90."[10] We would still agree with Westcott, however, when he says: "The letter may be placed in the critical period between A.D. 64, the government of Gessius Florus, and 67, the commencement of the Jewish War, and most probably just before the breaking of the storm in the latter year."[11]

[8]Alfred Wikenhauser, *New Testament Introduction*, trans. J. Cunningham (New York: Herder and Herder, 1960), p. 467.

[9]*Ibid.*, p. 469.

[10]Paul Feine and Johannes Behm, *Introduction to the New Testament.* Completely reedited by W. G. Kuemmel, trans. A. J. Mattill, Jr. (Nashville: Abingdon Press, 1966), p. 282.

[11]*Op cit.*, p. xlii.

C. Destination

The traditional view is that Hebrews was written to Jewish Christians in Palestine. But Theodor Zahn suggested it was the Jewish Christian group at Rome. The Jerusalem Christians were poor, and dependent on offerings from the Gentile churches. But Heb. 6:10 indicates that the readers of Hebrews often helped poor Christians. Some have thought that the Epistle was written to Alexandria. But this idea has found little support.

In 1836 it was first suggested that the Epistle was addressed mainly to Gentiles. A majority of Protestant scholars today hold this position, together with some Catholics. Wikenhauser writes: "It must be admitted that the balance of evidence favours denying that it was written to Jewish Christians."[12] Kuemmel agrees. But J. Cambier says: "However, the emphasis throughout the whole letter on the superiority of the new religious dispensation as compared with the old is better explained if we think of the Epistle as being sent to Judeo-Christians."[13] To us this argument seems unanswerable. We would agree with Donald Guthrie when he writes: "A definite balance in favour of a Jewish Christian destination must be admitted, if any credence at all is to be attached to the traditional title."[14] Everett F. Harrison says: "The Hebrew-Christian character of the epistle seems sufficiently demonstrated."[15]

"They of Italy salute you" (13:24) is more correctly translated, "Those who come from Italy send you greetings" (RSV). The Greek says "those away from" (*apo*). Taken with the fact that the first notice of Hebrews is in Rome (I Clement), this gives considerable support to the idea that the Epistle was written to Rome. This is the view of most scholars today. Guthrie and Harrison both leave the matter open. Harrison seems to favor somewhat a Palestinian destination.

D. Purpose

This depends, of course, on how we identify the readers. The traditional stance which Guthrie still describes as "the

[12]*Op. cit.*, p. 468.

[13]"The Epistle to the Hebrews," *Introduction to the New Testament*, ed. A. Robert and A. Feuillet, translated from the French by P. W. Skehan, *et al.* (New York: Desclee Co., 1965), p. 529.

[14]*New Testament Introduction: Hebrews to Revelation* (Chicago: Inter-Varsity Press, 1962), p. 29.

[15]*Introduction to the New Testament* (Grand Rapids: Wm. B. Eerdmans Publishing Co., 1964), p. 351.

most widely held view"[16] is that Hebrews was written to warn Jewish Christians against apostasy to Judaism. The Epistle seems clearly intended to show the superiority of Christianity to Judaism. The opening verses, as well as early chapters, assert the finality of Jesus Christ as God's final and perfect Revelation to mankind.

The key word of Hebrews is "better." Christ is better than the angels, than Moses, than Joshua. Christianity is a better covenant. It has a better rest, a better priesthood, a better altar and sacrifice. All of this would obviously be more significant for Jewish Christian readers than for Gentiles.

—Ralph Earle

[16] *Op. cit.*, p. 30

Outline

I. The Finality of Christ's Person, 1:1—4:16
   A. More than an Angel—a Son, 1:1—2:4
   B. Less than an Angel—a Man, 2:5-18
   C. Greater than Moses, 3:1-19
   D. The Indispensable Rest, 4:1-16

II. The Finality of Christ's Priesthood, 5:1—7:28
   A. A Perfect High Priest, 5:1-10
   B. The Need for Perfection, 5:11—6:20
   C. The Priesthood of Perfection, 7:1-28

III. The Finality of Christ's Passion, 8:1—10:25
   A. Christ and the New Covenant, 8:1-13
   B. The New Covenant and the Blood of Christ, 9:1-28
   C. The Way into the Holiest, 10:1-22
   D. The Obligations of the Holiest, 10:23-25

IV. The Finality of Our Profession, 10:26—13:25
   A. The Alternative to Faith, 10:26-39
   B. The Credentials of Faith, 11:1-40
   C. The Perseverance of Faith, 12:1-29
   D. The Way of Faith, 13:1-19
   E. Conclusion, 13:20-25

Section I The Finality of Christ's Person

Hebrews 1:1—4:16

A. More than an Angel—a Son, 1:1—2:4

1. *Our Speaking God* (1:1-2*a*).

The first four verses are one sentence and constitute the prologue of the Epistle. Here is affirmed the self-disclosure of God in a visible, historical Son, and the function of this Son in creation, revelation, providence, and redemption.

In the welter of confusion and the babble of many voices, sanity and certainty are possible only in the rediscovery that God has spoken. God is imminent in the affairs of men as well as transcendent. Jesus Christ is the Author and Source of the Christian faith; in confronting His person and earthly work we are confronting God.

a. God's past revelation (1:1*a*). The inspired writer is referring here, not to general revelation in nature and conscience, made to all men, but to special revelation, made to **the fathers,** i.e., the Hebrew nation and their spiritual progenitors. God's person, together with His holiness of character and sovereign will for His people, was revealed in "manifold portions and in many ways."[1] Though the times and methods varied greatly, the means was uniform—**by the prophets.** The writer to the Hebrews is determined to help his halting fellow Hebrews to hear God's full message spoken in and by His Son. It is a message far exceeding their insight thus far, a message of perfect redemption, and a message which in its very finality constitutes a solemn ultimatum.[2]

b. God's progressive revelation (1:1*b*). The self-disclosure

[1]Herman Edwin Mueller, *The Letter to the Hebrews, a Translation* (2nd ed.; Jennings Lodge, Oregon: The Western Press, 1945).

[2]"This midpoint in history, which the O.T. looks forward to and the writer reflects back upon, has broken the *Heilsgeschichte* into two halves. By saying, 'at the end of these days God spoke to us by a son' (1.2), he means that in the revelation through the Son the pre-eschatological period has come to an end and a new period in *Heilsgeschichte* has begun. It is also possible that H. L. MacNeill is right that when the writer says at the end of 1.2 that through the Son God 'made *tous aionas*,' he is thinking not of the world (cf. 11.13; 9.26), but the two ages, or economies, between which Christ is the midpoint. Phrases such as 'the time of the new order' (9.10) and 'the present period' (9.9) demarcate this age from the former one" (Sidney G. Sowers, *The Hermeneutics of Philo and Hebrews* [Richmond, Virginia: John Knox Press, 1965], pp. 92-93).

of God was progressive at least in the sense that the word of the prophets was cumulative. By **prophets** we may understand not only those who delivered oral messages, but the writers of the Old Testament books. What God said through Moses to the Israelites in the wilderness He also spoke to Ezra and his generation through the book of Moses. As a small stream becomes a mighty river, so did the Word of God become massive and full-orbed, sufficient to prepare the Jews and confirm these Hebrew Christians if they had had eyes to see and ears to hear. Jesus considered the Old Testament an adequate witness to himself (John 5:39-47).

c. *God's perfect revelation* (1:2*a*). The contrasting phrases "in time past" (1) and **these last days** are sufficient to dispose of any notion that God's revelation can be disassociated from datable, historical events. On the contrary, the events structure the truths derived from them. While attention is here focused on the recent revelation in a Son, this too is a concrete, historical event, indeed a Person, identified by every Hebrew Christian as Jesus of Nazareth. Here is the complete and culminating disclosure. Jesus Christ is God's full and final Word to man; everything prior is partial and preparatory, and everything subsequent is but the amplification and clarification of this Word. God speaks through the words of our Lord, but also through the events of His redemptive ministry, His conception and birth, His life, death, resurrection, and ascension.

2. *The Incarnate Son* (1:2*b*-3*d*)

a. His mission specified (1:3*d*). We attend to this first, because it is in the writer's mind subordinate (for the moment) to the identity of Christ's person. He states it very succinctly, not as a mission attempted, but as a mission accomplished: **when he had by himself purged our sins**, or more accurately, "having made purification of sins."[3] The Incarnation was necessitated solely by the fact of man's sin, and its single aim was man's redemption from sin. The full implications of this truth will be unfolded in the Epistle.

b. His person identified (1:2*b*-3). What is more urgent is that the Hebrew Christians shall see their Lord's humiliation as

[3]The addition of **by himself** in KJV is justified by the middle voice of the participle; but **our** (**our sins**) is not grammatically justified.

a profound but a brief interlude between His preexistent glory and its resumption. The Cross was an offense to the Jews, and even these Hebrew Christians were in danger of becoming ashamed of it, as the mark of weakness and defeat instead of triumph and power. It was imperative that they see the Cross in the light of the One who suffered on it. The redemptive power of His death was not only in the deed but in the identity of the Doer of the deed. Therefore in these sweeping introductory verses the brief reference to the Son's mission (3) is flanked by careful identification. Who is this Son?

(1) *The Agent of God's power* (1:2). In v. 2 we see His preincarnate position as the Agent of God's creative power: **whom he hath appointed heir of all things, by whom also he made the worlds.**[4] As Heir, Jesus is "lawful Owner" (Amp. NT). Jesus came not to negotiate with the devil but to defeat the usurper with his own weapon, death, and claim His own (2:8-15; I Cor. 15:24-25).

The agency of Jesus in creating the material universe is secondary (suggested by *dia*—**by**, lit., "through"—with the genitive) to that of the Father, which is primary. This is a difficult conception, and its full meaning eludes us. There is support here, however, for the doctrine that the Son is the eternal Logos (Word), at once the expressiveness and the means of expression of the Godhead. Even before creation, therefore, the Logos was that nature in God which was potential communication and concreteness. While not the demiurge of the Gnostics, the Logos was nevertheless the mediating link between a matter-space-time order and pure spirit. When these dual ideas of ownership (heir) and creativity are seen even dimly, the enormity of the sin of Christ-rejection becomes apparent (John 1:10-11).[5]

(2) *The Expression of God's essential Person* (1:3*ab*). It is clear that this Son is not only an Agent but an Aspect (we might say) of Deity itself. He cannot be disassociated from the essen-

[4]Cf. John 1:1-3; I Cor. 8:6; Col. 1:16-17.

[5]Literally v. 2 says that God hath spoken *in a Son*, or *in Son*. Chamberlain comments: "A qualitative force is often expressed by the absence of the article: *en tois prophetais* (Hebrews 1:1), 'in the prophets,' calls attention to a particular group, while *en huio* (Hebrews 1:2), 'in Son,' calls attention to the rank of the Son as a 'spokesman' for God. The ARV in trying to bring out the force of this phrase translates it, 'in his Son,' italicizing 'his'" (William Douglas Chamberlain, *An Exegetical Grammar of the Greek New Testament* [New York: Macmillan Company, 1960], p. 57).

tial being of the Father. First, as **the brightness of his glory** He perfectly reveals the majesty of God.[6] But more than this, He is **the express image of his person** (cf. Col. 1:15) or, as Mueller puts it, the "exact expression of His essential being." This is more than the image of God in which man was created, and certainly much more than the expression of God's holiness through His mighty acts; it is nothing less than the self-disclosure in visible, concrete form of God himself. But since we do not see in the incarnate Son the exact or full expression of the absolute attributes of immensity, aseity, immutability, or infinity, we may infer that God's essential being is primarily *holy personhood,* and in Jesus we see the exact expression of God's personality in His creative activity and redemptive love.[7]

(3) *The arm of God's sustaining providence* (1:3c). Not only is the Son the Agent of creation but He is the Agent of providence, **upholding all things by the word of his power.** Our Lord's power is not in His cleverness in manipulation, but solely in His spoken word. "I will; be thou clean. And immediately his leprosy was cleansed" (Matt. 8:3). "Then he arose, and rebuked the winds and the sea; and there was a great calm" (Matt. 8:26). Upon many such occasions, indeed throughout His entire ministry, this easy mastery of nature was displayed. His miracles were not the exercise of a special gift which God might temporarily bestow on a man; they were the exercising of His own prerogatives. As such they were but faint reflections of that larger control and supervision which maintains the intricate balance and precision in the universe. And He who is the Lord of the stars and planets is Lord of circumstances in our lives.

[6]Thayer says "reflects." Chamberlain says "the noun *apaugasma* (Hebrews 1:3), from *apaugazo,* could mean 'a ray of light flashed back as a reflection,' or 'a ray of light flashed from an object as an emission of light.' The problem of the interpreter then is, does the writer mean to say that Jesus is the 'effulgence' of God's glory, or the 'refulgence'? Only usage can decide this point. Philo's usage is divided. Calvin took it in the sense of 'refulgence.' The Greek fathers are unanimous for 'radiance,' 'effulgence,' in this passage" (*op. cit.,* p. 135).

[7]V. 3 is but an extension of the Logos concept, mentioned in reference to v. 2. This idea was not new to the Jews, at least the Alexandrian school. Parallel statements in Philo are very remarkable, as shown by Sowers, *op. cit.,* pp. 66 ff. However it is very significant that, while the Logos concept is present, the writer nowhere uses the term denoting Jesus; in fact he seems studiously to avoid doing so. His identifying title is Son, not Logos.

This lordship belongs essentially to the eternal Son. In the human nature of His theanthropic person He was subject to natural law, as a man: He suckled in infancy; He grew in stature and mental powers; He was hungry and weary; He suffered pain, both in body and in soul. Never did our Lord use His power to escape or soften the sharp bonds of His humanity (Matt. 4:3). As a Son born to a virgin He was subject to His Father's will, and learned "obedience by the things which he suffered" (5:8). But His essential lordship never altered. When He taught and acted He spoke and acted as a man, in constant deference to His Father. Yet at the same time He spoke and acted—whether in forgiving sins or healing bodies or raising the dead or stilling storms—in confident regality as Lord. The dialectic of the human and divine finds its synthesis in His own words: "I and my Father are one" (John 10:30).

This is the triple identity that the writer to the Hebrews so painstakingly seeks to establish at the very beginning of his discourse—*Agent in creation,* the *Logos of revelation,* and the *Lord of providence.*

3. *The Victorious Lord* (1:3e—2:4)

a. The throne resumed (1:3*e*). This divine Lord is the One **who . . . sat down on the right hand of the Majesty on high.** Here we have the main subject and predicate of v. 3. All else modifies, identifying His person and specifying His earthly work. The picture is one of triumphant exaltation. His mission is accomplished, and He takes His place as the Vicegerent of the Father (symbolized by the **right hand**). It is His rightful place, where He exercises full power of attorney (Matt. 28:18).[8]

b. His superiority to angels (1:4-14). The final assertion in the Prologue is that Jesus was thus demonstrated as **better than the angels** (4). This is a conclusion drawn from His resumed place at the right hand of the Father. Then the writer proceeds to prove his conclusion, in turn, from the OT. If the promised Messiah can be shown from the OT specifications to be more than an angel, the affirmation of His identity as the eternal Son will thereby be strengthened. Any objection by the Hebrews on scriptural grounds will thus have been removed, and the writer's own exposition of our Lord's person greatly buttressed. In v. 4

[8]Sowers says, "To sit at the throne of God in the Pseudepigraphical literature means participation in God's judgment over the world" (*op. cit.,* p. 82).

therefore we find His superiority demonstrated, and in 5-14 we find the claim that in the OT the superiority was predicted.[9]

(1) *Superiority demonstrated by events* (1:4). Mueller translates: "having become as much superior to the angels as He has inherited a name which surpasses them." The measure of His superiority, in other words, is the measure of the qualitative difference between Son and creature. The verbs here suggest *achievement,* admittedly, as an adoption subsequent to His obedience, and as a reward for it. The God-man, as such, viewed from the standpoint of His humiliation and earthly ministry, won the right to take the honored "place and rank" (Amp. NT). He became superior to the angels in the sense that He was declared to be such by His public victory. But while the right to resume this place was won, the **more excellent name** was inherited (v. 2, "heir of all things"), a possible reference to the Virgin Birth and Christ's preincarnate sonship.

(2) *Superiority proven by the Scripture* (1:5-14). In this passage there are six distinct quotations. The writer challenges his readers to name the angel to whom God has said, **Thou art my son, this day have I begotten thee** (5; Ps. 2:7).[10] The second

[9]The importance attached to this and the vigor with which the argument is presented is a strong indication that this Hebrew congregation must have been fascinated by the temptation to assign Jesus a place in the angelic order. This might indicate a Gnostic infection, to which an Alexandrian congregation, or any Hellenistic congregation of Jewish Christians, would most probably be exposed. It would be an attempt to preserve a rigorous monotheism but at the expense of the person of the Saviour. The inspired author of this Epistle will have none of it. He sees that if the Saviour is merely an incarnate angel, no matter what might have been His lofty rank, He was essentially a creature, and could never be associated with the Godhead. He perceives a grandeur and majesty in Jesus' person which alone can invest redemptive power in His blood, and which cannot be justly interpreted apart from a bold and radical identification with the eternal Logos, seen not as a demiurge but as a hypostasis in the very Godhead.

[10]Another probable reference to the Incarnation. Through the Virgin Mary, God quite literally begot the God-man. The many references to the beginning of Christ do not refer to His eternal place in the Godhead as the Logos. Hedegard says, "A well known German biblical scholar wrote many years ago: 'Nobody can *become* God—one *is* God, or is not.' Such statements should be pondered by those who hold adoptionist views and who think that the personality of Jesus was entirely human, but that He was deified after His earthly career and so should now be worshipped" (David Hedegard, *Ecumenism and the Bible* [London: Billing and Sons, Ltd., 1964], p. 13).

quotation (from II Sam. 7:14) is an application to Christ of a promise made initially to David concerning Solomon. The third, from the LXX, cannot be traced clearly in the OT, though there is a similar idea in Ps. 97:7; but the argument here is clear, that the angels of God would not be commanded to worship an equal. The quotation itself is introduced by a clear reference to the Incarnation: **. . . when he bringeth in the first begotten into the world** (6), or "when he brings the first-born Son again into the habitable world" (Amp. NT).[11]

Angels are **spirits,** mere "winds," and the angelic officers are as a mere **flame of fire** (7); but in sharpest contrast **the Son** reigns on a **throne . . . for ever and ever** (8).[12] **Righteousness is the sceptre**—the principle of government and basis of authority. This springs from the spotless holiness of the Son on the throne, who has **loved righteousness, and hated iniquity** (9). True character is revealed, not by pompous professions, but by secret preferences. What one loves and hates is the true index to his soul. The righteous King designs to implant this kind of holy affection and holy hatred in His subjects. This is the affectional aspect of Christian holiness. Because of our Lord's integrity the Father has exalted Him with **the oil of gladness above** His **fellows** (companions—possibly meaning earthly brethren; cf. 12:2).

The application of Psalms 102 to Jesus in vv. 10-12 is even a more radical and bold interpretation of the OT. This psalm is directed to Jehovah (Jahweh), the One whose name the devout Jew would not even pronounce; yet the writer to the Hebrews claims that this is a reference to our Lord. Either his argument here is utterly without sense or else he perceives by the Holy Spirit an OT application to Jesus which does not lie on the surface (cf. Luke 24:27). The passage itself is a reaffirmation of the unchangeable and eternal deity of Christ, in sublimely poetic language.

Finally he repeats the challenge—now with a statement from Ps. 110:1—given in v. 5 in the words, **But to which of the angels said he at any time?** This statement was used also by Jesus himself as a proof that the Christ was much more than David's son (Matt. 22:41-46). But while Jesus' emphasis was on the lordship of the Messiah, the emphasis of Hebrews is that only the

[11]Supported by Alford, *Expositor's Bible*, Vincent, Wuest.

[12]Ps. 45:6-7; 104:4.

Son, not an angel, was told to **sit on my right hand, until I make thine enemies thy footstool** (13). The announcement in v. 3 that Jesus "sat down . . ." is thus seen to be the fulfillment of prophecy. In contrast to the Son's place at the throne, angels are busy constantly ministering in a subordinate role to those **who shall be heirs of salvation** (14), i.e., Christian believers. It should be no small consolation to know that not only does the child of God have the Son and the Spirit as Advocates, but also the personal aid of angels.

In looking back we can see how in supporting his position concerning the Son from the OT the writer weaves into the fabric elements relating to our Lord's humiliation as a man and elements relating to His preincarnate and post-resurrection glory. But it is the one Person throughout. His argument completed, the writer shifts into the first of many hortatory applications.

c. *Therefore a superior salvation* (2:1-4). The real concern of the Epistle is now plain: Since the Saviour is more than an angel—a Son—it is doubly imperative that **we give the more earnest heed to the things which we have heard** (1). We might be careless about listening to the chatter of a neighbor but would pay the most rapt attention to the head of a state. So, if we value our souls, we are bound in greatest urgency to give that careful heed to the gospel which befits the majesty and importance of the Person whom the gospel presents. The present tense of **to give . . . heed** suggests the need for continued, watchful attentiveness. Otherwise we are in danger of drifting past these saving gospel truths. The KJV here is not accurate. It is not **lest . . . we should let them slip,** but lest we should "flow past," or "glide by" them (Thayer). The picture is that of a careless, drowsy boatsman in danger of drifting past the safe haven and being carried out to sea. The phrase in KJV **at any time** is rendered "in any way" (Amp. NT). There are many ways in which Christians are in danger of drifting.

The exhortation is clinched by simple logic: If the word of angels was **stedfast** (2; authoritative and binding), and placed its addressees under **just** (suitable) penalties for disobedience, **How shall we escape, if we neglect so great salvation?** (3)[13]

[13]Sowers says that **the word spoken by angels** (2) "can only mean the law. . . . Gal. 3.19 and Acts 7.38, 53 affirm the Jewish belief that the law was mediated by angels at Sinai. See Strack-Billerbeck at Gal. 3.19 for evidence of this belief in Judaism" (*op. cit.*, p. 77).

If it was serious to despise the law mediated by angels, it is far more serious to despise (by neglect) the salvation mediated by the Son, which has been delivered to men by confirming events and evidences everywhere as authenticating as those which confirmed the giving of the law on Mount Sinai (cf. 12:18-29). This salvation **began to be spoken by the Lord** (3), then was **confirmed** by the apostles and other disciples; and their testimony was supported by God's own **witness, both with signs and wonders, and with divers miracles, and gifts of the Holy Ghost**— "and with various powers and apportionings of the Holy Spirit" (Mueller)—**according to his own will** (4).

As a preaching text, 4 is of course applicable, by accommodation, to the unsaved. But its primary relevance is to Christians, and to them it can be applied with great power. The following developments suggest themselves.

"The Greatness of Salvation." **So great** suggests the inexpressible magnitude (cf. II Cor. 1:10; Rev. 16:18). Its greatness is seen in (1) The Lord who gave it, 3*b*—His person, His power, His passion; (2) The supernatural events which cradled it, 4; (3) The exceeding gravity of the peril from which it delivers us —from *sin* with its guilt, power, pollution, and eternal penalty, 7:27.

In "The Peril of Neglect" we see that (1) Christians are in danger of neglecting this great salvation (*a*) because it is yet largely invisible and spiritual, (*b*) because of the diverting influences of the world around us, (*c*) because of the unbelieving tendency of the carnal mind within man. (2) Christians are in danger of neglecting salvation by (*a*) ignoring the means of grace, (*b*) failing to share the gospel, (*c*) neglecting to obtain full salvation from inner sin.

"The Impossibility of Escape" suggests (1) The danger of spiritual atrophy which neglect brings, (2) The divine wrath that neglect merits (see context; also 6:4-6; 10:23-31; 12:12-29).

B. Less than an Angel—a Man, 2:5-18

1. *The Destiny of Man* (2:5-8)

Beginning with v. 5 there is a transition to a further exposition of the person and purpose of Jesus, with the emphasis now, not on His inherent sonship, but on the meaning and purpose of the Incarnation. While Jesus is not to be identified either with the angels or as an angel, He is to be thus identified with men.

a. The world to come (2:5). The clause **whereof we speak** clearly links the "great salvation" (3) and the presence of Jesus at the Father's "right hand" (1:3) with the future "earth habitation" (Mueller). It further suggests a trans-temporal scope of the subject matter and concern of the entire Epistle. The gospel of Jesus Christ not only is relevant to the present age but is the key to the ages to come, including the new heavens and the new earth. This cleansed and emancipated earth-world, which is the goal of all history, God has **not put in subjection** to the angels.

b. Its appointed Ruler (2:6-8*b*). The quotation from Ps. 8:4-6 reveals man's place in God's plan. In physical size, against the backdrop of the universe, he is insignificant; then why should God be **mindful of him?** (6) In rank and power he is inferior to the angels, but only temporarily (the Gk. of v. 7 indicates "for a little while"—Mueller). In spite of his physical smallness and his temporary **lower** rank God has crowned **him with glory and honour** (7) and **put all things in subjection under his feet** (8a).[14] The compass of man's predestined dominion is all-inclusive: **he left nothing** exempt (8*b*). Man's commission to subdue and rule this earth in God's behalf was concomitant with creation (Gen. 1:26-29). His attempted conquest of the natural order therefore is not displeasing to God, in and of itself, for it is part of the original assignment. But the assignment was spiritual as well as material, and therefore to pursue the material to the neglect and even rejection of the spiritual is sin. Furthermore, according to many theologians, man's assignment was to conquer the kingdom of Satan. Man was created to counteract the devil, says Oswald Chambers.[15] It is at least clear from Hebrews that man's commission was and is of cosmic and eternal magnitude.

c. His present impotence (2:8*c*). But man's rule has pathetically miscarried so far, for at the moment **we see not yet all things put under him.** Some things he has mastered fairly well, but in the spiritual realm he has dismally failed. This failure is not due to immaturity or insufficient time but to an intervening

[14]The clause **didst set him over the works of thy hands** is in the psalm, and included in KJV, but is not in the Greek text.

[15]Eric Sauer takes a similar position, claiming that man's supreme mission was to wrest control of this corner of the universe from the adversary and restore it to God. See *The King of the Earth* (Grand Rapids: Wm. B. Eerdmans Publishing Company, 1962), pp. 92-100.

catastrophe. The intended masters of Satan have become his captives.

2. *Fulfilled in Jesus* (2:8c-9)

There is a reassuring note of hope in the phrase **not yet.** The assignment has not been cancelled; it will yet be fulfilled. But not through the resources of the first Adam, for those resources are bankrupt. We may not see man as a conqueror now, **but we see Jesus** (9), the Second Adam, through whom a redeemed race will have not only a second chance but complete success.[16] This ringing declaration is the first use of the name **Jesus.** Up to this point the reference, while unmistakable, has been veiled: now all indirect allusion is laid aside and the sacred name heralded. Pilate brought Jesus forth, wearing the crown of thorns and the purple robe, and said, "Behold the man!" (John 19:5) But neither Pilate nor the multitude really beheld Him. They stared with eyes that could not see. Now the writer to the Hebrews directs their gaze toward Jesus in similar fashion, and with an intense desire that they shall see with clearer vision than either Pilate or the Jews at Jerusalem.

What Pilate uncomprehendingly proclaimed, this Epistle underscores with emphasis: Behold *the Man!* The One who was coequal with the Father before the world was, was himself **made** (for a short while) **a little lower than the angels.** Man's forfeited honor is fulfilled abundantly in this Man, for He is now **crowned with glory and honour,** at the Father's right hand, before the angels, and in the hearts of His disciples. But the crowning was by, "on account of" (*dia* with accusative), **the suffering of death.**[17]

[16]Since Jesus had ascended they could not see **Jesus** as the apostles had seen Him; the present tense suggests a clear mental view of a recent Person, thoroughly historical and intimately known; possibly the writer and some in the congregation addressed had been "eyewitnesses of his majesty" (II Pet. 1:16).

[17]Sowers reminds us, "That the present and realized fulfillment of Ps. 8 in Jesus is because He has been crowned with glory and honour in His suffering, and not because He has all things placed in subjection to Him. This subjection will take place in 'the world to come' (2.5)" (*op. cit.,* p. 81). Furthermore, the KJV connects the phrase **for the suffering of death** with the previous clause, thus making the phrase express the purpose of the Incarnation. A better exegesis connects the phrase with the following clause, thus indicating that precisely His death is the basis for His present glory and honor (Phil. 2:8-9).

It was His shameful death which was an embarrassment to the Hebrews; but they must understand that this is rather His glory and their hope. His death was not a tragic blunder but originated in God's **grace,** His compassionate determination to provide redemption. Its benefits are declared to be **for every man** ("every individual person"—Amp. NT). This certainly rules out a limited atonement, or any system which splits the intended merit of His death into common grace and saving grace; **for every man** implies universal equality. Furthermore, lest any attempt be made to depreciate our Lord's experience of death by misconstruing the word **taste,** it should be pointed out that this same word is used in Matt. 16:28; Mark 9:1; Luke 9:27; and John 8:52, where the full force of human death, entirely experienced, is implied. Dods says: ". . . actually experience death's bitterness."[18] Yet though the death is real, it is not an exact legal substitute, procuring the redemption absolutely of all men; His death was **for** ("in behalf of," *hyper* with ablative), i.e., He died to make possible the salvation of **every man.** This is substitutionary in an ethical sense rather than legal.

3. *The Purpose of the Incarnation* (2:10-18)

The clear statement of God's purpose is given in 9, but now the writer expands his thesis. The explanation is dual, and is found in two *hina*'s ("in order that") in the Greek text, translated: (*a*) **that through death he might** conquer Satan and free his subjects (14), and (*b*) **that he might be a merciful and faithful high priest** (17). But the writer first establishes the rationale of the Incarnation as a necessary basis for the accomplishment of these two objectives.

a. The kind of Saviour required (2:10-14*a*). The task is to bring **many sons unto glory** (10), i.e., to the full likeness of Christ and the full consummation of their redemption in heaven. But if this is to be done, **the captain of their salvation** must be made **perfect through sufferings.** This does not refer to the perfecting of our Lord's personal holiness, but to His qualifications as **captain** and File-Leader (cf. 12:2, where the same word is translated "author"). He is both Saviour and Example. He

[18]"The Epistle to the Hebrews," *The Expositor's Greek Testament,* ed. W. Robertson Nicoll (Grand Rapids: Wm. B. Eerdmans Publishing Company, n.d.), IV, 263.

goes before us, not only showing the path to glory, but clearing and making the way. Obviously in so doing He must suffer its ruggedness and its hardships. In His own person He must face the enemy and conquer. Only thus can a safe path be made for those who follow. This is not a captain who directs from behind the lines, and permits his men to do the fighting and dying, but One who goes ahead, and does the fighting and dying himself, in order that His followers may live, and be assured of victorious passage. Such imposition of sufferings is not cruel or irrational, unworthy of a great God; rather **it became him, for whom are all things, and by whom are all things** (10), to do it this way. The plan of salvation is to the greater glory of God himself, whose eternal wisdom and grace devised it.

The term **sufferings** in the plural suggests that Calvary is not alone intended but the many forms of suffering which belong to man as man, and those numerous agonies which our Lord knew from the manger to the Cross.

His kinship with us is twofold: (*a*) We are sanctified by Him and thus made like Him, and brought thereby into a wonderful fellowship and unity based on a moral likeness. (*b*) **Both he that sanctifieth and they who are sanctified are all of one** (11); i.e., they have one Father. Jesus, the God-man, by the Incarnation, now shares with man the fatherhood of God as Creator; by sanctifying His own disciples He shares with them the holiness of the Father. A family likeness is thereby established. This likeness to God through sanctification is the deeper meaning of sonship in the NT. Because of this family likeness, established (*a*) by His own participation in *human* nature, and (*b*) His impartation to them of *holy* nature, **he is not ashamed to call them brethren.**[19]

As proof of this assertion Hebrews quotes Ps. 22:22, and lifts out two brief phrases from Isa. 8:17-18.[20] Then the conclusion follows: Since the "children" and the "brethren" **are partakers**

[19]A discussion of sanctification at this point is not directly germane, as the reference is subordinate to the mainstream of thought, which is to establish the necessity of the Incarnation, if the Saviour is going to be qualified to do and be all that is required.

[20]None of the three is otherwise cited in the NT, and the application, especially of the Isaiah phrases, seems arbitrary. However the content of both passages was widely recognized by the Early Church as Messianic. See Sowers, *op. cit.*, p. 86.

of flesh and blood, he also himself likewise took part of the same (14). The word **partakers** (perfect of *koinoneo,* "to have in common") is vivid and strong, meaning that the brethren are mutual participants and fellow sufferers in the human situation; it would therefore be unthinkable for their captain to be a non-sharing suprahuman creature, detached from the human frame and uninvolved in the anguish of life.

b. The purpose of His death (2:14*b*-15). The Logos became man that He might die; He died that **he might destroy him that had the power of death, that is, the devil** (14). It was *by means* of His death (*dia* with the genitive) that Jesus was enabled to destroy the devil. His death was not incidental but both indispensable and dynamic. Two questions arise at once.

(1) In what sense did Satan have **the power of death?** It is clear from Hebrews that the death of Jesus not only had to do with man and his sin but with Satan and his power. Satan was not to be thought of as a mythological symbol of evil, but a person with power and authority in his own right, whose competitive kingdom of darkness was deeply involved in the primeval chaos, in man's predicament, and therefore in the purposes of the Incarnation and Crucifixion.[21]

The sense in which Satan had the power of death is difficult to determine. It must have included the death of man (15), and it is clear that the power is terribly final and inescapable apart from Christ's conquering death. The careful identification of this person as Diabolos, the Accuser, might suggest that as a prosecutor he legally demands death as punishment for man's sin. We must remember that God and Satan are opposing rulers in a life-and-death struggle, and man's sin gave to Satan a real advantage. This advantage might have been a demand that the divinely threatened penalty of sin be exacted to the full. But to exact it to the full would be ignominious failure with the human race; while to fail to exact the full death penalty would be a surrender of God's holy integrity by a broken word (I Cor. 15:

[21]**Power,** *kratos,* here means dominion, according to Thayer. A. T. Robertson comments: "Christ broke the power . . . of the devil over death (paradoxical as it seems), certainly in men's fear of death and in some unexplained way Satan had sway over the realm of death (Zech. 3:5 ff.)" (*Word Pictures in the New Testament* [New York: Harper & Brothers, 1932], V, 349.

56). Man's sin thus placed his Creator on the horns of a dilemma and gave to Satan a legal basis for pressing the claim of failure, either regarding man or respecting God's integrity. Satan does not perceive a third alternative, but exults because either horn of the dilemma will bring God into dishonor before angels and demons.

Others would see Satan's power of death, not as the power of a prosecuting attorney who believes he has an unbeatable case, but as the legal power of an executioner; i.e., Satan has legally obtained the right to kill. Eric Sauer sees the fall of Satan as the origin of death, and the explanation of death's introduction into the natural order of the world, long before the creation of man. In this view, man's sin brought the human race under the death-dealing power of Satan. War, famines, and plague could be among Satan's devices to destroy.

(2) In what sense was the Accuser "destroyed" through the death of Jesus? The word is from *katargeo,* "annulled, loosed." Satan was not annihilated, but his power was both broken in fact and legally cancelled, completely and finally (aorist subjunctive). Here was a third alternative to the dilemma which Satan could not foresee. The Incarnation lured Satan into defeating himself by his own weapon. By killing Jesus he forfeited his legal rights, for he killed One who had not sinned! And by the Resurrection the power of death was decisively broken. If Adam gave Satan an advantage in the cosmic struggle, Christ overturned it, and gave the advantage once for all to God. If Adam sold the human race into slavery to Satan, Christ delivered it. Admittedly this may sound like the ransom theory of the atonement, long since discarded by the Church as fanciful and primitive. But some such germ ideas as these are unmistakably in this passage of Scripture—and indeed to be found throughout the entire NT.

But there is in 15 a second half of the *hina* clause **(that through death)**. Christ died not only that the devil might be destroyed but that He might **deliver them who through fear of death were all their lifetime subject to bondage.** Grammatically these two purposes are coordinate, but in human experience man's **fear of death** must be related to Satan's **power of death;** therefore the destruction of Satan's power would in itself be the ground—or at least a partial ground—for the deliverance of Satan's victims. It is a complete deliverance from the "bound-in servitude" (Mueller) which resulted from their lifelong **fear of death.** This is a pitiful kind of bondage, a cringing subjection to a terror of dying, which shackles the entire human race. The **bondage** is broken by deliverance from the **fear.** Believers in Jesus know that death has been conquered by Christ's own death and resurrection. Hence, (*a*) the "sting of death," which is "sin" (I Cor. 15:56), has been removed by the atonement; therefore the basis of Satan's accusation has been cancelled (Rev. 12:10-11), and the judgment beyond death need not be feared. (*b*) Christ's resurrection guarantees their own; therefore confident, joyous hope displaces dark foreboding and un- Satan, and therefore they need not live in fear that he will be certainty. And (*c*) the power of death has been taken from able to kill them before their hour. They live rather in the assurance that their times are in God's hands.

c. *A plenary priesthood* (2:16-18). The Incarnation was necessary, not only that Jesus be perfected by suffering and death as a Saviour, but that He also be thus perfected as a High Priest. As a Saviour, He delivers from the power of Satan; as a High Priest, He delivers from the just condemnation of God. The same steps in the argument used in 9-15 are now taken again, but compressed. First His manhood is reaffirmed, this time specifically as an Israelite. **He took not . . the nature of angels** but **the seed of Abraham** (16). If He had been an angel He could not have had the kind of priestly ministry which is about to be described. Nor would universal manhood alone have sufficed; He must be a Hebrew. Jesus was one of their own race. **Wherefore** (17), i.e., this being so, it was proper for Him in all things **to be made like unto his brethren.** It would have been incongruous for Him to have descended from heaven as the Lion of the tribe of Judah, in full Messianic splendor, as some of the Jews imagined. Such a personage would have been too far removed from the Israelites in their sin and need to have been able to aid them in a priestly capacity. Only one like themselves in the full sharing of their human sufferings could **be** (become) **a merciful and faithful high priest in things pertaining to God.**

There are two aspects of Christ's priestly ministry: the Godward and the manward, the propitiatory and the pastoral.

(1) *The propitiatory* (2:17c). A high priest's primary task is to propitiate the holy God by dealing honestly and suitably

with the problem of sin. There can be no acceptable worship which ignores sin. The stain of high treason must be removed before fellowship and communion can be established between the Sovereign and His subject. This is the office of the Mediator —to represent God to the returning traitor, and the traitor to God, and execute the conditions of pardon specified by the Sovereign. This was certainly a familiar concept to the Hebrews, though it is still difficult for our Western minds to grasp. This Mediator between God and man is Jesus. His first office therefore as a merciful and faithful Priest is **to make reconciliation for the sins of the people.** The word translated **reconciliation** is *hilaskesthai,* "to expiate by oneself," in this case to satisfy personally the just requirements in behalf of another. God is propitiated (satisfied) by this expiation; therefore a reconciliation can be based upon it. It is not an expiation of the people but of the sins of the people. It is thus a cancellation, or pardon-procurement, of sins, and the sinners are freed from guilt and condemnation as a consequence. Clearly this is a reference to the priest's justifying function, not to a sanctifying ministry. The **people** are the worshippers, not unbelievers or the impenitent; the **sins** are whatever violations have accrued, either known or unknown.

(2) *The pastoral* (2:18). The causal coordinating conjunction **for** (*gar*) goes back to our Lord's likeness to His brethren (17). For not only is He thereby able as a High Priest to expiate sins, but **to succour them that are tempted,** inasmuch as He himself has **suffered being tempted.** The writer is still vindicating the divine plan which calls for a suffering Messiah. Jesus suffered, as a man, all the vicissitudes of life. He not only suffered the terrible experience of death, but He suffered the warfare of a moral being. He was no more removed by nature from temptation and its fierce struggles than He was from the buffetings of life and pain of death. He fought in the moral arena of manhood. And His were no sham battles or mock sparrings with a hired foe. He **suffered being tempted.** And this was part of His perfecting as Captain and as Priest—for how could a Priest truly sympathize unless He had stood where they stood? But since He understands by experience, **he is able to succour**—i.e., to run to the aid of those who cry for help (cf. 13:6; also Matt. 15:25; Mark 9:22, 24; Acts 16:9; 21:28; II Cor. 6:2; Rev. 12:16).

C. Greater than Moses, 3:1-19

The writer has established both the deity and the humanity of the Messiah, and the entire suitability of His suffering and death. **Wherefore** (in view of this), he now challenges his **holy brethren,** who share with him in **the heavenly calling,** to consider carefully **the Apostle and High Priest of** their **profession, Christ Jesus** (1).[22] This comparison is not in relation to angels, Adam, or Abraham, but to Moses. The voice of Moses had become virtually the voice of God in Hebrew thinking. An appeal to Moses settled all questions. The transfer of faith and allegiance from Moses to the Man of Galilee was very difficult, and the pressure to return to Moses was constant.

Moses' devotees could point to the miracles in Egypt, the mighty events of Sinai, and the leading out of the whole nation. Jesus' disciples could point only to local miracles on individuals, and a tiny motley band of despised followers. Moses died with dignity upon a mountain and was buried by angels (Deut. 34:9; Jude 9); Jesus was put to an ignominious and cruel public death by His enemies. The disciples of Jesus clung to His resurrection and a promise of future glory—a promise which thus far showed no signs of materializing. And the Resurrection was proof of superiority only to those who believed it. In the attempt which follows to prove that Jesus is greater than Moses it is noteworthy that the Resurrection is not appealed to. Rather the argument is based solely on the identity, already argued from their OT scriptures, of Jesus as the divine Son of God.[23] But regardless of approach, the writer is truly Pauline in his grasp of the complete eclipse of Moses by Christ. The question of the perpetuity of Moses' authority arose very early in the Church even at Jerusalem, and the first great council was convened to settle this issue (Acts 15). In their stern opposition to the tendency of the Judaizers to make Christianity a form of Judaism, Paul and the writer of Hebrews, if not the same person, were at least of the same mind.

[22]**Christ** is not in the Greek text.

[23]Chamberlain says, "The one article with 'apostle' and 'high priest' calls attention to the fact that both offices are bound up in one personality. 'Jesus' is an explanatory apposition to make clear who that personality is" (*op. cit.*, p. 55).

1. *The Basis of Christ's Superiority* (3:2-6*a*)

a. A superior appointment (3:2). The emphasis in this verse should not be placed on the fact that Jesus was **faithful** but upon the fact that God himself had **appointed him,** i.e., had "constituted" Him Apostle and Priest of the redemptive program. **Moses** too was **faithful in all his house** (God's house, not Moses'—see Num. 12:7), but his appointment was to a lower office in the divine economy. In *faithfulness* Hebrews concedes equal honor to Moses, but not in either *position* or *function.*

b. A superior worthiness (3:3-6*a*). Christ's appointment as Apostle and High Priest was justified by the identity of His person: His relationship to the household of God was that of Builder, not custodian; and by "builder" is meant not just the contractor or workman, but the *author,* the one who provides the house, as owner, architect, financier, constructor, and furnisher all in one person. Therefore Jesus is intrinsically **worthy of more glory than Moses** exactly in the same way and to the same degree **that he who hath builded the house hath more honour** (greater worthiness) **than the house** (3).

In 4-6*a* the inspired writer states plainly and boldly what he has just implied. The comparison between Jesus and Moses is not only that of Builder and house, but of Son and servant. He eases into this climax by the reminder that of course **every house is builded by some man** and the Author of **all things is God** (4), which would certainly include the particular house of which he is speaking. But in this **house**—or "household" of redemption —**Moses . . . was faithful . . . as a servant** (5), while **Christ** was faithful **as a son over his own house** (6*a*). Moreover, as a servant Moses was merely "a clerk for a witness of the things which were to be spoken" (Mueller). He was a humble civil servant whose task was to record what God did and said. In sharpest contrast Jesus was faithful **as a son over his own house.** In other words, the house that Moses worked in was Christ's, which means that Moses was a menial and temporary "clerk" under Jesus, the very One of whom these Hebrew Christians were tempted to be ashamed!

This was the uncompromising, radical claim of authentic Christianity. If the Hebrew Christians really saw this, the almost hypnotic power of Moses over their minds would be broken forever. The Moses cult would hold for them no further fascination. Moses had fulfilled his task and passed away; the

Son was not for a generation, but would rule the household of God forever. And this superlative greatness and incomparable superiority of Jesus was inescapable, if the writer had successfully demonstrated to them that the Suffering Servant of Isaiah and the Conquering Son must of necessity be one Messiah, Jesus. Since his arguments were based on their own Scriptures, and particularly the Septuagint, with which they were familiar, they must have felt the overwhelming weight of His case, and their hearts have begun to warm with a rekindled excitement about the Man Christ Jesus.

2. *The Implied Terms of the Christian's Security* (3:6b-19)

But Hebrews does not take such a revival for granted. Instead there is launched at once a lengthy application and exhortation which continues through c. 4. In the superiority of Jesus to Moses there are grave implications, chief of which is that the measure of this superiority is the measure of the peril of apostasy from Christ. In essence there is the same reasoning as was used in 2:2-4 respecting the comparative peril of rejecting the word spoken by angels and the word of the gospel. If the rejection of Moses by the Israelites in the wilderness resulted in their death notwithstanding the miraculous deliverance from Egypt, how much surer will be the final and eternal death of those who permit the infection of unbelief after once being united to Christ!

This sudden transition from the constructive argument to the personal application occurs sharply with the second clause of v. 6: **whose house are we.** The statement of an all-important, pivotal fact is followed by a warning (6c-11) and the warning is followed by a fervent exhortation (12-19).

a. A statement of fact (3:6b). There is a clear continuity between the house in which Moses participated and the present house of Christ. It is constituted of persons, not brick and mortar—**whose house are we**—which means that it is the household of the people of God in every age. The relationship of Christ as the *Head* is not new; but His *revelation* as Head is a new element. It was never Moses' household, but was always and will always be Christ's.

There was a time when the household could legitimately look to Moses as Christ's temporary deputy and chief steward; but now that Christ has been revealed, that time is forever past.

Christ has been openly disclosed as the Head; therefore from henceforth all eyes must be upon Him.

The term **house** cannot be diluted to include "camp followers" or unregenerate adherents of the faith. Its import is similar to the Church as the body of Christ, and in some respects to the Kingdom; but its central notes are *family* and *rule.* It is the family—or *new race*—of God's people ruled by God the Father and Christ the Son. One cannot join it, but he can be born into it by the second birth (cf. Gal. 6:10; Eph. 2:19; I Pet. 2: 1-10). The assertion **whose house are we** clearly acknowledges the regenerate state of the Hebrews who are being addressed.

b. A warning of forfeiture (3:6c). Membership in Christ's household is not unconditionally secure. The contingency is expressed by **if** (*ean*) with a subjunctive verb. This means that, while the warning is given hopefully, it is given with dead seriousness because of the real possibility that they may not hold fast. If they do not, their place in the household of God will be forfeited. No juggling of words can blunt the full force of this **if.**[24] The verb is strong (*kataschomen*—to hold down) and means to hold in a firm grasp, to have in full and secure possession (cf. 3:14; 10:23). To hold lightly and carelessly simply will not do.

But what is to be held so firmly? **The confidence and the rejoicing of the hope.** These are words expressing positive assurance and exultant buoyancy. The first, **confidence** (*parresian*), means freedom and boldness in speech (cf. 4:16; 10:19), indicating an open, unabashed enthusiasm about Jesus, with a readiness to declare one's faith. The closed mouth is a sign of a fearful heart. The second essential element of our faith that testifies to its vitality, which we must hold fast, is **rejoicing** (*kauchema*), a joyous exultation in the Christian hope, almost a holy boasting in the promises of the Lord. It is clear that security is not in past experience but in present victory, not in feeble but in triumphant faith, not in a grim and glum clinging to the Christian hope but in a vibrant possession that is on the offensive rather than the defensive. There is no safety—any more than there is satisfaction—in a tentative and tenuous Christianity.

[24]Robertson says: "This note of contingency and doubt runs all through the Epistle . . . The author makes no effort to reconcile this warning with God's elective purpose. He is not exhorting God, but these wavering Christians. All these are Pauline words" (*op. cit.*, p. 355).

How long must we thus maintain a dynamic, living faith? **Firm unto the end**—without wavering or relaxing our hold until the very close of our earthly probation.

c. *An admonition to faithfulness* (3:7-19). The balance of this chapter is difficult to unravel, as on the surface there seems to be needless repetition. The conditional nature of our participation in Christ is stated twice in the chapter (6, 14) each time followed at once by reference to the same OT passage (Ps. 95: 7-11). In the first use the entire passage is quoted, and it is made the basis for an immediate personal application (12-13). The second time only the essential idea is quoted; then the typological elements of the OT event (to which the Holy Spirit through the Psalmist refers) are dissected, and the central parallel of *rest forfeited by unbelief* is stressed. In these two divisions we discover a crescendo of emphasis, and in the second an advance in ideas which leads directly into the climactic c. 4, all of which makes the repetition purposeful.

(1) *The inspired warning and its timely relevance* (7-13). **Wherefore** (7)—because of the element of contingency in their relationship to Christ—the **brethren** are urged to **take heed** (12). The **wherefore** thus introduces the admonition of 12-13, not the quotation from Psalms 95; therefore the KJV is justified in treating the quotation parenthetically. It is the case of a preacher introducing a relevant passage of Scripture into his sermon as the springboard for his solemn application and charge. **As the Holy Ghost saith** (7)—note the high doctrine of inspiration implied here. The writer is not alone in declaring their peril, for the Holy Spirit has already given the exact warning to them in their Scriptures. It was not solely to that generation, for its principle is timeless. When God speaks, men are free to obey or to harden their hearts; when they harden their hearts, God rejects them, and they forfeit their opportunity. The Hebrew Christians are being reminded that in their own national history is a sad demonstration of this principle. Mueller renders the entire passage:

> *Today, if you shall hear His voice,*
> *Do not harden your hearts as in the indignation*
> *In the day of trial in the desert,*
> *For your fathers made trial during probation*
> *And saw my works forty years:*

Therefore, I was provoked with this generation
And said, Always they go astray in their hearts,
For, they will not acknowledge my ways;
So I swore in my anger,
Lest they will come in, into my rest.

The gist of the passage is: "You honor Moses. Do not forget that your fathers honored Moses too, and at first followed him, and with him were recipients of divine favor. But your fathers turned from Moses. In turning from him they were turning from God; hence God rejected them, and they scattered their bones in the wilderness. They who started for Canaan never reached Canaan. Now you are in peril of repeating their sin. You have followed Jesus—but now you are tempted to rebel. If you do, you will be rejecting God, and God will reject you; your place in the household of Christ will be lost."

With such a passage before them, they could not miss the seriousness of his plea: **Take heed, brethren, lest there be in any of you an evil heart of unbelief, in departing from the living God** (12). The necessity of constant alertness and diligence is, in various forms, a recurrent theme in this Epistle (2:1; 4:1, 11; 6:11-12; 10:23-25, 36-39; 12:1-3, 12-17). The warning here is not an accusation; it is not said that they *have* **an evil heart of unbelief,** but they are told to be watchful against allowing themselves at any future time to possess **an evil heart** (future tense of "to be," *estai*). The noun **unbelief** (*apistias*) means lack of trust and confidence; here it is used adjectively, and the phrase could be translated, *an evil, unbelieving heart.* Even if not deliberately chosen, a carelessly permitted state of doubt is **an evil heart,** now disposed, even though subconsciously, to all other forms of evil. There is a suggestion in the peculiar Greek construction of **in departing from the living God** that the heart becomes evil with unbelief when one begins to "stand aloof" from Christ (Amp. NT). The absence of the article (Gk., *a* **living God,** not *the*) could mean that the writer is pursuing his contrast between Christ and Moses. If standing aloof from Moses, who was merely a man, was so dire in its consequences, how much more would turning away from Christ, who is a living God, result in **an evil heart!**

As one means of preventing this they are told to **exhort one another daily** (13). The best defense is offense, and the best way of preserving one's own soul is to be watchful of the spiritual welfare of others. A strong sense of group responsibility is the mark of a healthy church. Christians are like live coals: together they feed each other's fire, and generate great heat; separated they soon cool and die. But this is not just idle social "togetherness," for eating and banter. There should be a deep tone of devotion and mutual concern permeating every gathering of believers, even so-called "social gatherings." Christians may be together in such a way as to mutually dissipate spiritual strength. They should see to it that in every hour of fellowship, whether at the table or in play or in home groups, something is included which will reinforce spiritual zeal and holy purpose.

The writer sees great significance in the quoted phrase **while it is called To day,** for he returns to it as a key to his exegesis in v. 15 and 4:7. He evidently understands **To day** to be the "day of opportunity"—a period of probation—for moral decision, which God gave to the Israelites under Moses, and which He now gives in Christ. He is saying to the Hebrews, The die is not yet cast. While the door is yet wide, and the options of moral agency are still open, **exhort one another daily,** for the time will come when **To day** will be forever past.

The peril which this daily exhortation is intended to prevent is their becoming **hardened through the deceitfulness of sin.** This is a settled obduracy, a stubborn frame of mind, which is around the corner for any Christian who permits himself, with a doubting heart, to drift away from personal love and loyalty to Jesus. It is a solemn thought that the human heart, even a heart once Christian, can congeal as cement, and lose its malleability. The danger is aggravated by the fact that the damage is done by the delusion of sin. Sin which is seen as sin can and will more readily be avoided. But when it is disguised as apparent good, the hardening process goes on unnoticed. Only keen alertness which is fully aware of the deceitfulness of sin can prevent this gradual hardening of the heart.

It is not clear whether the article *the* with **sin** (*hamartias*) is significant to the exegesis. If not, sin in the abstract is probably intended; i.e., sin by its very nature is delusive, and he who permits it, in any form, is bound to suffer the hardening effects. But if the article is intended to indicate some particular sin, the exposition may settle on these possibilities. (*a*) The writer may be referring to inbred sin, which makes every partially sanctified believer prone to drifting, and which can be counteracted only by vigorous diligence, and eradicated by entire sanctification. Or (*b*) he may be referring to the sin of unbelief, manifested by their tendency to be cool toward Jesus Christ. This seems to be their besetting sin (12:1). Its delusion lies in the fact that it appears to be simply the adoption of a cautious, sensible attitude. Or (*c*) it may be that the writer is using the term, not technically, but in its simplest etymological sense, *falling short.* In this case he is warning them to exhort one another to maintain unflagging devotion, lest they be deceived by that false sense of security which "falling short" engenders, and fatal hardening be the inevitable consequence.

(2) *Conditional security and its historical type* (3:14-19). At v. 14 the circular argument is back again at the point of departure. **For we are made partakers of Christ, if we hold the beginning of our confidence stedfast unto the end.** Again the giant **if,** this time with greater emphasis and stronger words. It is no longer merely *ean* but *eanper,* meaning *if indeed* or *absolutely if* we maintain our confidence. In v. 6 the Christian readers are designated constituent members of the household of Christ; now this is stated plainly as participation in Christ himself: **partakers of Christ** (*metochoi . . . tou Christou*). To understand the full strength of this word note how the writer uses it elsewhere: "oil of gladness above thy fellows" (1:9); "holy brethren, partakers of the heavenly calling" (3:1); "and were made partakers of the Holy Ghost" (6:4); "if ye be without chastisement, whereof all are partakers, then are ye bastards, and not sons" (12:8). There is no way this word can honorably be construed as nominal adherence or mere superficial profession!

The term **made** combined with **the beginning of our confidence** is remarkable. The first word is *ginomai,* "to become," in the perfect tense, indicating a present state based on a past but sustained action. Our state of salvation, based on our past conversion, is sustained in the present only if our confidence is maintained clear to the end of the Christian life. At the beginning it was fervent, committed, and cloudless. If this is not maintained, neither will our participation in Christ be sustained (Rev. 2:4-5).

The writer has already called attention to the No. 1 "case history" of such defection and forfeiture in their own national history. Now he repeats the crucial sentence, **While it is said,**

To day if ye will hear his voice, harden not your hearts (15). The **while** should be linked with **unto the end** in the previous verse. As long as God says, **To day,** our responsibility persists. The end will occur when probation ends, and it is no longer the **To day** of God's preferred salvation. Every time God speaks, at any point in the Christian life, the peril of hardening our hearts by stopping our ears is present. At each such crisis a fresh moral decision is made, and we either yield our hearts or harden them.

"Don't harden your hearts as your fathers did **in the provocation.**" As numerous as were the previous instances of grieving God, the particular **provocation** the writer has in mind is the refusal of the Israelites to enter Canaan at Kadesh-barnea (Numbers 13—14). In the next several verses, by a series of dramatic questions, the possibility of apostasy is established, and the responsibility squarely fixed.

The KJV misses the interrogative import of v. 16, and in so doing alters the meaning. *The Amplified New Testament* is more accurate: "For who were they that heard and yet were rebellious and provoked [Him]? Was it not all those who came out of Egypt led by Moses?" They started well but did not end well. It is possible to be a beneficiary of God's grace and an addressee of His promise, yet in the end be completely rejected. Why such stressing of this in writing to Christians? Because the same principles of divine equity which were operative then are operative now, with Christians equally as with OT Jews. So let us pinpoint these principles even further. **But with whom was he grieved forty years? was it not with them that had sinned, whose carcases fell in the wilderness?** (17) God's judgments are not capricious. He was indignant, not toward the innocent, but toward the guilty. These whose dead bodies littered the wilderness were not unfortunate pilgrims who floundered and by error missed the way; they were sinners. In this case the nature of their sin is not left in doubt. Outwardly their sin was the deliberate refusal to enter the land of Canaan. Inwardly it was unbelief. **And to whom sware he that they should not enter into his rest, but to them that believed not?** (18) Now notice his conclusion: **So we see that they could not enter in because of unbelief** (19)—not because God was unwilling for them to enter, or because He was unable to bring them in, but because their own unbelief cut them off. The kind of unbelief that is so fatal is clearly designated in v. 18

by **but to them that believed not.** The verb is *apeitheo* (*a* plus *peitho,* "to persuade") and means a deliberate refusal to allow oneself to be persuaded; to refuse to believe, and in refusing to believe, to refuse to obey. The perfect tense would suggest a settled state of unbelief resulting from a past major decision. They *would* not enter, and as a consequence they *could* not enter.

We may draw two conclusions. One is that unbelief and disobedience are but two sides of the same coin. The other is that the writer to the Hebrews is drawing a double analogy from Israelitish history. In part he is proving the peril and possibility of forfeiting eternal life in Christ by any degree of apostasy. But he is also perceiving in the land of Canaan a type of that spiritual assurance and rest which is God's calling for them in Christ, and which they are even now in danger of missing by dragging their feet. Refusal at *their* Kadesh will be as disastrous as the refusal of their forefathers, indeed infinitely more so. Just as the land of Canaan was a type of spiritual rest, so physical death in the wilderness was a type of spiritual death. It is to this greater peril of forfeiting their Canaan through the same kind of unbelief as the early Israelites forfeited theirs that he now turns in c. 4.

D. The Indispensable Rest, 4:1-16

This chapter could be called "Entering into His Rest," for such is its subject matter. The term "rest" is used nine times in these sixteen verses, eight times translating *katapausis* and once translating *sabbatismos.* The first word denotes a settled peace, or state of rest; and the second, found only here in the NT, means "Sabbath-state." This term "enter" in its various forms is found eight times in this chapter, all in connection with "rest."

This **rest** for **the people of God** (9) has often been understood as a second work of grace. Among the Quakers the terminology of Hebrews has been maintained and forms the basis of Philip Doddridge's stanza:

Now rest, my long divided heart;
Fixed on this blissful center, rest;
Nor ever from thy Lord depart,
With Him of every good possessed.

Among Wesleyans the Pauline terminology of entire sanctification is customary. The urgency of definite entrance is stressed in vv. 1, 6, 11, and in each case the form is aorist infinitive, which is punctiliar in import. There is no hint of a gradual or partial entry into God's rest. The central lesson is that history is being repeated; exactly where the Israelites were at Kadesh-barnea, these Hebrew Christians are now, except that the issues are more grave.

1. *A Similar Peril* (4:1-3)

Because of the historical example before us, we should **fear** ("have-an-anxious-dread"—Mueller), **lest a promise being left us of entering into his rest, any of you should seem to come short of it** (1). In respect to this **rest** a casual frame of mind, which is either indifferent or overly optimistic, is completely out of order. This is a life-and-death issue, on which should be concentrated the Christian's most intense and profound concern, that he not even appear to "be-staying-behind" (Mueller). The laggards are in danger as well as the outright rejectors.

That such a promise is left, or "reserved" for us (*kataleipo*, "to leave behind, reserve"; cf. Rom. 11:4), is confirmed in v. 2: **For unto us was the gospel preached, as well as unto them.** Literally it should read, "We were evangelized to the same degree —or as thoroughly—as they." The Israelites through Moses heard the good news of God's provision and will for them. So have we heard God's good news for us through Christ. **But the word preached did not profit them**—it did not result in ultimate and final benefit—not because it was not properly preached, but because **the word** was **not . . . mixed with faith in them that heard it.** Hearing the Word is not enough; it must be believed and obeyed. No matter how much faith is in the speaker, there must be voluntary faith in the hearer. Faith must be combined with the Word as a kind of spiritual catalytic agent, in order for the gospel to bring salvation.

Verse 3 is obscure as it stands in the KJV, yet we may be sure that its true meaning ties it coherently into the thought begun in v. 1. The key idea is in the expression "seem to come short" (lag behind). Again the writer is referring, by means of one short phrase, to Ps. 95:8-11. In harmonizing the seemingly disparate ideas of v. 3 we can begin by correcting the rendering of this brief quotation. It should read, "I sware in my wrath that they shall not enter into my rest" (see Ps. 95:11); the **if** in this case is erroneous and the "not" has been omitted. Next we need to see that the three clauses are coherent and meaningful only when interpreted in the light not only of the immediate context but of the context of the entire psalm from which the quotation is taken. Further, to get the idea, it is necessary to suggest that the present indicative verb of the main clause, **we . . . enter into** (*eiserchometha*), should be construed as futuristic, "we shall enter into."

Who? Those of us who **have believed** (aorist) shall **enter into rest.** We who confess to be Christians, having once accepted Christ in true faith, are eligible to enter into the rest which remains for "the people of God" (9), providing we do not forfeit our eligibility by hardening our hearts. For according to the divine decree they (the stubborn resisters, the backsliders) **shall [not] enter into my rest** (3*b* corrected). This ultimatum that believers may and rejectors may not enter is true **although** (in spite of the fact that) **the works were finished from the foundation of the world.** As the next verse explains, **my rest** is related to the cessation of God's creative works. The reference at this point to the completion of these works implies that God from the beginning has desired to share His rest with His people; but they cannot enter without the obedience of faith, and as long as they will not believe, they are excluded, no matter how long God has waited.

To see the possible further connection between this reference to the finished works of God and the previous line of thought we need to read Psalms 95 in its entirety. The Psalmist is magnifying the greatness of God in His creative handiwork, and challenging his hearers to worship. But God's works do not include coercion. His finished works are sufficient evidence of His power to lead His people into their Canaan. However, this must not be interpreted as assurance that, no matter what we do, He will manage to get us there anyway. On the contrary, this very evidence of God's greatness leaves us utterly inexcusable in our fearful unbelief; it justifies His wrath in declaring that in spite of all He has done hitherto He will not now take us in (cf. I Cor. 10:1-12).

These vibrant paragraphs are a desperate attempt to shake the Hebrew Christians out of their false security, by showing them that they possess no immunity to the hazards of spiritual hedging. Psalms 95 is interpreted as a warning directed to the people of God—including these Hebrews themselves—against rebellion at their Kadesh-barnea crossroads.

2. *A Spiritual Rest* (4:4-10)

In using Psalms 95 as a warning against false confidence, and especially against rejecting new light, the writer interprets **my rest** as the plan and provision of God for His people. This is a rest typified by Canaan, and the crisis of entering is typified by Kadesh-barnea. The disastrous consequences of failing to enter have been shown. Now in these verses the nature of this rest is disclosed.

We have already seen the relevance to this rest of the reference in v. 3 to God's finished works. This is amplified at once. The writer quotes Gen. 2:2 (but as usual without specifying the reference): **And God did rest the seventh day from all his works** (4). In some manner this fact is associated with **my rest** (5). **It remaineth** (6), i.e., for His people to enter.

Since the generation of Moses' day lost their chance **because of unbelief,** God in His mercy has declared through David another opportunity. There is another **To day,** even **after so long a time** (7). Plainly the writer sees in Psalms 95 a special prophecy for the gospel age, a prophecy containing both promise and threat.

Nor could God's true rest be said to have been given by Joshua (**Jesus,** 8, KJV) when he took the next generation into the Promised Land and settled them in their own houses, with their own vineyards and fields. For if that national **rest** had been what God intended, **then would he** (God, not Joshua) **not afterward have spoken of another day.** Joshua did give the Israelites rest of a sort (Josh. 22:4) and that in fulfillment of a promise (Deut. 31:7); but that political, civil, and material rest in Canaan was not *the* rest—it was only a type of that rest. **There remaineth** (is yet to be experienced) **therefore a rest to the people of God** (9). God's people, in the new **To day,** have an option on a rest which they do not yet know by experience, but which they may know—indeed must know—or cease to be God's people.

Note the three strands that are here woven together. Strand one: God's **rest** and His finished **works** are related. Strand two: God's **rest** is spiritual in nature, not nationalistic. Strand three: The **rest** is now available, in this new **To day.** But KJV misses the meaning at this critical point, for the Greek says *sabbatismos,* "a Sabbath-state." The rest which remains is a Sabbath-state of the soul—certainly not of the body, for daily labor continues necessary. And surely this is not a reference to the seventh-day Sabbath, as the Adventists teach; that would be as bad a reversion to types, and as complete a missing of the reality, as the Jews who could see nothing beyond materialistic prosperity and political autonomy in the Holy Land. The meaning is clinched by the immediate explanation: **For he that is entered into his** (God's) **rest . . . hath ceased from his own works, as God did from his** (10). Everything in this section has been moving toward this definitive proposition. This delineates the Sabbath-state which is the rest of God remaining for His people. As a climactic statement it is masterfully devastating to the very essence of their Judaistic inclinations. Whether Paul wrote it or not, nothing could be more Pauline (cf. Rom. 10:1-11; Gal. 3:1-6; 4:9-31; Col. 2:20-23). Their very strong tendency to revert to Moses, or at least cling to him and to Jesus with shared allegiance, was in itself evidence of a reluctance to relinquish all forms of self-effort and rely solely on the finished work of Christ.

Note the exact import. God did not cease from His works of providence or redemption, but of creation. The believer who enjoys perfect rest has likewise ceased from his own works of creation, not in the natural or material order, but in the spiritual order (John 6:62-63). The Israelites at Kadesh-barnea sized up their prospects of entering Canaan in the light of their resources, and of course despaired. Then when they saw their sin they "presumed to go up," but again in their own strength, and were overwhelmed by the Amalekites (Num. 14:40-45). So always is the bankruptcy of the purely human in the spiritual realm. It cannot be faith and works. That is the way of anxiety and frustration—not rest. But the place of "quiet rest, near to the heart of God" is the place of self-crucifixion, of total surrender of self to God, of complete abandonment of our vain efforts either to create the kingdom of God on earth or to create holiness within ourselves. We must not only submit but commit. "Let go and let God."

3. *An Immediate Duty* (4:11-16)[25]

a. If a final fall is to be avoided (4:11). There is distinct progress of thought in Hebrews, with interlocking transitions,

[25]Note the expository sermonic title and its development under *a*, *b*, and *c*.

rather than abrupt, radical shifts. Often a transition verse belongs with that which has just been said, as its conclusion, and equally with the new idea it introduces. Furthermore, these transition verses are repetitive, almost cyclic, in form and idea, yet each with a keynote signaling advance. So here: **Let us labour therefore to enter into that rest, lest any man fall after the same example of unbelief** (11). Both this verse and v. 1 speak of entering into the rest, and have a similar form: **Let us . . . lest.**[26]

But in v. 1 the exhortation is to "fear," in v. 11 to **labour.** In v. 1 the warning was against even *seeming* "to come short of it," i.e., against the peril of reluctance and spiritual sluggishness. In v. 11 the warning is against the inevitable, ultimate result of such sluggishness (cf. 2:3)—a final and irrevocable fall—such as befell the Israelites in the wilderness. Mueller renders the last clause, "fall not in the same pattern of obstinacy."

There is only one way to avoid this disaster, and that is for us to "be zealous and exert ourselves and strive diligently" (Amp. NT). No one drifts halfheartedly into rest. It must be seen as an indispensable sphere of living,[27] immediate entry into which demands our complete concentration.

It may seem incongruous to have just defined this rest as a cessation of works (10) and to follow by urging entry by labor. How can labor be the means of entering a rest which is the end of labor? Of one thing the NT assures us; it cannot possibly mean to work hard on earth in order to make sure of our rest in heaven.

One answer is to say that repentance is spiritual labor, but a labor which terminates in the rest of forgiveness and the rest from bondage to the works of iniquity (Matt. 11:28). We may note that consecration—self-crucifixion—is also a labor, intense

[26]In both verses the verb *erchomai,* "to go," is aorist infinitive—definitely punctiliar—and is followed by the preposition *eis,* "into." This cannot possibly therefore be an exhortation to labor "toward," as some construe it. Note also the four hortatory subjunctives in this chapter: 1, 11, 14, 16. See Chamberlain, *op. cit.,* p. 83.

[27]Notice that the rest is not something we seek and find, or struggle to obtain, but something we enter into, as the Hebrews into Canaan. It is therefore to be conceived as a sphere of being and way of life, a true Sabbath-state; not so much that which we possess as that which possesses us.

and painful, but which swiftly becomes the rest of spiritual resurrection power, of abiding in Jesus by the Holy Spirit, and of freedom from the tyranny of an imperious, unyielded self. It is a rest from the slave-driving of a materialistic value-system; a rest in which our works, our autonomy, our rights, our plans and ambitions and restless strivings, are surrendered decisively and habitually. This attitude may be so habitual that the surrender becomes a settled and happy frame of mind (Matt. 11:29-30).

It should be noted that the primary meaning of *spoudasomen* followed by an infinitive is not **labour** but "hasten, make haste," and is so used in II Tim. 4:9, 21; Titus 3:12. While the idea of striving is included inferentially, the temporal sense is probably the intended emphasis here, as being more in agreement with the tone of the context. This tone is the same sort of immediate challenge as shouted by Joshua and Caleb, "Let us go up at once, and possess it" (Num. 13:30); and it is the same tone of intense urgency and immediate duty which again and again characterizes this Epistle. He who is willing to wait until tomorrow to enter into rest will never enter.

In 3:17—4:11 we find "The Rest for the People of God." (1) There is a promised rest, 4:9; (2) We must make an effort to enter this rest, 4:11; (3) Faith in God's call is essential, 4:2; (4) Some have missed it—failed to enter in, 3:17—4:1 (John Knight).

b. Because God's word still requires response (4:12-13). These verses which speak so vividly of the searching word of God do not refer primarily to the written word in the Bible (though the written word is by no means excluded); nor can they be properly understood in detachment from the previous discussion, as if they constituted a sudden digression in thought. They are essential to the total exhortation. **For** (*gar*) means "because." The writer does not want to be understood as being excessively preoccupied with actions of the ancient Israelites. The point in the object lesson is that they were trifling, not with the word of Moses or Joshua, but with **the word of God** (12). This is precisely the point of this urgent exhortation. God's word as voiced in David, and as more recently preached by Christ and the apostles, is not a dead letter but **quick** (living). It is in force right now. It is not like an old, disused power line; it is live at the moment God is speaking. The particular word heard by the Israelites was the will of God for them concerning

Canaan, whereas the particular word now demanding their attention is God's word concerning Jesus, and the rest which He desires that they should find in Him.[28] This is the word which God has spoken to the world "in these last days" by a Son (1:2); it is the gospel message of eternal salvation through Christ which He spoke through our Lord's own teaching, the apostles' teaching, and confirmed by the display of His power in signs (2:3-4); this gospel message is the voice predicted in Psalms 95 for this new "To day" (3:15; 4:1-2, 7-8). All of this is what is meant by "the Word that God speaks" (Amp. NT).

This divine **word** is not only alive, but **powerful,** i.e., active in convicting, searching, disclosing. As a **twoedged sword** the gospel message so pierces the hearer that **soul and spirit** are divided; i.e., one's spiritual self is separated from one's soulish self. One may be religious—but not saved. One may be sensitive to man, but dead to God. He may be cultured and alert in mind and body, yet atrophied and dormant in spirit.[29] He may know aesthetic ecstasy but not spiritual joy. The world around, with which he communicates through the windows of the soul, may be quite real, but the world of God and Christ very unreal. Such deadness the gospel discovers and calls to one's attention.

This cutting, penetrating power also divides **joints and marrow,** a figurative suggestion, possibly, that the gospel finds us not just on the level of our visible personalities but on the level of our invisible selves. It is in the marrow that diseases of the blood lurk long before the bodily mechanism is noticeably affected. People may walk straight, yet the bones may be diseased within, as a tree may stand tall until a violent storm sends it crashing to the ground, revealing its rotten core. And in this painful self-disclosure, the gospel is a **discerner of the thoughts and intents of the heart.** We sort out a man's words and deeds; the gospel, as **a discerner** (a judge), searches his motives and secret imaginations, and in searching passes judgment. In fact, "there is no created-thing" (Mueller) **that is not manifest in his sight;** everything is **naked and opened unto the**

[28]Sowers is probably in error in supposing that v. 12 is a Philonic style reference to the eternal Logos; yet it is a reference to the incarnate Son (*op. cit.*, p. 67).

[29]Sowers observes: "Heb. is evidently referring to the cleavage in the soul into which in Philo's thinking the Logos penetrates till it reaches the 'soul's soul,' whose essence is spirit" (*op. cit.*, p. 69).

eyes of him with whom we have to do (13). The expression **of him** refers to Him who is the subject of our discourse. Since we cannot hide from God, we cannot bluff at our Kadesh-barnea. Our failure to enter His rest cannot be kept from Him; indeed, not even our secret unbelief and feet-dragging, or our secret hankerings after the "leeks and garlic" of Egypt.

c. *Because Jesus will help us* (4:14-16). These verses constitute both a continuation of the hortatory discourse on rest and a recapitulation and summary of the entire first four chapters. We shall consider first the discourse on rest.

Having called attention to the inescapable, searching light of God's Word, the writer now redirects attention to their desperately needed High Priest—Jesus, the Son of God. The God about whom he has been speaking is the same God who rejected their ancient fathers in holy wrath; He is not to be trifled with, and will equally reject them. Therefore they should be glad for their High Priest, and speedily take refuge in Him. The awful, incriminating revelation of their hearts by God's Word is ground for fear, but Jesus' high priestly ministry is ground for hope. Therefore **let us hold fast our profession** (14). Let us cling to our personal faith in and public confession of Jesus as our Saviour. **For we have not an high priest which cannot be touched with the feeling of our infirmities** (15). Literally, Jesus can "feel-along-with our enfeeblements" (Mueller).[30] The word **infirmities** (*astheneiais*) has a moral connotation in Hebrews (cf. 5:2), and means not just a physical weakness or a human limitation but a conscious feebleness and trembling in temptation. Our Lord understands us in this weakness too, for He **was in all points tempted like as we are.** Since He was himself tempted, He knows by experience what it means for us to be tempted. He was not tempted in every particular, or in every possible situation; e.g., He was not tempted as a husband, or father, or property owner, or employer, or soldier, for He was none of these. But He was tempted in the three basic areas of human susceptibility: body, soul, and spirit. He knew temptation in the realm of *bodily appetite,* in the realm of *human relationships,* and in the realm of *spiritual relationships.* Self—others—God: He was tempted at all three points. By what was He to be ruled? His desire for bread? His desire for acceptance? His

[30]The infinitive *sunpathesai,* from *sunpatheo,* "to suffer with," is active, not passive. Jesus has a fellow feeling for us.

desire for power?—or His loyalty to God? These are the pivotal questions of life, which every man must answer. Surely in these basic issues our Lord's temptations were an exact likeness (*kath homoioteta*) to ours.

But **without sin.** Although it is perfectly true that Jesus did not face temptation with the handicap of original sin, this is not the idea here. It is rather that Jesus did not once yield. He was perfectly triumphant. If He had not been tempted as we are, He could not sympathize with us in our many temptations; but if He had not also been perfectly victorious, He could not help us, but would rather be in need of help himself.

There is more than a hint here that the peculiar temptation then being experienced by these Hebrew Christians was specifically in the writer's mind. They were tempted to draw back, and thus to fail to enter into their promised rest. Jesus had had also His wilderness experience—in a sense, His Kadesh-barnea—and therefore knew what they were going through. He understands the wilderness of Satanic buffeting which follows the first glorious flush of faith. Therefore, while they must not even seem to draw back, neither must they cow in shame, or yield to the paralysis of despair, but **come boldly unto the throne of grace, that we** (they) **may obtain mercy** (forgiveness for wavering), **and find grace to help in** this **time of need** (16).[31]

These verses are also a summing up of the entire argument thus far in the Epistle. Jesus is a great High Priest, for He is not an angelic order of being, or coordinate in rank with Moses, but is the Son of God, the very One who "sat down on the right hand of the Majesty on high" (1:3), or, as expressed here, **passed into the heavens** (14). **The throne of grace** to which we are bidden to **come boldly** in prayer is the throne not only of God the Father but of God the Son; not only of the One whose word is law but the One who became Mediator and Intercessor. The Jesus of recent history and the Jehovah of the OT are seen to merge into one God at one throne. There, at that throne, our sins are both condemned and pardoned. There we find both justice and mercy. There we find renewed access to the rest that remains to the people of God. But all of

[31]Or "for timely help" (Mueller). The double use of **grace** (*charitos*) illustrates its double meaning: the throne of *divine unmerited favor* is the place to which we come boldly; there we obtain *divinely imparted energy*, or moral strength.

this is mediated by Jesus. Our boldness is only in and through Him. If Jesus is not the Son of God, at the Father's right hand, having totally fulfilled and thus displaced the Mosaic order, our boldness is but brash presumption. It is the Father through Jesus, and it is rest through Jesus, or not at all. Thus does the writer establish the finality of the person of Jesus Christ.

Section II *The Finality of Christ's Priesthood*

Hebrews 5:1—7:28

A. A Perfect High Priest, 5:1-10

While the priesthood of Jesus has already been affirmed, the emphasis has been on the identity of Jesus' person. Now the weight of the emphasis shifts completely, almost abruptly, to His role as High Priest.

The mediatorial ministry of Jesus as both Priest and Sacrifice underlies the whole of Romans, and is found also in I Tim. 2:5-6; I John 2:1-2; and is implicit in I Peter and elsewhere; but nowhere is this meaning of our Lord's earthly assignment so carefully unfolded as in Hebrews. The truth would be especially important to the Jews, whose very life, not only religious but (in the absence of a king) civil and national, revolved around their high priest. He was the symbol of their national unity and hopes.[1] For Jesus to be all this in their thinking and emotions would indeed be a radical change. A conversion to Jesus that would so completely displace the high priest at Jerusalem that what happened there would no longer seem either relevant or important would be drastic and thorough indeed. But Hebrews insists that nothing less than this is acceptable to God, or consistent with the actual facts of the case. Unless and until these Hebrew Christians see the divinely appointed priesthood of Jesus in its full, revolutionary implications, and are entirely weaned from their Aaronic ties, their Christianity will be inadequate and in the end they will be recaptured completely by the long tentacles of Judaism.

It is understandable that the Hebrew Christians should at first be captivated (and their attention preoccupied) by the Messianic role of Jesus as Prophet and King. He was the Son of David, whose return to the earth in power was momentarily expected. It is also necessary that they grasp His office as Priest, and see that this provides the key which will unlock the mystery of His strange death—indeed, of the whole of His first coming. His earthly life and death were not abortive, but fulfilled exactly their predestined function.

[1]See Sowers, *op. cit.*, p. 120.

In grasping the priestly nature of Christ's ministry they will also come to see the essentially spiritual nature of salvation. Jesus came, not to drive out the Roman army of occupation, but "to put away sin by the sacrifice of himself" (9:26). This is the great need which must be met before any others can be.

Furthermore, this concept of Jesus as Priest will prove to be the key to the OT. The meaning and purpose of the Mosaic-Aaronic sacrificial system can now be disclosed. The enigma of the "holiest of all" can now be solved.

But in this disclosure the writer to the Hebrews carefully shows that Jesus, as a new and final High Priest, inaugurated in His own person and work a new covenant, which included at its very heart a new depth of experiential redemption: a personal privilege of personal holiness approached symbolically under the old regime but now entered actually by those who see Jesus on the Cross, not as a Roman victim, but as the Sacrifice for man's sin.

All of this must be seen as constituting the heart of Christianity. Without this there is neither holiness of heart nor hope of heaven. Without this the vision of Jesus as Prophet and King is empty of effectual content. As Prophet, He would not rise above His OT predecessors or escape the venerable oblivion of history. As a King, He would fade into a poetic and ethereal symbolism. Therefore the exposition of Jesus as High Priest is not optional; it is imperative.

1. *The Requisites of Priesthood* (5:1-4)

The function of a **high priest** is clear. Those **taken from among men** in the usual Aaronic order are **ordained for men**; set apart for this one divine calling, to minister **things pertaining to God** (1). The primary purpose of such ordination is that someone might officially **offer both gifts and sacrifices for** (in behalf of) **sins.** Sin is the one thing which separates men from God and makes some sort of priestly mediation necessary.[2]

[2]The distinction between **gifts** and **sacrifices** is not clear. The text could be translated "gifts and also sacrifices for sins." In this case the priest would be expected to lead in worship, offering up the gifts of consecration and praise, and also to offer propitiatory sacrifices, that sins might be forgiven and the conscience eased.

To be properly qualified for this important function of mediation and religious leadership the high priest needs to be of such personal character that he **can have compassion on the ignorant, and on them that are out of the way** (2). Sowers says that **have compassion** (*metriopathein*) "was a philosophical term referring to the proper mean between excessive passion and apathy."[3] The priest must not be harsh and impatient; neither must he be indifferent and unconcerned. There must be sharp and profound moral concern coupled with an understanding sympathy. Out of this balance in the true judge will come a clearer discernment of degrees of guilt, in distinguishing between responsible and involuntary ignorance, between those who are **out of the way** ("deceived," Mueller) due to their own carelessness and those who have been led astray through their naïveté. The propriety of such moderation in priestly judgment lies in the obvious fact **that he himself also is compassed with infirmity** (cf. 4:15).

Because of this moral weakness in himself, the Aaronic high priest **ought, as for the people, so also for himself, to offer for sins** (3). He himself was not beyond the need of mediatorial aid. It is clear that the traditional order of high priests had an official superiority but not necessarily a significant moral superiority. In function they were above the people; in spiritual need they were but sinful men, on the common level. This likeness to the sinfulness of their people may have inspired their sympathy but it also circumscribed their power to elevate the people to whom they ministered.

A further qualification of a legitimate priesthood is now stated (4). A high priest was not a self-appointed functionary. God had specified that only Aaron and his descendants should serve in this office (Exod. 28:1; Num. 16:39-40; 17:1-13; 18:1), as far as the earthly Tabernacle and the worship of Israel were concerned. But in this verse the writer carefully ignores the Aaronic lineage; only **he that is called of God, as was Aaron,** can have a valid priesthood. In other words, Aaron was an example of a divinely authorized priestly order; but though the Israelites were bound to this Aaronic order, God was not. The writer is now about to affirm a new and superior order of high priest, equally ordained of God.

[3]*Op. cit.*, p. 121.

2. *The Qualifications of Christ* (5:5-10).

a. A divine ordination (5:5-6). In the one thing that counted, Christ's priesthood was as valid as Aaron's: it was just as truly a divine appointment. **So also Christ glorified not himself to be made an high priest** (5). The explanatory intent of the following clause in 5 is not clear in KJV, but the sense is given by the *Amplified New Testament:* He "was appointed and exalted by Him who said to Him, You are My Son, today I have begotten You."

But sonship does not necessarily mean priesthood. So now a new text is presented, **a priest for ever after the order of Melchisedec** (6). This will underlie the next three chapters, just as the text "To day if ye will hear his voice" is the guiding theme of cc. 3—4. The same God who in the Scriptures, through the Holy Spirit, claimed the Messiah as Son also proclaimed His priesthood.

b. A personal fitness (5:7-10). The purpose of the Incarnation was stated concisely in 2:9, then explained more expansively in the verses which followed. So here Christ's complete fitness as High Priest is summarized, then developed in detail in the following chapters. The one leading idea here is the part our Lord's sufferings played in qualifying Him perfectly to be the Author of our salvation. The Aaronic priests could sympathize because they too were prone to sin. Jesus' sufferings served a like purpose, but even more effectively, for suffering gives compassionate and constructive fellow-feeling far better than sinfulness, which is intrinsically debilitating, hardening, and dividing—not in any sense truly redemptive. However, far more significant than simply inducing sympathy, Christ's sufferings were essential to His perfection as High Priest; by which perfection He was enabled to become **the author of eternal salvation,** the very goal which the Aaronic priests could not reach. Note the factors in His perfecting.

(1) *The prayers He offered* (5:7). The **days of his flesh** were the days of His humiliation, when in His humanity He felt a very real sense of weakness and dependence, as evidenced by His habitual life of prayer. This prayer-habit reached its moving climax in the struggle in the Garden of Gethsemane, when He **offered up prayers and supplications.** Since it was the duty of high priests to offer (lit., "offer up") "gifts and sacrifices" (1),

Jesus made an offering too. This was not a formal presentation in the Temple, but a bitter, blood-sweat offering of prayer in the garden; not perfunctorily, but **with strong crying and tears.** We are awed in the presence of this anguish reflecting the intensity of His grief. The content of His earnest petition is in the next clause: **unto him that was able to save him from death.** He was wrestling with His Father for personal deliverance. The exact nature of this **death** has long puzzled commentators, as has also the following clause, **and was heard in that he feared.** Clearly a proper understanding of this latter statement will help us understand the former. Therefore let us attend to it first. More literally, Jesus "was heard because of His devotion," i.e., godly reverence and submission.[4] **Heard** (*eisakouo*) usually implies an affirmative answer (Matt. 6:7; Luke 1:13; Acts 10:34; I Cor. 14:21). But it cannot mean that here, except in the sense that the Father listened with compassion and sent angels to minister to Him. The cup of death was not removed, for which we can be eternally grateful.

What was this **death** from which He sought deliverance with such anguished intensity? Some have seen a significance in the preposition *ek,* and have translated the phrase "out of death" instead of **from death,** drawing from this the inference that He feared permanent death. This is hardly likely in view of Jesus' repeated predictions of His resurrection; and surely He knew the Scripture which promised, "Neither wilt thou suffer thine Holy One to see corruption" (Ps. 16:10; Acts 2:25-31). Moreover, one is reluctant to suppose that our Lord, after setting His face steadfastly toward Jerusalem, and stepping daily toward His passion with poise and deliberation, should now pray with such agony to escape physical death on the Cross.

It is more likely that His soul shrank from the spiritual aspects of that death, its identification with sin and its solitary loneliness, as the Father hid His face. In some profoundly mysterious sense Jesus must have suffered, even though briefly, the pangs of a lost soul. He who had never known the taint of sin,

[4]It is very questionable if the phrase can properly be given the sense of "heard in respect to the thing feared," as have Berkeley, Phillips, and others. Arndt and Gingrich concede that such an understanding is possible, but do not favor it. Since only this writer uses the word *eulabeias,* "fear," and in the other instance (11:7) it obviously means "reverence," it is hardly likely that it would mean "dread" here.

or the shadow of the Father's frown, or the least estrangement from the Father's fellowship, was now, in becoming sin in our behalf, to suffer all of these as integral elements of His **death.** It would be impossible for a holy soul to face such a prospect with equanimity.[5]

(2) *The obedience He learned* (5:8). By means of these very **things which he suffered** He **learned** the true meaning of **obedience.** Yet our Lord had never been disobedient, nor had He ever a disposition to be so. How then could He learn obedience? Only in the sense that obedience which costs extreme anguish takes on a new dimension. With Jesus, love for the Father had been such that obedience was always a delight. There was never any hesitation, or sense of a painful price. But here an obedience was demanded wherein the issues touched the Father-Son relationship itself, a requirement which in its very nature could not be a delight but more like a punishment. When obedience is easy it may well be suspect. Perhaps it is disguised selfishness, or simply a policy of expediency. But when obedience costs a broken heart, its lesson has been learned and its genuineness authenticated.

This our Lord had to learn by personal experience, drinking the cup clear to the dregs, even **though he were a Son.** If the Son was going to be a saving High Priest, adequate for all the needs of men, He had to go all the way and qualify in every respect. Only a High Priest perfectly submissive to God could properly represent God to man or represent man to God. The dignity of Christ's person as Son could not exempt Him from the humiliation of suffering, if He was to fulfill His calling as God's Suffering Servant (Isaiah 53). The thoroughness of obedience and extremity of suffering implied in this verse would tend to support the exposition of v. 7 that His prayer was not "heard" in the sense that He was not excused from the "cup."

Grammatically everything so far in vv. 7-8 is subordinate to the main subject and predicate, **learned he obedience.** The sense therefore is that, in spite of our Lord's "strong crying and tears," and in spite of the fact that the Father heard them, and in spite of the fact that Jesus was the Son, it was necessary that

[5]For an excellent discussion of the various interpretations of this verse see H. Orton Wiley, *The Epistle to the Hebrews* (Kansas City: Beacon Hill Press, 1959), pp. 180-86.

He suffer in order to learn by experience the full absoluteness of obedience.[6]

(3) *The perfection He attained* (5:9-10). **And being made perfect,** or when His qualifications as High Priest were entirely completed (*teleiotheis,* aorist passive participle of *teleioo,* "to execute fully"), **he became the author of eternal salvation unto all them that obey him.** This is the second main clause of this long sentence (7-10). Though grammatically coordinate, in substance it is the apex of the passage, indeed the thesis of the entire Epistle. The writer will elaborate details later, but in its connections here the proposition is clear. Christ's becoming a perfect Saviour was contingent upon His personal perfection through obedience. Becoming a Son was the corporate choice of the Triune God. Becoming a Saviour was the achievement of the Son, in facing up triumphantly to the full demands of His humiliation.

It is probably safe, in the light of the context, as well as the aorist participle (having been **made perfect**), to reject the notion that Christ's perfecting included His actual death. This would mean in effect that, having died on the Cross, **he became the author of eternal salvation.** Rather we should say that His perfecting corresponded with Aaron's consecration as a necessary prior qualification for the performance of His priestly function.[7] Christ's perfection was consummated in the garden when He said, "Nevertheless not my will, but thine, be done." This was the final sealing act in His consecration, and every subsequent consecration of believers includes a similar submission. Having been thus qualified freely, He proceeded to the Cross, where **he became** (aorist tense—punctiliar) **the author of eternal salvation.** In the deepest sense Christ was not a Saviour until He died and rose again. His saviourhood, while

[6]**Though** (*kaiper;* 8) simply doubles the intensity of the buildup of emphasis which the **and** (*kai*) of the previous clause begins.

[7]Cf. Sowers, *op. cit.,* p. 113. It is also a mistake to see in Christ's actual death a typological correspondence with the animal sacrifices by which Aaron and his sons were consecrated, as does Sower. Rather, a closer type of His death was the Passover lamb (Exod. 15:5; John 1:29; I Cor. 5:7). This lamb was perfected by being slain in the sense that its purpose was thus accomplished; but it also had to be perfect in the sense of being "without blemish" as a prior qualification for its acceptable use as the Passover sacrifice. It is in this sense, we believe, that Hebrews is referring to Christ's perfecting.

based on His identity as Son, is nonexistent apart from Calvary and the Resurrection.

As **author** Jesus is Creator and Source of eternal salvation, the very kind which the Aaronic priesthood could not even mediate, let alone create. Mueller translates **author** as the "one-causing" salvation. To weaken Christ's role with the indefinite article ("*an* author"),[8] just because the definite article is lacking in the Greek, is unpardonable. Its absence indicates in this case a qualitative force (cf. 1:2), as would be intended by the words: "He became father to the whole neighborhood."

The word order in the Greek is different from that in KJV which misses thereby a note of emphasis. Literally, Christ "became to all who obey Him Author of eternal salvation." To those who disbelieve and disobey, Christ becomes on the Cross, not Saviour, but Judge. The conditional element of salvation, and of Christ's atonement, is never for one moment lost sight of in this Epistle. Though the initiation and provision of salvation come from God alone, its personal implementation most certainly requires the cooperation of man.

It is this perfected Son who has been **called of God an high priest after the order of Melchisedec** (10). The prior, prophetic call of God is proof that Christ's mighty action as High Priest was valid, in the sense that it was in perfect fulfillment of the Scripture and in accordance with God's precise plan.

B. The Need for Perfection, 5:11—6:20

The writer desires now to expound in greater detail the biblical nature of a Melchisedecan order of priesthood, but he hesitates, for he is not sure that his readers have sufficient spiritual maturity to comprehend this admittedly difficult subject. For the second time therefore he turns aside from his main line of argument to devote his attention to their own spiritual state and peril. In this hortatory passage we have rebuke, exhortation, warning, and encouragement, in that order.

1. *The Dullness of the Immature* (5:11-14)

The writer has **many things to say** about this little known OT character, Melchisedec, for he is a key figure in understand-

[8]Cf. Sowers, *op. cit.*, p. 92.

ing Christ's high priesthood. However, they are **hard to be uttered,** i.e., difficult to explain, because these Christians **are dull of hearing** (11). They are not *becoming* sluggish in their spiritual appetite and understanding; they have already become so (perfect tense), and their present state is the result of some failure in the past. He shames them: When by this **time ye ought to be teachers, ye have need that one teach you again** (12). Probably plenty of them posed as teachers, but were not qualified to do so (cf. I Tim. 1:5-7). They had so lost their grip on the verities of the Christian faith that they needed a refresher course in the *ABC*'s of the gospel, **the first principles of the oracles of God.**[9] They have reverted to their spiritual infancy, instead of becoming men, and **are become such as have need of milk, and not of strong meat** ("solid nourishment," Mueller). This disgraceful state of affairs is due, not to lack of time, for apparently they were not recent converts, but to lack of application.

The contrasting marks of babyhood and manhood are summarized sharply in 13-14. The one whose diet is confined to **milk** is naturally **unskilful in the word of righteousness,** for the obvious reason that **he is a babe** (13); and spiritual babes are expected to be pupils, not teachers. The **word of righteousness** may mean the gospel itself or the teaching of the gospel, probably the latter, since they have already been told they ought to have reached the teaching stage (12). **But strong meat belongeth to them that are of full age** (14). The Christian truths —particularly the Christological perspective of the OT, which does not lie on the surface—can be grasped and taught only by mature Christians. Such mature persons are now defined as **those who by reason of use have their senses exercised** (fully trained) **to discern both good and evil.** Their **senses** refers to their "inner-perceptions" (Mueller). A skill in discernment is therefore the hallmark of maturity. **Good and evil** may be either ethical or doctrinal; probably both ideas are included, though the context would suggest an immediate emphasis on truth and error in relation to Christ and the Scriptures. But two things are clear: (1) perfection in this passage can be defined as maturity;

[9]**Oracles** means utterances (cf. 4:12-13), and probably here corresponds to the "word" of 6:1—the fundamental teachings of the gospel, including the teachings of Christ and the apostles and the Christological exposition of the OT.

and (2) professed "maturity" which lacks reliable insight into good and evil is spurious.[10]

The translation of *dia ten hexin* as **by reason of use** implies that maturity is a gradual attainment by means of practice. But this is not exactly accurate. *Hexin* as a noun is "habitude," or a condition of body or mind. The meaning could be: The fully mature are those who because of their advanced spiritual state have their spiritual faculties fully trained. In other words, a minimum level of spiritual maturity is a prerequisite to habitual practice, as the practice in turn both evidences the maturity and enlarges it.

2. *The Call to Perfection* (6:1-3)

The diagnostic rebuke now becomes an exhortation. **Therefore**—on account of the need for maturity if the "strong meat" I am about to give you is to be assimilated—**let us go on unto perfection** (1). Some support can be found in the passage for interpreting the writer here as urging that he and they will now proceed to the *subject* of perfection. But the weight of contextual evidence favors rather the assumption that *teleioteta,* "a state of perfection," is the fulfillment of the diagnosed need of *teleios* in the previous verses.[11] The subject matter, already announced, which he is eager to get into, is the Melchisedecan nature of Christ's priesthood. Perfection will be included in that discussion, in relation to Christ's superior accomplishments, but this is not the subjective state of maturity which he here calls **perfection.**

Vincent identifies the verb *pherometha* as passive, and translates, "Let us be borne . . ." Mueller translates, "Let us move into maturity." The preposition **unto** (*epi*) implies "an actual state of resting upon."[12] The kind of maturity now meant is a realizable state to which one may press quickly, if one is determined to do so. The Hebrews should have attained this

[10]Here too Hebrews is Pauline, for Paul also notes discernment as a mark of spiritual maturity (I Corinthians 2). Cf. Sowers, *op. cit.*, p. 78, fn.

[11]Thomas Hewitt writes: "An exhortation is now given urging the readers to move away from spiritual infancy and to go forward to spiritual maturity" (*The Epistle to the Hebrews,* "Tyndale Bible Commentaries" [Grand Rapids: Wm. B. Eerdmans Publishing Company, 1960], p. 103).

[12]Chamberlain, *op. cit.*, p. 121.

stage by now, and are chided for not having done so. They are here exhorted to correct their spiritual deficiency promptly.[13]

This interpretation and action is far better than the alternative, which is constantly having to repair our spiritual **foundation.** This foundation is threefold, and each of the three is twofold: First, *personal salvation*—(*a*) **repentance from dead works** (probably sinful works is intended) and (*b*) **faith toward God** (trust *in* God—*epi* again). Some people never get beyond the concept of daily sinning and daily repentance, plus daily struggle with doubt and darkness. Second, *church ritual*—(*a*) **the doctrine of baptism,** and (*b*) **laying on of hands** (2). Third, *eschatology*—(*a*) the **resurrection of the dead** and (*b*) **eternal judgment.** These items constitute virtually the whole of the gospel in many churches today, with the result that most Christians never reach beyond the first grade in spiritual matters.

And this resolute moving forward from first principles to perfection **will we do, if God permit** (3). Only God knows how serious is their declension from Christ. If the first works really need to be done over again, they are not yet qualified for an advanced stage. But even more serious—if their declension has actually become apostasy, then their unqualification has become disqualification. The tone of the passage now becomes ominous.

3. *Not a Call to Apostates* (6:4-8)

The writer is not willing to believe that these Hebrews have gone so far as apostasy (cf. 9); therefore he describes a hypothetical situation, as impersonally and objectively as possible. But while hypothetical as far as the argument is concerned, it is not the hypothesis of an impossibility, or of a possibility which is never reality; therefore the warning must be allowed to carry its full weight.

There is no **If they shall fall away** (6) in the Greek, but rather one word, *parapesontas,* "having fallen away." Christians who have fallen away cannot be renewed—this is the simple import. But this kind of "falling away" is more than the backsliding of a feeble Christian who has been tripped up by Satan. When used alone, *pipto* (many times in NT) means a falling prostrate of the thing or person himself, but when used with *para,*

[13]The hortatory subjunctive (**let us**), by which the writer identifies himself with them, can be understood as a polite form of speech.

as in this case (here only in NT), it implies a separation between the thing or person and something else, a falling from. This is not a stumbling in the Christian way, but a departure from it. The word as here used can refer only to a deliberate rejection of Jesus Christ. Westcott says: "The idea is that of falling aside from the right path, as the idea *hamartanein* is that of missing the right mark."

It is simply **impossible** (emphatic position) **to renew them again unto repentance.**[14]

It is impossible to stir them up toward repentance. If they have gone this far, they won't even lay again "the foundation of repentance" (1), in which case it is idle to talk about going on to perfection. God will no more "permit" (3) them to experience genuine perfection than He would permit the rebellious Israelites to go into Canaan.

The impossibility of renewal to repentance lies not only in the defiant and deliberate nature of the defection, but in the guilt which their shameful apostasy is constantly compounding: **seeing they crucify to themselves the Son of God afresh, and put him to an open shame** (6). Not only have they ceased to weep because He bled for them, but their callousness has become such that they willingly provide in their own persons a new cross for a re-crucifixion. "They nail up on the cross the Son of God afresh, as far as they are concerned" (Amp. NT). It may not be done crudely, with rabble and loud cry, but by gentle professors whose nails are the dialectics of classroom unbelief. As long as men who once knew Christ are now shaming Him openly by their apostasy, renewal of genuine religious repentance is both a moral and a psychological impossibility.

Scores of pages have been written seeking to blunt the cutting edge of this passage by minimizing and diluting the former experience of these apostates, making it appear that they were dabblers and "surreptitious tasters," rather than once regenerate persons. But such evasive juggling of plain words is not worthy of an exegete of God's holy Scripture, and makes suspect the doctrinal premise which requires such sidestepping.

[14]Some have made it read "renew them again until (or without) repentance." But both textual and exegetical support seems completely lacking. A. T. Robertson says it "bluntly denies the possibility of renewal for apostates from Christ (cf. 3:12—4:2). It is a terrible picture and cannot be toned down" (*op. cit.*, p. 375).

Let us note honestly the sort of persons the writer says are in danger of such apostasy.

It is impossible to renew again to repentance the apostates who were once **enlightened** (4), both as having **tasted of the heavenly gift** and as having been **made** (aorist participle, passive voice) **partakers of the Holy Ghost.** The **heavenly gift** probably means salvation through Jesus Christ.[15] **Partakers of the Holy Ghost** are *metoxous,* "associates, fellows" (1:9; 3:1, 14; 12:8; cf. Luke 5:7). There was a definite time in the past when they were made partakers of the grace of God. Here is an enlightenment which cannot possibly be confined to mere conviction or temporary religious enthusiasm.

These apostates were, further, those who **have tasted** both **the good word of God, and the powers of the world to come** (5). The word **tasted** (*geusamenous*), used twice in these verses, is a conscious experience ("have consciously partaken of," Vincent). It can no more be reduced to the "sampling" of the idly religious than can the same word be reduced to a superficial dallying when applied to the death of Jesus (2:9; cf. Matt. 16:28; Mark 9:1; Luke 9:27; John 8:52). These then were men who had experienced (*a*) the joys of salvation, (*b*) the fellowship of the Spirit, (*c*) the nourishment and satisfaction of the Word (either written or preached), and (*d*) the confirmation and reinforcement of the supernatural. These experiences are the normal privileges and constituents of regeneration. Believers who are thus regenerate are still in peril of apostatizing finally and irrevocably.

The bedrock nature of the issue at stake is settled beyond possible cavil by the illustration with which the warning is concluded. When the soil responds to the rain from heaven and the toil of the farmer by producing the intended harvest, it **receiveth blessing from God** (7). But if it produces nothing but **thorns and briers,** it **is rejected, and is nigh unto cursing; whose end is to be burned** (8). It is abandoned as worthless land, and "condemnation is at hand, the end of which is for burning" (Mueller). This is a sad end; for it is *souls* to which the analogy is fully applicable; if this be not so, the passage is meaningless.

[15]Marvin R. Vincent sees the **heavenly gift** as the Holy Spirit, who is thus the object of both the tasting and partaking (*Word Studies in the New Testament* [Grand Rapids: Wm. B. Eerdmans Publishing Co., 1946], IV, 445).

Here is plainly divine blessing the continuance of which is dependent on the returns yielded on the investment (Matt. 13:22).[16]

4. *The Hebrews Still Eligible* (6:9-15)

The writer is convinced that the Hebrew Christians have not backslid so far as described in 4-8; though wobbling and hesitant, they are eligible to press on to perfection. Therefore, **though we thus speak** (9) solemnly, it is with hope and not despair. The **better things** are in contrast to the shameful betrayal of Christ in 6 and the barrenness in 7-8. Of the Hebrews he expects the responses which belong to **salvation.** He reasons that **God** would not be so **unrighteous** as to disregard their **work and labour of love,** displayed so zealously in behalf of **his name** (10). This is a labor which they not only have performed **to the saints** in the past but are still performing. Whatever weakening may have occurred within, it has not become outwardly apparent in any slackening of humble service rendered to fellow Christians. Outwardly their fidelity is flawless. They may be sure that God also includes this in His total evaluation, and has not yet, therefore, rejected them.

a. The need for diligence (6:11-12). The writer's fervent **desire** (11) is that **every one** of them, without exception, continue to **shew** (display—prove; cf. 10, also Rom. 2:15; 9:17) **the same diligence to the full assurance of hope unto the end.** The word *spoudan,* **diligence,** is used as a verb in 4:11, "Let us labour." There the objective demanding diligence is rest; here it is **the full assurance of hope.** Their works were maintained, but some of the assurance had drained out of their hope concerning Christ's (and their) future triumph. Just as they have been "careful to maintain good works" (Titus 3:8, 14), so the same diligence should be expended in maintaining the joyous certainty of the final outcome of things (3:6-14). Having lost their gladness and buoyancy, they were moping around like resigned but doggedly loyal martyrs to a lost cause. This is a dangerously unhealthy spiritual state. If they are not diligent in this respect they will become **slothful** (12). It is always one or the other,

[16]The series of present tenses is significant. Here is land which repeatedly receives rain from heaven, and drinks it in—repeatedly absorbing it selfishly—and repeatedly is dressed by the laborer (prophets and priests), yet just as repeatedly and persistently gives nothing back; such land can only merit wrath in the end.

diligence or decadence. When a congregation has lost the glory and the fire, it will soon lose the truth and the way.

Rather, be **followers** (imitators) **of them who through faith and patience inherit the promises.** They are still eligible to inherit the promises, but will not remain so unless they diligently follow in the footsteps of those who have earned their right to that inheritance by obedient faith and endurance of every test.

b. The example of Abraham (6:13-15). This reference to Abraham serves three purposes.

(1) It introduces the idea of the oath as a double security for the promises. **For when God made promise to Abraham, because he could swear by no greater, he swear by himself** (13). The significance of this act is discussed in vv. 16-20; see comment there. Here, as is often done, the writer is introducing a new line of thought simultaneously with the conclusion of his previous emphasis.

(2) The reference to Abraham also serves to indicate one of the promises. Only the abstract is quoted, **Surely blessing I will bless thee, and multiplying I will multiply thee** (14). The full promise is in Gen. 22:16-18, and includes the Messianic reference, "In thy seed shall all the nations of the earth be blessed." The promise of great blessing upon the Hebrew people was a rock of hope to which every Jew clung. That promise was still good. This is the one point now being made. Later they will be shown that this is only one of the promises (plural, v. 12) and that this and all others are being fulfilled abundantly in Christ, but only in Him (exactly the line of interpretation taken by Paul in Gal. 3:5-9, 16-18).

(3) The most immediate purpose in these three verses is to illustrate what is meant by inheriting the promises "through faith and patience" (12). **And so** (you see what I mean) **after** Abraham **had patiently endured, he obtained the promise** (15). The patient endurance was Abraham's obedience in offering up Isaac. In this he met the supreme test of unflinching loyalty to God. It is the imitation of this kind of daring obedience that is being urged in v. 12. **The promise** being discussed, therefore, is not God's promise to Abraham of a son; that had been fulfilled. It was rather the promise of great blessing upon the Hebrew people. This was **the promise** Abraham obtained as a reward for his patient endurance. He did not see this great blessing; he only obtained the promise of it. Therefore we see the mean-

ing of the phrase "inherit the promises" in v. 12 (cf. c. 11). The idea is intriguing. Inheriting goods we are familiar with—a family business, name, or title, with its rights and privileges—may seem exciting. But inheriting promises seems unimportant, especially if they have been passed down through many generations and still appear unfulfilled. However, the writer is striving to show that these promises are by far the most priceless portion of their racial heritage, which they must not forfeit by slothfulness and unbelief.

5. *The Immutability of the Promises* (6:16-20)

The writer will now reason that they have every incentive to take heart and press on, since the promises are not only still valid, but backed by the greatest possible security, God's own oath. Reference was made to this in 13, but now further explanation is given.

a. God's oath (6:16-17). **For men verily swear by the greater** (16), i.e., someone greater than they, who can back them up, and also enforce fidelity to their word. **Such an oath** was a solemn affirmation before witnesses in the name of this higher person or power, which in Bible times was legally binding. No matter how men might squabble on an informal basis, once a promise or transaction was confirmed by an oath (**oath for confirmation**) the matter was considered settled, and **all strife** was ended. In this way, **to shew . . . the immutability of his counsel** (plan), God **confirmed it by an oath** (17). This oath was prompted by His willingness more abundantly to show the inviolability of His purpose. He went the "second mile," so to speak to prove the sincerity of His intentions. This was not unthropomorphic legend; it was rather God accommodating himself to man's way of doing and thinking in order to communicate. The Bible is full of this sublime humility of a mighty God. Naturally there would be absurdity in supposing that God swearing by himself added one whit to the integrity of His word, but it was an impressive mode of communicating **unto the heirs of promise** (lit., "the promise," which has already been quoted in 14). **The heirs** would include the Jews who qualified as spiritual heirs in Christ—and, according to Paul, believing Gentiles as well.

b. Our hope (6:18-20). God's purpose was **that by two immutable things, in which it was impossible for God to lie, we**

might have a strong consolation (18). The two unchangeable things were the integrity of God's own word in His simple promise and the self-imposed legal obligation of the oath. The **strong consolation** is the "strong assurance" (Mueller) which they are to diligently preserve (11). Their diligence therefore is not the feverish energy of the flesh in propping up faith; it is rather the devotion and concentration with which they keep ever before them the divine promises and the ground of their absolute security in them. The **we** who are entitled to this happy assurance are those **who have fled for refuge** (in Jesus) **to lay hold upon the hope set before us.**

Through Christ we have grasped Israel's hope anew. The **hope** is **an anchor of the soul, both sure and stedfast, and which entereth into that within the veil** (19). The content of the truly biblical Jewish hope was not in an earthly paradise with political domination of the world, as it was so often misconstrued; instead it was dwelling in the eternal presence of God. The deep hope of a spiritually minded soul was to penetrate the mysteries behind the veil (Lev. 16:2)—"a hope that reaches farther and enters into the very certainty of the Presence within the veil" (Amp. NT). Into this holiest of all our **forerunner is for us entered, even Jesus, made an high priest for ever**[17] **after the order of Melchisedec** (20). Jesus has gone into "the Holiest," not as a substitute for our access but as a **forerunner,** for we are to enter also. The writer will have much more to say about this "Holiest," and the way Christ opened for us. But now, having digressed long enough to incite them to greater diligence and to press on to spiritual maturity at once, he returns to the main thread of his argument, and takes up again the role of Jesus as High Priest, not of the Aaronic order, but **after the order of Melchisedec.** Undoubtedly the writer hopes that his exhortation has conditioned them to receive the difficult truths he wishes now to convey.

C. The Priesthood of Perfection, 7:1-28

It is wise to remind ourselves, as a sort of reorientation, of the writer's daring and revolutionary purpose. He is building

[17]"Having become an high priest"—the verb is perfect tense. He did not become a High Priest by taking His place at the right hand of the Father. Though there is an ongoing intercessory ministry (7:25), His office was assumed on earth.

an exegetical and logical position intended to shatter totally any remaining dependence on Judaism, as such. He must convince these Hebrew Christians of three things.

First, that the priesthood of Christ completely destroys and displaces the whole monolithic structure of Jewish priesthood and Temple worship. There can no longer be a temporizing with the concept of coexistence. The old bottles cannot hold the new wine, nor the old garment be patched up. The old is finished, abandoned by God, and it must be abandoned by Christians.

Second, Jesus Christ in His priesthood inaugurated a new covenant between God and His people, making the old covenant as obsolete as its ritualistic and priestly forms. This new covenant is the fulfillment of the typical meaning of the old, and likewise the fulfillment of the great OT predictions of such a replacement. It should therefore be no surprise to them, but should be embraced readily and with thanksgiving. This new covenant is qualitatively superior to the old in every respect, since it includes the substance instead of the shadow. This substance is essentially a personal perfection of the worshiper, described variously as rest, access into "the Holiest," and sanctification.

Third, the person and work of Christ are final, and cancel all other options. Having known Christ, they cannot go back. They cannot again find in Moses shelter from the wrath to come. To attempt to do so will result in judgments and eternal consequences far exceeding in woe anything that the race had experienced previously through disobedience.

In establishing this sort of case the writer's reasoning is thoroughly Jewish. Many elements have an affinity with Alexandrian Jewish Hellenism, as represented by Philo, yet others are compatible with the Rabbinical hermeneutics of Jerusalem. One point of agreement with both was his very high view of the OT as the divinely inspired Word of God. Nothing was superfluous or without meaning.[18]

But Hebrews differs from either Philo or the Palestinian

[18]His concept of Scripture as the "oracles of God" (5:12) means simply that "God is thought of [or in some passages Christ himself] as the direct speaker in the Scripture passages cited in 1:5, 6, 7, 13; 4:3; 5:5; 6:14; 7:17, 21 (cf. 5:6); 8:5, 8-12; 10:30, 37, 38; 13:5" (Sowers, *op. cit.*, p. 76). This may explain why he does not normally cite the human author or reference. Cf. also Sowers, *op. cit.*, pp. 82, 124.

Jews in the basic hermeneutical principle which underlies the whole letter, namely, that Christ is the key to the interpretation of the Jewish Scriptures. "For Hebrews," says Sowers, "the true meaning of the Bible is not unlocked by an inspired exegete, as in Philo's case, but rather by Christ toward whom the whole OT is directed."[19] He therefore sees proof texts which might not be recognized as such by an exegete looking through a different hermeneutical lens. But there is every reason to believe on both historical and theological grounds that in this he was faithful to the principle introduced by Christ himself on the walk to Emmaus (Luke 24:27) and which similarly structured the thinking of the apostles and the Early Church.

In the next several chapters, therefore, he interprets Christologically several texts. The first—and possibly the most crucial—is Ps. 110:4: "The Lord hath sworn, and will not repent, Thou art a priest for ever after the order of Melchizedek." On this verse will depend his polemic that Christ is legitimately a High Priest, appointed by God, but of a different and superior order than the Levitical, and hence displacing that Levitical order forever. He has already quoted the text (5:6) and referred to it twice (5:10; 6:20). He is now ready to enlarge.

1. *The Order of Melchisedec* (7:1-10)

The author reviews (1-2*a*) the basic facts given to us in Gen. 14:18-20. Then he begins an interpretation of the identity of this mysterious figure.

a. The pattern of his priesthood (7:2*b*-3). Significance is seen first in his name, **being by interpretation King of righteousness** (2). But importance is also attached to the fact that he is **King of Salem, which is, King of peace.** Here is typological correspondence with Christ at the outset in the subtle reminder that peace follows righteousness and cannot exist without it.

The delineations **without father, without mother, without descent, having neither beginning of days, nor end of life** (3), are to be understood in reference to the order of Melchisedec's priesthood, not his physical person. In the mind of a Jew, schooled in strict Levitical ideas, it was unthinkable that anyone should serve as a priest who was not of priestly parents, with

[19]*Op. cit.*, p. 79.

an unchallenged **descent** (genealogical record). Yet it was none other than the inspired writer Moses himself who labeled Melchisedec "priest of the most high God" (Gen. 14:18); and he was thus acknowledged even though all formal credentials were lacking. He had no official pedigree. There was no record of his birth date or the date of his death. In these respects he was **made like unto the Son of God,** who was equally without normal priestly pedigree.

The important thing to be emphasized is that this Melchisedec **abideth a priest continually.** Here is the fundamental proposition. All else is subordinate and delineating. First the facts of history are restated. Then the typological pattern is drawn, largely as an argument from silence. And the essential ideas which the writer will press are (1) this is certainly a non-Levitical order of priesthood, (2) a superior order, and (3) a priesthood which is characterized by perpetuity.[20]

b. The greatness of his priesthood (7:4-10). **Now consider how great this man** (lit., this one) **was, unto whom even the patriarch Abraham gave the tenth of the spoils** (4). The next two verses are obscure in the KJV, but a re-translation may clarify the meaning: "And admittedly they who are of the sons of Levi, having received the priesthood, have a commandment (or authority) to collect tithes from the people according to the law; these are their brethren, completely descended from Abraham. But he who is without genealogical record among them received tithes of Abraham, and blessed him who had the promises" (5-6).

The aim here is to show the superiority of Melchisedec's order of priesthood to the Levitical. Having implied that the spectacle of their father Abraham paying tithes to him proved this greatness, the writer quickly in 5 and 6 anticipates the possible rejoinder that Abraham also pays tithes to Levi through his descendants; therefore Levi is equally great. But this is a requirement of law, not a voluntary homage; and moreover, Levi himself is equally a descendant of Abraham, which makes it a

[20]Sowers understands Hebrews to ascribe the "for ever" of Ps. 110:4 literally to Melchisedec as well as to Christ. "Unlike mortal priests Melchisedec 'lives' (7:8)" (*op. cit.*, p. 124). But to suppose the historical man who met Abraham was literally without beginning of days or end of life would be to ascribe Godhood to him. It is not necessary so to interpret the Epistle (cf. Wiley, *op. cit.*, p. 232).

family matter, and thus "greatness" because of the "right" is cancelled out. But Melchisedec was completely an outsider, not entitled by law to collect tithes from Abraham as part of a utilitarian, domestic system; therefore for him to receive tithes was evidence of a special act of reverence on Abraham's part. In other words, Levi cannot claim equal greatness simply because he collects tithes, since the circumstances governing the act of tithing are so different.

Even beyond that, Melchisedec **blessed him that had the promises** (6). This is the clincher, for **without all contradiction the less is blessed of the better** (7). This would be self-evident; for the father blesses his son, the elder the younger, the priest the people, the king his subjects—never the other way around. The position of receiver is inferior to the position of giver, for receiving acknowledges weakness and need, whereas giving testifies to power and affluence. In paying tithes Abraham was paying homage—it was a religious act—while in receiving Melchisedec's blessing he was accepting the position of beneficiary. Hence on both counts he was proven subordinate to Melchisedec. Yet he is the very one who had been given by God promises of racial greatness and world usefulness through his own seed. Therefore the promises themselves could be said to be subject to the blessing of Melchisedec. If we but anticipate by seeing Jesus here as Melchisedec, we shall see the profound implication the Epistle is driving at from beginning to end.

The contrast between Levi and Melchisedec is carried yet further. The Levitical priests are **men that die**—they are mortal—but in that ancient case one received tithes **of whom it is witnessed that he liveth** (8). The "witness" seems to be inferential, based on Ps. 110:4. The logic is that if Christ's priesthood is to be forever, and at the same time according to the order of Melchisedec, than this order of priesthood must have been established forever. Therefore Abraham was paying tithes to one who represented, not a succession of priests, but a kind of priesthood which is perpetually vested in one ever-living Person. This kind of priesthood is obviously superior to the Levitical.

The writer now takes a final fling at the Levitical self-importance by resorting to a tongue-in-cheek twist. **And as I may so say** is the introductory phrase, literally, "So to speak a word." According to Chamberlain, this "introduces a hesitant statement. It indicates that the writer does not want to be understood literally";[21] therefore we cannot translate this statement into a serious principle applicable to the transmission of original sin. But here is a final rejoinder to the Levites' own rejoinder, using their kind of argument. If it could be said that Abraham paid tithes to Levi through his descendants—therefore Levi was as great as Melchisedec—it could equally be said that Levi paid **tithes in Abraham. For he was yet in the loins of his father, when Melchisedec met him** (9-10). This might be called a *reductio ad absurdum,* but surely an effective squelch.

It is apparent that the writer attaches great importance to the proposition that the priestly order of Melchisedec far eclipses that of Levi. To establish this polemical stake is to effectually secure his entire position, for this carries far-reaching implications respecting Christ. He now proceeds to state some of these implications, and in so doing is sounding the death knell to the whole Levitical system.

2. *The Old Order Displaced by the New* (7:11-22)

a. The impotence of the Levitical order (7:11). The various implications terminate in the basic question of **perfection,** which in this context is aptly defined as a "perfect fellowship between God and the worshipper" (Amp. NT). This is an exact delineation, seen from the conceptualism of "the Holiest." But it includes also (as seen from the conceptualism of the new covenant) personal sanctification, which alone can provide a moral basis for such fellowship. Both phases are expounded in due course. But now it is assumed that such perfection is of necessity, by its very nature, the goal and end of all religion. To the extent any system (including the Levitical) falls short of providing such perfection, to that extent it is inadequate and temporary.

The Jews supposed that their access to God through their Temple worship represented the high-water mark of possibilities. But if **perfection were by the Levitical priesthood . . . what further need was there that another priest should rise?** The logic is unanswerable. The parenthetical remark, **for under it the people received the law,** indicates that God gave the law to the Israelites through the mediation of this priesthood; therefore

[21]*Op. cit.,* p. 173.

its priests had whatever opportunity they would ever have to demonstrate the saving efficacy of their ministry. A divinely ordained priesthood mediating and administering a divinely given law— would not such a combination be adequate in achieving perfection? But the announcement of a new order proves that it was not. The Levitical order was not so intended or designed.

b. The annulment of the Mosaic law (7:12-19). But this carries with it a consequence equally jolting: **the priesthood being changed** (or "if the priesthood is changed," a conditional circumstantial participle), **there is made of necessity a change also of the law** (12). One implies the other. **For he of whom these things are spoken,** i.e., Jesus, came from **another tribe, of which no man gave attendance at the altar** (13), nor was permitted to do so, under penalty of death. That **our Lord sprang out of Juda** is well-known; but of this **tribe Moses spake nothing concerning priesthood** (14). Notice here that the writer is talking, not about Levi or Aaron, but about Moses. Back of the Levitical order of priesthood was the whole Mosaic law-system. If one collapsed, the other collapsed with it. If God made obsolete the Aaronic priesthood by a new priestly order, He also made obsolete the law-system by which the Aaronic priesthood derived its authority. Yet as shattering as this is, we must face it, for **it is yet far more evident** (indisputable) . . . **that after the similitude of Melchisedec there ariseth another priest, who is made, not after the law of a carnal commandment, but after the power of an endless life** (15-16). The text, Ps. 110:4, is proving to be an unyielding anvil on which the Mosaic system is being, not refashioned, but destroyed.

Two phrases in these verses must be especially noticed, **after the similitude of Melchisedec** (15) and **after the power of an endless life** (16). **After** (*kata*) means "according to." The word **similitude** (*homoioteta*) or "likeness" sheds light on *taxin*. This has been consistently translated **order** in KJV, as in the text (about to be re-quoted in 17), **Thou art a priest for ever after the order of Melchisedec.** Mueller ascribes to this word the meaning of "rank," and undoubtedly Christ's rank does supersede that of Aaron. But the idea of rank is not precisely the idea of Hebrews, and **order** comes closer. Here the writer is apparently using **similitude** as a synonym.

What is being taught is not so much a difference in rank as a radical difference in pattern or kind of priesthood. Hence the stress on its non-genealogical nature, but most of all on its perpetuity. And so the climactic fact, the **power of an endless life,** is set over against **the law of a carnal commandment.** Here is the central note of this new order, which is like that of its type, Melchisedec. This is why, also, the emphasis in interpreting the chapter should not be on the man Melchisedec, as a mysterious historical character, but on the order or kind of priesthood which he represents. If we try to ascribe 7:3 and 8 literally to the man, we are plunged into well-nigh inextricable difficulties, but if we ascribe them to the order which the man represents, we have no serious problem. We must remember that the one scripture which lifted Melchisedec out of obscurity to doctrinal significance (Ps. 110:4) attached that significance only to his role as a type of the priesthood of Christ. The important person in Ps. 110:4 is not Melchisedec but "Thou" (Christ). And the one idea inescapably conveyed is that the Messiah was to serve as Priest as well as King, a new kind of Priest, superseding and displacing the Aaronic order, as well as a new kind of King.

The writer finally reaches a blunt statement of what has been implicit all along: **For there is verily** ("there has come to pass") **a disannulling of the commandment going before** (the previous commandment) **for the weakness and unprofitableness thereof** (18). Through the superseding work of Christ the Mosaic law has become invalid. The **commandment** here corresponds to **the law of a carnal commandment** (16), which is **carnal** (fleshly) not in the sense of being evil, or of human origin, but in the sense that it concerns physical and external legalities, such as genealogies.[22] **Law** here would be "operation" (similar to **order, 17**), and thus the phrase would simply mean "not according to the pattern of these impotent and temporal externalities." The commandment prescribing priestly qualifications and activities is annulled (displaced, set aside) because of its inherent weakness. It was impotent in doing the main thing in man which needed to be done. **For the law** (of Moses, including the commandment governing the priesthood) **made nothing perfect** (19). It brought nothing to fruition, nothing to its proper level, neither the priests nor the people, neither the worship nor the worshipers.

We have cause for everlasting rejoicing in the fact that there follows one of the most pivotal adversative conjunctions in

[22]Sowers, *op. cit.*, p. 100.

the Bible—**but the bringing in of a better hope did.** While **did** is not expressed in the Greek, it is implied. In this case the sense of **a better hope** is a better basis or ground of hope. Under the old order there was law, but little to incite spiritual hope, for either holiness or heaven. But by this superior basis of hope (which is Christ) **we draw nigh to God.** Vincent says: "Christianity is the religion of good hope because by it men first enter into intimate fellowship with God. The old priesthood could not effect this."[23] Hope is a better incentive to prayer than is fear.

c. *The inauguration of a "better" testament* (7:20-22). The writer is continuing to draw out the implications of his text (Ps. 110:4). There are yet two more points to his exposition, both introduced by **And** (20, 23). The conclusion to be noted in vv. 20-22 is that **Jesus** was **made a surety of a better testament.** But the degree of superiority is based on the single fact, reviewed parenthetically in 21, that **those priests were made** (constituted priests) **without an oath** (21), but Jesus **not without an oath** (20). The writer has been considering the main proposition of his text, but now he draws out the significance of the first part. **The Lord sware and will not repent** (21). This emphasis is achieved forcefully by the use of two pronouns, *hoson,* **inasmuch as** (20), and its correlative, *tosouto,* **by so much** (22). Thus **inasmuch as** should be read with **by so much,** and it will be seen that the difference between priestly ordination without an oath-swearing (*horkomosias*) and with such an adjuring is the measure of the superiority of the new testament over the old. In the mind of the writer this difference is great, possibly due to two considerations: First the element of finality in the very nature of an oath-taking; and second, the nature of the One taking the oath. It is not God administering the oath to the Son, which in that case would be the Son promising to discharge His duties; it is God taking the oath himself, promising to establish the Son's individual priesthood forever. Such an obligation was never assumed in Aaron's case. And the **testament** (covenant) mediated by a prietst thus superior must in itself be equally superior. By the oath therefore Jesus becomes God's **surety** (pledge) of this new and better covenant.[24]

[23]*Op. cit.,* p. 463.

[24]Vincent says that the classic derivation of *enguos,* **surety,** implies one who gives security, and in reference to a wife, one who is plighted. "The idea underlying . . . is that of putting something into one's hand . . . as a pledge" (*op. cit.,* p. 464).

3. *A Perfect Salvation in a Perfected Saviour* (7:23-28)

The last point the writer draws out of his text is climactic. He has examined the various strands of truth in the Melchisedecan nature of Christ's priesthood; now he ties them together.

a. A perfect power to save (7:23-25). Not only does the contrast between the new priesthood (Christ's) and the old rest on the oath (or its absence) but on the fact inferred and confirmed by the simple facts of history. **They truly were many priests, because they were not suffered** (permitted) **to continue by reason of death** (23). **But this man** (Christ), **because he continueth ever, hath an unchangeable priesthood** (24). If Christ lives forever, His priesthood is forever—He "has the priesthood (which is) not-passing-away" (Mueller). There will be no other priest succeeding Him, to carry on His work and perhaps carry it further. He is the last. Therefore His priesthood is final and complete. **Wherefore** (because of this) **he is able also to save them to the uttermost that come unto God by him, seeing he ever liveth to make intercession for them** (25). The durative present tense of the infinitive *sozein,* **to save,** corresponds with the present participle, **ever liveth.** Because He ever lives He can ever save—every sinner in every generation, and in every situation of need. There is no exhausting of His resources. The power to save is in himself, and because He lives, the power is always there. Verse 16 spoke of "the power of an endless life." The nature of that power is now pinpointed—it is power to save men. The connection between His power to save and His intercession is also significant. He lives purposefully—"to plead their case" (Mueller).[25]

Christ secures for us not only deliverance from the sentence of death, which our sins deserve, but from the depravity of our nature. The word **uttermost** (*panteles*) discloses the degree of

[25]Of our Lord's intercession Vincent says, "The idea is not intercession, but intervention" (*op. cit.,* p. 465). Westcott comments, "Whatever man may need, as man or as sinful man, in each circumstance of effort and conflict, his want finds interpretation (if we may so speak) by the Spirit and effective advocacy by Christ our (High) Priest . . . in John 17 we find the substance of our highest wants and of Christ's intercession . . . the advocacy of Christ is both social and personal: for the church and for each believer, for one because the other" (*op. cit.,* p. 192).

this deliverance.[26] It is complete, without strings or reservations. It is not a "suspended sentence" or partial cleansing but a full justification and rectification (Rom. 8:14).

Subsequent discussions will show more clearly that perfect salvation from condemnation involves perfect salvation from all sin. Furthermore, this perfect power to save perfectly is the essence of the better testament—this also the writer will make clear.

Any sin in the believer's heart is proof of an imperfect salvation, and the defect must be either in the Saviour or in the believer. Since it cannot be in the Saviour, and certainly is not a deficiency in His promises or provisions, it must be a deficiency in appropriation. This truth is implied by the phrase that marks the one limitation of our Lord's power: Those who **come unto God by** (through) **him.** To bypass Jesus is to forfeit His salvation. His saving ability is confined to those who approach God on Calvary grounds, but it is not limited in its power within those who do so approach. Those who are yet defeated by sin have not yet come properly.

This passage suggests: (1) A living Saviour—**ever liveth;** (2) An adequate Saviour—**able also to save them to the uttermost;** (3) A restricted Saviour—**them . . . that come unto God by him.**

b. A perfected Person who saves (7:26-28). The writer has established the radical and revolutionary position inherent in

[26]The word translated **uttermost** is from *pas,* "all," and *telos,* "perfect," meaning perfect and complete. The word is used only here and in Luke 13:11, where it is found with the negative. This compound word is the strongest expression of thoroughness. It may well be translated "able to save them perfectly," referring not only to its durability, but to its immediate thoroughness. Christ's ability reaches down into the heart as well as out into eternity; He is able to save from sin now as well as from hell later, to cleanse as well as to sustain. Vincent says most emphatically: "all-complete . . . Not perpetually, but perfectly" (*ibid*).

Westcott says: "If Christ's priesthood had failed in any respect then provision would have been made for some other. But, as it is, the salvation wrought by Christ reaches to the last element of man's nature and life . . . the thought here is not of 'the world,' (John iii. xvii) but of believers: not of salvation in its broadest sense, but of the working out of salvation to the uttermost in those who have received the gospel. Thus the present (*sozein*) as distinguished from the aorist (*sosai*) has its full force. The support comes at each moment of trial." Speaking of the phrase *eis to panteles* he comments, "The old commentators strangely explained it as if it were *eis to dienekes—perpetually*" (*ibid.,* p. 191).

Ps. 110:4. Nothing more will be said about Melchisedec, but much more about the One whom the Father addressed in that remarkable pronouncement. Jesus is our High Priest, and He alone is sufficient for us because He alone has every requisite qualification. **For such an high priest became us** (26), i.e., was exactly suited to our every need. In what respects? He **is holy, harmless** ("without-evil," Mueller), **undefiled, separate from sinners, and made higher than the heavens.** Here are five marks. The first three witness to His personal qualifications and character: **holy** in heart, **harmless** in conduct, and **undefiled** in conscience. But the last two speak eloquently of the perfect accomplishment of His office—"having been separated" (perfect participle) **from sinners,** and "becoming" (present participle, middle voice) **higher than the heavens.** This separation probably is a reference to the eight-day solitude required of the high priest before making atonement once a year in the holy of holies. It is used figuratively here, for Christ's separation from sinners was moral, not social; it was lifelong, not temporary. Nevertheless the figure speaks of His full fitness for the supreme act of entering "the Holiest" in our behalf. As a consequence He is established in the supreme place of authority. Thus is epitomized both His *humiliation* and His *exaltation* (Isa. 52:13—53: 12; Phil. 2:9), and thus also is affirmed His *essential deity,* as every devout Jew would perceive (Ps. 108:5).

Because of His personal qualifications of character, He **needeth not daily, as those** other **high priests, to offer up sacrifices, first for his own sins, and then for the people's** (27). Here is a hint that the daily ritual of sacrifices was a necessary supplement to the great Day of Atonement because of continued daily sinning, as well as the insufficient efficacy of the annual atonement. But the stress here is that as far as Jesus was concerned such daily repetition was unnecessary. **For this he did once, when he offered up himself.** The **this** should be construed with the high priest's second sacrifice, i.e., for the people, since the first, i.e., **for his own sins,** was not needed. And **once** was enough, since the Sacrifice was himself. (Cf. 9:24—10:18.)

For the law maketh men high priests which have infirmity (28). Of this they have already been reminded (5:1-3). The word **infirmity** (*astheneian*) here, as in 4:15; 5:2; and 11:34, has a moral overtone, and speaks chiefly of the weakness which required those other high priests to offer sacrifices first for their own sins. It is a proclivity to sinning, which we can identify as original sin. *Having* ***infirmity,*** observes Vincent, is stronger than ***infirmity,*** which alone "might imply only special exhibitions of weakness, while *having infirmity* indicates a general characteristic."[27] This is the best the law can do—let sinners minister in a muddling sort of way to sinners—for until Jesus came there was no other choice.

But the word of the oath, which we have been expounding, **which was since the law,** i.e., came after, superseded, and outmoded the law, **maketh the Son, who is consecrated for evermore** (28). The Greek is elliptical here, but the KJV is correct in letting the main verb **maketh** ("constitutes"—Mueller) serve in both cases. But the KJV rendering of the last clause is not so clear. Literally it reads, "Son evermore having been perfected." Does it mean "having been made perfect forever" (Amp. NT), or is the Son constituted a Priest forever because He has been perfected? Mueller renders it with the latter sense, ". . . the law (has constituted) a Son, having been perfected, forever." Logically Christ's perfection should be seen as the antithesis of **infirmity.** There are comparison and contrast here, as the **but** shows. His superiority as High Priest consisted, in part, in the fact that He was free from the kind of infirmity which disqualified the Aaronic priests from a perfect (and therefore permanent) priestly ministry. But we must not make the antithesis so precise as to construe the perfect tense of the participle (having been perfected) as meaning that at a certain time in His life our Lord was freed or cleansed from sinful infirmity. Rather the exact content of His perfecting must be understood in the light of 5:7-9. By suffering and by obedience He was perfectly qualified to be the final and eternal High Priest.

It is evident that the writer to the Hebrews is advancing step by step to the very heart of Christ's work and ministry for us. His units of thought seem like interlocking chains, except there are often several chains being formed simultaneously. From another view his development seems telescopic. In each new section he introduces an advance truth, which he then draws out and elaborates in his next section. Christ was shown to be superior to angels as Son, superior to Moses as Captain, superior to Aaron as Priest, superior even to Abraham; and now this superiority is seen to issue in the inauguration of a superior covenant. Having stated this much in c. 7, he will proceed in c. 8 to elaborate on the rationale and nature of this new covenant.

[27]*Op. cit.*, p. 467.

Section III *The Finality of Christ's Passion*

Hebrews 8:1—10:25

A. Christ and the New Covenant, 8:1-13

1. *Introduction* (8:1-2)

The opening verse is an obvious signal that the writer has completed a stage in his discussion and is about to move on to another. He summarizes **the things which we have spoken** by the triple proposition: (*a*) **We have such an high priest. Such** (*toiouton*) is a qualitative pronoun. Chamberlain believes that in this case it serves as the antecedent to **who;**[1] but it is more likely that it is relative to the description just completed (7:26-28). It is linking what has just been said with that which is to follow. Now (*b*) it is this very High Priest **who is set on the right hand of the throne of the Majesty in the heavens** (cf. 1:3, 13; 2:9; 4:14; Matt. 26:64). He has been exalted by the Father to be Co-Ruler of the universe.[2] This is an absolute eminence. And third, (*c*) this High Priest is **a minister of the sanctuary** (2). Here is the transitional verse. The writer has just established our Lord's appointment and qualifications as High Priest; now he turns to examine the nature of His ministry. For a priest fulfills an office and performs a function. What does Jesus do? Where is the locus of His ministry? How does He fulfill it? What does His ministry accomplish for us? These are the questions to be answered in cc. 8—10, where the field of attention is shifted from His credentials to His work.

The noun **minister** (2) is in apposition to **who** (1), and the indefinite article **a** should be dropped, since He is not one minister among many. He is Jesus Christ, **minister of the sanctuary.** The designation is a compound word (*leitos,* "public,"

[1] *Op. cit.*, p. 48.

[2] Wiley says: "Hence we have the throne, the Majesty, and the heavens representing His kingly authority; and closely related, His priestly functions in the true tabernacle, likewise in the heavens. The words 'is set on the right hand of the throne' suggest a voluntary act, of One who takes His seat by virtue of a task accomplished or a purpose fully achieved; while the 'right hand' suggests the place of honor and power, as well as satisfaction and delight" (*op. cit.*, p. 262; cf. Sowers, *op. cit.*, p. 82).

and *ergon,* "work") and its primary meaning is a person of property who performs a public duty or service at his own expense—notably true of Jesus. In the NT it means officers, or official functionaries, administrators serving in behalf of others (Rom. 13:6; cf. *diakonos*).

Literally, **sanctuary** is plural, *ton hagion,* and should be rendered "the holies," possibly with reference to both the outer sanctuary and the holiest of all; though if this is feminine, it has special reference to the latter (Vincent). But in any case the place of His ministration is **the true tabernacle, which the Lord pitched, and not man** (2). The **tabernacle** (lit., "tent") is the place where God meets man and man meets God. The term also speaks metaphorically of the method by which this fellowship is arranged and consummated. The heavenly tabernacle corresponds to "heavenly things" (5); this is **the true tabernacle** (9:24) in the sense that it is reality and finality, whereas the earthly Tabernacle, while physically real and visible, was to the spiritual only typical and temporary. It was to the true what the shadow is to substance. The "heavenly things" is an expression not so much of a place as of a kind. The heavenly tabernacle is in contrast to the earthly as spiritual is in contrast to material. The earthly Tabernacle was rich in its material appeal to the senses, but impoverished in its ability to change or satisfy the soul in its personal relationship with God. The heavenly tabernacle, in contrast, is bereft of earthly pageantry and materiality, but consummate in its spiritual substance. Man may fabricate the outward and visible, making it very impressive and aesthetic; but God pitches—or provides—the spiritual.

2. *"A More Excellent Ministry"* (8:3-6)

Since a priest is ordained for the purpose of performing a priestly ministry, it is required, if He is to fill the role of priest, that Jesus **have somewhat also to offer** (3). But it cannot be material in nature. **For if he were on earth.** i.e., belonging to the earthly order of things, **he should not be a priest,** inasmuch as the earthly order is already manned by busy priests **that offer gifts according to the law** (of Moses) (4). Jesus does not belong to these.

For these men at Jerusalem **serve unto the example . . . of heavenly things** (5). That it is proper to thus downgrade the earthly system by calling it the pattern and shadow is proved by

God's admonishment to Moses, **See, saith he, that thou make all things according to the pattern shewed to thee in the mount. Pattern** here is *typon,* "type" or "cast"; in this case "design" or "plan." The design given in the mount was based on the spiritual prototype, hidden in God as a divine mystery, to be revealed in Christ. This means that the Tabernacle built by Moses in exact conformity to the heavenly design was a pattern-copy (*hypodeigmati*), i.e., a copy of the pattern, but only in the sense of a shadow cast on the ground by the heavenly reality. But if a faithful copy, each part both of structure and of ritual has its counterpart in Christ. This is exactly the assumption of the writer, and will be the basis of his exegesis later.

It is no wonder then that Jesus Christ would not fit at all into this copy-shadow economy, for His task is to turn shadow into substance. **But now hath he obtained a more excellent ministry** (6). As excellent as the Aaronic ministry was, because of its divine origins, Christ's is "still-more-excellent" (Mueller). In the next phrase the word **much** should be followed by a comma. The **by how much** (*hoso*) simply indicates that the measure of this greater excellence is the degree of superiority of the new covenant. **Also** belongs to what follows, i.e., **also he is the mediator of a better covenant.**

Six times in the NT, Jesus is said to be **mediator** (*mesites*) of the new covenant; three of these instances are in Hebrews (8:6; 9:15; 12:24). In the sense intended in this Epistle the emphasis is not on reconciliation, but upon negotiating and instituting. Yet Jesus was more than a verbal negotiator, or medium of communication. The deeper significance of His office of **mediator** will be noted at 9:15. The attention now should be kept focused on the **better covenant,** better because **it was established** (having been established) **upon better promises.** The promises are not better in the sense of being more dependable, but better in the sense of superior content. God promised better substance and better terms in the new covenant than had ever been promised in the old. This better substance is now indicated.

3. *A Better Covenant* (8:7-12)

Dispensationalists sometimes see numerous covenants made by God with His people, but the NT recognizes essentially only two: first, that which prevailed before Christ; and second, that which prevails since Christ. The OT records the history and operation of the old covenantal economy, while the NT expounds the new. Hebrews is the exposition par excellence, and a case could be made for the proposition that its basic theme is the new covenant—its meaning, means, and Mediator. The old covenant was inaugurated (officially, fully, and finally) by Moses (9:19-20), the new by Christ.

The concept of a divine-human **covenant** (*diatheke*) is not too complex to be readily grasped. It is a relationship with His people which God himself initiates, but which the people must ratify. It is a special relationship, setting the people of the covenant apart from all others, enabling God to say, **I will be to them a God, and they shall be to me a people** (10). It involves on the part of the people not only certain privileges but definite obligations, which they accept. God promises certain blessings, but on specified terms; thus the covenant assumes (in an inferential sense only) the nature of a contract, mutually agreed and entered into (see comments on 7:20-22 and 9:15-16).

a. The need for a better covenant (8:7-9). Before describing the new covenant the writer justifies it by reminding us of the limitations of the old: **For if that first covenant had been faultless, then should no place have been sought for the second** (7). In other words, the fact that God promises a new covenant proves that the old was inherently unsatisfactory. If it had been intrinsically adequate for God's purposes, He would simply have renewed it, instead of displacing it (13). But the fact is that in the Hebrew Scriptures there are promises of a new order. **For finding fault with them, he saith, Behold, the days come, saith the Lord, when I will make a new covenant with the house of Israel and with the house of Judah** (8; Jer. 31:31). In 7 he implies faultiness in the covenant; now in 8 he ascribes faultiness to the people. In the first case the idea is probably inherent limitations; i.e., there was limited efficacy in the first covenant, because of its preparatory nature. But the use of the word **fault** in 8 indicates blameworthiness, as is shown by the next verse: **Not according to the covenant that I made with their fathers in the day when I took them by the hand to lead them out of the land of Egypt; because they continued not in my covenant, and I regarded them not, saith the Lord** (9). Its limitations were inherent, as God knew from the beginning, but its complete breakdown was their fault.

What an exquisitely tender picture is the phrase, **when I took them by the hand to lead them out!** Surely the fault was not in

God! As a solicitous father, who with gentle care takes personal charge of his little ones, and nestles their small hands in his great one to lead them through danger and difficulty, so God nursed and sheltered the children of Israel. But this only compounds their blameworthiness. It is still further compounded by the fact that they did not have the excuse of literal children. They were a mature people who, although having suffered much, had demanded much, received much, and promised much.

Their crucial rebellion at Kadesh-barnea was the beginning of the end of the covenant; yet that was just one of many subsequent defections in the generations that followed. A better translation of 9*b* would be: "Because they abode not in My covenant, I also regarded them not." They did not remain at home, under the nuptial roof, but violated their vows as a rebellious and persistently wanton wife (Jer. 31:32). Therefore the time came when God rejected them.

b. *The substance of the better covenant* (8:10-12). In v. 6 is the assertion that the new covenant was based on "better promises." The possible significance of the plural will claim our attention later (9:15). But here only one promise is called to our attention—Jer. 31:31-34. Quoted from the LXX, Hebrews is essentially in agreement with the Hebrew text of Jeremiah, although in some details the OT version is richer. In some particulars also the Greek text used in Hebrews is closer to our OT than the KJV translates it. Note the following comparisons:

Jeremiah **(*Heb. text*)**	*Hebrews (KJV)*	***Gk. text*** **(*LXX*)**
(31) I will make . . .	same	I will consummate
(31) with the house of Israel . . . Judah	same	upon the house of Israel . . . Judah
(32) which my covenant they brake	because they continued not	abode not
(32) although I was an husband unto them	and I regarded them not	I also disregarded them
(33) the covenant that I will make	same	the covenant that I shall covenant
(33) the house of Israel; After those days, saith the Lord . . .	the house of Israel after those days, saith the Lord	same as KJV
(33) I will put my law in their inward parts	I will put my laws into their minds	same as KJV
(33) and write it in their hearts	and write them [pl.] in their hearts	engrave them [pl.] upon their hearts

Jeremiah (*Heb. text*)	*Hebrews* (*KJV*)	*Gk. text* (*LXX*)
(33) and I will be their God, and they shall be my people	and I will be to them a God, and they shall be to me a people	I will be God to them and they shall be people to me
(34) they shall teach no more	they shall not teach	they shall not at all teach
(34) his neighbour	same	countryman
(34) they shall all know me	for all shall know me	shall know me [perfect tense]
(34) I will forgive their iniquity	I will be merciful to their unrighteousness	I will be merciful to their iniquities [pl.]
(34) I will remember their sin no more	their sins and their iniquities will I remember no more	their sins I will in no wise remember [or, I will remember no more at all]

The reader will have to decide whether much or little should be made of these variations. Possibly the most radical discrepancy is in 32, where LXX and Hebrews make no mention of God's relationship to the nation as a Husband, but substitute the severe declaration of rejection—"I regarded them not." Other nuances will be noted below, but none of the variations alter the basic elements. The parties involved in the two covenants are the same, Jehovah on the one hand and Israel and Judah on the other. Here is a beautiful intimation of the essential unity of the descendants of Jacob, in spite of the rupture into the Northern and Southern kingdoms which still prevailed when God spoke this oracle through Jeremiah.[3] The designation of the Hebrew people as the addressees of the promise does not, of course, exclude the Gentiles who by faith are grafted into the true Israel (Rom. 11: 17-20). But this is not the writer's concern now. It is important that his Hebrew Christian readers see that God has a new plan for them.

(1) *Sanctification.* **I will put my laws into their mind, and write them in their hearts** (10). Here is a redemptive power not present in the old. Under the old covenant God promised to bless the people and they promised to obey His laws. But their promise, while sincere, did not reckon with their inner lawlessness of nature. As in a democracy laws without the support of the populace cannot be successfully enforced, so laws without the support of the heart will not be obeyed. The old covenant proved to be formal and external, because the laws were en-

[3]In v. 10, **Israel** should be understood as representing the whole people.

graved on tables of stone instead of on the fleshy tables of the heart. Conscience compelled a verbal agreement, for the people knew what they ought to do; but at too many points the standards of the law ran counter to their strong inner desires and propensities.

A holiness which is merely outward and formal cannot satisfy either God or man. There must be not only complete conformity *to* but affinity *with* the laws of God, in the very secret springs of man's being. Then the covenant will be kept; and best of all, kept joyfully. In contrast, laws which have been formally accepted but are incompatible with nature become odious and must be enforced by legal authority. Sanctions and officers are needed to compel some degree of outward obedience. This makes for tension and creates the unfortunate impression that righteousness is drudgery while only unrighteousness is "fun." People fail to see that the fault is not in the law but in the human heart.

Philo taught in Alexandria that the moral law buttressed with the sacrificial law had inherent power to purify the soul, and produce the character which it demanded.[4] Hebrews is a complete rebuttal of this position. The law only specifies what shall be done; it cannot impart the desire to do it. The law may induce the obedience of fear, but not the obedience of delight. This is why God through Jeremiah speaks in the personal pronoun, **I will put my laws . . . in their hearts.** He does not say He will establish another legal system which will prove more effective. Rather He will operate directly upon the individual worshiper, and supernaturally alter his nature (cf. Deut. 30:6). This we call sanctifying grace, and it is the very essence of the new covenant.

What are the laws which God will engrave? The answer can only be the basic standards of right and wrong. These standards were what human nature chafed against, and the sacrificial law provided atonement only for violations. In the OT the standards are epitomized in the Decalogue. In the NT these fundamentals are clarified, applied, amplified, summarized (cf. the great commandments and the Sermon on the Mount) but not essentially altered, and never abrogated. It is still God's **laws** that man is concerned with, and this is as true with the new covenant as with the old.

[4]See Sowers, *op. cit.*, pp. 100-101.

It might be difficult to prove a significant difference between **mind** and **hearts** as far as the exegesis in Hebrews is concerned. In 10:16 the two terms are inverted; this suggests that the writer thinks of the two clauses as a simple parallelism, and *mind* and *heart* as synonyms. In 8:10 the laws are inscribed in the heart, while they are put into the mind; but in 10:16 they are inscribed on the mind and put into the heart. Evidently the writer is emphasizing merely the internalizing of the law. It is to be thoroughly impregnated into man's moral and spiritual being, until the law of God is part of him, indeed, until it can be said to be the law of himself. When this is so, it will be as natural for him to obey it as it was before natural for him to disobey.

(2) *Adoption.* **I will be to them a God, and they shall be to me a people** (10). This was, up to a point, the relationship under the former covenant. But it was more an ideal than a living reality. Too often the relationship was punctuated by infidelity and saddened by divine judgments. But now it will be sound and stable.

Here is an incredible privilege, to be among those whom God is pleased to call "My people" (Jer. 31:33), and to be able to say with loving familiarity, "My God." This is a truly personal relationship, horizontally corporate, yet individually realized, and individually equal. Here are mutual regard, tender love, the thrill of belonging, and the thrill of possessing. To be one of the people of God is to possess not only God but also His people, so that the relationship is triangular. We may not only say, "My God!" but, "My people!" Under the new covenant this sacred ideal will be preciously and gloriously real.

(3) *Regeneration.* Why the certainty respecting such a stable and satisfying family relationship? Because it does not consist of a merely legal contract, but of a personal acquaintance. **And they shall not teach every man his neighbour** (countryman), **and every man his brother, saying, Know the Lord: for all shall know me, from the least to the greatest** (11). Although the promise is made to the racial Israel, the substance of the promise is such that its fulfillment will constitute a new race (Eph. 2:11-22), participation in which will be based, not on the old birth, but on the new birth. Only those who **know** the Lord in personal experience (Rom. 2:27) are in this reconstituted Israel. Here is plainly an implied participation based on regeneration and preserved by sanctification.

Exactly at this point was one of the inherent "faults" in the old covenant. Its transmission was by a community cultus and a racial line, rather than by the Holy Spirit. The perpetuation of the cultus depended upon a highly efficient and elaborate system of teaching—of children by parents, of neighbor by neighbor. It was thus more of a corporate tradition than a personal possession. Knowledge of God was more *about* than *with;* it was the kind that can be taught. This is secondhand, remote, unsatisfactory. It is not very stabilizing when the individual is taken out of the shelter of the socially cohesive situation, and transplanted to a hostile and alien soil. A few in every generation doubtless pressed their way through to some measure of personal acquaintance and fellowship with God, but the vast majority of Israelites (under the old order) were spiritually mere camp followers. Now under the new order, **all** (of the true Israel) shall know the Lord, **from the least to the greatest.**

Tragically, much modern religion is of the secondhand and formal variety. Whole nations today, as well as communities and families, are held to a nominal "Christianity" solely by the pressures and ties of a social cultus with its traditions, customs, and sacred rites. The vast majority in these homogeneous groups do not really know the Lord, any more than did Samuel as a boy in the Tabernacle. When such individuals are severed from their cultural and church roots and placed in a wicked city or an atheistic university, their moral ideals soon evaporate and their religious practices are soon abandoned.

(4) *Justification.* God will also be **merciful to their unrighteousness.** Jeremiah says plainly "forgive." The next clause expresses the thoroughness of this forgiveness: **their sins and their iniquities will I remember no more** (12). The **no more** (*ou me,* double negative) adds vigorous emphasis to the declaration. The sins of these who now know God, and have been brought into harmony with His law, are remitted absolutely and will never be charged to their account again. It would be incompatible with Hebrews as a whole, and certainly with the inner structure of this new covenant, to read into this forgiveness a blanket indulgence for the continued practice of sin. It rather is a forgiveness which is morally absolute because based on the blood of Christ, and is therefore no tentative easement based on animal sacrifices, and subject to the lifelong repetition of these sacrifices. This contrast will be the subject of his exegesis next, and the gist will

be twofold: (*a*) that the blood of bulls and goats can never (really) take away sins; and (*b*) these sacrifices can never bring full assurance to the worshiper's conscience that his sins are remitted. But genuine forgiveness accompanied by a cleansed conscience is both part and parcel of the new covenant, along with the fellowship of personal acquaintance and the power of personal holiness.[5]

Here are the four privileges provided in the new covenant: sanctification, adoption, regeneration, and justification. Though interrelated and interdependent, it is apparent that the core and the crowning glory of the NT is sanctification, without which the others cannot be preserved, and the absence of which spoiled all other blessings under the OT. Such inward holiness is the ideal and goal of all religion; but only in Christ and in the new covenant which it institutes is it actualized.

4. *A Displacing Covenant* (8:13)

Another doctrine of Philo, vigorously promulgated among the Alexandrian Jews, was that the Mosaic covenant was eternal. This, too, the author of Hebrews painstakingly refutes. He relies on the simple logic inherent in the adjective **new.** In saying, **A new covenant** (the Gk. says only **new,** *kainen*), God is automatically making **the first old.** Literally, He is antiquating it. The whole Judaistic system is now obsolete and fit only for the antique shop of the scholar's browsing. **Now that which decayeth and** becometh **old is ready to vanish away.** Mueller is more literal: "But, that which is antiquated and decadent (fading-with-age) is close to vanishing." If it is obsolete, it has served its day. It is time for a quiet demise and respectable burial. There is no value in trying to seek further shelter under a rotten tree about to fall, or to multiply canes to prop up decrepit old age. God is finished with it, and so must we be. The phrase **is ready to vanish away** is probably prophetic of the complete disappearance of the Jewish Temple system in A.D. 70, and so dates the writing of the Epistle before that collapse.

[5]The **for** (*hoti*) introducing 12 makes the verse subordinate, and means "because." There is thus seen to be a relationship between the fellowship involved in knowing God and the assurance of sins forgiven. Perfect fellowship is impossible as long as there are unsettled accounts. Either the *fact* or the *sense* of guilt will intervene like a dark cloud and blot out the face of God. Forgiveness therefore is not only a concomitant of regenerate life but indispensable to it as its logical ground.

B. The New Covenant and the Blood of Christ, 9:1-28

The finality of our Lord's superior priesthood, and of its essential ministry in displacing the old covenant with the new, has been established. Now the writer examines in detail the manner in which our Lord's ministry was accomplished, and exactly what it provided. The manner finds its dramatic uniqueness in the fact that Jesus was not only High Priest but Sacrifice, not only Offerer but also Offering.

1. *The Old Pattern of Divine Service* (9:1-10)

In addition to the Aaronic priesthood, the first **covenant** (though not in the Greek, **covenant** is implied by the previous verse) had two other essential components: (*a*) **ordinances of divine service, and** (*b*) **a worldly sanctuary** (1). There were rites prescribed for their worship, and regulations governing every minute detail. Not only was the form of worship prescribed, but the place in which the worship was conducted. The place is discussed first (see Chart *A*).

a. The worldly sanctuary (9:1-5). It was a **worldly** place in the sense that it was visible, material, and earthy, suitable for this world-order (John 4:20-24).

(1) *The outer sanctuary* (9:2). This designated place was a **tabernacle** (tent). Actually the text indicates two tabernacles. In **the first . . . which is called the sanctuary** (2; lit., "called holy") were **the candlestick, and the table, and the shewbread.** The **shewbread** consisted of twelve cakes representing the twelve tribes of Israel, kept always on the table as a perpetual memorial, or reminder of God's covenant with His people; and believed also to be a type of Christ, the Bread from heaven, to be eaten by the priests (all believers). On the opposite side of the room was **the candlestick,** the only source of illumination, since there were no windows. Here is a good picture of the justified heart: the inner light, fed by the oil of the Holy Spirit, and the daily bread of Christ within, by which we live.[6]

[6]According to Exod. 40:26 the golden altar of incense was also in the first sanctuary, whereas Hebrews locates it in the second (4). For further study see Exodus 25—26; 30; 40; *The International Standard Bible Encyclopoedia,* V, 2887; and H. Orton Wiley (*op. cit.,* pp. 282-83), who concludes: "Thus the golden altar was located in the holy place, but in its ritual associations it 'belonged to' the holy of holies." See also Amp. NT, fn.

(2) *The inner sanctuary* (9:3-5). The second **tabernacle,** or division of the total structure, was a chamber ten cubits (about fifteen feet) square **called the Holiest of all** (3). The veil separating this from the holy place is called **the second veil** because the holy place itself was separated from the outer court by a veil, which, as one approached the structure, would naturally be the first veil. The **Holiest of all . . . had the golden censer** (rather, "altar"), **and the ark of the covenant** (4). Only Hebrews lists three items in the ark, **the golden pot that had manna, and Aaron's rod that budded, and the tables of the covenant.**[7] Later we shall see that the ark represents the sanctified heart abiding in the presence of God (10:18-22). In this holy heart are three new covenant blessings: (*a*) the law of God (8:10; 10:16) means the enthronement of God's rule and rules, and the complete conformity of the moral nature to this rule. It involves the reconstruction of the moral image of God which was lost in the Fall, thus making righteousness of life not only possible but agreeable. (*b*) The supernatural fruit of the Spirit, now thriving on what was a lifeless stick, is symbolized by **Aaron's rod that budded.** (*c*) The abiding, inner strength of the living, indwelling Christ is pictured by the pot of **manna** (John 6:48-51; Eph. 3:14-21).

I. M. Haldeman thinks that the ark is a type of Christ,[8] but there are reasons why the **mercyseat** (*hilasterion*) more particularly represents our Lord. When we read that Christ has been "set forth to be a propitiation through faith in his blood" (Rom. 3:25), we discover the same word, *hilasterion,* which can mean either the means of propitiation or the place of propitiation.[9] Since the place of propitiation was the Cross and the means was Christ's blood, both meanings of the word converge in Him. As the **cherubims of glory** (God's presence) shadowed **the mercyseat** (5), so the mercy seat covered and completed the ark (it was the lid of the ark, closely and exactly fitted). Thus the holy soul finds its completeness only under the mercy seat. But the **mercyseat** is also a structural part of **the cherubims of glory;** it there-

[7]Exod. 16:33-34; 25:16; 26:34; 40:20; and Num. 17:1-11 imply the presence of the pot of manna and Aaron's rod with the tables of the law.

[8]*The Tabernacle Priesthood and Offerings* (Westwood, New Jersey: Fleming H. Revell Company, 1925), pp. 166 ff.

[9]W. F. Arndt and F. W. Gingrich, *A Greek-English Lexicon of the New Testament and Other Early Christian Literature* (Chicago: The University of Chicago Press, 1957), p. 376.

fore is the means of uniting God and the soul, and bringing the soul under the overshadowing of the divine wings. As this union depends on perfect union with the mercy seat, so the holiness of the soul and the divine overshadowing depend on being at once perfectly joined and perfectly subordinate to Christ. But this line of thought cannot be pressed too far here, since Hebrews declines to do so: **of which we cannot now speak particularly.** The writer is not planning to press the typological details of the furnishings.

b. The worldly ordinances (9:6-10). The writer's immediate aim is to show that the priestly ministry ordained for this earthly Tabernacle in the wilderness did not go all the way in meeting the need. It was inadequate. **The priests went always into the first tabernacle, accomplishing the service of God** (6). This was the prescribed sphere of their regular ministration, and it was the sphere of legal justification and ritualistic worship. It was external and formal, not at all like the intimacy of "the Holiest of All," such as when God spoke to Moses "face to face." Moses was admitted, but the priests were shut out; into that most holy place **went the high priest alone once every year** (7), on the tenth day of the seventh month (Tishri, our September-October). This day is now called Yom Kippur by the Jews. Even then the manner of the high priest's entering was so minutely prescribed, and the observance fraught with such peril, that it was as much a day of terror as of joy. He dared not enter **without blood, which he offered for himself, and for the errors**—sins of ignorance—**of the people** (cf. Leviticus 16). That the Aaronic high priest should be more circumscribed than Moses respecting **the holiest of all** would certainly imply that the Aaronic order was not God's intended way of breaking down the barrier to general participation in the blessings within the veil—**The Holy Ghost this signifying** (signifying this), **that the way into the holiest of all was not yet made manifest** (8).

The Levitical order by which these details were determined was not the invention of the postexilic priests, but an authentic segment of divine revelation, authored by the Holy Ghost himself. The restrictions and mystery surrounding **the holiest of all** were part of the lesson. By means of this lesson the Holy Spirit "means us to understand" (Phillips) that the whole Mosaic-Levitical system was a part-way system, and would remain such **while as the first tabernacle was yet standing,** or literally "while it has standing," i.e., an unimpaired standing or dignity. Naturally the literal tent had long ceased to stand, but that is not the intended sense here. The term **tabernacle** or "tent" is used figuratively of the whole system, which had valid standing and divine authority until Christ's death. During this whole era the mystery of **the holiest of all** was a closed book. And that which was practiced, both daily and annually, **was a figure** (9), i.e., a parable or comparison, not **for the time then present,** but "for the time now-at-hand" (Mueller). In Christ both the real meaning and the real fulfillment are being disclosed.

Within this **figure,** or parable, it was proper to offer up to God **both gifts and sacrifices.** But these were powerless to do the one thing that needed to be done; they **could not make him that did the service** (the worshiper) **perfect, as pertaining to the conscience.** They did not achieve the desired end in cleansing the conscience from uneasiness and guilt. The worshiper still lacked that which all worshipers everywhere crave—peace and assurance. There was an inherent impotency in animal sacrifices. The barest perfection achievable under this parabolic system consisted[10] **only in meats and drinks, and divers washings** (10). Whatever satisfaction was possible in meticulous observance of the sacrificial and ceremonial regulations was theirs; but as Paul discovered, that was altogether barren and unsatisfactory (Phil. 3:4-6).

What was the purpose of this system? To prefigure, as a parabolic type, the better system now found in Jesus, as we have already been told. Hence the old could not really be said to have failed; it served this purpose (Gal. 3:24), and was never intended to do more. The whole system was a set of **carnal ordinances, imposed** (omit the italicized **on them) until the time of reformation.**[11] Mueller renders it: "until a time of thorough-rectification." This is not a straightening, however, of the old system. It is a reference, rather, to that time when personal inner rectification, not possible in profound and thorough measure by means of external rites, becomes possible for all worshipers through the

[10]**Which stood,** italicized in KJV, is not justified (see A. T. Robertson, *op. cit.*, p. 397).

[11]The **carnal ordinances** (*dikaiomata sarkos*) is not the third item in the series, as KJV puts it. Rather this phrase (there should be no **and**) is in apposition to "gifts and sacrifices" (Robertson). The entire Levitical sacrificial and ceremonial system was imposed as a temporary measure—"to tide the worshippers over" (Amp. NT).

better covenant of Christ. The holiness which was only prefigured before becomes in Christ possible as reality.

2. *The Contrasting Service in Christ* (9:11-15)

a. His contrasting deed (9:11-12). **But Christ**—it is He who makes the great difference, both in the contrast of His action and in the superiority of His person. He had come as **a high priest of good things to come.**[12] His divine service as Priest is diverse from the Levitical both in the locale and in the sacrificial blood used.

As to the locale (the first point of contrast) His ministry takes place in **a greater and more perfect tabernacle, not made with hands** (11). Immediately follows the explanatory comment, **that is to say, not of this building,** or literally "this creation." The sanctuary with which Christ and His children have to do is not of this material order, visible, local, and destructible; it is rather a spiritual order of being. While Christ's death was physical and visible, its inner meaning was relevant to an invisible structure of reality, the kingdom of God. This is **more perfect** in many respects, but not the least, surely, are its permanence and universal accessibility.

The second point of contrast is in the blood used—not that **of goats and calves, but . . . his own** (12). Here also is a third contrast in the finality and once-for-all sufficiency of His single entry—**once into the holy place, having obtained eternal redemption for us.** "Having disclosed an eternal redemption," is Mueller's rendering. Eternal redemption is not unconditionally obtained, but made available.[13] The tense rendering poses a problem too. **Having obtained** places the crucial transaction prior to the entry into **the holy place.** In this case the atonement must be associated strictly with Christ's death at the altar of sacrifice, whereas in the Levitical plan the atonement was made not only by killing the animal but by taking the blood into the holiest (7). The rendering of RSV is more in harmony with the type: "thus securing eternal redemption." In other words, the redemption is

[12]Nestle (1958) has adopted the alternate reading *genomenon,* "having come." This would make the arrival of the new order of good things synchronize with the arrival of Christ.

[13]The middle voice of *heurisko* (as here) can mean "find (for myself), obtain" (Arndt and Gingrich), but if so intended here it would have to be "having obtained eternal redemption for himself." Phillips translates it "having won."

effected by His entry into the holiest as the climactic and integral part of the total redemptive act. As to what or where this **holy place** is, Robertson says it is heaven, and v. 24 supports this; but the emphasis is heaven conceived as "the presence of God" (24). This is more in keeping with the real symbolism of the earthly holy of holies, which signified, not heaven, but God's glorious presence, and an unimpeded relationship with God in His presence. Into this presence Jesus entered with **his own blood,** not literal blood, but with His blood-rights, having just died for men. And (the fourth point of contrast) into this sacred divine presence He **entered** to remain forever—not to hasten an exit, as did the Levitical high priest.

b. The contrasting benefit (9:13-14). There are not only the four points of contrast thus far noted, but there is also (fifth) the infinite contrast between the efficacy of Christ's blood and that of animals. The inherent value in animal blood would be virtually nil, but the inherent value of Christ's blood, the stainless God-man, would be incalculable. Yet this almost worthless blood of animals secured for the OT worshiper some benefits—**sanctifieth to the purifying of the flesh** (13). This sanctification was a restoration of their "external purity" (NEB) and their formal acceptability with God. They were again members in good standing of a holy race, God's chosen and consecrated people. Even this effect was not by virtue of the blood used, but through the act of penitence, worship, and obedience in seeking reconciliation by means of the prescribed sacrifices. Therefore the logic is: **For if the blood of bulls and goats, and the ashes of an heifer sprinkling the unclean** (13; cf. Lev. 16:3, 14-15; Num. 19:9, 17), will accomplish even this great boon, **how much more shall the blood of Christ, who through the eternal Spirit offered himself without spot to God, purge your conscience from dead works to serve the living God? (14)** The **how much more** is measured by the qualitative distance between malodorous, dumb creatures and God himself, their Creator. For this sacred blood of the Man Christ Jesus was elevated to infinite value by the fact that He performed His action **through the eternal Spirit,** not the Holy Spirit but His own spirit, the eternal Son.[14]

Now we note a sixth point of contrast. Whereas the sacrificial animals of the OT were helpless victims, this Lamb of God

[14]A. T. Robertson says: "Christ's own spirit which is eternal as he is," *op. cit.*, p. 400.

offered himself without spot to God. Jesus was not trapped into an untimely, tragic death; He gave himself willingly, knowing every moment that He had power to reject the Cross. Thus the intrinsic value of His blood was compounded by the ethical merit of His volitional act.

The vastly superior blessing offered to us by this holy and precious Blood is much deeper than a ritualistic purging, affecting one's standing; it affects the inner state—**purge your conscience from dead works to serve the living God.** The purging of the conscience here matches the perfecting of the conscience in v. 9. The impotence of animal blood is counterbalanced by the efficacy of Christ's blood, but again provisionally (Attic form of *kathario,* future tense, "shall purge"). In the blood of Jesus is adequate but conditional cleansing for all; but there is no automatic cleansing, accomplished unconditionally by the act of atonement. Faith appropriates the cleansing Blood, and faith solely in the Blood as the ground of our salvation will bring full consciousness of release.

That which is to be cleansed is the **conscience,** or moral consciousness ("souls"—Phillips). In spite of painstaking observance of the Levitical ceremonies, a sense of guilt and defilement still clutched the conscience of the worshiper; but in Jesus he may find perfect peace. He may know the sweet awareness of the eighty-four-year-old man who testified: "For the first time in my life I feel clean on the inside." Only the Holy Spirit can actually wash away all subjective sense of sin, and give a wholesome sense of clean newness; but this He does on the basis of the expiating merit of Christ's blood, and in response to faith in that Blood. Released, the believer is now able to worship the living God acceptably. The contrast between **living God** and **dead works** is striking. Sinful works which bring death to the soul unfit us either for fellowship with or service for the God whose being is holy life. Hence this purging of the conscience must of necessity include regeneration and initial sanctification (Eph. 2:1).

c. *The contrasting scope* (9:15*ab*). It was to make possible this deep-level purging that an entirely new covenant was instituted.[15] **And for this cause he is the mediator of the new testament (15).** In this new order of things Christ's one death

[15]**New** (*kainos*) means a new kind, marvelous and previously unheard of. Thus the new covenant is quite dissimilar to the old.

provides redemption for all **transgressions that were under the first testament,** thus canceling its claim upon them, and thereby justifying its termination. **They which are called,** i.e., who hear the gospel and obey, may in this way escape the bondage of the old order and share with believing Gentiles the promise of eternal life.

It is highly significant that Christ's death was for transgressions committed under the old covenant. One aspect of this is seen by Robertson: "Here there is a definite statement that the real value in the typical sacrifices under the Old Testament system was in their realization in the death of Christ. It is Christ's death that gives worth to the types that pointed to Him. So then the atoning sacrifice of Christ is the basis of the salvation of all who are saved before the cross and since."[16] But this is not all. The word **transgressions** (*parabasis*) is the strongest word in the NT for deliberate violation of known law, and always implies full guilt and liability to penalty.[17] The word is used only twice in Hebrews, here and 2:2, where we read that under the OT order "every transgression and disobedience received a just recompence of reward." The deliberate sinner could not escape punishment by the casual offering of an animal sacrifice. The sacrificial system was essentially for the sins of ignorance and omission, committed unintentionally by the upright Israelite. It was not an easy escape for the high-handed sinner, who had to be punished, in some cases by the death penalty. Since all were at times guilty of such sins, even if of the less serious forms, and often were unexposed and unpunished, it is understandable that the worshiper always suffered a lurking sense of condemnation.

This is the real crux of guilt and alienation from God. To meet this moral predicament there had to be better blood, better priesthood, a better covenant; and these are found in Christ and His death. Marvellous divine plan, that so blends justice and mercy at the Cross that now life can be offered to those deserving death! The phrase **by means of death** indicates that Christ's death, while not an exact substitute for theirs, was a ransom price acceptable in lieu of their death. Here is a new dimension of salvation: mercy is extended to include the overt, willful sinner, condemned under the old covenant. For him the old either had nothing to offer but death or was woefully inadequate. But

[16]*Op. cit.*, pp. 400 ff.

[17]Acts 1:25; Rom. 2:23; 4:15; 5:14; Gal. 3:19; I Tim. 2:14; II John 9, *et al.*

now he too may qualify for the promise of eternal inheritance. The only condition is that he be among the **called** ("who obey God's call," Phillips).

3. *The Attesting Blood* (9:15c-22)

Now the writer proceeds to show that just as Christ's blood provides a better purging within the new order, so does it serve to provide the necessary ratification for the new order.[18]

a. The promised inheritance (9:15c). The anchor post of this thought is the clause **receive the promise of eternal inheritance.** The new covenant relates to an **eternal inheritance,** of a spiritual and heavenly nature, not to the earthly and national inheritance to which the Jews had clung so tenaciously. That which is now at stake is the promise of this inheritance; its full actualization is not at once, but future. To **receive the promise** is to take it into one's hand, i.e., to lay claim, in Christ's name, to the provisions of the will. But in so doing the suppliant surrenders all claim to earthly power in exchange for an inheritance invisible and otherworldly but eternal and indestructible.

b. The death of the testator (9:16). The reference to "inheritance" reminds us that the covenant promising this inheritance in Christ is in the nature of a will.[19] There is a legacy included in the new decree. The death of our Lord was therefore not only a priestly necessity but a legal one as well, **For where a testament is, there must also of necessity be the death of the testator.** A legacy is made available only by the death of the benefactor who wrote it into his will. Here the One who died—plainly, Christ—is identified as the Testator, or Author of the covenant; yet elsewhere Yahweh is declared to be the Author (Jer. 31:33; Heb. 8:8). It is obvious therefore that the Christ who died is also the God who through Jeremiah said, "I will make a new covenant." As Son of Man, He is Mediator; as Son of God, He is Author.

[18]In c. 7 the never-ending life of Jesus as High Priest constitutes the guarantee of a new and better covenant. In c. 8 this better covenant is seen to rest also upon better promises. In c. 9 we see the cost of this new covenant—Christ's own blood. The writer moves in converging circles to the Cross.

[19]The word *diatheke,* "covenant," means last will and **testament** as well as a decreed plan. Only in a minor, and generally non-biblical sense, does it mean a contract or compact between equals (see Arndt and Gingrich).

c. The blood-rites of the first covenant (9:17-21). This principle is not only valid in Roman law—that a will **is of no strength at all while the testator liveth** (17). It was also not strange to the Mosaic order, for not even **the first testament was dedicated** (instituted) **without blood** (18). While no person died, animals were slain in lieu thereof, and their blood, by testifying that a death had occurred, could be used to ratify the covenant. When Moses had declared the terms of the divine decree, **he took the blood . . . and sprinkled both the book, and all the people** (19), **Saying, This is the blood of the testament which God hath enjoined unto you** (20). The **blood of the testament** is the blood that ratifies the covenant.[20]

Later, when the tent had been erected, and Aaron and his sons were installed, Moses **sprinkled** likewise **with blood both the tabernacle, and all the vessels of the ministry** (21; Leviticus 8). This later sprinkling should probably be considered as part of the first; it further consummated the old covenant which God had **enjoined** (20; imposed by authoritative commandment) upon them.

d. The heart of true religion (9:22). The necessity of blood-shedding, typifying life-giving, is summarized in v. 22. As far as ceremonial purification is concerned, of **things,** i.e., the Tabernacle and accoutrements of worship, **almost all things are by the law purged with blood.** But even more indispensable is atoning Blood for sinners. **Things** require sprinkling of blood when consecrated. But persons require forgiveness; and even though there may be exceptions respecting things, there are no exceptions in forgiveness, for **without shedding of blood** there **is no remission** at all.[21] This is the great difference between God's way and man's way, true religion and false. Man takes a slight view of sin, and scoffs at blood as inherently necessary to forgiveness. But by requiring blood God underscores the exceeding

[20]**The book** which Moses sprinkled was the "book of the covenant" which he wrote and then read to the people. After reciting it to the people orally, he received their united response, "All the words which the Lord hath said will we do" (Exod. 24:3-8). The terms were thus made clear twice before the blood sealed the covenant. The contents of the book were probably Exodus 20—23. Immediately after the institution of this covenant God called Moses to Mount Sinai again, this time to give him the pattern of the Tabernacle and the Levitical sacrificial system (Exod. 24:12 ff.).

[21]The word *haimatekchusias,* "blood-shedding," or outpouring, is a compound word found only here in the NT. The verb in this clause is *ginetai,* "becomes." Without blood-shedding no forgiveness occurs.

sinfulness of sin; and by providing the Blood, He discloses His infinite love. The sinner's own blood may be spared—even that of animals—for God has sacrificed His own "Lamb . . . which taketh away the sin of the world" (John 1:29).

4. *The Benefit of Better Sacrifices* (9:23-28)[22]

The thought of this section reaches a moving climax, as the writer summarizes the fruition and finality of our Lord's sacrifice for us. Nowhere does he use contrast more tellingly than here. The **patterns** are contrasted with the **heavenly things** (23); **holy places made with hands** contrasted with **the true** (24); the repetition of atonement **every year** contrasted with **once in the end of the world** (25-26); and the future **judgment** contrasted with coming **salvation** (27-28).

But the details must not lure our attention away from Christ. He is the majestic Lord who became both Priest and Sacrifice and is the center of attention in these verses, as He procures for us cosmic and eternal benefits. In this summing up, we are reminded that in fulfilling His ministry as Priest-Sacrifice our Lord was satisfying an inherent necessity. The necessity that **the patterns of things in the heavens should be purified with these** (blood-rites) is a reflection of the deeper necessity that **the heavenly things themselves** should be purified **with better sacrifices** (23). The earthly order of worship called **patterns** (*hypodeigmata*) was not the original model, but a token copy of the heavenly, and the word should in this case be thus rendered. It is the shadow, not the substance.[23]

Both **patterns** and the counterpart **heavenly things** are plural, for both schemas include a tabernacle as a locale, ordinances of service or worship, a priesthood for a mediatorial ministry, and assured benefits for the worshiper. The neuter *ta epourania*, **heavenly things**, really refers not so much to a place as to a dimension of reality, and could be rendered "heavenly realities" or spiritual things, and corresponds with the new covenant which is being discussed (cf. 8:2, 5; 9:11). The entire schema of the new covenant had to be purified as surely as the first covenant.

Any plan of redemption involving a holy God and unholy man must be consecrated and certified by the divinely prescribed

[22]Note the homiletical possibilities of 9:23-28, "The Wonders of God's Redemption." The theme is developed under *a*, *b*, and *c*.

[23]Cf. 8:5, where the word *hypodeigma* is translated "example"; the word "pattern" is a translation of *typon*, "type."

means. This is not an arbitrarily erected barrier; there is here a profoundly inherent propriety, indeed a moral necessity. For sin is already a barrier, thrown up by man, high and formidable. Man cannot remove it, or blithely climb over it, or set up loose and superficial terms of reconciliation to his own liking. Only God, the injured and dishonored Sovereign, can prescribe terms, and they must be of such a nature as to reflect the enormity of sin on the one hand and the awful holiness (as well as mercy) of God on the other.

If man and God are to be rejoined, it must be on a completely moral basis. God's love begets love, but in such a solemn context of Sinai fire and Calvary blood that the love which is begotten shall never be careless or presumptuous, but trembling with humility, awe, and penitence. Thus has it always been that God's redemptive pattern is crimson-hued. And even His final plan in Christ, called the new covenant, must be ratified, but **with better sacrifices than these** which were acceptable for the old covenant. In the one Person, Christ himself, and in His one death, and one entry into the holiest, are these better sacrifices to be found. They obtain for us incomparably better benefits, three of which are beautifully and concisely summarized in vv. 24-28.

a. Now—a perfect representation (9:24). The Levitical high priests went into **the holy places made with hands** (the two sanctuaries of the Tabernacle) for the purpose of serving in their mediatorial office as man's representatives before God. But they were only **figures of the true,** "the counterpart of reality" (Moffatt). The reality was the very throne of God. Here Christ entered **into heaven itself.** This is not only a spiritual sphere or dimension but a definite place, the very seat of the divine administration. It was there that Christ did and does represent us, **now to appear in the presence of God for us.** Since **presence** (*prosopo*) really means "face or countenance," the word stresses that this place of representation is not merely in the presence of God conceived as omnipresence, or His presence by means of the Holy Spirit, or His presence in special and accommodative glory as in the Temple, but the ultimate presence of God as an Individual and as the universal Ruler.

If this seems to localize and anthropomorphize God, we cannot help it. Though the reality eludes our finite minds, we cannot but think in the categories which the Divine Mind has furnished us. The aorist tense of *emphanisthenai,* **appear,** suggests not Christ's perpetual intercession (as in 7:25, where the verb is present tense, continuous), but His official representation as the culmination of His atoning deed. Green says, "to present oneself." Having finished the earthly phase of the mission, He presented himself to the Father as Son of Man. On earth He was God's Representative to man; now He returns as man's Representative to God, with five naked wounds as His credentials. What the high priest did in shadow in the holy of holies, Jesus did in substance for us in heaven. And He was accepted. But in accepting Christ, the Father accepts us.

b. Once—a perfect expiation (9:25-26). The contrast is not only between heaven and earth—the reality and the shadow—but between the conclusiveness of the one sacrifice under the new order and the inconclusiveness of the many sacrifices under the old. **Nor yet that he should offer himself often** (25) extends the thought of the previous verse by affirming that this crucial self-presentation before the Father does not need to be repeated, **as the high priest entereth into the** [earthly] **holy place every year with blood of others.** If our Lord's mediatorial deed were no more conclusive than the Levitical copy, **then must he often have suffered since the foundation of the world** (26). If the saving efficacy of His propitiatory act had been local, superficial, or temporary, frequent repetitions would have been necessary. The fantastic supposition is stated to show the incredible problem which any watering down of the infinite value of our Lord's deed would create. If He were not absolutely unique in person, priesthood, and as Offering, and entirely diverse from the Levitical order, the repeated death of Jesus would be a necessity, unthinkable though it may seem.

But now (this **now** parallels the "now" in v. 24) **once in the end of the world**—or "once (for all time) at the consummation of the eons" (Mueller)—**hath he appeared to put away sin by the sacrifice of himself** (26). Whereas the word "appear" in v. 24 refers to Christ's self-presentation in heaven, the word **appeared** here is from *phanerao,* "make manifest," and refers to His self-manifestation on earth. He disclosed himself to man as a Man for one purpose: **to put away sin.** This is not a verb but a noun, *athetesin,* "disannullment, voidance"; literally "for a voidance of sin." **Sin** is here used in the sense of guilt. Sin's claim on us can be cancelled; to make this possible was the object of Christ's mission. This achievement is precisely the basis of prevenient grace, for this is a racial boon. "The sacrifice of Christ dealt with sin as a principle: the Levitical sacrifices with individual transgressions."[24]

Christ accomplished his work **by the sacrifice of himself,** or "by means of" (*dia* with genitive, "through"). Here the sacrifice and the priestly ministration become one. The Levitical priests had only the **blood of others** (25). Jesus negotiated the atonement with His own. The Levitical priests struggled to live; He submitted to die, so great was His love for us. This sets Him forever apart from all lesser priesthoods. The infinite value of His divine person plus the supreme sacrifice of His self-offering makes an absolutely inexhaustible redemptive potential.

c. Coming—a perfect salvation (9:27-28). The weight of emphasis in this paragraph is carried by **once** (*hapax*). Christ has appeared only "once" for the purpose of making atonement (26). Only **once** is man **appointed to die,** with the **judgment** following (27). If the writer were intending to stress death as the inevitable appointment for every man, the word **once** would have been superfluous; furthermore we would have been compelled to inquire about the exceptions, as in the rapture (hinted at in the next verse). There is, instead, a further point of comparison here: **So Christ was once** for all **offered to bear the sins of many** (28). Christ's one self-offering for sin was final and nonrepeatable, not only on the ground of its inherent qualitative sufficiency but on the ground of the Incarnation. If man the sinner is sentenced to one earthly death only, then only one should be required of Man the Saviour.[25] So much for the comparison, which turns on the correlative **so** (*houtos*).

[24]Vincent, *op. cit.,* p. 492.

[25]The phrase **to bear the sins of many** is a quotation from Isa. 53:12, and clearly identifies Jesus with the Suffering Servant. The word *anenegkein* is aorist infinitive of *anaphero,* "to bring or take up"; in this case "more in the sense of take away" (Arndt and Gingrich). It is a technical term of the Levitical system; to "bear sin" was to suffer its full responsibility and penalty (Lev. 20:20; 22:9; 24:15; Num. 9:13). But the sin of the congregation was borne away by the live goat used on the Day of Atonement: "And the goat shall bear upon him all their iniquities" (Lev. 16:22). The same word is used in I Pet. 2:24 in reference to the vicarious sufferings of Jesus. He was both the slain goat and the live goat. As the slain goat He provided the Blood for atonement. As the live goat He bore away our sins "into the wilderness"—meaning that our guilt is taken away. The fact that it is "sin," singular, in v. 26, and **sins,** plural, in v. 28, does not alter the meaning, as long as we understand that in both cases the reference is to guilt. If we bear our sins, there is no hope. Jesus vicariously bore them for us, and thus bore our guilt from us.

Out of this comparison comes another sweeping contrast. Apart from Christ men who die have only the judgment to anticipate; but now, because the deed of the atonement is done, and needs never to be done again, they who choose to believe can anticipate a bright future beyond the grave. Christ's next action will be the gathering of those whom His blood has redeemed: **and unto them that look for him shall he appear the second time without sin unto salvation.** Three times in this paragraph we have the English word **appear,** but each is a translation of a different word in the Greek. Here it is the future passive of *horao,* "see"; the passive is "to be seen," to reveal oneself (Luke 1:11; Acts 2:3) and most surely includes the idea of a visible appearing (cf. Acts 1:11).

This second coming of the Christ will be **without** (apart from) **sin.** His future coming will add nothing to Calvary; it will offer no further degree of possible salvation from sin. For full salvation from sin we must look back, not forward, because sin is neither in physical environment nor in physical bodies but in men's hearts. The **salvation** which is yet promised, and which must await our Lord's return, is not from sin in the believer's heart. It is from sin's earthly and physical consequences—the curse, the scars, the seducing influence, the groaning of this enslaved creation—and from the probationary contingency of our earthly pilgrimage (Rom. 8:10-25). Holiness may be ours now, and unconditional, eternal security then. This will be the final stage of the great redemptive program (Acts 3:19-21; Rom. 13:11; II Pet. 3:10-14).

But final salvation is for a specified class: **them that look for him.** The present tense of the verb[26] suggests that instant readiness is evidenced by constant expectation. There is no shrinking or dread, but confidence and quiet joy. For Christians this is the future's supreme event, and its glorious prospect overshadows all else. They can never be quite at ease in a world with an absent Lord. Are we not then to understand that those who settle comfortably in this present order, as for a long stay, and forget their destiny and their coming King, will not be among the recipients of the great salvation? Possibly this restrictive clause sheds light on the **many** whose guilt is borne away. While racial guilt may

[26]*Apekdechomenois,* articular participle, present middle of *apekdechomai,* "expect, wait, or look for"—the precise word used by Paul in Phil. 3:20. See also Rom. 8:19, 23, 25; I Cor. 1:7; Gal. 5:5.

be put away in the sense that prevenient grace is operative, the actual sins are borne away only of the **many,** those whose affections are set on things above, and who keep on looking for their Lord's return.

C. The Way into the Holiest, 10:1-22

In c. 10 Hebrews is moving into its climax. Three main ideas in c. 9 are here brought to their final development and conclusion. First, we must not lose sight of the goal, which is free access **into the holiest of all** (9:8). Second, we must see that only the blood of Jesus can qualify us by purging our **conscience from dead works** (9:14). Third, we must keep in view the perpetual validity and finality of our Lord's once-for-all sacrifice (9:26). Although these are important pivots of thought in c. 9, the emphasis there is on the preparation, not of the worshiper, but of the holy places themselves. The new covenant as a testament had to be ratified, the new order officially instituted, and the "heavenly things" consecrated. All of that has been shown to be accomplished. Now the inspired writer returns to show that the same precious Blood which ratified the new testament and consecrated the new order also qualifies us for entry into the holiest. This qualification includes a justification which brings peace and a sanctification (both "initial" and "entire") which makes clean.

The writer's mood in c. 10 becomes dogmatic. He is gathering up the strands of evidence which he has been weaving, and declaring their meaning for the worshiper in a series of sharp, final conclusions.

1. *The Law Is a Dead End* (10:1-4)

The writer first reviews the utter impotence of the whole Mosaic sacrificial system. **For the law having a shadow of good things to come, and not the very image of the things, can never with those sacrifices which they offered year by year continually make the comers thereunto perfect** (1). **Can never!** That is blunt and unequivocal; therefore to cling hopefully to the Temple is entirely vain. This inability is proven by the very repetitiousness of these sacrifices; if they perfected the worshiper, why would he need to keep coming back? **For then would they not have ceased to be offered? because that the worshippers once purged should have had no more conscience of sins** (2).

The purging here explains the perfecting in v. 1. The sin offering has not perfected the worshiper unless it has purged him. This requirement includes much more than expiation (though it does include that), and certainly far more than ceremonial cleansing (the law was sufficient for that, 9:13); it includes a subjective cleansing of the worshiper himself. The word is *katharizo* (purify), and in this instance it is the perfect passive participle, with *hapax* (once); i.e., "having once been cleansed and kept clean." The perfect tense indicates an abiding condition based on a completed action. Only this kind of purging would result in having **no more conscience** (consciousness) **of sins** ("sense of sin," NEB.).

This is not a blanket covering which permits continued sinning without a disturbed conscience. The conscience is not chloroformed, nor is sinning licensed, or the moral law abrogated. But the need is for a purging which brings absolute peace respecting past sins and adequate power for avoiding continued sinning. This the Mosaic law could not do (9:9). On the contrary **in those sacrifices there is a remembrance again made of sins every year** (3). Every annual Day of Atonement was an agonizing reminder of both fresh sins and old sins. The sin problem was never really settled, the conscience never truly quieted. Why? Because **it is not possible that the blood of bulls and of goats should take away sins** (4). There is no redemptive power in animal blood; to suppose so is to grossly underestimate the nature and enormity of sin. The annual ritual of slaying the bull and the goat, and sending a second goat into the wilderness as a dramatic picture of carrying away guilt, was a prefiguring of the real cancellation and real cleansing which would someday be provided by better Blood. To persist in pinning hope on animal blood, which in itself is inherently worthless, is the height of folly. Salvation is simply not possible in that direction.

2. *The Law Is Displaced by a New Way* (10:5-18)

The writer has appealed consistently to the Scriptures. He here introduces a new passage (Ps. 40:6-8), but its use is overshadowed by the writer's direct appeal to the Triune God, Father (5-10), Son (11-14), and Holy Spirit (15-18). It is this Triune God who provides the new way into the holiest of all.

a. Authored by the will of God (10:5-10). **Wherefore** ("That is why," NEB) **when he cometh into the world, he saith, Sacrifice**

and offering thou wouldest not, but a body hast thou prepared me (5). In the act of coming into the world as Redeemer, Christ is saying to the Father, "Thou art not pleased with the present sacrifices, and Thou hast fitted Me to become a better one." The Son became incarnate for a redemptive purpose: through the Virgin Birth the Spirit fashioned in the womb of Mary a physical body which would become our Lord's instrument of sacrifice.

Actually, the quotation is from a psalm of David (40:6-8); but Hebrews interprets it as the words of Christ to God rather than the words of David. Or possibly the sense is that our Lord appropriates the words as finding their full meaning only in Him. Furthermore, the quotation is a condensed rendering of the LXX, not the Hebrew; this explains the substitution of **a body hast thou prepared me** in the place of "mine ears hast thou opened" (Ps. 40:6). The opening of ears may be understood as a synecdoche, using a part for the whole. But in any case the meaning is not essentially altered, but strengthened and clarified.

In burnt offerings and sacrifices for sin thou hast had no pleasure (6) is a parallelism to v. 5, and thus explanatory. Whole **burnt offerings**, representing consecration, and offerings **for sin** (*peri hamartias*) are not pleasing to God, even though He ordained them as a temporary means of worship, and their use is according to the law (8). God is not a sadistic Being who delights in the death of His creatures or in gory scenes of slaughter; but neither does He delight in the gory results of sin. Many non-ideal and unpleasant things are made necessary by the defiling and disrupting nature of sin, including the repugnant blood-shedding of the law and the infinitely more tragic blood-shedding of Christ.

The logic of the passage is simple, and Hebrews draws it out with perfect clarity. The fact that the annual sacrifices were not pleasing to God combined with the Son's announcement, **I come to do thy will, O God** (9), can spell only one conclusion: **He taketh away the first, that he may establish the second.** Christ's action is as completely the final and perfect will of God as the former system had not been the final will of God. **By the which will we are sanctified through the offering of the body of Jesus Christ once for all** (10). Basically, this is to say that Christ's once-for-all sacrifice as the ground and means of our sanctification finds its efficiency in the will of God the Father. God's will is the ultimate ground of our sanctification. The sovereignty of God underlies all. Here we look for the originating and initiating source. It is the "grace of God" that brings salvation (Titus 2:11).

The sanctification which is thus provided is not only ceremonial but inward and moral. We are not merely consecrated by the death of Christ, in the sense that His death brings us into a new and sacred relationship with God. This would be positional holiness only, and that had been available before. The weakness of the old order was at this very point—it offered nothing more than positional holiness.

The more thorough nature of this sanctification can be seen by noting three exegetical details. (1) It does not say that we are sanctified by a sovereign act of God's will, as the KJV might imply. The preposition is *en,* "in" or more properly "within." It is within the context of the will of God that we are sanctified. (2) It does not say that we are sanctified by the death of Christ, but **through.** Here the preposition is *dia,* with the genitive, meaning **through,** in the sense of a secondary agency. Our sanctification then is in the will of God and made possible by the deed of Christ. Our sanctification did not occur when Christ died, but was in that event made possible. Subjectively and immediately the work of sanctification is the work of the Holy Spirit (II Thess. 2:13; I Pet. 1:2). (3) The verb form *hegiasmenoi,* "having been sanctified," is perfect tense, which means that we, the worshipers, are, through Christ, in a state of sanctification resulting from a past sanctifying. But with most of these Hebrew Christians this was not yet subjectively a fact of experience. We may call this therefore a "perfect of prophecy," having a futuristic force. **Through the offering of the body of Jesus Christ** we are provisionally sanctified, and may be personally and inwardly sanctified.

b. Accomplished by the work of Christ (10:11-14). The will of God is implemented through a priesthood. The attempt to fulfill this function kept the Levitical priests standing **daily ministering and offering oftentimes the same sacrifices** (11). Not only once a year in the holiest of all did the high priest minister, but a whole battery of priests wore themselves out every day, repeating the same monotonous round. Their sacrifices were not only wearisome, but ineffectual, as has been shown already, but now reiterated: **which can never take away sins** (should be "sin," singular). Another dogmatic affirmation. The verb is strong, *periaireo,* to "remove utterly." **But this man** (Jesus), **after he had offered one sacrifice for sins for ever** ("perpetually [through the unceasing-continuance]"—Mueller) **sat down on the right hand of** the throne of **God** (12). In the Greek, vv. 11-12 are in an "on the one hand—on the other hand" form. The writer points to the ceaseless busyness of the many priests in the Temple on the one hand, then to the one Priest—**this man**—on the other hand, who for many sins offered one sacrifice, then **sat down.** The **standeth** contrasted with **sat down** makes a vivid picture of a task never finished over against a task fully and forever finished. In the one case the many sacrifices are never complete; in the other case the one sacrifice is so perfect that its efficacy is never exhausted. Quietly this successful High Priest waits expectantly "until His enemies should be made a stool for his feet" (13, RSV).[27] The ultimate conquest of all evil and every opposing force will issue from the one deed at Calvary. Its power is sufficient for the total task of redemption.

In v. 14 the redemptive depth of this power for believers, available now, is concisely yet comprehensively summarized: **For by one offering he hath perfected for ever them that are sanctified** (14). The tenses here need careful study. "We have been sanctified and still are" is the proper rendering of the perfect tense of v. 10. But in this verse it is **perfected,** which is perfect in tense, while the articular participle *tous hagizomenous,* "who are being sanctified," is present tense. A definite and complete sanctification is declared to be the divine will, in fact a state already experienced by the "we" of v. 10. Therefore the present participle of v. 13 must be interpreted as an iterative present; hence, those that are from time to time being sanctified, one after another. All who are experientially sanctified in every generation are equally **perfected for ever** by the **one offering.**

To be **perfected** does not mean to be completed in character beyond need for further growth. It means, rather, to be brought to an experience of reality and a state of fulfillment in heart relationship with God which the old order could not offer. It is perfection in the sense of being brought to a designed and desired level. That level is indicated by the term *sanctification.*[28] To be **perfected for ever** is not to be made unconditionally established and secure in this "sanctification." The phrase simply declares in the strongest language possible that all who from time to time

[27]Another quoting of Ps. 110:1. See also 1:3, 13; 8:1.

[28]No better descriptions of the content of sanctification can be found than Eph. 1:4 and I Tim. 1:5 (RSV).

are sanctified are sanctified perfectly by means of this one offering. The effects of the offering in the soul of the worshiper are as perfect (complete and satisfactory) as the offering itself, and these effects are perpetually available. "The Blood will never lose its power."[29]

c. Affirmed by the witness of the Spirit (10:15-18). Not only is our sanctification the will of the Father, and its perfection the work of the Son, but its accomplishment is the prediction of the Holy Spirit. **Whereof** (concerning the perfection of the sanctified) **the Holy Ghost also is a witness to us** (15). This is often construed to mean the inner witness of the Holy Spirit to the believing seeker at the point of sanctification; but while there is such a witness, that is hardly the thought here. The **witness** rather is the inspired prophecy of Jeremiah, already quoted (8:8-12), delineating the content of the new covenant. The significant point of this **witness** is v. 17: **And their sins and iniquities will I remember no more.**[30] The RSV (supported by others) gives a clearer rendering than KJV:

> "And the Holy Spirit also bears witness to us; for after saying,
> 'This is the covenant that I will make with them
> after those days, says the Lord:
> I will put my laws on their hearts,
> and write them on their minds,'
> then he adds,
> 'I will remember their sins and their misdeeds no more.'
> Where there is forgiveness of these, there is no longer any offering for sin" (15-18).

It is clear that the particular portion of the Spirit's witness which is especially relevant at the moment, and therefore especially appealed to, is the finality of God's forgiveness, which confirms the finality of our Lord's one offering. Literally, God is being quoted as saying, "I will be reminded no more" (Mueller). In the old system there was a "remembrance again made of sins every year" (3). But the terms of the new covenant distinctly repudiate such annual memorials. "I don't want to be reminded,"

[29]For full and helpful discussion of v. 14 see Wiley, *op. cit.,* pp. 324-28.

[30]This is implied by the preposition *meta,* **after,** followed by the large ellipsis between vv. 16 and 17; but made even clearer in v. 18 by the importance attached to the forgiveness sentence (see Robertson, *op. cit.,* pp. 409-10).

God says. There is no need, since a perfect atonement, adequate for all sins in either direction from the Cross, makes possible an absolute remission. Such remission makes needless any more offering for sin. Sin under the blood of Jesus needs no further blood.

Thus by appealing to the Spirit the writer further proves the finality and efficacy of the one sacrifice to perfect "for ever them that are sanctified." But while v. 17 is his "punch line" in proving this finality, the important relation of the absolute remission of v. 17 to the inward sanctification of 16 must not be overlooked. Whose sins are forgiven and forgotten? Those who have had God's laws (by God's own grace) put **into their hearts** and written **in their minds.** These are not presumptuous professors who persist in sin, or even double-minded believers, but those who are remembering the law and obeying it from their heart, as the law not only of God but now of their own redeemed nature. The unlimited forgiveness is dependent on the experiential reality of the inward rectification. These therefore are the sanctified who have been "perfected for ever." Their justification is perfected forever, and their holiness perfected forever. Both are perpetually available privileges through the exhaustless power of the one sacrifice!

The argument is finished. The writer has shown the finality of our Lord's person, priesthood, and passion. The nature and superiority of the new covenant have been expounded, and the old covenant shown to be obsolete and invalid. Now he makes a hortatory application, and in so doing puts his finger on the central aim of the new order and the objective of his exposition: the way into the holiest.

3. *We Therefore Have Boldness to Enter* (10:19-22)

Having therefore, brethren, boldness to enter into the holiest by the blood of Jesus . . . let us draw near (19, 22*a*). The main predicate in these four verses is **let us draw near;** all else is subordinate. Before this pivotal clause everything is controlled by **having therefore,** and points to Jesus as the **new and living way** (20) of access to the holiest. After this main clause the attention is directed to the necessary personal qualifications for entering. But it will be proper to divide it by verses.

a. The rent veil (10:20). Let us remember that the writer set his sights on the way into the holiest in 9:8, where he declared that "the way into the holiest of all was not yet made manifest." But now the way is both open and disclosed. This way is **new** in the sense that it is newly made. **New** (*prosphaton*) literally means "freshly killed"; here is a way of entrance that never gets old. It is **living** in the sense that it is perennially valid, never outdated; but especially in the sense that it is effectual.[31]

This way **he hath consecrated for us** (20). The act of instituting (aorist tense) is the very deed the writer has been discussing. But Christ has instituted this way **through the veil, that is to say, his flesh. Veil** is *katapetasmatos*, "curtain," from *katapetannumi*, "expand." **The veil,** therefore, is a sort of spiritual "iron curtain" which not only separates but "expands" in the sense of emphasizing the distance between God and man. The original type in the Tabernacle is referred to in 9:3, while the spiritual prototype is mentioned in 6:19. There the entry "into that within the veil" is described as "the hope set before us" and Jesus is said to have entered for us as our "forerunner." The prospect was thus affirmed, but the writer was not yet ready to state the way, which would turn hope into faith and faith into fact. In this keystone verse, however, Jesus is not simply the "forerunner" through the veil, but **his flesh** (human nature) *is* **the veil.** This is a radically new concept, highly figurative, the interpretation of which needs the illumination of Matt. 27:51: "And, behold, the veil of the temple was rent in twain from the top to the bottom."

One interpretation sees **the veil** as a type of Jesus primarily. This would explain the fact that in the Tabernacle the veil was exquisitely beautiful, with emblems interwoven of both humanity and deity (Exod. 26:31-33). Haldeman comments: "So long as Christ walked the earth in His beautiful and perfect humanity, He shut men out from God."[32] Jesus only as a perfect Example would bring condemnation, not salvation, for He would bring into bold relief the impassable gulf between man's sinfulness and that spotless purity requisite for fellowship with the holy God. If the **veil** is to become a **way,** it must be sacrificed; it must be rent. The saving efficacy of the broken body and shed blood was in the perfection of our Lord's total human life and nature, a fit

[31]Dods says: ". . . not as a way that abides (Chrys., etc.) nor as leading to eternal life (Grotius, etc.) nor as a way which consists in fellowship with a Person (Westcott), but as effective, actually bringing its followers to their goal" (*op. cit.*, p. 346; cf. 4:12).

[32]*Op. cit.*, p. 127. See also pp. 123-40.

and acceptable substitute, the "just for the unjust." But as the Blood speaks more of expiation, and is the basis of our justification (His physical life as the cost of our spiritual life), so the body of Christ (v. 5; His human nature) is more particularly associated with the way into the holiest. It speaks not of His life given for us, but His human nature being made available to us, that ours might be a transformed nature (Titus 2:14). Thus there is not only expiation, but sanctification; not only the way into the first sanctuary, with the rights of pardon, but the way into the second, with the rights of inner holiness—complete oneness with God.

An alternate (and maybe preferable) interpretation of **the veil** is to see it as a type of man's sinfulness, which disqualified him from access to the holiest of all. In this case Jesus was that nature—that **veil**—by spiritual identification. He assumed in His own body the unworthiness of that nature and carried it to the Cross (Rom. 6:6; 8:30). This broken body at the Cross released power for the rending of man's sinfulness: (1) "From the top"—man's efforts in altering his nature are vain; only God can do it; (2) "to the bottom"—a thorough and complete destruction of the sinful nature is the provision; it was not torn halfway (Rom. 8:4). But either interpretation of Christ as **the veil** brings us out to the same place: the hindrance is removed, and we have full access into the holiest.

b. The royal Priest (10:21). The rending of Jesus' flesh as a sin offering was not the end, for He arose and ascended to the Father's right hand, where "he ever liveth to make intercession for us" (7:25). We have a **high priest** (lit., "a great priest") **over the house of God.** Not only does this Priest provide the "new and living way," but He is at hand to escort us in, and stand with us as our Surety. The "way" is "living" because the Way-Maker and Way-Guide is living. The fact of Christ's priesthood and its relation to our redemption the writer has already presented in 4:14—7:28. The great major truths of the Christian faith demand action. He refers back to them as the ground of the worshiper's privilege and obligation.

c. The right approach (10:22). Because of Christ's death, for both pardon and perfection, and because of His perpetual priesthood, which is an assurance of ever-available help and mercy, the writer with both exaltation and anxious concern makes his compelling appeal: **Let us draw near** (22).

But the exhortation is not indiscriminate. It is as true as it ever was that there is a prescribed way to enter, and the privilege is restricted to qualified worshipers. The "new . . . way" provided requires a right way to use it. (1) There must be **a true heart.** This is simple and sincere dedication to the perfect and complete will of God. A divided, unyielded, or lukewarm heart will be repelled. (2) There must also be **full assurance of faith.** The word *plerophoria* means "full conviction," firm persuasion, "engendered by faith."[33] These great foundation truths of the gospel must be believed so deeply that our approach to the holiest will be with unhesitant boldness and confidence.[34] Weakness of faith is the Achilles' heel of these Hebrew Christians, and to cure this weakness almost the entire balance of the Epistle will be devoted. But these two requirements—consecration and steadfast faith—are the human conditions which must be met at the crisis of entire sanctification.

(3) But back of these twin requirements for immediate entry are two prior qualifications: **having our hearts sprinkled from an evil conscience, and our bodies washed with pure water.** These highly symbolic clauses speak of the justification and regeneration without which one is not eligible to enter the holiest of all. Implicit here is the priesthood of all believers. No priest would dare approach the inner sanctuary without having had the sprinkling of blood, shed at the great altar, and a careful washing at the great brazen laver. The blood was for the expiation of sins, and the water was for cleansing of filth. Haldeman says, "The laver at the door of the Tabernacle is the symbol of regeneration."[35] But now, though figurative language is used, those who would enter as ministering and worshiping "priests" must have the substance, not the shadow. In the old economy, blood-sprinkling was external (9:13, 19, 21); here it is internal, in the heart (I Pet. 1:2). The washing of our bodies with pure water is as figurative as the sprinkling; therefore this cannot refer to water baptism. That would be a reversion to the formal and external straitjacket from which Christ has extricated us. To see nothing but material water here is to be still imprisoned in Judaism. No water is pure enough to cleanse the acquired depravity of our earthly life.

[33]Vincent, *op. cit.*, p. 501.

[34]See 6:11 for a similar Greek phrase.

[35]*Op. cit.*, p. 236. See also John 15:3; Eph. 5:25-26; Titus 3:5; I John 3:5.

It is now necessary to come to grips with a basic issue which to some minds may still seem unsettled. The interpretation has been developed with the understanding that the holiest of all is primarily holiness of heart rather than heaven as a future abode. Heaven is not only a place, but a sphere of divine grace, and like the kingdom of God (Luke 17:21), is "within you." Hebrews indicates that "heaven itself" is the spiritual counterpart of the earthly Tabernacle (both sanctuaries, 9:24). Yet according to Paul we now may sit together in "heavenly places" (Eph. 1:3; 2:6). Hebrews also admonishes us to come "boldly unto the throne of grace," the very throne shared by the Son, and the very august presence into which Christ has entered beyond the veil. The only way the priests could ever approach the tabernacle type of this throne was by entering within the veil. How do we "come boldly" to this throne? By prayer and faith, which would suggest that time and space are not barriers in the heavenly sphere. The throne of God is where the suppliant is. By the Spirit, the Father and the Son are brought nigh. The unfolding of the writer's exposition strongly indicates that for the believer the holiest of all is not a future state or a far-off location, but an abiding place with the Triune God into which we may enter now, and in which we may live. Notice:

(1) It is in the ark that the tables of law are; and the essence of the new covenant is the engraving of this law on our hearts. This we may experience (cf. Rom. 8:2-4).

(2) There also are the rod that budded and the pot of manna, emblems of the indwelling Christ and the fruit of the Spirit, both of which are the characteristic norm of Christian holiness now (Eph. 3:16-20).

(3) There also are the mercy seat and the overshadowing wings of the divine presence. This secret place with God may be the home of our souls now.

(4) The climax of Hebrews is the affirmation that we have "boldness to enter into the holiest" (19), or "an open-confidence for the way-into the Holy Place" (Mueller). Vincent says: "Lit. *for the entering of the holiest . . . Eisodos* in N.T. habitually of the *act of entering.*"[36]

(5) Since the weight of evidence indicates that boldness is our purchased right for immediate entrance, we should under-

[36] *Op. cit.*, p. 499.

stand **Let us draw near** in this light. It is hardly plausible that the confident entry urged in v. 19 should now be toned down to a respectful and hopeful approach, as would be expected if a future heaven were the holiest of all. Furthermore, the Greek does not imply such hesitancy. The word *proserchometha*, "let us come," is exactly the same as used in 4:16, "Let us therefore come boldly unto the throne of grace." This throne is symbolically within the veil, not outside; and we are not told merely to **draw near,** stopping expectantly at a safe distance, but to "come to" (see also 7:25; 12:18, 22).

There is sufficient reason, therefore, to believe that the exhortation **Let us draw near** is an urgent plea to enter immediately into heart holiness, into that intimate relationship with God and state of inward rectitude which was not the norm under the old economy, but which has now been made equally and freely available to all qualified worshipers. It is this which constitutes the personal and experiential realization of the essential heart of the new covenant. The appeal would lose its true urgency if a mere contemplation of heaven were intended. But to interpret the tone of urgency seriously is to see its connection with a like appeal in 4:11, "Let us labour therefore to enter into that rest, lest any man fall after the same example of unbelief."[37]

D. The Obligations of the Holiest, 10:23-25

While the Jewish high priest "drew near" only once a year, and that never "boldly," it is the privilege of believers to abide in the holiest. But it is not a privilege without its demands, and it is not an "experience" which is once-for-all and non-forfeitable. Its terms must be kept, and its obligations discharged. (Note the homiletical outline of 1, 2, and 3.)

1. *An Unwavering Profession* (10:23)

In being urged to **hold fast the profession of our faith without wavering** we are reminded that an open and public identification with God's plan in Christ must never be relinquished. The present tense suggests the necessity of continuing to voice our faith, and to do it without becoming apologetic or hesitant. For one thing, others need the steadying influence of our steadfastness. Furthermore, our own maintenance of victory is at stake.

[37]See Wiley, *op. cit.*, pp. 331-34.

When we honor God by affirming our confidence in His integrity, He honors us by deepening our assurance.

The usual word in the Epistle for "faith" is *pistis,* whereas the word used here, *elpis,* means "hope." According to Thayer it was the LXX equivalent of the Hebrew word for "trust," and in the NT came to have the Christian sense of "joyful and confident expectation of eternal salvation."[38] The faith with which they entered the holiest (v. 22) might be said to be the faith of *appropriation,* while *elpis* is the faith of *expectation.* One promise, that of the new covenant, is fulfilled, as appropriation becomes realization. But there was yet much unrealized. The promise of the Second Coming (9:28) was yet ahead. It was confidence in this particularly which they must keep on professing—**for he is faithful that promised.**

2. *An Unceasing Provocation* (10:24)

The true holiest of all, enjoyed now by faith, involves a certain corporate and social responsibility. Ancient priests never entered in groups or pairs, but always singly. There is a profound sense in which we too must go alone. It is in solitary loneliness, with God shut in and all the world shut out, that we are sanctified wholly. We are sanctified as individuals, and in the holiest of all we learn to find the sustenance for our souls in God, not in people. Nevertheless this God-dependence is not intended to foster a remoteness from our fellows. There is a rugged moral individualism which is of the very essence of true holiness; but that kind of individualism which is inconsiderate, and cannot work with others, is not only a caricature but a counterfeit. In addition to our steadfast profession of faith, therefore, **let us consider** (present tense—keep on considering) **one another to provoke unto love and to good works.** Let us study one another for the purpose of inspiring and inciting love and good deeds. When instead we provoke each other to grief, anger, or discouragement, with its accompanying neglect of good works, it is because we have not been sufficiently considerate. We have been thoughtless instead of thoughtful. We have not given proper attention to the personality needs of another and to the finesse of our approach. It is amazing the way some Christians inspire their fellows both to be better and do more, while others keep people around them

[38]*Op. cit.,* p. 205.

in an almost constant state of irritation and obstinacy. In actual fact, the sanctified Christian should quickly demonstrate that now, for the first time, he is in a state of grace wherein he can really forget himself in his concern for others.

3. *An Undeviating Practice* (10:25)

To his exhortation to ceaseless mutual consideration the writer adds: **Not forsaking the assembling of ourselves together.** Faithful preservation of that fellowship which can develop only in corporate worship is one of the means of "provoking" each other. Therefore we should attend the means of grace regularly if for no other reason than out of "consideration" for others. But such faithfulness is also one of the "good works" to which we are to incite them—and surely we can do this in no better way than by example. The sad acknowledgment, **as the manner of some is,** would imply that some of these Hebrew Christians no longer felt it necessary to attend the church services. This might be prompted by a mistaken piety, which supposed that solitary worship was better; or a religious conceit, which imagined that the need for corporate worship had been outgrown; or a decline in spiritual fervor, which resulted in sheer indifference. But regardless of the reason, carelessness in our attendance upon the means of grace is fatal, both to our influence and to our own souls. Entry into the holiest does not annul our need for the church, nor does it grant us any special privileges of exemption from our corporate obligations. The practice of assembling regularly is not dispensable but indispensable to holiness.

Only by meeting together can we fulfil the positive duty of **exhorting one another.** The word *parakaleo,* "exhort," has many synonyms: invite to come, call for, call upon, admonish, persuade, entreat, implore, encourage, console. What a gracious, many-sided ministry! We are not called to go to church to criticize, rarely to rebuke, but always to encourage. From the pulpit should come this comforting and encouraging note; and this should be the tone of our public testimonies and personal greetings. For this we do not need an "exhorter's license"!

This tender, faithful concern for one another should increase as we contemplate the Second Coming: **and so much the more, as ye see the day approaching.** The closer we believe His coming to be, the greater is our responsibility to each other. The apostasy of the times should put us on special guard against slackness, both in ourselves and in our brethren.

Section IV *The Finality of Our Profession*

Hebrews 10:26—13:25

A. The Alternative to Faith, 10:26-39

The triple exhortation of the previous paragraph is the peak of the Epistle, inasmuch as the doctrinal exposition has been building up to this climactic point. From here on the practical and personal implications and obligations are urged upon the readers. The Christ-way is at present essentially a faith-way, in contrast to the visible and colorful cultus of the past, with its sensuous appeal, and the visible and concrete Kingdom of the future. This faith-way is an interim between past sight (which only tantalized) and future sight (which will consummate all). But the faith-way, if thoroughly accepted, will be entirely satisfactory, as it brings immediate spiritual blessings in the holiest, and quickens hope for "the Day drawing near" (v. 25, RSV).

1. *Devotion or Disaster* (10:26-31).

The earnest exhortations to "draw near," to "hold fast," and to "provoke" one another to love, and to do so with an accelerated fervor as we "see the day approaching," are in view of the terrifying consequences if we fail to do so. **For if we sin wilfully** (deliberately) **after that we have received the knowledge of the truth, there remaineth no more sacrifice for sins** (26), or, "no longer a sacrifice left-over" (Mueller). God has no additional means of atonement held in reserve, for the benefit of those who elect to reject Christ. The Levitical sacrifices are obsolete and no longer acceptable. Christ's sacrifice will not be repeated. And there is no third route to heaven. All non-Christian religions are ruled out, as are all forms of humanistic gifts of culture and ritual. No Christ-substitute is of any saving value. The deliberate sinning against which we are warned is a failure to go all the way in the full obligations of discipleship after having the knowledge of the truth of the new covenant and salvation in Jesus. It is the view that Christ may be *a* way but not the *only* way; we can find other covering for our sin, and our failure to obey the admonitions of vv. 22-25 does not really matter.

But not so. The only thing remaining, i.e., "now left," is a

certain fearful looking for of judgment and fiery indignation, which shall devour the adversaries (27). This is a definite and sure expectation of God's terrifying judgment and blazing wrath. "When God prepares a hammer it will not be made of silk." In Egypt there was a midnight wail in every home that despised the blood. Later on, the death penalty was inescapable when one despised Moses' law. God has annulled this through Christ (7:18), but men had no right to do so, and those who attempted it, going after "other gods," were to be stoned "till they die" (Deut. 17:1-7), utterly **without mercy** (28). If rejection of Moses and his law was so serious, **Of how much sorer punishment, suppose ye, shall he be thought worthy** who apostasizes from Christ? (29) Since he has shown them so convincingly and inescapably the infinite superiority of Christ and His deed, he challenges them to figure it out for themselves. If they will but think soberly they will know that ex-Christians, for whom so much more has been done, and who have so much more at stake, will deserve as much worse punishment than a rebel against Moses as Christ is more worthy of loyalty than Moses.[1]

This deserving of punishment is seen in its true magnitude when we recognize what the apostate has done. First, he has **trodden under foot the Son of God** (29). This is a picture of extreme scorn. We trample on what we consider of no impor-

[1]Robertson calls this an argument "from the less to the greater," and cites Moffatt as saying such an argument "is the first of Hillel's seven rules for exegesis" (*op. cit.*, pp. 413-14).

The inference here is that the punishment for Christ-rejection will be much more severe than for Moses-rejection. Naturally a question arises. What could be worse than dying "without mercy"? If one so deliberately sinned as to warrant the death penalty, such penalty would presumably be inflicted without benefit of priestly and sacrificial mediation; hence the transgressor would die unforgiven—die, i.e., without divine mercy as well as without the mercy of men. And if he died as a lost soul, was his lostness any less than that of a Christ-rejector? Are there degrees of "lostness"? There are three possible answers. First, Jesus clearly taught degrees of punishment, based on degrees of light and opportunity (Luke 12:46-48). Second, He also taught that to reject Him exceeded in sinfulness all previous rebellion and wickedness, and would precipitate greater wrath (Matt. 11:20-24; 12:41-42; 21:33-41; 23:34-38). But third, we may be reading into the OT account of punishment an ultimate and eternal significance which is not there. The death penalty could have been a public necessity, not a testimony of eternal destiny. Personal repentance may have been possible, with or without atoning sacrifices. Possibly 9:15 is relevant here; even Matt. 10:28, and possibly I Pet. 3:18-22.

tance. The apostate reaches for this world, and joins with the world in trampling, not just Jesus of Nazareth (as he may think), not just the Man of Galilee (as again he may suppose), but the eternal Son of God. Second, he has **counted the blood of the covenant, wherewith he was sanctified, an unholy thing.** Not so much unholy, as common and ordinary—no better than any other blood. This Blood of the new testament, by which one has in the past been made holy, is now denied. "How are the mighty fallen!" (II Sam. 1:19) One may fall from the highest spiritual eminence to incredible depths. But whether backsliders or still pagans, preachers and theologians who declare that Jesus' blood was no different in its eternal value and saving power from that of any other man are guilty of this very sacrilege. Third, the apostate has **done despite unto the Spirit of grace.** He has "insulted" (Phillips), "thus profaning" (Amp. NT), the Spirit. The phrase **the Spirit of grace** (*to pneumatas charitos*) is probably not a subjective genitive (as assumed by NEB), but an objective genitive, meaning the Spirit who imparts grace (Amp. NT). All of the inward movings of our spirits Godward through the years of prevenient grace, all the release and cleansing and power of both justification and sanctification, all the spiritual joy and renewal and glow of the divine favor and the divine enablings are the inward miracle-working of the Holy Spirit. To insult Him is suicide (6:4; Mark 3:28-30).

How do men change so deplorably? First, by spiritual failure —failing to enter the holiest of all, to hold fast the profession of faith, to provoke unto love and good works, and to meet together for worship, service, and fellowship (19-25). Then doctrinal declension is the inevitable next step. The intellect follows the heart. An alienated heart will produce a treacherous and disloyal mind. When the soul is darkened by sin, the mind will be clouded by confusion and uncertainty. The incredible apostasy described in v. 29 implies the denial of the doctrine of the Son of God, the doctrine of the sanctifying Blood, and the doctrine of the Spirit of grace; for Christianity is both doctrine and experience. It is fatal to sever the two, or magnify one at the expense of the other. And it is dangerous to tamper with the "faith which was once delivered unto the saints" (Jude 3; also Gal. 1:23; 3:23; Phil. 1:27). Total apostasy is never expected; it gradually overtakes the one who begins by apostasy at one point. When we whittle down the gospel we soon whittle it away.

The deadliness of such sin ought to be clearly seen by these

Hebrew Christians, **For we know him that hath said, Vengeance belongeth unto me, I will recompense, saith the Lord** (Deut. 32: 25). **And again, The Lord shall judge his people** (30; Deut. 32: 36; Ps. 135:14). They are dealing with the God of their Scriptures, the God they profess to believe in. Furthermore, they claim to be His people, which leaves them totally without excuse. Then comes a solemn exclamation: **It is a fearful** (terrible) **thing to fall into the hands of the living God** (31), i.e., for adverse judgment. From God's hands there will be no escape and no appeal. The God whose hands led the children of Israel in the wilderness (8:9), who stretched out His hands daily to "a disobedient and gainsaying people" (Rom. 10:21), whose "hand is not shortened, that it cannot save" (Isa. 59:1), will by those same hands bring down the proud, and uproot the mighty, and cast the wicked from His holy presence into outer and eternal darkness. The wrath of God is His eternal and holy antipathy toward sin. His love has provided an escape from sin, and thus an escape from the wrath. If this escape is rejected, there is no other: the wrath must consume. Love can offer Calvary, but it cannot alter the disjunction between holiness and sin. If God cannot win us by Calvary, will He save us by force? No, if we will not be saved by the nail-pierced hands, we cannot be saved from the hand with the drawn sword. "Behold therefore the goodness and severity of God" (Rom. 11:22).

2. *Remember Past Steadfastness* (10:32-34).

The tone changes abruptly from stern warning to a personal almost pleading appeal, based on a nostalgic recall of better days **But call to remembrance the former days, in which, after ye were illuminated, ye endured a great fight of afflictions** (32) Following their spiritual enlightenment, which would include an open confession of Christ, they found themselves bitterly contested at once by both demonic and human foes. **Endured** means not only that they suffered this ordeal, but suffered it patiently and came through victoriously. These sufferings were both personal and vicarious. They were at times "publicly exposed to abuse and affliction" (RSV), and other times they were involved in sharing like experiences with their fellow Christians: "being partners with those so treated" (33, RSV). They literally entered into one another's burdens, and gave to each other mutual support and encouragement. They specifically **had compassion** (suffered with, sympathized with) those who were imprisoned for their faith (34).[2] While they were not themselves cast into prison, their material goods were plundered and confiscated. Yet so great was their spiritual fervor that they **took joyfully** such loss, **knowing in yourselves that ye have in heaven a better and an enduring substance** (34; Matt. 6:19-20). Their inner assurance of spiritual realities was strong enough to loosen worldly ties and transfer personal affections. When our sole treasure is in the "here and now," and our faith in the future is feeble, we cannot rejoice when persecution uproots us. This rejoicing was not because their goods were taken, but because their material goods did not constitute their real wealth; that was reserved for them in perfect security, untarnishable by time and untouchable by oppressors.

But apparently the situation was now eased. Instead, however, of prospering spiritually as the Palestinian churches did (Acts 9:31), their improved fortune was accompanied by a spiritual decline. The writer hopes that a reminder of these better days in the past, when their faith was more costly but their fellowship closer and their souls more radiant, will spark a spiritual renewal.

3. *The Faith-Way Is Not Optional* (10:35-39)

In view of (*a*) the awful consequences of apostasy, and (*b*) the triumphs of faith in the past, it is not reasonable to give up now. **Cast not away therefore your confidence** (35). **Confidence** (*parresian*) is the same word translated "boldness" in v. 19 (cf. also 3:6; 4:16). Their past boldness in loyal confession of Jesus and their God-given boldness to live in the holiest should not be tossed aside for social or temporal advantage. All the world's barter cannot equal **the great recompence of reward** (in the world to come) which belongs to their bold fidelity. God will compensate: **For ye have need of patience** (perseverance; cf. 12:1), **that, after ye have done the will of God, ye might receive the promise** (36). The **will of God** which is to be **done** (aorist tense) is explained in vv. 19-25. Instead of retreating, they should advance boldly into the holiest, and persevere therein. In the holiest they will by faith experience the fulfillment of the "better promises" (8:6) respecting the new covenant, and will enjoy complete renovation by the inwardly inscribed law. Only such believers will receive the fulfillment of that other promise that

[2]**Of me in my bonds** has comparatively weak textual support.

Jesus will return (9:28; John 14:1-3; *et al.*). It is clear that obedience regarding the holiest is indispensable if one would qualify to meet the Lord.[3]

That the promise now in mind is the coming of the Lord is at least suggested by the following verse: **For yet a little while, and he that shall come will come, and will not tarry** (37).[4] This application is harmonious with v. 25, and with the second half of the quotation: **Now** (but) **the just** (My righteous one) **shall live by faith: but if any man draw back, my soul shall have no pleasure in him** (38).[5] In spite of the certainty, expressed in terms of immediacy, Christians in the meanwhile "walk by faith, not by sight" (II Cor. 5:7). No matter how precious and experiential privileges in the holiest may be, the holy life is still a life of faith. The full glories of redemption in Christ are yet future, and therefore yet invisible. For earthy, flesh-and-blood beings, this invisibility is a constant test and drain, because the present earth by contrast is so glaringly visible and so suffocatingly near. It is easy to "shrink back" (Phillips) from a life that at so many points denies an earth which can be seen in order to qualify for a world

[3]It is possible to see *poiesontes*, "having done," as a constative aorist, in which case the obedience required to qualify for seeing the Lord embraces the total Christian life, from initial conversion to the end of probation, and includes not only entering the holiest but the possession therein of patience. This would certainly rule out fixation of security by any one initial act of obedience.

[4]V. 37 presents a needling problem. The writer is here combining a brief temporal phrase from Isa. 26:20 with ideas from Hab. 2:3, following the LXX, as usual. The use of the phrase **a little while** is not interpretative of Isa. 26:20, but is simply applied to the particular event described by Habakkuk. That prophecy seems more relevant to Christ's first coming than to His second. Furthermore, *mikron hoson hoson*, **a little while**, adds to the problem, since it literally is *a very, very little while*. The deliberate accent is on extreme brevity. If the reference is actually to the Second Coming as assumed above, it is necessary to see **yet a little while** as a timeless principle, or constantly valid viewpoint. The writer, as a man, might have misunderstood, and expected an immediate return of the Lord. But the Spirit, who prompted the adoption of the phrase, intended this to be the momentary expectation of every generation. Thus His coming is always "imminent." And from the standpoint of the God to whom a "thousand years [is] as one day" (II Pet. 3:8), and from the standpoint of eternity, the delay is indeed but a moment of time.

[5]The singular *dikaios mou*, "my righteous one," reminds us that the Church does not live a collective faith, but by the individual faith of its members. The middle voice, *zesetai*, **live**, would suggest the rendering: "The just man shall maintain life within himself by his faith."

that cannot be seen.[6] But God has **no pleasure** in those who **draw back,** because it is the action of both worldly-mindedness and unbelief.

Faith believes in the reality of the invisible, in the greater value of the spiritual, and in the God who has promised that in Christ the invisible shall become visible and the spiritual become concrete. It is this kind of faith which makes fellowship in the Spirit possible. Stoutly and hopefully the writer assumes their resolute oneness with him: **We are not of them who draw back unto perdition; but of them that believe to the saving of the soul** (39). We are not of the hypocrites or those who make a "stealthy retreat" (Robertson). That would be at the cost of one's eternal soul. Only those **that believe** (*pisteos*), i.e., those belonging to the believers (genitive case), will finally be saved. Clearly, according to this passage, one cannot be a backslider and a believer at the same time.

B. The Credentials of Faith, 11:1-40

It would be natural for the Hebrew Christians to wonder if the faith-way was either necessary or valid. Their Jewish hopes for a Messianic kingdom were not eradicated by the acceptance of Jesus, but were rather transferred to Him. Since their materialistic concept was not fulfilled by His first coming, it became attached to His second coming. As long as they expected this to occur very soon—certainly within their lifetime—they had in that hope sufficient incentive to endure persecution and loss patiently, since they would soon be revenged, vindicated, and restored to earthly power. But when time dragged on with deepening trouble, yet no sign of His coming, they began to experience misgivings. Was Jesus after all their Messiah? Was their sacrifice worthwhile? Inevitably it is easier to begin coming to terms with the world when one ceases to be sure of his reason for conflict with the world.

This hope for a glorious future, while perfectly valid within itself, was mixed with remnants of Jewish nationalism and other

[6]The expression also means those who conceal their testimony as Christians. Cf. Acts 20:20, 27, where Paul testifies that he did not hold back, or conceal, any needed truth because of cowardice. The fact that **if any man draw back** is a third-class condition indicates that drawing back, while not certain, is a possibility. Hebrews is not wasting words warning against hypothetical possibilities which God would never permit to become actual.

serious misapprehensions. Jesus himself, and later Paul, had tried to disabuse the minds of disciples of such lingering misundertandings. They taught, first, that the future glories were essentially spiritual, and that the real reason for following Jesus was the eternal salvation of the soul, not a selfish desire to be "in on things" when His world rule was set up. Second, that the return of Christ in power was not to be expected at once, but there would rather be an intervening period of indefinite duration. During this time their attention should be preoccupied, not with the hope of the Second Coming, but with the evangelization of the world.

Pentecost succeeded in thoroughly shifting the enthusiasm of the Early Church from an earthly, visible rule to the preaching of the gospel, that Christ might indwell the hearts of men by faith. They never lost sight of their "hope," but it became more spiritualized, and certainly more subordinate to their immediate task. Pentecost replaced a materialistic vision with a thoroughgoing spiritual conceptualism. They saw now that the arena of struggle was moral and spiritual, not political or material; that sin and Satan were the real enemies, and holiness (now) and heaven (later) were the real objectives; that the power was neither the sword nor the oration, but the Word, the Blood, and the Spirit.

This fuller understanding had someway not reached through to these Hebrew Christians. Their Pentecost had not come. They were yet double-minded. In this state the temptation was strong to scorn a faith-way, that seemed to be ineffectual. Jesus was no longer visible, and the promise of His return had not been fulfilled. Would it not be better to walk by sight rather than faith, to return to Moses and the Temple? Better to have something concrete and visible than to cling doggedly to a faith in what seemed to be a never-never land of uncertainty and nebulous hope. In the throes of this struggle they were in peril of repeating the error of their fathers (Exod. 32:1).

The elementary necessity of faith, as an integral part of the divine plan, has been implicit in the Epistle all along, occasionally coming to the fore. But now the writer turns to this theme with undivided attention. He must show that the faith-way is superior, not inferior, and that it is effectual, not ineffectual. To do this he advances in c. 11 the credentials of faith, by explaining its nature, and by showing that as a divine requirement the faith-way is not new, but as old as the history of God's people. By it all the righteous in the stream of special revelation were what they were.

If they had not been men of faith, the present generation would have had no rich Hebrew heritage to enjoy.

1. *The Meaning of Faith* (11:1)

The writer begins with a general proposition concerning the nature of faith. **Now faith is the substance of things hoped for, the evidence of things not seen.** The word **faith** (*pistis*) can mean belief, trust, fidelity, firm persuasion, or firm conviction. But in the Bible it always finds its object in God. Biblical faith is not belief in self or man but in God. The constant use of the dative of means ("by faith") in this chapter does not ascribe any magical power to faith itself, but simply sees that faith is the means by which we receive *from* God, the spring of our service *for* God, and the only acceptable basis of a satisfactory relationship *with* God.

The proposition of v. 1 therefore, while not defining **faith** strictly, shows (*a*) its relation to hope, and (*b*) its relation to the invisible. The rendering **substance** is not quite the sense. Rather, *hypostasis* is "a being set under." In this case it means the confidence that our hopes are valid, and the ground for their becoming realized. Faith stands under the **things hoped for** and preserves them for us. If we lose our faith, our hopes will not materialize. Someone has said: "Faith is the title deed." The mere *feeling* of assurance, however, may not be a safe title. That only is safe assurance which is faith in the promises of God, regardless of personal feeling.

Also the proposition indicates the relation of faith to the invisible order of reality. Again the translation **evidence** can be misleading, for faith of itself proves nothing. Strictly, it is true, the word *elengchos* does mean "proof." But here it is used in the sense of "entire persuasion," so complete that further proof is needless. We see things by faith which we cannot see with the natural eye. Phillips catches the intended meaning in its simplicity. "It [faith] means being certain of things we cannot see." Faith therefore is much more than wishful thinking or wistful hoping.

2. *The Assurance of Faith* (11:2-3)

It was in this kind of faith that **the elders** (ancient fathers) received **a good report,** i.e., "were given assurance" (2). The most fundamental general attestation received by faith (by them but shared by us—we) is our understanding **that the worlds were framed by the word of God, so that things which are seen were not made of things which do appear** (3). There is here implied the epistemological principle that faith is a means of knowledge. Much of our knowledge comes by faith in some authoritative person or source of information, rather than by personal presence and verification. We are sure of divine creation but we were not there to see it. Even more germane to the writer's defense of faith is the stated metaphysical fact, not only that the "universe was fashioned by the word of God" (NEB), but that in this creative act the "visible came forth from the invisible" (NEB). Therefore the real world, in the most ultimate sense of reality, is not the phenomenal order but the invisible order. What seems real to our physical senses is actually only a product of that which to our senses seems unreal. Faith therefore is not a fairy-fancy, in a make-believe world, but the exact opposite; it penetrates through the superficial world of appearance to lay hold of the fundamental and eternal reality behind the appearances. Faith therefore is not a concession to the kindergarten level of religion, but is integral to mature religion, and is at the heart of a sound philosophy.[7]

3. *The Righteousness of Faith* (11:4-5)

a. The faith-way of righteousness (11:4). Not only do we acquire knowledge by faith, but faith is the means of receiving assurance of divine approval as well. Abel illustrates the acquisition of righteousness by faith and God's witness thereto, while Enoch illustrates the preservation by faith of this relationship with God clear to the end of life. **By faith Abel offered unto God a more excellent sacrifice than Cain, by which he obtained witness that he was righteous, God testifying of his gifts** (4). God's witness to Abel that he was righteous was in itself an evidence (a testimony) to (not **of**) the acceptability of his gifts. **By which** refers not to **faith** but to **sacrifice**. It was the **more excellent sacrifice** which became the ground of acceptance. By this act **he being dead yet speaketh**; thus we are reminded that faith simply in the goodness of God does not justify anyone. Faith justifies indirectly, not directly. It approaches God through a sacrifice. Faith is active in its perception both of God and of sin,

[7]The preposition **through** at the beginning of v. 3 in distinction from the usual "by" in this chapter reflects no difference in the Greek.

and in its confidence that God is eager to be propitiated. Faith is therefore placed in the sacrifice as a valid approach and also in God's willingness to accept the sacrifice; but faith does not assume that God is indifferent to the means of approach.

The faith of humanism assumes that it needs no sacrifice, but it brings no peace. It is the faith of pride and presumption. Evangelical faith approaches God by way of Calvary. The superiority of Abel's sacrifice[8] was both in his humble spirit and in the substance of his sacrifice (Gen. 4:3-4). Modern Cains, too, need to know that the bloodless offerings of self-righteous men, the labor of human hands, and the achievements of human culture purchase no access to the favor of God. Sin has made all of that invalid as a basis for divine-human at-one-ness. There must be blood, and only the blood of God's holy Lamb will do. Let us offer it by faith, and we too shall know the inner witness of righteousness.

b. The faith-walk of righteousness (11:5). From Enoch we learn that it is both possible and necessary to maintain this faith-relationship throughout earthly probation. **By faith Enoch was translated that he should not see death.**[9] The word **translated** (*metetethe*) is literally "transposed," as from a lower key to a higher (same word in 7:12). In Acts 7:16 it is used in reference to transferring Jacob's corpse from Egypt to Sychem in Canaan. The affirmation that he **was not found** suggests that for days his family and friends searched for him, but in vain, for God had transposed his life to a celestial key. But the outward transposition was justified by the inward transformation. Behind the gift of wings was a godly walk (Gen. 5:24). This was not the rapture of a sinner, but a saint, **for before his translation he had this testimony, that he pleased God.** God's Spirit witnessed that all was well; no last-minute adjustments were needed. Here again the part faith played was indirect—faith, in itself, cannot translate anybody to heaven. But Enoch's walk with God was by faith, and the translation was God's sovereign reward for his faithfulness in so walking.

[8]Lit., "more sacrifice." Its greater excellence is implied in the Greek rather than stated.

[9]The use of *tou* with the infinitive does not in this case mean purpose, but result. God did not translate him in order to exempt him from death, but his exemption was the result of God's act. See Robertson, *op. cit.*, V. 420.

4. *The Substance of Faith* (11:6)

Now a great faith principle is clearly stated. It is first asserted negatively: **But without faith it is impossible to please him.** If Enoch had not kept believing, he would not have kept receiving the assurance that he pleased God. This is an inescapable but simple law of the Kingdom. God must have subjects who have confidence in Him as God—and this includes His wisdom, His goodness, and His power. To doubt is to slander. To trust is to honor. All other tributes are insults if the tribute of faith is lacking. We are not kept by feeling but by faith, because only by believing God can we be pleasing to God.

The principle is next amplified positively: **for he that cometh to God must believe that he is**—this is the intellectual stance of theism. It is a personalistic theism—**he** is, not "Being" is. But men may believe that God exists and still have neither communication nor communion with Him. Therefore theoretical theism must become the humble trust **that he is a rewarder of them that diligently seek him.** Here is a dual confidence: first in God's attentiveness to seeking men, and second in the integrity and benevolence of God's character. He will reward the seeker, and the reward will fully match the need (Luke 11:9-13). Only such confidence makes possible a meaningful and personal relationship. But such confidence does not dispense with diligent seeking. God's rewards of saving grace are not promiscuously and indiscriminately scattered. The relationship must be interpersonal—two-way. Man must want God, not only for His gifts, but for His own sake, and want Him enough to seek Him out. Man must take some initiative too, as evidence of sincere desire.

In v. 6 we see "How to Get Something from God." (1) Purity of motive, **seek him**—His presence, His will, His glory; (2) There must be earnestness of purpose, **diligently seek**—seek sincerely, openly, persistently; (3) There must be simplicity of faith, **believe that he is, and that he is a rewarder**—a faith reflected in diligent seeking, a faith that stakes everything on the integrity of God, a faith that declares itself.

5. *The Work of Faith* (11:7)

By faith Noah . . . prepared an ark (Gen. 6:8-9, 13-22; 7:1). However, the initiative was not human but divine: **being warned of God.** The name of God is not given but implied by the participle, *kramatistheis,* "having been divinely apprised and warned" (cf. 8:5). **Moved with fear** indicates the inward motivation. How is faith compatible with fear? Simply by reason of the fact that the fear was generated by his implicit confidence in the Word of God. He believed a flood was coming, and was electrified into action by the appalling prospect of being caught unprepared. The result of his faith-action was **the saving of his house.** When men believe God and act accordingly, salvation results, both physically and spiritually, in the lives of others.

6. *The Obedience of Faith* (11:8)

When the "father of the faithful" **was called to go out into a place which he should after receive for an inheritance,** he **obeyed.** This too was **by faith** inasmuch as (*a*) there was a background of faith-acquaintance with God himself; (*b*) he believed this impression was the voice of God; (*c*) he believed there was such a place if God said so; (*d*) he believed God would protect him en route and after arrival; (*e*) that God would identify the place in His own way and time; and (*f*) that God's promise to give him the land would surely be fulfilled (Gen. 12:1-4). This is the kind of faith that both prompts obedience and is proved by it. Achieving faith, which does exploits for God, is always a matter of simple obedience, with God taking the initiative. But the faith must be strong enough to obey even when God keeps us in the dark about some details we would like to know. Abraham did not know where he was going, only the direction. No relief map was displayed, only the promise, "I will shew thee" (Gen. 12:1). Some people never accomplish anything for God because they will not obey a step at a time; they want too much advance information. They want to eliminate from obedience all mystery, uncertainty, and apparent risk. But this would mean the elimination of faith as well.

7. *The Sojourn of Faith* (11:9-10)

After Abraham arrived, **he sojourned in the land of promise** (9); literally, "he became a sojourner." He settled in the land, not as owner or conqueror, but as an alien, **as in a strange country;** i.e., not as his own, but as belonging to another. He did not brandish a sword and proclaim his rule; he took nothing into his own hands. This too is the faith-way: to let God fulfill His promises in His own time and manner. We do not have to force issues or precipitate wars to bring about His will. Weak faith is always biting its nails.

Quiet, patient trust was demanded of Abraham for a long time, and not only from him but from his son and grandson, Isaac and Jacob, **heirs with him of the same promise.** Three generations of heirs, living **in tabernacles** (tents), not cities or houses, but as outsiders in their own land! Were they ever tempted to wonder if they had been mistaken, or if God had forgotten, or was too slow? In God's order of things the real state of affairs is often hidden. David was king in God's mind years before he was king in the minds of the people. But faith can wait, for it sees the facts behind the circumstances. It does not have to shout; neither does it abandon hope and drift into despair. This example of Abraham was perhaps given to shame these Hebrew Christians who were getting panicky because not all the promises in Christ had yet materialized.

Abraham may have admired the Canaanitish cities, but he did not envy them, **For he looked for a city which hath foundations, whose builder and maker is God** (10). He "awaited the city having the foundations [of eternal reality], where the architect (*director of works*) and builder (*public worker*) (is) God" (Mueller). He could afford to wait; for long after the Canaanitish cities would have crumbled into dust, God's city would stand. We too can afford to wait.

8. *The Progeny of Faith* (11:11-12).

Faith also was the key to Sarah's miraculous conception: **because she judged him faithful who had promised** (11). True, when she first heard the prediction she "laughed within herself" (Gen. 18:12), for at her age she knew that in the natural the idea was absurd. But her gentle laugh of amusement sobered into firm faith when the Lord rebuked her, and in the end became a laugh of holy joy (Gen. 21:6). Her confidence in God enabled her to receive supernatural strength for the experience.

Through the faith of both Sarah and Abraham, God was able to make good His promise, given first before Isaac was born and then reaffirmed after Abraham was tested at Mount Moriah (Gen. 15:5; 22:17): **Therefore sprang there even of one, and him as good as dead** (lit., already impotent), **so many as the stars of the sky in multitude, and as the sand which is by the sea shore innumerable** (12). But not only is the Hebrew race the progeny of faith, but Gentile believers also, since "they which are of faith, the same are the children of Abraham" (Rom. 4:9-25; Gal. 3:7-9).

9. *The Confession of Faith* (11:13-16)

Biblical faith always looks forward as well as upward, and embraces eternity as well as time. The writer has briefly noted the faith-life of the patriarchs, to whom the promises were given. Now he reminds us that they did not abandon faith because the promises did not materialize overnight. **These all died in faith, not having received the promises** (13). Naturally the form is changed from *pistei,* "by faith," to *kata pistin,* "according to faith." They did not die by faith, but they died **in** the **faith,** believing God to their last breath. They had been given **the promises,** but had not received the fulfillment (same word in 10:36). The promise of a son (Isaac) had been fulfilled; evidently, therefore, **the promises** on which they kept their eye and by which they lived and died were larger than this one. The birth of Isaac was but a token of the fulness to come.

In 13-16 we see that "The Confession of Faith" includes:

a. The possession of vision—**but having seen them afar off,** or, "from afar." This was the seer's insight into the future. They sensed that the vision God had given them was for a far-off day. But they were big enough to see the whole, not just the parts, and see ahead, not just the present; they were willing to be tiny parts in God's larger plan. They knew the God who gave the vision would not die when they did.

b. A persuasion of value—**and were persuaded of them, and embraced them.** They were not only convinced that the promises were "good," but gave themselves completely to the superior values they represented. The two phrases are a dual rendering of one word, *aspasamenoi,* "having saluted," and means in this case "having embraced mentally," having welcomed "to the heart or understanding."

c. A profession of pilgrimage—**and** (having) **confessed that they were strangers and pilgrims on the earth.** Here are revealed a depth of perception and largeness of view in the patriarchs not often recognized. Their vision extended beyond Canaan. They were not only wanderers in the promised land of Palestine, but **strangers** and sojourners **on the earth. For they that say such things declare plainly that they seek a country** (14), i.e., a fatherland; and obviously they do not consider either Canaan or their ancestral land of Mesopotamia to be that true fatherland. Surely, **if they had been mindful of that country from whence**

they came out, they might have had opportunity to have returned (15). The significance of the imperfect tense in both main verbs is missed by KJV (the subjunctive idea of **might** is not in the Gk. text). It should read: "And if indeed they had kept remembering that (land) from which they had gone out, they would continually have had opportunity to return."[10] The chronic backward look produces the habitually backward foot. When men want to "bend back" (*anakampsai*), their eyes will discover plenty of ways and reasons. To be **mindful** is to "fix the thoughts upon," to make mention, to speak of. If people do not want to backslide, they had better keep the past out of both their imagination and their conversation. If God is willing to forget, we had also better forget.

These OT saints, however, were not even glancing back; they were too enamored with the future. **But now they desire a better country, that is, an heavenly** (16). Literally, "they stretch themselves out," so great is their intense devotion. That the patriarchs had a concept of heaven—or at least a spiritual theocracy—is plainly stated, for the contrast is not only with the old land but with the country where they were now wandering as nomads. Canaan was nice, but it did not fulfill the inner revelation which God had given to them. They may have seen in the land a type of the Kingdom, as they saw in Isaac a type of the Messiah and an earnest of the blessing which should be to all the families of the earth. Possibly this is the reason they were willing to be counted as aliens in the land; they never felt really at home anyway. It is sad that their descendants lost the vision (as these Hebrew Christians were in danger of doing), and settled down with fierce attachment to an earthly land. Pilgrims are not overly occupied with possessions; and greedy possessors soon cease to be pilgrims. As C. S. Lewis says: "Many a man thinks that he is finding his place in the world, when in reality it is finding its place in him."

Because of their spiritual-mindedness **God is not ashamed to be called their God: for he hath prepared for them a city.** Some who profess to believe in God are a discredit to Him by their miserable earthbound souls. But not so with Abraham, Sarah, Isaac, and Jacob (Exod. 3:3-16); from them He was glad to receive the appellation **God.** He has in Christ prepared a city—

[10]Chamberlain, *op. cit.,* p. 197.

a sure and eternal dwelling place (John 14:1-4; Rev. 21:2). Because they looked forward in faith, they are as benefited by Christ as we who look forward in faith, though ours is reinforced with the added knowledge of Calvary, which leaves us with no excuse at all for missing the Holy City.

10. *The Test of Faith* (11:17-19)

There is sublime and yet poignant trust in perfect faith, as exhibited in Abraham when he, being **tried** (put to the proof), **offered up Isaac** (17). The writer deliberately bears down on the intense severity of this test: **he that had received** (welcomed, received with joy) **the promises offered up** (was in the act of offering up) **his only begotten son**—the very one **of whom it was said, That in Isaac shall thy seed be called** (18). To one of lesser faith, this would have loomed as a complete dashing of hopes. But Abraham's poise had a simple explanation: **Accounting that God was able to raise him up, even from the dead; from whence also he received him in a figure** (19). That is, figuratively speaking, Isaac was a gift of life out of death; the God who performed one miracle in the fulfillment of promise could perform a second one. The expression **was able** does not ascribe to Abraham certainty that God *would* but that He *could.* This was the only solution Abraham could see; but so great was his trust in God's integrity that he felt perfectly safe to obey absolutely and leave the ways and means to God. It is important to observe that Abraham surmounted this trial because Isaac had never become an idol.

In this passage we see "Faith Tested and Triumphant." (1) Faith is tested (*a*) when the sacrifices demanded seem unreasonable, (*b*) when the mysteries of providence remain unsolvable, (*c*) when the promises of God seem unrealizable; (2) Faith triumphs because (*a*) it believes in God's greatness in spite of difficulties, (*b*) it trusts in God's goodness in spite of appearances, (*c*) it obeys God's orders in spite of consequences.

11. *The Confidence of Faith* (11:20-22)

Faith gives to its possessor the eyes of the seer, and a quiet confidence in the future of God's people. This is demonstrated in Isaac, who **by faith . . . blessed Jacob and Esau concerning things to come** (20; cf. Gen. 27:27-29, 39-40). It is also seen in

Jacob . . . who blessed both the sons of Joseph on his dying bed (21; cf. Gen. 48:11-20).[11] Joseph exemplifies this still further: **By faith Joseph, when he died, made mention of the departing of the children of Israel; and gave commandment concerning his bones** (22; cf. Gen. 50:24-25). He wanted no remains left in Egypt. In all three examples the confidence in the future was based on faith in the integrity of God's promises. Here was vision which transcended both their own fortunes and their own generation. They saw themselves as part of a great plan, links in an unfolding chain of divine history.[12] Their faith was undisturbed by the lack of fulfillment in their lifetime—added rebuke indeed for these wobbling Hebrew Christians!

12. *The Courage of Faith* (11:23)

It was faith that enabled Amram and Jochebed to hide **Moses, when he was born . . . three months . . . because they saw he was a proper child; and they were not afraid of the king's commandment** (Exod. 2:2 ff.). The commandment was that every male infant should be cast into the river (Exod. 1:22). But this child was perceived by the parents to be **proper,** i.e., beautiful. The adjective "princely" would better convey the idea. All fond parents think their child is exceptional; there is a hint here, however, of a prophetic insight that this child had a special destiny. This vision and faith gave the parents courage to believe that God would assist them in circumventing the cruel injunction of the king. They **were not afraid** (lit., were not terrified or intimidated). When the babe became so noisy at three months that they could no longer keep his presence secret, they prepared a floating cradle and appointed his big sister, Miriam, baby-sitter. Instead of casting him into the river they put him on the river, believing that if God had a special plan for him He could someway manage his preservation. And He did, in a manner "stranger than fiction."

[11]The next clause should be, "and worshipped upon the top of his staff," from the LXX. This corresponds to Gen. 47:31: "And Israel bowed himself upon the bed's head." Leaning is implied in the LXX version, and worship is implied by the Hebrew. As to whether it should be **staff** or "bed," Robertson says, "The Hebrew word allows either meaning with different vowel points" (*op. cit.*, p. 425).

[12]He who would write a Christian philosophy of history should begin with this chapter.

13. *The Choice of Faith* (11:24-26)

The early years are sometimes more important than the later years in a child's life. Fortunately Moses' mother had him when he was most plastic, and must have schooled him well in the knowledge of the one true God. As a youth he weighed the simple, God-fearing lives of his mother's people and the glittering but corrupt life at court. **By faith Moses, when he was come to years, refused to be called the son of Pharaoh's daughter** (24). It was a clear-cut and final disavowal, as the aorist tense would suggest. He broke with the Egyptian royalty once and for all, **choosing** (lit., having chosen) **rather to suffer affliction with the people of God** (25). The outward, courageous refusal was the result of a previously made inward decision. The ability to make up one's mind, and to settle always on the right side, is the mark of strong character. Again the writer is shaming these Hebrew Christians for their weak wavering.

The cruel oppression and hardship suffered by his people Moses well knew; he was not naively ignorant. But he weighed their sufferings over against **the pleasures of sin,** because he perceived that the sufferers were **the people of God,** therefore were inwardly superior, and would come out best in the end, while **the pleasures of sin** were but **for a season.** Thus the advantages of the Egyptian court were seen to be both superficial and temporary. His choice, therefore, was prompted by his standard of value: **Esteeming the reproach of Christ** ("the stigma that rests on God's Anointed," NEB) **greater riches than the treasures in Egypt.** The stigma is still there! Modern religionists try by every conceivable means to destigmatize the Christian way, but we may be sure that to the extent they succeed in making Christ palatable to the natural man, to that extent they have fashioned a false and imaginary Christ. What concept did Moses have of **Christ** (lit., the Christ)? Probably not a clear concept, but his knowledge that the Hebrews were the people of God doubtless also included a dim knowledge of a promised Anointed One (I Cor. 10:1-4). Though his mind may have been hazy as to details, his faith was sure, so sure that on it he was willing to risk both his present and his future.

Baring Moses' heart still further, the writer explains that his system of value was structured in large measure by his ability to look ahead: **for he had respect unto the recompence of the reward** (26). Literally, the word *apeblepen,* "he was looking," means "look off from all other objects and at a single one." The imperfect tense indicates that this was not a romantic and flighty interest, but a steadfast gaze. He kept on looking with fixed and earnest attention; inevitably the Egyptian glitter completely faded from view. The secret always of escaping the siren charms of the world is to look far enough ahead to perceive duration and consequence.

By faith therefore Moses was able to perceive the real issues of life. On the surface it looked as if he were choosing between pain and pleasure, but in reality it was between godliness and sin. Superficially it seemed to be a choice between his mother and Pharaoh's daughter, but in reality the choice was between Christ and the world. He appeared to be choosing between poverty and Egypt's treasure; but actually it was between heaven and earth. It seemed to be between the desert and the throne; underneath, it was between immortality and oblivion.

Furthermore, **by faith** he was able to distinguish the passing from the permanent. The *passing* included (1) the suffering of God's people, (2) **the pleasures of sin,** (3) **the treasures in Egypt,** (4) **the reproach of Christ.** The *permanent* included (1) **the people of God,** (2) the person of **Christ,** (3) the payment of **the recompence.**

In 24-26 we see "The Qualities of Strong Faith." (1) It perceives the superiority of spiritual and moral values over sensual and temporal blessings, 25-26; (2) It is sure that the lasting values are on the side of Christ and the people of God, 24, 26; (3) It chooses to surrender a passing advantage for a permanent gain, 25-26.

14. *The Endurance of Faith* (11:27)

By faith he forsook Egypt, not fearing the wrath of the king (27). According to Exod. 2:11-15, Moses' youthful exodus was a real flight, prompted by a fear. It is more likely therefore that Hebrews is here referring to the dignified and deliberate departure forty years later. The word *katelipen,* **he forsook,** simply means to relinquish, to leave behind, and does not necessarily imply flight. In his youth Moses' faith was strong enough to make the basic and ultimate choice, but it needed the maturing of the desert and the burning bush to become panic-proof. The secret of his poise was that **he endured, as seeing him who is invisible.** He bore stoutly the threatenings and duplicity of the cornered

Pharaoh, and was fortified because faith sees the **invisible;** not only the invisible order as such, but the "Invisible One" (masculine singular). Faith has a spiritual radar which unbelief lacks (II Kings 6:16-17; Dan. 3:23-25). But the great distinguishing mark of biblical faith is that it is fixed on a personal God, not some impersonal law or power.

15. *The Exodus of Faith* (11:28-31)

True faith always gets out of Egypt. It never stays. Actually v. 27 is both a preface and preview of this section, which consists of sketching the high points of the migration from Egypt to Canaan. The history here is not all bright; shameful unbelief checkered the story, with tragic consequences. Elsewhere in the Epistle the Hebrew Christians have been sharply reminded of this. But attention now is on the fact that the nation would never have been freed from slavery, and would never have acquired Canaan, if it had not been for those who had faith. Every major step forward was a victory of faith. Doubt chalked up no advances.

a. The Passover (11:28). The first essential preparatory step in the Exodus was the Passover. **Through** (or by) **faith he kept the passover, and the sprinkling of blood.** The object was to escape the sword of him **that destroyed the firstborn.** This act of divine judgment was not only necessitated and justified by Egyptian stubbornness, but it was symbolic of that eternal death which is endemic to spiritual Egypt. Similarly the lamb slain was symbolic of that future Lamb of God, who should take away the sin of the world (John 1:29). There is no escape, either from Egyptian bondage or Egyptian darkness or death, without the sprinkling of blood. But notice, life is dependent not just on the blood shed, but the blood applied. Shed blood alone would have protected no one. There was salvation only as the blood was sprinkled individually on the individual lintel and two side posts of the individual home (Exod. 12:23). The truth applies equally to the blood of God's Lamb. It is only as faith appropriates and the Spirit works that the Blood saves.

b. The Red Sea (11:29). **By faith they passed through the Red sea as by dry land.** For details see Exod. 14:22-27. The faith now is ascribed to the people, as well as to Moses. In this event we see the difference between faith and presumption. It does not lie in what is done but on what authority. Israel acted on divine command, but the **Egyptians assaying** (lit., taking a try, or making trial) **to do** the same thing **were drowned.** The same action may be proper and successful, or presumptive, fanatical, and disastrous, depending on the presence or absence of God. "With God, over the sea; without Him, not over the threshold."

c. *The walls of Jericho* (11:30). Moses is dead; no longer can the Israelites depend on his faith. But that faith was shared by his protegé Joshua, and to some extent by the whole nation. This was a new generation, which had profited at least in some measure from the debacle of their fathers. Though the river Jordan had been crossed, Jericho blocked their path at the very gateway to the Promised Land, actually more formidable than the fears of Kadesh-barnea. But **by faith the walls of Jericho fell down.** How can faith bring down high walls? Psychological, subjective effects of faith are explainable, but faith sends out no thought waves possessing objective, physical power. Faith achieves its object mediately, not immediately, by way of (1) human obedience, and (2) the power of God. The walls therefore fell down only after they were compassed about seven days.[13] "Faith without works is dead" (Jas. 2:26). But the "works" must be prescribed by God, not by man.

d. *The convert*[14] *Rahab* (11:31). According to Rahab's own testimony to the spies sent out by Joshua (Josh. 2:1-21), her people knew the recent history of the Israelites, and because of this their hearts were paralyzed by fear. What was there in her fear that made it faith? (1) She perceived the plan of God; (2) she accepted the plan of God and adjusted to it; (3) she acted on her new allegiance, even at the risk of her life; (4) she gathered her family and hung out the scarlet thread (Josh. 2:18; 6:25). In the scarlet thread given to Rahab can be seen a type of that longer "scarlet thread" which runs from Genesis to Revelation as the badge of the people of God. James cites Rahab as

[13]For more on Jericho, see George Frederick Wright's article in *The International Standard Bible Encyclopaedia*, III, 1592.

[14]It is not certain at all that Rahab was an immoral woman; the word in the original Hebrew may only have meant (as in her case) "innkeeper." If on the other hand she was an evil character, we are reminded that saving faith will bring harlots into the Kingdom while unbelief will keep "the good" people out. See Adam Clarke, II, 10 ff. Also many believe Rahab to be the Rachab of Matt. 1:5, which would make her an ancestress of David and of Christ. See Adam Clarke, *ibid.;* also Lightfoot, *Horae Heb,* on Matt. 1:5. Such an assumption, of course, implies gaps in the genealogy as given by Matthew.

an example of being justified "by works" (Jas. 2:25). There is not the slightest incongruity here; nor will anyone suppose such if he sees the true nature of biblical faith. The principle of action in faith is illustrated here as in v. 30.

16. *The Conquests of Faith* (11:32-35*a*)

And what shall I more say? Is it necessary to go on detailing the laurels of faith to brace up these Hebrew Christians? In the interests of space the writer condenses the exploits of the OT into a compact summary. Without enlarging, he mentions **Gideon . . . Barak . . . Samson . . . Jephthae . . . David also, and Samuel,** and **the prophets** (32). All are Israel's heroes. Not all were equally worthy, but all achieved immortality because in the hour of crisis they rose up as men of faith. God can do more with 300 men of faith (Gideon's band) than with 32,000 whose hearts tremble with fear and doubt. Having listed a few famous names, the writer enumerates some of the mighty deeds wrought by faith: **subdued kingdoms, wrought righteousness** (worked out righteous solutions), **obtained promises** (33). In this case the *fulfillment* of **promises** is meant (same word in 6:15; Rom. 11:7). **Women received their dead raised to life again** (35*a*). This was faith triumphing over death.[15] Verses 33*b*-34 list some of the more dramatic and sensational exploits, but easily overlooked is the more important conquest of faith: **out of weakness were made strong** ("strengthened-with-power"—Mueller). But the layman, preacher, missionary, church, and nation must first feel and acknowledge their weakness, then resolutely look to God and God alone. At this point He can infuse them with power (I Sam. 14:6; Jas. 4:6-10), and use a "worm" to "thresh the mountains" (Isa. 41:14-15). But by far the deepest weaknesses and the highest mountains are moral. When a weak character is transformed into a spiritual and moral giant by the power of faith—that is the great miracle.

17. *The Triumph of Faith* (11:35*b*-38)

In the middle of v. 35 a sharp corner is turned with the words: **and others were tortured, not accepting deliverance.** The writer

[15]The mothers of I Kings 17:17 ff. and II Kings 4:8-37 witnessed *anastaseos,* a resurrection, but faith looks ahead to a *kreittonos,* "better resurrection." Any resurrection now would be temporary and merely physical. Ahead of the believer is a resurrection which is total, permanent, and celestial (I Corinthians 15).

has been reciting the heroic achievements of faith; now he moves to her patient sufferings. This is not a lower but a higher key in the symphony of faith, though the tone is hushed and reverent. The allusion in these verses is to men and women in the history of God's people who could have saved their lives by renouncing their faith. They chose rather to renounce life itself, even at the cost of agony, that **they might obtain a better resurrection.** This is the supreme mark of authentic faith: it is not so concerned about what happens this side of death as about what happens the other side. True faith reaches beyond every present denial, and through every earthly barrier. Its strength does not rest in visible proofs and miraculous deliverances, but comes from communion with God himself. It therefore transcends the need for sensory supports. Because faith is sure of God in Christ it is sure of the final outcome. It is a weak faith that will not believe except it "see signs and wonders" (John 4:48).

Too often we find ourselves saying: "Things are beginning to improve—my faith is rising." Real faith rests in the integrity of God when things are getting worse instead of better. The supreme test of all is the moment of agony when we know that God could deliver us if He would, and He does not; when the scourge lashes, the prison locks, the saw tears the tender flesh—and God allows it. Fair-weather faith soon vanishes before the onslaught of such soul-shaking tempests. If faith is relevant only to being happy and prosperous in this world, it is a feeble and worthless crutch of selfish earthliness. True Christian faith, by contrast, finds its greatest triumph, not in the visible exploits, but in a quiet confidence and poise when there are no encouraging circumstances. The brightest faith is faith that is bright when right is vanquished, when wrong is on the throne, and life seems completely irrational. Surely it can be said of such OT saints: **Of whom the world was not worthy** (38).

18. *The Report of Faith* (11:39-40)

All of these noble victors, **having obtained a good report** (having been assured) **through faith, received not the promise** (39). *The Amplified New Testament* renders it: "Though they won divine approval by [the help of] their faith, [they] did not receive the fulfillment of what was promised." The same affirmation was made of the earlier patriarchs in v. 13. The reason for the delay is now stated: **God having provided some better thing**

for us, that they without us should not be made perfect (40). This **better thing** cannot refer to heaven, for they will share that with us on an equal basis.

The **better thing** can refer only to probation and privilege. Our post-Pentecost advantages are in the "rest," "perfection," "sanctification," and access to the holiest which the writer has been discussing. This Epistle is unmistakably clear in teaching that a level and quality of personal salvation are made possible by the events of Good Friday, Easter, and Pentecost which were not available before. The dispensation of the Holy Spirit is a real advance, not only in method of redemptive outreach and in revelation of truth, but in the area of accessible spiritual attainment. Such a depth of redemption, effected in the new covenant, was foreseen under the old regime but not enjoyed. This was evidently the prize which their faith laid hold of. But simultaneous with our present spiritual blessings, they have now "caught up" with us and enjoy them in heaven. In this sense they are now **made perfect;** their souls' deliverance is consummated. But while their faith reached for blessings beyond the grave, ours must lay hold of at least the earnest of those blessings now, while yet in life. To prod these Hebrew Christians into so doing has been the aim of the entire Epistle.

C. The Perseverance of Faith, 12:1-29

1. *Resources in Christ* (12:1-4)

The writer, having proved so eloquently that the necessity of living by faith is no ground for self-pity, but rather is a way trod by their ancestral heroes, now "pounds the pulpit" with a resounding **Wherefore** (*toigaroun*). This is a doubly strengthened form of the particle *toi,* combining *toi, gar,* and *oun:* "Well then!" (It is used only here and in I Thess. 4:8.) He has been pointing at their fathers; now he points squarely at them (but with the first person plural pronoun): **Seeing we also are compassed about** (surrounded) **with so great a cloud of witnesses,** we are under immediate obligation to change both our attitude and action. The **also** associates us with those in 11:39. The **witnesses** are not mere observers in the stands, curious to see how we will do, but testifiers that they have made it, so we can too. In number they are a vast **cloud** of boosters, one great "cheer squad." The picture is that of a great amphitheatre. The onlookers are all friends, and we are challenged by them to succeed in the race. We can, if we do certain simple things: **Let us lay aside every weight, and the sin which doth so easily beset us.** This is the negative admonition, and concerns qualifying for the race. Unnecessary encumbrances which will wear us out and slow us down, no matter how innocent in themselves, must be stripped off, just as a runner divests himself of superfluous clothing.

Equally imperative is putting off, *ten euperistaton hamartian,* the "easily or constantly environing sin." The adjective is used only here in the NT. RSV's phrase, "sin which clings so closely," is apt, but its ignoring of the article (following Moffatt) is not justified, for a specific sin was in the writer's mind (see Phillips; NEB, including footnote; Amp. NT). Turning the singular into plural and rendering it "sins," as does *Living Letters,* is without excuse. The habitual practice of sinning is not in mind here; it is rather a tendency or fault which is hard to shake loose, but which will mean their ultimate defeat if they do not. Robertson identifies this as apostasy from Christ; but if so it could only be incipient. A chronic tendency to unbelief, which constantly exposes them to apostasy, is more compatible with the previous chapter and in fact the entire Epistle. But such a chronic tendency is simply an evidence of the carnal mind, and one of its characteristic manifestations. Evidently this may and must be laid aside, put off, completely and entirely. This differs from an earthly runner, who expects to return and take up his garments and treasures again. It is once-for-all divestment, for in the Christian race there is no finish line this side of the grave.

The positive instruction is, **And let us run with patience the race that is set before us (1).** But let us also get the grammar straight. KJV and RSV both give us two **let us** pleas, when in reality there is only one, *trechomen,* **let us run.** The first instance is an aorist participle, *apothemenoi,* and should be translated, "Having laid aside . . . let us run." Furthermore, in contrast to the definiteness and finality of the laying aside, the running (present tense) must be ceaseless—"Let us keep on running." Patience (*hypomones*) means "constancy, perseverance." The prize is not for the good starters but for the good finishers. An initial spurt of speed does not entitle the Christian to a nap later on. For **the race that is set before us** ("laid-down-before us," Mueller) embraces the whole of life, and is a contest to the finish with sin, the flesh, and the devil. Fortunately, however, it is a contest which not only one but every entrant may win.

For this life-run, and for the decisive discarding of sin which we must do now if we would stand any chance of winning finally, there is adequate grace in **looking unto Jesus** (2), our Living Saviour. He is our ever-present and available Resource for strength and steadiness. Here is another participle, also dependent upon **let us run;** it therefore tells us how to run successfully. And since it is present tense, we learn that this is a condition which we must continue to meet all along the way. When our eyes stray from Jesus, our feet wobble from the course marked out. The word is "looking away" (same as Phil. 2:23), meaning from other people, other things, even from the "cloud of witnesses," to Jesus alone.

The logic of such a constant gaze is the fact that Christ is **the author and finisher of our** ("the," NEB) **faith.** This whole faith-plan and method finds in Jesus its prime **author,** or "File Leader" (cf. 2:10; translated "Prince of life," Acts 3:15). He is not the **author . . . of our faith** in the sense that He has created and implanted it by the unilateral operation of the Holy Spirit. But He can be said to be the Author of our personal faith in the sense that He is its Object, its Inspiration, its Ground, and that it would be impossible without the total redemptive action of the Son. The sense of Captain (as in 2:10) must be included too, in carrying out the imagery of a race. He is the Captain of the team; we look to Him for orders and leadership.

He is also the **finisher** (*teleioten*) of the faith. He was perfected through suffering (2:10); the faith-way (and inferentially, our faith) is perfected by this perfected Saviour. In one sense He perfected it at Calvary; in another sense by the Resurrection; in us He perfects it by chastening (5 ff.) and by holiness (14 ff.); in the ultimate sense He will consummate the faith by His second coming and our glorification. He perfects by rounding out, completing, supplying all parts, at whatever stage perfecting is needed. He perfects our regeneration, our sanctification, our Christian maturity, and our final salvation.

His power of example and His sufficiency as a source of grace are now expounded more specifically: **who for the joy that was set before him endured the cross, despising the shame.** The reproach of the Cross, its shame and social stigma, was becoming an embarrassment to these Christians; their avowed Messiah had died on a hated Roman cross as a common criminal. But the One who suffered the shame most of all—Jesus himself—despised it completely. To be overwhelmed by the social shadow of the Cross was to lose a true perspective. He was able to endure and despise it because of the certain outcome—the joy that would follow the sufferings. Confidence in tomorrow sustains for today. This is the attitude these Hebrews should take. They should be far more ashamed of their own cowardly cross-evasion than of His cross-bearing. Since now He is Lord, **set down at the right hand of the throne of God,** there is an absolutely secure future for them if they believe—but an equally certain judgment for them if they become turncoats.

He further incites them to steadfastness by pleading with them to **consider him that endured such contradiction of sinners against himself** (3)—i.e., "such grievous opposition and bitter hostility" (Amp. NT)—**lest ye be wearied and faint in your minds** (souls). Their trials and persecutions had not matched His. **Ye have not yet resisted unto blood, striving against sin** (4). This should have made them wince. Evidently these Christian Hebrews had come through their persecutions with little loss. They may have lost possessions (10:34), but they had shed no blood, as had Jesus, and even some of those cited in c. 11.

2. *Incentives in Chastening* (12:5-11)

The writer now turns to an appeal to scripture, on which he develops a Christian philosophy of suffering. The basic thesis is that their sufferings should be interpreted as chastening, and chastening as an evidence of sonship and divine favor—therefore not an occasion for discouragement but for encouragement.

a. The biblical premise (12:5-8). Under the pressure of adverse circumstances it is easy to forget the relevant portions of God's Word, which ought to comfort and steady us in this very time of need (Ps. 119:49-52, 105-7). **And ye have forgotten the exhortation which speaketh unto you as unto children,** he chides. The following admonition is from Prov. 3:11-12, LXX (cf. Rev. 3:19): **My Son, despise not thou the chastening of the Lord, nor faint when thou art rebuked of him** (5). In general, **chastening** (*paideias*) has reference to discipline, training, and instruction (pediatrics and pedagogy are modern terms based on *pais*); in this context the unpleasant side of discipline is in view. In v. 6 scourging is specified, implying corporal punishment—the use of the rod. Our Heavenly Father believes in the advice

He has given to earthly fathers in the Word (Prov. 13:24). Modern pedagogy, which has eliminated the rod, has not produced better children. Someone has said, "If the psychology of permissiveness were right we would be a nation of saints." To **despise** this is to "neglect, regard slightly, make light of." If we take a wrong attitude toward discipline, we forfeit the benefit.

Such chastening is not an expression of God's displeasure but His favor. **For whom the Lord loveth he chasteneth** (6). If therefore you are experiencing chastening, you should take comfort and reassurance in the fact that God is simply dealing **with you as with sons** (7). What a high privilege to be treated by God as His sons! Better to be chastised by God than pampered by the devil! The rhetorical question, **For what son is he whom the father chasteneth not?** implies that since this is expected of earthly fathers as the normal course, we should not be surprised when God as Father acts in conformity with His proper role. It also implies that all human sons are faulty, so much so that an absence of chastening might imply a lack of true fatherly interest, even true fatherly ties: **But if ye be without chastisement, whereof all are partakers, then are ye bastards** (illegitimate children), **and not sons.** Too much prosperity and smoothness in life may be a bad sign. This should be remembered when some modern charlatans preach a religion of "health, wealth, and prosperity." God is interested in saving souls and developing strong character, not just in seeing to it that "a pleasant time is had by all." What can we conclude so far?

(1) That the reverses and adversities of life are either sent or permitted by God for their disciplinary value.

(2) All of us need such discipline; therefore it should be embraced with humility and gratitude, rather than resentment and disquiet.

(3) That we are not alone in such experiences, for they are universal to the children of God, and should be expected.

(4) That they are the surest possible evidence, not of God's disinterest, but of His profound interest and concern for us as individuals—members of the royal family.

b. The parental example (12:9-10). Moreover, the writer says, since we have had this kind of correction from our earthly fathers and **gave them reverence: shall we not much rather be in subjection unto the Father of spirits, and live?** (9) The parental duty of careful and strict child training was universally acknowledged among the Jews, and disrespect and rebellion were almost unknown. Surely therefore they should have no trouble in seeing the far greater and even more logical propriety of accepting the same from God, **the Father of spirits,** from whom our eternal life is derived. Men are fathers of the flesh; God is our spiritual Father (John 1:12). The family relationship is spiritual, though as real as physical relationship with earthly fathers. This phrase does not necessarily imply biblical support for "creationism" as a theory for the origin of individual souls. It is simply an affirmation that our relationship with God is more fundamental to the inner man and more eternal in nature than is our relationship with our human fathers.

There is yet another reason for extending to God even greater respect: Our earthly fathers were faulty in their administration of discipline, but such bungling can never be ascribed to God. **For they verily for a few days chastened us after their own pleasure** (10); or "according to the thing seeming good to them."[16] The verse does not imply that they inflicted punishment just to feel good themselves, but according to their judgment at the time; and often their methods were not the most conducive to the desired end. Such failure cannot be ascribed to God: **but he for our profit** (*epi to sumpheron*); the phrase should probably be rendered, "by that which is appropriate."

The exact end is spelled out: **that we might be partakers of his holiness** (lit., "for the sharing in of His holiness"). This is God's supreme aim and wish for man, and is the objective of all His redemptive deeds. We may not share God's natural attributes which belong solely to Deity—as omniscience, omnipotence, etc. But we may be like Him in holiness, since this is a moral quality possible (through grace) to all personal moral agents. And this is a sufficient—and the only sufficient—basis of fellowship (I Pet. 1:14-16).

c. *The "peaceable fruit"* (12:11). Holiness is the aim, and chastening seems to be one of God's methods. But the aim of the method is not always obvious; neither is the effectiveness of the method always immediately apparent. **Now no chastening for the present seemeth to be joyous, but grievous.** While in the throes of the suffering, Christians have a hard time seeing anything to shout about. They may be unable to perceive any "rhyme or reason" at all, and only a strong faith can "in every

[16]Robertson, *op. cit.*, p. 436; cf. Phillips.

thing give thanks" (Rom. 5:1-5; Phil. 4:4-6; I Thess. 5:18; Jas. 1:2-4; I Pet. 1:5-7). But though the full meaning of our sufferings may never be disclosed in this life, the spiritual benefit within ourselves will gradually become apparent: **afterward it yieldeth the peaceable fruit of righteousness**—not to the nonparticipants, and academic theorizers, but **unto them which are exercised thereby.** Only the sharers in the suffering share in the personal profit. The perfect tense of **exercised** indicates completion: the ordeal is past; the lesson over. God brings us *into* but He also bring us *through*—though some tunnels are longer than others, and some seem very long indeed. In contrast to **exercised,** the term **yieldeth** is present tense, suggesting a continuous reaping of benefit. The word means to render back. It thus is a yielding of returns on an investment, or a harvest on the seed sown. **Righteousness** ("holiness," v. 10) is itself **the peaceable fruit** (same word, Jas. 3:17). The **fruit** of **chastening,** which is **righteousness,** is **peaceable** in the sense that it imparts peace and belongs to peace (Rom. 14:17).

Assuming that **righteousness** and "holiness" are used synonymously in these verses, we may conclude that the *partaking* (10; aorist infinitive—punctiliar, indicating a definite possession) of the holiness is brought about gradually by means of chastening.[17] There is herein a significant inference, but also one or two questions. The inference is that this holiness is a subjective state of character, not merely an imputation. Imputed righteousness (or holiness) belongs to justification, and is given solely on the ground of the atoning Blood and appropriating faith. It does not in the least depend on the cleansing, refining influences of sufferings.

The questions are: (1) To what extent are we to share God's holiness? Obviously only in a reflective and partial sense, though real, not fictitious. Obviously also, in a progressive sense, as we "pursue" it (v. 14) and walk in the light. But complete holiness is intended at once at least in the sense of the exclusion of sin (v. 1).

(2) Is chastening the only way of producing holiness in us? By no means. There is a degree of holiness which is ours in regeneration; subsequently, another degree imparted by the Spirit in fulfillment of the new covenant (10:10-17). No prolonged

[17]No contradiction here. The punctiliar idea is that of definiteness and completeness, but does not always mean instantaneity.

suffering is needed for this, or indeed will ever effect it. This is indeed that fellowship of holiness—that life "near to the heart of God" in the holiest—into which we may enter by faith (10: 19-25). That holiness which is the aim of chastening is particularly related to maturity rather than purity.[18]

Finally (3), How can suffering make us more holy? It cannot, directly. It does so only indirectly, as we let God's grace sanctify the suffering and thus use it to deepen our understanding, enlarge our sympathies, strengthen our faith, stabilize our purpose, spiritualize our perspectives, sweeten and mellow our attitudes, and thus make us in character and personality more Christlike. The benefits of chastening are not automatic. They may never accrue—certainly will not if we rebel and apostatize. We must "trust and obey"; we must submit to the molding hand of the Potter if we are to benefit from chastening.

3. *Diligence in Holiness* (12:12-17)

The writer has explained that chastening is a ground for exultation, not gloom. Now he exhorts the Christians to act accordingly.

a. Holiness in the life (12:12-13). **Wherefore lift up the hands which hang down, and the feeble knees** (12). Snap out of the posture (both literally and figuratively) of discouragement. Let the hands be lifted up in praise, extended out to the needy, and put under the burdens of life. There is work to do. Let the knees cease to tremble with fear, and stand like men (Eph. 6:10-13). **And make straight paths for your feet** ("straight, *orthas,* wheel tracks"—Robertson), **lest that which is lame be turned out of the way** (13; cf. Prov. 4:26, LXX; Isa. 35:3). It is not quite clear whether the **lame** (*to cholon*) refers to the personal weakness of the believer's spiritual foot which is in danger of being turned aside (*ektrape*) (as assumed by RSV, Phillips, NEB) or whether it is a weak Christian, as a member of the body of Christ, who is in danger of being diverted completely by the crooked paths of older believers. Some interpret the passage as referring to individuals: "Let no lame souls be dislocated, rather set them right" (Moffatt); "Graphic picture of concern for the weak" (Robertson). On the other hand the singular neuter gender suggests the impersonal **that which;** the *ektrape,* **turned**

[18]See Wiley, *op. cit.,* pp. 390-93.

out, is interpreted by some as (in this case) a medical term meaning "in order that what is lame may not be dislocated."[19]

In either case it is best not to lose sight of the highly metaphorical nature of this verse, as referring, not to persons, but to aspects of the Christian life. As hands are a metaphor of service, and knees are a picture of attitude (whether courageous or anxious), so feet are a picture of the Christian's daily walk. If that walk is wobbly and crooked, our own weaknesses will be made worse and our influence on others will be damaging. God desires healing instead; but neither our own souls nor our influence will be healed unless we correct what is wrong in our lives. Repentance is the prerequisite for soul health.

b. Holiness in the heart (12:14). Verse 14 extends the thought and further explains it; there is no break in the mood or emphasis. **Follow peace with all men** (cf. Ps. 34:14). The imperative **follow** (*diokete*) means in this case to run swiftly to reach the goal. The reference is not primarily to a path or way which is to be followed, but to a certain intensity of energy in doing what needs right now to be done. The same word is translated "follow after" and "press" in Phil. 3:12, 14, but there it is relevant to an ultimate goal ("the prize" at the end of the race). Here in Hebrews the pursuit commanded is relevant to an immediate goal.

The first immediate goal is **peace with all.** If we are to lift up hanging hands, stiffen sagging knees, and straighten out our way of life, we must begin with dislocated personal relationships. This is certainly not a blanket admonition to pursue a policy of appeasement with evil or fraternization with the wicked, but to seek immediately a state of reconciliation where peaceable relations have been sinfully disrupted, and to maintain that state of interpersonal peace which belongs to righteousness.

And holiness, without which no man shall see the Lord indicates that the peace sought must be compatible with holiness. Certainly a weak compromise with evil would not meet this requirement. The Greek is perfectly clear that the qualifying clause **without which** belongs to **holiness,** not **peace.** Insofar as getting right with men is part of becoming holy, the peace can be said to be included. But our honest efforts to seek peace may be thwarted by the obstinacy of the other person; therefore

[19]Arndt and Gingrich. Cf. RSV, Phillips, NEB, Vincent.

success in this endeavor is not an absolute necessity for seeing God, but success in obtaining holiness is.

It is impossible to limit the vision of God which is here at stake to a spiritual comprehension now, though this is of course included. The word **see** (*opsetai,* future tense of "to see with the eyes") metaphorically refers in this case to being admitted into intimate and blessed fellowship with God in His future kingdom (cf. Thayer, Matt. 5:8). Moffatt says that without it "no one will ever see the Lord." Let us make no mistake about it: our final salvation hinges on holiness. It is perfectly clear therefore that this must be a kind of holiness which is possible now, since death may claim us the next hour. Its pursuit is not a lifelong, never-quite-successful effort. This might be the case had the Greek made the seeing dependent upon the pursuing; but it is rather dependent on the holiness. The implication is that the right kind of effort will lead at once to the indispensable holiness; any persisting unholiness will prove that the command to **follow** has not been obeyed as intended.

What then is this **holiness** (*ton hagiasmon*)? It differs from *hagiotetos,* "holiness" (of God) in v. 10, in which we are made to share through chastening. That is genitive singular of *hagiotes,* which is a quality noun, meaning that the quality of holiness is inherent in God's nature.[20] In v. 14, however, the word is from *hagiasmos,* an action noun, meaning the state resulting from an action, a being-made-holy, or a becoming-holy (Arndt and Gingrich), and is a word peculiar to biblical and Christian literature. Only Christianity has the concept of becoming holy in this sense. In the NT the word is used consistently in reference to a state of grace available to believers.[21] In five cases it is rendered "holiness," and in five cases it is rendered "sanctification." This noun form is used in Hebrews only here, but forms of the verb *hagiazo,* "to sanctify," appear seven times (2:11, twice; 9:13; 10:10, 14, 29; 13:12). God *is* holy, but fallen man must *become* holy. Holiness is original with God, and may be imparted by God. With man holiness is derived from God, and momentarily dependent on His grace.

(1) It is a definite work of grace, as a study of the tenses will indicate.

[20]The only other NT use of this word (II Cor. 1:12) is in textual doubt.

[21]Rom. 6:19, 22; I Cor. 1:30; I Thess. 4:3-4, 7; II Thess. 2:13; I Tim. 2:15; Heb. 12:14; I Pet. 1:2.

(2) It is a subjective, personal, realizable state (rather than simply an imputed state), or the command to pursue it would be meaningless. In c. 10 holiness is presented in relation to the high priestly work of Christ, and in relation to the new covenant; in c. 12 it is presented from the side of man's responsibility in its obtainment.

(3) It is the fruit of definite surrender in the believer's life (Rom. 6:19, 22).

(4) It is the immediate will of God (I Thess. 4:3).

(5) It is a work of God's grace by which believers are enabled to maintain moral purity (I Thess. 4:4, 7).

(6) Its source is Jesus Christ and His blood (13:12; I Cor. 1:30).

(7) Its accomplishment is the primary ministry of the Holy Spirit (I Thess 4:18; II Thess. 2:13; I Pet. 1:2).

(8) If this holiness is related to the holiest, as its antitype, then the exercise of faith is included in its pursuit (10:22).

(9) This holiness begins in regeneration, since (*a*) repentance is a concomitant to the principle and practice of holy living; (*b*) a concomitant of regeneration is initial sanctification or cleansing from acquired depravity; (*c*) the spiritual life reived in regeneration is itself holy; (*d*) the believer is hallowed and consecrated imputationally by virtue of his relationship to God as Father and Christ as Saviour: hence he can be said to be holy ethically, initially, and positionally.

(10) But the believer's holiness cannot be complete, i.e., thorough, until all competing and incompatible unholiness is excluded. To pursue such full holiness is the command of v. 14. But its pursuit involves the immediate: (*a*) putting off of excess weights and the besetting sin, 12:1; (*b*) perfect faith in Jesus as the sole Finisher as well as Author of the "faith," (12:2); (*c*) submission to God's will for us, including His chastening (12:5-11; Rom. 6:13; 12:1-2); (*d*) correction of our attitudes, relationships, and manner of living, insofar as that lies within our power (12:12-14*a*; II Cor. 6:17—7:1).

c. *Holiness in the Church* (12:15-17). The command *to follow* is the main verb of vv. 14-16, and grammatically governs the whole. **Looking diligently** is a present active participle, by which we gather that the action of the **looking** coincides with the action of *following*. That, too, is present tense; i.e., the pursuit of holiness, its obtainment, its maintenance, and its out-living is a continuous obligation of believers, both as individuals and as churches. While pursuing our own holiness, therefore, we are also to be constantly concerned about the spiritual welfare of those around us in our fellowship. **Looking diligently** (*episkopountes*) is the task primarily of the elders (I Pet. 5:2, same word used), but in a lesser sense of the entire church. It is derived from *episkope* (Eng., "episcopal"), "inspection, investigation, visitation." We have a responsibility toward one another. Christian love does not demand an excessive policing, but neither does it include a presumptive confidence that never says, "How is it with your soul?"

In turn, the participle **looking diligently** governs three subordinate subjunctive clauses,[22] each beginning with **lest any.** In the perils warned against, each represents an advanced stage in degeneration and apostasy, the second and third growing out of the first.

(1) We are to watch, first, **lest any man fail of the grace of God (15)**. This is the fundamental peril, and the fundamental failure. Sometimes this failure is interpreted as a falling from the grace of God, in which case the warning would be against backsliding. But here the word *hysteron* is from *hystereo,* "to be behind" (4:1—"come short"). Of this verse Thayer says: "fail to become a partaker" of holiness, which is the *sine qua non* of fitness for heaven. The danger here is not so much open rebellion as near-obedience. In v. 14 the command is to strive. Well-meaning people may fall short of holiness by failing to arouse themselves. "Holiness doesn't have wheels," as Samuel Brengle said; it will not come to us. We must devote ourselves to its obtainment with earnest desire and unswerving determination. Lazy Christians who can be easily denied will be denied.

(2) The peril which lurks in this basic failure is expressed in words from Deut. 29:18, LXX: **lest any root of bitterness springing up trouble you.** The **bitterness** is more than unpleasant; it is poisonous. The **root** is the person who falls short of holiness, which threatens the health of the church. But it is also the **root of bittetrness** in him, which is the carnal nature. No one can be a **root of bitterness** in his church relationships unless he has a **root of bitterness** in his heart. It is this very spirit of

[22]The third is subjunctive in sense, though the verb form is omitted.

selfishness, ill will, and sourness, often hiding behind a facade of amiability, which constitutes the believer's carnal-mindedness. It is the removal of this spirit which is the precise objective in the urgent command to seek holiness. Every believer who fails to press on to holiness is a threat to the well-being of the church: **and thereby many be defiled.** One carnal Christian can spread poison and wreak havoc through the whole body. The phrase **springing up** is especially apt, as the Greek pictures a "quick process" (Robertson). Mueller translates it "shooting up." There is always danger of an eruption on the part of unsanctified believers, causing a disruption of fellowship and service.

(3) But carnality, yielded to rather than eradicated, is always increasing, in one direction or another. **Lest there be any fornicator, or profane person, as Esau, who for one morsel of meat sold his birthright** (16). The bitter Christian is typified by the "elder brother" in the parable of the prodigal son. Esau, on the other hand, typifies grosser manifestations of carnality. The Christian who is unsanctified may degenerate from the elder-brother type to the Esau type—often does, in fact. Or he may stay in the church as a respectable member, spewing out poison by a bad spirit. His sins will not so much be sins of the flesh as sins of the spirit (Jas. 3:8-18; III John 9). Or the Christian who fails to press on to holiness may never go through the bitterness stage, but gradually drift into the tragic selling of Esau.

When one neglects holiness, he will next despise, and ultimately sell it cheaply for self-gratification. One form of self-gratification is indicated by **fornicator,** strictly, a "male prostitute," but in this case anyone who is promiscuous and self-indulgent in sexual activity. The writer may have been using **fornicator** in the figurative sense of idolatry so common in the OT. In either case Esau's total collapse in the crisis was the result of habitual self-indulgence before the crisis. The other form of self-gratification is *secularism.* Esau's sin was not profanity (necessarily) as we use the term today, but the sin of treating sacred things as common. **Profane** (*bebelos*) comes from *belos,* "threshold," that which is walked on as people go in and out, merely an instrument of convenience. When people want to use God instead of being used by God, when they turn the church into a tool for personal advancement, they are dangerously on Esau-ground. The full-blown sin is reached when they finally surrender spiritual values for material, when the church and vital spirituality are sacrificed to satisfy their lust for more and more things, or more and more pleasure. The secularist and materialist are twins. Both put material, sensual, and earthly values ahead of spiritual and eternal values.

In 15-16 we see "Holiness, the Safeguard." Only thorough holiness will safeguard the church from: (1) **The disruption of fellowship,** 15; (2) **The corruption of morals,** 16*a*; (3) **The destruction of religion,** 16*b*. The seed of all these—bitterness, fornication, worldly-mindedness—is in every unsanctified heart. Therefore constant emphasis on holiness is not only justified but demanded by the simple facts of our human situation.

In reference to the destruction of religion, the term destroy is defined as "to reduce to naught or take away the powers and functions of something so that restoration is impossible" (*The New Century Dictionary*). How true of Esau! **For ye know how that afterward, when he would have inherited the blessing, he was rejected: for he found no place of repentance** (change of mind), **though he sought it carefully with tears (17).** Esau may have found repentance unto eternal salvation, but not to the re-acquirement of the birthright.[23] Some transactions are irreversible. There is a point of no return in spiritual things too, beyond which tears are powerless to effect change. The morsel of meat will soon be gone, but the consequences of its choice never. For the believer, death is the final dividing line, the sealing of the irrevocable transaction. To persist in selling holiness, which is our birthright, for the pottage of this world will finally settle our doom. There is hope for the backslider, but no hope for the absolute apostate, and no "second chance" after death.

4. *An Awful Ultimatum* (12:18-29)

The emphatic word is *gar*, **for,** or "because." This is the explanation for the tone of urgency and the pronouncement of finality in the previous section. Think of whom and what you are dealing with, and the reasonableness of the plea will become apparent! The mood changes from exhortation to the most solemn warning. The argument is again in the form of contrast; first negative, then positive—**ye are not come (18-21), ye are come (22-29).**

a. Not Mount Sinai (12:18-21). This time the confrontation is not with the Lawgiver at Sinai—as frightening as that was, ac-

[23]Another interpretation is: "no way to change his father's mind."

companied by **the sound of a trumpet, and the voice of words** (19), with the dire threatenings, such as to cause even Moses to exclaim, **I exceedingly fear and quake** (21). That was **the mount that might be touched** (18), symbolizing a visible, earthly theocracy, given as a "schoolmaster" to prepare the nation for Christ. It was a temporary and preparatory order. Yet disregard even of that, temporary though it was, warranted stoning to death. For the entire historical account see Exod. 19:1-25.

b. But Mount Zion (12:22-29). But **ye are come** to that permanent order of God's kingdom among men for which Mount Sinai was but an advance notice. There the law was given; here it is perfectly fulfilled. There God was Lawgiver; here He is Law Administrator, in unhindered absolute sovereignty. Every recalcitrant will is removed. Without holiness we would not fit into this regime of absolute control; this is the implication. In this heavenly order all unholiness is instantly repelled.

The imagery is majestic, yet it reflects reality. All the truths carefully unfolded in the Epistle are here gathered up in one great symphonic crescendo. The place is **the city of the living God, the heavenly Jerusalem** (22). The orchestra is **an innumerable company of angels,** and the choir, singing the song of the Lamb, is **the general assembly and church of the firstborn,** including **the spirits of just men made perfect** (23; holy men glorified in heaven). On the throne is **God the Judge of all,** and at His side is **Jesus the mediator of the new covenant.** Redeemed men have come also **to the blood of sprinkling, that speaketh better things than that of Abel** (24). Better indeed! **The blood** of Abel here alluded to was not his own (shed by Cain) but that which he offered, by means of which he "obtained witness that he was righteous," and by which "he being dead yet speaketh" (11:4). His blood therefore spoke of justification by faith, but Christ's blood speaks not only of justification but sanctification.

Therefore, **See that ye refuse not him that speaketh** (25). Do not refuse the "better things" of which He speaks, for in refusing them you will be refusing Him. Note the peremptory command. The writer has laid aside his kid gloves, and is speaking sharply and bluntly. It is high time they stopped their dangerous foolishness, **For if they escaped not who refused him that speaketh on earth, much more shall not we escape, if we turn away from him** (and His offer of holiness) **that speaketh from heaven.** When He spoke at Sinai the earth was shaken, but through Hag. 2:6 He promised, **Yet once more I shake not the**

earth only, but also heaven (26). There is going to be a sifting and sorting and reshuffling of the whole universe. Both material and spiritual realms will come under review, for destruction or reforming. There will be in this **once more** (finale of history) **the removing of those things that are shaken** (i.e., the "shakeable" things of creation), **as of things that are made** (fabricated for this world order), **that those things which cannot be shaken may remain** (27). God, Christ, the Church, holiness, love—these things are unshakeable. They will remain eternally, and he who has appropriated them so into himself by grace that he has been assimilated into them (not pantheistically but spiritually) will remain too.

In this age sometimes called "post-Christian," when old values are challenged and venerable institutions are crumbling, it is well for the Christian to remember that, when the nations rage and would seek to dethrone God himself, "he that sitteth in the heavens shall laugh" (Ps. 2:4). Nothing is more ludicrous, as well as tragic, than the puny defiance of men, whose silly pride is mocked by their frailty. An unfinished manuscript was found after the death of Author Albert Payson Terhune. The writing had stopped with the prophetic word: "God will write the final sentence." And that final sentence will not be the epitaph of the Church, but the confirmation of the pronouncement of our Lord that "the gates of hell shall not prevail against it" (Matt. 16:18).

Wherefore we receiving a kingdom which cannot be moved, let us have grace (lit., let us keep on having grace)—all that God makes available to us (4:16)—**whereby** (thus) **we may serve God acceptably with reverence and godly fear** (28). There can be no acceptable service if we slight or neglect to appropriate any measure of the justifying, sanctifying, and keeping grace which is ours through the blood of Jesus. **For our God is a consuming fire** (29; cf. 10:31; Deut. 4:24). He will either consume sin in us or He will consume us in our sin.

D. The Way of Faith, 13:1-19

The faith-way of the Christian religion certainly includes perseverance in holiness on the part of the believer. The consequences of failing to thus persevere are ultimate and final. The Epistle has solemnly voiced the maximum warning. The last chapter now is a sort of denouement. It contains no new warning, but gathers into one several strands of final admonition, both practical and doctrinal. Casual reading might give the impression that we have here only an assortment of diverse ideas with little coherence. But closer attention will show an ethical emphasis divided by a very pertinent doctrinal parenthesis (8-15); then a conclusion which contains not only some personal remarks, but a fittingly climactic benedictory prayer.

1. *A Way of Practical Holiness* (13:1-7)

a. Love toward the brethren (13:1). The topic sentence of this paragraph is the opening admonition: **Let brotherly love continue.** This term **brotherly love** (*philadelphia*) was chosen by William Penn to express the foundation principle of his colony, and became the name of America's fourth largest city. This is the social expression of *agape*—the good fellowship and happy camaraderie that is consistent with the *agape* love which God has put in their hearts (Rom. 12:10; I Thess. 4:9; I Pet. 1:22; II Pet. 1:7). This love must be permitted to **continue** (*meneto*, abide) at all costs. Whatever else is lost or gained, this kind of love must be "at home" among them.

b. Kindness toward the stranger (13:2). The same word *philia*, "love," which in v. 1 is combined with "brethren" is here combined with *zenos*, "stranger." Don't let the warmth of your affection and hospitality be a cliquish thing, confined to your immediate circle of fellow believers, but **entertain strangers** too (6:10): **for thereby some have entertained angels unawares** (Genesis 18—19). This does not require that we treat every passing tramp as an honored guest, but it does mean that there are unexpected and hidden rewards in a generous spirit of hospitality, which extends to outsiders as well as insiders. Our kindness may not uncover any angels, but may contribute to the making of saints.

c. Compassion toward sufferers (13:3). We are also to **remember them that are in bonds**, as if we ourselves shared their bonds (cf. 10:4). There can be no true empathy if we merely shed crocodile tears at home. We must enter into the sufferings of others by prayer, writing, visitation, at times civil or financial aid. Though **in bonds** probably means prisoners, bonds of illness which confine people in hospitals or as invalids at home also need to be remembered. We are to be considerate of whoever suffers adversity, of any kind, as **being yourselves also in the body.** Superior good fortune at the moment is no ground for smugness, and certainly no evidence of heavenly favoritism; nor is it a guarantee for the future. Being **in the body** is to be equally exposed to all the hazards which belong to life on earth. Christians are often supernaturally protected, but not always. They are not immune to disease or exempt from suffering. Why God allowed James to be killed by Herod but miraculously spared Peter, and why He permits all other such apparent inequities, is a mystery hidden in His inscrutable but flawless sovereignty.

d. Carefulness toward moral standards (13:4). The Greek has no verb here, so it is literally "honorable marriage among all." This therefore can be understood as a statement of fact: **Marriage is honourable,** or as a command: "Let marriage be honorable," in which case the second phrase (also without a verb) could be a qualifying parallelism: **and the bed undefiled.** The only honorable marriage is the marriage undefiled by unfaithfulness. Rather than **but,** the reading should be: *for* **whoremongers** (unmarried fornicators) **and adulterers** (married fornicators) **God will judge,** both in this life and in the next. Forbidden pleasure will in the end prove costly indeed. We cannot please God without observing strictly a thoroughly Christian standard of sexual purity and marital fidelity.

e. Independence toward money (13:5-6). **Let your conversation** (lit., way of life) **be without covetousness.** The word *aphilargyros* is not the usual term for **covetousness,** and literally means "without love of money" (same word, I Tim. 3:3). How important is the love element in Christian holiness! Two kinds of *philia,* "affection," are *enjoined* in 1-2. Here is a kind to be studiously *avoided.* "Keep your life free from love of money" (RSV) and the things money will buy. Rather, **be content** (be sufficed, satisfied) **with such things as ye have** (cf. I Tim. 6:5-11; the Bible has many such warnings). Restless eyes and feverish desires are incompatible with rest of soul and incongruous with a profession of holiness. If we would be satisfied with fewer things and less pretentious houses, we would have more poise, more quietness of spirit, more inward happiness, and certainly more time for prayer, worship, service, and the cultivation of the finer values in life. Even Christians are too often little better than affluent, well-fed barbarians, with little appreciation for the culture of mind and soul.

The key, of course, is the depth of our love for and faith in God. Christians can learn to be content with limited material advantages if they really believe His word, **I will never leave thee, nor forsake thee,**[24] and really prefer the possession of His presence to the possession of things. An assurance of the divine presence is the best pledge of security. **So that we may boldly say, The Lord is my helper, and I will not fear what man shall do unto me** (6; cf. Ps. 118:6). Here is the antidote to fear: not the forced boldness of one "whistling in the dark," but the firm confidence of one who is willing to stand up and declare his faith (Rom. 8:31-39).

f. Veneration toward deceased leaders (13:7). The KJV implies a present-tense situation, but virtually all modern versions interpret this as a reference to past leaders. The aorist of *elalesan*, **spoken,** as well as other nuances in words and phrasing, bear this out. Literally the verse should read: "Be mindful always of those who (were) ruling you, whose faith you should continually imitate, examining carefully the outcome of (their) way of life."[25] Their way of life was a faith-way, and a way of practical holiness —that which the writer is now delineating. The final outcome of their way of life was good fruit, not evil. It is not memorials that the church needs, or even memoirs, if filed and forgotten. The church is always in need of careful study of the lives and teachings of past leaders in order that they may be still followed, and their way of life, and the faith which sustained it, be transmitted to each succeeding generation. Too many think it smart to debunk and belittle the past. But only as we line up with our founding fathers can we steer a straight course for the future. Instead of despising them, we should be inspired by their devotion, and assiduously strive to match them in greatness of soul.

2. *A Way of Absolute Loyalty* (13:8-16)

Verse 8 is a transition sentence, introducing an important doctrinal digression.

a. Jesus the Christ (13:8-9). This section reminds us once again that, in all our holy living and religious activities, **Jesus Christ** is the Source and the Center. The connection with

[24]"A free paraphrase of Gen. 28:15; Deut. 31:8; Josh. 1:5; I Chron. 28:20" (Robertson, *op. cit.*, p. 445).

[25]For **remember** (*mnemoneuete*) cf. use of same word in 11:15, 22.

the previous verse is not as the KJV might imply; i.e., Jesus is not "the end [or subject] of their conversation," for we have seen that "end" means "outcome" and "conversation" means "way of life." Jesus is the Object and constant Focus of their faith; we are to follow Him. The faith by which we live must not for one moment or to any degree be shifted from Jesus to anything else. We are not to turn to a new asceticism or the old ritualism, and certainly not to be deluded by novel doctrines which come along.

True Christian holiness is thoroughly Christ-centered. For only Jesus is unchangeable and eternal—**the same yesterday, and to day, and for ever** (8). First Jesus of Nazareth was the Christ; let this be fixed firmly in our thinking. Then what **Jesus Christ** was **yesterday** in the days of His flesh (2:3; 5:7), and what He is **to day** at the Father's right hand, He will be **for ever.** As God's Revelation, He is final and will never "be superseded or supplemented" (Moffatt). Because we have in Christ the one Foundation, the one Cornerstone, the one sure Anchor, **be not carried about with divers** (many-colored) **and strange** (unheard of, I Pet. 4:12) **doctrines** (9). To be **carried about** (*parapheresthe*) is to be "swept along" (Jude 12), to be led away, misled, seduced. Unsanctified and immature Christians, especially young would-be intellectuals, are too easily impressed by the novel and heterodox. Whatever is new excites them; the old bores them. But Jesus is both old and ever new; let them dig deep enough spiritually and they will find in Him a perennial Source of excitement. He is Truth. Any doctrine which weakens His hold on their hearts, or His authority over their minds, is untruth.

It is a good thing that the heart be established with grace, i.e., rendered constant and unwavering by means of (dative) **grace.** The grace of God, which is both the favor of God extended through the atonement and a divinely imparted ability to be holy, is mediated solely through Jesus Christ. To turn from Christ is to forfeit grace (Titus 2:11-14). The particular alternative to the grace-way which enticed these Hebrews was the attempt to become morally and spiritually strong **with meats,** or "rules of diet" (Phillips). The reference is to the complex dietary system of Judaism, which some felt Christians were still under obligation to observe. But the writer reminds them of the vanity and impotence of such legalistic observances by simply pointing out that they **have not profited them that have been occupied therein,** i.e., that walked by these strict rules. The inability of asceticism to sanctify is historically apparent (Gal. 3:3; 4:9-10; Col. 2:16-23).

b. Jesus the Crucified (13:10-14). The great altar at the door of the sanctuary (see Diagram *A*) was the true center of Judaism, as on it the animal sacrifices were made. It therefore symbolized the whole Mosaic system, including the dietary rules. It stood—in the days of the Tabernacle, then in Solomon's Temple, Zerubbabel's, and finally in Herod's—as the one way to approach God, the one hope of pardon and life. Now the writer reminds them, **We,** too, **have an altar,** the Cross, on which Jesus was offered as the sacrificial Lamb. But our **altar** cannot be shared with Herod's altar: **whereof they have no right to eat which serve the tabernacle** (10). The "eating" is as metaphorical as the altar; hence the sense is to partake of or share in.

The **right** is denied all who worship in the Temple. Such a right is to be understood in the sense of both permission and ability. Since the Cross has fulfilled and abrogated the Temple, persistence in the Temple is tantamount to rejection of the Cross. Some Jews thought they could have the benefits of Jesus without discontinuing their age-old Temple practices, and for a while a certain amount of overlapping was tolerated. But intrinsically the two are incompatible, and failure to see this is blindness to the meaning of the Cross. It is to reduce the Cross to a complement of the Mosaic altar, whereas in fact it is a total displacement. Therefore the writer is dogmatic: it must be one or the other.

In the Epistle it has been carefully shown that Jesus' death answers to the sin offering at all major points. Now a further identity is specified: **For the bodies of those beasts, whose blood is brought into the sanctuary by the high priest for sin, are burned without the camp** (11; cf. Leviticus 4). Nothing was eaten by anyone. There was a complete removal. The main function which the animal represented in this was absolute separation from the sin—both its guilt and its presence. Our Lord fulfilled the details of the typical atonement in this respect too: **Wherefore Jesus also, that he might sanctify the people** (the worshippers) **with his own blood, suffered without the gate** (12). He suffered unto death, willingly going to Golgotha, not only because He was rejected in Jerusalem, but because He desired and the Father desired that He be a perfect Sin Offering. His body was "burned" without the gate. He suffered this severance from the city—i.e., this total break with all earthly powers and systems, even Jewish—in order **that he might sanctify the people with his own blood.**

The connection between His ability to sanctify and His suffering outside **the camp** (13) is probably no more than His deliberate fulfillment of the complete requirements of the sin offering. In other words, He desired to qualify His own blood as the sanctifying agent in every possible respect. The sanctification which is the glorious objective has already been expounded. It embraces more than consecrations and ceremonial cleansing, which were possible under the old order. It includes the complete renovation of the worshiper, a cleansing which establishes in him the substance of the new covenant. Mueller says: ". . . make the people holy." This is effected **with** (not by) His blood, as could be said if unconditional expiation only were intended. **With** (through) is indicated by *dia* with the genitive, expressing secondary agency. The Blood is the procuring cause of the sanctifying activity of the Holy Spirit. The **people** would be instantly recognized by these Hebrew readers as the people of God, for a parallel is being drawn between the Christian altar and the Jewish. As only the circumcised could benefit from the Jewish altar, so only those initiated into the household of God by repentance and faith could be eligible for the full sanctifying benefit of Christ.

As Jesus broke with the Judaic Jerusalem (concerning which He had been tempted in the wilderness) in order to make us holy, so must we break with every vestige of Judaism if we are to be made holy.

As far as separation is concerned, the cost of appropriating holiness can be no less than the cost of providing it. **Let us go forth therefore unto him without the camp, bearing his reproach** (13). We must identify ourselves with Jesus in His shame and obloquy, if we would be identified with Him in His future kingdom. Since Jesus despised the shame, so must we (12:2). There is no holiness to be had in the Jerusalem of obsolete religious systems, any more than in the Athens of human philosophy, or the Rome of human laws. The source of holiness is the Cross. To it we must go. There comes a time in every Christian's life when he must tear himself away from the security of human walls and the solace of human comfort and the hope of human temples and abandon himself solely to the cross of Christ. But not a cross in the abstract; not unto *it,* but unto **him.** The Cross without the dying-living Christ is only a sentiment. But to Him let us cling, and with Him let us stand (Gal. 6:14).

In the cross of Christ I glory,
Towering o'er the wrecks of time.

It is vain to look back to Jerusalem for security: **For here have we no continuing** (abiding) **city, but we seek one to come** (14). The Jews supposed that Jerusalem was eternal (misinterpreting certain promises), but soon it would be destroyed by Titus (A.D. 70).[26]

Affection and hope placed in any city or culture or system of this world order are misplaced. But "we seek after the one (which is) to be" (Mueller). The more intensely occupied we are with this search, the less excited we will be about present cities, all of which tend to become modern Babels.

c. *God, the Author of all* (13:15-16). As vv. 13-14 are complementary, so are 15-16. Together they remind these Hebrews that, while animal sacrifices on the old altar are no longer obligatory, there are sacrifices which peculiarly belong to the believer's identification with the new altar. First, *the sacrifice of praise:* **By him** (Jesus) **therefore let us offer the sacrifice of praise to God continually, that is, the fruit of our lips giving praise to his name** (15). Let us "keep on [present tense] offering up praise." We are always in debt to God, and should always be grateful. But this gratitude must be expressed. As a loving wife wants to hear her husband say he loves her, so does God look for us to give voice to our thankfulness and our devotion. The second half of the verse is explanatory of the first. Praise is the proper **fruit**—the natural and appropriate product—of **lips** that confess Jesus as Lord. If we take Christ's **name,** i.e., if we profess to be Christians, the least we can do is to demonstrate it by open and habitual thanksgiving (Ps. 50:14, 23). This is a sufficient rationale for public testimony meetings. Christians who receive but do not give back in oral praise, both publicly and privately, soon become spiritual Dead Seas, briny and poisonous. A silent, secret loyalty to Jesus is not acceptable.

Second, the *sacrifice of good works.* In the conjunction **but** (*de*) is a warning not to suppose that verbal expressions of praise constitute one's total obligation to offer sacrifices in the new order. There is an outward obligation as well as upward. The spiritual must be authenticated by the social. Piety and charity

[26]"Vincent rightly argues that the Epistle must have been written before the destruction of Jerusalem" (A. T. Robertson, *op. cit.,* p. 449).

must go hand in hand (Jas. 1:27). **But to do good and to communicate forget not** (16). The word **communicate** (*koinonias*) is here a noun, and generally would mean, "Be not forgetful . . . of fellowshipping" (Mueller). This is compatible with the writer's general counsel elsewhere (10:25); but in this connection, as in II Cor. 9:13, the idea intended is a loving concern for fellow believers which gives practical and monetary aid (Jas. 2:15-16; I John 3:17). This too belongs to our absolute loyalty to Jesus.[27] However, when the writer concludes with the clause, **for with such sacrifices God is well pleased,** the **such** probably includes the sacrifice of praise as well as the sacrifice of benevolent deeds. With animal sacrifices God was utterly weary, but of these Christian expressions of gratitude and love God will never tire.

3. *A Way of Humble Submission* (13:17-19)

Verse 16 is transitional, for by it the thought is smoothly switched back from the parenthetical doctrinal discussion (8-16) to the main line of emphasis on the faith-way of practical holiness (1-7). As v. 7 instructed them to maintain an attitude of proper veneration for past leaders, v. 17 clearly commands obedience to present leaders. **Obey them that have the rule over you, and submit yourselves.** The word **obey** here has the peculiar sense of allowing oneself to be persuaded (reminiscent of James's mark of true wisdom: "easy to be entreated"). **Submit** (*hupeikete*) conveys a similar idea: "yield, fig. give way, submit to someone's authority" (Arndt and Gingrich). One may not always agree with one's leaders; one may even debate an issue with them. But if they are urgent, even adamant, the follower is the one who gives in. As yielding the right-of-way in traffic is often the better part of valor, so yielding to our God-called and God-ordained leaders is the better part of religion. The ability to submit graciously, with neither snap-back, poutiness, or haughtiness, is the sure mark of bigness. And it is likewise a mark of the Spirit-filled life (Eph. 5:18-21).

The reasonableness of this duty of humble submission is seen in the nature of our leaders' responsibility: **for they watch for**

[27]Systematic "communicating" to the poor was part of essential early Methodism. But we must not confine the idea only to charity, for Christians are obligated to "communicate" to the total needs of Christ's Church. Public offerings are as acceptable and pleasing to God as public praise services. When the pastor says, "Let us worship the Lord with our tithes and offerings," he is on solid biblical ground.

your souls, as they that must give account. "For they seek continuously and sleeplessly for your spiritual welfare, because God will expect an accounting from them" (paraphrase). Phillips says: "They are like men standing guard over your spiritual good, and they have great responsibility." Our leaders are under subjection to authority too. They did not ask for the job of shepherding our souls. They were assigned to the task by God himself. For us to ignore them is to thwart them in the fulfillment of their mission, and cause their task to be **with grief** (groaning, cf. Rom. 8:26) and not **with joy.** Their task is heavy enough at best! Let us not add to it. Even more seriously, in despising them we despise God, who has placed this responsibility upon them. Those laymen in our day, therefore, who desire to whittle down the authority of the clergy, and who are seeking to erase the line between clergy and laity, would do well to ponder this passage, and remember that the ecclesiastical order which elevates the clergy in the Church was not invented by the clergy; it was established by God.

But the passage also demands just the hint of an addition. Obedience is obligatory only to clergymen who are truly called of God, who do **watch for** our souls, and whose chief cause of either joy or grief is the spiritual welfare of their people. Clergymen who bear the office only, whose chief concern is feathering their own nests, who are more excited about sports than souls, and who know nothing of groaning over the lost and the wayward, have no claim to the divine rights vested in the true Christian ministry.

In the two rather pathetic, pleading verses which follow, the writer reveals the other side of the coin. Preachers are not supermen, but very human and weak, unable to bear their terrific responsibility in their own strength. They not only have rights but needs, and one of them is the prayer support and loving confidence of their people, as well as their obedience. **Pray for us: for we trust we have a good conscience, in all things willing to live honestly** (honorably; 18). Whoever may have written this, it is impossible to read it without thinking of Paul (II Cor. 1:11 ff., 17 ff.; I Thess. 2:18). There is here a fear of being rejected, a fear that his treatise may be spurned because of prejudice fed by slanderous reports. Paul was never very popular with the Judaizers, who seem to be in the saddle in this Hebrew congregation. **But I beseech you rather** ("the more urgently," RSV) **to do this, that I may be restored to you the sooner** (19).

He has faith that their prayers will make a difference in the time of his deliverance. If preachers have an obligation to laity, how great also is the obligation of laity to preachers! For their prayers have power to expedite the work of the ministry by making strong the hands of the minister.

E. Conclusion, 13:20-25

1. *A Benedictory Prayer* (13:20-21)

There is no more sublime prayer than this, constituting as it does a reverent yet exultant epitome of the Epistle. **Now the God of peace**[28] **that brought again from the dead** (out from among the dead) **our Lord Jesus, that great shepherd of the sheep, through the blood of the everlasting covenant** (20), **make you perfect in every good work to do his will, working in you that which is wellpleasing in his sight, through Jesus Christ; to whom be glory for ever and ever. Amen** (21). The sentence spans both verses, but in v. 20 we find the subject (with modifiers), while in v. 21 we have the predicate. A condensed paraphrase could be (*a*) May the God who has acted so marvellously for us (20), (*b*) act commensurately within us (21), (*c*) through Jesus Christ.

a. **God** is the subject of the sentence and the Agent of the implied petition. The God who is thus indirectly addressed is He who restored to life (same word, Rom. 10:7) **that great** (strong emphasis, cf. 4:14; 10:21) **shepherd of the sheep** (20).[29] The phrase **through the blood of the everlasting covenant** apparently modifies **that brought again,** in which case the preposition *en* is better translated by "in" or **through** (KJV), than "by" (RSV, Phillips, NEB). The Resurrection took place "in the sphere of" or in the total context of **the blood of the everlasting covenant.** If Christ's blood had not been **the blood of the . . . covenant** there would have been no Resurrection. It is noteworthy that the writer did not in his Epistle attempt to prove the Resurrection and then work back from there. Instead he proved the identity of Jesus as Son and High Priest, whose blood inaugurated the new covenant, atoned for sin, and made provision for all re-

[28]A Pauline phrase used six times (Rom. 15:33; 16:20; II Cor. 13:11; II Thess. 3:16; Phil. 4:9).

[29]A prophetic figure well-known to these Bible-believing Hebrews (Ps. 23:1; 80:1; Isa. 40:11; Jer. 31:10; Ezek. 34:23; 37:24).

demption blessings. Acceptance of the Resurrection quite naturally follows. In historical theology, it is questionable if a denial of the Resurrection has ever been associated with an evangelical perception of the atoning Blood.[30]

b. The prayer is that this God may **make you perfect in every good work to do his will, working in you that which is wellpleasing in his sight** (21). In v. 16 we were told the kind of sacrifices which are well pleasing to God. Here the writer refers to an inward work of grace that is well pleasing to Him. God is pleased to receive the right kind of service from us, but also to perform a work in us (Rom. 12:2). This which God does must be the foundation for what we do. The participle **working,** (*poion*) is present, synchronizing the action with the action of the main verb, **Make you perfect.** But whether it is solely explanatory or supplementary depends on whether "us" is the right reading or **you.** In other words, does it say: **Make you perfect . . . working in you** (KJV), or does it say, "Make you perfect . . . working in us . . ." (NEB, Mueller, Goodspeed)? Nestle's *Text* gives *hemin,* "us," and the textual support for this seems overwhelming. If this is correct, then NEB makes good sense: "Make you perfect in all goodness so that you may do his will, and may he make of us what he would have us be." This supposes two prayers in the one: a prayer for their perfecting, and a general prayer for the whole Church.

The prayer for their perfecting must now be pinpointed. Chamberlain says **make . . . perfect** (*katartisai*) is volitive optative, which gives the sense of a prayer: "May (God) . . . adjust thoroughly." Usually in Hebrews **perfect** is a translation of *teleios* in some form. The word *katartizo,* however, is used in the Epistle only here and in 10:5 ("a body hast thou prepared me") and 11:3 ("the worlds were framed"). RSV and Phillips say

[30]The wording not only of KJV but also other versions seems to attach the phrase **through the blood** to the **make you perfect** of the next verse, implying that God makes us perfect by means of the Blood. While in a certain sense this is surely true, the other interpretation of this particular passage, given above, seems to be demanded by the Greek word order. The **great shepherd** is declared by name in the appositional phrase, **our Lord Jesus,** lit., "the Lord of us, Jesus." In the Greek this does not follow **that brought again from the dead,** as in KJV, but stands at the end of the verse. The God who alone can act redemptively, therefore, is the God and Father of our Lord Jesus Christ, and what the Father does for us and in us is done on the ground of Christ as both the sacrificial Lamb and the living Shepherd. See Wiley, *op. cit.,* pp. 428-29.

"equip"; Mueller says "prepare (refit)"; Goodspeed says "fit." Now notice RSV: "Equip you with everything good that you may do his will." Clearly this is spiritual equipment for the full, unhindered performance of the will of God. "With everything good"!—a pure heart by the infilling of the Holy Spirit; and the aorist tense suggests a full and completed divine action. What an apt description of entire sanctification as a second definite work of grace! And this blessing is **through Jesus Christ; to whom be glory for ever and ever. Amen.**

2. *Personal Greetings* (13:22-25)

Following this final flight in noble prayer, the writer swiftly brings the Epistle to a close. First, his pathetic personal plea for acceptance expressed in vv. 18-19 is renewed, now more directly: **And I beseech you, brethren, suffer** (bear with) **the word of exhortation** (22). He appeals to their patience by adding that "it is after all a short letter" (NEB). Then he apprises them of some good news concerning the release of Timothy, and promises: **with whom, if he come shortly, I will see you** (23). Evidently Timothy would have to travel some distance to join the writer; and the writer is planning to see the addressees of his letter, which would suggest a specific congregation or at least locality. They are directed to greet all their leaders **and all the saints** (24). **They of Italy salute you** (see Introduction).

Finally: **Grace be with you all. Amen** (25). This writer, as does Paul, sees grace as man's summum bonum. No greater gift can he wish for them in his parting greeting.[31]

[31]The subscription, "Written to the Hebrews from Italy by Timothy," is not in the text.

Bibliography

I. COMMENTARIES

ALFORD, HENRY. *The New Testament for English Readers,* Vol. II. London: Rivingtons, 1866.

BARCLAY, WILLIAM. *The Epistle to the Hebrews.* The Church of Scotland, n.d.

BROWN, JOHN. *An Exposition of Hebrews.* London: The Banner of Truth Trust, 1961 (reprint).

DODS, MARCUS. "The Epistle to the Hebrews," *The Expositor's Greek Testament,* Vol. IV. Edited by W. ROBERTSON NICOLL. Grand Rapids: Wm. B. Eerdmans Publishing Company, n.d. (reprint).

HEWITT, THOMAS. *The Epistle to the Hebrews,* "Tyndale Bible Commentaries." Edited by R. V. G. TASKER. Grand Rapids: Wm. B. Eerdmans Publishing Company, 1960.

MOULTON, W. F. *Hebrews,* "Layman's Handy Commentary." Edited by CHARLES JOHN ELLICOTT. Grand Rapids: Zondervan Publishing House, 1957 (reprint).

MURRAY, ANDREW. *The Holiest of All.* London: Oliphants Ltd., 1962 (reprint).

PINK, ARTHUR W. *An Exposition of Hebrews,* 2 vols. Grand Rapids: Baker Book House, 1963.

ROBERTSON, ARCHIBALD THOMAS. *Word Pictures in the New Testament,* Vol. V. New York: Harper and Brothers, Publishers, 1932.

ROBINSON, THEODORE H. "The Epistle to the Hebrews," *The Moffatt New Testament Commentary.* Edited by JAMES MOFFATT. London: Hodder and Stoughton Limited, 1953 (reprint).

VINCENT, MARVIN R. *Word Studies in the New Testament,* Vol. IV. Grand Rapids: Wm. B. Eerdmans Publishing Co., 1946 (reprint).

WEISS, BERNHARD. *A Commentary on the New Testament,* Vol. IV. Trans. by GEORGE H. SCHODDE and EPIPHANIUS WILSON. New York: Funk & Wagnalls Company, 1906.

WILEY, H. ORTON. *The Epistle to the Hebrews.* Kansas City: Beacon Hill Press, 1959.

II. OTHER BOOKS

The Analytical Greek Lexicon. New York: Harper and Brothers, n.d.

ARNDT, W. F., and GINGRICH, F. W. *A Greek-English Lexicon of the New Testament and Other Early Christian Literature.* Chicago: The University of Chicago Press, 1957.

CHAMBERLAIN, WILLIAM DOUGLAS. *An Exegetical Grammar of the Greek New Testament.* New York: The Macmillan Company, 1960.

HALDEMAN, I. M. *The Tabernacle Priesthood and Offerings.* Westwood, New Jersey: Fleming H. Revell Company, 1925.

MUELLER, HERMAN EDWIN. *The Letter to the Hebrews, a Translation.* Jennings Lodge, Oregon: The Western Press, 1940.

SAUER, ERIC. *The King of the Earth.* Grand Rapids: Wm. B. Eerdmans Publishing Company, 1962.

SOWERS, SIDNEY G. *The Hermeneutics of Philo and Hebrews.* Richmond: John Knox Press, 1965.

THAYER, JOSEPH HENRY. *Greek-English Lexicon of the New Testament.* Grand Rapids: Zondervan Publishing House, 1963 (reprint).

THIESSEN, HENRY CLARENCE. *Introduction to the New Testament.* Grand Rapids: Wm. B. Eerdmans Publishing Company, 1943.

The General Epistle of

JAMES

A. F. Harper

Introduction

The Epistle of James is known as one of the General Epistles of the New Testament. The designation is given to these books because they were written as circular letters for reading by a number of churches. This is in contrast to most of Paul's Epistles, which were addressed to specific churches or to individuals.

A. Authorship

The writer identifies himself only as "James, a servant of God and of the Lord Jesus Christ" (1:1). There were several prominent men of the New Testament called James. However, there is strong evidence for the view of many Bible scholars that the author was the head of the church in Jerusalem (Acts 15:13). Paul refers to him as "James the Lord's brother" and numbers him among the "apostles"[1] (Gal. 1:19). In Gal. 2:9 he characterizes James as one of the "pillars" of the Church.

This James is mentioned twice in the Gospels (Matt. 13:55; Mark 6:3). In both places he is listed as one of the brothers of Jesus. He apparently did not become a follower of our Lord until after the Resurrection. He was among those early disciples who, in the Upper Room, waiting for the descent of the Holy Spirit, "continued with one accord in prayer and supplication" (Acts 1:14).

James's ability and faith soon gave him a place of prominent leadership among the early Christians. When Peter left Palestine (Acts 12:17), James seems to have taken over leadership of the Jerusalem church. Three years after Paul's conversion he visited the leaders at Jerusalem and there saw "James the Lord's brother" (Gal. 1:19). In Acts 15, at the conference regarding admission of Gentiles to the Church, James was the presiding officer. On the same visit to Jerusalem, Paul and Barnabas were given the right hand of fellowship by "James, Cephas, and John" (Gal. 2:9). On his last visit to Jerusalem,

[1]The Greek of the passage is ambiguous (cf. Joseph B. Mayor, *The Epistle of St. James* [New York: Macmillan and Co., 1892], p. xxvii). Many scholars feel that the real meaning is that Paul did not see any of the apostles except Peter. He did, in addition, see James, who was not an apostle.

when Paul gave his report, "James; and all the elders were present" (Acts 21:18).

From a man in this position of responsibility and authority we would expect a general pastoral letter of practical counsel concerning matters affecting the spiritual life of the Church. This is what we find in the Epistle.

B. Destination

James addressed his letter "to the twelve tribes which are scattered abroad" (1:1). These would be Christians who had formerly been Jews and who had been scattered by the early persecutions of the Church. Probably the salutation would include also Jewish Christians won to Christ by Paul and other missionaries where churches were established in Gentile cities. In most of these churches there was at least a nucleus of Jewish believers who accepted Christ as a result of the preaching in their synagogues.

C. Date

There is no evidence in the Epistle itself or from external sources that gives much help in determining exactly when the letter was written. Some conservative scholars argue for a date as early as A.D. 45, others as late as A.D. 62. The earlier dates are premised on the fact that in the Epistle the author makes no mention of the problem of the admission of Gentiles into the Church. We know that James was deeply concerned with this matter at a later time. Those who propose the later dates point out the relatively settled condition of the Church reflected in the Epistle. James was too little concerned with laying foundations and stressing evangelical doctrines to have been writing to an infant Church. Thus the content of the letter argues that the Epistle would have been written later than the letters to the Galatians and the Romans, in which the author dealt with fundamental doctrinal issues. The essential point is not the exact year but the period. If, as it seems, James was martyred in A.D. 63, the Epistle was, of course, written before this date.

D. Purpose and Character

The Epistle was designed to foster practical Christian living just as were the ethical sections of Paul's letters. The time was far enough removed from the earliest days of the Church that undermining attitudes and practices were beginning to appear.

James speaks out against these evils with earnestness and a holy severity, exhorting Christians everywhere to remain true to the teachings and practices of the faith.

It is often noted that James is the most characteristically Jewish book in the New Testament. Because of this feature and because of the emphasis upon godly behavior, the book is akin to the wisdom literature of the Old Testament. Due to his concern for social justice, James is often called the Amos of the New Testament. There is in the Epistle also a marked similarity to the teachings of Jesus in the Sermon on the Mount. This would perhaps be expected because James was brought up in the same boyhood environment as Jesus and was in close touch with Him during the years prior to our Lord's public ministry. Hayes writes, "James says less about the Master than any other writer in the NT, but his speech is more like that of the Master than the speech of any one of them."[2]

James' deep concern for the practical outcomes of Christian faith seems at times to make him an opponent of Paul's emphasis on salvation by faith alone. It was this emphasis which caused Martin Luther's derogatory comment that the Book of James was "an epistle of straw." But Luther was wrong. James' position is not an attack on salvation by faith; it is a protest against hypocrisy. James wants the world to know that faith is a transforming force. Salvation by faith results in holy living. This does not contradict Paul's teaching—it complements it. The two emphases are the two facets of a full-orbed Christian faith—redemption and holy living.

Tasker has a fitting evaluation of the unique function of the book. "This Epistle would seem to be of especial value to the individual Christian during what we might describe as the second stage in his pilgrim's progress. After he has been led to respond to the gospel of grace, and come to have the joyful assurance that he is a redeemed child of God, if he is to advance along the way of holiness, and if the ethical implications of his new faith are to be translated into practical realities, then he needs the stimulus and the challenge of the Epistle of James."[3]

[2]"James, Epistle of," *The International Standard Bible Encyclopedia,* ed. James Orr, *et al.* (Grand Rapids: Wm. B. Eerdmans Publishing Co., 1943), III, 1,964.

[3]"The General Epistle of James," *The Tyndale New Testament Commentaries,* ed. R. V. G. Tasker (Grand Rapids: Wm. B. Eerdmans Publishing Co. 1957), p. 11.

Outline

I. Introduction, 1:1

II. Steadfast in the Faith, 1:2-27
   A. The Christian Attitude Toward Trials, 1:2-4
   B. The Prayer for God's Best, 1:5-8
   C. True Riches, 1:9-11
   D. Understanding Trial and Temptation, 1:12-18
   E. Responsive to Divine Truth, 1:19-27

III. Christian Standards of Value, 2:1-13
   A. A False Measurement of Men, 2:1-4
   B. A True Measurement of Men, 2:5-7
   C. The Rule That Is Always Right, 2:8-13

IV. Works Follow True Faith, 2:14-26
   A. When Faith Is Not Faith, 2:14-17
   B. An Objection Answered, 2:18-19
   C. Proofs from Hebrew History, 2:20-26

V. Christian Speech, 3:1-12
   A. Responsibility of Teachers, 3:1-2*a*
   B. Right Use of the Tongue, 3:2*b*-5*a*
   C. Tragedies of the Tongue, 3:5*b*-6
   D. The Untamable Tongue, 3:7-8
   E. Cleanse the Heart to Control the Tongue, 3:9-12

VI. The Wisdom of God, 3:13-18
   A. Wisdom Is as Wisdom Does, 3:13
   B. Wisdom That Is Carnal, 3:14-16
   C. Wisdom from Above, 3:17-18

VII. A Call to Christian Holiness, 4:1-17
   A. The Inner Cause of Conflict, 4:1-4
   B. God Wants a Holy People, 4:5-10
   C. The Evil of Evil Speaking, 4:11-12
   D. Recognize the Presence of God, 4:13-17

VIII. Judgment on the Ungodly Rich, 5:1-6
   A. Woe Pronounced, 5:1
   B. Selfish Hoarding, 5:2-3
   C. Dishonest Accumulation, 5:4, 6
   D. Selfish Satisfaction, 5:5

IX. The Second Coming, a Hope for Christians, 5:7-12
   A. Christ Is Coming Again, 5:7-8
   B. Pressures Tempt Us to Impatience, 5:9
   C. Examples of Patience, 5:10-11
   D. Swearing Forbidden, 5:12

X. Prayer, Faith, and Reclamation, 5:13-20
   A. Prayer and Praise, 5:13
   B. Prayer and Faith for Healing, 5:14-18
   C. Reclaiming the Backslider, 5:19-20

Section I *Introduction*

James 1:1

A. The Writer, 1:1

Letters in the first century customarily opened with the name of the writer, followed by the name of the recipient and a formula of greeting in the exact order as they appear here. The writer identified himself simply at **James.** Probably no further explanation was needed for the Christians of that day. They would recognize at once James of Jerusalem, the recognized leader of the Church. (See Intro., "Authorship.")

B. The Writer's Credentials, 1:1

With true Christian spirit James commended himself to his readers, not as the head of the Church, but as **a servant of God and of the Lord Jesus Christ.** The term **servant** (*doulos*) is literally a bond servant or slave. This meaning would be understood when used in relation to men. However, when used in reference to God, Jewish readers would understand it as meaning worshiper.[1]

It is sometimes noted with derogatory overtones that Christ is referred to only three times in this Epistle (1:1; 2:1; 5:8). It can be assumed that the reason was not disinterest on the part of James, but rather the assumption that Christian readers would know the basis of his message. In any case, there is a clear declaration of supreme Christian loyalty in the apostle's opening sentence. **A servant of God** was a familiar Old Testament phrase. James adds to it the distinctively New Testament dimension—a worshiper of **the Lord Jesus Christ.** It is a man who serves God and accepts the deity of Jesus who writes this letter.

C. The Recipients, 1:1

The letter is addressed **to the twelve tribes which are scattered abroad.** In Jewish terms **the twelve tribes** meant Israel

[1]W. E. Oesterley, "The General Epistle of James," *The Expositor's Greek Testament,* ed. W. Robertson Nicoll (Grand Rapids: Wm. B. Eerdmans Publishing Co., 1956), IV, 419.

as a whole. As James used the term, it would refer to Jewish Christians. (See Intro., "Destination.") It seems probable that while James had converted Jews in the focus of his attention, the words would include the whole of spiritual Israel, i.e., all Christians everywhere.

D. The Greeting, 1:1

Greeting (*chairein;* lit., rejoice) was the usual formula in letters of the first century, as in that of Claudius Lysias to Felix (Acts 23:26). The only other place in the New Testament where this form is used is in the letter which James wrote following the Jerusalem conference (Acts 15:23). This fact lends internal support to the view that James wrote the Epistle which bears his name.

Section II Steadfast in the Faith

James 1:2-27

A. The Christian Attitude Toward Trials, 1:2-4

My brethren (2) was a term that early Christians brought over from their Jewish background. The **brethren** here addressed would include Gentile as well as Jewish Christians. The closing word of 1, "greeting" (rejoice), is picked up in the **joy** of v. 2. It is as if James were saying, "I wish you *joy;* and you must account as pure *joy* all the troubles into which you may fall."[1] **Temptations** (*peirasmoi*) has the double sense of outward trials and inner temptations. In this context the translation "trials" (NASB) is the correct meaning.

We are given no choice as to whether or not we shall have trials; probably God could not trust us to choose what is good for us! We cannot decide whether to have them; we can only choose what shall be our attitude toward them. Here we are given God's counsel, "When all kinds of trials and temptations crowd into your lives, my brothers, don't resent them as intruders, but welcome them as friends!" (Phillips) Nevertheless, the troubles are not to be of our own making. It is not when we inflict suffering on ourselves but when we **fall into** it that we may regard it as placed in our way by God, and are to look upon it as a source of joy rather than sorrow.[2]

Being glad because you hurt is a difficult assignment! But this is God's counsel here given to us, and the writer hastens to explain it (cf. Rom. 5:3-5; I Pet. 1:6-7). The "blood, sweat, and tears" of the Christian life are for a purpose. They are one of the means by which we grow into the likeness of God. The athlete can find joy in the rigor of his training as long as he keeps the winning of the race in view. The Christian can find joy, even in trials, when he sees those trials as a means of achieving Christlikeness. He may at times draw so close to God that in his trial he can even **count it all joy.** In this counsel James is echoing the teaching of our Lord himself (Matt. 5:11-12).

The **all joy** may be set over against the **divers** (various)

[1]Alfred Plummer, "The General Epistles of St. James and St. Jude," *The Expositor's Bible* (New York: A. C. Armstrong and Son, 1903), p. 62.

[2]*Ibid.*, p. 63.

temptations. If the trials are manifold (ASV), God's triumphing grace is even more abundant. The Christian's attitude is to be better than mere endurance; it is to be a triumph. If we only doggedly set our jaws, grit our teeth, and hold on with a downcast spirit, we have not yet reached the attitude that God's Word here points out to us. Our burdens may be heavy but we must not let all of our energy and effort be swallowed up in enduring what we have to endure. If our troubles do not do us good, they do us harm. While we bravely bear the burdens that we must bear, there can also be joy in the Lord: joy in spite of those burdens; deep happiness as we realize that the burdens cannot crush us; an overwhelming sense of fellowship with Christ as He carries the heavy end of the load; real joy in the fact that through these trials we share in "the fellowship of his sufferings" (Phil. 3:10) and are being fashioned into His likeness.

The trying of our **faith** (3) strengthens our patience, and Jesus said, "In your patience ye shall win your souls" (Luke 21:19, ASV). James does not give us this counsel on pure personal authority. **Knowing this** means, Find out for yourselves. The tense of the verb suggests progressive and continuous action —continually finding out. The apostle tells us, Keep trying to be joyful in steadfastness and see if it is not the best way to manage your trials.

And why should one keep trying? Tasker answers: "That the Christian may be **perfect and entire,** pressing on to the complete and the fully balanced life of holiness."[3] This is the will of God for the Christian. The admonition points to a holiness representing the highest goal of Christian maturity. But that maturity is not to be expected apart from fulfilling our Lord's command and His provision for reaching this high country of holiness. The word **perfect** is the same word that Jesus used when He instructed His followers, "Be ye therefore perfect, even as your Father which is in heaven is perfect" (Matt. 5:48).

In 1:2-6 we see some of the fruits that grow when we try to cultivate "Joy in the Midst of Trial." (1) **Patience,** 3; (2) Prayer —**ask of God,** 5; (3) **Faith,** 6.

B. The Prayer for God's Best, 1:5-8

The closing thought in 4, "wanting" (lacking), is picked up by **lack** in 5. And there is a further connection. James has just

[3]*Op. cit.*, p. 41.

given to his fellow Christians an exceedingly difficult assignment: "Dear brothers, is your life full of difficulties and temptations? Then be happy" (1:2, LL). Bede interprets the connection between these verses as the natural question of the believer, "How am I to see trial in this light, and make this use of it? It needs a higher wisdom."[4] James knows the answer to that question: **If any of you lack wisdom, let him ask of God** (5).

1. *The Nature of Wisdom* (1:5)

What is the wisdom for which James exhorts his brethren in Christ to ask? It is more than knowledge, and it is beyond any natural human attainment. Robertson writes, "With James wisdom is the right use of one's opportunities in holy living. It is living like Christ in accord with the will of God."[5] Mayor compares this prayer for wisdom to St. Paul's prayer for the Spirit.[6] Moffatt writes of wisdom, "It came to mean a life which interpreted the divine law as the rule for faith and morals; the emphasis fell on moral and spiritual requirements. . . . What James means by it is the divine endowment of the soul by which the believing man recognizes and realizes that divine rule of life called righteousness"[7] (cf. 1:20; 3:17-18). Knowling is more specific in his interpretation: "St. James . . . assigns this high place to wisdom as he learnt to know it not only in the Book of Wisdom . . . but in men 'full of the Holy Ghost and wisdom,' Acts vi. 3, and as he may have seen it in Him, 'a greater than Solomon' . . . Who is described as 'filled with wisdom, Luke ii.40."[8] Knowling quotes Beyschlag as interpreting **wisdom** in the thought of St. James to be "that gift of God which makes a man ready for every good work . . . as not essentially different from that which is called in a parallel passage the gift of the Holy Spirit, Luke xi. 13."[9]

[4]Quoted in Mayor, *op. cit.*, p. 35.

[5]*Studies in the Epistle of St. James* (New York: George H. Doran Co., 1915), p. 63.

[6]*Op. cit.*, p. 36.

[7]"The General Epistles of James, Peter and Judas," *The Moffatt New Testament Commentary,* ed. James Moffatt (New York: Harper and Brothers Publishers, n.d.), p. 11.

[8]"The Epistle of St. James," *Westminster Commentaries*, ed. Walter Lock (London: Methuen and Co., 1910), p. 9.

[9]*Ibid.*, p. 9.

2. *The Gift of God* (1:5)

The evidence certainly points to the view that this **wisdom** of which James writes is the best gift that God has to give to His people. It is the gift of himself through His Holy Spirit. Jesus reasoned, "If a son shall ask bread of any of you that is a father, will he give him a stone? . . . If ye then, being evil, know how to give good gifts unto your children: how much more shall your heavenly Father give the Holy Spirit to them that ask him?" (Luke 11:11, 13) The **wisdom** for which a follower of Christ ought to ask—this "right use of one's opportunities in holy living," this "divine endowment of the soul by which the believing man recognizes and realizes . . . righteousness"—the writer believes to be the promised gift of the Holy Spirit.

Wisdom for all future decisions of the Christian life is not given in a moment of time, but He who is the Source of all wise Christian choices is promised as a gift from God to those who ask for His presence. Of the promised Holy Spirit, Jesus said, "When he, the Spirit of truth is come, he will guide you into all truth" (John 16:13). If a man lacks what it takes to live the Christian life, **let him ask of God, that giveth to all men liberally, and upbraideth not; and it shall be given him** (5). When James spoke of the divine generosity, he may have been recalling our Lord's words, "God does not give the Spirit in sparing measure" (John 3:34, Weymouth).

3. *A Gift Received by Faith* (1:6*a*)

If any man lacks the power to face his trials with joy, "let him ask of God" and **let him ask in faith.** If our asking be rewarded, it must be absolutely sincere. Do we really want the kind of help that God chooses to give us or do we secretly hope for an easier way? Do we have faith enough in the wisdom of God and in the love of God to let Him transform us into persons like himself through the gift of himself? This gift, like every spiritual gift from God, comes by faith: "He that cometh to God must believe that he is, and that he is a rewarder of them that diligently seek him" (Heb. 11:6). **In faith** "implies prayer . . . that asks for wisdom . . . that by it the petitioner is made the complete Christian he ought to be."[10]

[10]R. C. H. Lenski, *The Interpretation of the Epistle to the Hebrews and of the Epistle of James* (Columbus: Wartburg Press, 1946), p. 530.

4. *The Gift of a Unified Soul* (1:6b-8)

The divided heart is not the way to triumph in trial. If we are only halfhearted, we get only half help—or less! We shall be like **a wave of the sea** (6), at one time rushing toward the shore of faith and hope, at another rolled back into the ocean of unbelief. In our dealings with God there must be no double-mindedness, wanting partly our own way and partly God's way. Such instability is the mark of **a double minded man** (8; Gk. *dipsychos*, lit., two-souled), a man of divided affections and unsubdued will, wishing to secure both worlds.[11] It is this double-mindedness which keeps a man from finding joy in his trials, and it is the same disposition that will block him from getting the help that he needs from God. A man must believe with all his soul that there is help in God. On the basis of this unwavering faith a man may count on receiving the gift he seeks—**it shall be given him** (5). And the gift itself is the very singleness of heart that one seeks to manifest in the asking:

A heart resigned, submissive, meek,
My great Redeemer's throne,
Where only Christ is heard to speak,
Where Jesus reigns alone (Charles Wesley).

C. True Riches, 1:9-11

Verses 9-11 have no direct connection with 5-8 but they relate back to the theme of 2-4. Among the trials that the Christian of the first century faced were the hardships of poverty, together with exploitation by the rich and powerful. **The brother of low degree** (9) is a poverty-stricken Christian, one of "my brethren" (2), and not just a poor man. **The rich man** (11) seems to be the man who trusts in his riches and is therefore not a true follower of Christ. However, commentators differ on this point. If the rich man is a wealthy and ungodly person, 10-11 are a stern warning of the tragic end of an ungodly life. If, on the other hand, **the rich** (10) are wealthy Christians, these verses are an equally stern warning to converted men against dependence upon material wealth.

[11]Andrew McNab, "The General Epistle of James," *The New Bible Commentary*, ed. F. Davidson, *et al.* (Grand Rapids: Wm. B. Eerdmans Publishing Co., 1953), p. 1119.

1. *Origin of True Joy* (1:9-10*a*)

The Christian **brother** (9) can rejoice even under the grind of poverty. He does not enjoy the deprivations that he suffers, but he has a source of true joy that lifts his spirits above material limitations. The exaltation is what fellowship with Christ does for a man's sense of worth in the sight of God. When a man knows that he belongs to Christ, and has learned to count important the spiritual values of life, he does not need many material advantages to be a satisfied and joyful man. (Cf. Phil. 4:10-13.)

2. *Failure of False Security* (1:10*b*-11)

Likewise, the only source of true joy for **the rich** (10) is that he shall be **made low.** This humiliation is the reorientation of values that comes to a rich man when he follows Christ. The rich man who remains a disciple soon learns what his Master taught: "A man's life consisteth not in the abundance of the things which he possesseth. The life is more than meat, and the body is more than raiment" (Luke 12:15, 23).

James illustrates the short-term security of all material and merely human resources with a familiar biblical figure (cf. Isa. 40:6-8; I Pet. 1:24). **The flower of the grass** probably refers to the bright Palestinian wild flowers growing in the pasture lands (cf. "lilies of the field," Matt. 6:28). The **burning heat** (11) would be familiar to all who had been residents of Palestine. It was the hot east wind from the Syrian desert (see map 2) which could turn green pastures to brown in a single day. **The grace of the fashion of it perisheth** is graphically translated, "The flower withers, its petals fall, and what was lovely to look at is lost forever" (NEB). James drives home his point: **so also shall the rich man fade away.** The expression **in his ways** implies that the rich man referred to is the ungodly rich man who trusts in his riches. The words may mean the journeys of a wealthy trader, and thus suggest his feverish activities in acquiring wealth.

It has been noted that Paul draws his metaphors from human activity—building, husbandry, athletic contests, and warfare. James, on the other hand, like Jesus, prefers scenes of nature: "wave of the sea" (1:6), "flower of the grass" (1:10), "fierce winds" (3:4), wood kindled by "a little fire" (3:5), "the course of nature" (3:6), "every kind of beasts, and of birds" (3:7), "a fountain" (3:11), "the fig tree" (3:12), the "fruit of the earth" (5:7), and "the heaven gave rain" (5:18).

D. Understanding Trial and Temptation, 1:12-18

The word **temptation** (12) has two general meanings. The first of these indicates afflictions, persecutions, or trials from providential circumstances. It is in this sense that James uses the word in the earlier part of the chapter and in v. 12. Fearful lest his readers misapply to inward temptation what he had said about outward trials, James discusses in 13-18 the more generally understood meaning of the term as solicitation to sin.

1. *Reward for Steadfastness* (1:12)

Verse 12 is not closely related to 11 but it continues the discussion of trials in 2-4. James here asserts that the man who faces trials with courage and joy is the **blessed** (happy, cf. 5:11) man. The word is reminiscent of the Beatitudes (Matt. 5:10-12), and is found frequently in the Old Testament (e.g., Ps. 1:1-3) and also occurs in I Pet. 3:14; 4:14. **The crown** was used by the Jews to represent the highest happiness. Here **the crown of life** may refer to some specific Old Testament passage, e.g., the Septuagint rendering of Zech. 6:14: "The crown shall be for those who endure." **Endureth** is to be understood as facing trials in the manner recommended in 2-4. It has been rendered, "Happy the man who remains steadfast under trial" (NEB). **When he is tried** carries the meaning "when he hath been approved" (ASV; cf. Rom. 14:18; 16:10; II Tim. 2:15). The ultimate goal of the Christian is life eternal. It is a quality of life that begins here and now, but its culmination lies beyond the grave. This goal is here called **the crown of life,** a symbol of what is expressed in the words "Well done, thou good and faithful servant" (Matt. 25:21).

2. *Temptation Does Not Come from God* (1:13)

The stresses of moral choice bring a "crown of life" when one faces them steadfastly, but they can also raise questions in the mind. When this happens, one has moved from the area of trials into the field of temptation. James has in mind the man who seeks an excuse for his failure to be steadfast—who says, This temptation is too hard for me; God is to blame for sending it.

The author says, Let no man who feels an impulse to commit sin say, **I am tempted of God** (13). God permits trials to make us strong, but He never entices us to do evil. God is a holy God; His whole plan of redemption was designed to destroy sin. Because of His very nature God cannot be tempted by evil; to encourage one of His creatures to sin would be a violation of the purpose for which He gave His only Son. God permits the possibility of evil and its sometimes attractive forms in the moral world but He does not wish us to yield to the temptation.

3. *Temptation Comes from Within* (1:14)

James knew the supernatural powers of the devil at work in the world (cf. 3:6) but he here seeks to drive home a man's personal involvement and responsibility for sins committed. The lure to evil is within our own natures. It is somehow entwined with our freedom. The issue is, Would I rather be free, tempted, and have the possibility of victory, or be a "good" robot? The robot is without temptation but it also does not know the dignity of freedom or the challenge of conflict, and it knows nothing of the exhilaration of battles won.

James says a man **is drawn away of his own lust.** This word *epithumia* ("desire," RSV) can have a neutral meaning, neither good nor bad. Thus H. Orton Wiley writes: "All appetite is instinctive and unreasoning. It knows nothing of wrong, but simply craves indulgence. It never controls itself, but is subject to control. Hence St. Paul says, 'I keep under my body, and bring it into subjection: lest that by any means, when I have preached to others, I myself should be a castaway' (I Cor. 9:27)."[12] This is perhaps the sense in which James uses the word here.

However, in most instances in the New Testament, *epithumia* has connotations of evil. If this be the meaning here, when a man is drawn away from a straight course, it is by a wrong desire. Tasker writes, "This verse, in fact, so far from being opposed to the doctrine of original sin, substantiates it. James would undoubtedly have agreed with the statement that 'the imagination of man's heart is evil from his youth' (Gn. viii.21). Lustful desires, as our Lord so clearly taught (Mt. v.28), are themselves sinful even when they have not yet issued in lustful actions."[13] If this interpretation be accepted, there is here a further dimension to the origin of temptation. Wrong desires may be wrong not only because they are uncontrolled but because, apart from the Holy Spirit's sanctifying presence, they are carnal.

[12]*Christian Theology* (Kansas City: Beacon Hill Press, 1943), III, 49.

[13]*Op. cit.*, pp. 46-47.

4. *The Tragedy of Indulged Desire* (1:15)

In 14 **lust** probably refers generally to any enticement to evil. The language, however, is most commonly associated with inducement to sexual sin. James picks up this figure in 15 to trace the course of evil from a wrong thought indulged, to a sinful act, to God's judgment on the sinner. A wrong thought **hath conceived** when we have given it the consent of the will. Then follows the act itself. **When it is finished** refers not so much to the completed act of one sin, but rather to the accumulation of evil deeds that constitutes a sinful life. Phillips interprets the verse thus and links it to 16, "And sin in the long run means death—make no mistake about that, brothers of mine!"

5. *God Gives Only Good* (1:16-17)

Verse 16 is often treated as a transition from the thought of 13-14 to that of 17-18. The turn is sharp, **Do not err.** Do not wander so far in your thinking as to believe that any trial or any temptation comes from an evil purpose on God's part. God gives only what is good—and He is the Source of all good things. God has made us the kind of persons that we are, and when creation was completed He saw that "it was very good" (Gen. 1:31). Moffatt translates the first part of 17, "All we are given is good, and all our endowments are faultless."

The Father of lights (17) doubtless has a double reference. It refers to God as the Creator of the lights of the physical universe—sun, moon, and stars. But He is also the Father of all our spiritual illumination and blessings. James here contrasts the hourly changes in the sun and moon with the unchanging character of God. The lights in the heavens may change from hour to hour and cast shadows where they had previously given light. But in God's character there is "no variation, neither shadow that is cast by turning" (ASV). He is immutable. It follows as an assured consequence of God's unchanging character that in His dealings with us "there is never the slightest variation or shadow of inconsistency" (Phillips).

6. *The Glory of God's Plan* (1:18)

Does **us** refer to the writer and the readers as men or as Christians? Commentators differ on this point. The truth is significant in either case. If we understand **us** to be men created in the image of God, the meaning is clear. God made us the way we are—**of his own will** He did it. The reason for our freedom, testing, perplexities, and moral problems involving choice is that we should be like Him—**a kind of firstfruits of his creatures.** He created us free to choose the evil and free to choose the good in order that we should be in a measure the creators of our own spirits, the crowning glory of His creative **word** (cf. Heb. 11:3).

We may, however, with firm exegetical evidence understand **us** to refer to the Christian Church. Robertson titles his discussion of this verse "The New Birth." God, who is our Father through creation, is also our Father through redemption. Men redeemed from sin are the crowning glory of God's purposes for human life—"the first specimens of his new creation" (Phillips). **The word of truth** is thus understood to be the truth of the gospel. Knowling goes further and asserts: "We cannot forget that our Lord (John xvii, 17-19) speaks of 'the word' which is truth, that by it the disciples are to be sanctified."[14] God's final purpose is to bring us victoriously through our tests; to make us like himself in holiness and in love.

E. Responsive to Divine Truth, 1:19-27

Wherefore[15] (19) is the link to the preceding paragraph. In 18, James had spoken of "the word of truth" through which men are born of God. Since this divine Word has brought us to God, we must continue to be guided by it as we live for Him. An open, receptive spirit to God's Word and to the guidance of His Holy Spirit is always the way to make progress in the things of God. A rebellious, fighting, or complaining spirit does not work **the righteousness of God** (20). This continuing responsiveness to the truth of God is the tie that binds together the exhortations of 19-27.

1. *Lay Aside Hasty Speech* (1:19*abc*)

Hayes reminds us that James does not have much to say about sins of the flesh, so characteristic of first-century Gentiles. Rather he warns against those sins to which the Jews were more

[14] *Op. cit.*, p. 26.

[15] For **wherefore . . . let every man be,** the oldest MSS. have, "Ye know this," or, "Know this." Even so, it may be interpreted as a transitional phrase. Cf. NEB, Phillips, NASB.

prone—pride, impatience, and other sins of the temper and tongue.[16] So here the apostle quotes three precepts likely to have been familiar to his readers, **Let every man be swift to hear, slow to speak, slow to wrath** (19). Because he is about to give a sharp warning, James prefaces his words with an expression of deep affection and in it identifies himself with his hearers—**my beloved brethren.** It seems best to regard the hearing and speaking in a general sense, rather than to restrict the meaning (as some do) to hearing and speaking the gospel message. James later (21-25) deals specifically with man's relationship to the saving "word."

Zeno points out that a man has two ears but only one mouth; he should therefore listen twice as much as he talks. There is a close connection between hearing and speaking; also between speaking and wrath. He who listens most intently best understands his fellowman; understanding leads to considered speech and to the soft answer that "turneth away wrath." Quick speaking, on the other hand, often produces grievous words that "stir up anger" (Prov. 15:1).

2. *Lay Aside Wrath* (19*d*-20)

Anger almost always hurts both our fellowman and ourselves. Carnal anger always does. Therefore we are to be **slow** to anger (19) of any kind and to lay aside entirely anger that **worketh not the righteousness of God** (20). This **righteousness of God** means right conduct, i.e., doing what God wills (cf. Matt. 6:33). Not only does carnal anger move one to unloving conduct and so displeases God, but such angry behavior in a professed Christian raises doubts in the minds of observers and thus slows the progress of God's kingdom. Poteat comments: "The only anger which a man is justified in loosing is an anger like Christ's (cf. Mark 3:5), which is not the expression of private petulance but of public resentment against behavior or actions which cause others to suffer without blame on their part."[17]

Robertson outlines the truth of v. 19 thus: (1) Brilliant listening, 19*a*; (2) Eloquent silence, 19*b*; (3) Dull anger, 19*c*-*f*.[18]

[16]*Op. cit.*, III, 1562.

[17]"James" (Exposition), *The Interpreter's Bible*, ed. George A. Buttrick, *et al.* (New York: Abingdon-Cokesbury Press, 1951), XII, 31.

[18]*Op. cit.*, pp. 89-92.

3. *Lay Aside All Evil* (1:21)

Here we encounter another **wherefore,** which prompts us always to ask, "What is it there for?" James has just been speaking of wrath and its relationship to the will of God. His mind now moves to the broader context of God's will and man's evil. **All filthiness and superfluity of naughtiness** fails to convey clear truth to the reader today. Phillips has, "Have done, then, with impurity and with every other evil." NASB renders it, "Putting aside all filthiness and all that remains of wickedness." **Lay apart** (*apothemenoi*) is the aorist tense and suggests a clean break with everything that is contrary to the will of God. Robertson compares the meaning to Paul's figure of putting off the "old man" of sin and putting on the "new man" of righteousness (Eph. 4:2; Col. 3:8). He comments, "Surely evil runs riot unless it is checked and taken out root and branch."[19] **Superfluity of naughtiness** (*kakia,* wickedness) is not to be understood as "more than necessary." Wickedness "in the smallest measure is already excess."

The putting off of all evil is the condition for the subsequent reception of the **engrafted word** (better, "implanted," RSV). Moffatt carries out the figure of the seed and soil thus, "Make a soil of humble modesty for the Word which roots itself inwardly with power to save your souls." Knowling observes that " 'the word' so described is scarcely distinguishable from the indwelling Christ."[20] This is the word **which is able to save your souls.** "It brings a present salvation here and now (John 5:34); it is a new life of purity. It helps in the progressive salvation of the whole man in his battle with sin and growth in grace (2 Tim. 3:15). It leads to final salvation in heaven with Christ in God (I Pet. 1:9). The gospel is the power of God unto salvation (Rom. 1:16)."[21]

4. *Act on the Word* (1:22-25)

James is nowhere closer to the teachings of his Brother and Lord than in the emphasis of this passage. Jesus declared, "Not every one that saith unto me, Lord, Lord, shall enter into the kingdom of heaven; but he that doeth the will of my Father which is in heaven" (Matt. 5:21). James echoes this teaching

[19]*Ibid.*, p. 94. [20]*Op. cit.*, p. 30.

[21]A. T. Robertson, *op. cit.*, p. 95.

in imperative[22] form, **Be ye doers of the word, and not hearers only, deceiving your own selves** (22). James probably had in mind the setting of a typical early Christian congregation with its synagogue style of worship. The leader read Old Testament passages and New Testament writings for the edification of the listening people. Mayor suggests that we may take the imperative here to mean not simply "be" but rather, "show yourselves more and more."[23]

The man who hears the truth but does not accept it and shape his life by it is like a man looking at his image **in a glass** (23; mirror) but paying no attention to what he sees. The purpose of a mirror is to show us what we are—to reveal to us any marks of dirt that need to be cleansed away or signs of disease that need to be healed. **His natural face** is literally "the face of his birth." Ross observes, "The mirror of the Word of God reveals man to himself; it shows him that there is something seriously wrong with the nature which he brought into the world with him."[24]

There are tragic results when a man knows the right and fails to do it. In 24 the Greek perfect tense in **goeth his way** indicates the permanence of the result. This man "goes away and does not return."

In 25, James continues the figure of a mirror but his figure cannot convey the whole truth. A mirror reflects only the face in front of it, but God's Word shows us both what our human nature is and what is the divine ideal for us. **The word** in 22 is here called **the perfect law of liberty.** This is a law that sets forth what we must do, but it is a **law of liberty.** God's law for men is not enforced by external compulsion but is freely accepted as the desire and aim of those who are guided by it. We are assured that he who **looketh into . . . and continueth therein . . . shall be blessed.** Phillips says, "The man who looks . . . and makes a habit of so doing . . . wins true happiness." As we con-

[22]"The writer of this epistle speaks as one having authority. . . . His official position must have been recognized and unquestioned. He is as sure of his standing with his readers as he is of the absoluteness of his message. . . . There are 54 imperatives in the 108 verses of this epistle" (ISBE, III, 1562).

[23]*Op. cit.*, p. 64.

[24]"The Epistles of James and John," *The New International Commentary on the New Testament* (Grand Rapids: Wm. B. Eerdmans Publishing Co., 1954), p. 40.

tinue to concentrate on "the glory of the Lord" revealed in His Word, Paul declares, we "are transformed into the same likeness, from glory to glory" (II Cor. 3:18).

5. *Religion—False and True* (1:26-27)

In 22-25 we have seen the Christian's obligation to learn and do the whole will of God. Here we have a particular application. Verse 26 goes back to the theme of controlled speech introduced in 19 and discussed at length in 3:1-18. The phrase **seem to be religious** (26) is a bit misleading. The Greek, *dokei,* means "seem in his own estimation." It is not the hypocrite but the self-deceived of whom James is writing; the next clause, **deceiveth his own heart,** makes this clear. The word **religious** (*threskos*) refers to religion in its outward forms and ceremonies. The writer is here concerned with those whose religion consists of ritual but lacks holiness. *Living Letters* gives a striking paraphrase: "If anyone says he is a Christian but doesn't control his sharp tongue, he is just fooling himself and his religion isn't worth much."

In 26 the failure is an uncontrolled tongue. In 27 if a man fails, it is at the points of indifference to human need and "the contagion of the world's slow stain." James is not here giving a complete definition of the Christian religion. What he discusses is not the whole, but rather two indispensable parts of **pure religion and undefiled** (27). Social concern and holy conduct are the body of which the indwelling Christ is the living Soul. Knowling[25] points out that the two titles nicely balance the two clauses that follow:

Before . . . the Father—To visit the fatherless and widows.

Before God—To keep himself unspotted from the world.

James uses the term **world** in a sense employed elsewhere in the New Testament. It is the "order" or sphere of human life separated from God because it no longer is an expression of His will.

[25]*Op. cit.,* p. 36.

Section III *Christian Standards of Value*

James 2:1-13

In this section James returns to a fuller treatment of his concern, expressed in 1:9-11, for a proper Christian attitude toward wealth. His warning is clearly in line with Jesus' own emphasis that we cannot at the same time be the servants of God and the servants of money (cf. Matt. 5:24). James's warning is supported also by Paul, "For the love of money is the root of all evil" (I Tim. 6:10). The problem is as old as man, but James's admonition is also as relevant today as a doctor's counsels for regular physical examinations to detect early symptoms of cancer.

A. A False Measurement of Men, 2:1-4

James's specific concern is that a Christian congregation shall not seek to court the favor of the wealthy *for the sake of their wealth.* Are these words today addressed directly to a suburban, middle-class church? Are they addressed to a new congregation striving to gain a foothold in the community? Do they speak to us when we are seeking to attract people who can pay the budgets? All of these are worthy goals but the Bible bids us beware! James would warn us not to show partiality toward upper-income people when they come, nor to give them preferential treatment *in our efforts to win them.* When we do we are not like Jesus.

1. *The Command* (2:1)

Verse 1 should be read as a command in line with the imperative nature of the Epistle.[1] But James begins his word of reproof where all effective reproof must begin—he identifies himself with those whom he reproves. He writes to **my brethren** (1) and "my beloved brethren" (5). As a wise church leader, James asks his readers to evaluate their conduct in the light of their supreme Christian allegiance—**the faith of our Lord Jesus Christ.** The expression **have not the faith** means "as you hold the faith." These were Christian men and women to whom James was writing. They were well aware of the meaning of the Christian faith—the religion that Christ had brought into the world. **Respect**

[1]Cf. footnote on 1:22.

of persons is partiality; the exhortation is, "Show no prejudice, no partiality" (Amp. NT). Phillips puts the exhortation graphically: "Don't ever attempt, my brothers, to combine snobbery with faith in our glorious Lord Jesus Christ!"

2. *The Illustration* (2:2-4)

These verses are today a kind of Christian ethics for church ushers! However, in the first-century Church they were probably addressed, not to an usher, but to any member of the congregation who had a choice seat for the service. Perhaps James had observed this kind of preferential treatment in the Jerusalem church or in some neighboring congregation that he had visited. The **assembly** (2; Gk., *synagogue*) would be the place where the Christians—probably a mixed group of converted Jews and Gentiles—met to worship. It is the same term used for the Jewish synagogues. This was a word and a form of worship that the Early Church borrowed directly from its Hebrew ancestry. It should be noted, however, that this is the only place in the New Testament where a Christian congregation is called a "synagogue."

The **man with a gold ring** and the **poor man** were, we may assume, visitors and not regular members. There is difference of opinion as to whether they were Christian or non-Christian visitors. This, however, does not change the spiritual truth of the passage. The attitudes shown toward the men were wrong in either case. And if the well-dressed man were the kind of person described in 6-7, even if a member, his profession of religion had done little to transform his life. The unchristian act was to immediately judge the worth of the man by the appearance of his apparel. The **gold ring** would indicate a man of senatorial rank or a Roman nobleman. During the early years of the empire only such men had the right to wear such a ring. **Goodly apparel** signifies a white toga. This was often worn by a candidate seeking political office.[2] **Respect** (3) should be understood as paying special attention to the man of prosperous appearance. In the synagogue chairs or other seats were usually provided for the elders and scribes. A place of honor on these seats would be offered to a person of rank. Persons of lesser rank would stand,

[2]Bo Reicke, "The Epistles of James, Peter, and Jude," *The Anchor Bible*, ed. William Foxwell Albright and David Noel Freedman (New York: Doubleday and Company, Inc., 1964) XXXVII, 27.

or be seated on the floor. **Under my footstool** may be read "at my feet" (RSV).

Are ye not then partial in yourselves? (4) has two possible interpretations. Some take it to mean making distinctions between members and thus dividing the church. *The Amplified New Testament* thus renders it, "discriminating among your own." Others interpret the phrase as simply a parallel thought to the last half of the verse. The NEB renders the entire verse, "Do you not see that you are inconsistent and judge by false standards?" **Judges of evil thoughts** is better "judges with evil thoughts" (RSV), i.e., thinking thoughts with wrong motives. Here were judges who were using wrong standards of measurement. What kind of evil thoughts were these misguided Christian brethren thinking? (1) That fine clothes are marks of fine men and that shabby clothing means shabby character. (2) That wealth is a guide to the worth of persons. (3) That financial standing should make a difference in acceptance in the church. (4) That social and economic "caste systems" are acceptable to Christ and are appropriate to His Church.

B. A True Measurement of Men, 2:5-7

The writings of James are varied in style. Often he writes short sentences that remind us of proverbs. But here he is as careful as Paul in lining up his sequences of argument.

1. *God's Choice of the Poor* (2:5-6*a*)

Hearken (5) means, "Wait a minute, pay attention." It is comparable to Jesus' use of "verily, verily" (cf. John 3:5). James here reproves his fellow Christians, but it is the reproof of love for **my beloved brethren.** He is sensitive to the mistreatment of **the poor** and to the often callous and inhuman actions of the rich (cf. 5:1-6). But he does not defend the poor because of their poverty nor attack the rich because they are wealthy. Rather his defense and attack are both based on other facts. Admittedly he recognizes these facts as generally true of the respective classes.

James's argument is that **ye have despised** (6) those whom **God** has **chosen** (5). "It is not that God has limited His choice to the poor, but that, as a matter of history, they have been His first choice (see Lk. i.52; I Cor. i.26)."[3] Nor has God's choice

[3]Tasker, *op. cit.*, p. 58.

been arbitrary. It is simply a fact that the poor and the oppressed prove more responsive to the gospel than do the wealthy who depend upon the power of their money. In any case, James makes it clear that the poor of whom he speaks are those who are **rich in faith, and heirs of the kingdom which he hath promised to them that love him.**

2. *Man's Poor Choice of the Rich* (2:6b-7)

Favoring the rich and snubbing the poor simply does not make sense for Christians. John Calvin commented that it is odd to honor one's executioners and in the meantime to injure one's friends! It was probably wealthy Jews to whom James had reference. In his native Palestine, he had seen the rich Sadducees oppress the Church (Acts 4:1-4); and may have been familiar with Paul's experiences in Gentile cities (Acts 13:50; 16:19).

Three specific charges are levelled against the rich men whose favor the church sought to gain. Oppression and court trials are the first two; blasphemy is the third. In all of them James appeals to the reader's own knowledge and sense of fitness. "Is it not the rich who oppress you and personally [lit., they themselves] drag you into court? Do they not blaspheme the fair name by which you have been called?" (NASB) **By the which ye are called** (7) is literally "which has been called upon you." The reference points to the experience of baptism in which the **worthy name,** i.e., the name of Christ, was invoked upon them. The writer's use of **that . . . name** instead of God or Christ seems to reflect his Jewish training in which there was always so great a reverence for God that they hesitated to speak the name of Deity.[4]

C. The Rule That Is Always Right, 2:8-13

1. *The Royal Law* (2:8)

In this paragraph (8-13) James brings us back, as we must always be brought back when we evaluate the character of our conduct, to a basic rule for the Christian—**Thou shalt love thy neighbour as thyself** (8). We shall always **do well** if we always do as we would like others to do to us if conditions were reversed.

This law for the guidance of Christian conduct is **according to the scripture.** It is quoted from the Old Testament (Lev. 19:

[4]Oesterley, *op. cit.*, IV, 440.

18) and reaffirmed in the teachings of Jesus (Matt. 22:39). It is **the royal law** because it is the word of our Lord; it is **the royal law** because when it is kept in deed and in truth we cannot break any of God's laws governing our relationships with our fellowman. The keeping of this law is the keeping of all.

2. *Partiality Is Sin* (2:9-11)

The author is moving toward the conclusion of his argument: If Christians observe the law of love they will be pleasing to God, but when they show partiality they are committing sin. In 9-11 he anticipates a possible objection. "Why make so much of this matter of respect of persons? It is only a single offense, and it is surely not to be taken seriously."[5] This objection James refutes by pointing out that to break any part of the law is to break the whole law.

a. Any sin breaks God's law (2:10). What does James mean when he affirms that if a man **offend in one point, he is guilty of all** (10)? He certainly does not mean that breaking one commandment is as bad in its consequences as breaking all ten. Nor does he mean that the consequences of a minor failure are as serious as the results of flagrant sin. Some of the more extreme Stoics declared that the theft of a penny was as bad as killing your parents. But James was a Christian and not a Stoic. Jesus taught that a man must love God with all his heart. Any sin is evidence that my love for God is something less than complete. Any sin is therefore as bad as another in the sense that it breaks my fellowship with God. If that sin is not forgiven and that fellowship is not restored, a man has severed his vital union with God. In this sense a man **is guilty of all:** keeping all of the other commandments is of no value in satisfying God so long as I reject His will for my life at some one point. In this sense a man is "guilty of all in breaking *the whole law,* though not *the whole of the law,* because [he] offends against *love,* which is the fulfilling of the law."[6] A man cannot commit the sin of willfully despising human personality and be pleasing to God any more than he can violate another commandment and still retain God's favor.

b. Partiality is serious (2:11). In v. 9, James has said that if we show partiality we **are convinced** (convicted) **of the law as**

[5]McNab, *op. cit.,* p. 1121.

[6]Amos Binney and Daniel Steele, *The People's Commentary* (New York: Nelson and Phillips, 1878), p. 631.

transgressors. He now seeks to show how serious this transgression is. The same God who said, "Thou shalt not commit adultery," commanded, "Thou shalt not kill"—and this kind of personality destruction is murder. James here reflects Jesus' extension of the commandment against killing (cf. Matt. 5:21-22). To be angry at a man is devastating; to hold a person in contempt is, in God's sight, one form of committing murder. Men can be destroyed by a wrong attitude as effectively as by a physical blow.

3. *Live in the Light of God's Judgment* (2:12-13)

We cannot please God in this life if our conduct violates the golden rule. When we face the Judgment Day the same rule will be in effect. Therefore James exhorts, "So speak and so act, as those who are to be judged by the law of liberty" (12, NASB).

The Christian is not under the law of Moses. Since Christ came we are under **the law of liberty** (12). We are freed from the petty details of the old law, but we shall be judged by Christ's law—"Thou shalt love the Lord thy God with all thy heart, and with all thy soul, and with all thy mind. . . . Thou shalt love thy neighbour as thyself" (Matt. 22:37, 39). This is both sterner and milder than the Mosaic law. "It will be a deeper-going judgment than that of man, for it will not stop short at particular precepts or even at the outward act, whatever it may be, but will penetrate to the temper and motive. On the other hand it sweeps away all anxious questioning as to the exact performance of each separate precept. If there has been in you the true spirit of love to God and love to man, that is accepted as the real fulfilment of the law."[7]

The stern side of New Testament judgment is clearly stated, **He shall have judgment without mercy, that hath shewed no mercy** (13). Jesus supports this position in Matt. 6:14, "For if ye forgive not men their trespasses, neither will your Father forgive your trespasses." But even so, God is still a God of mercy, **and mercy rejoiceth against judgment,** i.e., "triumphs over judgment" (RSV).

In the light of these truths one can only pray, "Search me, O God, and know my heart: try me, and know my thoughts: and see if there be any wicked way in me" (Ps. 139:23-24). Let me

[7]Mayor, *op. cit.*, p. 87.

not sin by being partial to the rich or by despising the poor, even under nicer names. Teach me to judge my conduct in the light of Thy Word. Let me not be guided by my own fears or by the prejudices of the day in which I live. Lead me in the paths in which I ought to go; then shall I come before Thee unafraid. In Jesus' name I ask it. Amen.

Section IV *Works Follow True Faith*

James 2:14-26

This section has often raised questions in the minds of Bible readers because it seems to contradict the teaching of the Apostle Paul concerning faith and works. In his Epistles to the Romans and Galatians, Paul teaches that one cannot be saved by works; he receives salvation by faith and by faith alone. In this passage James asserts that faith alone is not sufficient for salvation, and that to be effective, faith must be accompanied by works.

The contradiction is only apparent. Bible students are agreed that the two inspired authors were giving the same words different meanings. When James uses the word faith he means merely an intellectual assent. When Paul speaks of faith he means a belief that carries with it the consent of the will. When Paul speaks of works he refers to the works of the law, i.e., the works of Jewish legalism which can never save the soul. When James speaks of works he refers to the good deeds which flow naturally from a heart filled with love to God and love to man.

It is evident that Paul is in substantial agreement with the teachings of James, for he too emphasizes that knowledge without action is useless. He writes, "For not the hearers of the law are just before God, but the doers of the law shall be justified" (Rom. 2:13). It has been said that Paul insisting on faith only, and James on works also, stand not face-to-face, fighting each other, but back-to-back, fighting opposite foes; they are both on the same side, although for a time they look and strike in opposite directions.

In this section James deals with the interaction of faith and works in the Christian life. His basic thesis is that if one professes to have faith and does not accompany it with works his faith is worthless. This section, like 2:1-13, is a closely reasoned presentation. The thesis is stated in 14-17; in 18-20, James answers an objection; in 21-25 he offers scriptural proofs; and in 26 gives a summarizing statement.

A. When Faith Is Not Faith, 2:14-17

1. *Worthless Profession* (2:14)

As in 2:1, James prefaces and softens his rebuke by identifying himself with his readers. He writes to **my brethren (14)**.

The faith to which he objects is not really recognized by James as true faith. It is a profession but not a reality. What benefit is it **though a man say he hath faith, and have not works?** Phillips gives the correct sense of the second question, "Could that sort of faith save anyone's soul?"

2. *A Parable* (2:15-17)

Verses 15-16 have been described as a "little parable" with the application given in 17. John uses similar argument: "But whoever has the world's goods, and beholds his brother in need and closes his heart against him, how does the love of God abide in him?" (I John 3:17, NASB) James's impatience with an impractical faith comes through sharply in the paraphrase, "If you have a friend who is in need of food and clothing and you say to him, 'Well, goodbye and God bless you, stay warm and eat hearty,' and then don't give him clothes or food, what good does that do?" (LL) Clarke comments, "Your saying so to them, while you give them nothing, will just profit them as much as your professed faith, without those works which are the genuine fruits of true faith, will profit you in the day when God comes to sit in judgment on your soul."[1]

Such a faith **is dead** (17)—inwardly dead as well as outwardly inoperative. It is not only fruitless, but it has no inherent vitality capable of producing fruits of righteousness. The evidence of its deadness is that it is **alone**—it has no accompanying deeds.

The specific mention of **sister** (15) is taken by Ross as evidence against the theory held by some, that we have in James a pre-Christian document of Jewish origin. He writes, "Sisters must receive equality of treatment with brothers in the Church of Him with whom there is neither male nor female (Gal. 3:28)."[2] **Naked** (*gumnoi*) is to be here understood as ill-clothed (cf. Matt. 25:36).

B. An Objection Answered, 2:18-19

At this point James introduces the views of an imaginary opponent who objects that faith can exist apart from works. **A man may say** (18) implies that a well-known argument is

[1]*The New Testament of Our Lord and Saviour Jesus Christ* (New York: Abingdon-Cokesbury Press, n.d.), II, 811.

[2]*Op. cit.*, p. 51.

being presented. James does not argue for the priority of works over faith; he only insists that there is no valid Christian faith apart from works of righteousness. The apostle says, I claim faith *and deeds as well!* To the man who says that faith and works may exist independently James can only reply, "Show me your faith apart from your works, and I by my works will show you my faith" (RSV).

In v. 19, James correctly cites belief in the one true God as the central tenet of the faith held by his opponent. This was basic to Jewish faith as shown by one of their writers: "Whosoever prolongs the utterance of the word One (Deut. vi.4) shall have his days prolonged to him." But belief in God is also the foundation of Christian faith (cf. I Cor. 8:6; Eph. 4:6).

Some would put the first part of 19 into question form, "So you believe that there is one God?" (Phillips) James responds, **Thou doest well** (19). So far so good—but this is neither far enough nor good enough: **the devils** (*daimonia,* demons) **also believe, and tremble.** Faith alone—in the sense of recognizing God without responding to Him in obedient action—is a religion that even demons can have (cf. Matt. 8:29; Mark 1:24). But such faith is not saving faith; they only **tremble** ("shudder," NASB). "Their faith is shown by their terror, an emotion of self-interest, but that does not save them."[3] John Wesley comments on those who have such limited faith: "This proves only that thou hast the same faith with devils. . . . they . . . tremble at the dreadful expectation of eternal torments. So far is that faith from either justifying or saving them that have it."[4]

C. Proofs from Hebrew History, 2:20-26

James now turns to proofs that should carry the greatest weight with his readers—evidence from the Scriptures, which they accepted as authoritative. In both instances the Old Testament persons were moved to action by their faith in God rather than by mere sentiments of natural human kindness.

1. *Introducing the Evidence* (2:20)

The expression **Wilt thou know?** (20, lit., Do you wish to know?) introduces this new turn in the argument. The question

[3]Moffatt, *op. cit.*, p. 41.

[4]*Explanatory Notes upon the New Testament* (London: Epworth Press, 1941 [reprint]), p. 862.

seems to imply a reluctance that borders on perversity in the man questioned. Do you really want unanswerable proof? is the correct sense. **O vain man** means a "foolish" (RSV) or empty-headed man. Trench says such a man "is one in whom the higher wisdom has found no entrance, but who is puffed up with a vain conceit of his own insight."[5] James here repeats his basic premise that **faith without works is dead** ("barren," RSV; lit., without work, inactive). Such lifeless faith produces nothing of any importance.

2. *The Argument from Abraham* (2:21-24)

Verse 21 speaks of **Abraham** as being **justified by works.** This seems to be a direct contradiction of Paul, who wrote that "Abraham believed [had faith in] God, and it was counted unto him for righteousness" (Rom. 4:3; cf. Gal. 3:6). Both James and Paul appeal to the truth in Gen. 15:6 in support of their arguments. The reconciliation is to be found in the specific events in Abraham's life to which Paul and James respectively referred; also in the sense in which they used the term **justified** (21).

Paul refers to Abraham's faith at the time that God promised to give him a child (Gen. 15:1-6). The faith that commended him to God was a faith that accepted God's promise with no supporting proofs. James, on the other hand, referred to Abraham's faith when he **offered Isaac his son upon the altar** (Gen. 22:1-19). "James is here speaking not of [the] original imputation of righteousness to Abraham in virtue of his faith, but of the infallible proof . . . that the faith which resulted in that imputation was real faith. It expressed itself in such total obedience to God that thirty years later Abraham was ready, in submission to the divine will, to offer **Isaac his son.** The term **justified** in this verse means in effect 'shown to be justified.' "[6]

The inseparable interplay of Christian faith and action is made clear in a recent translation of 22: "You see that faith was working with his deeds, and as a result of the deeds, faith was perfected" (NASB). If we accept James's evidence, we must admit his conclusion: "So you see, a man is saved by what he does, as well as by what he believes" (24, LL).

The expression **Abraham our father** (21) is sometimes used to support the argument that the recipients of this Epistle were Jewish, or at least all were of Jewish origin. But the concept of

[5]Quoted in Ross, *op. cit.*, p. 53.

[6]Tasker, *op. cit.*, pp. 67-68.

Abraham as the "father of the faithful"—Gentile as well as Jewish—was a Christian concept of the first century (cf. Rom. 4:16; Gal. 3:7-9).

In support of the reality of Abraham's righteousness, James points out that **he was called the Friend of God** (23). In II Chron. 20:7, Abraham is called God's "friend for ever"; and in Isa. 41:8, God calls Israel "the seed of Abraham my friend." This expression, **Friend of God,** seems to mean "that God did not hide from Abraham what He proposed to do (see Gn. xvii.17). Abraham was privileged to see something of the great plan which God was working out in history. He rejoiced to see the day of Messiah (see Jn. viii.56)."[7]

3. *The Evidence from Rahab* (2:25)

James selected **Rahab the harlot** (25) to follow Abraham the faithful in his Old Testament proofs that faith does not function apart from works. In this grouping he is supported by the author of Hebrews (cf. Heb. 11:17-19, 31). James seems to be pointing out that the principle he has been arguing is a universal one and that there can be no exceptions. He cites Rahab, who was "a gentile, a woman, and a prostitute."

In Hebrews, the writer points out that Rahab's action was "by faith." James would not deny it, but he here insists that she was **justified by works** in the sense that her actions were proof of her faith. "She believed in God, and evidenced her faith by the trouble she took in receiving the scouts and assisting them to escape, at the risk of her own life. No mere belief this!"[8]

4. *The Closing Summation* (2:26)

Like a lawyer before the jury or a debater before an audience, James gives a summation of the argument he has been presenting from 14 through 25. "Just as a human body without a spirit is lifeless, so also faith is lifeless without obedience" (26, Weymouth). When body and spirit are separated, death and decay result. Similarly when faith and its "works of obedience" (Amp. NT) are separated, faith dies. Moffatt notes the close relationship of the truth here declared, to the principle that James establishes in 4:17, "Therefore to him that knoweth to do good, and doeth it not, to him it is sin."

[7] *Ibid.*, p. 69.

[8] Moffatt, *op. cit.*, p. 45.

Section V *Christian Speech*

James 3:1-12

This section is complete in itself and deals with the ever-practical problem of the Christian and his use of the tongue. While these verses are self-contained, they are also related to the rest of the Epistle. James's broad theme of Christian behavior includes the Christian's behavior at the point of speech. The author picks up for full development here one of the germ ideas in 1:19, "Let every man be . . . slow to speak." The transition from the theme of 2:14-26 is a natural one; James is concerned about the *words* as well as the *works* of the Christian.

A. Responsibility of Teachers, 3:1-2*a*

The sense of v. 1 is stated clearly by Moffatt: "My brothers, do not crowd in to be teachers; remember, we teachers will be judged with special strictness." It was apparently the eagerness among early Christians to assume the role of **masters** (teachers) that prompted James to write this section of his letter. For best understanding of the passage Lenski reminds us that "we should think of the early churches in which any members might speak in the meetings. First Corinthians 14:26-34 is instructive: any brother might contribute some word; yet Paul lays down restrictions: it must be for the purpose of edifying only, must occur in due order, two or three only are to speak, and the women must keep silent. James has the same ideas."[1]

Again, James identifies himself with his readers, **my brethren.** These admonitions are not intended to forbid any Christian doing what he can do to guide others in Christian life and conduct. They are meant to remind us of our responsibilities rather than to deter us from our duties. The warning is directed to the opinionated and to those who are seeking prestige (cf. Matt. 23:8-10). James is saying: Don't be eager for the task of directing the lives of others, because this task carries heavy responsibilities. He who is a teacher is assumed to have greater knowledge; such added light demands added living. If we fail

[1]*Op. cit.*, p. 599.

we shall receive the greater condemnation because we have less excuse for failure.

The apostle reminds us that **in many things we offend all** (2). A better translation is, "We all make many mistakes" (RSV). We are all likely to stumble (cf. I Cor. 10:12); we are all too subject to error and too prone to mistakes to voluntarily increase our hazards by assuming the role of guides. Wesley comments, "Let no more of you take this upon you than God thrusts out; seeing it is so hard not to offend in speaking much."[2]

B. Right Use of the Tongue, 3:2*b*-5*a*

James started his discussion of Christian speech in connection with the responsibilities of teachers. Here, with the phrase **if any man,** he broadens the application to all Christians.

1. *A Guiding Principle* (3:2*b*)

James uses the device of repeating words to gain emphasis. "Offend" in 2*a* is followed by **offend** in 2*b*. He says if we **offend not in word**—if we do no wrong by our speaking—we are to be classed as **perfect** men. He who can rightly control his words can properly **bridle** (guide or control) all of his conduct. This is probably not meant as a literal statement because a man could keep his speech under control and yet sin in other ways. James is using a kind of proverb—a generalization to emphasize the key place of speech in the Christian life. It is comparable to Jesus' assertion, "By thy words thou shalt be justified, and by thy words thou shalt be condemned" (Matt. 12:37).

What does James mean by **a perfect man?** The adjective **perfect** (*teleios*) normally refers to the purpose or function of the noun modified. In this setting it would mean "those who fully attain to their high calling."[3] The Christian who is Christian in his speech is fully pleasing to God. He is **a perfect man** in the sense that Jesus commanded His disciples to use straightforward speech (Matt. 5:37) and then said, "Be ye perfect, even as your Father which is in heaven is perfect" (Matt. 5:48). In the light of this truth a Christian can only join in the prayer of the Psalmist, "Let the words of my mouth, and the meditation of my heart, be acceptable in thy sight, O Lord, my strength and my redeemer" (Ps. 19:14).

[2]*Op. cit.*, p. 864.

[3]Oesterley, *op. cit.*, IV, 422.

2. *Some Illustrations* (3:3-5*a*)

The word "bridle" (2) turned James's thought to the illustration of **bits in the horses' mouths** (3). **The tongue is a little member** (5), but he reminds us that the size of the instrument is no true measure of the significance of our words. Three striking figures are used to arouse the reader to this truth. The first two illustrate the positive values of controlled speech. **The bits in the horses' mouths** (3) are small things but by use of the bit, literally by controlling the tongue of the horse, we guide the animal and accomplish our purposes. The **helm** (4; rudder) is **very small** in comparison to the ship, but by controlling the helm **the governor** (pilot) guides the ship safely.

In both illustrations the writer shows that some very small things can produce some very significant results. So it is with our speech: "The human tongue is physically small, but what tremendous effects it can boast of!" (Phillips)[4] Although the effects of speech are often out of proportion to the size of the tongue, these effects may be wholesome and constructive. Control is the key, and such control is our Christian duty.

C. Tragedies of the Tongue, 3:5*b*-6

James's third figure contrasting the size of the cause and the extent of the effect also introduces the idea of the tragic results of uncontrolled speech: **Behold, how great a matter** (lit., forest) **a little fire kindleth! And the tongue is a fire** (5-6). It is the wicked tongue which James now describes. Easton translates, "That world of unrighteousness, the tongue, is set among our members."[5] This fire destroys with its heat and **defileth the whole body** (6) with its smoke. The conflagration ignited by an uncontrolled tongue is caused by the devil; **it is set on fire of hell. The course of nature** is interpreted to mean: "The orderly course of human affairs is set on fire—made destructive to mankind—by evil tongues."[6]

[4]This interpretation of 5*a* assumes that the sentence belongs with the preceding verses. Those who relate it to 5*b* and 6 give the words an evil connotation, e.g., "It is a great boaster" (NEB, margin).

[5]"The Epistle of James" (Exegesis), *The Interpreter's Bible,* ed. George A. Buttrick, *et al.,* XII (New York: Abingdon-Cokesbury Press, 1951), 47.

[6]*Ibid.,* p. 48.

"You and I do not exist merely as separate entities. Each of us is not a house that is set off by itself. . . . James thinks of us as houses that are set together in a great city. A fire that is kindled in any one house will spread and become a great conflagration."[7] The sense of the whole verse is strikingly clear in *Living Letters:* "And the tongue is a flame of fire. It is full of wickedness and poisons every part of the body.[8] And the tongue is set on fire by hell itself, and can turn our whole lives into a blazing flame of destruction and disaster."

D. The Untamable Tongue, 3:7-8

The figure of fire raging out of control suggests a new comparison. The introductory **for (7)** indicates a further explanation of the tragic results of uncontrolled speech. Wild beasts of all kinds have been tamed and made to serve man's good, **but the tongue can no man tame; it is an unruly evil** (8). The reference to the domestication of beasts appears to be an allusion "to the dominion originally given to man over the inferior creatures, which has not been lost, as has the control of the tongue."[9] In v. 7 the author again shows his love for repetition and alliteration: every **kind** (*physis*) **of beasts** has **been tamed** by **mankind.** The unruly tongue is **full of deadly** (death-bringing) **poison** (cf. Ps. 58:4; 140:1-3). Some interpreters understand this passage to mean that one man cannot control the tongue of another. However the entire context seems to show clearly that James is speaking of self-control. **No man** can tame his own tongue because its motivation to evil comes from powerful impulses not of his own choosing—the tongue is set on fire by hell.

E. Cleanse the Heart to Control the Tongue, 3:9-12

In vv. 3-8, James has been writing of the tongue and the human nature of fallen man. At v. 9 a new dimension is introduced as the apostle discusses the speech of believers—**my brethren** (10). "Language is the expression of man's thoughts and a revelation as to whether he is dominated by self-will or by obedi-

[7]Lenski, *op. cit.*, p. 606.

[8]Some interpret **the whole body** in 6 and in 2 as referring to the Church —the whole body of believers. While the context generally suggests the individual person, there are clear indications of the consequences of speech that reach out and affect the lives of others.

[9]Binney and Steele, *op. cit.*, p. 633.

ence to God's will."[10] A double-talking tongue is as incongruous in a Christian as a fresh-and-salt-water spring in the earth (11), or as a **fig tree** (12) bearing olives.

1. *A Moral Contradiction* (3:9-10)

Of the expression **Therewith bless we God** (9) Lenski writes, "The readers, no doubt, still followed the Jewish custom of adding: 'Blessed be he!' whenever they named God."[11] This was an appropriate expression of reverence for every early Christian. Yet what was happening among them? Forgetting our Lord's second great command (Matt. 22:36-39), and provoked by anger, they were cursing their fellowmen, who **are made after the similitude of God,** i.e., made in the image of God (cf. Gen. 1: 26-27).[12] Under New Testament teaching even a mumbled curse or an angry mood toward a fellowman is a contradiction of our Christian profession (cf. Matt. 5:22). In Christian men **these things ought not so to be** (10) because these attitudes and acts are unlike God.

2. *An Unnatural Condition* (3:11-12)

Such a contradiction in conduct is as unnatural as it is immoral. The interrogative word **Doth** (11, *meti*) expects a strong "no" as an answer. The sense is, "You certainly do not suppose, do you?" No one visiting salt springs such as those found near the Dead Sea would expect to find salt water and fresh water coming from the same source. If it did, the salty water would spoil the fresh; the bad would spoil the good.

The orchard and the vineyard teach the same truth. "As is the root, so will be the fruit." Jesus had reminded His hearers that men do not "gather grapes of thorns, or figs of thistles" (Matt. 7:16). James echoes this truth when he asks, **Can the fig tree . . . bear olive berries? either a vine figs? (12)**

3. *A Divine Remedy*

When James declares, "These things ought not so to be" (10) in followers of Christ, he knows that there is a solution to this unnatural condition and this moral confusion. That solution is

[10]McNab, *op. cit.*, p. 1122. [11]*Op. cit.*, p. 611.

[12]Wesley comments, "Indeed we have now lost this likeness; yet there remains from thence an indelible nobleness, which we ought to reverence both in ourselves and in others" (*op. cit.*, p. 864).

found in "the wisdom that is from above" (v. 17); it is found in the freedom from double-mindedness that comes when a man asks "in faith, nothing wavering" (1:5-8). James is speaking the truth when he says that no man can tame his own tongue—but God can do it! Jesus asked, "How can ye, being evil, speak good things? for out of the abundance of the heart the mouth speaketh. A good man out of the good treasure of the heart bringeth forth good things: and an evil man out of the evil treasure bringeth forth evil things" (Matt. 12:34-35). Elsewhere our Lord's counsel is clear, "Cleanse first that which is within . . . that the outside may be clean also" (Matt. 23:35). When the inner life is cleansed and controlled by the Holy Spirit, the Christian's speech can be disciplined in ways that are pleasing to God. The tongue, unruly though it be, is caged in the mouth, and God can give grace to close the cage when it ought to be closed!

The following lines are a fitting conclusion to this section:

. . . Make it pass,
Before you speak, three gates of gold:
These narrow gates. First, "Is it true?"
Then, "Is it needful?" In your mind
Give truthful answer. And the next
Is last and narrowest, "Is it kind?"
And if to reach your lips at last
It passes through these gateways three,
Then you may tell the tale, nor fear
What the result of speech may be (Beth Day).[13]

[13]Written about 1850. Quoted by Poteat, *op. cit.*, XII, 49.

Section VI *The Wisdom of God*

James 3:13-18

A. Wisdom Is as Wisdom Does, 3:13

This section has only a loose connection with the immediately preceding verses. Perhaps the **wise man** (13) can be thought of as the fountain of sweet water, unmixed with bitterness (11), or as the tree whose nature is such that it produces "good fruit" (12, 17). But fundamentally the writer's thought connects with 1-2*a* where he gives counsel to Christian teachers—or would-be teachers—in the Church. The ever-practical James applies the test of goodness to Christian leaders, and more broadly to all who would call themselves Christians. Seneca said, "Wisdom teaches us to do, as well as to talk." *The New English Bible* reflects the meaning of v. 13 accurately: "Who among you is wise or clever? Let his right conduct give practical proof of it, with the modesty that comes of wisdom."

The truly **wise man . . . endued with knowledge** (*epistemon*) is the man who knows God. The wise man of the Old Testament wrote: "The fear of the Lord is the beginning of wisdom: and the knowledge of the holy is understanding" (Prov. 9:10). This is the meaning that James employs (cf. 1:5). **A good conversation** is "his good life" (RSV). **His works** would be specific results or actions growing out of his good life. All such good actions are to be performed **with meekness of wisdom,** i.e., with the humility that is born of being Christlike.

B. Wisdom That Is Carnal, 3:14-16

The transition to 14 is to be found in the idea of "meekness" (13). Those who have **bitter envying and strife in your hearts** (14) are without humility. The lack indicates that they do not have the **wisdom** of God from which meekness springs. This "jealousy and selfish ambition" (RSV) is **in your hearts**—the central core of the person, from which actions originate (cf. Matt. 15:19). James says: If you find this kind of spirit, "do not pride yourselves on it and thus be in defiance of and false to the Truth" (Amp. NT). The apostle may be using **the truth** in its customary sense. However, in view of the specialized meaning he gives the term in 1:18 and 5:19 it can be understood to be synonymous with the gospel. Thus "men are warned against expressions and deeds which contradicted 'the faith of our Lord Jesus Christ' " (2:1).[1]

This wisdom (15)—the wrong spirit that James described in 14—**descendeth not from above.** Jealousy and selfish ambition are not the fruits of a God-filled life. There is a downward progression in the apostle's description of the origin of these attitudes. Such a spirit is **earthly** in contrast to heavenly. It reflects concern for passing values instead of concern for the things of God (cf. John 8:23; Phil. 3:19). This spirit is **sensual.** The American Standard Version has a marginal reading, "natural" or "animal." "The Greek is *psychikos* which describes man as he is in Adam (i.e., 'natural') in contrast to *pneumatikos,* ('spiritual')."[2] The term is sometimes taken as almost equivalent to "carnal" or at least to "fleshly."[3] James reaches the ultimate in describing the evil attitudes of selfishness and strife when he calls them **devilish** (*daimoniodes*), i.e., proceeding from Satan and resembling the spirit of demons.

Paul declares that "God is not the author of confusion" (I Cor. 14:33). James corroborates the truth by pointing out that where Satanic forces are at work **there is confusion** (16). **Envying and strife** confuse the man who harbors them, until he cannot think clearly nor act intelligently. These twin evils also corrupt and confuse all social relationships where they are present in the attitudes and actions of men. Phillips renders the verse, "For wherever you find jealousy and rivalry you also find disharmony and all other kinds of evil."

C. Wisdom from Above, 3:17-18

James now returns to a description of the wisdom that he commended to his readers in 13. **The wisdom that is from above** (17) is an expression found in rabbinical writings, but James adopted it and put his own enriched meaning into it. It is another word for the life of God in the soul of man. Adam Clarke calls it "the pure religion of the Lord Jesus, bought by his blood, and infused by his Spirit."[4]

[1]Knowling, *op. cit.,* p. 86. [2]McNab, *op. cit.,* p. 1124.

[3]T. A. Moxon, "Natural," *Dictionary of the Bible,* ed. James Hastings, *et al.* (New York: Charles Scribner's Sons, 1937), p. 647.

[4]*Op. cit.,* II, 817.

The eight elements of wisdom listed in 17 are comparable to Paul's nine fruits of the Spirit (Gal. 5:22-23). James lists purity first probably because the gift comes from a holy God. Such wisdom is **pure,** "unmixed with evil." This divine purity (cf. I Pet. 1:22) is sometimes regarded as the equivalent of single-heartedness—a sincerity which would exclude all double-mindedness, the divided heart (1:8; 4:8), the eye not single (Matt. 6:22).[5] As a result of this cleansing, man's nature becomes as similar to that of God as it is possible for the finite to resemble the infinite. **Peaceable** looks at the Spirit-filled life from within; it describes the Christian's inner state of mind, whereas the traits that follow describe what outsiders may observe.

The first of these outward manifestations is **gentle** (ness). This is not so much tenderness as a spirit of fairness in contrast to unreasonableness. **Easy to be intreated** is a closely related virtue; it is being open to persuasion and hence ready to be guided. However, some see in it a more positive trait, describing the man who wins his way by gentleness. The genuine man of God is **full of mercy and good fruits** (17) in contrast to "every evil work" (16) that originates from a carnal wisdom.

The last two traits are negative in form. The word translated **without partiality** (*adiakritos*) occurs nowhere else in the New Testament. It means "unambiguous" (Moffatt), "without uncertainty" (RSV), "straightforward" (NEB). In our relationship with others we are to be sincere, without a hint of dishonesty and with no concealment of facts. This is, of course, close to the meaning of James's next statement, that God's people are to be **without hypocrisy.**

In v. 18 the author promises a concluding blessing to those who serve God and His cause without selfishness and strife. The language is difficult and translations vary, but Moffatt gives an accurate and clear rendering: "The peacemakers who sow in peace reap righteousness." **Righteousness** is the **fruit** of seed that is **sown in peace.** The spirit of our Christian witness is almost as important to the progress of the Kingdom as is the truth that we proclaim. The writer here echoes the teaching of our Lord when He said, "Blessed are the peacemakers: for they shall be called the children of God" (Matt. 5:9).

[5]Knowling, *op. cit.*, p. 88.

Section VII *A Call to Christian Holiness*

James 4:1-17

The opening note of chapter 4 is in sharp contrast to the close of chapter 3. There James spoke of the peace of the heavenly wisdom; here he deals with the strife of carnal conflict. Moffatt uses this striking transition: " 'But how speak of peace to you,' James tells his churches, 'you wrangling, worldly crew? To your knees before God!' The thunder of his call to repentance rolls through verses 1-10."[1]

A. The Inner Cause of Conflict, 4:1-4

"Wars without come from wars within." Here is the truth that James would drive home to his readers. He was addressing himself to a spiritual problem existing within the circle of believers. He is still speaking to "my brethren" (1:2; 2:1; 3:1, 10; 4:11). These were professed Christians but they were not getting along very well as followers of Christ. Within their own fellowship there were envy and strife (3:14). In an appeal to conscience James asks, **From whence come** (these) **wars and fightings among you?** (1) Are they not due to a war being waged in your own spirits?

1. *Wrong Desires and Spiritual Disaster* (4:1-2b)

James gives an affirmative answer to his own question, but he knows it is the same answer his readers will hear from an accusing conscience. You have set your hearts on what the world can give you and as a result you are in trouble. Worldly desires conflict with each other. These **lusts that war in your members** (1) disturb your own peace of mind. You covet what you cannot have without injury to another, so you fight and kill and thus spread the conflict to others. The basic trouble is that you allow unholy desires to possess your spirits. Those desires if uncleansed and unchecked lead to spiritual disaster.

In view of 3:14 it is best to interpret **kill, fight,** and **war** figuratively. It is not probable that these actually occurred in the

[1]*Op. cit.*, p. 55.

Christian community. Also both James and his Christian readers would be familiar with Jesus' interpretation that to harbor the evil desire was, in God's sight, to violate the commandments (cf. Matt. 5:21-22). Most modern translators punctuate v. 6 to give two balanced sentences, e.g., "You lust and do not have; so you commit murder. And you are envious and cannot obtain; so you fight and quarrel" (NASB).

2. *Refusal of God's Will* (4:2c-3)

These Christians suffered inner tensions and outward conflicts because they refused to pray. In their feverish struggle to get what they wanted they had drifted so far from God that they did not take time to talk to Him about it. James says, **Ye have not, because ye ask not** (2). Wesley comments, "And no marvel; for a man full of evil desire, of envy or hatred cannot pray."[2] Even when they went through the motions of prayer James says, **Ye . . . receive not, because ye ask amiss.** Self-centered prayers that ignore the will of God bring us no enduring satisfaction. Had they prayed sincerely, God would have helped them. He would have changed their desires where those desires were wrong. It is impossible to maintain a selfish spirit in the presence of God. As we draw close to Him we are more and more inclined to say, "Not my will, but thine, be done" (Luke 22:42). But until we pray, and until we yield, we go on with the inner war, the outer conflict, and the utter unhappiness.

3. *Break with the World* (4:4)

The words **Ye adulterers and** are not found in the older Greek manuscripts. We should interpret **adulteresses** figuratively as Jesus used the term when He called the disloyal and unfaithful people of His day an "adulterous generation" (Matt. 12:39). The expression **know ye not** assumes that the readers are familiar with this truth but are ignoring it. **The world** here, as elsewhere in the New Testament, means all that men think and do that ignores God and is contrary to His will. In ringing words James declares that God's people must make a clear-cut choice between God and all un-Christlike attitudes. If we belong to God, the friendship of the world must go. If we hold on to any evil way, cherishing it as a friend, we make ourselves **the enemy of God**

[2]*Op. cit.*, p. 866.

and we no longer have a biblical basis to believe that we are in saving relationship to Him.

B. God Wants a Holy People, 4:5-10

1. *The Yearning God* (4:5-6)

The interpretation of verse 5 has always been found difficult. The King James translation is grammatically correct but it is not the only possibility. Most modern translations and commentators agree that the verb **dwelleth** (*katokisen*) is the word used in the New Testament to indicate the presence of God's Spirit. They therefore give the verse an entirely different interpretation, such as: "He yearns jealously over the spirit which he has made to dwell in us" (RSV). If this interpretation be correct, it is clear that James is through with his chastening of evil conduct and has begun his appeal for repentance. By cherishing friendship with the world we may backslide and lose God out of our lives. But this does not occur easily. God is a jealous God, who will brook no rivals. But when we were converted He gave us a new spirit. God yearns over this new life in the soul. He uses every effort to check us when we grow careless. He wants that life to increase, for He wants us to be wholly His own.

There is no specific Old Testament passage that corresponds to the last half of v. 5. By the words **the scripture saith,** James cites, not a quotation, "but a summary of Old Testament teachings: God wants all of a person, our undivided loyalty" (Berk., fn.).

God yearns over our divided affections and our resulting friendship with the world. He longs for the fullness of His Spirit to control our lives; He calls us to come to Him and submit to His ministry. God gives this special help to those fitted by their humility to receive it. To prove his point James quotes Prov. 3:34 exactly as it occurs in the Septuagint (cf. I Pet. 5:5). The words, **He giveth more grace** (6), are in the Greek "a greater grace." Knowling comments: "The best meaning appears to be that the Spirit of God bestows upon those who submit to the Divine will, and surrender themselves to it entirely, richer supplies of grace to effect that complete surrender to the yearnings of the Divine love, and to count all things as loss in response to it."[3] **God resisteth the proud,** because as long as we

[3] *Op. cit.*, p. 101.

have confidence in the worth of our own unspiritual, worldly, sinful attitudes—as long as we think them satisfactory—God can do nothing for us. But He **giveth grace unto the humble,** because when we are humble we are ready to admit our wrong spirit and our need of help.

2. *The Way of Blessing* (4:7-10)

McNab has given a superb summary introduction to this passage:

> Having contrasted the proud and the humble, and the divine attitude of resisting the one and bestowing grace on the other, James proceeds to set forth the abiding secret of victory in the war against worldliness and sin. It consists of two activities, submission to God and resistance to the devil (7). Herein are blended perfectly the true activities of faith and works. By faith we submit to God in a fuller, deeper surrender to His will and cease to fight against Him. In the act of submission we are prepared for conflict with the evil one; and at the same time our powers of resistance are strengthened and multiplied. See also I Pet. v. 8, 9.
>
> There now follows a series of practical injunctions which have special application to those who are seeking the way of God more perfectly. . . . The clean hands symbolize our activities; the pure heart represents the very citadel of our personality.[4]

a. Submit to God (4:7-8*a*). God is ever eager to woo us from the love of the world to a deep and abiding love for himself. But, eager as He is, God cannot create in us a spirit akin to His own until we ourselves seek for His Spirit. In this passage we are urged to exert ourselves in order to achieve this deeper life. James uses the imperative mood in his verbs: **Submit yourselves . . . Resist the devil** (7); **Draw nigh to God . . . Cleanse your hands . . . purify your hearts** (8); "Be afflicted, and mourn, and weep" (9); "Humble yourselves" (10). If we are to receive this greater grace, we must act.

Submit yourselves therefore to God (7) means fully and gladly to seek His complete will for our lives. But if we do this we must **resist the devil.** "The devil knows well enough that his greatest hope of drawing Christians away from a wholehearted and voluntary submission to God lies in appealing to their wounded pride. . . . [He] is constantly saying to the Christian, 'Why keep so closely to the narrow way and the humble path? Why not be more self-assertive? Why not express yourself as

[4]*Op. cit.*, p. 1125.

fully as you can, and find power and enjoyment in that self-expression?"[5]

On **Draw nigh to God** (8) Ross comments: "Draw nigh unto God, as those who long to come into the closest possible relation to Him, in contrast to those who are His enemies and who keep at a distance from Him. God will then draw nigh unto you, to visit you with His salvation (Ps. 106:4)."[6]

b. Clean hands and pure hearts (4:8*b*). How shall we draw nigh for this uttermost salvation (cf. Heb. 7:24-25) that God has for His children? James's reply is, **Cleanse your hands, ye sinners; and purify your hearts, ye double minded** (8). "That sharp term 'sinners' . . . is meant to pierce the conscience of the reader, and such also is the intention of the other sharp term which balances it, 'ye double minded.' The double-minded, as in 1:8, are those who are divided in their hearts' love between God and the world."[7] Hands stained by acts of sin need cleansing; hearts tainted with love for the world need to be purified. God has grace for both.

On **purify your hearts** Knowling says, "The verb . . . is used of spiritual cleansing: cf. I Pet. i.22; I John iii.3."[8] Adam Clarke, dean of Wesleyan commentators, writes, "*Separate* yourselves from the world, and consecrate yourself to God: this is the true notion of sanctification. . . . There are, therefore, two things implied . . . 1. That he separates himself from evil ways and evil companions, and devotes himself to God. 2. That God separates guilt from his conscience, and sin from his soul, and thus makes him internally and externally *holy*. . . . As a man is a *sinner*, he must have his *hands cleansed* from wicked works; as he is *double-minded*, he must have his *heart sanctified*. *Sanctification* belongs to the *heart*, because of *pollution of the mind; cleansing* belongs to the *hands*, because of *sinful acts*."[9]

c. The open door to God (4:9-10). In these two verses James returns to the theme of 6-7. He who comes to God must come in repentance and humility. The exhortation, **Be afflicted, and mourn, and weep** (9), shows the right attitude toward past unfaithfulness. There is no sin in good humor. The **laughter** of

[5]Tasker, *op. cit.*, pp. 92-93.
[6]*Op. cit.*, p. 80.
[7]*Ibid.*
[8]*Op. cit.*, p. 104.
[9]*Op. cit.*, II, 820.

which James speaks "was the unseemly laughter and merriment of the friend of the world, the sport of the fool."[10] He has in mind the gay pleasure-seeker of 5:5. All such persons should turn their merriment into **mourning.** The word **heaviness** (*katepheia*) denotes a downcast look expressive of sorrow. The writer calls on "sinners" to adopt the attitude of the publican who could only confess that he was a sinner and would not even lift up his eyes to heaven (Luke 18:13). Of the "double minded" Tasker writes, "So long . . . as sin is active in the believer's own life and is working its havoc in the lives of others, the mourning of penitence . . . must be among the Christian's most deeply felt emotions."[11]

The open door to God is always found by following James's exhortation: **Humble yourselves in the sight of the Lord** (10). Then we experience the effect of the gracious promise, **and he shall lift you up.** The figure came from the behavior of oriental mourners and penitents who lay on the ground and rolled in the dust. When they felt assured and pardoned, they arose, brushed off the dust, and dressed in clean garments. "We are humbled in the sight of God. But such a sense of humiliation, so far from being a cause of despair, is the essential condition of our exaltation. . . . Such exaltation is for the Christian both an immediate and a more distant reality. All who submit to the will of God, at any stage in their spiritual pilgrimage, are *ipso facto* exalted."[12] The poet rejoiced:

Jesus offers this blest cleansing
Unto all His children dear,
Fully, freely purifying,
Banishing all doubt and fear;
It will help you, O my brother,
When you sing and when you pray.
He is waiting now to give it;
It is for us all today (L. L. Pickett).

In 4:1-10 we see "Cleansing for Carnal Christians." (1) Evidences of carnality, 1-4; (2) God yearns to give "a greater grace," 5-6, ASV; (3) The way of blessing, 7-10.

[10]Knowling, *op. cit.*, p. 105.
[11]*Op. cit.*, p. 95.
[12]*Ibid.*, p. 97.

C. The Evil of Evil Speaking, 4:11-12

Moffatt places these two verses after 2:13, "restoring 4:11-12 to what seems to have been its original place" (Moffatt, fn. at 2:13). There is a certain logic in this proposal; for in 2:8-13, James was discussing the "royal law" and its observance. But such a rearrangement of the text is not necessary. Robertson comments, "It is quite possible that James here merely recurs to the subject of the loose tongue. . . . He has 'one word more' on this burning topic . . . an extremely difficult subject to say the last word about."[13] The connection with the preceding passage is the fact that when a Christian begins to drift away from God he begins to grow critical of his brethren. Three times in one verse James reminds his readers of their obligations as Christian brothers, **brethren . . . brother . . . his brother** (11). When love subsides, our brethren suffer.

James reminds us that he who speaks evil of his brother finds himself in trouble with God. **The law** of which the writer speaks is "the royal law" (cf. 2:8). When I violate God's law of love, I set myself up as a judge and say in effect: God's law is not a good law. Thus the real evil of evil speaking rests in a sinful pride that refuses to accept and obey the law of God. In v. 12, James seeks to awe and shame the evil speaker with the enormity of his sin. "He alone, Who made the law, can rightly judge among us. He alone decides to save us or destroy. So what right do you have to judge or to criticize others?" (LL) The writer is not here condemning legitimate human judgment. In v. 11 he has made it clear that evil judging is speaking evil of another. James's warning echoes that of Jesus, "Judge not, that ye be not judged" (Matt. 7:1).

D. Recognize the Presence of God, 4:13-17

This section relates to what precedes it at the point of an unchristian attitude toward material gain (2) and to James's previous discussion of pride and humility (6-7, 10). The Jews of the Dispersion (see Intro., "Destination," and comments on 1:1) settled in the cities of the Roman Empire. In this environment they became merchants and traders. Among those converted to Christianity there would be found numerous persons of these occupations (cf. Lydia, Acts 16:13-15). It was probably

[13]*Op. cit.*, p. 212.

to such traders that James addressed this passage. These were Christians who had failed to see, or who had forgotten, the real meaning of Christian faith in life and business. To all such persons the apostle says: Recognize the reality of God.

1. *Ignoring God* (4:13-15)

Go to now (13) is somewhat comparable to the Aramaic expression "Ah you!" (lit., Woe unto you). The sin of these men was not in planning for the future, but in failing to consider God in their plans. We are reminded of the foolish man in Jesus' story who said to himself, "Thou hast much goods laid up for many years; take thine ease" (Luke 12:19). James reminds us that no man can safely leave God out of account. If our lives are consciously submitted to Him, we seek His counsel. Even if we do not willingly submit our plans to Him, we must always take into account the stubborn fact that our times are in His hands.

The apostle reminds us all, **Ye know not what shall be on the morrow** (14). Moffatt makes it emphatic—"You who know nothing about tomorrow." A tiny clot of blood in the brain may cause instant and unexpected death. The heart, concealing an unknown weakness or driven too hard, may cease to beat. The Psalmist wrote, "My days are like a shadow that declineth" (Ps. 102:11). James echoes the truth: **Life . . . is even a vapour, that appeareth for a little time, and then vanisheth away. Life** (*zoe*) means natural life. Aristotle used the two verbs **appeareth** (*phainomene*) and **vanisheth** (*aphanizomene*) to describe the appearance and disappearance of a flock of birds as they pass across the sky.

No Christian—indeed no intelligent sinner—ought to be presumptuous about tomorrow's lease on life. A man whose life "is hid with Christ in God" (Col. 3:3) always has the attitude, **If the Lord will, we shall live, and do this, or that** (15). Some devout Christians take this passage quite literally and say: "The Lord willing, I will see you next week." In their letters they write: "I expect to come, D.V." (Latin, *Deo volente,* God willing). It is a fine, Christian custom and to be practiced if one can do so thoughtfully and sincerely. But even the formality may miss the heart of James's admonition. Robertson writes: "James does not, of course, mean that one should always say these words. That gets to be cant or mere clap-trap. It becomes repellent to hear one use the name of God flippantly and constantly. . . . The thing that matters is for us to have the right attitude of heart toward God, not the chattering of a formula. . . . God should be the silent partner in all our plans and work, to be consulted, to be followed whenever his will is made known."[14] Mayor comments on **we shall live, and do this:** "The boaster forgets that life depends on the will of God. The right feeling is, both my life and my actions are determined by Him."[15]

2. *From Neglect to Opposition* (4:16)

How far can a man go in neglecting God without passing across the line into downright opposition? This is the issue here involved. Thus far it seems apparent that James has been rebuking thoughtlessness rather than conscious sin. But the mood here shifts further toward self-sufficiency. **But now** (16, *nun de*) means: You ought to take God into your plans, but *the facts are* that you do not—and you take a measure of satisfaction in your self-sufficiency. Phillips interprets the meaning clearly: "As it is, you get a certain pride in yourself in planning your future with such confidence. That sort of pride is all wrong."

3. *Sins of Omission* (4:17)

Verse 17 may be taken as a concluding exhortation to the theme of 13-16. "Those to whom the words have been addressed had, to some extent, erred through thoughtlessness; now that things have been made quite plain to them, they are in a position to know how to act; if, therefore, in spite of knowing now how to act aright, the proper course is neglected, then it is sinful."[16] But this truth has more than local reference. The words are reminiscent of Jesus' teaching, "And that servant, which knew his Lord's will, and prepared not himself, neither did according to his will, shall be beaten with many stripes" (Luke 12:47). In a real sense v. 17 applies to much that has gone before in the entire Epistle (cf. 1:22; 2:14; 3:1, 13; and 4:11). Phillips gives an excellent interpretive paraphrase: "No doubt you agree with the above in theory. Well, remember that if a man knows what is right and fails to do it, his failure is a real sin."

[14] *Ibid.*, pp. 220-21. [15] *Op. cit.*, p. 141.
[16] Oesterley, *op. cit.*, IV, 464.

Section VIII *Judgment on the Ungodly Rich*

James 5:1-6

This section dealing with God's judgment upon the wealthy follows naturally from 4:13-17, where James discusses doing business and getting gains without including God in the plans. There is, however, a marked change in the atmosphere of the Epistle. In 4:13-17 it is the merchant of the Dispersion whom James has in view; here it is the rich landowner of Palestine.[1] In chapter 4 the writer holds out hope for repentance and improvement; here there is only a forecast of doom. Elsewhere in the Epistle it is Christian "brethren" who are addressed; here it is obviously the ungodly.

How shall we account for this striking interlude in the letter? The best explanation is that James here uses a rhetorical device known as an apostrophe. Using this literary technique, a speaker or writer appears for a moment to turn away from his audience and address directly some other person or thing. Obviously the apostrophe is meant for the benefit of the real audience rather than for those thus imaginatively addressed. The apostle's stern warning to the ungodly rich was meant to encourage the poor to whom he was writing. Also perhaps to warn them against envying the wealthy (cf. Psalms 73). It is possible that James envisioned his written message as sometimes falling into the hands of some persons in this very class of men and they would thus be warned. We believe that the Holy Spirit meant the words for the wider influence that they have found in our Bible—an influence certainly beyond the thought of James when he was moved by the Holy Spirit to write them.

A. Woe Pronounced, 5:1

Neither here nor elsewhere in the New Testament are the rich denounced simply because they are rich. Rather, God warns against the temptations to which the wealthy are especially

[1]Only in Palestine would field laborers have been hired help; elsewhere in the Roman Empire the fields were worked by slaves.

prone. It is not all rich men to whom James speaks but only the kind whom he describes—the ungodly rich. In 1:10 he has another message for wealthy Christians. **Rich men** (1) are apt to say to themselves, "Eat, drink, and be merry"; but God says, **Weep and howl for your miseries that shall come upon you.** When God speaks, it is well to listen.

B. Selfish Hoarding, 5:2-3

James here points to the evil of riches that are selfishly hoarded rather than spent or invested for purposes that God can approve. In one of the books of the Apocrypha[2] we read, "Lose your money to a brother and friend, and let it not rust hidden beneath a stone" (Sirach 29.10). The judgment spoken of in this section has not yet arrived at the time that James is writing, but it is so certain that James speaks with a prophetic note. The literal meaning of the Greek is that these miseries are already in the process of coming upon them. **Your riches** (2) probably refers to agricultural wealth such as grain, wine, or oil which was stored but also subject to spoilage (cf. Luke 12:16-20). Expensive **garments** and coins were the chief forms of oriental wealth. The fabrics were naturally subject to destruction by moths. The **gold and silver** (3) would not actually rust, but they would tarnish, and thus give clear evidence of misuse by hoarding.

These results of hoarded wealth are testimony against the owners. The moth holes and tarnish said eloquently that here was wealth not being used. James sees this decay of the money as extended to the owners. Like some infectious agent that would destroy both metal and men, the rust has begun its cancerous work in the bodies of the self-centered rich. Its infection burns their flesh as if **it were fire.** The expression **the last days** (3) seems clearly to refer to the consummation of time and the day of judgment.[3] There seems to be in the last sentence of v. 3 a play upon ideas and words. The rich who hoarded treasures for their own last days will discover that those treasures have become a fire in **the last days** of final judgment. "Their rust . . . will eat your flesh, since you have stored up fire" (RSV, margin).

[2]The apocryphal books were used in the Early Church for illustrative and inspirational help but were not accepted as a basis for doctrine.

[3]For a different view see Adam Clarke, *op. cit.*, II, 824.

C. Dishonest Accumulation, 5:4, 6

God is as much concerned with how we earn our money and how we spend it as He is with how much we put into the collection plates. Verse 4 condemns those who grow wealthy by exploiting the labor of others. There is here a Hebrew parallel structure common in Old Testament poetry in which the second thought repeats the first in slightly different form. In the first clause it is **the hire of the labourers** that **crieth.** In the second clause it is **the cries of them that have reaped** that have **entered into the ears of the Lord.** The language reflects God's Old Testament law for the laborer: "Pay him his daily wages before sundown, for he is in need, and his heart is set on it; lest he cry out to the Lord against you, and it become sin in you" (Deut. 24:15, Berk.). **Lord of sabaoth** is usually translated "Lord of Hosts" (cf. RSV, NEB). *Jahwe Sabaoth* was an ancient Israelite name for Jehovah.

Verse 6 reflects dishonest wealth acquired through fraudulent court actions. In 2:6, James referred to the rich who "draw you before the judgment seats." **He doth not resist you** probably means that he has no adequate legal defense. In the courts the influential rich have "condemned and ruined" (Phillips) the poor man who could not afford the fee for a lawyer or a bribe for the judge. The helplessness of the victim only increases the guilt of the oppressor. When the desire for wealth will make a man take another's living, or his actual life, greed has become murder.

D. Selfish Satisfaction, 5:5

The evil of v. 5 is but another facet of the selfish spirit reflected in 2-3. Riches condemn all who use them for purely personal pleasure. *Living Letters* paraphrases the words accurately: "You have spent your years here on earth having fun, satisfying your every whim." There are various interpretations of the phrase **in a day of slaughter** (cf. Jer. 12:3). The differences hinge on the meaning of the preposition. **In** (*en*) may mean "in," "on," "at," or "by." Matthew Henry saw in the phrase a reference to the Jewish feast days when many sacrifices were slaughtered. "Ye live as if it was every day a day of sacrifices, a festival; and hereby your hearts are fattened, and nourished to stupidity, dullness, pride and insensibility, to the wants and afflictions of others."[4] In view of James's reference to a coming day of judgment it seems to fit the context best here to translate *en* as "for." Thus one recent translation interprets the meaning: "You have lived on earth in wanton luxury, fattening yourselves like cattle—and the day for slaughter has come" (NEB). Moffatt emphasizes and sharpens the concept: "as for *the Day of slaughter.*" The finality and doom of this entire section is summarized by Moffatt: "You must pay with your lives for the wanton indulgence that has cost your victims their lives, the victims of your social and judicial oppression."[5]

[4]*A Commentary on the Holy Bible* (Chicago: W. P. Blessing Co., n.d.), VI, 1303.

[5]*Op. cit.*, p. 70.

Section IX *The Second Coming, a Hope for Christians*

James 5:7-12

In this section James turns again to address his **brethren** (7). The theme is God's overruling providence as applied to the Christian. Verses 1-6 tell us that God will finally punish unforgiven sinners. Here the Scripture assures us that He will, in His own time, also fully reward the faithful follower of Christ.

A. Christ Is Coming Again, 5:7-8

James does not try to prove the doctrine of the Second Coming, nor even to announce it. He takes it for granted as a living hope in the Early Church. He cites the imminence and reality of our Lord's **coming** (*parousia*) as a reason for Christians to be steadfast—**Be patient therefore, brethren, unto** (until) **the coming of the Lord** (7).

Two kinds of patience are suggested. The first says, **Be patient** (7)—do not be quick to retaliate against the wrongs inflicted upon you by such men as are described in 1-6. The second says, **Be ye . . . patient** (8)—patiently accept God's delay in the timing of our Lord's return.

The illustration of seedtime and harvest was drawn from Palestinian experience. **The husbandman** is the farmer, and the **fruit of the earth** the grain crop. It was **precious** because the lives of the farmer and his family depended on it. In Palestine the grain is planted in the fall and gets the **early . . . rain** toward the end of October. It gets the **latter rain** in March and April, just before it ripens. During this entire time the farmer waits in patience. The reason for his patience is his confident hope of the crop.

James interprets his own parable: **Be ye also patient; stablish your hearts: for the coming of the Lord draweth nigh** (8). Our Lord's coming was a great source of hope to the early Christians. Does it today stir our expectancy as it ought to do? Tasker writes: "If the Lord's return seems to us to be long delayed, or if we relegate it to such a remote future that it has no effect upon our outlook or our way of living, it is clear that it has ceased to be for us a *living* hope; and it may be that we have allowed the doctrine that 'He will come again with glory to judge both the quick and the dead' to be whittled away by scepticism, or to be so transmuted into something else, such as the gradual transformation of human society by Christian values, that it has ceased to exercise any powerful influence on our lives."[1] To the extent that we allow this to happen, we cease to be New Testament Christians.

B. Pressures Tempt Us to Impatience, 5:9

The focus here shifts from patience with sinners outside of the Church to patience with one another inside the Church. Some wag has written:

To walk in love with saints above
Will be a wondrous glory;
But to walk below with saints you know—
Well, that's another story!

In times of hardship, patience is strained and we are tempted to **grudge** (9; lit., groan, hence complain or grumble) "against one another" (NASB). James warns Christians against finding fault with each other, **lest ye be condemned.** The near coming of Christ is a warning against Christian failure as well as a consolation to Christian steadfastness. Moreover, **the judge standeth before the door.** Christ's return is near; He is to be the Judge of all men; therefore we need not take up the role of judging others either out of the Church or in it (cf. Matt. 7:1-5).

C. Examples of Patience, 5:10-11

Examples of godliness are always encouraging to the Christian. James probably had in mind Jesus' words: "Blessed are ye when men shall . . . persecute you . . . for my sake. Rejoice . . . for so persecuted they the prophets which were before you" (Matt. 5:11-12). That is why he says, **We count them happy** (11, we call them blessed). "We, like Jesus, pronounce a beatitude on the prophets who were such patient men."[2] James thus reminds us of our privilege as well as our suffering. If we suffer for God, we walk in a goodly company. Why were the prophets, rather

[1]*Op. cit.*, p. 120.

[2]Lenski, *op. cit.*, p. 655.

than Jesus himself (cf. I Pet. 2:21), selected by James as examples of patient endurance? Mayor considers several possibilities, the last of which is that "James wishes to fix their thought on Him rather as the Lord of glory than as the pattern of suffering."[3]

From the patiently suffering prophets who had **spoken in the name of the Lord** (10), James turns to a man who has been called "a world example" of patience. This is the only reference to Job in the New Testament, although James assumes that his readers are familiar with the story: **Ye have heard of the patience of Job** (11). The patience of the prophets was an attitude of long-suffering toward their fellowmen who persecuted them. The word used to describe the **patience** of Job (*hypomene*) means endurance.[4] The unique patience of Job was his determination to endure whatever misfortunes came to him without losing his faith in God. The phrase **the end of the Lord** means "the goal of the Lord." The apostle knew that God's final purpose is always blessedness for the man who endures. Probably quoting from the Psalms, he concludes, "The Lord is deeply sympathetic and merciful" (11, Berk.; cf. Ps. 103:8; also Exod. 34:6).

D. Swearing Forbidden, 5:12

The admonition of this verse seems on the surface unrelated to the context. There is, however, a connection with the thought of 9. Under the pressure of circumstances there is a tendency to speak explosively and to use God's name carelessly in hasty and irreverent oaths. It is perhaps in relation to 9 that James says: **But above all things**—i.e., above all unguarded forms of emotional and complaining speech—**swear not.** In this command the writer is quoting closely the words of Jesus (Matt. 5:34-37; see comments, BBC, VI, 77).

Neither James nor Jesus intended to forbid serious or official oath-taking enjoined in Scripture (cf. Deut. 6:13; 10:20; Isa. 65:16; Jer. 4:2; 12:16). They both were concerned about irreverent use of God's name and warned against dishonest speech that required an oath to support every assertion. The way to avoid offense of this kind is always to use simple and straightforward speech—**let your yea be yea; and your nay, nay.**

[3]*Op. cit.*, p. 151. [4]*Ibid.*, p. 152.

Section X Prayer, Faith, and Reclamation

James 5:13-20

The continuity and interrelationship of these closing verses of the Epistle are not entirely clear. They are therefore interpreted in different ways. Some consider them essentially unrelated, and title the section simply "Closing Admonitions." But careful reading shows that there is a logical progression as James here speaks to the spiritual needs of Christian men.

A. Prayer and Praise, 5:13

In verses 7-12 the apostle had been exhorting his readers concerning their Christian demeanor in the face of affliction. **Afflicted** (*kakopathei*) here has the same meaning as "affliction" (*kakopatheias*) in 10. In trial, as in every circumstance of life, the Christian's highest duty and his greatest privilege is communion with God. James therefore writes, **Is any among you afflicted? let him pray.** So that his readers might keep a proper perspective, and remember God in life's happy hours also, he adds: **Is any merry? let him sing psalms.** Praise is the sound that should arise from our lips when life is joyful; and there should be praise even under pressure when we remember the goodness of God (cf. Eph. 5:18-20). **Sing psalms** is too narrow a translation of the Greek; it came into the Authorized Version probably through the custom of psalm singing prevalent in England in 1611, when this translation was made. Nearly all the newer translations have "sing praises." Reicke reminds us that there is a place for gospel songs as well as for Christian hymns. He says: "Here it is worth noting that Christian singing is supposed to be the medium of the light and joyful as well as more serious sentiments."[1]

B. Prayer and Faith for Healing, 5:14-18

One form of affliction is illness, which probably accounts for the theme of this paragraph.

[1]*Op. cit.*, p. 57.

1. *The Privilege of Divine Healing* (5:14-15*a*)

Prayer in times of illness is both our duty and our privilege in Christ. We probably should observe this Christian practice more than we do. James says, "If anyone is ill" (14, Phillips) **let him call for the elders of the church; and let them pray over him.** The **elders** were leaders recognized or appointed in the local congregation as early as A.D. 40-50 (cf. Acts 11:30; 14:23). Their function was somewhat similar to that of the pastor today. To **pray over him** meant to pray standing over the sickbed. A secondary meaning of the word **over** (*epi*) would permit the reading pray *about* him rather than *above* him.

The practice of **anointing him with oil** in connection with healing is mentioned in only one other place in the New Testament (Mark 6:13). With us such anointing serves as a symbol of obedience to the admonition of God's Word and probably as a form of encouragement to the faith of the sick. In New Testament times it may have been a natural medicinal treatment used in cooperation with prayer. We know that anointing the body with oil was a common medical practice in first-century Palestine. The verb **anointing** (*aleipsantes*) means literally "having anointed." Moffatt envisions the action as smearing the patient's body with oil. It seems clear, however, that if the anointing was a use of a natural means of healing, it had also a spiritual significance, for it was to be administered **in the name of the Lord.** In any case, James assures us that it is **the prayer of faith** ("prayer offered in faith," NEB) that **shall save the sick, and the Lord shall raise him up** (15).

The Bible teaches the doctrine of divine healing, and we ought to seek to offer the prayer of faith for the healing of the sick. However, providential means and agencies when deemed necessary should not be refused. Those who know not Christ must resort to medicine and surgery without prayer. We who trust Him may use every good gift that modern science has given us, and at the same time commit our healing entirely to His sovereign power.

Easton comments: "The writer leaves this promise without qualification, although both he and his readers know perfectly well that not all cases of sickness will be healed; here as always when the efficacy of prayer is taught, the condition, 'if it be God's will,' is to be tacitly understood. Nonetheless, everyone knows that where intense and vivid faith exists—and that such was the case when James was written may be taken for granted—extraordinary cures occur."[2]

2. *Healing and Forgiveness* (5:15*b*-16*a*)

Among the Jews, illness was usually attributed to sin. Jesus rejected this view as a universal principle (John 9:1-2) but elsewhere suggested what we know to be a fact, that very often sin is the cause of a specific illness (cf. John 5:14). In such cases the man seeking healing is assumed also to be penitent for his sin and would be seeking forgiveness. In 16 the order of prayer is reversed. Here a man is admonished, "Confess your sins to one another, and pray one for another, *so that you may be healed*" (16, NASB, italics mine). When a man comes to God sincerely with any need, he receives help. Such help increases his faith in God, and he is likely to find help for other needs as well.

Easton[3] points out that the admonition, **Confess your faults one to another** (16), is not to be taken as a universal Christian practice, but rather to be understood in its context, the confession being made by the sick man and the prayer by the visitors. Though this seems to be a reasonable interpretation, the grammar permits a broader exegesis. It is certainly true that to acknowledge when we have done wrong and to offer mutual prayers of intercession greatly strengthens the whole spiritual life of the church, and thus opens the way for increased blessings from God.

3. *Effective Prayer* (5:16*b*-18)

When may we expect our prayers to bring answers from God? James makes it clear that prayers of this kind must come from **a righteous man** (16), i.e., one who is in right relationship with God and man. One translation of the last sentence of 16 is: "The effective prayer of a righteous man can accomplish much" (NASB). The only prayer of the unrighteous that God promises to hear is the prayer of penitence. Based on the word translated **effectual fervent** (*energoumene*), Mayor writes of his own interpretation: "We are tempted to regard as passive the forms which are usually assumed to be middle, and so to get the force here of prayer *actuated or inspired by the Spirit,* as in Rom. viii.26 . . . (so Benson 'inspired,' Macknight 'inwrought prayer,' Bassett, 'when energized by the Spirit of God.')"[4]

[2]*Op. cit.,* XII, 71. [3]*Ibid.* [4]*Op. cit.,* p. 165.

Every man who prays knows that there are times when the Holy Spirit thus helps him in his prayer. But James cautions us to remember that men who get their prayers answered need not be superhuman saints, different from the average man. The writer here gives an Old Testament example of prayer as he had previously given examples of faith in 10-11. "Elijah was a man of like nature with ourselves" (17, RSV. Cf. I Kings 17:1; 18:1, 42-45).[5] He was a man exactly like us—with the same resources available from God that are available to us. Any true Christian who serves God like the elders is encouraged to pray the prayer of faith. James's admonition to pray for healing of the sick and his illustration of Elijah's prayer for rain assure us that God answers prayer in the natural realm. Prayer not only changes us, but through it God also changes things.

C. Reclaiming the Backslider, 5:19-20

James opens his concluding exhortation as he had opened his first, **Brethren** (19); it is the last time he used this tender appeal in his letter. Three strands of thought tie these verses to the preceding passage. (1) There is a continuation of the theme of sin and confession in 15-16. (2) Dealing with a sick penitent was only one method of evangelism, because not all sins lead to physical illness. (3) While not explicit, we may assume that James conceived of this ministry of restoration as being carried out with the same "fervent prayer" of which he had just been writing.

The Epistle carries much stern warning and sharp reproof, but it is evident here as elsewhere that the author's ultimate goal is to correct and to set right those who are in danger. For James, a brother in danger is a brother to be recovered. In the words **Let him know** (20) he assures every Christian of the importance of this task and how far-reaching are its consequences. To **err from the truth** (19) is to turn away from faith in Christ and from obedience to Him. For other passages equating **truth** with

[5]There is a slight difference in the stated duration of the drought. James says **three years and six months.** Jesus also used the same figure (Luke 4:25). The OT account says "in the third year" (I Kings 18:1). The figure of three and one-half years appears to have become a popular expression indicating the length of trouble in apocalyptic teachings (cf. Dan. 12:7; Rev. 11:2).

saving faith see John 1:17 and Rom. 1:18. The clause **one convert him**[6] is better rendered "someone brings him back" (RSV).

The terms **one** (19) and **he** (20) make it clear that this ministry of loving personal evangelism is the duty and privilege of all Christians, not just "the elders of the church." When James speaks of **any of you** (19) and **the sinner** (20) he helps us to remember our Lord's concern for the one lost sheep and the one prodigal son. For all of his social teaching, James does not lose sight of the supreme value of the individual soul. When we recover a Christian from backsliding, as when we lead a man to Christ, we **save a soul from death**—from spiritual death in this life, and from eternal death hereafter (cf. John 5:24).

The last words of the Epistle, **and shall hide a multitude of sins,** are drawn from Prov. 10:12, as are Peter's words in I Pet. 4:8. Whose **sins** are thus hidden? The applications in these two other places give the clue to the meaning here. In Proverbs the sins covered are social consequences. Just as hatred stirs up strife, so love covers, or prevents, these evil results. Peter urges charity (love) because love covers, or prevents sins of anger and retaliation in the other person. In both instances the action of the righteous man has basic reference to the sins of the other persons involved. So here we understand that it is the sins of the erring man and the social evils resulting from his sins that are covered. The New Testament is clear in its teaching that no man is saved by any "works of righteousness"—not even by the gracious work of guiding the wandering back to Christ. Our sins are covered only by faith in our Lord Jesus Christ. But there is grace for us and for the backslider. Charles Wesley wrote:

Plenteous grace with Thee is found,
Grace to cover all my sin.
Let the healing streams abound;
Make and keep me pure within.

The letter closes without a farewell greeting. Moffatt comments that it ends "abruptly but not inappropriately." James's closing note is a climactic emphasis on New Testament evangelism. "No duty laid upon Christians is more in keeping with the

[6]The word **convert** (*epistrepho*) is the same word that Jesus used with Peter after he had denied his Lord. "When thou art converted [*epistrepsas*], strengthen thy brethren" (Luke 22:32).

mind of their Lord, or more expressive of Christian love, than the duty of reclaiming the backslider."[7]

Doremus Hayes writes of this entire Epistle: "All who are long on theory and short on practice ought to steep themselves in the spirit of James; and since there are such people in every community and in every age, the message of the Epistle will never grow old."[8]

[7]Tasker, *op. cit.*, p. 142. [8]ISBE, III, 1567.

Bibliography

I. COMMENTARIES

Binney, Amos, and Steele, Daniel. *The People's Commentary.* New York: Nelson and Phillips, 1878.

Clarke, Adam. *The New Testament of Our Lord and Saviour Jesus Christ,* Vol. II. New York: Abingdon-Cokesbury Press, n.d.

Easton, Burton Scott. "James" (Exegesis). *The Interpreter's Bible.* Edited by George A. Buttrick, *et al.* Vol. XII. New York: Abingdon-Cokesbury Press, 1951.

Henry, Matthew. *A Commentary on the Holy Bible,* Vol. VI. Chicago: W. P. Blessing Co., n.d.

Knowling, R. J. "The Epistle of St. James," *Westminster Commentaries.* London: Methuen and Co. Ltd., 1910.

Lenski, R. C. H. *The Interpretation of the Epistle to the Hebrews and of the Epistle of James.* Columbus: Wartburg Press, 1946.

Mayor, Joseph B. *The Epistle of St. James.* New York: Macmillan and Co., 1892.

McNab, Andrew. "The General Epistle of James," *The New Bible Commentary.* Edited by F. Davidson, *et al.* Grand Rapids: Wm. B. Eerdmans Publishing Co., 1953.

Oesterley, W. E. "The General Epistle of James." *The Expositor's Greek Testament.* Grand Rapids: Wm. B. Eerdmans Publishing Co., 1956.

Poteat, Gordon. "James" (Exposition). *The Interpreter's Bible.* Edited by George A. Buttrick, *et al.* Vol. XII. New York: Abingdon-Cokesbury Press, 1951.

Reicke, Bo. "The Epistles of James, Peter, and Jude," *The Anchor Bible.* Edited by William Foxwell Albright and David Noel Freedman. Vol. XXXVII. New York: Doubleday and Doran, 1964.

Robertson, A. T. *Studies in the Epistle of St. James.* New York: George H. Doran Co., 1915.

Ross, Alexander. "The Epistles of James and John," *The New International Commentary on the New Testament.* Grand Rapids: Wm. B. Eerdmans Publishing Co., 1954.

Tasker, R. V. G. "James," *The Tyndale New Testament Commentaries.* Edited by R. V. G. Tasker. Grand Rapids: Wm. B. Eerdmans Publishing Co., 1957.

Wesley, John. *Explanatory Notes upon the New Testament.* London: Epworth Press, 1941 (reprint).

II. OTHER BOOKS

Earle, Ralph, *et al. Exploring the New Testament.* Kansas City: Beacon Hill Press of Kansas City, 1955.

Harrison, Everett F. *Introduction to the New Testament.* Grand Rapids: Wm. B. Eerdmans Publishing Co., 1964.

TENNEY, MERRILL C. *New Testament Survey.* Grand Rapids: Wm. B. Eerdmans Publishing Co., 1961.

WILEY, H. ORTON. *Christian Theology.* Vol. III. Kansas City: Beacon Hill Press of Kansas City, 1943.

III. ARTICLES

HAYES, DOREMUS ALMY. "James, Epistle of," *The International Standard Bible Encyclopedia.* Edited by JAMES ORR, *et al.* Vol. III. Grand Rapids: Wm. B. Eerdmans Publishing Co., 1943.

KERR, C. M. "James," *The International Standard Bible Encyclopedia.* Edited by JAMES ORR, *et al.* Vol. III. Grand Rapids: Wm. B. Eerdmans Publishing Co., 1943.

MOXON, T. A. "Natural," *Dictionary of the Bible.* Edited by JAMES HASTINGS, *et al.* New York: Charles Scribners Sons, 1937.

The First Epistle of

PETER

Roy S. Nicholson

Introduction

The First Epistle of Peter has been described as "The Epistle of Hope," "The Epistle of Courage," and "The Epistle of Hope and Glory." It could also be called "The Epistle of Holy Living," for it emphasizes the fact that holiness of life is more important than deliverance from suffering. Its most dominant lessons are that God's true children will be subjected to undeserved suffering, but that despite such persecutions, through the grace and power of God they may remain steadfast; and that they will conduct themselves as becomes holiness regardless of any situation which may confront them. The Christian way, Peter reminds them, is one of holiness like that exemplified by Christ during His earthly sojourn.

A. Authorship

This Epistle claims to be from the hand of Peter, the apostle, and was universally accepted as such by the Early Church. Renan is quoted by Marcus Dods as writing that the First Epistle of Peter was "the most anciently and the most unanimously cited as authentic."[1] Bishop Thomas A. Horne says that the genuineness and authenticity of I Peter "were never disputed."[2] Both the external and the internal evidence strongly argue its Petrine authorship.[3]

Concerning the authorship of I Peter, Charles Bigg declares boldly: "There is no book in the New Testament which has earlier, better, or stronger attestation."[4] Most scholars today agree that Peter wrote this Epistle. The principal uncertainty, however, concerns the part Silvanus had in its writing (cf. 5:12).

B. To Whom Addressed

This "encyclical" letter was evidently intended for the whole body of Christians inhabiting the region which comprised Asia

[1] *An Introduction to the New Testament* (6th ed.; New York: Thomas Whittaker, n.d.), p. 198.

[2] *A Compendious Introduction to the Study of the Bible* (Nashville: Lane and Scott, 1850), p. 342.

[3] Ralph Earle, *et al., Exploring the New Testament* (Kansas City: Beacon Hill Press of Kansas City, 1955), pp. 399-400.

[4] *The Epistles of St. Peter and St. Jude* ("The International Critical Commentary"; New York: Charles Scribner's Sons, 1905), p. 7.

Minor north of the Taurus Mountains. They were probably Paul's converts and included both Jews and Gentiles. Some consider that the Jews were in the majority. Others think there were more Gentiles than Jews (cf. 1:14; 2:9-10; 3:6; 4:3). Dods says that Gentile converts to Christianity always acquired some familiarity with the Old Testament teachings and some knowledge of its personalities. His conclusion is: "It may indeed be accepted as certain that the letter is addressed to all Christians dwelling in the regions named. And that the Christian churches of these districts were composed of Gentiles and Jews may also be accepted as certain."[5]

Stephen W. Paine suggests that some to whom this letter would come may have been Gentiles who heard Peter's sermon at Pentecost (cf. Acts 2:9) and "had doubtless gone back to their home territory as spiritual colonists."[6] Andrew F. Walls suggests that this letter was sent to that part of Asia Minor which was not evangelized by Paul. His view assumes that Paul's letter to the Galatians was sent to those living in South Galatia.[7]

Bo Reicke's view is that those in the south Galatia region are not mentioned because they were already more closely related to the church at Antioch than to the Roman congregation.[8] Some authorities declare that I Peter is addressed to the same persons as those to whom James wrote, since they were dispersed and were surrounded by cruel hardships and fiery temptations. This Epistle may have been written before the officially instituted state persecution, but during a time when the Christians were facing social ostracism inspired by fanatical Jews and hostile pagans. It appears that these believers were suffering because: (*a*) they were Jews; (*b*) they were Christians; and (*c*) they were considered by the Jews as apostates.[9]

John H. Kerr quotes Canon Cook as saying that the general and special injunctions in I Peter equally justify the conclusion

[5]*Op. cit.*, pp. 203-4.

[6]"The First Epistle of Peter," *The Wycliffe Bible Commentary*, ed. Charles F. Pfeiffer and Everett F. Harrison (Chicago: Moody Press, 1962), p. 1443.

[7]"Introduction," in Alan M. Stibbs, *The First Epistle General of Peter* ("Tyndale New Testament Commentaries"; London: Tyndale Press, 1959), p. 64.

[8]"The Epistles of James, Peter and Jude," *The Anchor Bible*, ed. William F. Albright and David N. Freedman (New York: Doubleday and Company, 1964), p. 77.

[9]Charles R. Erdman, *The General Epistles, an Exposition* (Philadelphia: The Westminster Press, 1918), p. 52.

"that so far from having Israelites exclusively before his mind, the large-minded baptizer of Cornelius gave his deepest and most earnest thought to a body in which there is neither Jew nor Gentile, in which Christ is all in all."[10]

C. Date and Place of Writing

There is a wide divergence of opinion regarding both the time and the place of the writing of this Epistle. Lack of space allows only bare mention of sources where these points are considered in detail, and brief citation of the conclusions of conservative scholars.

As to the date, W. H. Bennett, after having carefully considered the objections to the Petrine authorship and a date at which Peter could have written it, concludes that "the date will be about A.D. 64-66."[11] Earle suggests the date as being A.D. 64.[12] E. G. Selwyn discusses the question of the date at some length and places it in the latter half of A.D. 63 or the first half of A.D. 64.[13] William Barclay's conclusion is that it was written shortly after the great fire at Rome during Nero's reign, and incident to the first persecution of the Christians.[14] Therefore it seems reasonable to date the book A.D. 63-65.

The place from which I Peter was written arouses as much controversy as its date. "Babylon" (5:13) has been interpreted three different ways. A few contend that it was written from a small city by that name in northern Egypt which was the site of a Roman military outpost. A considerable body of scholars zealously assert that it was written from Babylon on the Euphrates River in Mesopotamia. Most authorities feel that it was written from Rome, which Peter enshrouded in an allegorical expression. The general testimony of antiquity, which carries significant weight, is that it was written from that city. Eusebius, Jerome, and others definitely state that I Peter was written in Rome.

Kuhn declared that the reference can only be to the imperial capital. He cites as his reasons "the general application to Rome

[10]*An Introduction to the Study of the Books of the New Testament* (13th ed.; New York: Fleming H. Revell Company, 1939), p. 271.

[11]*The General Epistles, James, Peter, John and Jude* ("The Century Bible"; Edinburgh: T. C. and E. E. Jack, 1901), p. 43.

[12]*Op. cit.*, p. 400.

[13]*The First Epistle of St. Peter* (London: Macmillan and Co., 1961), pp. 56-63.

[14]*The Letters of James and Peter* ("The Daily Study Bible," 2d ed.; Philadelphia: The Westminster Press, 1960), p. 194.

in early exegesis, with only a few dwindling exceptions; [and] the lack of even a hint that Peter ever stayed or worked in the land of Babylon, as distinct from the solid historicity of his stay and martyrdom in Rome."[15] Beare takes the adverse view that it was written from the area to which it is addressed, by a presbyter who used a pseudonym.[16] But consensus is that it was written from Rome.

D. Nature and Style

Recent discussion on I Peter has centered about whether or not it is a letter, a liturgy for a baptismal service, a combination of these two, or a baptismal discourse.[17] It is definitely epistolary in form. Its introduction, greeting, and closing have the marks common to an epistle.[18] It frequently exhibits "digressions, recapitulations, repeated emphases, and spontaneous outpourings in the form of ascriptions, invocations, and so on."[19]

The style of writing expresses the vehemence and fervor of Peter's spirit. While it denounces no special heresies, it reveals the full knowledge which Peter had of Christianity. He writes with the strong assurance and conviction of the truth of his teachings. The references to Christ's life and teachings are unobtrusive, yet plain. The Epistle abounds with references to Peter's own experience, yet he who was chief man in the apostolic circle exhorts and testifies without appearing to command. Nevertheless Merrill C. Tenney calls attention to "a continuous chain of commands" consisting of thirty-four imperatives which indicates that Peter was "speaking from his heart, not writing a formal essay."[20]

Joseph Benson quotes Blackwall's statement that Peter wrote with "that quickness and rapidity of style, with that noble neglect of some of the formal consequences and niceties of grammar, still preserving its true reason and natural analogy . . . that you can

[15]"Babylon," *Theological Dictionary of the New Testament,* ed. Gerhard Kittel, trans. Geoffrey W. Bromiley, I (Grand Rapids: Wm. B. Eerdmans Publishing Co., 1964), 516.

[16]Francis W. Beare, *The First Epistle of Peter* (Oxford: Basil Blackwell, 1947), p. 31.

[17]Paul S. Rees, *Triumphant in Trouble* (Westwood, N.J.: Fleming H. Revell Company, 1962), pp. 16-17.

[18]Reicke, *op. cit.,* p. 74.

[19]Philip E. Hughes, "I Peter," *Christianity Today,* I, No. 9, 39.

[20]*New Testament Survey* (Grand Rapids: Wm. B. Eerdmans Pub. Co., 1961), pp. 351-52.

scarce perceive the pauses of his discourse, and distinction of his periods. A noble majesty, and becoming freedom, is what distinguishes St. Peter: a devout and judicious person cannot read him without solemn attention and awful concern."[21]

Selwyn sees in I Peter a blending of the *priestly*, the *prophetic*, and the *mystical* elements in "a mood of serene authority" which permeates the entire Epistle, and "is not the less effective because it is unobtrusive."[22]

E. The Aim of the Epistle

In earnest tones Peter urges the dispersed Christians to fortitude, patience, hope, and holiness of life in the face of hostile mistreatment by their enemies. Merrill C. Tenney succinctly expressed the aim as being to show Christians "how to live out their redemption in a hostile world."[23] This involved the proper performance of all personal, civil, and religious duties. Only by that means could they enjoy divine approval and refute the false and slanderous accusations their enemies brought against them because they would not engage in the common idolatrous practices of those among whom they resided.

Adherence to the principles of Christ inevitably causes Christians to be persecuted to some extent, and on occasion the persecution becomes very severe. Peter, knowing how fierce and fiery persecution could become, urges them, in the light of assured glory beyond the ordeal of suffering, to maintain their Christian faith despite undeserved reproach, persecution, or even death. Christians can be "triumphant in trouble."

"Peter knows it. He wants his Christian friends in Asia Minor to know it—and to demonstrate it."[24] Faithfulness to Christ's principles amidst their fiery trials would establish them in holiness and assist them to appreciate their future inheritance, which is radiant with the visible glory of Christ. There is no effort to deny persecution, but the aim is to remind them that persecution patiently endured issues in blessedness and glory.

F. The Theology

The theology of I Peter is very simple and bears a marked resemblance to the sermons in the Book of Acts and the theology

[21]*The New Testament of Our Lord and Savior Jesus Christ. With Critical, Explanatory, and Practical Notes*, II (New York: George Lane and Levi Scott, 1852), 603.

[22]*Op. cit.*, p. 3.

[23]*Op. cit.*, p. 352.

[24]Rees, *op. cit.*, p. 9.

of the very early Church. Those interested in the theology and ethics of this Epistle are referred to Selwyn[25] and Barclay.[26] The former has a very extensive treatment of these subjects. The Epistle's Christology is clear. It stresses the "Servant Motif" set forth in Isaiah 53 but does not omit emphasizing Christ's subsequent exaltation. The eschatological hope is kept in sharp focus, with "the horizon of glory ever hovering over the suffering saints as they continue their pilgrimage." Macknight calls attention to "some deep mysteries"[27] found in this Epistle. These do not, however, obscure the remarkable beauty of its Christian teachings which prove that the gospel they had received was "the true grace of God" wherein they were to remain steadfast (5:12).

G. Similarity to Paul's Epistles

One source of objections to the Petrine authorship of this Epistle is some similarity of language and structure between it and some of Paul's Epistles, particularly Romans and Ephesians. There are, however, very clear instances of Peter's individuality. This Epistle agrees with Peter's personal characteristics and his speeches as recorded in the Book of Acts. I Peter has some similarities to portions of John's writings as well as to Paul's, but it has not been suggested that Peter imitated John.[28] The German scholar Gotthard Victor Lechler declared: "We rather adhere to the view that now and again words of Paul floated before the mind of Peter, believing this to be quite consistent, however, with the spiritual independence of Peter; for it is rash to make apparent resemblances of this kind a reason for assuming forthwith a want of independence or the contradiction of views. . . ."[29]

[25]*Op. cit.*, pp. 64-115. [26]*Op. cit.*, pp. 166-68.

[27]James Macknight, *The Apostolical Epistles* (Philadelphia: Thomas Wardle, 1841), pp. 603-8.

[28]Cf. John McClintock and James Strong, *Cyclopedia of Biblical, Theological and Ecclesiastical Literature* (New York: Harper and Brothers, 1894), VIII, 16-17.

[29]*Apostolic and Post-Apostolic Times*, translated by A. J. K. Davidson, II (Edinburgh: T. and T. Clark, 1886), 136, note.

Outline

I. Introduction, 1:1

II. Holiness Purposed, 1:2-12
   A. The Divine Trinity Involved, 1:2
   B. A Well-grounded, Living Hope, 1:3
   C. A Glorious Inheritance, 1:4-5
   D. A Steadiness in Trials, 1:6-9
   E. A Challenge to Men and Angels, 1:10-12

III. Holiness Commanded, 1:13-16
   A. A Command That Requires Attention, 1:13-14
   B. A Command Based on God's Character, 1:15
   C. A Command Enforced by the Highest Motive, 1:16

IV. Holiness Provided, 1:17-21
   A. A Standard of Judgment, 1:17
   B. An Infinite Cost, 1:18-19
   C. An Eternal Plan, 1:20
   D. Appropriation by Personal Faith, 1:21

V. Holiness Experienced, 1:22-25
   A. Purity Through Obeying the Truth, 1:22*a*
   B. Purity Through an Operation of the Spirit, 1:22*b*
   C. Purity Expressing Itself in Fervent Love, 1:22*c*
   D. Purity Assured by God's Word, 1:23-25

VI. Holiness Exemplified, 2:1—3:17
   A. Things Laid Aside, 2:1
   B. Desire for the Word of God, 2:2-3
   C. Offering Spiritual Sacrifices, 2:4-5
   D. A Transformed Character, 2:6-10
   E. Abstinence from Fleshly Desires, 2:11-12
   F. Submission to Civil Authorities, 2:13-16
   G. Fulfillment of All Ethical Obligations, 2:17
   H. Patient Endurance of Undeserved Suffering, 2:18-20
   I. "The Imitation of Christ," 2:21-25

J. Propriety in Marital Relationship, 3:1-7
K. The Discharge of Social Obligations, 3:8-14
L. A Consistent Testimony, 3:15-17

VII. Holiness Triumphant, 3:18-22
A. Suffering Does Not Thwart God's Purpose, 3:18
B. A Parenthesis: Christ's Descent into Hades, 3:19-20
C. From Suffering to Glory, 3:21-22

VIII. Holiness Superior, 4:1-19
A. Dedication to God's Will, 4:1-2
B. Surmounting Misunderstanding, 4:3-6
C. Sobriety and Watchfulness, 4:7
D. Charity Toward Offenders, 4:8
E. Demonstrating Hospitality, 4:9-10
F. God's Glory in All Things, 4:11
G. Sharing Christ's Sufferings, 4:12-16
H. No Fear of God's Examination, 4:17-19

IX. Holiness in Action, 5:1-9
A. Official Relationships in the Church, 5:1-4
B. Personal Relationship to the Entire Fellowship, 5:5-7
C. Constant Resistance to the Adversary, 5:8-9

X. Holiness and Eternal Glory, 5:10-11
A. God Initiates the Call to Holiness, 5:10*a*
B. The Goal Is Eternal Glory, 5:10*b*
C. Holiness and Hope Tested by Suffering, 5:10*c*
D. A Process with Eternity in View, 5:10*d*
E. The Doxology, 5:11

XI. The Conclusion, 5:12-14
A. A Letter with a Purpose, 5:12
B. Salutations from the Church, 5:13
C. The Token of Brotherhood, 5:14*a*
D. A Prayer for Peace, 5:14*b*

Section I *Introduction*

I Peter 1:1

The author of this letter identifies himself as **Peter, an apostle of Jesus Christ.** In II Pet. 1:1 he speaks of himself as "Simon Peter, a servant and an apostle of Jesus Christ." For a further study of Peter's designation as "Simon" and "Cephas," cf. John 1:40-42. Doremus A. Hayes described Peter as "A Likeable Man . . . A Hasty Man . . . A Going Man . . . A Loyal Man . . . A Rock Man . . . A Growing Man . . . and The Apostle of Hope."[30]

This Epistle is addressed **to the strangers scattered throughout Pontus, Galatia, Cappadocia, Asia, and Bithynia**—all provinces south of the Black Sea (see map 1). These **strangers** are members of the Christian Church who have been called out from the world (cf. Matt. 24:22, 24; Rom. 8:33), and "reside as aliens" (NASB) in the territories designated. For a fuller discussion of the questions on the authorship and destination of I Peter see Introduction.

[30]*The New Testament Epistles, Hebrews, James, First Peter, Second Peter, Jude* (New York: Methodist Book Concern, 1921), pp. 121-45.

Section II Holiness Purposed

I Peter 1:2-12

A. The Divine Trinity Involved, 1:2

1. *The Question of Election* (1:2*a*)

The question of election poses a problem for the Christian Church because of the conflicting interpretations of ancient and modern theologians on the subject. That the Bible does teach election, none can deny. Benjamin Field[31] describes three kinds of scriptural election: (1) The election of individuals to perform some particular and special service (Deut. 21:5; I Sam. 2:27-28; Jer. 1:5; Luke 6:13; Acts 9:15); (2) The election of nations or bodies of people to eminent religious privileges (Deut. 4:37; 7:6; 10:15; Isa. 41:8-9); (3) A personal election of individuals to be the children of God and the heirs of eternal glory (1:2; II Thess. 2:13-14). This latter election does not imply an "exclusion of others from like precious blessings; nor does it render their final salvation irrevocably secure; they are still in a state of probation, and their election, through unbelief . . . may be rendered void and come to nothing."[32]

"God's election and predestination . . . are His gracious provision for and purpose to save all who savingly believe on the Lord Jesus Christ, and not an arbitrary predetermination of those who can believe."[33]

2. *The Holiness Purposed* (1:2*ab*)

Their election was **according to the foreknowledge of God the Father;** i.e., according to "God's comprehensive knowledge of His own plans and working, so that foreknowledge is practically equivalent to His deliberate and far-seeing purpose."[34]

[31]*The Student's Handbook of Christian Theology* (new ed.; New York: Hunt and Eaton, 1889), pp. 181-87.

[32]*Ibid.*, p. 184.

[33]W. T. Purkiser, *et al., Exploring Our Christian Faith* (Kansas City, Mo.: Beacon Hill Press of Kansas City, 1960), p. 90. See also pp. 274-80.

[34]Bennett, *op. cit.*, p. 186.

The **sanctification** here purposed includes both the process and the result of that operation of the Holy Spirit whereby man's heart is cleansed from moral evil, and self is totally adjusted to the will of God. God's eternal purpose is that man shall be like Him (cf. Eph. 1:4). In that moral condition He created man (cf. Gen. 1:26-27). There is a crisis aspect to this divine work so that in an instant "the heart is cleansed from all sin, and filled with the pure love of God and man" (John Wesley). The holiness here purposed is wrought by the Holy Spirit, who administers the "estate of grace" provided through the blood of Jesus Christ. It is not an absolute perfection which precludes the possibility of improvement, but it is the restoration of the divine image to the soul of man so that both his character and his service are acceptable to God. It is fitness for life and service and not finality in the sense of being a non-improvable state. It gives to life purity, power, beauty, and symmetry.[35]

3. *The Guarantee of Its Attainability* (1:2)

This sanctification originates with **God the Father.** It is provided by the redeeming death of Jesus Christ. It is wrought by the effective operation **of the Spirit.** This involvement of the Trinity indicates the importance of such inward, personal heart cleansing, and guarantees its realization when man completely abandons himself to the will and service of God and exercises appropriating faith in the merit **of the blood of Jesus Christ.** Peter's salutation to these Christians indicates his faith that the personal enjoyment of the **grace** of imparted holiness results in **peace** being **multiplied.**

B. A Well-grounded, Living Hope, 1:3

In writing to Christians who were experiencing fiery trials and unbelievable hardships Peter not only reminded them of the purpose and power of God revealed in the salvation secured for them by the Trinity (v. 2), but encouraged them to face the future with holy boldness, because their salvation would be perfected. **Blessed be . . . God,** who, as the **Father of our Lord Jesus Christ,** "is the ultimate source of our regeneration; and, through his resurrection guarantees our future blessedness; and meanwhile, keeps us safely through the dangers of this present life."[36]

[35]See Purkiser, *op. cit.*, pp. 350-89.

[36]Bennett, *op. cit.*, p. 188.

Chapter one deals mainly with faith as the groundwork and support of obedience and patience. Faith establishes Christians in believing; obedience directs them in doing; and patience comforts them in suffering. Their faith is to be grounded on their redemption and salvation by Jesus Christ, the inheritance of immortality bought by His blood for them, and the evidence and stability of their right and title to it.

As **the resurrection of Jesus Christ from the dead** was the first step toward His glory and to that exaltation which followed, so regeneration is "the foundation and first step unto all those privileges of a Christian that follow upon the state of grace."[37] Furthermore, the resurrection of the Lord Jesus is "the foundation stone of our hope . . . confirmation of what he declared as truth when he lived . . . a proof of the immortality of the soul . . . a pledge that all who are united to him will be raised up."[38] The death of Christ manifests His love. His resurrection manifests His power and ability to save. Therefore His resurrection is fundamental to the Christian's hope and confidence. Peter, as an eyewitness to the fact of our Lord's resurrection, followed his salutation to the dispersed Christians with a doxology that exhibits "the content and basis of the Christian hope," which permeates the New Testament, namely, the "hope of the resurrection of the dead." It is based on the triumph of Christ over death, and looks outward from man and upward to God, fixing man's eye on God. The "Godward look is the secret of the Christian hope."[39]

C. A Glorious Inheritance, 1:4-5

The "abundant mercy" of God (v. 3) reveals His beneficent character, which is the source of the Christian's hope. "The resurrection" of Christ attests to God's acceptance of His sacrifice and is the ground of His mediatorial exaltation. The central object of the believer's hope is **an inheritance incorruptible, and undefiled, and that fadeth not away, reserved in heaven for you, who are kept by the power of God through faith unto salvation.**

Being children of God, believers are heirs of God. An inheritance awaits them. Unlike fading earthly treasures, this

[37] Albert Barnes, *Christianity Today,* Vol. I, No. 14, p. 23.

[38] *Ibid.*

[39] William Barclay, *More New Testament Words* (New York: Harper and Row, 1958), pp. 42-46.

spiritual inheritance is **incorruptible.** It retains its perfection unchanged because it contains no seeds of decay. It is **undefiled,** "incapable of being itself defiled, or of being enjoyed by any polluted soul."[40] Instead of fading it remains in perpetual freshness and never decays in its value, sweetness, or beauty. It is kept absolutely secure for the believers who are being **kept** for it. This eternal, spiritual inheritance which persecution is powerless to touch encourages believers to stand fast in the faith regardless of their sufferings.

This requires faith in the power of God, who guards against all enemies. He has the ability to preserve any believer who commits himself to divine power. This is the efficient cause of preservation while man's faith is the effective means. In this instance **faith** refers to being **kept** rather than **faith unto salvation.** The **salvation** referred to is final salvation in heaven. This **salvation is ready to be revealed in the last time.** It is not something to be prepared hereafter or now in the course of preparation and therefore "liable never to be realized, but an accomplished fact, ready and waiting to be manifested at the right moment."[41] There is security for the believer. It is *for eternity,* but it is not unconditional security. It requires faith, which involves mental assent and personal commitment.

D. A Steadiness in Trials, 1:6-9

That joy and grief may coexist in the Christian life is revealed by the greatness of the purpose of salvation and the preciousness of the wonderful Saviour. Peter assures his readers that there is an "inheritance" awaiting Christians and that these manifold temptations which caused suffering are allowed in order to prove that their faith is real. Steadiness in these crises, though it might appear that they were being **tried with fire** (7), would mean approval by the Lord himself with **praise and honour and glory at His appearing.** The problem of suffering has always puzzled Christians, but the path to glory leads through opposition. Moreover, trials and sufferings "seldom go single, but are manifold and come from different quarters" (Matthew Henry). This process purifies the soul by the separation of any dross and

[40]Wesley, *et al., One Volume New Testament Commentary* (Grand Rapids: Baker Book House, reprinted ed., 1957), *ad loc.*

[41]Bennett, *op. cit.*, p. 190.

the display of the soundness of the Christian's faith in and love for Jesus Christ.

In this Epistle, Peter is fulfilling his Master's commission: "Strengthen thy brethren" (Luke 22:32). He had seen Jesus, but it is probable that no one in the churches addressed had ever seen Him. Peter commends them for believing in the crucified, risen, and unseen Christ, and for their love which is the fruit of true faith. Steadiness despite fiery trials would enable them to **rejoice with joy unspeakable and full of glory: receiving the end of your faith . . . the salvation of your souls** (8-9). Their steadiness under persecution would prove the reality of their faith and so strengthen them that human language could not express their joy at being saved from all sin and fitted to enjoy the blessings that Christ will bestow upon the faithful at His return.

E. A Challenge to Men and Angels, 1:10-12

The **salvation** of which **the prophets have enquired and searched diligently** (10) is directly the product of **the grace** of God: His unmerited and undeserved favor which man was impotent to secure for himself, but without which he was hopeless. The source of this revelation which the prophets foretold was **the Spirit of Christ** (11), the Holy Spirit. The salvation prophesied is now declared to be an experienced fact with indescribable glories awaiting those who are "kept by the power of God through faith" (v. 5).

At Pentecost, and later, Peter referred to the prophets (cf. Acts 2:16-21, 25-31; 3:24). Their great subject was the grace that God had provided for the world in the gift of salvation to all who would believe in Jesus Christ (cf. John 3:16; II Pet. 3:9). The prophets who enquired and searched diligently revealed the deepest kind of interest in the subject of which they wrote and spoke. The salvation they foretold so far transcended anything they knew or had experienced that they were "like miners searching after precious ore, after the meaning of the prophecies which they delivered."[42]

The prophets centered their interest about the **time the Spirit of Christ . . . did signify, when it** (He) **testified beforehand the sufferings of Christ, and the glory that should follow** (11). They wanted to know both the exact time and the nature of the time.

[42]Wesley, *op. cit., ad loc.*

"They wanted to know more than they wrote, and to understand better what they did write."[43] They desired to know the conditions and circumstances under which Christ would appear. These men of God were also baffled by the nature and relation of the sufferings and subsequent glories associated with Messiah's coming. They, as well as these dispersed Christians, were baffled by the problem of how sufferings and glories could be reconciled. How much time must elapse between them? Interest in God's gracious purpose was so great that **the angels desire to look into** (12) this mystery. The most that was revealed to the prophets was that the things they ministered were **not unto themselves.** They were the administrators of an estate which the believers in Christ should enjoy.

> Verses 10-12 effectively clinch the Apostle's appeal for constancy and cheerful endurance of trials. Salvation was worth waiting for, seeing it was the realization of the teaching of the prophets, and had awakened intense interest in prophets and angels. The Christians might be persecuted and despised, yet they were "the heirs of all the ages"; for them inspired men had laboured through past centuries, and in their own days. For a while they had to suffer; they did not know how long their trials would last, or how long they might have to wait before they were delivered by the new revelation of Christ. . . . Christians might well bear patiently their uncertainty as to times and seasons, seeing that they shared this ignorance with angels (Mark 13:32) who knew even less of the gospel than the readers of the Epistle.[44]

But of this they were assured: their present sufferings would give way to future glories if they maintained a steadfast faith in Jesus Christ, their Saviour and Example.

[43]Nathaniel M. Williams, "Commentary on the Epistles of Peter," *An American Commentary on the New Testament* (Philadelphia: The American Baptist Publication Society, 1890), p. 17.

[44]Bennett, *op. cit.*, p. 195.

Section III *Holiness Commanded*

I Peter 1:13-16

A. A Command That Requires Attention, 1:13-14

In view of this great salvation with its living hope and incorruptible inheritance, men cannot escape the obligation to live holy lives. Uncertainty and delay must not beguile them back into the old life from which they had been saved. **Wherefore gird up the loins of your mind, be sober** ("perfectly composed," Berk.), **and hope to the end for the grace that is to be brought unto you at the revelation of Jesus Christ** (13), i.e., at His second coming. They must prepare for action, bracing themselves for an effort by fully concentrating on their circumstances and obeying the commands of God. They were not to allow their minds to dwell upon worldly solicitations, fears, and prejudices. Success in the Christian life requires the cooperation of the intellect with the moral and spiritual faculties. To be prepared for the Lord's return they must be **obedient children** (14), not conformed to the manners and morals of those about them. Their character and conduct must be compatible with their Christian faith. Phillips renders 14*b*, "Don't let your character be moulded by the desires of your ignorant days." Since they have been "begotten . . . again" (v. 3), they partake of the nature of their Father, which is holiness (cf. Matt. 5:48). This new way of life requires abandonment of what they once were and did, and transformation into what they had not been.

B. A Command Based on God's Character, 1:15

The negative side of holiness is set forth in v. 14. The positive side is here set forth in the same idea of fashioning oneself after a new pattern. **But as he which hath called you is holy, so be ye holy.** God calls; it is man's duty to respond. God gives the Pattern; it is man's responsibility to adopt it. God is the Model of all holiness (cf. I John 2:6). The high privilege and glorious destiny of the "elect" (v. 2) obligate them to follow diligently the example of the Holy One who called them (cf. Eph. 5:1).

What is in the heart will be manifest in the life. Hence true holiness will reveal itself in every phase of daily living: **In all manner of conversation.** "Be holy in every department of your lives" (Phillips). "Be holy yourselves in all your conduct" (RSV). True holiness is vitally related to all civil, religious, personal, and public aspects of life—to all human relationships. Holiness and ethics cannot be separated, for true ethical conduct is patterned after the character of God.

C. A Command Enforced by the Highest Motive, 1:16

The holiness of God is the supreme motive for man's holiness: **Be ye holy; for I am holy** (16). God's command to be holy (cf. Lev. 11:44-46; 19:2; 20:7, 26) shows that He purposes that those whom He calls shall be His very own possession, unshared by any other. He is their Father; heaven is their home (cf. v. 4); and their life on earth is a sojourn (cf. v. 1). Therefore their character which fits them for heaven must be like His own (cf. II Cor. 3:17-18). This fitness is not attained by a ritual separation from impurity, nor by a formal consecration to divine service, but by the impartation of the holiness of God through Christ (cf. Heb. 12:10; 13:12; I John 1:7). Through personal appropriation of the promises and provisions of the atonement, believers are made "partakers of the divine nature" (II Pet. 1:4).

Holiness is God's choice for the moral condition of man. Because of God's nature it is *right* that man should resemble Him. He is the Creator. Because of man's nature it is *possible* for him to resemble God. The possibility of being holy determines our duty to be holy. When we consider the nature of God, the will of God, the call of God, the command of God, the promises of God, the provision and power of God, and the eternal purposes of God, the inevitable conclusion is that without holiness we cannot please Him (cf. Heb. 12:14).

Section IV *Holiness Provided*

I Peter 1:17-21

A. A Standard of Judgment, 1:17

The holiness of God creates reverential awe in all true believers. He is not only our **Father** but also our Judge. His holiness guarantees that His mercy shall not become an indulgence or His justice a tyranny. **Without respect of persons** (impartially) He **judgeth according to every man's work.** All sin is infinitely offensive to God, who from His holiness hates sin, from His goodness inclines to rescue man from sin, by His wisdom understands how salvation from sin may be accomplished, and by His power is able to achieve it. Therefore, since holiness is a basic attribute of God and is consistent with His purpose for man, all earthly sojourners should live in fear lest in the day of judgment they be condemned by a holy Judge who cannot excuse sin or approve an unholy being. Such reverential fear is the very opposite of the indifference to holiness and the carnal security which characterize so many who profess to be Christians. It is a moral impossibility for man to love God and knowingly reject holiness, which brings him back into a fulfillment of all that belongs to his nature as God made it.

B. An Infinite Cost, 1:18-19

Both the infinite cost at which redemption was made possible and the impartial judgment of God upon all men enforce the duty to be holy. **Ye were not redeemed with corruptible things, as silver and gold . . . but with the precious blood of Christ.** Silver and gold, though highly treasured by man, are **corruptible**, and will pass away (cf. v. 7). Eternal values are here under consideration. Many still live by the **vain . . . tradition** received from their ancestors, and expect salvation through "a heartless routine of ritualism," or good works. In the case of the Jews, they trusted to their earthly relationship as "children of Abraham" for salvation. The Gentiles placed their hope in the many gods of polytheism, whose favor they thought could be had with silver and gold. In either case their mode of life was sanctioned by conventional religion and morality.[45]

The word **redeemed** is a favorite figure of the work of Christ. Its chief point lies in "the payment of a price, the unhappy state of the sinner and the deliverance."[46] The objective in this redemption is not only to deliver from eternal misery but from the love and power of sin. Wuest points out that silver and gold are in diminutive form, "referring to little silver and gold coins which were used to buy slaves out of slavery."[47] But believers know that their deliverance is not provided by a **corruptible** ransom. Admission into an incorruptible inheritance cannot be secured by such means. It is by **the precious blood of Christ.** This is Peter's first use of the word **precious,** which occurs several times in his Epistles. Redemption is costly, for it is by the sacrificial death of Christ, whose blood is held in high honor; it is "costly, essentially and intrinsically precious because it is God's blood (Acts 20:28), for Deity became incarnate in humanity. For that reason it is highly honored by God the Father."[48] The infinite cost and the inestimable benefit of salvation supply a new cause for man to aspire to holiness in character and conduct.

C. An Eternal Plan, 1:20

The provision of a plan for salvation was not a new thing, or an afterthought with God. The whole system under which the Jews had been brought up had this as its meaning. Through types and shadows, prophets and priests God sought to prepare them for this "event in eternity," when Christ became incarnate, was crucified, resurrected, and glorified. But before the foundation of the world God had chosen us "in him . . . that we should be holy" (Eph. 1:4). Thus "the personality and work of Christ were neither the natural result of the world's development nor the suddenly formed decree of God in time."[49] But He **was manifest** in the fullness of God's time. "The Christian dispensation, the point and period in history of Christ's coming, is here regarded as the climax and consummation of the previous ages (cf. Heb.

[45]Cf. Bennett, *op. cit.*, p. 200. [46]*Ibid.*

[47]*First Peter in the Greek New Testament* (Grand Rapids, Mich.: William B. Eerdmans Publishing Co., 1942), p. 42.

[48]*Ibid.*, p. 43. See also Purkiser, *op. cit.*, c. XII.

[49]Lange, *Commentary,* "I Peter," p. 24.

1:1-2; 9:26.)"[50] (See also Rom. 16:25-26; Gal. 4:4-5; Eph. 1:9-10; 3:9-11; Col. 1:26; II Tim. 1:9-10; Titus 1:2-3; Rev. 13:8.)

D. Appropriation by Personal Faith, 1:21

By him, the Incarnation of God and our only Mediator, we **believe in God, that raised him up from the dead, and gave him glory.** "Without Christ we should only dread God; whereas through Him we believe, and hope, and love" (Wesley). Our **faith and hope** rest in God alone. He is not a god such as the heathen knew, nor even the God whom Israel knew as the Deliverer from Egypt, but the God of supreme power and glory, the "Father of our Lord Jesus Christ" (v. 3; cf. Acts 2:22-36).

Only through Christ can man be saved (cf. Acts 4:12). For this salvation to become a personal reality there must be appropriating faith (cf. Heb. 11:6), which includes intellectual assent to the fact that the death, resurrection, and glorification of Christ provide salvation. There must also be personal commitment to Christ, to the end that the benefits of His atonement may be imparted to the soul by the Holy Spirit. God has, by resurrecting and exalting Christ, demonstrated His acceptance of Christ's person and work, so that in the light of Christ's redeeming death, and God's acceptance of His sacrifice in our stead, we are challenged to come to God in **faith and hope** which are sustained by grace in spite of suffering (cf. vv. 3, 13, 21).

[50]Alan M. Stibbs, "The First Epistle General of Peter," *Tyndale New Testament Commentaries,* ed. R. V. G. Tasker (London: The Tyndale Press, 1959), p. 92.

Section V *Holiness Experienced*

I Peter 1:22-25

A. Purity Through Obeying the Truth, 1:22*a*

Believers are called to holiness (cf. I Thess. 4:7), which involves obedience to the truth. Jesus Christ declared: "I am the . . . truth" (John 14:6). He also prayed the Father that His followers might be sanctified "through thy truth: thy word is truth" (John 17:17). "The Word of God, functioning in the believer's heart as truth and light, is the formal cause of sanctification."[51] The process of purification may be said to have begun when the truth concerning Christ was first accepted and one submitted to its requirements. Bennett considers **the truth** not so much the specific rules laid down by Christ and His apostles as "a comprehensive term embracing all the means by which the will of Christ is made known—his teaching and example, the influence of his character and work, and of his Spirit. . . . Submission to such an authority would involve complete separation from all that was unworthy in their former life."[52]

The process has the crisis of cleansing in view. Before and after that crisis there must be continued obedience to the truth. This is "not a long-drawn-out and never-completed process of growth,"[53] but is an instantaneous experience attested by the witness of the Holy Spirit and "the fruit of the Spirit" (Gal. 5:22-23). This purification is both negative, laying aside all evil (cf. 2:1), and positive, putting on the good and growing therein. It is something in addition to that begun in regeneration (cf. v. 3), and involves moment-by-moment response to the Spirit's revelation of the will of God.

B. Purity Through an Operation of the Spirit, 1:22*b*

The divine Agent in the purification of the heart is the Holy Spirit (cf. Acts 2:1-4; 15:8-9; Rom. 15:16; II Thess. 2:13; II Pet. 1:2). "Though the Greek [of Acts 15:9] is not identical, the meaning is essentially the same as 'having purified your souls,'

[51]Purkiser, *op. cit.*, p. 361. [52]Bennett, *op. cit.*, p. 202.

[53]See Purkiser, *op. cit.*, c. XVII, for a full treatment on "Crisis and Process in Sanctification."

which Peter here says is the result of 'obedience to the truth' (1:22)."[54] "The Spirit," says John Wesley, "bestows upon you freely both obedience and purity of heart."

The purification of the heart is an internal and subjective work; therefore as a spiritual operation it requires the agency of God's Spirit. So intimately is He associated with the application of the merits of Christ's atoning death for the sanctification of the heart that He is generally referred to as the Holy Spirit. It is also His work to witness that the cleansing is a reality (cf. I John 3:24; 4:13).

C. Purity Expressing Itself in Fervent Love, 1:22*c*

The product of a pure heart is **unfeigned love of the brethren.** The new nature expresses itself in "unhypocritical" (NASB, margin) love because the heart has been cleansed from selfishness and hatred. This love for one another is fervent, or earnest and constant, "with the faculty of loving stretched to its full energy." There is nothing superficial or merely sentimental about it, because it is from a heart "pure from any spot of unholy desire or inordinate passion" (Wesley). Walls declares the Greek word *ektenos* does not suggest warmth, but "full intensity," or in an "all-out" manner.[55] This is possible because the purified have a new source of life, a new nature, and a new power by which to translate duty into action.

D. Purity Assured by God's Word, 1:23-25

Jesus himself described the beginning of the Christian life as being **born again** (23; cf. John 3:1-8). Sinners are "dead in trespasses" (Eph. 2:1); hence they need a renewal of life or a spiritual rebirth. Peter described it as "begotten . . . again" (v. 3), and Titus as "the washing of regeneration" (3:5). By it Christians enter into a new relationship as "sons of God" (I John 3:1-2). The spiritual nature of this new relationship is seen in that it is **not of corruptible seed,** as is true in all human generation, **but of incorruptible, by the word of God.** This new birth is effected by the Spirit of God (cf. John 3:5-8), through the medium of the

[54]John Wick Bowman, "The First and Second Letters of Peter," *The Layman's Bible Commentary,* ed. Balmer H. Kelly (Richmond: John Knox Press, 1959), p. 131.

[55]*Op. cit.,* p. 44.

living and eternal truths of the gospel message (I Cor. 4:15), which **abideth for ever.** The "living word" and the "living hope" (v. 3) are vitally related.

Sanctification begins in regeneration. "The new life principle imparted by the Holy Spirit is the principle of holiness."[56] Thus we speak of it as initial sanctification, which is partial rather than entire. But **the word of the Lord** which **endureth for ever** (25) assures that entire sanctification is realizable as a crisis experience after regeneration, a point on which Peter, Paul, and John perfectly agree (cf. Eph. 1:13; I Thess. 5:23-24; I John 1:7, 9). The truth regarding holiness rests on secure foundation.

On **all flesh is as grass** (24), Wesley comments: "Every human creature is transient and withering as grass. *And all the glory of it*—His wisdom, strength, wealth, righteousness. *As the flower*—The most short-lived part of it."[57] But **the word** (25)—good tidings by which believers are brought into a new spiritual life and relationship—**endureth for ever.** God's purpose, which He will accomplish despite Satanic opposition and human frailty, is to create children who will be like Him.

[56]Purkiser, *op. cit.*, p. 341. [57]*Op. cit.*, p. 876.

Section VI *Holiness Exemplified*

I Peter 2:1—3:17

A. Things Laid Aside, 2:1

This section begins the ethical emphases upon the Christian life. Holiness is more than a doctrine and an experience; it is a life. This section (2:1—3:17) indicates the conduct expected of those who have appropriated the high privileges of c. 1. These elect people, on a pilgrimage through a hostile world, must exemplify the spirit of holiness in order to recommend the gospel to the unconverted among whom they sojourn. The things required make for Christian consistency.

The exhortation of v. 1 is an amplification of the principle of love in 1:22. Five things are to be laid aside, because they are inconsistent with that pure love. **Malice** is ill will, the inclination to injure one's neighbor or to make others suffer. **Guile** is deceitful cunning or trickery in order to gain advantage over others. **Hypocrisies** are counterfeit acts in which one pretends to be or do something which he is or does not. **Envies** indicates jealousies which really are concealed malice, or ill will; they spring from hearts that are "displeased at and depreciate the ability, prosperity, performance, or reputation of others."[58] The term **evil speakings** is malice in words, which insinuates, defames, backbites, and carries injurious tales.

Augustine is quoted as saying: "*Malice* delights in another's hurt; *envy* pines at another's good; *guile* imparts duplicity to the hearts, *hypocrisy* (or flattery) to the tongue; *evil speakings* wound another's character." The Greek verb and tense—**laying aside**—indicate a definite action against any and all sin at the time of their conversion, so that there is no place for any sin in the life of a Christian. Marvin L. Galbreath quoted Paul S. Rees as saying: "Every sin that has survived the shock of conversion must go."[59]

[58]D. D. Whedon, *Commentary on the New Testament* (New York: Hunt and Eaton, 1890), V, 200.

[59]*James and Peter,* "Aldersgate Biblical Series" (Winona Lake, Ind.: Light and Life Press, 1962), Leader's Guide, p. 63.

B. Desire for the Word of God, 2:2-3

Again the negative and the positive aspects of the Christian life are set in contrast. In v. 1 there were hindrances to be cast off. Here, **as newborn babes** (2), who had experienced a complete change of life and character, they are to **desire,** or intensely long for, **the sincere,** unadulterated and undiluted, spiritual **milk of the word.** They must make progress; the surest way to relapse into sin is to not press on in holiness. These had a genuine regeneration (cf. 1:3, 23). The nourishment afforded by the true doctrines of the gospel would enable them to **grow** "in faith, love, holiness, unto the full stature of Christ" (Wesley).

Only as Christians feed on God's Word will they grow. Nothing can substitute for it. An explanation of many cases of arrested development among God's people is that so few have really **tasted** (3), or proved by personal attention to their devotional life, **that the Lord is gracious;** or as some translators prefer, "how sweet the Lord is" (cf. Alford). The growing soul must "take time to be holy."

C. Offering Spiritual Sacrifices, 2:4-5

In 1:23, Peter contrasts a carnal seed and a spiritual seed; here he contrasts a spiritual temple of born-again believers with the stone Temple at Jerusalem. Through Jesus Christ, the **living stone,** and our relation to Him as **lively** (living) **stones,** alive unto God through Christ, we **are built up a spiritual house** (5), "an habitation of God through the Spirit" (Eph. 2:22). Our relation to Christ is one of moment-by-moment communion and dependence by faith. Our Lord was **disallowed . . . of men** (4) who rejected Him as a vile blasphemer, but He **is chosen of God, and precious.** Finite man rejected Him, but the infinite God chose Him as the "chief corner stone" and singled Him out for that honor.

As living stones, those who compose this **spiritual house** (5) are not cold, rigid, and lifeless, as was the material of the earthly Temple building. They, by the indwelling Spirit, are the **house** (or habitation) of God. And not only do they compose the house but as **an holy priesthood,** consecrated to God and holy as He is holy (1:15), they minister in it, offering up **spiritual sacrifices,** their "souls and bodies, with all their thoughts, words and actions" (Wesley) in contrast to bulls, goats, and lambs of the old economy. The believers' sacrifices are **acceptable to God** because they are offered **by** (or through) **Jesus Christ,** their great High Priest, the perfect Sacrifice and Propitiation for the sins of mankind, and our Advocate with the Father (cf. I John 1:1-2; Heb. 4:14-16).

D. A Transformed Character, 2:6-10

Peter draws from Isa. 28:16 for this quotation (6-8), but since it is not an exact quotation of either the Hebrew or the LXX some suppose it to have been quoted from memory. Stibbs suggests that Isa. 28:16; Ps. 118:22; and Isa. 8:14 are "combined to express the full truth" of this metaphor.[60] The principal truth is that the unique position of Christ as the **chief corner stone** of His new habitation was foreseen and foreordained (**elect**) of God, **and he that believeth on him shall not be confounded** (6), "disappointed," "put to shame" (NASB), for in Christ he will find that his confidence is well-placed.

On the other hand, Christ, who is **precious** (a precious value) to those who believe, becomes three things to the disobedient and the unbelieving: (*a*) **the head of the corner** (7), to rebuke their scorn; (*b*) **a stone of stumbling** (8), against which they hurt themselves if they carelessly pass Him by; and (*c*) **a rock of offence,** bringing shame and eternal ruin upon those who **stumble** over Him by refusing to submit to the influence of the gospel, and thus resist His power and authority. Their destruction is **appointed,** not arbitrarily, but in justice because of their rejection of mercy and truth.

In vv. 9-10 there is another contrast, between the believers' present (9) and their past (10). It is a real condition, not merely an ideal. They are **a chosen generation** (9), selected out of the world and by their new birth given a new relationship; **a royal priesthood,** wherein each believer by the complete identification of his will with God's will shares His royal authority and can approach God directly through Christ. They are **an holy nation,** or people, because called by a holy God and cleansed by the Spirit (cf. 1:22); **a peculiar people** ("God's own people," RSV; "a purchased people," Wesley).

The divine purpose is that by the contrast between the holiness of the new life, **his marvellous light,** and the evil of the old **darkness** out of which they were redeemed, they should **shew forth the praises of him who . . . called** them into this new life.

[60]*Op. cit.,* p. 101.

Their testimony is all the more remarkable because **in time past** they **were not a people** (cf. Hos. 1:10; 2:23), **but are now the people of God** (10) by the threefold right of creation, preservation, and redemption. They who once **had not obtained mercy . . . now have obtained mercy,** not through personal merit, but by the grace and the abundant mercy of God (cf. 1:2-3).

E. Abstinence from Fleshly Desires, 2:11-12

Here Peter begins another series of exhortations. Earlier (1:13—2:10) he had revealed concern for the believers' relations to Christ and to one another. In this series (2:11—4:6) he is concerned about their relations to the outside world. This preliminary exhortation warns that there are **fleshly lusts, which war against the soul** (11). Wesley speaks of their sojourning in a strange house (the body), and being **pilgrims** in a strange country (this world). Therefore they are to abstain from whatever is of the nature of this strange house in which they dwell temporarily, or this country through which they are passing. We are not to understand from this that the body or human life on earth are essentially evil. They are evil only insofar as they come into conflict with the will of God for **the soul.**

The Christians were misrepresented and mistreated because they refused to worship heathen deities and join in sensual idol feasts. Peter says they must scrupulously avoid everything which would hurt the body, hinder the soul's development, destroy mutual love, or weaken their Christian witness. Their **conversation** (entire life) must be **honest among the Gentiles** (12), commending itself by its virtues to the moral judgment of even non-Christians. Long before the Christian era Plato had written concerning "the immortal battle between right and wrong."[61] Despite false and reckless slanders that the Christians were evildoers, a scrupulous investigation of their lives and characters would convince their detractors of the Christians' consistency, and might lead the **Gentiles** (heathen) to believe in Christ. At any rate honesty would compel them to **glorify God,** i.e., praise the Christians' God, after whom they patterned their conduct. Verse 12 may reflect what Peter heard Christ say in the Sermon on the Mount (cf. Matt. 5:16). **The day of visitation** would be the day "when the Spirit influences them" (Berk., fn.).

[61] *Against the Atheists,* Lewis' ed., 1845, p. 68, l. 12.

F. Submission to Civil Authorities, 2:13-16

The Christians' allegiance to Jesus as heavenly King subjected them to persecution on the false charge of disloyalty to earthly governments. Although Christians are "strangers and pilgrims" (v. 11), they are to be submissive to the civil powers, which "instrumentally . . . are ordained by men; but originally all their power is from God" (Wesley). Peter knows that saints make the best citizens. Their submission is **for the Lord's sake** (13). Cooperation with those authorities which promote the general welfare of mankind commends the gospel to all good citizens; therefore Christians must avoid being "contentiously conscientious" in refusing to do what it would not be sinful to do.

This submission extends **to every ordinance of man,** "every institution ordained for men" (RSV, fn.), or "every man-made authority" (Phillips). Selwyn translates it "every fundamental social institution, i.e., the state, the household, the family," and reminds that, whereas Paul (cf. Rom. 13:1-7) refers to the *origin* of the state, Peter refers to its *functions*, both of which are divinely ordained.[62] This submission unto **the king, as supreme,** means the Roman emperor, who at the time Peter wrote is generally acknowledged to have been Nero. **Unto governors** (14) would refer to subordinate representatives of the supreme authority. Their obligation was to maintain the government by **the punishment of evil doers** who refused allegiance and rebelled against the civil authority, and by **the praise of them that do well.** Having warned against giving any just cause for punishment as "evildoers" (v. 12), Peter now stresses obedience to civil authority. This is a general rule, but there are exceptional cases when "human ordinances conflict with the dictates of the conscience enlightened by the Holy Spirit."[63] In such instances Peter himself is an example of what is to be done (cf. Acts 4:19-20; 5:29).

The obedience which true holiness exhibits fulfils **the will of God** (15), which always involves blameless living. Such **well doing** will **put to silence the ignorance of foolish men.** In modern parlance it "squelches" the slanderous babblers who repeat false accusations against the Christians. In this connection, Peter warns against any trace of the heresy that because we are free in Christ we can act as we please (cf. II Pet. 2:18-19; Jude 3-4). Although Christians are **free** from slavish fears and dedicated to

[62]*Op. cit.*, p. 172.

[63]Bennett, *op. cit.*, p. 216.

the service of God, they must not use their **liberty for a cloke** (16; excuse) for wrongdoing, such as sedition or self-indulgence. Rather, their freedom in Christ should be the occasion of willing service to God and His representatives in the Church and society.

G. Fulfillment of All Ethical Obligations, 2:17

In four short commands Peter states principles which if heeded will avert much trouble and fulfil man's ethical obligations. **Honour all men.** This means that all men will be given the esteem they deserve as being created in God's image, redeemed by His Son, and designed for a place in His kingdom. There are different circumstances of life, but the Christian renders to each the regard and treatment to which he is entitled. Obedience to this plain command will deal a mortal blow to all racial conflicts. **Love the brotherhood** requires a special attitude toward the corporate body of believers, not only as individuals but as a fellowship. Correct relations with non-Christians requires the observance of proper rules of conduct (cf. 1:15; 2:12); but within the Church, life is more a matter of right attitudes and feeling than of rules. This kind of love is possible only between fellow Christians. **Fear God.** Peter ascended from men in general to men of spiritual relationship, and from them to God himself. He is to be regarded with such reverential awe and humility that man's greatest fear will be that he displease Him. This fear produces loyal, loving service to God and the Church. On **Honour the king,** see comments on 13. The fear of God requires proper regard for the civil authorities He ordains; but when claims to obedience conflict, His claim supersedes that of any human authority.

H. Patient Endurance of Undeserved Suffering, 2:18-20

This exhortation enlarges upon that of 13. Peter accepted the fact of the institution of slavery and the organization of society into households which included varied degrees of **servants** (18) ranging from slaves to employees. Some of the **masters** were **good and gentle,** kind and considerate, while others were **froward** (despotic and unjust). Regardless of the master's disposition the servant was to be obedient and submissive **with all fear** (respect). Verse 19 makes it clear that Christian servants were to be motivated by the desire to prove faithful to God's requirements and loyal to their superiors, rather than by fear of punishment.

It is a display of grace rather than "natural heroism or philosophic pride" (Williams) when **a man for conscience toward God** (19) endures undeserved mistreatment in a Christian spirit, **suffering wrongfully,** in order to maintain the sense of God's presence and blessing. This is an echo of the Sermon on the Mount (cf. Matt. 5:10). But there is no glory if the sufferings, however severe or how patiently borne, are due to the servant's faults. Peter is saying that when after having done that which is good and kind one meets with undeserved suffering and takes **it patiently, this is acceptable with God** (20), "finds favor with God" (NASB). What happens to one is not as important as how he reacts to it, for the reaction reveals his true character.

I. "The Imitation of Christ," 2:21-25

Christians are called to follow Christ, to be holy (1:15-16), and if necessary to suffer wrongfully (v. 19). They must go where He goes and share His lot, whether it be to the glorious Mount of Transfiguration or to sorrowful Gethsemane and Calvary. The apostles never promised that following Christ would exempt one from suffering, even unjust suffering (cf. Acts 14:22; I Thess. 3:3-4), **because Christ also suffered for us** (21). Since He suffered vicariously to redeem us, gratitude should compel us to suffer for Him. Following Christ involves cross-bearing (cf. Mark 8:34) and tribulation (cf. John 16:33), in which He is our **example.** In v. 21 we have a double metaphor: **an example,** i.e., written copy set by the master to be carefully followed as a pattern by the pupils; and a walk to emulate, suggested by **that ye should follow his steps** (footprints). The ideas involve complete identification with our Lord's personal innocence, patient submission, and uncomplaining meekness.

Our suffering Lord **did no sin, neither was guile found in his mouth** (22). He was above reproach in act and word. When **he was reviled** (23; slandered and blasphemed), He never threatened in revenge. **When he suffered** the ignominious shame at His arrest and crucifixion, **he threatened not; but committed himself** ("His cause," ASV) **to him that judgeth righteously.** His submission, which was voluntary, not only fulfilled the will of God but furnished His followers a principle and an example. He believed that God would vindicate and reward innocence.

Matthew Henry suggests that v. 24 is added lest it be gathered from vv. 21-23 that Christ's death was designed only for an example of patience under sufferings, when there is a more glorious design and effect of it. **Who his own self bare our sins in his own body on the tree** (24) clearly declares the substitutionary nature of His death. *We* deserved to suffer the consequences of our sins: pain, death, humiliation—all the punishment sin entails —but *He* did this for us **in his own body** as an act of the Incarnation (cf. Lev. 5:1, 17; Heb. 10:5-10).

Peter had once remonstrated with Jesus when He foretold His death (cf. Matt. 16:21-23). But now he knows that all hope of eternal life and salvation lies in our Lord's sufferings and His death. Paul describes how we may be wholly delivered from the guilt and power of sin (cf. Romans 6). Peter describes the purpose: **that we, being dead to sins, should live unto righteousness.** The expression **by whose stripes ye were healed** indicates Christ's humiliation and extreme suffering (cf. Isaiah 53), by which men are saved. Stibbs[64] quotes Theodoret as saying that this "is a new and strange method of healing; the doctor suffered the cost, and the sick received healing."

The sad past of these Christians is revealed as sheep going astray (25) from truth, holiness, and happiness; and so they were lost, unprotected, exposed to perils. Their life "lacked a guide, a guardian, and a goal"[65]; consequently they were straying farther and farther away. **But** they **are now returned,** through the influence of divine grace, to find Christ as a Physician to heal them, a **Shepherd** to lead and feed them, **and Bishop** (watchful Guardian) to care for their **souls.**[66] Thus Christ's sufferings made Him a perfect Example for all suffering saints in all ages. His sufferings were borne without sin, with patience, and as man's Substitute.

J. Propriety in Marital Relationship, 3:1-7

Peter has shown that divine grace is sufficient to save, to sanctify, and to sustain through suffering. Now he shows that it is sufficient for social relationships. Continuing the idea of subjection (cf. 2:13, 18), Peter passes to the relation between **wives** and **husbands** (1), not women and men in general. Citizens are to submit to civil authority, servants to their masters, and Christian wives are to be obedient and loyal to their own husbands, even though their husbands should **obey not the word,** i.e., are

[64]*Op. cit.*, p. 12. [65]*Ibid.*

[66]See Whedon, *op. cit.*, p. 205; and Stibbs, *op. cit.*, p. 122.

not Christians. This command does not imply the wife's personal inferiority nor obligate her to participate in anything which violates her Spirit-enlightened conscience or the dignity of her human rights.

Marriage is a divine institution, and incompatibility of religion does not justify the dissolution of the marriage bond (cf. I Cor. 7:10-14). The subordination of the wife to the husband was ordained by God (cf. Gen. 2:7, 21-22) and it is to be maintained in love by the woman as a helpmeet for man. On the other hand, the superiority of the husband is to be maintained in tenderness. "In her subordination Eve was not restive, and in his superiority Adam was not exacting. . . . Christianity restores the husband and the wife to the right relation. 'Authority, kindly exercised, and subordination, quietly acknowledged, promote the development of the affections.' "[67]

The glorious aim is that the unbelieving husbands **may . . . be won by the conversation** (conduct) **of the wives** as **they behold** their **chaste conversation coupled with fear** (2). The wife has a holy fear of doing anything which would create an obstacle to her husband's conversion. This leads to a "delicate, timorous grace, afraid of the least air, or shadow of anything that hath a resemblance of wronging it in carriage or speech or apparel."[68] "The eloquent language of pure conduct and respectful demeanor . . . such silent persuasion of a becoming behavior" challenges the husband to consider what makes the difference. Her sermon without words would convince him that "Jesus must be the Messiah, or his wife could not have been so chaste!"[69] **Without the word** (1) has been interpreted, "may without argument ['without a word,' RSV] be won over by the conduct of their wives" (Berk.).

"The Dress Question" is handled by a principle that is often overlooked: True attractiveness is not by **that outward adorning of plaiting the hair** (3) for ornamental purposes, **and of wearing of gold** ("by way of ornament," Wesley), **or of putting on of apparel** for the gratification of pride and vanity; but it is the winsomeness of a Christian character, which **is not corruptible** (4).

[67]Willams, *op. cit.*, p. 42.

[68]"The Epistles of Peter, John and Jude," *Layman's Handy Commentary*, ed. Charles John Ellicott (Grand Rapids, Mich.: Zondervan Publishing House, 1957 [reprint]), p. 64.

[69]*Ibid.*

An "incorruptible inheritance" (1:4) must be matched by an incorruptible character, which exhibits **a meek and quiet spirit.** "A meek spirit gives no trouble willingly to any; a quiet spirit bears all wrongs without being troubled" (Wesley). Another describes this as "the spirit which neither worries other people, nor allows itself to be worried."[70] One so adorned is never out of fashion in the sight of God.

Some have always tended toward extremes in dress.[71] The trend today is to sin by wearing too little clothing. Heart holiness is the remedy for the love of outward adornment. The extreme disregard for personal appearance which some show is not a mark of superior piety. Holy women strive always to be unblamable in behavior, regarding both their attitude toward dress and respect and courtesy toward their husbands, **even as Sara** (6), **whose** spiritual **daughters** must follow her example. Regardless of the detailed prohibitions which some see in these verses, four principles must govern the Christian's dress: (1) It must be *neat,* not slovenly. (2) It must be *simple,* not gaudy. (3) It must be *modest,* properly clothing the person. (4) It must be *economical* and consistent with Christian stewardship. The last part of v. 6 has been translated, "And you are now her children if you do right and let nothing terrify you" (RSV).

Husbands (7) also have the duty of living with their wives **according to knowledge** ("understanding," Berk.) as equals. Their obligations are equal, for they are **heirs together of the grace of life.** As the physically **weaker vessel** the wife is entitled to reverent regard and respectful treatment from him to whom she is subordinate. Domestic disharmony growing out of disagreements and ill feelings is to be avoided, that their **prayers be not hindered.** Holiness produces right attitudes and proper actions between husbands and wives (cf. I Thess. 4:3-7).

K. The Discharge of Social Obligations, 3:8-14

In terse, simple language five exhortations concerning living harmoniously in the Christian community are given. They must all **be . . . of one mind** (8), united on principles and **having compassion one of another,** i.e., sympathetic. Since all belong to one family they must **love as brethren,** being **pitiful** (tenderhearted)

[70]Bennett, *op. cit.,* p. 224.

[71]See *Juvenal,* Sat. VI, 492-504; Barclay, *op. cit.,* pp. 261-63; Wuest, *op. cit.,* pp. 73-80.

toward the afflicted, and **courteous** (showing respect and love) toward equals and inferiors. Attention to these commands prevents the spirit of retaliation which returns "insult for insult" (NASB). Having been **called** to **inherit a blessing** (9), they know that insults and abuses cannot really harm them. They may feel the hurt, but by refusing to retaliate and by blessing their detractors they not only imitate God but demonstrate concern for the salvation of their persecutors.

Vv. 10-12 are quoted from the LXX of Ps. 34:12-16. He that would "make life amiable and desirable" (Wesley) must **refrain his tongue from evil** (10), not only slanderous speech, but rash and provocative statements. Under provocation by others he will **eschew** (avoid) **evil** (11) dispositions and actions by swerving aside from them. He has taken Christ as his Model and is resolved to **seek peace and ensue** (pursue) **it** with all men (cf. Rom. 12:18; Heb. 12:14), even when it seems that they desire contention instead of peace. Since the believer's attention is focused upon the will of God for his life, he is assured that **the eyes of the Lord are over the righteous** (12). God is not "unconscious of the needs of his people nor indifferent to the sins of those that do evil."[72]

Those who live according to Christ's principles can rely upon God's protection (cf. Rom. 8:23-39). Experience proves that malicious and violent men may and do persecute those who love the good and do it, but Christians are not to overrate their danger (cf. Luke 12:4) "and in their terror forget that there [is] a protecting Providence."[73] Peter is very anxious that persecuted Christians shall not be ensnared in sin by provocation and undeserved suffering at their enemies' hands and thus forfeit God's protection. If one's suffering is **for righteousness' sake** (14), it issues in happiness (cf. 2:19; Matt. 10:12).

L. A Consistent Testimony, 3:15-17

The secret of courage and success in meeting opposition is to **sanctify the Lord God in your hearts** (15). That means to enthrone Christ in the heart as the supreme Lord, who though innocent suffered for the guilty and is entitled to preeminence in all things (cf. Col. 1:18); to acknowledge Him as holy; to fully trust His wise providences with all sincerity; and to love Him

[72]Erdman, *op. cit.*, p. 73.

[73]Bennett, *op. cit.*, p. 230.

with a love inspired by a correct theology which invests His death "with atoning significance."[74]

We must always **be ready** to meet the ridicule of critics and the honest inquiries of those who seek the truth. Peter may be writing out of the bitter recollection of his failure on the night of Christ's betrayal. The **answer to every man that asketh . . . a reason of the hope** involves a rational account of the basic truths of Christianity and a convincing refutation of false accusations. Such an answer requires **meekness and fear** as well as **a good conscience** (16). To be effective the testimony must be supported by a godly life; must be given with firmness, yet free from any trace of defiance or disrespect to inquirers, and proceed from a heart that is conscious of the Divine Presence. In Peter's day when Christians were looked upon as evildoers, and accused of heretical religious views and bad morals, their best defense was not vehement argument but **good conversation** [conduct] **in Christ,** the silent witness of a holy life centered in the Lord Jesus.

If the will of God be . . . that ye suffer (17) indicates that it may be His will for us to suffer. This may be true of those whose lives are holy, whose defense is logical and complete, whose faith has been demonstrated to be reasonable, and whose innocence has been vindicated. But even so, **it is better** to suffer for doing good deeds than to provoke ill treatment by unchristian conduct and attitudes. The highest form of suffering is not that which one deserves, but that which comes because he is doing good. One commentator feels that v. 17 is not a mere truism or axiom of Christian ethics, but "a profound warning, owing to an urgent need . . . not to gain the glory of martyrdom through stubborn opposition to the power of the state."[75]

[74]Selwyn, *op. cit.*, p. 193.

[75]Reicke, *op. cit.*, p. 108.

Section VII *Holiness Triumphant*

I Peter 3:18-22

A. Suffering Does Not Thwart God's Purpose, 3:18

In this passage Jesus Christ is presented as "the supreme example of one who suffers for well-doing." He **suffered for sins, the just for the unjust, that he might bring us to God** (18). His sufferings were voluntary and vicarious, for He "made atonement by suffering *in the stead* of those for whom he offered himself a sacrifice . . . one righteous man for a world of the unrighteous."[76]

The central idea is undeserved suffering. But if suffering leads to death, that is not the end. Christ was **put to death in the flesh** ("as a man," Wesley), **but** was **quickened** (raised from the dead) **by the Spirit,** resurrected to life both by "His own Divine power, and the power of the Holy Ghost."[77] The reference to Christ's death and resurrection draws a contrast between what Bennett describes as "the limited and subordinate nature of the suffering, and the infinite glory and power of Christ in his exaltation. His death was brought about by natural causes . . . but his resurrection was supernatural. . . . it was connected with the unique spiritual endowments of Christ . . . and enabled him to bring to God those who believed on him (cf. 1:3)."[78]

B. A Parenthesis: Christ's Descent into Hades, 3:19-20

Verses 19-20 form a parenthesis between 18 and 21 and constitute what is generally conceded to be one of the most difficult NT passages to interpret. It has been made the basis of such unscriptural doctrines as purgatorial sufferings and posthumous salvation.

A careful study of the voluminous literature on this passage reveals that each commentator has his own solution and interprets it according to his theological predilections. Some of the interpretations are as follows:

1. Christ, in His preincarnate state, preached to the spirits

[76]Whedon, *op. cit.*, p. 209. [77]Wesley, *op. cit.*, p. 882.

[78]*Op. cit.*, pp. 233-34.

now in prison. This was done by the Holy Spirit in the preaching of Noah, but only Noah and his family believed and were saved.

2. He preached to the victims of the Flood who turned to God before they perished in the mighty waters of the Deluge.

3. He went in His spirit into the realm where only spirits could go, and proclaimed the righteousness of their judgment because they did not believe the preaching of Noah.

4. He went in the power of the Spirit and proclaimed himself Victor, and led the OT saints ("prisoners of hope," Zech. 9:12) on high (cf. Eph. 4:8-10), thus separating the paradise section of Hades from that of the wicked spirits.

5. He went in the non-corporeal mode of His existence, upon which He entered immediately after His death, and proclaimed victory over the defiant and destructive fallen angels whose seductive power polluted the antediluvian world and caused the Flood (Gen. 6:1-8). His proclamation of victory over all evil was bad news for the evil spirits.

6. He went in His spirit, not bodily form, between His crucifixion and resurrection, and proclaimed the gospel message, to set free those who once were disobedient but believed on Him after their death at His preaching.

These interpretations differ on four main points only outlined here but on which fuller treatment will be found in the references given below. Those differences concern: (1) the *time* when this preaching may have occurred; (2) the *subject matter* of this preaching; (3) the *persons* preached to; and (4) the *result* of this preaching. A study of the reference materials will convince one of Dr. Paul S. Rees's conclusion that "no consensus as to its interpretation appears anywhere on the horizon."[79]

Of this we may be certain: "The passage holds out no hope for the impenitent, it forbids the notion that those who during their earthly life refuse the Gospel of God's grace may have a second chance in the world beyond, and may be ultimately saved."[80]

[79]*Op. cit.*, p. 91.

[80]William G. Moorehead, *Outline Studies in the New Testament, Catholic Epistles* (New York: Fleming H. Revell Company, 1908), p. 67. Concerning the several interpretations of this passage see Stibbs, *op. cit.*, pp. 140-43; Selwyn, *op. cit.*, pp. 197-208, 314-62; Bennett, *op. cit.*, pp. 234-37; Bigg, *op. cit.*, p. 162; Barclay, *op. cit.*, pp. 279-87; Whedon, *op. cit.*, pp. 209-14; Wuest, *op. cit.*, pp. 92-109; Hayes, *op. cit.*, pp. 176-82.

God's plan and purpose prevailed in Noah's day when eight souls were saved "in the flood" (Phillips), or "were brought to safety through the water" (NEB). Whether many or few believe our testimony and even if *we* are persecuted for righteousness' sake, this divine principle stands out: In His own time God will deliver the righteous and punish the wicked. The disobedience of the antediluvian world led to damnation, but the faith and obedience of Noah resulted in his salvation and that of his family.

The death and resurrection of Christ suggest that for those who lose their lives for His sake death is the entrance into a wider sphere of activity, for after His quickening **he went and preached unto the spirits in prison; which sometime were disobedient . . . in the days of Noah** (19-20). Whatever the full meaning of these verses, Christ's descent into Hades was "the first stage of His exaltation."[81]

C. From Suffering to Glory, 3:21-22

Verse 21 should be translated: "And corresponding to that, baptism now saves you—not the removal of dirt from the flesh, but an appeal to God for a good conscience—through the resurrection of Jesus Christ" (NASB).

The resurrection of Jesus Christ: who is gone into heaven, and is on the right hand of God marks the transition from suffering to glory. Believers may have to suffer (17) but if they maintain a good conscience toward God by living a separated life, as they pledged to do at their baptism, they have God's pledge and the proof of His past works to insure that theirs is a well-grounded hope. **The right hand of God** is the highest place of heavenly honor. It is the place of Christ, whose death redeemed man (cf. v. 18). In His glorious exaltation His supremacy is acknowledged by **angels and authorities and powers**—"all orders both of angels and men" (Wesley). Peter's inference here and in 5:1 is that those who retain steadfastness of faith despite any suffering experienced for Christ's sake (cf. 4:13) shall share the triumphs and the glories with which Christ was crowned for the suffering of death (cf. John 17:24; Phil. 2:5-11; Rev. 3:21). Therefore no suffering saint should have fears about his future. All suffering for righteousness' sake will be followed by unspeakable glory.

[81]Purkiser, *op. cit.*, p. 170.

Section VIII Holiness Superior

I Peter 4:1-19

A. Dedication to God's Will, 4:1-2

In various ways Peter has stressed preparation for suffering (cf. esp. 3:13-17) which is inescapable. Christ is our Example in *undeserved suffering* (cf. 3:18-22). Here in vv. 1-6 separation from sin is cited as one of the causes of persecution. Since **Christ . . . suffered for us in the flesh** (1), Christians must **arm** themselves **with the same mind** to suffer patiently whatever is the will of God. This not only means identification with Christ in spirit and in purpose, but in abhorrence of sin. Peter here uses the phrase **suffered for us in the flesh** to indicate our Lord's death. In parallel fashion he uses the phrase **he that hath suffered in the flesh** to refer to our death to sin (cf. Rom. 6:2-4). He does not mean that suffering as such saves men. Identification with our Lord's death means that the Christian has **ceased from sin.** He is in the world, but not of it. He is in the body, but having broken all relation with sin, he no longer patterns his life after **the lusts of men** (2) who are actuated by the depraved nature. Instead of conforming to the moral standards of the old life, his life now has a new directive, **the will of God,** and a new dynamic, the power of the Holy Spirit (cf. Rom. 6:1-13; 8:1-13).

B. Surmounting Misunderstanding, 4:3-6

The life of holiness which is complete identification with "the will of God" (v. 2) is brought into sharp contrast with **the will of the Gentiles** (3), or the lax morality which characterized their lives in **the time past.** Too much of life had already been devoted to disgusting forms of impurities, vile passions, evil desires, drunkenness, wild conduct, **and abominable idolatries,** which not only were unbecoming for Christians but "outraged the sense of common decency."[82]

Regarding any and all sin, there is but one course open to Christians: definite separation—not isolation, but separation in spirit and in practice. When Christians adopt the customs of the world, they absorb the spirit of the world. When they repudiate

[82]Cf. Wuest, *op. cit.*, p. 112; Bennett, *op. cit.*, p. 243.

its customs, they must be prepared to receive the world's opposition. The degree of its misunderstanding, misrepresentation, and mistreatment of Christians often indicates the effectiveness of their separation and witness. Those who **run not** (4) with their former associates, refusing to participate in their old **excess of riot,** will be treated with contempt; but this must not provoke them to return to the old life. There is not only a past from which they have been saved, but there is an "inheritance . . . reserved" for them (cf. 1:4) if they prove faithful. However, before that is bestowed upon them they must all—**the quick** (living) **and the dead** (5), believers and unbelievers—**give account to him that is . . . judge.** He will vindicate the righteous who suffer unjustly, but He will punish the unrighteous. The fact of accountability to a holy Judge is an incentive to holiness of heart and life.

The preaching of **the gospel . . . to them that are dead** (6) has (as 3:18-22) occasioned endless controversy, but Whedon's comments are clear, and they interpret this verse in the light of the clear teaching of the entire Bible. "The plain meaning is that the gospel was preached to men when living, who are now dead; just as it would be perfectly correct to say that it was preached to saints in glory, or to souls that are in perdition; meaning that it was preached to them when here on the earth. The aorist shows its cessation."[83]

C. Sobriety and Watchfulness, 4:7

Earlier Peter referred to "the last time" (1:5), "the appearing of Jesus Christ" (1:7), and "the revelation of Jesus Christ" (1:13). He looked upon the close of the dispensation as being **at hand.** The second coming of Christ, the resurrection of the dead, and the judgment were considered as being so near that they were urged as powerful incentives to holy living and encouragement to believers in their afflictions. The brevity of time left to them demanded discretion, self-control, "sound judgment and sober spirit for the purpose of prayer" (NASB). "Irrational and restless excitement makes true prayer impossible."[84]

Peter may have penned these words with sad recollection over the occasion when "fear, idle curiosity, restless excitement, and neglect of duty" caused him to fail to watch and pray and he denied his Lord. However long our Lord may delay His return, Christians must keep ready and be alert to the wiles of the

[83] *Op. cit.*, p. 216.

[84] Bennett, *op. cit.*, p. 246.

devil, who seeks to gain an advantage over them (cf. II Cor. 2:11; 11:14-15; Eph. 6:11).

D. Charity Toward Offenders, 4:8

Holiness is practical, and manifests itself in proper social relationships. "The greatest thing in the world" is love (cf. I Corinthians 13). If there is pure love to God, there will be **fervent charity among** themselves. This (cf. 1:22) is a stretched-out love, which gives out to others instead of being self-centered. This love is a matter of first importance and requires cultivation. Where love prevails, all other duties are performed. And if there be a **multitude of sins,** charity will **cover** them, as with an overspread mantle. The motive in "covering" is not to conceal the offense or to deny its reality, but to forgive it and thereby quench strife and keep down further sin. They were to keep their mutual love "at full strength, because love cancels innumerable sins" (NEB), and is the very essence of a good and pure life.

E. Demonstrating Hospitality, 4:9-10

Where there is watchful living there will be worthy living. This means that one uses whatever he may possess, however humble and meager, to meet the needs of fellow Christians. In Peter's day this could have meant those who had been driven from their homes by persecution or were making a long journey. Christians are to be hospitable **without grudging,** even if it imposes a burden on them, for complaining about its cost robs of the blessing of sharing with one's brethren.

The motive behind this generosity is love: love to the needy brother, and love to the Heavenly Father, from whom we receive every good gift (cf. I Cor. 4:7). One's gifts or talents are not for use as he selfishly desires. They are a trust from God to be employed as He intended for **good stewards** (10) to use them: to bless others. Such service is a *ministry* whether it be of talents, money, influence, or other blessings that God has so bountifully given; and all have received some gifts that can be shared (cf. Romans 12 and I Corinthians 12).

F. God's Glory in All Things, 4:11

As if to illustrate his meaning of ministering one's stewardship (v. 10), Peter specifies two items: (1) Speaking publicly for the Lord in proclaiming His Word, and (2) Rendering service to others out of one's personal means. **If any man speak, let him speak as the oracles of God** means that one is to declare God's doctrines as communicated to him by the Spirit of God, in agreement with the Word of God. He is to teach the whole body of divine truth as revealed in the Scriptures. He is to depend upon God and speak in gravity and with authority. "He that . . . does not enjoin practical holiness to believers, does not speak as the oracles of God" (Wesley).

If any man minister, let him do it as of the ability which God giveth. Whatever service is rendered is to be given remembering that all we have comes from God. It is the goodness of God that supplies wisdom of mind, strength of body, and material resources. Whenever a man entirely consecrates himself and his all, God will **be glorified through Jesus Christ,** the Mediator through whom God ministers the ability. Since man's chief end is to glorify God, the loving and faithful performance of his duty redounds to the glory of God, **to whom** is due the **praise** and **dominion for ever and ever. Amen.** Some say that **to whom** refers to God, and others that it refers to Christ. Since Christ is one with the Father (cf. John 10:31) and is given similar adoration in Rev. 1:6, this doxology is perfectly in order if it be ascribed to Christ.

G. Sharing Christ's Sufferings, 4:12-16

Again Peter returns to a dominant theme: the suffering of Christians. As followers of Christ they expect to share His glory; consequently they should also expect to share His sufferings. They are not to think it **strange** or be bewildered at **the fiery trial** (12). This is not a mere happenstance. Nor is it simply Satan trying to persuade them that if they sustained a special relationship to God (cf. 1:2-4; 2:9-10) such sufferings would not happen to them. Their "ordeal by fire" has a divine purpose, although at the time they might not understand it. Peter had previously referred to the fire test of their faith which issued in glory (cf. 1:7). As **partakers of Christ's sufferings** (13), they are to rejoice, not in the fact that they suffer, but because they experience it as Christ's representatives. The immediate suffering came because the Christians called Jesus the Son of God and worshipped Him as the supreme Sovereign instead of worshiping the emperor. The degree of their rejoicing should be increased by the intensity of the persecutions they endured. The joy which they now have despite their sufferings will give way to **exceeding**

joy—when his glory shall be revealed, i.e., when they shall see Christ and His rule shall be supreme. At that time these sufferers shall leap for joy in triumphant exultation.

Peter was concerned that the insults and persecutions they experienced be **for the name of Christ** (14), and because of a life consistent with His teachings. *Reproach* and *glory* are set in contrast. Contemptuous treatment inflicts greater suffering upon some sensitive souls than physical abuse or the destruction of their property. Hence the allusion to Christ's assurance of blessings upon suffering for His sake (cf. Matt. 5:11). **The spirit of glory and of God** gives fortitude to face suffering without shrinking.[85] The indwelling Spirit assures suffering Christians of their participation in perfected glory at Christ's coming. The meaning of 15-16 is: Let no one dishonour Christ by suffering just punishment for crimes against men; no one is blessed if he is suffering for his own fault. Rather let a man glory in punishment inflicted because he is a Christian.[86]

The warning against suffering **as a murderer . . . thief . . . evildoer . . . busybody** (15) need not shock one if he remembers the general state of society at that time. Some of these believers' past lives may have been as bad as that of the Corinthians whom Paul described (cf. I Cor. 6:9-11). There were instances where criminals, in order to conceal their nature and the real cause of their punishment, professed to be Christians, and made it appear that they were punished on that account. The **busybody in other men's matters** is one who "steps out of his own calling, and makes himself a judge of others" (Wesley). The Christians were considered by their enemies to be hostile to civilized society in that they were accused of trying to compel non-Christians to conform to Christian standards. That would create civil commotion which could produce mob violence (cf. Acts 19:21-41).

Those who **suffer as a Christian** should **not be ashamed; but . . . glorify God** (16). At this time the term **Christian** had become the name by which the heathen sarcastically described Jesus' followers (cf. Acts 11:26; 26:28). The Jews who rejected Jesus as the Christ would not call His followers Christians. Renan, quoted in Ellicott, said: "Well-bred people avoided pronouncing the name, or, when forced to do so, made a kind of apology."[87]

[85]See Wuest, *op. cit.,* pp. 118-22.
[86]Bennett, *op. cit.,* p. 250. See also Ellicott, *op. cit.,* pp. 103-4.
[87]*Op. cit.,* p. 104.

Apparently the Christians themselves did not yet use this designation, but wore it as a badge of the highest honor when their enemies applied it to them. What Peter exhorted them to do (v. 16) he himself had practiced (cf. Acts 5:29-42, esp. v. 41).

H. No Fear of God's Examination, 4:17-19

In the present trials and sorrows Peter sensed the beginning of a protracted period of **judgment** (17). Justice requires judgment and God has appointed a righteous Judge (cf. Acts 17:31) who knows accurately every man's intentions as well as his actions. He is the believers' hope (cf. 1:3, 21). They sustain a precious relationship to Him and He to them (cf. 1:18-21; 2:7). The pattern which God seems to follow in discipline and judgment begins with His own people (cf. Isa. 10:12-13; Jer. 25:29; 49:12; Ezek. 9:6), in order to reveal who stands the test. The "ordeal of fire" through which the Christians were passing might seem terrible, but it was to purge them and enable them to glorify God.

If true believers found it difficult to endure their testings, they should remember that the doom of **them that obey not . . . God** far exceeds the worst that Christians are called upon to endure, or can imagine. Their prospect is hopeless. And lest any readers be tempted to seek relief from persecution by renouncing the Christian faith, Peter reminded them that something far worse awaits the disobedient, whether they be heathen persecutors or disloyal professing Christians.[88] If the righteous Judge will not overlook the faults of His dutiful followers, but disciplines them to purify and fit them for glory (cf. Heb. 12:5-10), how awful must be His wrath upon the willful rebel! Peter's question about **the ungodly and the sinner** (18) definitely discounts the assertion of some that he allows the possibility of posthumous salvation in 3:18-22 and 4:6.

When suffering is the instrument of divine discipline, and when it is not for personal wrongdoing, it is **according to the will of God** (19), and should be borne in a right spirit. Such sufferers are charged to "keep on doing what is right and trust yourself to the God Who made you, for He will never fail you" (LL).[89] Since God created the soul and gave it new life in Christ, He will be faithful to fulfil His promises to protect His own possession. Holiness thus delivers the believer from the fear of God's examination of either his character or his conduct.

[88]Cf. Beare, *op. cit.*, p. 168.

[89]Cf. Wuest, *op. cit.*, p. 123.

Section IX *Holiness in Action*

I Peter 5:1-9

A. Official Relationships in the Church, 5:1-4

The elders (1) were mature church officials who acted as overseers; they had definite administrative and pastoral duties. The contrast with the "younger" (v. 5) indicates a simple form of church government at the time Peter wrote. Wise administration of church affairs is vital to the purity and preservation of the Church, and doubly so when persecutions impose peculiar responsibilities upon its leaders. **I . . . am also an elder.** Peter may have considered his apostleship as a kind of eldership, or he may have served as an elder in the church where he lived. In modesty he refers to his apostleship in a matter-of-fact way as **a witness of the sufferings of Christ,** about which he had so much to say. The description of his official relationship is such as becomes holiness. There is neither self-exaltation nor disparagement, nor any hint of primacy, such as some have claimed for Peter.

He was also **a partaker of the glory that shall be revealed** when Christ returns to earth. Peter was on the Mount of Transfiguration and there saw our Lord's glory. He observed the glorious, infallible proofs of His resurrection and heard the angel's promise that Christ would return. He had been given a special commission which he was endeavoring to fulfil (cf. Luke 22:32; John 21:15-17), of which this Epistle is proof.

The pastoral responsibility of these elders is described as being to **feed the flock of God** (2). The word "tend" comprehends the meaning better than **feed.** The shepherd's duty has been described as threefold: to provide pasture, paths to the pasture, and protection along the paths to the pasture. Thus it involves more than preaching. **The flock** is the Church. It belongs to God as His purchased possession. Once its members were as straying sheep but they have "now returned unto the Shepherd and Bishop" of their souls (cf. 2:25). The shepherd is to instruct and guide the flock into cheerful obedience to God's whole will. **The oversight** to be exercised involves three particulars stated negatively and positively. (1) As to the spirit of this service, it is **not by constraint, but willingly.** Leadership of the church was so hazardous in that day that it could cost the leader's life. Even so, he was not to do this work unwillingly as if it were a burden, or consider it as a compulsory professional duty. Instead this was a ministry to which God had appointed him, and called for cheerful obedience. (2) As to the motive of this oversight, it is **not for filthy lucre, but of a ready mind**—not as a hireling who hopes to gain money. The elders had a right to expect material support from those to whom they ministered in spiritual things; but their motive should not be from a "constitutional love of gain," which "is a disqualification for the Christian ministry."[90] Consider its effect on Judas Iscariot! (3) As to the manner in which oversight is to be exercised, it is not **as being lords over God's heritage, but . . . ensamples to the flock** (3). The leaders must never be tyrannical and forget the rights of the people entrusted to their care. They are not to dominate as arrogant Diotrephes (III John 9-11), but lead by the power of a holy life. The undershepherd must never forget that he is not **the chief Shepherd** (4).

The leader's earthly compensation may be insignificant, but **when the chief Shepherd shall appear** (cf. 4:13), he shall have his imperishable reward (cf. 1:4-5), **a crown of glory,** "the bliss of heaven, the chief element of which is the life of God poured out into the soul through Christ";[91] "a never-ending share in His glory and honor" (LL).

B. Personal Relationship to the Entire Fellowship, 5:5-7

Again Peter introduces the principle of submission. It is implied in vv. 3-4, but is emphasized in v. 5. There is divergence of opinion as to whether **younger** (5) means juniors as to age or lower in rank. Some understand it to mean the laity of the Church as distinct from the ministry; and others, those who are younger in the Christian way. Wuest suggests that it may very well refer to guilds as organizations composed of younger people within the Church, for there were such organizations in the Greek cities of Asia Minor.[92]

The emphasis on submission to duly constituted leadership is always in order, but especially in times of stress when there is a tendency on the part of some individuals and groups to feel that the leadership is "not sufficiently vigorous in its reaction to the

[90]Williams, *op. cit.*, p. 68. [91]*Ibid.*, p. 70.
[92]*Op. cit.*, p. 126.

crisis."[93] The **elder** must serve; the **younger** must **submit;** but all are to **be clothed with humility.** This garment is to be so securely fastened that nothing can strip it from us. Humility produces a proper attitude toward one another and toward all Christian duties, however menial they may be. This seems to allude to our Lord's girding himself and washing the disciples' feet (cf. John 13:1-9)—an occasion when impetuous Peter learned a valuable lesson in humility.

The divine attitude toward the proud is a challenge to cultivate humility and submission. "God sets his face against the arrogant" (NEB), as in battle array, for pride has set them against God's mighty hand. But **the humble** who faithfully submit to Him and trust His purpose, power, and providences have no cause for distressing anxiety—the sin of worry. Their reliance is in Him to whom belongs their care. He watches everything that concerns them, has all things under His control, and is not forgetful. **He careth for you** (7) assures us that we are "his personal concern" (Phillips). In due time, when He sees fit to do so, He will exalt us, either by removing the trouble or by taking us to himself. Why be distracted by anxiety, since He has you safe in His own keeping? This reliance upon God and His promises does not exempt us from the duty to be watchful against temptation, or to bear one's share of personal responsibilities (cf. Gal. 6:4), but it does remove "the fret of care."

C. Constant Resistance to the Adversary, 5:8-9

Worry is condemned but watchfulness is commanded. **Be sober** (self-controlled), **be vigilant** (8); sound the true shepherd's alarm against a dangerous foe. These verses reflect Peter's personal encounter and bitter experience with Satan (cf. Luke 22: 31-46). His true nature is vividly described as; (1) **your adversary,** the opponent of God, His eternal purpose, and all that is good. Satan is the adverse party, or prosecutor, in cases before the Judge. He is the "accuser of the brethren" (Rev. 12:10), charging false and calumnious things against the saints. Any lapse into sin, however produced, enables him to convict them and secure their punishment; therefore perpetual vigilance and earnest effort are imperative (cf. 1:13; 4:7). He is also called (2) **the devil,** who accuses, slanders, tempts, and seduces. His

[93]Beare, *op. cit.*, p. 176.

wiles vary from appearing as a subtle serpent or an angel of light, to (3) **a roaring lion,** bloodthirsty, violent, insatiable for prey, always on the prowl, **seeking whom he may devour.** This crafty foe is not vaguely stalking for prey; he "is eying all the Christians in turn to see which he has the best chance of"[94] swallowing up, both soul and body.

The Christian's attitude toward this diabolical personality must be steadfast resistance **in the faith** (9). He who plagues the saints and stops at nothing in his opposition to God, truth, and holiness may be overcome by the power of God and spiritual armament (cf. Eph. 6:11-18). Orthodoxy is not enough. Human wisdom is insufficient (cf. I Cor. 10:12), and cowering fear leads to man's defeat. But he may be overcome by complete reliance on God as the great Deliverer (cf. vv. 6-7), by maintaining unshaken trust in divine aid, and by undeviating loyalty to Christ (cf. Rev. 12:11).

The extent of these Satan-inspired afflictions (cf. Job 1—2) extends to all the **brethren that are in the world.** The entire Christian brotherhood experiences the **same** sufferings and persecutions. Therefore we must not consider our afflictions as indications of God's disfavor or proof that He has forgotten us (cf. v. 7). The fact that other believers were experiencing tribulations proved that the readers were not singled out for exceptional sufferings (cf. Acts 14:22; I Cor. 10:13; I Thess. 1:6; 3:4), and that their troubles were no more severe than those of Christians in other parts of the world. Being part of a brotherhood of sufferers should encourage them to **resist** the devil, and thereby "shew forth the praises of him who hath called" them "into his marvellous light" (2:9).

[94]Ellicott, *op. cit.*, p. 113.

Section X Holiness and Eternal Glory

I Peter 5:10-11

A. God Initiates the Call to Holiness, 5:10*a*

Another encouragement to resist the devil is that **the God of all grace . . . hath called us** (10) unto holiness, which is a preparation for the glory that He has in store for the overcomers. He is the Source and Giver of all needed grace for every occasion. He has saving, sanctifying, sustaining, satisfying, and stabilizing grace which is all-sufficient (cf. II Cor. 12:9-10). For sins He has the grace of pardon and forgiveness. For sin He has the grace of cleansing and purity of heart. For sickness He has the grace of healing. For sorrow there is the grace of His comforting presence and precious promises. For stress He has the grace of peace that "passeth all understanding" (cf. Phil. 4:6-7). He has enough grace, and more than enough, to meet every need (cf. II Cor. 9:8). The fact that He has called us is proof of His grace; and the sufficiency of His grace assures us of all that is needed for daily, holy living.

B. The Goal Is Eternal Glory, 5:10*b*

The call originates in the grace of God, for by grace "alone the whole work is begun, continued, and finished in your soul" (Wesley). Those called must respond by obedient acceptance and faithful use of the grace so freely offered through the merit of **Christ Jesus,** through whom alone we are made partakers of His great salvation (cf. 1:2-3). Anything which separates from Him destroys our hope of life and glory (cf. John 15:5-6).

The goal in all this is that we may share **his eternal glory,** for which holiness is the preparation (cf. Matt. 5:8, 28; Heb. 12:14). And as was true in the Master's experience, the road to glory lies through tribulations and the fires of persecution. These, however, are of short duration, while the **glory** is **eternal** (cf. II Cor. 4:17; Heb. 11:25-26).

The fullness of what is in store for the overcomer cannot be known, but someone has suggested that it includes:

A love that cannot be fathomed,
A life that cannot die,
A righteousness that cannot be tarnished,
A peace that cannot be understood,

A rest that cannot be disturbed,
A joy that cannot be diminished,
A hope that cannot be disappointed,
A light that cannot be interrupted,
A strength that cannot be enfeebled,
A purity that cannot be defiled,
A beauty that cannot be marred,
A wisdom that cannot be baffled,
Resources that cannot be exhausted.[95]

C. Holiness and Hope Tested by Suffering, 5:10*c*

The problem of suffering, introduced at 1:6-9 and repeatedly mentioned throughout this Epistle, has baffled philosophers and theologians through the centuries. Job wondered why the righteous suffered. David was perplexed by this problem (cf. Psalms 73, esp. vv. 12-17). It baffled Christ's disciples (cf. John 9:1-3). It perplexes believers today. But God purposes that it shall turn "for a testimony" (Luke 21:13). Despite what one may not understand or be able to explain, suffering *is* compatible with a holy life (cf. Isa. 48:10; Dan. 11:35; 12:10). Instead of meaning that the sufferer is under God's wrath, it may mean that God has chosen him to demonstrate His grace and power. Suffering produces a unity with and nearness to God that cannot come otherwise; it enlarges life and teaches sympathy with other sufferers. Above all, it teaches the cost of our redemption (cf. 1:18-19; 2:21-24; 3:18).

Peter was concerned lest his Christian readers be victimized by self-pity, which is of Satanic origin (cf. Matt. 16:23). If they began to think that no one else suffered as they did or had such a hard lot, their faith and love would wane. Satan would then get an advantage and exploit it through questions as to whether God dealt fairly with them. A recent author says that life reaches its greatest fulfillment in that suffering which elevates one to an overview that enables him to grasp the ultimate as well as the immediate meaning of suffering.[96]

D. A Process with Eternity in View, 5:10*d*

Despite the fact of a crisis of cleansing, or entire sanctification, there must be constant improvement, enlargement, and

[95]Quoted by J. Allen Blair, *Living Peacefully* (New York: Loizeaux Brothers, 1959), p. 249.

[96]Wayne E. Oates, *What Psychology Says About Religion* (New York: Association Press, 1958), pp. 102-3.

spiritual maturation to properly fit one for service. This does not imply that there has not been a thorough cleansing. Rather, it shows that there is need for a process which develops and matures the gifts, graces, and fruit of the Spirit, and thereby assists one to better control the human element involved.[97]

God's process of preparing us to share in His glory is to **make . . . perfect,** i.e., repair and thus make perfect any defect which appears during the ravages of persecution, so that we are fitted to serve Him perfectly. Selwyn's comment on the Greek word translated **perfect** deserves attention.[98] Since all our enduement is from God, He himself shall be our fitness, if we trust and obey Him. He will also **stablish,** so that nothing shall cause us to waver or be shaken. We shall be confirmed or made steadfast in faith and duty. If there is a display of weakness, He will **strengthen.** Testings reveal not only the possession of some strength, but the need and possibility of more strength, which God bestows by giving inward power to overcome every foe. Furthermore, if the ground on which one stands seems to tremble, the divine promise and process is to **settle,** i.e., to give a sure footing. Peter, "the rock man," keeps the idea of a solid foundation, security, and stability before the suffering Christians.

E. The Doxology, 5:11

He is "the God of all grace" (v. 10), who himself furnishes abundant grace to keep us through affliction. He provides all needed strength and influences of the Spirit by which acceptable service may be rendered to God and man. Since **glory and dominion** belong to Him **for ever and ever,** all should acknowledge it and give to Him the glory that is due His name. **Amen.**

[97]Cf. Purkiser, *op. cit.,* pp. 351, 367.
[98]*Op. cit.,* p. 240. See also Rees, *op. cit.,* pp. 135-36.

Section XI *The Conclusion*

I Peter 5:12-14

A. A Letter with a Purpose, 5:12

One of the problems associated with I Peter is the part **Silvanus, a faithful brother,** had in its writing. (See Introduction.) It is generally agreed that the reference is to Silas, Paul's associate on many important occasions, and who shared some of the critical experiences which befell him (cf. Acts 15; 16:19-40; I Thess. 1:1; II Thess. 1:1). He was one of "the chief men among the brethren" in the Jerusalem church (cf. Acts 15:22) and "a prophet" (Acts 15:32). The words **I suppose** do not imply lack of confidence, but indicate that Peter's judgment was based on personal knowledge of the character and worth of the man—"as I regard him" (RSV).

This letter was brief in comparison to what he would have preferred to write them by way of exhortation, encouragement, and instruction in view of their circumstances. A careful study of its doctrinal contents will show that it is, nevertheless, an important letter. In exhorting them Peter also used entreaty, encouragement, and consolation. **In testifying** he gave the personal account of an eyewitness of those things which they had heard from others and which they had believed. As an actual observer he was competent to assure them that the faith whereon they stood is **the true grace of God.** No questions arising out of their afflictions nor any Satanic suggestion that their faith was misplaced should entice them from this **true grace.** Their present suffering was but a passing incident of their earthly sojourn on the way to glory.

B. Salutations from the Church, 5:13

This verse has occasioned considerable conjecture as to the place and the person referred to. The italicizing of **church that is** shows that they are not in the original Greek. The feminine verb permits the translation, "She that is in Babylon." This feminine singular with which the name of **Marcus** is connected, and who is described as **my son,** cause some to conclude that Peter's wife joins in the salutation. However the consensus of most commentators is that the church and John Mark, a spiritual son (cf. Acts 12:12; 13:5; 15:37, 39), send the greetings. As to the place, the most likely interpretation indicates Rome (see Introduction) as the city from which Peter wrote. However the assertion that Peter founded the church at Rome and was its bishop for several decades is historically baseless. **Babylon** was often used symbolically for Rome (cf. Rev. 17:5, 9). The tenor of the claims of later Roman bishops for Peter's primacy is contrary to what he wrote concerning church leadership (v. 3). But the tradition that Peter was in Rome in the A.D. sixties is early and strong, and should not be discounted. For **elected together with you,** read "chosen together with you" (NASB).

C. The Token of Brotherhood, 5:14*a*

The **kiss of charity** with which they were to greet one another was a token of Christian brotherhood. It evidently was a common custom in the Early Church (cf. Rom. 16:16; I Cor. 16:20; II Cor. 13:12; I Thess. 5:26), signifying mutual affection. At one time it was a part of the regular ceremony of public worship. But it became subject to abuse and in time an Early Church father wrote about "another—an impure—kiss full of venom pretending to holiness."[99] Eventually the custom was restricted to men kissing the men, and women the women. Today the spirit of this token of brotherhood is expressed in Western lands by a cordial handshake.

D. A Prayer for Peace, 5:14*b*

It is significant that Peter, the Apostle of the Jews, closes this letter with the Hebrew benediction of **peace,** while Paul, the Apostle of the Gentiles, closes his letters with "grace" (e.g., II Thess. 3:17-18). The **peace** which Peter wishes to them is peace "in all the fullness of its meaning"—peace with God and peace with all men, which included peace among themselves. What a consolation to know that in times such as theirs and ours **all that are in Christ Jesus** can have a peace which transcends "trouble, turmoil, tempest, tension"![100] **Amen.** So may it be with you!

[99]Wuest, *op. cit.*, p. 133.

[100]Rees, *op. cit.*, p. 143.

Bibliography

I. COMMENTARIES

BARCLAY, WILLIAM. *The Letters of James and Peter.* Second Edition. "The Daily Study Bible." Philadelphia: Westminster Press, 1960.

BEARE, FRANCIS W. *The First Epistle of Peter.* Oxford: Basil Blackwell, 1947.

BENNETT, W. H. *The General Epistles: James, Peter, John and Jude.* "The Century Bible." Edited by W. F. ADENEY. Edinburgh: T. C. and E. C. Jack, 1901.

BENSON, JOSEPH. *The New Testament of Our Lord and Saviour Jesus Christ, with Critical, Explanatory and Practical Notes,* Vol. II. New York: Carlton and Phillips, 1856.

BIGG, CHARLES. *The Epistles of St. Peter and St. Jude.* "The International Critical Commentary." New York: Charles Scribner's Sons, 1905.

BOWMAN, JOHN WICK. "The First and Second Letters of Peter," *The Layman's Bible Commentary.* Edited by BALMER H. KELLEY. Richmond: John Knox Press, 1959.

CAFFIN, B. C., *et al. I Peter.* "The Pulpit Commentary." Edited by H. D. M. SPENCE and JOSEPH C. EXELL. Reprint Edition. Grand Rapids: William B. Eerdmans Publishing Company, 1950.

CLARKE, ADAM. *The New Testament of Our Lord and Saviour Jesus Christ,* Vol. II. New York: Abingdon-Cokesbury Press, n.d.

ERDMAN, CHARLES R. *The General Epistles: An Exposition.* First Edition. Philadelphia: Westminster Press, 1918.

HUNTER, ARCHIBALD M., and HOMRIGHAUSEN, ELMER G. "The First Epistle of Peter." *The Interpreter's Bible,* Vol. XII. Edited by GEORGE ARTHUR BUTTRICK, *et al.* New York: Abingdon-Cokesbury Press, 1957.

MACKNIGHT, JAMES. *The Apostolical Epistles.* Philadelphia: Thomas Wardle, 1841.

PAINE, STEPHEN W. *The First Epistle of Peter.* "The Wycliffe Bible Commentary." Edited by CHARLES F. PFEIFFER and EVERETT F. HARRISON. Chicago: Moody Press, 1962.

REICKE, BO. "The Epistles of James, Peter and Jude." *The Anchor Bible.* Edited by WILLIAM F. ALBRIGHT and DAVID N. FREEMAN. New York: Doubleday and Company, 1964.

SELWYN, E. G. *The First Epistle of St. Peter.* London: Macmillan and Company, 1961.

STIBBS, ALAN M. *The First Epistle General of Peter.* "Tyndale New Testament Commentaries." Edited by R. V. G. TASKER. London: Tyndale Press, 1959.

WESLEY, JOHN. *Explanatory Notes upon the New Testament.* New York: Carlton and Phillips, 1855.

———, *et al. One Volume New Testament Commentary.* Reprint Edition. Grand Rapids: Baker Book House, 1957.

WHEDON, DANIEL D. *Commentary on the New Testament,* Vol. V. New York: Hunt and Eaton, 1890.

WILLIAMS, NATHANIEL M. *Commentary on the Epistles of Peter.* "An American Commentary on the New Testament." Edited by ALVAH HOVEY. Philadelphia: American Baptist Publication Society, 1890.

II. OTHER BOOKS

ARNDT, W. F., and GINGRICH, F. W. (eds.). *A Greek-English Lexicon of the New Testament and Other Early Christian Literature.* Chicago: The University of Chicago Press, 1957.

BARCLAY, WILLIAM. *More New Testament Words.* New York: Harper and Row, 1958.

BLAIR, J. ALLEN. *Living Peacefully.* New York: Loizeaux Brothers, Inc., 1959.

DODS, MARCUS. *An Introduction to the New Testament.* Sixth Edition. New York: Thomas Whittaker, n.d.

EARLE, RALPH, *et al. Exploring the New Testament.* Kansas City: Beacon Hill Press of Kansas City, 1955.

FIELD, BENJAMIN. *The Student's Handbook of Christian Theology.* New Edition. New York: Hunt and Eaton, 1889.

GALBREATH, MARVIN L. *James and Peter.* "Aldersgate Biblical Series." Leader's Guide. Winona Lake: Light and Life Press, 1962.

KERR, JOHN H. *An Introduction to the Study of the New Testament.* Thirteenth Edition. New York: Fleming H. Revell, 1939.

MCCLINTOCK, JOHN, and STRONG, JAMES. *Cyclopedia of Biblical, Theological and Ecclesiastical Literature,* Vol. VIII. New York: Harper and Brothers, 1894.

MOOREHEAD, WILLIAM G. *Catholic Epistles.* "Outline Studies in the New Testament." New York: Fleming H. Revell, 1908.

PURKISER, W. T., *et al. Exploring Our Christian Faith.* Kansas City: Beacon Hill Press of Kansas City, 1960.

REES, PAUL S. *Triumphant in Trouble.* Westwood, N.J.: Fleming H. Revell Company, 1962.

TENNEY, MERRILL C. *New Testament Survey.* Grand Rapids: William B. Eerdmans Publishing Company, 1961.

WUEST, KENNETH S. *First Peter in the Greek New Testament.* "Wuest's Word Studies." Grand Rapids: William B. Eerdmans Publishing Company, 1942.

The Second Epistle of

PETER

Eldon R. Fuhrman

Introduction

A. Authorship

Although there has been strenuous controversy regarding the authorship of this Epistle, there can be no doubt that the author explicitly and repeatedly identified himself as Peter. The comparative lack of early historical attestation for the genuineness of the Epistle is more than compensated for by an abundance of internal evidence. The writer calls himself Simon Peter (1:1). He states that the Lord had showed him the imminence and manner of his own death (1:14). He claims to have been an eyewitness of the Transfiguration (1:16-17), and records the heavenly voice heard while present with Christ "in the holy mount" (1:18). The writer mentions having written an earlier Epistle to the same people (3:1), and speaks of his "beloved brother Paul" as if he were intimately acquainted with him and his writings (3:15-16). Since these autobiographical allusions accord with other biblical sources of information about Peter, the case is strengthened for believing he is the Epistle's author.

Much has been made of the fact that the Second Epistle is written in poorer Greek than the First. But this can be accounted for by the suggestion that Peter had Silas as a secretary for the First (I Pet. 5:12), whereas he himself wrote the Second in prison.

The only alternative to affirming Peter's authorship of this Epistle is that of deliberate forgery. However, as H. C. Thiessen once pointed out, "if II Peter is a forgery, then we have here a forgery without an object, without any of the ordinary marks of forgery, and without any resemblance to undoubted forgeries."[1] Since there is no conclusive historical evidence against Petrine authorship, since the alternatives raise more doubts and questions than they solve, and since the Christian earnestness, apostolic tone, and autobiographical allusions harmonize with other sources of information about Peter, he is here accepted without reservation as the author of this letter.

B. Occasion for Writing

The Second Epistle of Peter claims to be a companion letter to an earlier one sent to the same readers (3:1). This means that it was directed to Jewish and Gentile Christians in northern Asia

[1]*Introduction to the New Testament* (Grand Rapids: Wm. B. Eerdmans Publishing Co., 1942), p. 288.

Minor; that is, "to the strangers scattered throughout Pontus, Galatia, Cappadocia, Asia, and Bithynia" (I Pet. 1:1; see map 1). These then are the ones who have obtained "like precious faith" with Peter and the other apostles.

Between the writing of the two letters a change of circumstances had taken place among these people. Whereas the first letter had been written to prepare them for suffering, perhaps at the hands of an unfriendly government (1:7; 2:12-15; 3:14-17; 4:3-4, 12-16; 5:8-10), the second letter warns against the encroachments of false teachers (2:1-3, 10-15, 19-22; 3:3-7, 15-17). These false teachers are likened to the false prophets who arose among the people in Old Testament times, whose teachings are characterized by deception, arrogance, caricature, scorn, and earthly-mindedness. For such Peter prophesies a sure and early doom, as well as for all who succumb to their pernicious influence. It is worthy of note that these false teachers made their greatest effort and appeal among recent converts to Christ, who had not attained to sufficient maturity and stability to ward off their enticements (2:18-20). To these people Peter addressed an encouraging word to persevere in their faith (1:12; 3:1-4, 17-18) and a warning as to their judgment and doom if they returned to their former lusts (1:9; 2:20-22). Such conditions, along with the anticipation of his soon-coming death (1:13-15) and the return of Christ (3:3-13), made for a strong sense of urgency in Peter's letter to them.

Peter does not say where he was when he wrote this letter, but at least some of the relevant data suggest Rome. He was expecting his death soon (1:14). Tradition sometimes claims that Peter and Paul may have labored together in Rome before becoming martyrs during the reign of Nero.[2] For this view there is some internal evidence as well (3:1, 15).

C. Date

The date of writing is bound up in the matter of Petrine authorship, which is here accepted as true. It follows then that, if Peter wrote this Epistle, he did so after writing I Peter (II Pet. 3:1), after Paul had become well-known among Christians of that

[2]For more extended discussion of this matter, see M. C. Tenney, *New Testament Survey* (Grand Rapids: Wm. B. Eerdmans Pub. Co., 1961), pp. 36 ff.; S. A. Cartledge, *A Conservative Introduction to the New Testament* (Grand Rapids: Zondervan Publishing House, 1941), p. 175; E. F. Harrison, *Introduction to the New Testament* (Grand Rapids: Wm. B. Eerdmans Publishing Co., 1964), p. 481; A. E. Barnett, *The New Testament, Its Making and Meaning* (New York: Abingdon-Cokesbury Press, 1946), p. 271.

day (3:15-16), on the eve of an outbreak of heretical teaching (2:1-3), and shortly before Peter's death (1:14-15). As a result of these internal evidences, the date of writing usually is placed in the period of A.D. 65 to 67. The following statement by Merrill C. Tenney is the consensus of a number of reputable New Testament scholars:

> It was his [Peter's] last extant work sent shortly before his death to the churches with which he had communicated in his first epistle. The threat of persecution seems to have passed away, for the suffering of Christians is not stressed at all. Perhaps if the epistle were dispatched from Rome about A. D. 65 to 67, Peter realized that the disturbance which originally threatened to affect the provinces had proved to be local in its scope: new problems had arisen that demanded attention; the danger to his churches was now less from without than it was from within.[8]

D. Distinctive Characteristics of Second Peter

One distinctive feature of this letter is the number of oft-used words in Peter's vocabulary. There are ten references to *right, righteous,* or *righteousness* (1:1, 13; 2:5, 8 twice, 9, 15 twice, 21; 3:13), and seventeen references to *knowledge* and *understanding* (1:2, 3, 5, 6, 8, 12, 14, 16, 20; 2:9, 20, 21 twice; 3:3, 16, 17, 18). Sixteen references are made to Jesus Christ as Saviour, Lord, and Master (1:1, 2, 8, 11, 14, 16; 2:1, 9, 11, 20; 3:2, 8, 9, 10, 15, 18), and five to godliness (1:3, 6, 7; 2:9; 3:11) in contrast to ungodliness (2:5-6; 3:7). The five calls to remember (1:12, 13, 15; 3:1, 2) point to Peter's teaching that, added to the knowledge of Jesus Christ as Saviour and Lord, there need to be frequent reminders to advance in a life of righteousness and godliness, lest Christians lapse into ungodliness. This is well summarized in the last two verses of the letter: "Ye therefore, beloved, seeing ye know these things before, beware lest ye also, being led away with the error of the wicked, fall from your own stedfastness. But grow in grace, and in the knowledge of our Lord and Saviour Jesus Christ" (3:17-18).

Another distinctive of this letter is the heavy reliance upon the transfiguration of Christ as a validation of the prophetic and apostolic message (1:16-18). Peter regards the Incarnation as the very epitome of the meaning of the person and work of Christ. He is the central Figure of prophecy (1:19-21), the very Pattern and Program of truth. Hence it is no surprise that before launch-

[8] *Op. cit.*, p. 368; cf. also Cartledge, *op. cit.*, pp. 174-75; Harrison, *op. cit.*, p. 401; Thiessen, *op. cit.*, p. 291; A. T. Robertson, *Word Pictures in the New Testament* (New York: Harper and Brothers, 1933), VI, 144.

ing into an exposé of false teachers, Peter reminded his readers of his own place at the Mount of Transfiguration. As a result he did not hesitate to denounce as pernicious heresy untruth that was sure to destroy Christian piety and purity (2:1-2, 11, 13-14, 18-19).

The discerning reader also is impressed with the large place Old Testament history has in this letter. The fall of angels (2:4), the Flood (2:5; 3:5-7), the destruction of Sodom and Gomorrah (2:6), and Lot's deliverance (2:7) are cited in rapid succession as proof that God's acts in the past underwrite the certainty of prophecy for the future. Peter is very sure that prophecy is the history of the future, whether he is talking about false prophets foreshadowing false teachers, or local judgments foreshadowing the final judgment, or scoffers of the past foreshadowing the scoffers of the present and future.

Peter's apocalypticism, present in his first letter also, is a distinguishing mark of the Second Epistle. In contrast to the theory that all history moves by steady and uninterrupted strides, Peter insists that the Flood, happening with sudden and catastrophic awesomeness, was nothing less than a terrifying intervention of divine judgment. He writes also that God will once again intervene in judgment, only this time by a fiery holocaust. For such an impending judgment Peter insists upon immediate readiness, lest his readers be caught unawares (3:11).

Finally, it is a unique feature of this letter to acknowledge the writings of a fellow apostle as having the status of Scripture. Even though the "beloved brother Paul" wrote "some things hard to be understood, which they that are unlearned and unstable wrest . . . unto their own destruction," yet he is a valid interpreter of "the longsuffering of our Lord" by reason of "the wisdom given unto him." Thus Peter puts Paul's writings alongside "the other scriptures" and thereby accords them a place in the canon, a deserved recognition indeed.

E. Theological Emphases

In keeping with the general teaching of Scripture, Peter asserts the righteousness of God as the basis for obtaining the "precious faith" common to all "through the knowledge of God, and of Jesus our Lord" (1:1-2). Likewise Peter affirms the depravity of fallen mankind, describing it as "the corruption that is in the world through lust" (1:4). Deliverance from the effects of the Fall comes by the knowledge of God and by becoming a partaker of the divine nature through faith (1:4-5). This deliverance is preserved by an active application of the faith principle to the promotion and enlargement of the Christian life (1:5-11).

In the second chapter Peter reiterates a teaching found often in Scripture, i.e., the sure and final doom of all who walk in an ungodly way (2:4-9). This is true even though some may have enjoyed brief liberation from "the pollutions of the world" before becoming entangled and overcome again (2:18-22). Likewise, the emphasis upon the Lord's return in judgment, as taught by Peter in 3:10-13, is a matter held in common with the rest of Scripture.

At the same time, however, Peter contributes some theological teaching that is not presented anywhere else with equal explicitness. His declaration that "prophecy came not in old time by the will of man: but holy men of God spake as they were moved by the Holy Ghost" (1:21), is one of the most definitive passages on inspiration in the New Testament. In unequivocal terms, Peter declares that Old Testament prophecy is not the work or word of man, but the Word of God, and that it is to be accepted as "a light that shineth in a dark place" (1:19).

Also, Peter's eschatological teaching answers the perplexing question of the seeming delay in the Lord's return. To those who may have been disappointed that the Lord had not returned in their day, and to the scoffers who could not conceive of any interruption in the orderly process of nature, Peter answered by pointing out that God had broken the uniform processes of the past by a flood and would do so again by fire. The delay of Christ's return was not due to a false prophecy, but was rather a sign of God's desire to give man a longer opportunity to repent (3:8-9). Nevertheless the divine control of the end-time is as sure as the divine initiation of the beginning.

Although there may be some allusions to the experience of Christian holiness (1:3-4), the main emphases are upon its expression (3:11-14) and expansion (1:5-11). Also, Peter waxes indignant against false teachers whose strategy was to exploit holy things for their own evil purposes (2:10-18). Perhaps the lack of spiritual stability on the part of those deceived (2:14, 18-22) was due in part to their lack of the full measure of inward sanctity, but Peter does not say this explicitly. Rather, he attributes their extreme susceptibility to the misleading influences of false teachers and to their being relatively new in the Christian life (2:14, 18, 20-22). This is one more reason for the spiritual regimen enjoined (1:5-11), and besought (3:17-18).

Although explicit references to entire sanctification are not as numerous here as in some other parts of the New Testament, it is against the backdrop of understanding Christianity as a holy religion that Peter writes. The knowledge of God has a holy effect upon man (1:4). The steadfast pursuit of Christian discipline intensifies the knowledge of holy things (1:8-11). The majesty and glory of Jesus Christ made the site of the Transfiguration a "holy mount" (1:18). The Holy Spirit moved upon holy men to declare the prophecies of the Old Testament (1:20-21). It is away from a holy walk that heretical teachers have turned some recent converts to Christianity (2:21), thus bringing upon themselves the judgment and wrath of a holy God (2:9-10). It is the word of holy prophets and apostles that warned of scoffers (3:2-3), and nothing short of a life of "holy conversation and godliness" is adequate for the future (3:11-12). Thus Peter admonishes us to be found of the Lord "in peace, without spot, and blameless" (3:14)—hallmarks of a holy life in any age.

Outline

I. Salutation, 1:1-2
  A. The Addresser, 1:1*a*
  B. Those Addressed, 1:1*b*
  C. The Acknowledgment, 1:2

II. The Grace and Knowledge of God, 1:3-21
  A. Exhortation to Christian Growth, 1:3-11
  B. A Call to Remembrance, 1:12-15
  C. The Truth of the Prophetic Word, 1:16-21

III. Grace and Knowledge Imperiled by False Teachers, 2:1-22
  A. False Teachers Foretold, 2:1-3
  B. False Teachers Reserved for Punishment, 2:4-10*a*
  C. False Teachers Characterized, 2:10*b*-16
  D. False Teachers and Their Victims, 2:17-22

IV. The Promise of Christ's Coming, 3:1-18
  A. Denial of the Lord's Coming, 3:1-7
  B. Delay of the Lord's Coming, 3:8-10
  C. Demands of the Lord's Coming, 3:11-13
  D. Diligence Needed for the Lord's Coming, 3:14-16
  E. Concluding Summary and Exhortation, 3:17-18

Section I *Salutation*

II Peter 1:1-2

A. The Addresser, 1:1*a*

The author introduces himself as **Simon Peter, a servant and an apostle of Jesus Christ.** Peter is known in the New Testament by four names: Peter (Matt. 16:18), Simeon (Acts 15:14), Simon (John 1:41), and Cephas (John 1:42). **Simon** is the Greek form of the Hebrew proper name, Symeon, and was the name by which Peter was known to his friends in everyday life. Cephas is the Aramaic synonym of the Greek *Petros,* which is translated into English as **Peter;** and it means a stone or rock.[4]

The word translated **servant** (*doulos*) literally means one who was in entire bondage to another. Paul refers to himself by the same word in Rom. 1:1 and Titus 1:1.[5] As an **apostle,** Peter stressed the fact that he had been sent by **Jesus Christ,** and therefore spoke with special authority.[6]

B. Those Addressed, 1:1*b*

Peter addressed himself **to them that have obtained like precious faith with us,** which is translated in the RSV, "to those who have obtained a faith of equal standing with ours." The Greek word here (*isotimos*) is a compound adjective (*isos,* equal; *time,* honor, price) and is used only here in the New Testament.[7] Hence the faith which these people have obtained is equal in honor and privilege with that of Peter or any of the apostles. Peter refers to those who once had been Gentiles as now having a faith equal to Jews, for both are saved **through the righteousness of God and our Saviour Jesus Christ;** that is, through faith in Jesus Christ, who is truly righteous (I John 1:9). The righteous God and Jesus Christ are the same person, as Paul

[4]J. A. Huffman, *Golden Treasures from the Greek New Testament* (Winona Lake: Standard Press, 1951), p. 106.

[5]Gerhard Kittel, *Theological Dictionary of the New Testament,* trans. G. F. Bromiley (Grand Rapids: Wm. B. Eerdmans Pub. Co., 1964), II, 261-80.

[6]G. C. Morgan, *Peter and the Church* (New York: Fleming H. Revell Co., 1938), pp. 11 ff.

[7]A. T. Robertson, *op. cit.,* p. 147.

notes in Titus 2:13, "Looking for that blessed hope, and the glorious appearing of the great God and our Saviour Jesus Christ."

It is evident then that, whereas the First Epistle was addressed to those of the Dispersion (I Pet. 1:1), this letter was more general, having in mind especially those who had once been despised but who are now given citizenship in the kingdom of God. Peter had learned his lesson concerning the equal privileges of Gentiles with Jews and, despite a brief lapse (Gal. 2:11-14), taught accordingly (Acts 11—15).

C. The Acknowledgment, 1:2

Not only does Peter accept these Gentiles as Christians, but he also acknowledges that **grace and peace** have been given to them, and he prays that it may **be multiplied . . . through the knowledge of God, and of Jesus our Lord.** Thus Peter wishes that this beneficent state may increase, and he explains how it comes to pass. **Grace and peace** increase as we move forward in our **knowledge of God,** for Christian experience is never static.

The word for **knowledge** in the Greek is *gnosis,* but Peter adds the prefix *epi,* which means "additional, full, certain, sure, and personal."[8] Wesley refers to it as "the divine, experimental knowledge of God and of Christ."[9] Peter is teaching here that Christianity means nothing less than a rich and growing personal knowledge of God by reason of our relationship to Jesus Christ. Such knowledge is not mere abstract speculation, because it is of a living Person. Here is a distinct characteristic of this Epistle, and, as was noted in the Introduction, a matter of repeated emphasis. The admonition to "grow in grace, and in the knowledge of our Lord and Saviour Jesus Christ," is Peter's final word (3:18). The apostle's emphasis on the grace and knowledge of God is everywhere present, either by implication or by explicit reference, in each section of the body of the Epistle.

[8]J. H. Thayer, *A Greek-English Lexicon of the New Testament* (New York: American Book Company, 1889), p. 237.

[9]*Explanatory Notes upon the New Testament* (London: The Epworth Press, reprinted 1958), p. 890.

Section II *The Grace and Knowledge of God*

II Peter 1:3-21

A. Exhortation to Christian Growth, 1:3-11

The prayer for the multiplication of grace and peace through the knowledge of God and Christ (2) is now to be treated by Peter in a systematic manner. In logical order he notes the divine resources, the steps involved in growth, the benefits, a call to remembrance, and the assurance that growth in the knowledge of God is growth in truth.

1. *A Review of the Divine Resources* (1:3-4)

The apostle makes an extraordinary claim concerning Christ. It is **his divine power** (which) **hath given unto us all things that pertain unto life and godliness** (3). Peter had seen the power of Christ calm the stormy sea and enable him to walk on the water (Matt. 14:22-23); he had heard the resurrected Christ make the claim that all power was given to Him in heaven and on earth (Matt. 28:18); he had received the power of Christ into his life by the sanctifying baptism of the Spirit of Pentecost (Acts 1:8; 2:4); and he knew, with Paul, that Christ was the power of God (I Cor. 1:24). Hence, as Wesley said, "There is a wonderful cheerfulness in the [exhortation]."[10]

The word for **power** (*dynamis*) indicates a steady, dynamic energy residing in Christ by virtue of His nature as divine.[11]

Not only is there power in Christ, but it is that same power that has made available **all things that pertain unto life and godliness.** His gifts are granted for the purpose of helping us live godly lives; that is, lives that veer more and more toward God and holy things. However, this power is made available to mankind only **through the knowledge of him that hath called us to glory and virtue.** Here the mediatorial work of Christ at the right hand of the Father (Heb. 1:13) is recognized.

Included in the **all things** given are **exceeding great and precious promises** (4), that is, promises which are superlatively great and of inestimable value. These are so great, in fact, that

[10]*Ibid.*

[11]Thayer, *op. cit.*, pp. 158-60.

by believing them we may actually escape **the corruption that is in the world through lust** and reach the zenith of human expectation, becoming **partakers of the divine nature.** Such is the meaning of fellowship with God in Christ by the Holy Spirit!

The core idea of these two verses is that within the divine nature there reside moral and spiritual energies (power) sufficient to make for life and piety. These energies are expressed in terms of specific promises. In order for man to have life and piety, he must realize within himself these very energies which reside in the Godhead. This takes place as a result of a faith relation to those promises. Through faith we receive a knowledge, a partaking, a communion in the **divine nature** as shared with man by God in Christ. When this happens, man is saved from **corruption**—an exalted privilege indeed! He is brought into communion with God—an even greater privilege—and ushered into the ethical sphere to which Peter turns our attention next.

2. *Responsibility for Supplementing Faith* (1:5-7)

Far from being quiescent or passive, the faith principle actually launches one into the throes of endless ethical endeavor: **And beside this, giving all diligence, add to your faith virtue** (5). As the RSV says, "For this very reason make every effort to supplement your faith with virtue." Faith is the root of the Christian life; works are the fruit of faith; or, to use another analogy, faith is the foundation upon which to build the edifice of love. As Wesley said, "Our diligence is to follow the gift of God, and is followed by an increase of all His gifts."[12]

The word **add** means to supply or superadd. It comes from a compound word *epichorigeo,* meaning "to join to, to furnish one thing after another, so that there be no want or chasm," and was used in Grecian arts with the meaning "to lead a chorus." Thus Peter urges us to add one thing after another in a beautiful order until the chorus is complete and the Christian life is fully equipped with every virtue. And each grace gained helps bring to perfection the other graces.

Virtue means excellence, courage, or moral goodness. It is valor accrued in the discharge of Christian duty. This is moral power developed by standing true in the test.

The next step upward is to add **knowledge**—the knowledge of God, of divine things in general; that is, a seasoned moral

[12]*Op. cit., ad loc.*

wisdom that comes as a result of living by faith. And to this is added **temperance** (6), which is self-control, both inward and outward, in the use of all things lawful.[13] To this is added **patience,** which in the original language means endurance or steadfastness in faith during trial and suffering[14] (Rom. 5:3-5). This, as developed in faith, leads on to **godliness,** which, according to Cremer, means "the recognition of dependence upon the gods, the confession of human dependence, the tribute of homage, which man renders in the certainty that he needs their favour."[15] Thus, in Christian usage it means piety, reverence, a state of soul in which the individual seeks to conform to the mind of God in all things, by the power of the Holy Spirit within. It follows, then, that on the basis of piety one supplies **brotherly kindness,** which means "love to a brother in the Christian faith,"[16] and refers back to I Pet. 1:2, 13, 22; 2:7; 3:7; 4:10. It is admonished by Paul (Rom. 12:10) and John as well (I John 4:20-21).

The entire process comes to climax and completion when to brotherly love is added **charity** or agape-love, which manifests itself not only to the Christian community but also to God, to all mankind, "and to the whole creation, animate and inanimate."[17] It is what Wesley called "the pure and perfect love of God and of all mankind."[18]

3. *The Results of Supplementing Faith* (1:8-11)

Peter insists that **if these things be in you, and abound,** four results will follow. They could be called "The Blessings of Growing in Grace." (1) Increased fruitfulness—we **shall neither be barren** (idle) **nor unfruitful in the knowledge of our Lord Jesus Christ**, 8; (2) Sustained perspective, enabling us to continue to **see afar off,** 9; (3) An assured perseverance—**for if ye do these things, ye shall never fall,** 10; and (4) A promised promotion

[13]Marvin R. Vincent, *Word Studies in the New Testament* (New York: Charles Scribner's Sons, 1908), I, 679.

[14]R. H. Strachan, "Second Epistle General of Peter," *The Expositor's Greek Testament* (Grand Rapids: Wm. B. Eerdmans Publishing Co., n.d.), V, 126.

[15]*Biblico-Theological Lexicon of New Testament Greek* (Edinburgh: T. & T. Clark, 1896), p. 524.

[16]W. F. Arndt and F. W. Gingrich, *A Greek-English Lexicon of the New Testament* (Chicago: The University of Chicago Press, 1952), p. 866.

[17]Strachan, *op. cit.*, p. 127. [18]*Op. cit.*, p. 891.

into the everlasting kingdom of our Lord and Saviour Jesus Christ, 11.

If we fail to add to our faith we shall become idle, and spiritual failures. Thus both positively and negatively, strong injunctions bear upon the Christian believer to **give diligence** to make his **calling and election sure** (10). The faith-principle leads inevitably into the faith-process, and both are for the sake of the continuing faith-perspective of our final promotion into the faith-promised Kingdom. Here are the clearly stated "principles of preservation"[19] which no Christian can neglect, except at the peril of the soul's eternal well-being. A human condition, **if ye do these things,** is to be met before the divine promise, **ye shall never fall,** is fulfilled.

B. A Call to Remembrance, 1:12-15

Strong reasons prompted Peter to alert his readers to the need of perseverance. (*a*) He would **not be negligent to put** them **always in remembrance of these things** (12). Even though they were well **established in the present truth** ("the truth which is present with you," NASB), diligent practice in that faith would lead on to higher truth which must be embraced also. (*b*) He saw the power for continuing progress of **putting** them **in remembrance** (13) of what they already knew. (*c*) In the light of his impending death he was concerned to put these counsels into the permanent form of writing in order that, after his death, they might have them **always in remembrance** (15). Thus three times Peter said he would have them to be **in remembrance** (12, 13, 15). And still another strong reason follows, namely, (*d*) the truth of what was believed, which is noted in 16-21. **I think it meet** (13; i.e., fitting). **Tabernacle** (13-14) would be Peter's earthly body.

C. The Truth of the Prophetic Word, 1:16-21

The strong call to action is followed by an equally strong affirmation that **we have not followed** out **cunningly devised fables** (16; artfully formed myths devised by human cleverness), such as were common among the heathen, **when . . . the power** (*dynamis*) **and coming** (*parousia*) **of . . . Christ** were **made**

[19]G. C. Morgan, *The Analyzed Bible* (New York: Fleming H. Revell Co., 1908), p. 291.

known. Peter, James, and John were **eyewitnesses of his majesty** at the Transfiguration (cf. Matt. 17:1-13). These men were influenced to the end of their ministry by that vision. James died a martyr for his testimony; John said they beheld His glory (I John 1:14); and Peter insisted that they heard God say, **This is my beloved Son** (17). Thus their vision of Christ's majesty and God's voice affirming Christ's sonship were true evidences that distinguished the incarnation of the Second Person of the Godhead from the spurious claims of heathen myths about the descent of their gods to earth.[20]

To these evidences Peter adds a third: **We have also a more sure word of prophecy** ("And we have the prophetic word made firmer still," Amp. NT). Interpreters disagree as to whether Peter meant (1) that the **sure word of prophecy** was a better evidence than what was seen and heard on the Mount of Transfiguration, or (2) that the Transfiguration scene confirmed the Messianic prophecies and made clear the deity of Jesus Christ as God's beloved Son. Vincent holds to the former and Robertson to the latter.[21] Strachan translates it in a way that honors both positions. "Thus we have still further confirmation of the words of the prophets, a fact to which you would do well to give heed, as to a lamp shining in a murky place, meant to serve until the Day break, and the Day-star arise in your hearts."[22] Either way the net effect is the same. The prophetic word is attested as true by the transfiguration of the Son, wherein Christ's power to triumph over sin and death is declared, and His coming again in honor and glory is previewed. Thus the prophetic word, with its central reference to the Messiah of promise, is **a light that shineth in a dark place.** It was such before, during, and after Christ's first coming; it is ever such **until the day dawn, and the day star arise in your hearts** (19).

But Peter adds a final reason for affirming the truth of the prophetic word—its divine origin. **Knowing this first**—that is, recognizing this truth above all else—**that no prophecy of the scripture is of any private interpretation**—proceeds from the prophet's own knowledge or invention, or was the offspring of calculation or conjecture.[23] This seems to be a reference to the

[20]Vincent, *op. cit.*, p. 685. [21]*Ibid.*, p. 687; Robertson, *op. cit.*, p. 157.

[22]*Op. cit.*, p. 131.

[23]Adam Clarke, *The New Testament of Our Lord and Saviour Jesus Christ* (New York: Abingdon-Cokesbury Press, n.d.), II, 883.

methods of some false teachers to disparage the Old Testament as merely the works of men. As Robertson points out, it is the prophet's grasp of the prophecy, not that of the readers, that is presented here, because "no prophecy of Scripture comes out of private disclosure."[24] This is not to say, however, that the ordinary believer cannot confidently interpret the Bible without the help of professional scholars. Rather, it is to say that, since Scripture was given by the agency of the Holy Spirit (21), it must be interpreted with the assistance of the Holy Spirit. This is Peter's answer to those who interpreted Scripture so as to make it serve their own ends.[25] Divine illumination is the necessary corollary of divine inspiration. Otherwise, private prejudice rules and the enemy of all error, the Holy Scripture, is used in the defense of error.

The reason for the statement in 20 is found in 21. **For** (*gar*) **the prophecy came not in old time by the will of man.** That is, true prophecy is not of private origination nor the result of human impulse. If the previous verse denies man the ultimate right to interpret Scripture according to his own proud cleverness or sinful prejudice, the present verse denies that the presence of Scripture in our midst is due to human initiative. **But** (i.e., in contrast to the wrong idea about the origin of Scripture) **holy men of God spake . . . moved by the Holy Ghost** (21). Scripture came into being because "men moved by the Spirit spake from God" (RSV). (The best texts omit **holy,** and read "from God." Thus it is correct to render it as "men moved by the Spirit spake from God.")

The word for **moved** (*pheromenoi,* the present passive participle form of *phero*) means "impelled, moved upon, carried, or borne along."[26] Thus the divine initiative in producing Scripture was actualized by the determining and constraining influence of the Holy Spirit on select human agents. This is strong evidence for the plenary inspiration of the Holy Scriptures, and their entire trustworthiness as a result. Men spoke because the Spirit impelled and not vice versa. A supernatural influence was brought to bear upon divinely chosen men, in consequence of

[24]*Op. cit.,* pp. 158-59.

[25]E. E. Cochrane, *The Epistles of Peter* (Grand Rapids: Baker Book House, 1965), p. 87.

[26]Arndt and Gingrich, *op. cit.,* pp. 862-63. Cf. Cremer, *op. cit.,* p. 688; Thayer, *op. cit.,* pp. 650-51.

which that which they uttered, orally and then in writing, was altogether dependable and authoritative.[27]

Yet it must not be overlooked that the word for **men** (*anthropoi*) appears at the end of the Greek sentence. This gives it a position of emphasis and brings the human agent into prominence. It was the Holy Spirit who **moved;** it was **men** who spoke. This gives the Scripture a relatedness and a relevance to men that could not have been so apart from the use of human agency. Thus Paul could say that "all scripture is given by inspiration of God, and is profitable . . . that the man of God may be perfect" (II Tim. 3:16-17). These inspired writings, as confirmed by the incarnate and transfigured Christ, give Peter, and us, the needed assurance that Christianity is a divinely revealed religion, that it is trustworthy and authoritative, and that its truthfulness may be acted upon with all confidence in the power of a forward-moving faith.

We see in 19-21 "The More Sure Word of Prophecy": (1) It has the power to illuminate, 19; (2) It must not be interpreted according to private views and opinions, 20; (3) It did not originate by human impulse, but by the impelling and moving work of the Holy Spirit, 21.

[27]A helpful discussion of this passage is given by Carl F. H. Henry in an article entitled "Inspiration" in *Baker's Bible Dictionary,* pp. 286-89.

Section III *Grace and Knowledge Imperiled by False Teachers*

II Peter 2:1-22

A. False Teachers Foretold, 2:1-3

Having referred to the misuse of the "prophecy of the scripture" (1:20), Peter proceeds to expose the peril of **false teachers.** In the manner of the **false** (pseudo) **prophets** in Old Testament times (Deut. 13:1-5; Isa. 28:7; Jer. 6:13-14; Ezek. 13:9-10; Mic. 3:11) these persons **privily** (secretly, like a traitor in the camp) **shall bring in** (into the Church) **damnable heresies**—that is, "heresies marked by destruction."[28] By such heresies the **false teachers** are "disowning the very master who bought them, and bringing swift disaster on their own heads" (NEB).

Vincent notes that the word translated **heresies** means a choice. Thus, "a heresy is, strictly, the choice of an opinion contrary to that usually received; thence transferred to the body of those who profess such opinions, and therefore *a sect.*"[29] The nature of these sectarian movements is to propagate heretical teachings, to prey on existing congregations for their adherents, and to create divisions, thus disrupting the work of Christ in the world, and "turning the grace of . . . God into lasciviousness" (Jude 4). No wonder, then, that heretical teaching has been a prime tool of Satan to sow seeds of discord and to stifle the progress of world evangelism (Matt. 13:24-30). No wonder, either, that the apostles denounced it in vehement fashion, for heretical teaching is usually the insidious enemy of holiness and righteousness! Such heresy is dangerous because the sanctification of the human spirit is by the belief of the divine truth (II Thess. 2:13). Thus, to believe a lie, however innocently propagated, is to incur the risk of eventual damnation (II Thess. 2:9-12). The strong affinity between heresy and depraved morality, as seen in this chapter, illustrates the reciprocal encouragement each gives the other—both of them acting as cause and effect. The criterion for detecting heresy in Christian teaching is whether or not it denies the lordship of Jesus Christ. Such teaching is

[28]Robertson, *op. cit.*, p. 160.

[29]*Op. cit.*, p. 689.

either a deliberate or an unintended repudiation of revealed truth, accepting contradictory positions in its stead.

The fact **that many shall follow their pernicious ways** (2; "lascivious doings," RSV) is evidence that the heart of man, apart from divine grace, is exceedingly prone to corruption and error. Deceived people cause **the way of truth** (to) **be evil spoken of.** The danger is ever present because of the effort of false teachers to **make merchandise** (take advantage of) God's people by **feigned** (forged) **words.** The **covetousness** (3; insatiate craze) of the heretical leaders has been interpreted by some as the desire for financial gain, and by others as the eagerness to win followers. In either case the motivation is self-centered instead of Christ-centered. To both leaders and followers, Peter gives warning of a **judgment** that **now of a long time lingereth not** and of a **damnation** (destruction) that has long been gathering momentum but is now impending.

B. False Teachers Reserved for Punishment, 2:4-10*a*

The end of false teachers, in terms of "judgment" and "damnation" (3), is a statement of prophecy, but it is as sure as history. Peter cites four examples, three of retribution and one of preservation, to enforce his argument of things to come. **If God spared not the angels that sinned** (4); and if He **spared not the old world, but saved Noah** (5); and if He **burned the cities of Sodom and Gomorrha into ashes** (6); and if He **delivered just Lot** (7), then **the Lord knoweth how to deliver the godly out of temptations** (trials), **and to reserve the unjust unto the day of judgment to be punished** (9). The form of judgment may be casting **down to hell** (*tartarosas,* only here in NT)[30] and delivering **into chains of darkness** ("pits of nether gloom," RSV), as in the case of fallen angels; or by **flood,** as was true of the world of Noah's day; or by turning **cities . . . into ashes,** as Sodom and Gomorrah. But the fact of judgment upon sinful persons is sure. To this list Peter adds false teachers and their victims, who, if they do not repent (3:9), will perish in judgment also (3). This class of persons is described as "those who indulge the flesh in its corrupt desires and despise authority" (10, NASB).

The judgment of God is not only sure and severe, but also selective. Some angels did not fall; Noah and his immediate fam-

[30]*Tartarus* was the Greek name for a subterranean place lower than Hades where the wicked dead were punished.

ily were saved; Lot was saved out of Sodom. Thus the Lord knows who is doomed and who is to be delivered, and He knows how to keep each for his proper eternal abode. **The eighth person** (5) means "with seven other persons" (RSV). Phillips' rendering of v. 7 is, "Lot, remember, was a good man suffering spiritual agonies day after day at what he saw and heard of their lawlessness."

C. False Teachers Characterized, 2:10*b*-16

1. *Audacity* (2:10*b*-11)

Peter indicates that false teachers are characterized by being **presumptuous** (10; excessive in daring) and **selfwilled** (possessed of a self-loving and a self-sufficient attitude), who do not tremble to **speak evil of** (blaspheme) **dignities** ("the glories of the unseen world," Phillips). In contrast **angels,** who excel **in power and might** (11), do not pronounce a **railing accusation** (blasphemous judgment) even **against them** (evil angels) **before the Lord** (cf. Jude 9).

2. *Animality* (2:12-14)

The reason for the audacity of false teachers is found in their animality. **As natural** (irrational) **brute beasts** (12), they are born for capture and destruction like beasts of prey. Their brutishness is evidenced in the fact that they **speak evil** (blaspheme) **of the things that they understand not** (matters of which they are ignorant). They pose as spiritual experts when in reality they are ignorant of the things of God. Alas for them, they **shall utterly perish in their own corruption.** In their destroying they shall surely be destroyed; being unrighteous they **shall receive** the wages of iniquity (13). But Peter has not finished. Their animality is expressed further in counting it pleasure **to riot** (revel) even **in the day time.** Such professing Christians are **spots . . . and blemishes** on the Christian community. The last part of 13 has been interpreted, "deceiving you by living in foul sin on the side while they join your love feasts as though they were true men" (LL). Because their **eyes** are **full of adultery** (14), they cannot see a woman without lustful thoughts toward her. In fact they are so far enmeshed that they **cannot cease from sin** (are unable to stop sinning), because they have by **covetous practices** actually trained their hearts in evil desires.

No wonder, then, that they are **cursed children** ("under a curse," Phillips). They are under God's curse now, and are heirs of doom in the world to come.

3. *Avarice* (2:15-16)

To their audacity and animality Peter adds a third sin—their avarice. They **have forsaken the right way** (15), because they **loved the wages of unrighteousness;** "they have plunged into Balaam's error for pay" (Jude 11, NEB). The comparison of the false teachers to Balaam is indicative of their motives (cf. Numbers 22—23). Balaam earnestly desired the money which Balak would have given him for cursing Israel. He refrained from taking it only because he **was rebuked for his iniquity** (by) **the dumb ass** (16). These false teachers, however, had no such external hindrance, and lacking inner compunction, they were ready to accept "gain from wrong doing" (RSV).

D. False Teachers and Their Victims, 2:17-22

To say that false teachers are like **wells without water,** or **clouds that are carried with a tempest,** for whom is **reserved** "the fate of gloomy darkness" (17),[31] is to speak of their disappointing emptiness. To say of these teachers that they **speak great swelling words of vanity,** and that **they allure through the lusts of the flesh** (18) with the **promise** of **liberty,** although **they themselves are the servants of corruption** (19), is to speak of their depraving enticements. To both teacher and follower, Peter speaks a solemn word of warning. For those who have **escaped** the miasma of sin **through the knowledge of . . . Christ,** and **are again entangled therein . . . the latter end is worse . . . than the** first (20). To know the way of righteousness is to know the way of responsibility. Thus for one who has known the joy of salvation to **turn from the holy commandment** (21) is to sin against more light, and hence to be liable to more punishment than he would have been formerly. To go from conversion to reversion is like a dog that **is turned to his own vomit again** (cf. Prov. 26:11), or like **the sow that was washed to her wallowing in the mire** (22). Such is the determined end of those who persistently turn away from Christ after once having known Him.

[31]Strachan, *op. cit.*, p. 140.

Section IV *The Promise of Christ's Coming*

II Peter 3:1-18

Turning from the libertines and their victims, Peter proposes once again to rouse his readers to serious reflection on the words spoken by the holy prophets, and by the apostles of the Lord. The readers' minds were **pure** ("sincere," ASV) but still they needed to **be mindful.** No state of grace this side of heaven exempts men from the need of repeated reminders of the truths of the Christian message, and all of this becomes the more urgent in the light of Christ's imminent return to earth.

In Peter's time, as now, there were varied reactions to the message of Christ's return. Some denied that it would happen; others wondered about the delay; still others believed it, but perhaps failed to give sufficient heed to its demands for a holy life, and to its call for diligence in Christian pursuits. To each of these Peter gave a timely word, insisting as he did so that the unity of Scripture, with its centrality upon Christ, made it possible to appeal to both Old and New Testaments for his authority and urgency.

A. Denial of the Lord's Coming, 3:1-7

Although the denial of the Lord's coming is a sin of unbelievers, the believer is affected by their ridicule. Consequently Peter deemed it necessary to remind his readers that both **the holy prophets** and **the apostles of the Lord and Saviour** (2) had said that this event would take place.

One of the marks of the **last days** (3) will be the coming forth of **scoffers** (mockers), men who are **walking after their own lusts** ("whose only guide in life is what they want for themselves," Phillips). Such men will attempt to demolish sound doctrine by ridicule. "What has happened to his promised coming? Since the first Christians fell asleep, everything remains exactly as it was since the beginning of creation!" (4, Phillips) This kind of comment is a sample of their mockery.[32] The nub of the argument is that, if Christ had not come by their time, He would never do so.

[32]Arndt and Gingrich, *op. cit.*, p. 255.

Peter's handling of the problem included a reminder of the word previously spoken concerning this mockery by those who denied the doctrine of Christ's second coming. It also shows how he used the Word of God in refuting their ridicule. Whether sooner or later, Jesus Christ would come again. This had been specifically promised at His ascension (Acts 1:10-11), and the promise was well fortified by a theistic and supernaturalistic philosophy of history reflected in vv. 5-7. Peter's reasoning is that those who deny Christ's second coming "deliberately forget this fact: that God did destroy the world with a mighty flood, long after He had made the heavens by the word of His command, and had used the waters to form the earth and surround it. And God (this same God) has commanded that the earth and the heavens be stored away for a great bonfire at the judgment day, when all ungodly men will perish" (LL).

It is noteworthy that the doctrine of Christ's coming again became a battleground between the contending forces of naturalism and continuity on one hand and those who believed in the supernatural and the revealed on the other. In taking the biblical position, that creation does not necessarily mean endless continuance, Peter went a step further to point out that along with creation and continuity there has always been change. This is a stabilized universe, thanks to God's eternal changelessness, but it is not static. The universe owes its origin and ongoing to **the word of God** (5), which is vital and dynamic! Moreover, God's initiative in creating is proof that He can intervene in what He has created. This has already happened at Christ's first coming in the Incarnation. Thus the only logical end of the argument of unbelief, in denying the Lord's second coming, is to deny the first one also. Their denial, then, was not based on solid philosophy, or a clear-eyed perspective of history. It was based rather upon their hatred of anything supernatural, because they resented any interference to **walking after their own lusts** (3). Such is the enmity of the carnal mind against God (Rom. 8:5-8).

This answer to these who discounted the coming of Christ gave Peter an opportunity to expound some precious truths concerning God's Word. It is a creative Word (5) but it is also a destructive Word, so far as ungodliness is concerned (6). It is a Word that starts (5) and sustains creation (7), and also can stop it (6-7). It brings consternation to the wicked (5-6, 10) and comforting counsel to the beloved (1, 8, 14, 17). It speaks of God's transcendent power and being (5-10) and of His immanent participation in human affairs (9). It tells of divine forbearance and divine faithfulness. It relates the past (6) to the present (7) and the future (10). It insists that creation, judgment, and renewal in the yesterdays (5-6) is proof enough of the possibility of another such cycle in the tomorrows (7, 10, 12-13). It claims that divine activity (5-7) is the basis of human responsibility (9-12, 14). It assures us of the triumph of righteousness (13) and the truth of holiness (11, 14). No wonder our Lord insisted that "man shall not live by bread alone, but by every word that proceedeth out of the mouth of God" (Matt. 4:4)!

B. Delay of the Lord's Coming, 3:8-10

"Where is the promise of his coming?" is the question the unbeliever asks. "When is the Lord coming?" is a question for believers. Some who do not *deny* are nonetheless perplexed by the *delay*.

To the question, "Why Does the Lord Delay His Second Coming?" Peter gives a fourfold answer: (1) Delay does not mean the denial of God's word, **for the day of the Lord will come,** 10; (2) Delay does not mean the reversal of God's word, for **the Lord is not slack** (tardy, late)[33] **concerning his** purposes, 9; (3) Delay is an evidence that God exists eternally—**One day is with the Lord as a thousand years, and a thousand years as one day,** 8; (4) Delay means that God is extending mercy; He is **not willing that any should perish, but that all should come to repentance,** 9.

Although the Lord will not come one day *sooner* than the appointed time, for **one day is with the Lord as a thousand years** (8), yet it is always *soon,* for with God **a thousand years** (is) **as one day.** We are told that **the day of the Lord will come as a thief in the night** (10; cf. Matt. 24:43; I Thess. 5:2, 4; Rev. 3:3; 16:15). At that time **the heavens shall pass away with a great noise** ("shall disappear with a great rushing sound," NEB), **and the elements** (the elemental particles by which the universe is constructed)[34] **shall melt with fervent heat, the earth also and the works that are therein shall be burned up.** Whatever be the mystery as to when and how "all these things shall be dissolved" (11), the certainty remains: **The day of the Lord will come** (10).

[33]Vincent, *op. cit.*, p. 705.

[34]Wilbur M. Smith, *This Atomic Age and the Word of God* (Boston: W. A. Wilde Co., 1948), p. 131.

C. Demands of the Lord's Coming, 3:11-13

As is true everywhere in Scripture, Peter's objective is to do more than inform the mind or satisfy human curiosity; it is to incite to ethical endeavor, to inculcate the highly moral response of faith—action in terms of obedient love. Hence Peter says, **Seeing then that all these things shall be dissolved** (*luomenon,* present passive participle, but used to describe something in the future),[35] **what manner of persons** (what sort of men) **ought ye to be in all holy conversation** (manner of life) **and godliness** (piety)? Here is another illustration of the close tie between belief in the Lord's coming and the call to holiness. Anything short of holiness of heart and life spells a deficiency of preparation for the **coming of the day of God** (12).

Closely allied to the persons we ought to be is the perspective we ought to have. **Looking for** (expecting) **and hasting unto** (running toward) **the day of God.** Apparently Christians can hasten the day of God by helping to fulfill those conditions without which it cannot come—preaching the gospel to the whole world (Matt. 24:14), and calling men to repent and be converted (Acts 3:19). Such assiduous labor helps Christians to **look for** (expect) **new heavens and a new earth** (13). Our labor is encouraged further by the promise we ought to believe—the promise of a world **wherein dwelleth righteousness.** Whatever perplexities there are in the present, the future "has its home" in righteousness (Isa. 65:17 ff.; 66:22; Rev. 21:1). Believing this makes it easier to endure the vexations of unrighteousness now. Thus, as Strachan points out, "the parousia is both judgment on the wicked and triumph for the kingdom."[36]

These words were written by Peter long before the atomic age, but his description of a "great noise," of "elements" melting, etc., fits strikingly into the atomic vocabulary. Whether or not God will use atomic destruction to abolish the present order of things is impossible to say. Some think so.[37] At any rate, it is clear that there is a divine determination to bring an end to the sinful order on earth by a fiery, purifying baptism, and to prepare it for righteousness only.[38] The new creature in Christ, as described by Paul (II Cor. 5:17), is an earnest of the whole new heavens and new earth as affirmed by Peter.

[35]Strachan, *op. cit.,* p. 145.

[36]*Ibid.,* p. 146.

[37]Wilbur M. Smith, *op. cit., passim.*

[38]Huffman, *op. cit.,* p. 148

D. Diligence Needed for the Lord's Coming, 3:14-16

In a manner similar to his previous admonition (11), after another emphasis on the apocalyptic nature of "the day of God" (12), Peter repeats the emphasis on the need for personal holiness. **Be diligent** ("Do your utmost," NEB) to **be found of him in peace** (14), so you "may meet Him without terror, being sprinkled with His blood and sanctified by His Spirit."[39] This means we must be **without spot,** without moral and spiritual defilement (Eph. 5:27; Jas. 3:6; Jude 23), **and blameless,** in sincerity, without blemish or defect.[40] Verse 15*a* has been interpreted, "And remember why He is waiting. He is giving us time to get His message of salvation out to others" (LL).

This descriptive call to personal purity is followed by an appeal to study the letters of **our beloved brother Paul** (15) plus **the other scriptures** (16). Obviously Peter was acquainted with these writings too, and referred to them as *tas loipas graphas,* "the rest of the Scriptures."[41] The fact that some **wrest** (twist) them **unto their own destruction** did not mean they were to be avoided. Rather, it meant they were to be studied and applied with greater care and exactness. It is impossible to determine how many of Paul's Epistles are referred to here, but Robertson thinks Peter may have read every one of them within a month or two of their writing.[42] At any rate, Peter insists that on the question of the return of Christ he and Paul are in agreement in their teaching.

Speaking of the **unlearned and unstable** who twist the Scriptures to their own ruin, Strachan points out that the word **unlearned** (*amatheis*) "signifies not so much 'unlearned' as 'uneducated'; a mind untrained and undisciplined in habits of thought, lacking in the moral qualities of a balanced judgment."[43] The second word, **unstable** (*astariktoi*), "refers more to conduct, those whose habits are not fully trained and established."[44] The obvious and basic reason for "driving a straight furrow" in the Word of God (II Tim. 2:15, NEB) is to assure a sound Christian experience. This is to be followed by a diligent and prolonged search for truth united with a life of conscientious devotion and ethical behavior.

[39]Wesley, *op. cit.,* p. 899.

[40]George A. Turner, *The Vision Which Transforms* (Kansas City: Beacon Hill Press of Kansas City, 1965), p. 134; cf. also Thayer, *op. cit.,* pp. 31-32.

[41]Strachan, *op. cit.,* p. 147.

[42]*Op. cit.,* pp. 178-79.

[43]*Op. cit.,* p. 147.

[44]*Ibid.*

E. Concluding Summary and Exhortation, 3:17-18

The final two verses contain the essence and theme of the entire Epistle: (1) **Beware** (be on your guard) **lest ye . . . fall** (17); (2) **But grow in grace, and in the knowledge of our Lord and Saviour Jesus Christ** (18). A distinct peril has been noted; **Beware!** A call to progress has been sounded; **Grow!** False teachers and their teachings are in antagonism to the Church. The answer to their threat is to advance in the **grace** and **knowledge** of Christ. To be occupied in growing will help keep us from being overcome. To witness to the *power* (1:16) of our Lord Jesus Christ will give Him **glory . . . now;** to believe in the *coming* (1:16) of our Lord will enable us to give Him **glory . . . for ever. Amen.**

Bibliography

I. COMMENTARIES

CLARKE, ADAM. *The New Testament of Our Lord and Saviour Jesus Christ,* Vol. II. New York: Abingdon-Cokesbury Press, n.d.

COCHRANE, E. E. *The Epistles of Peter.* Grand Rapids: Baker Book House, 1965.

STRACHAN, R. H. "The Second Epistle General of Peter," *The Expositor's Greek Testament.* Grand Rapids: Wm. B. Eerdmans Publishing Co., n.d.

WESLEY, JOHN. *Explanatory Notes upon the New Testament.* London: Epworth Press, 1958 (reprint).

II. OTHER BOOKS

ARNDT, W. F., and GINGRICH, F. W. *A Greek-English Lexicon of the New Testament and Other Early Christian Literature.* Chicago: University of Chicago Press, 1952.

BARNETT, A. E. *The New Testament, Its Making and Meaning.* New York: Abingdon-Cokesbury Press, 1946.

CARTLEDGE, S. A. *A Conservative Introduction to the New Testament.* Grand Rapids: Zondervan Publishing House, 1941.

CREMER, H. *Biblico-Theological Lexicon of the New Testament.* Edinburgh: T. and T. Clark, 1896.

HARRISON, E. F. *Introduction to the New Testament.* Grand Rapids: Wm. B. Eerdmans Publishing Co., 1964.

HUFFMAN, J. A. *Golden Treasures from the Greek New Testament.* Winona Lake: Standard Press, 1951.

KITTEL, G. *Theological Dictionary of the New Testament.* Translated by G. W. BROMILEY. Grand Rapids: Wm. B. Eerdmans Publishing Co., 1964.

MORGAN, G. C. *The Analyzed Bible.* New York: Fleming H. Revell Co., 1908.

———. *Peter and the Church.* New York: Fleming H. Revell Co., 1938.

ROBERTSON, A. T. *Word Pictures in the New Testament,* Vol. VI. New York: Harper and Brothers, 1933.

SMITH, W. M. *This Atomic Age and the Word of God.* Boston: W. A. Wilde Co., 1948.

TENNEY, M. C. *New Testament Survey.* Grand Rapids: Wm. B. Eerdmans Publishing Co., 1961.

THAYER, J. H. *A Greek-English Lexicon of the New Testament.* New York: American Book Co., 1889.

THIESSEN, H. C. *Introduction to the New Testament.* Grand Rapids: Wm. B. Eerdmans Publishing Co., 1942.

TURNER, GEORGE ALLEN. *The Vision Which Transforms.* Kansas City: Beacon Hill Press of Kansas City, 1965.

VINCENT, M. R. *Word Studies in the New Testament,* Vol. I. New York: Charles Scribner's Sons, 1908.

III. ARTICLES

HARRISON, E. F. "Apostle," *Baker's Dictionary of Theology.* Grand Rapids: Wm. B. Eerdmans Publishing Co., 1960, pp. 57-59.

HENRY, CARL F. H. "Inspiration," *Baker's Dictionary of Theology.* Grand Rapids: Wm. B. Eerdmans Publishing Co., 1960, pp. 286-89.

The First Epistle of

JOHN

Harvey J. S. Blaney

Introduction

A. Prescript

The First Epistle of John is not an Epistle in the same sense as the Epistle to the Hebrews or those of Peter and James. Neither is it a letter in the style of the letters of St. Paul. It has been called an essay, a treatise, a tract, and a sermon. While it is difficult to name, it has all the marks of the work of a pastor whose purpose was the building up of his people in the faith. Other portions of the New Testament have this same purpose, but this Epistle stands out by itself. Its distinctiveness does not rest upon either its purpose or its style of writing, nor its contents, but upon the intense passion of the author. John's intimate acquaintance with his readers made unnecessary any personal salutation or reference, and his fervid love which is everywhere evident made him bold, even abrupt, in his manner of expression. "The spirit of . . . John is an imposing spirit; and one feels himself almost oppressed by the majesty of the thoughts of this Epistle, which are like heavenly music in the reader's ears."[1]

No other book of the Bible treats so many doctrines so concisely and so well. From sin and its confession through atonement and cleansing on to the life of Christian holiness, the author presents the claims of the gospel so clearly that "the wayfaring men, though fools, shall not err therein." However, it is not doctrine for the sake of a system of theology, but doctrine as the basis of fellowship with God and a life of perfect love. Theology comes to life in the children of God. The author was the last writer of the New Testament, and into this Epistle he poured the distillation of a life of communion with his risen Lord and of intimate knowledge of the other books of the New Testament. True, his memory served him well—he had *seen*, and *heard*, and *handled* "the Word of life"—but it was memory raised to the level of spiritual perception and relived in the realm of the Spirit.

"In the estimation of deeply spiritual minds the First Epistle of John holds the highest place in that series of inspired writings which constitute the Bible."[2] John Wesley called it "the deepest

[1]Erich Haupt, *The First Epistle of John* ("Clark's Foreign Theological Library"; Edinburgh: T. & T. Clark, 1893), LXV, xl.

[2]Daniel Steele, *Half Hours with St. John's Epistles* (Chicago: The Christian Witness Co., 1901), p. xxi.

part of the Holy Scripture." Robert Law saw in this Epistle three tests of life: the theological test, whether we believe that Jesus is the Son of God; the moral test, whether we are living lives of righteousness; and the social test, whether we have love one for the other.[3] The Epistle seeks to make real in the life of believers the prayer of Jesus in John 17:15, "I pray not that thou shouldest take them out of the world, but that thou shouldest keep them from the evil."

B. The Epistle and John's Gospel

Even the casual reader must be aware that the ideas of the Epistle and the Gospel, as well as their ways of expression, are similar. Dr. James Moulton says that no one with the faintest instinct of style would detach the Johannine Epistles from the Fourth Gospel.[4] To B. F. Westcott the Epistle "is so closely connected with the Fourth Gospel in vocabulary, style, thought, and scope that these two books cannot but be regarded as works of the same author."[5] William Alexander says, "The two documents not only touch each other in thought, but interpenetrate each other; thus the Epistle is constantly *suggesting* questions which the Gospel only can answer."[6]

The great similarity between the two may be seen by the comparison of a few parallel passages, the reference to the Epistle being placed first in each pair: 1:1 and 1:1; 1:2 and 3:2; 1:2 and 1:1; 1:6 and 8:12; 2:3 and 14:15; 2:5 and 14:21; 2:6 and 15:5; 2:8 and 13:34; 2:25 and 17:2. Rather extensive comparisons are given by Hayes[7] and Stott[8] for those who wish to pursue the matter more thoroughly.

C. Authorship and Date

Such close similarities, however, by no means guarantees unity of authorship. The Epistle has shared in the prolonged dis-

[3]*The Tests of Life* (Edinburgh: T. & T. Clark, 1909), p. 209.

[4]A. S. Peake (ed.), *A Commentary on the Bible* (New York: Thomas Nelson and Sons, n.d.), p. 592.

[5]*The Epistles of St. John* (London: Macmillan and Co., 1892), p. xxx.

[6]*The Epistles of St. John* ("The Expositor's Bible," ed. W. R. Nicoll; New York: Funk and Wagnalls Co., 1900), p. 75.

[7]D. A. Hayes, *John and His Writings* (New York: Methodist Book Concern, 1917), pp. 163-72.

[8]J. R. W. Stott, *The Epistles of St. John* ("The Tyndale New Testament Commentary"; Grand Rapids: Wm. B. Eerdmans Publishing Co., 1964), pp. 24-40.

cussion over the authorship of the Gospel and in the present uncertain results of that discussion among scholars. Until the sixteenth century no one seems to have doubted that the First Epistle and the Gospel were by the same author.

The arguments for the traditional view by A. E. Brooke have become more or less normative.[9] The opposite view is held by C. H. Dodd.[10] Both men agree that the ideas of the two writings as well as their ways of expression are similar. Brooke concludes that it is impossible to prove a common authorship as against imitation or similarity produced by common education in the same school of thought. But he finds no adequate reasons for setting aside the traditional view which attributes the Epistle and the Gospel to the same author—it remains the most probable explanation of the facts.

On the other hand Dodd feels that he can find evidences of difference in authorship by showing divergences of thought in the Epistle. In three ways the Epistle stands closer to popular Christian beliefs than does the Gospel: in respect of eschatology, of the significance attached to the death of Christ, and of the doctrine of the Holy Spirit. He presents his answers in the form of doubts and impressions and concludes that the Epistle was written by a disciple of the fourth Evangelist, and a diligent student of his work.

Both of these great scholars express indecisive conclusions from all their available evidence, and this inclines one to say that the chief value is not to be found in the study of the *authorship* of either the Gospel or the Epistle of John. It further inclines one to the traditional position of a single author, and this is the position taken by the present writer. A similar view is expressed by David Smith, who quotes J. B. Lightfoot for support. He says, "It is beyond reasonable doubt that the Epistle and the Gospel are from the same pen. 'The identity of authorship in the two books . . . though not undisputed, is accepted with such a degree of unanimity that it may be placed in the category of acknowledged fact.' "[11]

The argument necessary to establish the disciple John as this single author, even on a probable basis, is too long and involved

[9]*A Critical and Exegetical Commentary on the Johannine Epistles* ("The International Critical Commentary"; New York: Charles Scribner's Sons, 1912), pp. i-xix.

[10]*The Johannine Epistles* ("The Moffatt New Testament Commentary"; New York: Harper Brothers, 1946), pp. xlvii-lvi.

[11]"The Epistles of St. John," *The Expositor's Greek Testament* (New York: Hodder and Stoughton, n.d.), V, 154.

for the space here allowed. The whole problem has been surveyed quite thoroughly in my introduction to the Gospel of John in *The Wesleyan Bible Commentary*.[12] The conclusion is that no evidence has successfully dislodged the Apostle John from his traditional place as the author, and there is little fresh evidence to keep the discussion alive. John is still quite firmly established as the author of both the Gospel and the Epistle. The date of First John shares its berth with the Gospel. Probably written the latter of the two, it would be dated in the middle of the last decade of the first century, about A.D. 95.

D. Characteristics

St. John was a man of keen insight. He looked at every situation and every truth as from a great height where only the primary distinctions are seen and important cleavages are noticeable. His is a vision of perspective, the view of things fundamental. For instance, he draws a line between the world and the Church, between the sons of Satan and the sons of God. Yet he does not say that all sinners are equally sinful—sin ranges from worldly-mindedness to the sin unto death. Similarly, he sees the Christian life as one of perfect love. Yet some are borderline Christians while others are truly indwelt by the Spirit of God.

John is not unmindful of the finer nuances of truth when he fails to deal with them. By treating issues which, when settled, will incorporate other and lesser issues, he reveals a closeness to the mind of Christ and is almost inexhaustible in his implications.

This Epistle is marked by contrasts—light and darkness, life and death, saint and sinner, love and hate, Christ and antichrist.

First John is one of the most difficult books of the New Testament to analyze. If the author had an organized plan by which he wrote, it was one of inner feeling and harmonious thought rather than of formal organization. The Epistle is a work of art which reveals its form only through the responses of the one who studies it, and this has given rise to a variety of outlines. The transitions from one subject to another are not distinct but are like the "changes of dissolving views," like the developing panorama of an evening sunset which enriches the imagination and fills the soul of the beholder with spiritual riches and contentment.

[12]H. J. S. Blaney, "The Gospel According to St. John," *The Wesleyan Bible Commentary*, IV (Grand Rapids: Wm. B. Eerdmans Publishing Co., 1964), 359-64.

The Moffatt New Testament Commentary organized the Epistle around three topics: "What Is Christianity?" (1:5—2:28), "Life in the Family of God" (2:29—4:12), and "The Certainty of the Faith" (4:13—5:13). *The Cambridge Bible for Schools and Colleges* finds two main topics: "God Is Light" (1:5—2:28), and "God Is Love" (2:29—5:12). Robert Law found in it various *Tests of Life.* Some commentators do not try to outline the Epistle. The accompanying summary analysis is offered only as a set of convenient impressions around which to build the commentary.

Outline

I. Introduction, 1:1-4

II. Fundamentals of the Gospel, 1:5—2:29
   - A. The Message of Life—God Is Light, 1:5-7
   - B. From Sin to Life, 1:8-10
   - C. That You May Not Sin, 2:1-2
   - D. The Test of Obedience, 2:3-6
   - E. The Test of Life, 2:7-8
   - F. The Test of Love, 2:9-11
   - G. Children, Fathers, Young Men, 2:12-14
   - H. Love of the World, 2:15-17
   - I. The World Passes Away, 2:18-26
   - J. Dwelling in Christ, 2:27-29

III. Character of the Children of God, 3:1-24
   - A. God's Children, 3:1-3
   - B. A Definition of Sin, 3:4-6
   - C. Children of God Versus Children of the Devil, 3:7-8
   - D. Sinlessness, 3:9-12
   - E. Love and Hate, 3:13-17
   - F. Love Revealed in Action, 3:18-24

IV. Source of Sonship, 4:1—5:12
   - A. Truth and Error, 4:1-6
   - B. Love Is of God, 4:7-12
   - C. God Is Love, 4:13-21
   - D. Faith Is the Victory, 5:1-5
   - E. Eternal Life, 5:6-12

V. Conclusion, 5:13-21
   - A. The Ground of Assurance, 5:13-17
   - B. Spiritual Knowledge, 5:18-21

Section I *Introduction*

I John 1:1-4

This introductory paragraph of the Epistle is exceedingly complex in structure and as a consequence does not readily yield the meaning of the writer. It gives the impression that the author was so "full of his subject," so overwhelmed by the truth he sought to express, that his thoughts became crowded and his expression complicated. This is not characteristic of John's style.

The subject of the first sentence is **we** (1), an "editorial we" which is used repeatedly throughout the Epistle. Here the reference is to the early ministers of the gospel, of whom John was probably the one longest to survive. The verb is **declare** (3), and the object is **the Word of life** (1). Simply stated the author is saying, "We declare to you the Word of life."

The five dependent clauses of v. 1 are descriptive of the object: **That which was from the beginning, which we have heard, which we have seen with our eyes, which we have looked upon, and our hands have handled,** is identical in meaning with **the Word of life.** The parenthetical sentence of v. 2 also speaks of the same object. This is the Word (*Logos*) of the introduction to John's Gospel, and of course refers to Jesus.

But this analysis is only partially correct. It is not exactly **the Word** which John declares but something about (*peri*) **the Word.** This fact is borne out in v. 2, where it is **the life** which had made its appearance and which John had seen and was testifying to. And so, more precisely, the object of John's declaration is the **life** which was the possession of the Logos and which emanated from Him. Further evidence of this is found in the neuter pronoun, **that,** used four times in v. 1. In John's Gospel both life and light are said to be in the Logos. "And so here, when the writer says that the Life was with God and was disclosed to us, we need not suppose that he means anything substantially different from what is said in the Prologue to the Fourth Gospel."[1]

It would be wholly proper to say that John was writing what was known—what had been revealed—about Christ. In other

[1]Dodd, *op. cit.*, p. 2.

words, he was declaring the gospel of Christ. The gospel was the revelation "that Jesus is the Christ, the Son of God," and that those who believe may "have life through his name" (John 20: 31). He was not writing a complete Christology, but had something very important to say concerning the life which is in Christ and which He imparts to His followers.

On this basis, the hearing and the seeing and handling of **the Word of life** was more than the identification of Jesus by an eyewitness. It was John's anthropomorphic way of also proclaiming that he and the other disciples—even the whole Church—had recognized in Jesus the eternal life of the Deity. He thus sought to combat the Docetic notion that Jesus was phantomlike and not real. But his primary aim was not polemical; it was theological and devotional.

Both **the Word of life** and the gospel which John preached were **from the beginning** (1), before creation and before the Incarnation. John had **heard** Christ in the deepest sense of the term—he had heard His sermons and teachings, but he also had heard His message of **eternal life** (2). He had **seen** Christ as a man but he also had seen who He was—the Son of God. Such sight—and insight—may come to one involuntarily as the result of evidential circumstances. But John also **looked upon** Him, and "that implies deliberate and perhaps pleasurable sight."[2] The handling is reminiscent of the demand of Thomas for sensory evidence of the reality of Christ's post-resurrection body and thus becomes a reference to the fact of the Resurrection.

The parenthetical phrase of v. 2 is a revised repetition of what has preceded it. The emphasis is upon **the life,** and this life could be known only because it **was manifested.** No man by searching can find it; it can be seen and known only by revelation. **Life** which was **from the beginning** was also **with the Father.** And it is **eternal life.** It is not proper to equate this life solely with everlasting life, because eternal (*aionion*) is qualitative rather than quantitative. "It can only mean 'belonging to the age' of which the writer is speaking or thinking and so comes to mean possessed of the characteristics of that age. If the 'age to come' is supra-temporal, then *aionios* denotes that the subject which it qualifies has this characteristic."[3]

[2]A. Plummer, *The Epistles of St. John,* "The Cambridge Bible for Schools and Colleges" (Cambridge: University Press, 1911), p. 72.

[3]Brooke, *op. cit.*, p. 6.

Wherever John uses the term "life" it has this eternal quality implicit in its meaning. This is illustrated by the designation of Jesus as "the way, the truth, and the life" (John 14:6), and by His statement, "I am come that they might have life, and that they might have it more abundantly" (John 10:10). This **life was manifested** by Christ for the redemption of man. It is a quality of life which Christ himself possessed and which He imparts to all those who believe in Him. It is this life which distinguishes the "sons of God" from the "world" (3:1). The message of the Epistle concerns this life, and John follows in the path of his Master in proclaiming it. He spoke of that life which he himself shared in fellowship with God **the Father, and with his Son Jesus Christ** (3). He wrote as he had preached, that his readers might also share the fellowship, the evident result of which is fullness of joy.

This then is the primary purpose of John's Epistle, that we may have fellowship with God through sharing the life of Christ and that "our joy may be made full and may remain so."[4] This fellowship is best understood in terms of eternal life.

John's concept of **life** also has light to shed on the meaning of the Resurrection. To describe the post-resurrection life of Christ as a renewal of life taken from Him in death is inadequate, if not inaccurate. The body which revived was different from the one wrapped for burial; it was "a spiritual body" (I Cor. 15:44). But life, such as we are speaking of, was untouched by the crucifixion experience. It was unbroken, untarnished, and undisturbed. It passed through the tomb, just as it had passed through the rigors of the Incarnation, unsullied and whole. While we have said that **eternal life** does not primarily connote endless duration, we must also say that its quality is a survival quality which, in temporal terms, is like God himself, "from everlasting to everlasting." Death does have a sting and there is nothing pleasant to be said about it. But life of this sort transcends both life and death as we commonly know them—transcends them and absorbs them.

This is the heart of the Easter message, the glorious fact of eternal life, demonstrated in the Resurrection. It is not that Christ came back to life but rather that He arose from the dead. To the Christian this means that the **fellowship** (*koinonia*) that **we have with God and share with one another cannot be broken**

[4]Plummer, *op. cit.*, p. 76.

or destroyed by suffering and death. Indeed, the fellowship of life is most meaningful when these experiences must be endured.

Fellowship with the Lord and fellowship with the brethren constitute the ground of one's highest **joy.** And one's **joy** is made **full** or complete through unbroken fellowship.

John's use of the term **life** has something to say about the Incarnation. The life of the Christ child, which He shared with the Father and which made Him the Son of God, wrapped itself in humanity without losing its eternal quality. The Virgin Birth was the entrance into humanity of that **life** which John heard and saw and handled rather than the formation of a new life by natural processes.

Section II *Fundamentals of the Gospel*

I John 1:5—2:29

A. The Message of Life—God Is Light, 1:5-7

Here we encounter one of the paradoxes for which John is noted. According to v. 2 his subject was "eternal life." Now he introduces what appears to be a new subject and says, **This then is the message which we . . . declare unto you, that God is light** (5). If consistency be a virtue, perhaps we must seek a deeper consistency below the surface, or a higher type in the lofty thought of the writer. We meet here John's habit of approaching his theme from various angles. This makes for difficult analysis but for rich rewards. All of his thoughts are interlocked; but as the apostle passes from one to the other and back again, with the shuttle of lofty inspiration, he weaves a pattern of rare beauty and profound insight.

God is light. This is the gospel condensed to its briefest expression. Another similar metaphorical statement, "God is love," appears in 4:8 and 16. John has elsewhere used still another such term, "God is spirit" (John 4:24, lit.). The three statements taken together represent some of the most momentous statements ever made concerning the nature of God. "God is spirit"—in His essential nature. **God is light**—in His self-revelation to man. "God is love"—in His redemptive, healing work of salvation.

God is a revealing God. **Light** is the third word in these first verses of the Epistle having reference to the revealing nature of God. The first is "Word" (*logos*), then life (*zoe*), and now light (*phos*). All three are also used by John in the prologue of his Gospel, beautifully combined in the verse, "In him [the *logos*] was life; and the life was the light of men" (John 1:4). In both Gospel and the Epistle **light** is set in direct contrast to **darkness.** Herein is the purpose of God's self-revelation—that **darkness** might be invaded and challenged by the **light.**

Both **light** and **darkness** are spiritual terms denoting the opposite qualities of holiness and sin. God is Light, Holiness, and Purity, and it is of the nature of light to reveal itself. But light cannot be revealed to anything incapable of receiving it. God has revealed himself *through* the physical world but not *to* it. Revelation can come only to rational beings capable of making a choice. They can accept or reject a given revelation. "Only man is capable of light, that is, can so receive the nature of the Logos pouring toward him, that he himself shall be consciously transformed into it."[1]

God has revealed himself for the purpose of imparting His life and light to man, so that man's character may be brought into correspondence with the divine nature. No man can have fellowship with God—the fellowship of shared eternal life—while still living in darkness. If man claims to have such fellowship but actually lives a life untouched by the light, he deceives himself. John declares such a man is a liar. It is not a matter of opinion, nor of testimony, but of the truth of God's self-revelation. A man who chooses the sphere of darkness in which to live does not know fellowship with God and with His children.

This truth is self-evident. If we **walk in the light** (7), we cease to walk in the darkness. The result is a life that is cleansed from sin and brought into fellowship with God through Christ. This can be as assuredly known as the previous experience of walking in darkness. To John both darkness and light are very real. One's life will manifest the change, and to testify to it is but telling the truth.

It would seem logical for John to conclude that we thus have fellowship *with God.* Some ancient manuscripts have this reading, but the better translation is, **We have fellowship one with another.** Our experience with God can be tested in terms of its effect upon our relationship to other Christians.

This revealed light of God is analogous to the sun, which dispels darkness. That figure, however, does not fit John's thought. Earlier he said that "the darkness has not overcome it" (John 1:5, RSV), but he never says that the light has entirely overcome the darkness. The world is still in the darkness of sin and there is no promise that such darkness will be destroyed as long as time lasts. A better analogy is that of a great searchlight which pierces the darkness and makes a path through it. And so John speaks of walking in the light even in the midst of surrounding darkness. But the darkness cannot overcome the light; he who walks in the light enjoys fellowship with the Father and with His Son, Jesus Christ, and a mystic union with Christians of all ages.

It is a mistake to think that all which John implies here can be attained on one occasion or in response to a momentary total

[1]Haupt, *op. cit.*, p. 25.

surrender to God. Jesus said, "Follow me." Only those who begin to follow and continue to walk in the light can experience the results spoken of. This speaks of a walk to be pursued, a life to be lived, a fellowship to be enjoyed, and a cleansing to be experienced.

These observations should not be thought to militate against the idea of cleansing as distinguished from the idea of forgiveness. If we are able to discern John's thought thus far, he has been speaking of what we may term the "inner man" rather than his outward conduct, although that is not excluded. "This connection of thought itself shows that *katharidzein* must not be understood of the forgiveness of sins past, but of sanctification. . . . *Pasa hamartia*, every sin, is much too comprehensive a word for the sins of the past; it signifies not 'all our sins' but 'all that is called sin.'"[2]

The expression **the blood of Jesus Christ his Son** is a clue to what John is emphasizing. He writes to people who understand this language as a reference to the final master-stroke of God in the redemptive process. In terms of God's self-revelation the blood of Christ includes a number of precious truths in its meaning. First, it says that God revealed himself in the man Jesus. Second, God became *man*. This means that He not only "took upon him the form of a servant, and was made in the likeness of men" (Phil. 2:7), but He also became man, fusing His nature with that of mankind in a way never known before. In creation man was made in the image of God. In redemption God was made in the image of man. Something marvelous happened to the human race at the Incarnation. God revealed himself *in* mankind as well as *to* men. In the third place, God himself suffered for the sins of the world. God suffered in Jesus, because Jesus was God the Son.

This is part of what it means for God to have revealed himself redemptively. He revealed himself creatively in nature, including man. But redemptively He revealed himself primarily in man and for man. This does not mean that all men will thereby be saved eternally any more than the image of God in which man was initially created could save him from the Fall. It does mean that the conscience of man since Calvary is a Christian conscience, whether obeyed or suppressed. It means that Christlikeness is the highest moral standard known to man, even though

[2]*Ibid.*, p. 42.

like Saul of Tarsus he kicks against its pricks. It means that "the Light, which lighteth every man" has come into the world.

B. From Sin to Life, 1:8-10

Verse 8 repeats the thought of 6 and carries it further. **If we say that we have no sin** (8) we make a false assumption. This is worse than lying (6); it is self-deception. And it is self-destructive unless one sees his mistake and repents. "To 'have sin' is not merely a synonym for to commit sins . . . 'Sin' is the principle of which sinful acts are the several manifestations."[3] Brooke argues this interpretation against those who hold that the same phrase, "have sin," found in John 15:22-24, means guilt for sin. And he concludes: "The 'sin' which had got its hold, in consequence of their rejecting Him in spite of what He had done among them, had conceived and brought forth hate."[4] Sin, not truth, is the controlling principle in such persons.

If we confess (9) corresponds to v. 7. The hypothetical individual in this verse acknowledges the fact of the inner principle of sin which produces sinful acts and a guilty conscience. He responds to the light of God revealed in him and acknowledges the darkness which controls him. When one confesses his sins he learns by experience the true nature of God; he learns what it means to say that "God is light." He finds that God **is faithful** to His own purposes for which He revealed himself in Christ. God cannot deny himself; He must be true to His own nature.

God is also **just** (*dikaios*, righteous), and this is in reference to man and his sin. Men are tempted to retaliate in kind when others mistreat or perpetrate evil against them. But not so with God. All the injustice and failures of man cannot provoke God to be unjust in response to genuine confession of sins. John wishes to make it clear that no charge of injustice or unrighteousness can successfully be brought against God.

But in the work of redemption God does much more than vindicate His moral justice. "The revelation in Jesus Christ shows that God is *dikaios* as He acts along the line of His saving power by making faith in Jesus Christ the condition of receiving His deliverance."[5] There is a saving quality to the justice or

[3]Brooke, *op. cit.*, p. 17. [4]*Ibid.*, p. 18.

[5]James Moffatt, *Grace in the New Testament* (New York: Ray Long and Richard R. Smith, Inc., 1932), p. 218.

righteousness of God. It is demonstrated in those who "walk in the light," those who *confess* their sins.

John's concept of salvation parallels his concept of sin. Sin is something which we can control—something one chooses to accept or reject, but sin is also something which controls us. It is both an evil act and the propensity toward such action. For the act of sin, John prescribes forgiveness; for the propensity to sin, he offers cleansing.

Forgiveness and cleansing do not represent to John the whole substance of the salvation experience. They are part of the processes by which one comes into the new life of light and love. They are two doors—perhaps double doors—through which one passes from the life of sin and sinning into the life of fellowship with God and His people. They do not, however, constitute John's main emphasis because he is here more concerned with product than with process. This is why he so strongly emphasizes the Godlike qualities of life, light, and love.

Verse 10 corresponds to v. 8. **If we say that we have not sinned** is a broader and more general phrase than either **if we say that we have fellowship** or **if we say that we have no sin.** John is saying, "If we say we have never sinned." This is a denial of the very fact of sin, the reason for the atonement, the occasion for God's self-revelation to man. This attitude is the most reprehensible of all, because it makes God **a liar.** It is the sin above all other sins—the sin of arrogance and pride, which places the wisdom of man above that of God. This is the fruit of the first recorded temptation: "Hath God said . . . ? Ye shall not surely die" (Gen. 3:1, 4).

His word is not in us is a repetition of **the truth is not in us** (8). Truth and God's word come with the light, and he who walks in darkness is governed by neither.

The repeated **we** refers to the group of Christians to whom John wrote, of which he was a part, perhaps the pastor or superintendent. The apostle does not hold the sinful state to be normative for the Christian, for he wrote in order "that ye sin not" (2:1). He could say that they were liars and made God a liar by claiming to be free from sin, because the possibility of sinning is always present and because some of their number had become party to the antichristian spirit and had backslidden. The possibility of sin does not mean its probability. John's emphasis is upon the positive Christian virtues of fellowship, walking in the light, forgiveness, and cleansing rather than upon the negative elements of walking in darkness.

It would not be true to John's thought to so equate walking in the light and repenting of sin as to make both continuously necessary to the Christian life. The confession of sins is the beginning of walking in the light—the turning of one's back on the darkness of sin. And there is a repenting which needs not to be repented of, a turning from darkness to light that does not have to be repeated, even though the possibility of sinning is always present. However, this possibility of sinning should not be construed to mean the actual existence of sin.

There is a kind of perfectionism which is rightfully termed heresy—the claim that one can be freed from the propensity to sin in such a manner as to make it impossible to commit any act of sin. It is difficult to identify any such teaching even among the most radical of the holiness teachers. While some may occasionally make this claim, it is mostly expressed by critics of the Wesleyan theological position on sin and salvation. The possibility of committing sin remains, for Christians must live in a sinful world, they can be tempted, and they are beset by human weaknesses of many kinds. But this situation is not incompatible with walking in the light. It is God's light, not their own. The truth is found in the ancient formula, "It is possible not to sin," rather than, "It is not possible to sin."

The problem involves the understanding of the nature of sin. Any act of wrongdoing, however inadvertent and loathsome to the doer, must be labelled sin in the broad sense of the term. The most saintly of people are liable to sin under this definition. John says that "all unrighteousness is sin" (5:17). He also says that "whosoever abideth in him sinneth not" (3:6); and, "He that committeth sin is of the devil" (3:8). Being a Christian will not of itself guarantee that a man may not kill another in an automobile accident. But no fair-minded man would accuse him of being a murderer and thereby impugn his righteous character, for motives must always be considered. John therefore establishes the definition of sin as a willful act by a responsible person.

There is no desire here to dismiss a problem by oversimplifying it. Armed conflict, mental unbalance, lack of judgment in untried circumstances, cultural patterns, and many other elements of modern living prevent a clearly defined distinction between the sin which one has chosen and a wrong which circumstances have thrust upon him. The final judgment alone will give the answer. But a distinction between willful and involuntary evil is present in John's thought and it is a most necessary theological dogma.

Sin, as John uses the term, includes both the propensity and the act. Repentance involves the acceptance of guilt and is therefore a willful thing. John never attributes responsibility for sinful acts where there has been no responsible choice.

C. That You May Not Sin, 2:1-2

In the midst of John's treatment of sin he speaks an assuring word to the faithful—**My little children** (1). This is an affectionate expression, often used in reference to the relationship between teacher and students. This may have been John's immediate use of the term. But it has a deeper meaning, a reference to the fact that Christians experience fellowship with God as the result of the new birth (John 3:3). They therefore resemble their Heavenly Father in both purpose and action.

That ye sin not comes as a necessary challenge to the antinomianism described above, in which freedom from sin is considered not only impracticable but also impossible. John seems to sense that his teaching on repentance and forgiveness might lead to this kind of doctrine and life. And so he states without equivocation that the hallmark of the Christian life is the absence of sin. This should be the goal and the heart desire of every child of God. It is also an attainable goal because of **these things** of which John wrote—the self-revelation of God, the provision for fellowship with Him and with His people, the promise of forgiveness and cleansing through walking in the light, and the efficacy of the blood of Jesus Christ. "The writer's object is to produce 'sinlessness.' And this is not a fruitless aspiration after an ideal which cannot possibly be realized, for the means of dealing with the sin which he desires to combat is at hand."[6]

The need for such exhortation is an acknowledgment of a certain tension under which the Christian life is lived. There is the conscious assurance that a sure remedy has been provided for sin in a man's heart and life, both in principle and in action. Over against this there is the haunting consciousness that one is still liable to fall. This is not the state described by Paul as

[6]Brooke, *op. cit.*, p. 23. See Steele, *op. cit.*, pp. 243-61.

"another law in my members," "that, when I would do good, evil is present with me" (Rom. 7:23, 21). It is, rather, the tension between spirituality and humanity. It is the necessary risk which every man runs who strives to follow the clear beam of God's revealed light while inhabiting a perishable body in a world of darkness and sin.

In the expression **that ye sin not** (*hina me harmartete*), the "aorist suggests definite acts of sin rather than the habitual state, which is incompatible with the position of Christians who are in truth what their name implies."[7] John is not saying that Christians cannot sin nor that they will not sin, but that they should not sin.

If any man sin refers in this instance to the Christian overtaken by sin rather than to the habitual, willful sinner. It is possible in this sense to sin "unwillfully." One may succumb because the sinful forces are stronger than he is. He may be deceived or trapped because of ignorance. Or he may go astray through carelessness. In any case restoration is readily available in the person of Jesus Christ. But this glorious knowledge should not lessen one's sense of the blackness of sin and the dangers of sinning.

In the previous chapter the remedy for sin was spoken of in terms of confession resulting in forgiveness and cleansing and establishing a fellowship of the children of God. In the present context the remedy is expressed in terms of the personal, redemptive work of Christ. Three characteristics are attributed to Him and these stand in apposition to "the blood of Jesus Christ." It might be said that they serve to explain what is meant when the Blood is used metaphorically for the total redemptive work of Christ. He is called an **advocate, the righteous,** and **the propitiation.**

We have an advocate (*paracleton*). This noun is used in the New Testament only by John. In the Gospel he speaks of the Holy Spirit as "another Comforter" (*paracleton;* John 14:16), showing that the Holy Spirit operates as Christ's Agent in the world. The term **advocate** has a variety of meanings found in the history of its use. The paraclete is one who is sent for, one who is called to help, one who comforts, one who intercedes. The word itself "denotes merely 'one called in to help.' In the Epistle the idea of one who pleads the Christian's cause before God is

[7]*Ibid.*

clearly indicated, and 'advocate' is the most satisfactory translation."[8]

Jesus Christ is here called **the righteous.** Previously God himself was termed "just" or righteous (*dikaion;* 1:9). This supports John's assertion that Christ is the Son of God, the Revelation of the person of God. The term **righteous** refers not so much to the vindication of Christ's moral character as to the saving quality of His activity. Very simply, John has here said that, when the Christian falls into sin, a plea for help brings Christ to his side to save him. As truly man and truly God, Christ is able to represent each before the other. He can intercede for man before God because "He needs no advocate for Himself."[9]

Christ is **the propitiation** (*hilasmos;* "expiation," RSV) **for our sins.** In the KJV and RSV translations, there are two interpretations of the same word, both or either of which may carry John's meaning. **Propitiation** carries the idea of placating or pacifying one who has been wronged. The question then arises whether it is God or man who must be pacified. The Old Testament's sacrificial system was not instituted to appease the wrath of God against sinful man, although it is often interpreted in this way. Rather, it was given as a sign of man's faith in God, a vehicle by which he returned from his estrangement from God in repentance and hope of forgiveness. **Propitiation** has to do with the reconciliation of man to God rather than of God to man. This position is true to the Gospel of John, where God is depicted as sending Christ because of His great love for the world of sinful men. God redeems man because of His love, not because of anger or hatred.

Thus Christ's work of redemption, His becoming man and dying on the Cross, turned the tide of man's rebellion and reconciled him, the prodigal, to God, the waiting Father. This must be thought of in a very real, yet provisional sense. Mankind, in Christ, the God-man, has been reconciled to God, but men individually and collectively must come and experience their reconciliation by repentance and a willingness to walk in the light (1:7, 9). Otherwise the doctrine of reconciliation leads one inevitably to legalistic universalism. And this is not John's teaching.

[8]*Ibid.*, p. 26. See also Hastings, *Dictionary of the Bible*, III, 665.

[9]*Ibid.*, p. 27.

Expiation, on the other hand, carries the idea of removal or forgiveness. It is through the work of the incarnate Son of God that the remedy has been provided for man's sin problem. Jesus Christ is God's Agent for man's salvation. The cognate term *hilasterion* refers to the mercy seat, the place of reconciliation or meeting between God and man. In Christ alone can salvation be found. This coincides with John's previous thought: The blood of Jesus Christ, God's Son, "cleanseth us from all sin" (1:9).

Perhaps both of these terms are necessary for an adequate understanding of John's thought. To the Christian, before whom he holds the standard of sinlessness, he also holds up Christ, the righteous Advocate, in whom alone can be found reconciliation with God and the removal of all sin.

But lest he be misunderstood, John hastens to add that this divine remedy is **for the sins of the whole world** of men, not just for stumbling Christians. The provision which restores a Christian is the same which pardoned and cleansed him in the first place. All who will "walk in the light" may know the same reconciliation and fellowship which only God's children know.

John speaks to us of a responsible God, but also of responsible man. The Father has made full provision for the restoration of man, His noblest creation. He did not relinquish His responsibility when man fell into sin. But neither did He abrogate man's freedom and personal responsibility when He provided salvation in Jesus Christ. The greatness of man can be seen even in his ruined state. He may have allowed the powers of evil to dominate him, yet at the same time he is no groveling worm in the dust, neither has sin robbed him of that power of choice which originally differentiated him as man instead of a puppet. Nor does God treat man other than as the noble creature He first created. He was made to function in an upright position, physically and intellectually. In matters of salvation God expects man to stand up and be counted; to stand and say his piece; to stand and choose; to deliberately walk in the light or continue to walk in darkness. The hope of salvation rests in the atoning work of Christ, but it also rests to a necessary degree in man's native ability to choose his own destiny.

D. The Test of Obedience, 2:3-6

Hereby we do know that we know him (3). In c. 1 confession and walking in the light on man's part, coupled with forgiveness and cleansing on the part of God, result in fellowship with God, with Christ, and with the saints of the Church. In the present section the result of the restoring work of Christ is to **know him.** To the Greeks, knowledge of ultimate reality came through rational contemplation, and to the Gnostics it came as the result of a mystical experience. To John, ultimate knowledge is the knowledge of God in Jesus Christ and is to be obtained through the processes of being saved from sin. Those who enjoy God's fellowship also know Him. The apostle writes in order that we may **know that we know him,** that "we may be sure that we know him" (RSV). "We learn to perceive more and more clearly that our knowledge is genuine through its abiding results in a growing willingness to obey."[10] This knowledge is related to the fellowship of 1:7, which is the result of partaking of life in Christ. In his Gospel, John says: "And this is life eternal, that they might know thee the only true God, and Jesus Christ, whom thou hast sent" (John 17:3). "In the Fourth Gospel it is made perfectly plain that to know God is to experience His love in Christ, and to return that love in obedience."[11]

If we keep his commandments we have passed one test which validates our knowledge of God. Two other tests are suggested later (3:14, 24). This does not mean that every man who keeps the laws of God is a Christian; many observe Christian principles of living because they are right and promise the greatest rewards—men are honest because "honesty is the best policy." It does mean, however, that the affections are set upon the moral precepts of the gospel and thus become the basis of obedience to God's laws.

The term **his commandments** does not here refer to the Ten Commandments alone. To **keep his commandments** equals to keep **his word** (5), and this means the truth of God as it is in Christ. It means to strive continually to be more and more like Christ—**to walk, even as he walked** (6). "To know about Christ, to understand the doctrine of His person and work is mere theory; we get to know Him and to know that we know Him by practice of His precepts."[12] In the words of Jesus himself, "Not every one that saith unto me, Lord, Lord, shall enter into the kingdom of heaven; but he that doeth the will of my Father which is in heaven" (Matt. 7:21). "Emotionalized religion with-

[10]Brooke, *op. cit.*, p. 30.
[11]Dodd, *op. cit.*, p. 31.
[12]David Smith, *op. cit.*, p. 174.

out discipline becomes sentimental, and intellectualized religion becomes sterile . . . Moral discipline is the path to Christian character."[13]

Keeping God's commandments is parallel to walking in the light. The results promised are only for those who "keep on keeping on." We know Him when we desire above all things to be obedient to Him, and as we continue to keep His word our love for God is perfected. (See also 2:15; 3:17; 4:12; 5:3.) The Greek *teteleiotia* "means 'has been made perfect and remains so.' Obedience, not feeling is the test of perfect love."[14] God's commandments have all been prompted by love, and the only appropriate response is the response of love. Our fellowship with God is a fellowship of love. "In itself it is not a startling or revolting thought, that the love of God should dwell in us in its full measure and in its simple perfection."[15] "In a sense it is God's love throbbing in our bosoms, because it is originated, or rather occasioned by Him. But in an important sense it is human, because it is the activity of our spiritual susceptibilities unfolding according to the laws of the mind as gratitude toward a benefactor."[16]

If a man and woman can know what it is to so love each other that they will seal that love in the bonds of matrimony and be true to it "until death do us part," it is not too much to expect the professing Christian to love God with an undivided allegiance. Paul said that "love is the fulfilling of the law" (Rom. 13:10). And the moral law of God revealed in both the Old and the New Testaments was confirmed by Jesus. Our Lord's command is, "Thou shalt love the Lord thy God with all thy heart, and with all thy soul, and with all thy mind" (Matt. 22:37).

E. The Test of Life, 2:7-8

The better reading for **Brethren** (7) is "Beloved" (*agapetoi*). John uses this endearing term because of the importance of what he has to say, and to gain the sympathetic attention of his readers. In using the terms an **old commandment** and a **new commandment,** it seems clear that he is speaking of one com-

[13]Paul W. Hoon, "First John" (Exposition), *The Interpreter's Bible,* XII (New York: Abingdon Press, 1957), 230.

[14]Plummer, *op. cit.,* p. 91.

[15]Haupt, *op. cit.,* p. 70.

[16]Steele, *op. cit.,* p. 34.

mandment in two aspects rather than of two commandments. On the surface it would appear that it had been given in the Old Testament and was therefore old, and reiterated in the New Testament and was therefore new. On this basis it could only be the commandment of love, as summarized by Jesus in Matt. 22: 37-40.

This commandment had been given **from the beginning.** The phrase could mean from the beginning of creation, from the first giving of the Mosaic law, or from the beginning of the apostolic age, when Christians had first received the gospel. The second is possible, because the Fall broke a love relationship between God and man and the institution of the Mosaic dispensation sought to restore it. The commandment to love both God and one's fellowman became new when it was given afresh by Jesus under new circumstances and to achieve a new bond which the law was unable to establish.

However, the third interpretation is preferable and of greater meaning. At the beginning the Church had received the commandment of love, and now John is reaffirming the truth of this commandment. It was **old** because it was the only law by which they had been living the Christian life. "It was old but not obsolete, ancient but not antiquated."[17] It was **old** as John looked back upon it, but it was **new** when given and **new** at every stage of emphasis. At the time of the last Passover, Jesus said to His disciples, "A new commandment I give unto you" (John 13:34). Erich Haupt sees in this incident a distinctiveness in the way in which Jesus demonstrated His love. At this period in His ministry He acted out of the fullness of His love. He acted not as Lord and Teacher but as a Servant, and He acted in wholly unexpected ways. To the disciples at the foot-washing He exhorted them to do as He had done (John 13:15); shortly after, when He spoke of the new commandment, it was to say that they were to love one another as He loved them (John 13:34). Only in the latter part of His life and ministry did Jesus hold himself up as a Pattern for His disciples to follow. Previously they had practiced love as a duty, but henceforth they were to love as He loved, spontaneously from the heart. This corresponds exactly to what John says in our present passage—that the Christian "ought himself also so to walk, even as he walked." Perhaps in the back of John's mind was the thought that it was in His

[17]Plummer, *op. cit.*, p. 93.

passion that Jesus urged imitation of His manner of loving. If this be the case, it leads to a better understanding of the new commandment. John was following the thought pattern of Jesus himself.[18]

Thus John was doing more than describing the law of love, saying that it was old yet ever new. His purpose was much deeper. He was warning against the natural human tendency to become formal and duty-bound in our service to God and man. When obedience replaces spontaneous love, then the commandment of love indeed is old—as old as creation, as old as Sinai, as old as any age which has lost its first love. Obedience must not be a substitute for love but an evidence of it, even as it is a test of one's true knowledge of God.

Which thing is true in him and in you (8) means its truth has been demonstrated in both Christ and in Christians. The commandment of love is valid because it proves itself when put to the test. "The darkness is on the wane, the true light is showing its power; *therefore,* I bid you to walk as children of light."[19]

F. The Test of Love, 2:9-11

John has exposed the fallacy of the claims of some members of the group who were not truly Christian. He did so in regard to fellowship (1:6), to sin (1:8), to sins (1:10), and to knowledge of God (2:4). In each case he challenged heresy with truth. He does the same thing here in regard to love—**He that saith he is in the light, and hateth his brother, is in darkness even until now** (9). The apostle has drawn contrasts between light and darkness, truth and falsehood; and now between love and hate. In these terms he points up inconsistency between profession and conduct, as well as errors in theology. No man can do better than he knows; but in this case there had been a willful ignorance, brought on by failing to walk in the light and to keep love fresh. Darkness had blinded the eyes. Unmindful of what had happened, they were living in the past, a bright past, in which they gloried while the darkness engulfed them.

Doubtless this kind of person was in the minority. But the problem was real in the Church, and John had to cope with it. To the main body of the "beloved" he wrote, **He that loveth his brother abideth in the light, and there is none occasion of**

[18]Haupt, *op. cit.*, pp. 72-81. [19]Plummer, *op. cit.*, p. 93.

stumbling in him (10). He neither stumbles nor falls into the darkness, nor does he cause others to fall by the way. Heretical teachings and their advocates have always appealed to a disproportionate number of the Church and its leaders. Truth is less spectacular but it is of the stuff of eternity.

G. Children, Fathers, Young Men, 2:12-14

These verses present two problems: the classes of people addressed and the change of tense in the verb "to write."

There are two sets of triplets here, each consisting of **little children, fathers** and **young men.** In the first the Greek word used for **little children** is *teknia* and in the second it is *paidia.* The difference in meaning between the two is only slight, and John probably did not intend to make any. In other places in the Epistle where either of the two words is used (2:1, 28; 3:7, 18; 4:4; 5:21), the whole body of readers is probably meant. The order of **children, fathers,** and **young men** is illogical if John were speaking of age-groups. **Little children** is an affectionate term for all of those addressed. He divides them into two groups—**fathers** and **young men.** This division may be by age or by spiritual maturity, since age and maturity are usually contrasted with youth and immaturity, although not always so. At the same time, all may in a real sense be included in each of the three categories.

The change of tenses is less easily understood. Nestle's Greek text has *grapho* (I write or I am writing, present indicative) three times and *egrapha* (I wrote or I have written, aorist) three times. The KJV here, being a translation of a less accurate Greek text, has **I write** four times and **I have written** twice. The RSV has "I am writing" three times and "I write" three times, regarding "the aorist as 'epistolary,' equivalent to a present."[20] The NEB has "I write" in the first triplet and "I have written" in the second.

A number of interpretations of the change from the present to the aorist have been suggested. Alfred Plummer lists seven.[21] Three are more plausible than the others. First, the "I write" may have reference to the Epistle and the "I wrote" to the Gospel of John. This is Plummer's own choice, and of course rests upon

[20]Amos N. Wilder, "First John" (Exegesis), *The Interpreter's Bible* (New York: Abingdon Press, 1957), XII, 230.

[21]*Op. cit.*, pp. 98-99.

the prior acceptance of the unity of authorship of the two works. Second, in the use of the aorist "the writer turns back in thought to that part of the letter which he had already finished."[22] Third, "in the present . . . the apostle has in view the passing act in which he is engaged: in the aorist . . . the Epistle is in his mind represented as finished; he speaks historically of the intellectual conception of the Epistle which preceded the actual . . . writing."[23] Either of the first two explanations is preferable to the third.

John wrote to his **little children, because your sins are forgiven for his name's sake** (12). Forgiveness is not the whole of salvation from sin, but it is the entrance to the Christian life, the beginning of walking in the light in Christian fellowship. In Hebrew the name always stands for the character of an individual. **For his name's sake** is a way of saying that they were forgiven through the atoning work of Christ.

We have seen that **little children** are divided into **fathers** and **young men.** In like manner forgiveness of sins has two aspects: **fathers** may suggest knowledge of Christ, and **young men** strength to be victorious over evil and over Satan himself.

In the second triplet John wrote because his **little children** had known the Father, a reiteration of "ye have known" in v. 13. He then breaks this knowledge of the Father into two elements: knowledge of the Son and victory over the devil. The Christian life has both the theoretical and the practical sides to it. Forgiveness of sins and the knowledge of God (3) are the foundations of the **young men,** who would naturally be in the prime of life. But a victorious walk with God. Strength to overcome is attributed to more pertinently, fellowship with God, in all of its expressed ramifications, keeps both young or old in the prime of spiritual life and vigor. Walking in the light of obedience to the will of God and having the Word of God abiding within make one strong against all of the forces of evil.

H. Love of the World, 2:15-17

Those who aspire to the high standard of Christian living described by John must be done with **the world** and **the things that are in the world** (15). This is because the world is in darkness and God's people walk in the light. There is a seeming con-

[22]Brooke, *op. cit.*, p. 41. [23]Haupt, *op. cit.*, p. 95.

tradiction between this restriction and John's own statement that God loves the world (John 3:16). It would seem that we are told not to love the very world which Christ died to save and of which all people are a part. But "the world which the Father loves is the whole human race. The world which we are not to love is all that is alienated from Him, all that prevents men from loving Him in return . . . The world which we are not to love is His rival."[24] "They were to shun no place and no man; they were to love all places and all men; but in all places and among all men, there would be a world which they were not to love."[25] This **world** is the system of life which has been established by unregenerate man under the influence of evil. It can without argument be said of this system that, **if any man love the world, the love of the Father is not in him.** "One heart cannot contain two loves so hostile to each other as the love of light and the love of darkness."[26] "God alone is worthy to be completely loved."[27] "No man can serve two masters . . . Ye cannot serve God and mammon" (Matt. 6:24).

The things that are in the world which the Christian is told not to love cannot mean all the objects which go to make up the world. The expression is identical in meaning with **all that is in the world** (16). By this "we may understand the element that makes the world the world, its fundamental determination and nature."[28] There follows, not a catalog of what goes to make up the world, but three essential marks of worldliness: **the lust of the flesh, and the lust of the eyes, and the pride of life.**

Some writers have found in these a parallel to the three temptations of Jesus in the wilderness, but it is difficult to carry such parallels to meaningful conclusions. **The lust of the flesh** is sensuality; not the temptation to satisfy a legitimate appetite, as with Jesus in the wilderness, but the desire for the unnatural such as "gluttony, drunkenness, and the irregular intercourse of the sexes."[29] "The evil significance of the phrase lies in 'lust,' not in 'the flesh.'"[30] This finds its illustration in the eroticism which is spread by picture and word and voice throughout the

[24]Plummer, *op. cit.*, p. 107.

[25]F. D. Maurice, *The Epistles of St. John* (London: Macmillan and Co., 1881), p. 129.

[26]Steele, *op. cit.*, p. 46.

[27]Hoon, *op. cit.*, p. 238.

[28]Haupt, *op. cit.*, p. 100.

[29]Maurice, *op. cit.*, p. 129.

[30]Law, *op. cit.*, p. 149.

advertising and entertainment world. Its danger lies in that it goes under the name of love. It knows no standard other than its own satisfaction. It is essentially selfish, irresponsible, and self-consuming. **The flesh** (*sarx*) "denotes human nature as corrupted by sin."[31]

The lust of the eyes is unlawful, "prurient curiosity." This lust involves what one does not have. **The lust of the flesh** involves what one has and uses to evil ends. "They are related as the desire for enjoyment, and the enjoyment of what is desired, but in such a way that the egoistic element is prominent."[32] The **lust of the eyes** involves not only the eye but also the mind and the imagination. It can seek satisfaction through the media of literature and art, and perhaps is the more pronounced when unsatisfied; its complete satisfaction would include yielding to the lust of the flesh. This kind of lust is "the tendency to be captivated by the outward show of things, without inquiring into their real values."[33] "Our author, looking upon contemporary society from a Christian standpoint, and judging it with a deeper seriousness, sees it as the very incarnation of this pretentious, self-glorifying spirit."[34]

The world which **passeth away** (17) is the world which Christians are not to love. It is true that John speaks later in eschatological terms of the last time (2:15), Christ's coming (2:28), Christ's appearing (3:2), and of the day of judgment (4:17). These may imply the end of the world, when "the heavens being on fire shall be dissolved, and the elements shall melt with fervent heat" (II Pet. 3:12). But here the apostle is not speaking of what will happen to the physical world. John is thinking of the world of godlessness. The life which man has constructed in self-esteem and in defiance of God has no permanent survival power. The twentieth century, more than any previous time, gives powerful testimony to both the transience of all temporal things and the possibility that man may destroy the civilization he has created, including himself. The ways of sin are strewn with the seeds of their own destruction.

The world also passes away in terms of the progress of personal history. Time flies and everything changes. The pride and revelry and lustful activities of youth and middle age soon lose their attraction when age comes on, and **"the years**

[31]Brooke, *op. cit.*, p. 48
[32]Haupt, *op. cit.*, p. 107.
[33]Dodd, *op. cit.*, p. 41.
[34]*Ibid.*, p. 42.

draw nigh, when thou shalt say, I have no pleasure in them" (Eccles. 12:1).

In contrast, **he that doeth the will of God abideth for ever.** Here, too, John is speaking in moral rather than physical terms. That man who is in the world but not of it survives all that passes away by virtue of the life which he possesses through Christ. We do not have a direct contrast here between the world which is temporary and the man who is eternal because of doing God's will. John could have directly contrasted the world and the kingdom of God. But then he would have had to contrast the Christian and the sinner, virtually saying that the sinner will also pass away. John does not say this, but he does attribute immortality to the eternal (spiritual) life which men receive through Christ. He seems to say that men can live one of two kinds of life on earth—the one kind will survive and the other will not.

I. The World Passes Away, 2:18-26

The last time (18) should be translated "the last hour" (RSV, NEB, and others). Similar phrases occur elsewhere in the New Testament (John 11:24; Acts 2:17; I Pet. 1:3; Jude 18) and find their counterpart in "the day of the Lord" in the Hebrew prophets. Some writers are bold to say that John thought "the history of the world . . . was about to be drawn to a close."[35] This finds some support in the Book of Revelation. Others interpret it as meaning "the time immediately preceding the return of Christ to judge the world."[36] Steele says, "This expression denotes a crisis and not the end of the world."[37] John saw this crisis as precipitated by the persecutions of the Christians which brought the Church and the Roman Empire into a struggle to the death. As far as the apostle could see, history would not continue its accustomed course. He could not give particulars because they were not revealed to him. But his faith told him that the righteous would survive and the sinful world would be destroyed. God could not be defeated in such a contest.

Evidence of **the last time** is the appearance of **many antichrists.** These were not world leaders or rulers whom the world had gone after, but they were former church members who had

[35]R. R. Williams, "The Letters of John and James," *The Cambridge Bible Commentary* (Cambridge: University Press, 1965), p. 30.

[36]Plummer, *op. cit.*, p. 65. [37]*Op. cit.*, p. 50.

denied **that Jesus is the Christ** (22). They were those **who went out from us, but they were not of us** (19). "The severing of the connection showed that such membership had never been anything but external."[38] They were the product of the crisis in which many fell away. While John speaks of an **antichrist** that **shall come** (18), of which the people had heard, he does not describe him. His **antichrist** falls short of Paul's "son of perdition, who opposeth and exalteth himself above all that is called God" (II Thess. 2:3-4). Of the Pharisees who were against Him, Jesus said, "Ye are of your father the devil" (John 8:44).

In contrast to the antichrists are those who follow Christ. Of the Christians, John says, **Ye have an unction** (20); literally, You have an anointing (*chrisma*) **from the Holy One.** "Just as the Antichrist has his representatives, so the Anointed One, the Christ, has His."[39]

The anointing with oil under the Mosaic covenant accompanied the consecration of only priests and kings and prophets. Under the Christian dispensation the anointing with the Holy Spirit is the privilege of all. The result of the gift of the Holy Spirit is knowledge. This is a restatement of 2:3, and the knowledge here could mean the knowledge of Christ. But its meaning seems to be broader than this. The phrase **Ye know all things** is more correctly translated, "Ye all know." The meaning seems to be that all true Christians have the knowledge of truth as it is revealed in Christ. The apostle had spoken of the Holy Spirit as the "Spirit of truth" (John 14:17), who, when He comes, "will guide you into all truth" (John 16:13). He here is saying that through the anointing of the Holy Spirit men have a sure knowledge—not of historical or scientific or even theological truth, but of salvation truth.

John had written to the Christians because they recognized the truth when it was presented to them. He would not cast his pearls before swine—the antichrists. There come times when it is folly to press the claims of the gospel upon certain people. John says it is because they are liars and want to hear only that which is untrue.

No lie is of the truth (21); i.e., truth contains no falsehood.

[38]Brooke, *op. cit.*, p. 53. See "Antichrist," by Otto C. Piper, *A Handbook of Christian Theology* (New York: The World Publishing Co., 1958), pp. 13-17.

[39]Plummer, *op. cit.*, p. 110.

Because they accepted falsehood, John could give them no truth. The denial of **Jesus** as **the Christ** (22) and of God as His **Father** had made them unfit to hear the truth. The denial of the one was the denial of the other (23). More than that, it was the denial of the Incarnation. To John the Incarnation is the primary dogma of Christian theology—it is central, around which all other dogmas gather and out of which they grow.

Apparently, the antichrists had been actively engaged in trying to **seduce** (26; deceive) the Christians. John had exposed them until they were persuaded to leave the Church. He urges the Christians to continue as they had **from the beginning** (24) in the hope of the **promise** of **eternal life** (25). This life is both a present possession and a future hope.

J. Dwelling in Christ, 2:27-29

John expressed the relationship between the Christian and his God in terms of **the anointing** (27). God abides in the Christian through the continuing presence of the Holy Spirit, and by the same token the Christian abides in God. In a similar expression Jesus said to His disciples, "Abide in me, and I in you. . . . I am the vine, ye are the branches" (John 15:4-5). This emphasizes the closest kind of fellowship where both parties are actively engaged in its continuation.

The Holy Spirit is present as a Teacher, and therefore **ye need not that any man teach you.** John does not mean that all human instruction can be discarded, else he would never have written these words of instruction. Rather, in the strongest language he is saying that Christians do not depend upon such "wisdom" as the Gnostics claimed to possess. It was this deceptive philosophy that John was warning against. The similarity of the claim to special sources of knowledge by both the Church and the false teachers made the apostle's exhortations of great importance to Christians of the first century.

The Holy Spirit is the "Conservator of orthodoxy." He is the Teacher of unadulterated truth; He is therefore the Guarantor that our abiding relationship to God is one of intelligent understanding as well as of emotional attachment. "The experience of eternal life meant growth in truth as well as possession of truth."[40] "As truth is appropriated their fellowship with the Divine grows and becomes more real."[41]

[40]Hoon, *op. cit.*, p. 250. [41]Brooke, *op. cit.*, p. 61.

Furthermore, **little children** must **abide in him** (28). There is something for them to do, as in any personal relationship and in any process of learning. "What they were taught at the first gave the standard by which all later developments must be measured . . . They must abide 'as He taught them.' The earliest teaching had not been superceded by a higher and altogether different message, as the Gnostics would have it. They needed no further teaching."[42]

A new motive is now added for remaining in true fellowship. Because it is the "last hour," Christians must be ready to meet Christ **when he shall appear.** Two qualities should characterize them at that time—they should **have confidence, and not be ashamed.** The first "means especially the fearless trust with which the faithful soul meets God."[43]

For **not be ashamed** the RSV has "not shrink from him in shame at his coming." Let each man who professes to have met Jesus Christ so "walk in the light," so "keep his commandments," so "abide in him," so be taught of the Spirit, that he may have nothing in his life to be ashamed of either here and now or at His coming.

Verse 29 uses two Greek verbs for **know**—*oida,* "know," and *ginosko,* "learn to know."[44] We can read thus: **If ye know that he** (Christ) **is righteous**—and you do if you are taught by the Holy Spirit—you will come also to **know that every one that doeth righteousness is born of** God.

A new, yet related thought is introduced here. Through the understanding given by the Holy Spirit the true Christian can determine if another is a true Christian. This is discerned by observing whether his actions are righteous or not. The Christian will be like his Master, "Jesus Christ the righteous" (2:1); he will "keep his commandments" and will walk even as Christ walked.

John does not talk of justification by faith as does Paul, although belief in the person and work of Christ is paramount. A man becomes a Christian by receiving eternal life from Christ. For this reason John does not need to argue against works-righteousness as did Paul. In simple fact, what a man does and

[42]*Ibid.,* pp. 62-63. [43]Plummer, *op. cit.,* p. 117.

[44]J. H. Thayer, *A Greek-English Lexicon of the New Testament* (Edinburgh: T. & T. Clark, 4th ed., 1914), p. 118.

how he acts are very closely associated with his salvation. The emphases of the two apostles are different but they would agree that righteous deeds must follow one's initial conversion. "By their fruits ye shall know them" (Matt. 7:20)—know that they are born of God, born anew from above.

Section III *Character of the Children of God*

I John 3:1-24

A. God's Children, 3:1-3

Behold, what manner of love (1) is more than a simple imperative, calling for attention. This is a genuine exclamation of amazement mixed with gratitude. The pronoun *potapos* (**what manner** or what sort) "never serves . . . to indicate merely external greatness . . . but always that which is internal."[1] It refers to the quality of God's love, the fact that it is given to those who are both unlovely and unworthy. "The love of God in Christ is foreign to this world: 'From what far realm? What unearthly love?' "[2] The wonder of this love is more than that it is a manifestation of God's grace; the wonder is that it has been given to man.

John specifies that it is **the Father** who gives His love—not "our Father," as Jesus taught His disciples in the Lord's Prayer. The apostle never uses the term "your Father." **The Father** here has the significance of God, the Father of Jesus Christ. God has demonstrated His love to us in the Son. Earlier God revealed himself as "light" (1:5), now as **love,** which becomes virtually the theme of the remainder of the Epistle. The marvellous thing is that this love has been given to us and as a result we have become the children of God. Christians are products of the love of God, while mankind in general is the result of the creative activity of God. Not only have we been **called the sons of God,** but we are so in fact. "And so we are" (*kai esmen*) should be added to the King James Version at this point, because it is in the oldest and best Greek manuscripts.

Paul employs the term "sons" (*uioi*) in a legal sense, using the analogy of adoption rather than generation. To John we are "children" (*tekna*) of God by the new birth, and this is the closer relationship.

Therefore (as a result of which) **the world knoweth us not.** Believers call us children of God, but the world does not recognize us as such at all. "Augustine compares the attitude of the world toward God to that of sick men in delirium who would do

[1]Haupt, *op. cit.*, p. 153.

[2]Smith, *op. cit.*, p. 182.

violence to their physician."[3] **Because it knew him not,** neither Christ as the Son of God nor the love of God manifested in Christ, the world cannot identify Christians as such. This was demonstrated in the life and death of Jesus, who was treated as a man to be destroyed. In part it was because the deity of Jesus was veiled—and the sonship of Christians is also obscured by their humanity. "We have this treasure in earthen vessels" (II Cor. 4:7). But John attributes this blindness of the world to its inherent nature (see 2:15 ff.).

Beloved, now are we the sons of God (2). This repetition with the added time element **now** sets up a contrast between the present and the future of the children of God. They have not yet benefited fully from the provisions of the atonement. The children must grow and develop—and still the unknown future stretches out ahead: **it doth not yet appear what we shall be.** The contrast points to a qualitative as well as a quantitative difference between the **now** and the **not yet.**

The difference will be apparent when He shall appear—"at his coming" (2:28). **We know that . . . we shall be like him; for we shall see him as he is.** This statement may be taken in several ways. Most certainly we shall be like Him then because in a real sense we are like Him now. Others understand that "we shall be like Him because we shall see Him." This presumes that the vision of God will make us like Him.

There is much to be said for both of these positions. The glorious fulfillment of our sonship is the blessed hope of the Christian. Such hope cannot be entertained by one whose life is lived in sin.

This expectation is the reflection of a life of purity while at the same time it motivates one to keep himself pure: **Every man that hath this hope in him purifieth himself** (3). No man can thus keep himself pure by his own will and effort, but he can continually walk in the light; and this light—the revealed truth of God in Christ—serves as the purifying ray. The light will search a man's innermost being and it will burn its way into his very conscience and will. John further dares to assert that we are pure **as he is pure.** He can make this bold assertion because it is God who does the cleansing. It is because of this purifying that **we shall be like him.**

[3]Plummer, *op. cit.*, p. 121.

B. A Definition of Sin, 3:4-6

John now returns to his discussion of sin. Having acknowledged the possibility of the Christian committing sin (2:1), he must dwell on the subject at greater length. His interest is practical, although theological concepts of sin are not lacking. He has defined or described sin as both action and motivation (1:8-9)—and both find a cure in the "blood of Christ." This dual concept of sin persists in the present paragraph: **Whosoever committeth sin transgresseth also the law: for sin is the transgression of the law** (4). A somewhat more lucid translation is, "To commit sin is to break God's law: sin, in fact, is lawlessness" (NEB). Sinning is contradictory to dwelling in Christ, which is the experience of the Christian. The spirit of lawlessness is also contradictory to keeping God's commandments. For John's use of the word commandment, see comments on 2:3-6. Here it would be proper to say that **sin is the transgression of the law** of love. Lawlessness grows out of hatred as obedience originates in love. When one acts from any other motive than that of love he acts selfishly, irresponsibly, and in denial of the value and selfhood of other persons involved. To purposely injure another in any way—physically, mentally, spiritually, or socially—is to act contrary to the law of love; it is to sin. "Love worketh no ill to his neighbour: therefore love is the fulfilling of the law" (Rom. 13:10).

Church history reveals that some of the greatest atrocities have been committed by one segment of the Church against another, usually over some difference in belief or interpretation. Some Christians, observing the injunction, "Love not the world," have included the unconverted people of the world, and sometimes many of the beauties and joys of living. Behind this attitude is hidden a feeling of self-attained superiority attached to the chosen people of God. It is akin to the claim of the Gnostics to a "superior enlightenment" which "placed them above the moral law."[4]

All evangelistic effort is both pseudo and futile where the world which is being evangelized is not also loved.

John writes like this because **in him** (Christ) **is no sin** (5) and Christians are to be like Him. God never makes demands to which we cannot attain; He always provides the capability. John says, **Ye know that he was manifested to take away our sins.**

[4]*Ibid.*, p. 123.

C. Children of God Versus Children of the Devil, 3:7-8

While actions motivated by love are normative for the Christian, they do not always come about automatically. Christian love has been demonstrated by Christ and, to a degree, it has been received when one becomes a Christian. But the life of love must also be learned. One can be deceived about living by the law of love. If we would be thoroughly persuaded of it and live by it, we must guard our minds against those who would deceive by word or action, and fortify ourselves with the knowledge of the truth. John declares, **He that doeth righteousness is righteous** (7). Love is a mental comprehension and assent as well as an emotional experience. The last portion of v. 7 repeats 2:29. But John here adds a point for emphasis. **He that committeth sin is of the devil** (8). This does not mean that if a Christian should sin inadvertently—which John has allowed to be possible (2:1)—he belongs to the devil in the way that the Christian belongs to God as a son. John means that insofar as one's life is not motivated by love to obey God, it is motivated by a readiness to respond to the overtures of Satan. Or he may mean that the one who *habitually* sins is among those of whom Jesus said, "Ye are of your father the devil, and the lusts of your father ye will do" (John 8:44). "Like the rest of the New Testament, John has no doubt that behind the rebel wills of men there is a master-rebel, who sinned before they were in being ('from the beginning'), and who, as the enemy of all good, is called the devil, the slanderer, or Satan, the adversary."[5]

The devil has always been the worst of sinners. But Christ came to **destroy the works of the devil.** To **destroy** the devil's works means what John had already said in terms of personal forgiveness, cleansing, and being brought into fellowship with God. This can occur gloriously in the life of the individual even now. There is hope that it will take place in its totality at some future time, though as yet the works of the devil are plentiful and visible.

D. Sinlessness, 3:9-12

Again John emphasizes what he has said before, **Whosoever is born of God doth not commit sin** (9), but here the apostle adds **and he cannot sin.** This is a moral and ethical impossibility, not a

[5]Charles Gore, *The Epistles of John* (New York: Charles Scribner's Sons, 1920), pp. 144-45.

literal one. According to God's nature, one who is born of Him cannot sin, because **his** (God's) **seed remaineth in him.** This **seed** ("God's nature," RSV; "the divine seed," NEB) refers to the eternal life which God has promised to those who obey Him and abide in Him (2:25). Another way to express this truth is to say that he whose life is governed by the law of love—love for God and for his fellowman—**cannot sin,** because he cannot, at one and the same time, both love another and intentionally sin against him.

Here, then, is a further test for determining who are **the children of God** and who are **the children of the devil** (10). **The children of God** do not sin, while **the children of the devil** continue to sin. They are opposite groups in the sense that the one is possessed by the Spirit of Christ and the other by the spirit of antichrist; they are parallel in the sense that every "creature endowed with free will can choose his own parent in the moral world."[6] In this tenth verse "reference is no longer made to the regenerate ground of nature which is the principle of all religious development, but to the ethical position which the regenerate have acquired, of course always on the ground of that divine principle."[7]

Another test of the validity of one's claim to being a child of God is that he love his brother. This is the best illustration of doing **righteousness**—a favorite expression in the Epistle—because it is observable. **Brother** here refers to a brother Christian, representative of all Christians, rather than of all men. A mutual love is required—**that we should love one another** (11). But "a mutual love between Christians and the world is, according to verse 13, impossible, since the world must hate us."[8] Cain, who **slew his brother** (12), is the perfect antithesis of the one who loves his brother. The mention of Cain's story here is the more significant because the cause of the quarrel was a religious disagreement. "The violent deed was only the last expression of that antipathy which righteousness always calls out in those who make evil the guiding principle of their life."[9]

E. Love and Hate, 3:13-17

John has been emphasizing the opposing character of love and hate. It is natural—if not always manifest—for Christians

[6]Plummer, *op. cit.*, p. 128. [7]Haupt, *op. cit.*, p. 194.
[8]*Ibid.*, p. 203. [9]Brooke, *op. cit.*, p. 92.

to love one another. It is just as natural for people of the world to hate the Christian. One might have expected John to emphasize the love of Christians for the sinful world (John 3:16) in response to the world's hatred of the Christian. And because he did not do so it might be concluded that love for the world of mankind is not to be enjoined upon the Christian. But this is an argument from silence that has no weight. John's subject is the evidence of Christian character rather than the evangelistic concern which the Church should manifest. Love for **the brethren** (14) is a better piece of evidence than love for the sinful world, because if one cannot love "the children of God," how could he be expected to love the "children of the devil"?

Love of the **brethren,** then, becomes a criterion for judging that one has been converted from sin. "Life and love are two aspects of the same fact in the moral world, as life and growth in the physical: the one marks the state, the other the activity."[10] But he who does not have love does not have life—**he abideth in death.** More than this, he is **a murderer** (15), like Cain. This is strong language but it is patterned after that of Jesus in Matt. 5:28. The motive is always prior to the overt act. And he who has murder in his heart cannot at the same time be the possessor of eternal life.

The prime example of love is found, of course, in Jesus. **Hereby perceive we the love of God** (16). The phrase **of God** is not found in the Greek text. Read "hereby perceive we love" —love in its essence, love in its highest expression. Love which will not give, even to the fullest extent of one's life and possessions, is not real love. Genuine love starts with sharing **this world's good** (17) ("enough to live on," NEB). It starts with loving one's brother as himself and goes on to loving him better than oneself—**we ought to lay down our lives for the brethren** (16). "John scorns mere talk about loving and demands the deeds and truth of love as evidence of spiritual life."[11] This is the essence of the law of God—the new commandment that we are admonished to keep. Verses 14*b*-15 have been rendered: "The man without love for his brother is living in death already. The man who actively hates his brother is a potential murderer, and

[10]Plummer, *op. cit.,* p. 131.

[11]R. E. O. White, *Open Letter to Evangelicals* (Grand Rapids: Wm. B. Eerdmans Publishing Co., 1964), p. 92.

you will readily see that the eternal life of God cannot live in the heart of a murderer" (Phillips).

One should not stop without observing the relationship between love and suffering which is so evident in the death of Christ. Earlier (1:5) John said that "God is light"—He is revealing. Now he is gradually leading up to saying (4:8) that "God is love"—He is healing. There is great healing value to be found in suffering, especially in accepted, vicarious suffering. Real love will suffer, will yearn over another in need, will go even to death's door with him—love "suffereth long, and is kind." For **shutteth up his bowels of compassion** (17) read "shuts up his heart against him" (NEB).

F. Love Revealed in Action, 3:18-24

To ease the thrust of sharp words and to maintain communication with his hearers, John again comes back to his most endearing term, **my little children** (18). He has raised some difficult questions and stated some propositions which, if taken literally, could cause embarrassment and circumstances even more dire than the situation involved. Must the Christian give his life for others—be like Christ in this respect—in order to demonstrate his love? Does John mean that one must always help a brother Christian who is in need, even when he himself may be in equally straitened circumstances? Should the Christian buy shoes for another man's children while his own children go about in bare feet? Should one give freely and without question to strangers? Wesley said in answer to such questions, "Give and lend to any so far (but not farther, for God never contradicts himself) as is consistent with thy engagements to thy creditors, thy family, and the household of faith."[12]

The dilemma caused by the concept of dying and giving is too often solved by settling for verbal expressions of love, even expressions of pity for the poor and letters of condolence for those in need. John knew this and warned against it. **Let us not love in word,** he said, **neither in tongue** (18). He means that we should **not love in word** as the only expression of our love, **but in deed and in truth.** He might have said, "Do not love by words," as love's only expression. Deeds are always necessary, while verbal

[12]*Explanatory Notes upon the New Testament* (London: The Epworth Press, 1950), p. 34.

expressions of love can be dispensed with, provided one loves in truth, "the inward actuality of love."[13] **In truth** is set in contrast to **in word.** The deed must always be accompanied by the truth. "Let us put our love not into words or into talk, but into deeds, and make it real" (Moffatt).

The dilemma may also bring about a certain lack of confidence on the part of the Christian as to whether he has given proper expression to his love, or whether his love is genuine. How can one know that he is **of the truth?** (19) How can he be reassured in his heart? How shall he be kept free from self-condemnation? The answer is found in a personal knowledge of one's relationship with God. **We know** is a cornerstone of John's witness to the gospel. Assurance of being **of the truth** is the hallmark of the Christian.

The answer given by John is made more clear by attaching the first portion of 20 to the previous verse, reading thus: "By this we shall know that we are of the truth, and reassure our hearts before him whenever our hearts condemn us; for God is greater than our hearts, and he knows everything" (RSV). God is greater in the sense of tenderness and understanding. "The worst that is in us is known to God . . . and still He cares for us and desires us," and "He 'readeth everything'—sees the deepest things, and these are the real things. This is the true test of a man: Is the deepest that is in him the best?"[14] The answer to any feeling of condemnation, whether it be real and deserved or a false sense of guilt from a confusion due to surrounding circumstances, is found within one's own heart. The heart is what we usually think of as conscience (so the NEB).

We can paraphrase John's statement in this way. When our hearts condemn us we can be reassured in either of two ways. If the condemnation is unwarranted, God knows and does not himself condemn us. Not every sense of guilt is the result of disobedience to the will of God. Sometimes it is the result of confusion, or fear, or certain types of mental disorders which give rise to guilt feelings. Did John detect symptoms of neuroses among the "beloved"? Whether the sense of guilt arises from committed sin or from mental disturbances, **God . . . knoweth all things.** He knows the deepest and sincerest intent of the heart and will separate the real from the imaginary.

[13]Haupt, *op. cit.*, p. 215.

[14]Smith, *op. cit.*, p. 187.

In like manner, **if our heart condemn us not, then have we confidence toward God** (21). Those who teach that one cannot have a clear conscience before God—that a claim of conscious forgiveness and cleansing is a sign of pride, itself the prime sin —have not rightly understood John. It is possible to have a conscience "void of offence" and a strong sense of sonship in God—and this John declares. Forgiveness can be as real as guilt.

Confidence in God and faithfulness in prayer are always closely related. That is why John wrote, **Whatsoever we ask, we receive of him** (22). We have confidence **because we keep his commandments, and do those things that are pleasing in his sight.** This does not mean that the Christian life is always easy. "The command of Jesus is hard, utterly hard, for those who try to resist it. But for those who willingly submit, the yoke is easy, and the burden is light."[15] The things that are pleasing to Him may not always be pleasant to do. To love "in deed and in truth" is much more than doing the occasional favor that comes to hand and is easily accomplished. It is doing that which we know He wants us to do, even though we know that it will cost us dearly. In this kind of assurance Bonhoeffer returned to Germany during World War II to share the sufferings of his people and died a martyr to his faith. Such a life of obedience is a parable of God himself becoming man to bear man's sins on the Cross. This is why obedience to God's will is the ground of our assurance and the foundation of believing prayer.

To love "in deed and in truth" (18) is to be in God's employment, giving the cup of water, doing God's will, responding to His call. In various ways God asks all Christians to serve Him, but He calls some men particularly to the Christian ministry. Traditionally this calling has been fulfilled through the regular channels of the Church, by preaching and pastoral ministering, by becoming a missionary, or by other full-time activities in the framework of the organized Church. But there is a more universal sense of the Christian's vocation. It is the day-by-day response of our love to the needs of others as we encounter them.

This expression of obedient love is first of all the acceptance that one is an ambassador of Christ under all circumstances. He is not called always to follow a prescribed method of witnessing but he is called to manifest the attitude and deportment of a

[15]Dietrich Bonhoeffer, *The Cost of Discipleship* (New York: The Macmillan Co., 1963), p. 40.

representative of the gospel. This entails a sensitive awareness of what is becoming to a man of God and an openheartedness to the leadings of the Holy Spirit. Then there will follow the response of Christian love, the word fitly spoken, the deed of kindness, and the standing in Christ's stead in the midst of the world. It is easy to settle for less—shunning the difficult for that which is pleasant. It is strange how we sometimes equate Christian joy with the doing of only those things which we find to our liking. Christ never promised that Christian service would be always enjoyable. Neither did He promise that His followers would be spared the pain and hardship which are parts of normal life on this earth. But He did say that the man who is motivated by love in what he finds at hand to do will not count the cost. Length of life and material things may of themselves be evil unless they be made to serve the dictates of Christian love.

At this point one's spirit rises to the preaching point. Let Christ be our Example and our Pattern (Phil. 2:5-8). He (1) "made himself of no reputation, and took upon him the form of a servant" deliberately and by choice. Or as Phillips translates it, He "stripped himself of all privilege by consenting to be a slave by nature." Then (2) "being found in fashion as a man," whether in joy or pain, in favor or in disfavor, in pleasure or in weariness, among friends or among enemies, He (3) "became obedient"—"living a life of utter obedience" (Phillips)—to the will of God, even though it led to death on the Cross. This is the "cost of discipleship."

Whatsoever we ask, we receive. This verse as well as John 14:14, "If ye shall ask any thing in my name, I will do it," is often quoted so as to give the impression that prayers may be verbalized in such a way as to ensure their answer. Prayer that springs from an obedience to Christ, that knows no turning back, does not need to have its answer guaranteed. This verse does not mean that everything one can think to ask for will be granted him. The **whatsoever** refers to what John is discussing—the things pertaining to one's relationship with God. The apostle is showing how a man may live in the assurance that the grace of God, though it be "costly grace," will be abundantly supplied. The most effective asking or praying one can do is done by a life of willing obedience.

Verses 23-24 emphasize what John has said before. The commandment is **to believe on the name of . . . Jesus Christ** (23). This is theology but much more than theology. It is dogma come alive; it is believing enough to stake one's life on the name—the character—of Christ. The commandment is to **love one another, as he gave us commandment** by His own example of love unto death. The commandment is not one from an external authority, but rather one of personal participation—not that of a general who orders his soldiers to charge but one who leads them into battle.

In 2:28, John exhorted his readers to abide in Christ. Added here is the promise of Christ abiding in the Christian. In addition, the ministry of the Holy Spirit is introduced as a new theme. The whole passage resembles portions of Christ's last discourse to His disciples (John 14—17). As in those chapters, God and Christ and the Spirit dwell in the Christian. This is not muddied theology but rather genuine Christian experience, and also one of the clearest scriptural references to the Trinity.

Section IV Source of Sonship

I John 4:1—5:12

A. Truth and Error, 4:1-6

"One of the gifts that according to St. Paul is brought to the Church by the true Spirit is precisely the discerning of spirits (I Cor. 12:10)."[1] John puts it this way: **Beloved, believe not every spirit, but try the spirits whether they are of God** (1). From this point his argument proceeds to show that confession of Jesus Christ as the incarnate Son of God is evidence that God's Holy Spirit is working through a man. "This demonstration is so conducted as to set over against the Holy Spirit, who testifies of Christ and for Christ, the spirit of the world and of Antichrist, which not only opposes this witness, but diffuses the opposite lie."[2]

There are many spirits in the world, both good and bad, and some standard of judging them must be found. There is **the Spirit of God** (2) and the **spirit of antichrist** (3), each possessing and manifesting himself through men. Matthew speaks of "false Christs, and false prophets" (Matt. 24:24). Those to whom John here refers are doubtless those in 2:18-27 who are termed "many antichrists," who "went out from us, but . . . were not of us." He who "denieth that Jesus is the Christ" is a "liar," who also "denieth the Father and the Son."

There is a diabolic supernatural power, as well as a righteous supernatural power, working in the world and in the lives of men. There are also false prophets who make evil out of good. Some are to be found in the church—those who substitute institutionalized religion for the vitality of the Spirit of Christ, and those who substitute a humanism for the gospel of Christ. There are found also in the world those who exchange love for God for love of power, "political saviors who incarnate demonism that palpably partakes of evil."[3] "The variety and the popularity of contemporary false prophets should not surprise us; it is still true that 'the world listens to them' (5). In every age the lie contends against

[1]Stephen Neill, *Christian Holiness* (New York: Harper and Brothers, 1960), p. 86.

[2]Haupt, *op. cit.*, p. 241.

[3]Hoon, *op. cit.*, p. 272.

the truth, evil against good, false prophets against true prophets, the spirit of Antichrist against Christ."[4]

The true prophet **confesseth that Jesus Christ is come in the flesh** (2). **Jesus** refers to His human nature and **Christ** to His divine nature, and thus the two together become the expression of the Incarnation. **Is come in the flesh** must not be construed to be the same as "come into the flesh." "Christ did not descend . . . into an already existing man, but He came in human nature; He 'became flesh.' "[5] John is saying that the Incarnation is not only the central focus of the gospel but that it also gathers within its total significance the other great doctrinal truths such as the Virgin Birth, the Crucifixion, and the Resurrection. The Incarnation is the essential creed of Christianity; on this doctrine all else which calls itself Christian stands or falls.

In a sense, then, we are saying that this is a creed but much more than a creed. It is a formulation of faith, but it is also a historical fact that **Christ is come in the flesh.** The Christian religion is grounded in a historical event, in the crowning act of God in redemption. God became man. His relation with man is thus active and dynamic. To confess to the Incarnation is to enter into this activity of God, to become involved in what God has done and is doing, to be a partner and thus a living witness to the Christian doctrine of salvation. Forgiveness is more than a legal release from guilt; it is partaking of new life in Christ and being energized for active participation in the kingdom of God on earth.

In contrast to the false prophets, John says, **Ye are of God** (4), and, **We are of God** (6). **The world** (5) listens to the false prophets but it will not listen to what John has been teaching. Nevertheless, God listens and thereby confirms its truth: **Hereby know we the spirit of truth, and the spirit of error** (6). **The spirit of truth** is the Spirit of God.

The Christian participates in the Incarnation by the indwelling of the Spirit. This is the "abiding" dealt with in c. 3 and also in v. 13 of the present chapter. This is the "Comforter," "the Spirit of truth," whom Jesus promised to His disciples, saying, "He dwelleth with you, and shall be in you" (John 14:17). In this way John builds a solid case by which the Christian may be assured of his relationship with God and can distinguish between truth and error.

[4]*Ibid.*, p. 273. [5]Plummer, *op. cit.*, p. 142.

There is here a beautiful flexibility within rigidity. Christian doctrine is as uncompromising as truth itself; at the same time, according to John, it demands conformity at only one inclusive point—the Incarnation. Do we dare to follow him in this? He set up one standard and only one, while the Church has multiplied its dogmas, and these have led to division rather than to unity. A return to the Incarnation as truly central and utterly essential in both creed and experience would return the Church to the gospel in its dynamic simplicity. Think what would happen if this great principle of love were put into effect in the world of men and of nations! The results are assured, **because greater is he that is in you, than he that is in the world** (4). John emphasized that which was central in doctrine and essential in experience in order to achieve that which was spiritual in content.

B. Love Is of God, 4:7-12

Verses 1-6 are an enlargement of the first part of the text found in 3:23: "That we should believe on the name of his Son Jesus Christ." The second half of the text, "and love one another," is developed in the present section.

One of the results of the gift of the Spirit is brotherly love. In 2:7-11 this theme is discussed as the result of walking in the light. In 3:10-18 it is treated as a particular mark of the Christian. In the present passage "it appears as a gift of the Spirit of God, a contrast to the anti-christian spirit, and above all as an effluence from the very Being of God."[6] These might be called the threefold ground of perfect love.

Let us love one another (7), is more than an exhortation. It flows naturally from the statement that **love is of God.** Such love does not depend upon the quality of its object. If a man has fellowship with God, is born of God, and walks in the light, he will invariably love others because **love is of God.**

While John probably has reference to love for the Christian community, love for men in general cannot be excluded. Love then becomes a test of one's relationship with God. The apostle does not say that everyone who is born of God manifests love, but rather that **every one that loveth is born of God, and knoweth God.** By this "he certainly does not mean that in every person

[6]*Ibid.*, p. 146.

who feels some surge of emotional love—man for woman, mother for child—there is the sign of the God-given love, indicating God-given life. There may be some links between the most elementary forms of love . . . and the divine love, but that is not what our writer is thinking about."[7] A distinction must be marked between what we call natural love and Christian love, although the difference is not always readily discernible. I once knew a man, a vocal unbeliever, who demonstrated over a period of years a love and devotion to his invalid wife which I have never seen surpassed among Christians. The only answer to the dilemma which this observation raises is that this love was manifested in no other aspect of his life. Perhaps this is the distinction we seek.

It is easier to understand **He that loveth not knoweth not God; for God is love** (8). This expression, **God is love,** parallels John's former statement, "God is light" **(1:5)**. It "expresses not a quality which He possesses, but one which embraces all that He is."[8] This is not the same as to say that "love is God." To John's thinking, expressions of love by man are less than Christian if they are not grounded in God's revelation of himself in Jesus Christ. "If we take the two definitions [God is light and God is love] together, we reach the result that no action of God is conceivable which has not for its aim the demonstration of love."[9] This writer continues, "If, then, light and love are as inseparable [in] the divine nature as form and matter [in] any material thing, then it follows that every one who is born of God must be a partaker of this light and of this love."[10]

John has spoken several times of one's relationship with God being a relationship of knowledge (2:4, 13-14; 3:6; 4:7). In his statement, **God is love,** he speaks of a true knowledge of God, of the very nature of God, and not knowledge *about* God. That nature was manifested in Jesus Christ. It is especially manifested **toward us (9)** (believers) because we have received it. Where there is no reception there is no revelation. Those who walk in the light are able to know that **God is love.**

Verse **9** shows us that the love of God in Christ had an object. Christ was its vehicle while man was its object of contact in the

[7]R. R. Williams, "The Letters of St. John and James," *The Cambridge Bible Commentary* (Cambridge: The University Press, 1965), p. 48.

[8]Plummer, *op. cit.,* p. 147.

[9]Haupt, *op. cit.*, p. 258.

[10]*Ibid.,* p. 259.

world. "God so loved" that He **sent his only begotten Son into the world, that we might live through him.** In Christ we see the love of God. Through Christ we experience that love. "Only when the Christ for us is really the Christ in us, do we exhaust the meaning of [God is love]."[11]

God's love for man is not a response to our love. The response is ours. Our love depends upon and is the result of His love. In Christ, God loved the unlovely, the estranged sinful creature called man, and made reconciliation with him. (See note on 2:2.) It need only be said here that in the Incarnation God did not make himself favorably disposed toward man. That could have been accomplished by much easier means as is amply demonstrated in the Old Testament. But by becoming man God reconciled man to himself—He did what man himself could not do.

In v. 11, for the second time in this chapter, John uses the endearing term **Beloved** (*agapetoi*). It attracts devoted attention and has in it the force of an entreaty. **If God so loved us**—and He did—**we ought also to love one another.** God's love serves not only as a sufficient example but as a stimulating cause. Our love should flow naturally from God's love which we have experienced.

No man hath seen God (12). This seems at first to be an intrusion into the train of thought. The author is probably warning his readers not to try to know God in any way other than he is describing. Many have sought to find God and many have claimed to know God in clearer perspective than in the Christian Church. John is saying that all such attempts have failed. One may learn some things about God through searching, but the Father cannot be really known except through His self-revelation as love in Jesus Christ.

The validity of our relationship with God is shown in brotherly love, because love can come only from God. "What a wonderful truth this is, that God's love for us shall be *in* us, and become our love for others."[12] By our love for one another we know that God through His Spirit **dwelleth in us.** And by the exercise of that love, **his love is perfected in us** (12). It is not God's love for us that is perfected. "Anything that is complete in its kind

[11]*Ibid.*, p. 262.

[12]Thomas Cook, *New Testament Holiness* (London: The Epworth Press, 1958), p. 52.

is perfect."[13] Rather, "When God's love to us comes to be in us, it is like the virtue which the loadstone gives to the needle, inclining it to move toward the pole."[14] The meaning in this last clause in 12 is that our love for the brethren is brought to its most complete expression.

C. God Is Love, 4:13-21

The first four verses of this section are a review of what has gone before. Verse 13 sums up 1-12 and parallels 3:24. Verses 14-16 summarize 1-6 and 7-12. In these verses (13-16) the author reasserts the bases of the Christian's assurance. The first is the gift of **his Spirit** (13). Here is the Divine Presence whom Jesus said He would ask the Father to send to His followers (John 14: 16). This presence of the Holy Spirit is a deeply satisfying subjective witness that we belong to God. John next shows "its complement in the external testimony to Christ as Savior":[15] **We have seen and do testify that the Father sent the Son to be the Saviour of the world** (14). This refers us back to the earlier claim that the Incarnation is the central Christian dogma. Thus one's assurance has both a subjective and an objective character.

In 16 the author reverses the order—putting the objective evidence first—when he says that **we have known and believed the love that God hath to us** ("for us"), and which has been perfected in us. John says: "We have known, it has become plain to us, that divine love has taken up its dwelling in us; and, after we have come to know this, we have also believingly apprehended it."[16] The content of the Christian confession "is nothing less than the love of God, manifested in the incarnate life, and the death, of Jesus."[17] The essence of knowing God in personal experience is the possession of the love of God within. **He that dwelleth in love dwelleth in God, and God in him** (16). The indwelling of the Holy Spirit (13, cf. 3:24) is also the indwelling of love, which results in brotherly love (11). "The natural man can neither believe nor love. In his fallen and unredeemed state he is both blind and selfish. It is only by the grace of the Holy Spirit, who is the Spirit of truth and whose first-fruits is love (Gal. v. 22) that man ever comes to believe in Christ and to love

[13]George Peck, *Christian Perfection* (New York: Carlton and Lanahan, 1842, 4th ed.), p. 25.

[14]Cook, *op. cit.*, p. 76, from Lange.

[15]Dodd, *op. cit.*, p. 115.

[16]Haupt, *op. cit.*, p. 271.

[17]Dodd, *op. cit.*, p. 116.

others."[18] The effective cause of all our love is the fact that **God is love.**

In 7-8 the concept that "God is love" is associated with the knowledge of God. In the present context it is associated with the nature of God. **Love** (*agape*) denotes essence and is said to dwell in the Christian as a result of a mystical experience with God. It must not be thought of as something which comes in from the outside to reside as a separate entity; nor is it a gift which can be removed as easily as it was given. Rather, it is a kind of fusion of God's nature with man's nature, in a living experience.

This is the experience of perfect love, the second work of grace, which is the hallmark of the Wesleyan theological tradition. This is Christian perfection, and John is one of the most powerful advocates in the Scriptures of such an experience of union with God. For the Christian, this is dwelling in love and dwelling in God, and God in him. It is the love of God dwelling in us, which love must be perfected in us. It is not the Christian as a person apart from God who is made perfect, but rather God's love is made perfect within him.

Since God is perfect and love is His nature, in what sense must His love in us be perfected? The answer must be seen in the purpose for which that love is given. God does not pour His love in us to be consumed upon ourselves. Love turned in upon itself is self-destructive. God loves us in order that we may love others. His love in us is perfected when it becomes brotherly love (2:5; 4:12). Seldom does the apostle speak of our love for God, and when he does so, it is only obliquely (4:10, 19-20). For John the three aspects of love are that God loves us, His love dwells in us, and we love the brethren.

This experience of perfected love gives us boldness **in the day of judgment** (17). In this respect we are like Christ: **because as he is, so are we in this world.** Whether it be the final judgment or the day-to-day judgment which one faces here, the man who is motivated by love does not fear it: **There is no fear in love; but perfect love casteth out fear** (18). This love which casts out fear is best seen in Christ on the Cross. "Fellowship with God is at the same time the perfected indwelling of the divine love in us;

[18]J. R. W. Stott, *The Epistles of John,* "The Tyndale New Testament Commentaries" (Grand Rapids: Wm. B. Eerdmans Publishing Co., 1964), pp. 165-66.

both of these, however, make us like Christ; according to this conformity to Him shall we be finally judged; and if we have it, we have also confidence at the last day."[19]

Speaking to this point Bengel says, "Men's condition is varied: without fear and love; with fear without love; with fear and love; without fear with love."[20] Fear carries with it the expectation of retaliation, the certainty of judgment. "We can love and reverence God simultaneously (cf. Heb. v. 7), but we cannot approach Him in love and hide from Him in fear at the same time."[21] "The presence of fear is a sign that love is not yet perfect,"[22] **but perfect love casteth out fear.** Fear gives way to confidence and assurance when, and only when, love is perfect (*teleia*), when it "penetrates and fills the whole life and being of man."[23]

We love him, because he first loved us (19) sums up what was begun at v. 8. **Him** (*humeis*) is not found in the Greek and should be read, **We love.** This does not exclude love for God but it broadens the concept to include love for others. The verb **love** (*agapomen*) may be either indicative (we love) or hortative subjunctive ("let us love," as v. 7). The best translations favor the indicative. "The thought is that the amazing love of God in Christ is the inspiration of all the love that stirs in our hearts. It awakens within us an answering love—a grateful love for Him manifesting itself in love for our brethren."[24] Moreover, "our love owes its very origin to God's love, from which it is an effluence."[25]

Turning now to the form of questioning which he used in the first chapter, John again sets up a test of love. If one does not love **his brother whom he hath seen, how can he love God whom he hath not seen? (20)** The apostle does not mean to degrade love for one's brother in comparison to one's love for God. Rather, he is saying that our love for God finds its test of validity in our love for others. Perhaps this is why, up to this point, John has not directly made mention of our love for God.

[19]Haupt, *op. cit.*, pp. 269-70.

[20]*Gnomon of the New Testament*, trans. by C. T. Lewis and M. R. Vincent (Philadelphia: Perkinpine and Higgins, 1880), II, 802-3.

[21]Stott, *op. cit.*, p. 169.

[22]Brooke, *op. cit.*, p. 125.

[23]Haupt, *op. cit.*, p. 279.

[24]Smith, *op. cit.*, p. 192.

[25]Plummer, *op. cit.*, p. 153.

It is nonexistent if it is not accompanied by brotherly love. "My deeds of charity to my neighbor may indeed and must spring from love to God; but there are no means of testifying our love to Him in act, to Him as invisible, or to Him in and for Himself, without such a mediating element."[26]

This is so because God has commanded **that he who loveth God love his brother also** (21). Verse 21 may be a reference to the summary of the Mosaic law as loving God with one's whole heart and his neighbor as himself (Lev. 19:18; Deut. 6:5; Luke 10:27). John thinks of the commandment as the commandment of love (see comments on 2:7-8). Love, being of the very nature of God, contains its own motivation to self-expression toward others. It is of the nature of love to express itself. Yet, because man at his best is still human and fallible, the injunction to love his brethren in both word and deed must be set continually before him.

The love of God perfected in one's heart and life must find its expression in his love for others, "first, because it is only in loving our brother whom we see . . . that we can exercise the very love wherewith God has first loved us . . . secondly, because in loving our brother, we are obeying the commandment of Him whom we profess to love . . . thirdly, because in loving our brother we love one who is begotten of God."[27]

Behind John's thinking at this point stands the form of a man, the God-man, our elder Brother, who is the primary object of the love of all those who are born of God. The apostle may have been thinking: If we do not love Christ, whom we have seen and heard and handled (1:1-3), how can we love God, who can be seen only in Christ? He does not speak of our love for Christ, who is the focus of God's love for man. But certainly John would say that our love for both God and man presupposes our love for Christ. "In many respects we may be very imperfect, but if we love God [and man] with all the capacity we actually possess, we are Christianly perfect according to the Scriptures."[28] Thomas Cook further says "the only perfection possible on earth is a perfection of love, of motive, of intention."[29]

[26]Haupt, *op. cit.*, p. 283.

[27]Robert S. Candlish, *The First Epistle of John* (Grand Rapids: Zondervan Publishing House, n.d.), p. 433.

[28]Cook, *op. cit.*, p. 61.

[29]*Ibid.*, p. 10.

D. Faith Is the Victory, 5:1-5

In the clause **whosoever believeth** (1), the subject of the verb is *pas,* "all" or "everyone." It is a much stronger term than if the author had merely said "he." The verb is *pisteuon,* "believe." In previous passages where similar tests are employed (4:2, 15) the verb is "confess" (*homologei*). This term was used as a verbal expression of faith to give outward evidence that men were truly Christians. In the present chapter it is the inner witness of divine sonship that is in question, and so the verb for believing is used. A mere understanding and verbal statement of truth does not include all that is involved in being a partaker of the life of God in Christ. That which is outward must become inward. With the mouth man confesses, but with the heart he believes.

However, these two concepts should not be put in contrast the one to the other. "In confession the believer takes his stand, commits his life, declares what he believes to be true, affirms his ultimate loyalty, and defies every false claim upon his life. The confession of faith is the seal of faith and the courage of faith."[30]

Such confession as John demanded on the part of Christians was necessitated by the Gnostic errors with which they then wrestled. The Church was forced to take its stand on primary issues, and it was important that its beliefs be put into understandable terms. There are evidences of these early creedal formulations throughout the New Testament, resulting not only from defense against heresies but also from preaching and teaching needs.[31] This was a natural growth within the Church because worship demands some forms for expression of faith. "What cannot be thought through critically and expressed with reasonable clarity cannot demand the allegiance of man's whole being. Understanding is necessary for man's full commitment. Hence faith must be spoken and made intelligible."[32]

All of the creedal formulations of the New Testament are Christological, because the Church sought to understand and rightly express its faith in the Christ. These statements developed from the simple "We believe" in the second and third centuries to the demand for confessional statements as necessary for salva-

[30]John H. Leith (ed.), *Creeds of the Churches* (New York: Doubleday and Co., 1903), p. 5.

[31]See Rom. 1:3-4; 10:9; I Cor. 8:6; 12:3; 15:3-7.

[32]Leith, *op. cit.,* p. 1.

tion in the sixth century. Here is reflected the tendency of the Church to move from simplicity to complexity and from freedom to conformity—from faith in Christ as the Son of God to the acceptance of fixed dogmatic forms as the ground of orthodoxy. It tends to be a move from confession based upon inner faith to a confession of mental assent requiring no necessary inner persuasion. Here we see the human tendency to stray from the substance to the form, from that which is primary to that which is secondary. It can be found wherever stated intellectual positions—concerning miracles, modes of divine inspiration, interpretation of the Scriptures, observances of rites and rituals, manners of form and deportment—rather than genuine expressions of faith are made normative for faith and salvation.

John would draw us back from a process which tends to cut the nerve of true Christian faith. He places his finger on the auricle and ventricle of the heart of the gospel. He asks for no more than an inner, personal faith in Christ as the Son of God witnessed before the world—the love of God in the heart working itself out to a needy world.

This is a lesson in values, placing things in their proper order and putting emphases where they belong. Here also is a lesson in freedom. Nothing is so free and untrammeled as personal faith and love. "If the Son therefore shall make you free, ye shall be free indeed" (John 8:36). No man is free unless he is free to believe and to love.

To believe that **Jesus is the Christ** (1), in John's language, is to be **born of God.** It is to love God and therefore to love others. To love God is to keep His commandments (2:4-8), and this is evidence that we love the children of God (3:23). Our love for God can be recognized only as we manifest it in love for the brethren (3:16). To sum up: **This is the love of God, that we keep his commandments: and his commandments are not grievous** (burdensome) (3). This does not mean that God's laws are of small moral weight. They are not burdensome to the Christian because "all difficulty lies simply in the relation between the thing concerned and the power of the person concerned."[33] The one who is joined to Christ by faith finds that His yoke is easy and His burden is light.

To John, **the world** (4; cf. 2:15) is opposed to God and thus to God's people and is therefore something to be contended with and defeated. The Christian is already a victor over the sinful

[33]Haupt, *op. cit.*, p. 292.

world by virtue of his having believed in Christ as the Son of God. By that same faith, maintained and confirmed, the world is overcome. But we must remember that this faith gathers up within its significance the concepts of walking in the light, of being forgiven, of abiding in Christ, of possessing the Holy Spirit, and of loving God.

To overcome the world means to be victorious in one's own life over all that makes the world what it is in its opposition to God. It means to successfully keep the injunction "that ye sin not" (2:1).

But this faith also includes love of the brethren, and so the victory is a victory of love. Love of the brethren overflows and strives to make "children of God" of those who are "children of the devil" (3:10). Evangelism that evangelizes is **victory** over the world of the highest sort. Where love is the weapon, salvation the missile, and eternal life the aim, victory is resurrection, rather than destruction, and overcoming becomes winning. The best way to destroy an enemy is to win him to one's own cause. In this way Christ was "manifested, that he might destroy the works of the devil" (3:8). The Christian's total relationship to Christ and to the world, which involves the greater portion of the Epistle up to this point, is summed up in the concept of faith—in the words of Paul, it is a "faith which worketh by love" (Gal. 5:6).

E. Eternal Life, 5:6-12

This First Epistle of John opened with a declaration concerning Christ, the "Word of life" (1:1). There followed a description of the inward relationship of the Christian to God and to his brethren, and a further discussion of the external evidence of that relationship in loving deeds toward God and man. This is a love relationship based upon faith in Christ as the Son of God. It is a sharing in "the Word of life"—"that eternal life, which was with the Father, and was manifested unto us" (1:2) through the Son. It is the fellowship (*koinonia*) of which John spoke earlier, into which he sought to bring those to whom he wrote and which he and the other apostles shared. "And truly our fellowship is with the Father, and with his Son Jesus Christ" (1:3).

This is "the *koinonia* of the Spirit [3:24; 4:13]. It is a religious community sharing through the Holy Spirit the supernatural life of Christ."[34] It shares a "common life" with a

[34]Lindsay Dewar, *The Holy Spirit and Modern Thought* (New York: Harper and Brothers, 1959), p. 204.

"common purpose,"[35] a common faith in Christ with a common love for the brethren, the inward and outward aspects of the Christian life through the indwelling of the Holy Spirit. Theologically, this may be called the Christology of the Spirit in the life of the Church.

One of the most prominent ideas in John's writings is that of **witness** (6; *martyria*). The gospel is a gospel of witness.[36] In The Revelation, John "bare record [*emartyresen*] of the word of God, and of the testimony [*martyrian*] of Jesus Christ" (Rev. 1:2). The First Epistle begins with the author's witness, "That which we have seen and heard declare we unto you" (1:3), and now toward the close John presents the witness of God himself—the witness of God to Christ through the Spirit. It is **the witness of God** (9) and **it is the Spirit that beareth witness, because the Spirit is truth** (6).

The present section has a textual problem in the latter portion of 7 and the first portion of 8. These few words are recognized by New Testament scholars as a gloss, a marginal comment which crept into the text during some early translation. A distinction between the witnesses **in heaven** (7) and **in earth** (8) as found in the KJV is without significance in John's thought. The two verses as complete in the original should read, **For there are three that bear record . . . the spirit, and the water, and the blood: and these three agree in one,** or "these three are in agreement" (NEB).

There is one primary Witness—the Holy Spirit. Throughout the Christian centuries the Spirit has been manifest in every successful witness of the Church to Jesus Christ. The Church has suffered from the extreme of ecclesiasticism on the one hand where the creeds were substituted for the voice of the Spirit and the other extreme which makes "the claim that the inward voice of the Holy Spirit takes precedence over the external word of Scripture, or the dicta of prelates."[37] Somewhere between the two, John places the witness of the Spirit, firmly grounded in the truth that Jesus is the Christ, the Son of God. This truth often tends to become secondary in an emphasis on either one or both extremes.

[35]*Ibid.* [36]See Plummer, *op. cit.*, p. 160.

[37]Henry P. VanDusen, *Spirit, Son, and Father* (New York: Charles Scribner's Sons, 1958), p. 82.

The other two witnesses of **water, and the blood**—the baptism and the crucifixion of Christ—are subsidiary to the Spirit in that they do not contain their own authority. There have been many other baptisms and many crucifixions, and even the baptism and death of the Christ were virtually unnoticed in secular annals; but the Spirit-inspired history of the Church has kept these two great events alive and made them witnesses to the deity of Jesus Christ.

The water, and the blood have been given many interpretations. The one already mentioned, equating them with the Baptism and Crucifixion, is the most tenable. Another suggests the Baptism and the Eucharist, while a third suggests the water and blood which flowed from the side of Jesus at the Crucifixion. A fourth interpretation makes **the water, and the blood** refer to purification and redemption.[38]

A Gnostic heresy of John's time held that Jesus was only a man "upon whom the Christ descended at the baptism and from whom the Christ departed before the cross."[39] John sought to refute this teaching by saying that Christ came not only by water but also through blood, and this he gives as a witness to our Lord's deity. Christ's public ministry began at His baptism and concluded with His crucifixion. "The Crucifixion was the consummation of the Incarnation. It was not a mere incident in the life of an ordinary man."[40] Phillips makes v. 8 crystal-clear: "The witness therefore is a triple one—the Spirit in our own hearts, the signs of the water of baptism and the blood of atonement—and they all say the same thing."

This testimony should not be difficult to accept because it **is the witness of God** (9). Since we are so inclined to accept what others tell us as evidence, we may surely accept this witness of the Spirit. Moreover, the Christian has the corroborating witness within his own heart, because he has become a partaker of the eternal life of God. He who does not believe the testimony of God to the deity of Jesus **hath made him** (God) **a liar** (10) and branded himself as not being a Christian. **He that hath the Son**—has believed the testimony described above—**hath** eternal **life** (12). He who does not believe does not have life, and this whole discussion has no real meaning to him.

[38]Plummer, *op. cit.*, pp. 157-59; Brooke, *op. cit.*, pp. 132-34.

[39]Stott, *op. cit.*, p. 178.

[40]Brooke, *op. cit.*, p. 133.

Section V *Conclusion*

I John 5:13-21

A. The Ground of Assurance, 5:13-17

John elsewhere suggests several reasons why he wrote this Epistle, but, as in the Gospel, he leaves the main purpose until the end. In the Gospel he wrote in order that men "might believe that Jesus is the Christ, the Son of God; and that believing ye might have life through his name" (John 20:31). It was written in order to bring men into this experience of eternal life. The Epistle is written to those **that believe on the name of the Son of God** (13). In the light of this statement the last portion of 13, **that ye may believe on the name of the Son of God,** is probably a gloss and should be deleted as in the RSV and the NEB. It is not reasonable that John wrote to believers in order that they might become believers. His purpose in writing was a single purpose and very simply expressed, **that ye may know that ye have eternal life.** The Gospel, then, was written in order that men might have life, and the Epistle in order that they might know that they have it. The key words of the Epistle are *assure, confidence, know,* and *believe,* as well as *life, love,* and *faith.*

In v. 14, John writes, **And this is the confidence that we have in him.** Three times previously John has spoken of **confidence** (*parresia*): twice in connection with the day of judgment (2:28; 4:17) and once in connection with prayer (3:21). "Thus two more leading ideas of the Epistle meet in this recapitulation, boldness towards God and brotherly love; for it is love of the brethren which induces us to pray for them."[1]

This **confidence** or "boldness" which comes from the knowledge of possessing eternal life results in a confidence in respect to prayer for the brethren. **If we ask any thing according to his will, he heareth us.** This **any thing** refers not to every request that we make, however proper it may be; it refers, rather, to anything concerning the salvation of a **brother** (16). Here is intercessory, importunate prayer. There are two limitations: first, it must be **according to his will.** It is "active identification with

[1]Plummer, *op. cit.,* p. 166.

the divine will, the lifting up of our wills to God's desires, not the persuasion of God's will to fulfil our desires."[2] But it is not always possible to know just what God's will is. In the words of Paul, "We know not what we should pray for as we ought: but the Spirit itself maketh intercession for us with groanings which cannot be uttered" (Rom. 8:26). Nevertheless, in general we know that it is God's will that all shall share in eternal life and become sons of God.

In the second place our prayers are limited by those for whom we pray—the brethren. Verses 15-17 probably refer basically to one who has sinned inadvertently (2:1-2) and for some reason persisted therein. This one is still termed **a brother** and means one belonging to the community of believers but at the same time living unrighteously (17).

John makes a distinction between kinds of sinning—some are **unto death** and some are not. The **sin unto death** is not a particular sin, but habitual sinning. "We must get rid of the idea . . . that 'sin unto death' is a sin which can be recognized by those among whom the one who commits it lives. . . . He implies that some sins may be known to be 'not unto death:' he neither says nor implies that all 'sin unto death' can be known as such."[3]

Sin unto death is sinning wilfully, and if it is "persisted in, it must lead to final separation from the Divine life."[4] There is also a sinning which is **not unto death.** The difference lies in the set of the soul. It may be illustrated by a man on a ladder. One cannot determine his true condition until he learns if he is moving up or down. Some men in sin are struggling to get out while others allow themselves to sink deeper. God knows the difference and we are assured that **he shall give him life for them that sin not unto death** (16).

Some commentators have used this passage to teach the unpardonable sin. There is here no suggestion or implication of a sin or a habit of sinning that God will not forgive. John says that a man may depart from God and keep on going until he can no longer hear God; he can walk in darkness until he is out of reach of the light. But the apostle's main topic here is prayer, intercessory prayer, a close corollary to brotherly love.

This kind of prayer is praying in faith, asking anything, everything for the brethren, but leaving the results to the will

[2]Hoon, *op. cit.*, p. 298.

[3]Plummer, *op. cit.*, p. 167.

[4]Brooke, *op. cit.*, p. 146.

of God, who knows what is going on. And lest it be thought that the uncertainty on the part of the one who prays seems to cast doubt upon the fact of sin or to treat it lightly, he says that **all unrighteousness is sin** (17). Sin is also "the transgression of the law" (3:4). It is best that we do not know what goes on in the heart of a brother; we would be either too severe or too easy on him. It is not our place to know and to judge. It is our part to pray. God will do the rest.

John's formula for intercessory prayer is a good one: (1) Pray for the brethren; (2) Pray in faith; (3) Pray knowing that God hears us; (4) Pray in the knowledge that God will answer according to His will.

B. Spiritual Knowledge, 5:18-21

The idea of confidence is here buttressed by the certainty of adequate knowledge. This theme of the dependability of our spiritual knowledge occurs earlier, and in v. 13 it is stated as the prime purpose of the Epistle. It is knowledge of God (2:3), of the possession of eternal life (3:14), and of all things necessary for salvation (2:20); it comes from obedience to God (2:3), from the possession of love for the brethren (3:14; 5:13), and is attested by the indwelling Holy Spirit (3:24). This knowledge is more than an intuition because it can be tested in the experiences of life.

Now in closing the Epistle the writer reemphasizes these facts of Christian knowledge—facts concerning the Christian's relationship to Satan and to Jesus Christ. "We have in these last verses a final emphasis laid on the fundamental principles on which the Epistle rests: that we through the mission of the Lord Jesus Christ have fellowship with God; that this fellowship protects us from sin, and establishes us in a relation of perfect opposition to the world."[5]

The declaration, **Whosoever is born of God sinneth not** (18), is a reemphasis of 3:9. The reason for this victory over sin is, **He that is begotten of God keepeth himself, and that wicked one toucheth him not.** But a difference of one letter in the Greek serves to alter the meaning and to leave the wrong impression. The better manuscripts have *auton* (him) rather than *eauton* (himself), so that it should read, "He that is begotten of God keepeth him." Also, the change from the perfect of the

[5]Haupt, *op. cit.*, p. 345.

verb for **born** and **begotten** (*gegennemenos*) to the aorist (*gennetheis*) assists in the proper translation: "He who was born of God keeps him, and the evil one does not touch him" (RSV, NEB). It is Christ, the begotten of God, who keeps the Christian. "Our security is not our grip on Christ but His grip on us."[6]

"In addition to his offices Victor (vss. 4-5), Redeemer (1:7; 3:5, 8, 16; 4:10, 14), Advocate (2:1), Revealer (2:20; 5:6-8), Teacher (2:27), Jesus may be conceived as Defender or Keeper."[7]

The second fact of which the Christian has sure knowledge is **that we are of God, and the whole world lieth in wickedness** (19). John uses the plural **we,** including himself with all other Christians. All the grounds of knowledge previously stated support and confirm the fact **that we are of God.** In stark contrast to this, the "world is in the power of the evil one" (NASB). The concept of **world** here is more inclusive than in 2:15; in addition to the meaning there, the word here includes the people who are controlled by the evil world system. "It is clear therefore that the severance between the Church and the world ought to be, and tends to be, as total as that between God and the evil one."[8]

The third affirmation goes far beyond the other two, which are based upon it. It has to do with Jesus Christ. **We know that the Son of God is come, and hath given us an understanding** (20). "Both revelation and redemption are His gracious work. Without Him we could neither know God nor overcome sin . . . The Christian religion is both historical and experimental."[9]

He **hath given us . . . understanding**—the power to comprehend, the capacity to know—**that we may know him that is true.** It is through Christ that we have been able to recognize with "a continuous and progressive apprehension"[10] the things which we know. We possess what we have been made able to receive, and we know that which we are able to comprehend because of Christ.

All that we know is summed up in **we . . . know him that is true.** We know God in personal experience. We know that He is real **and we are in him** who is real. God is the Father of Jesus Christ, in whom has been revealed eternal life. We have eternal

[6]Smith, *op. cit.*, p. 199.
[7]Hoon, *op. cit.*, p. 300.
[8]Plummer, *op. cit.*, pp. 170-71.
[9]Stott, *op. cit.*, p. 194.
[10]*Ibid.*, p. 195, quoting Westcott.

life when we are in God, Father and Son, "because he hath given us of his Spirit" (4:13).

John closes the Epistle with his favorite term of affection, **little children.** His final exhortation seems almost out of place because he has not before spoken of it: **Keep yourselves from idols** (21). The verb is not the same as in 18 and should be translated "guard" (RSV). The warning is to be alert against that which was a present danger. In Ephesus "every street through which his [John's] readers walked, and every heathen house they visited swarmed with idols in the literal sense."[11]

Here is the last great contrast of the many found in this Epistle, between the living God and lifeless gods. This contrast climaxes the central purpose of the apostle, who sought to build faith in his people even in the midst of a "faithless and perverse generation" (Matt. 17:17). How well he succeeded is a matter of history.

But John in this Epistle still speaks today because he gives voice to the living Word of God. How well he succeeds in this task depends on how well we hear and how well, under God, we make today's history. Amen!

[11]Plummer, *op. cit.*, p. 173.

The Second Epistle of

JOHN

Harvey J. S. Blaney

Outline

Live in Love and Obedience

A. Salutation, 1-3
B. The Message, 4-11
C. Conclusion, 12-13

Live in Love and Obedience

II John 1-13

A. Salutation, 1-3

The author calls himself **the elder** (1; *presbyteros*), although he did not identify himself in this fashion in the First Epistle. The term means essentially one of superior age. It is probable that he thus acknowledged his position among the churches in his charge as the revered, elderly teacher and preacher which we know John to have been.

The letter is addressed to **the elect lady** (*eklekte kuria*, "the lady chosen of God," NEB) **and her children.** Two interpretations have made proper names out of the Greek and thus refer it to an individual: (*a*) Electa, the Beloved, and (*b*) the elect Kuria. The more probable meaning is that **the elect lady** has reference to a local church; **her children** (cf. 4) would then refer to the church members. This short letter is addressed to a church and her members from a sister church and its members (13). It was written by **the elder** who at that time was associated as leader with the sending church.

There seemed to be need of the assertion **whom I love in the truth.** Perhaps the persons mentioned in 10 had showed no disposition of Christian love. The attitude of the author was a "love which is exercised in the highest sphere, which corresponds to the truest conception of love."[1] This affection was shared by **all** other Christians who knew the church. Knowing the truth as it has been revealed in Christ induces brotherly love. They all belonged to the fellowship (*koinonia*) of the saints.[2]

[1]Brooke, *op. cit.*, p. 170.

[2]See comments on I John 2:3.

For the truth's sake (2) refers to the truth as it is revealed in Jesus Christ. This would be the eternal life which the believers had received. John boldly asserts that this truth **shall be with us for ever.**

The greeting, **Grace be with you, mercy, and peace** (3), is "not a wish but a confident assurance."[3] " 'Grace' is the *favour* of God toward sinners; 'mercy' is the *compassion* of God for the misery of sinners; 'peace' is the result when the guilt and misery of sin are removed. 'Grace' is rare in the writings of John; elsewhere only John i:14, 16, 17; Rev. i:4, xxii: 32."[4] For the remainder of the verse see comments on I John 3:23; 4:9, 15.

B. The Message, 4-11

I rejoiced greatly (4) probably reflects a contrast to the disappointment so often experienced in John's association with the churches. This joy was his reason for writing. The members were **walking in truth** as they had **received . . . commandment from the Father.**

Most of the truths in this short Epistle are found in I John in more elaborated form. The **new commandment . . . that we love one another** (5) is the same **as ye have heard from the beginning** (6). See comments on I John 2:7-8 and 3:23.

The **deceivers** (7) are doubtless those against whom John warned in the previous Epistle (cf. I John 2:18-23) but the term **deceivers** (*planoi*) is not used by him elsewhere. It means a vagabond or tramp and thus a corrupter or deceptive person.[5] John uses the related cognate verb meaning "to lead from the right way," in I John 1:8; 2:26; and 3:7.

These **deceivers** are identified by their failure to confess or witness to the Incarnation—they **confess not that Jesus Christ is come in the flesh.** The RSV renders it, "the coming of Jesus Christ in the flesh." This has been interpreted by Dodd as referring to the Second Coming.[6] However, it appears more evidently a reference to the test of discipleship already discussed in I John 4:2-3. This kind of **deceiver** is also **an antichrist.**

Look to yourselves (8), is a warning similar to Heb. 2:1. The reason for the admonition is **that we lose not those things which we have wrought, but that we receive a full reward.** It is not certain if the verbs should be in the first person **(we have**

[3]Smith, *op. cit.*, p. 201.
[4]Plummer, *op. cit.*, p. 177.
[5]Thayer, *op. cit.*, p. 515.
[6]*Op. cit.*, p. 149.

wrought) or in the second ("you have wrought"). "The meaning is this: 'Take heed that these deceivers do not undo the work which Apostles and Evangelists have wrought in you, but that ye receive the full fruit of it.' "[7]

Whosoever transgresseth (9), though possibly not the best translation, still catches the general meaning. "Anyone who goes ahead" (RSV) or "anyone who runs ahead too far" (NEB) are more accurate. Weymouth has an excellent translation of the entire passage: "No one has God who, instead of remaining true to the teachings of Christ, goes beyond it."

"St. John does not here condemn theological progress . . . Theology is to God's revelation in Grace as Science is to His revelation in Nature."[8] As science continues to discover new things in the created universe, theology continues to discover more of "the treasures which are hidden in Christ. . . . A theology which is simply old is dead; a theology which is simply new is false . . . We must maintain 'the teaching of the Christ.' "[9] Anything which denies the redemptive activity of God the Father and Jesus Christ the Son is untrue and unchristian. There are no "Christian atheists"; the term itself is a contradiction. **He that abideth in the doctrine of Christ,** even while he explores its unfathomable depths, **hath both the Father and the Son.**

If there come any unto you (10) continues to speak of the deceivers. John tells the members of the church not to allow such teachers into the congregation nor to assist them in their labors. "This counsel of the Apostle must be read in the light of local circumstances."[10] It cannot be rightfully used as authorization for rejecting everyone who does not agree with us. On the other hand, neither should we so localize it that we condone an easy tolerance. The touchstone of Christian truth is the Incarnation. It is Christlike to be merciful to all men, seeking to save them. It is anti-Christlike to harbor heresy. "Charity has its limits: it must not be shown to one man in such a way as to do grievous harm to others; still less must it be shown in such a way as to do more harm than good to the recipient."[11] We must "try the spirits whether they are of God" (I John 4:1). **For he that biddeth him** (the deceiver) **God speed is partaker of his evil deeds** (11).

[7]Plummer, *op. cit.*, p. 181.
[8]Smith, *op. cit.*, p. 202.
[9]*Ibid.*, pp. 202-3.
[10]*Ibid.*, p. 203.
[11]Plummer, *op. cit.*, p. 182.

C. Conclusion, 12-13

John had **many things** of which he wished **to write** (12). Perhaps in this short Epistle we have in capsule form what he wrote more fully in the First Epistle. Dodd comments: "We may . . . take it for granted that the Presbyter really is looking forward to a visit which will give opportunity for personal discussion of this thorny situation."[12] If such a hope is realized, his **joy** will be **full.**

The Epistle closes with greetings from the members of the church from which John wrote: "The children of your Sister, chosen by God, send their greetings" (13, NEB). **Amen.**

[12]*Op. cit.*, p. 153.

The Third Epistle of JOHN

Harvey J. S. Blaney

Outline

Church Builders and Destroyers

A. Salutation, 1-2
B. The Message, 3-12
C. Conclusion and Benediction, 13-14

Church Builders and Destroyers

III John 1-14

A. Salutation, 1-2

The elder (see comments on II John 1) writes a personal note to **Gaius,** the **beloved**—the affectionate epithet being repeated three times (2, 5, 11)—**whom I love in the truth** (1). John's wish for his beloved brother concerned his material and bodily welfare, but John should not be accused of being a materialist. Knowing as he did that Gaius lived according to the truth in Christ, he could wish no greater blessing than that his friend should **prosper and be in health** (2), **even as** his **soul** was prosperous. Would to God that this wish could become the model prayer for all who confess the name of Christ!

B. The Message, 3-12

John's source of knowledge concerning Gaius was some visiting **brethren** (3). Their testimony was reliable, for they were **brethren** indeed. It was that **the truth** dwelt in their mutual friend, Gaius, and that he walked **in the truth.** As elsewhere in John's writings, **truth** refers to receiving the revelation of God in Christ and the sharing of His eternal life. In v. 4 we see a clear reflection of the Christian minister's concerns and his satisfactions: **I have no greater joy,** said John, **than to hear that my children walk in truth.**

These brethren were **strangers** (5) to whom Gaius had rendered meaningful Christian service in his usual manner. He was consistently faithful, and these visiting brethren had recognized this quality and commented upon it to the apostle. They especially noted that Gaius' service was a work of his loyal devotion to **the church** (6).

We know no more of Gaius than what is here recorded, but his character is revealed in three respects: (1) He was a true Christian; (2) He served the church through love; (3) He did not fail in his hospitality to strangers. Such men are the salt of the earth, pillars of the church, whose lives are more eloquent testimonies to the gospel than ever mere words could be.

John gently urges Gaius to continue his good work. Of these brethren, the apostle writes: "Please help them on their journey in a manner worthy of the God we serve" (6*b*, NEB). Here is an appeal to Gaius' high sense of Christian courtesy, his regard for the fellowship of the saints, his knowledge of God as revealed in Christ, and his ability to recognize the true spirit of Christianity even in strangers.

These itinerant preachers were known to John although they had not previously been known to Gaius. **They went forth** (7) in the name of Christ, trusting for their support from God's people. The fact that they took **nothing of the Gentiles** ("pagans," NEB; "heathen," RSV) does not necessarily mean "that the Gentiles offered help which these brethren refused, but that the brethren never asked them for help."[1]

This reported action is not intended to be a statement of policy of the Early Church. Verse 8 is rather simply an appeal for the Christians to assist these traveling evangelists. By so doing they would become fellow workers in **the truth.** Every true minister of the gospel is worthy of support from the church. It should not be considered wages for work done, but rather the releasing of the minister from the task of supporting himself and his family so that he might be free to do the work of the Lord. Any church which does not support its pastor in this fashion is falling short of its Christian responsibility. It must, of course, be recognized that there are new and small congregations who find this impossible, but the obligation still rests upon the church in the larger sense. The Christian denomination which makes no adequate provision for the support of the ministers whom it ordains is placing an unjust burden upon those from whom they expect so much.

[1]Plummer, *op. cit.*, p. 189

Diotrephes (9), in contrast to Gaius, loved **to have the preeminence,** and refused to recognize the apostle, who was apparently the superintendent. He perhaps even destroyed the letter that John had written to **the church.** Four additional things are said of this "dog in the manger" church member. He spoke against John with **malicious words** (10); he refused to welcome **the brethren** as had Gaius; he sought to prevent those who followed the example of Gaius' hospitality; and he sought to have them voted **out of the church.**

Diotrophes comes close to representing the antichrists of I John 2:18-19 who had gone out from the church. Perhaps the only difference was that Diotrophes remained in the congregation. He apparently held an official position, but his words were **malicious** (*poneros,* evil) and senseless. He would not recognize (*epidechetai*) the authority of John nor **receive** (same Gk. word, *epidechetai*) **the brethren,** who may have been sent out by John. Gaius was perhaps the pastor and Diotrephes the leading church member.

A word may well be said concerning the tension which sometimes arises between the pastor and strong laymen. This is especially significant when the pastor is young and perhaps less talented natively, and even less well-educated, than a lay member of the church. In this circumstance much Christian grace must be exercised by both parties lest the body of Christ be infected with evil and destroyed.

In v. 12 brief mention is made of **Demetrius,** who may have been a member of the church but more probably was the bearer of the letter (cf. 9) and the leader of the brethren whom Diotrephes had refused to receive. Demetrius was much like Gaius in his attitude and reputation in the church.

C. Conclusion and Benediction, 13-14

The close of this Epistle is very similar to that of II John (see comments on II John 12-13). This may suggest that they were written about the same time, but there is no reason to think that the letter referred to in 9 was II John. The apostle hopes that **I shall shortly see thee** (14), probably by visiting the church. At that time, he will not forget what Diotrephes has been doing (10)—a warning of discipline.

Peace be to thee (14), was the usual and meaningful Christian blessing. The **friends**—not identified—sent greetings to the church. John asks also to be remembered to the members individually. Perhaps his use of **friends** suggests only those members who were faithful to God and loyal to their leaders.

This short letter is a gem of a treatise on personal relationships in the church. The *koinonia* of the First Epistle was not easily attained or maintained in the first century—perhaps no easier than today. But the ideal has been shown us and the way to attain to it. It is the way of perfect love. Fellowship can be built upon no other foundation, but in love we become "fellow-helpers to the truth" (8).

Bibliography

A. COMMENTARIES

BENGEL, JOHN ALBERT. *Gnomon of the New Testament.* Translated by ANDREW R. FAWCETT. Fourth Edition. Edinburgh: T. & T. Clark, 1860.

BROOKE, A. E. *A Critical and Exegetical Commentary on the Johannine Epistles.* "The International Critical Commentary." Edited by C. A. BRIGGS. New York: Charles Scribner's Sons, 1912.

CANDLISH, ROBERT S. *The First Epistle of John.* Grand Rapids: Zondervan Publishing House, n.d. (reprint).

DODD, C. H. *The Johannine Epistles.* New York: Harper and Brothers, 1946.

GORE, CHARLES. *The Epistles of St. John.* New York: Charles Scribner's Sons, 1920.

HAUPT, ERICH. *The First Epistle of John.* Translated by W. B. POPE. "Clark's Foreign Theological Library." Edinburgh: T. & T. Clark, 1893.

HOON, PAUL W. "First John" (Exposition). *The Interpreter's Bible.* Vol. XII. New York: Abingdon Press, 1957.

MAURICE, F. D. *The Epistles of St. John.* London: Macmillan and Co., 1881.

PLUMMER, ALFRED. *The Epistles of St. John.* "The Cambridge Bible for Schools and Colleges." Cambridge: The University Press, 1911.

SMITH, DAVID. "The Epistles of St. John." *The Expositor's Greek Testament.* New York: Hodder & Stoughton, n.d.

STEELE, DANIEL. *Half-hours with St. John's Epistles.* Chicago: The Christian Witness Co., 1901.

STOTT, J. R. W. *The Epistles of John.* "The Tyndale New Testament Commentaries." Grand Rapids: Wm. B. Eerdmans Publishing Co., 1964.

WESLEY, JOHN. *Explanatory Notes upon the New Testament.* London: Epworth Press, 1950.

WESTCOTT, B. F. *The Epistles of St. John.* London: Macmillan and Co., 1892.

WILDER, AMOS N. "The First, Second, and Third Epistles of John" (Exegesis). *The Interpreter's Bible*. Edited by GEORGE A. BUTTRICK. Vol. XII. New York: Abingdon Press, 1957.

WILLIAMS, R. R. *The Letters of John and James*. "The Cambridge Bible Commentary." Cambridge University Press, 1965.

B. OTHER BOOKS

BONHOEFFER, DIETRICH. *The Cost of Discipleship*. New York: The Macmillan Co., 1965 (Revised and Unabridged Edition).

COOK, THOMAS. *New Testament Holiness*. London: The Epworth Press, 1958 (15th ed.).

DEWAR, LINDSAY. *The Holy Spirit and Modern Thought*. New York: Harper and Brothers, 1959.

HAYES, D. A. *John and His Writings*. New York: The Methodist Book Concern, 1917.

LEITH, JOHN H. *Creeds of the Church*. New York: Anchor Books, Doubleday and Company, 1963.

MOFFATT, JAMES. *Grace in the New Testament*. New York: Ray Long and Richard R. Smith, 1932.

NEILL, STEPHEN. *Christian Holiness*. New York: Harper and Brothers, 1960.

PECK, GEORGE. *The Scripture Doctrine of Christian Perfection*. New York: Carlton and Lanahan, 1842.

PIPER, OTTO. *God in History*. New York: The Macmillan Co., 1939.

THAYER, JOSEPH H. *A Greek-English Lexicon of the New Testament*. New York: Harper and Brothers, 1889 (Corrected Edition).

VAN DUSEN, HENRY P. *Spirit, Son, and Father*. New York: Charles Scribner's Sons, 1958.

WHITE, R. E. O. *Open Letter to Evangelicals*. Grand Rapids: Wm. B. Eerdmans Publishing Co., 1964.

WOOD, J. A. *Christian Perfection*. Chicago: The Christian Witness Co., 1921.

The Epistle of

JUDE

Delbert R. Rose

Introduction

A. Authorship

Since Jude (an anglicized form of Judas and Judah) was a common name in biblical times, how are we to identify the author of this Epistle? Of the six different Judes (Judases) in the NT, only two can be seriously considered as the likely author—Judas the apostle ("not Iscariot"—John 14:22) and Judas the brother of Jesus (Matt. 13:55).

Some consider this Epistle as written by an unknown Jude, and the phrase "brother of James" (Jude 1) as a later interpolation to heighten the Epistle's authority. A few regard the letter as pseudonymous.[1]

Authorship problems become further complicated when some scholars—in both Roman Catholic and Protestant circles—regard Judas the apostle (Thaddaeus—Lebbaeus) the same man as Judas the brother of Jesus. They interpret "brother" in Mark 6:3 (cf. Matt. 13:55) in a very wide sense, as meaning "kinsman" or "relative." This view regards the Epistles of both James and Jude as authored by apostles, the sons of Alphaeus and a certain Mary who was a close relative of the Virgin. This viewpoint does not do justice, however, to Mark 3:31 and John 6:70—7:5, which clearly indicate that, after the twelve apostles had been selected, Jesus' own brothers still did not believe on Him.

If Judas the apostle had authored this letter, would he not have appealed to his own apostleship, especially in the light of his aim to combat heresy (17)? And if James ("the brother") were an apostle, ought not Jude to have honored him as such, especially if wanting his letter to have the maximum acceptance and authority?

This writer concurs with Guthrie that after weighing the various views—ancient and modern—"the balance of probability" rests on the side of Jude the brother of Jesus as the most likely author of this letter.[2]

[1]J. C. Beker, "Letter of Jude," *The Interpreter's Dictionary of the Bible*, ed. George A. Buttrick, *et al.*, II (New York: Abingdon Press, 1962), 1009.

[2]*New Testament Introduction: Hebrews to Revelation* (Chicago: Inter-Varsity Press, 1962), p. 229. See also Zahn, A. T. Robertson, Lenski, and Cranfield.

B. Purpose

With every intention of writing an exposition of "our common salvation" (3, ASV), Jude felt constrained to change his aim and issue "a tract for the times." His Epistle is an urgent exhortation (3) aimed at fortifying the Church against certain heretics appearing within her ranks. "The *purpose* of Jude is the same as the main purpose of Second Peter: to warn against teachers of heresy and urge steadfastness in the faith."[3]

Jude's immediate purpose was clearly practical, yet it was deeply rooted theologically. He refers to the heretics' attitude toward such matters as grace, sin, Christ, sex, angels, authority—divine and human—Christian unity, and "last things."

While pointing to judgment to come upon perverts and apostates, Jude persuades his readers to wage a vigorous "defense of the faith" by intensifying spiritual disciplines for themselves (20-21) and evangelistic concern for others (22-23).

Two prominent evils—not unrelated in many instances—plagued the Church in the late apostolic and post-apostolic times: (1) antinomianism and (2) Gnosticism. Jude writes with each error in view—at least in its incipient form.

1) The antinomians claimed grace had liberated them from moral law. They reasoned that, since grace can forgive any sin, it does not really matter what one does, for grace will abound the more where there is great sin (cf. Rom. 3:8; 6:1, 15). In this way the heretics turned the grace of God into an excuse for bold immoralities (4, 18-19). Across the centuries antinomians have repeatedly arisen within the Church. And "there are still many," writes William Barclay, "who in their heart of hearts trade upon God's forgiveness, and who make the grace of God an excuse to sin."[4]

2) "Gnosticism took a bewildering variety of forms, but basically it teaches salvation through knowledge (*gnosis*)"[5] instead of through a saving faith in Jesus Christ. Its underlying assumption was that the universe is dualistic, composed of matter (which is inherently evil) and of spirit (which is essentially and absolutely good). Consequently Gnosticism could not accept

[3]Bo Reicke, *The Epistles of James, Peter, and Jude* ("The Anchor Bible"; Garden City, New York: Doubleday & Company, Inc., 1964), p. 192.

[4]*The Letters of John and Jude* ("The Daily Study Bible"; Philadelphia: The Westminster Press, 1960), p. 189.

[5]F. F. Bruce, "The Gospel of Thomas," *Faith and Thought:* Journal of the Victoria Institute, Vol. 92, Number 1 (Summer, 1961), p. 4.

"in their fullness the biblical doctrines of creation, incarnation or resurrection."[6] The Gnostics therefore denied the unity of the Godhead and the uniqueness of Jesus Christ as the *only* Mediator of creation, revelation, redemption, and judgment (4, 14-15, 24-25, ASV). For them sin had no real "moral seriousness," and hence there was no real necessity for the atoning work of Christ as the only way to pardon and purity.[7]

Jude's Epistle is an exposure of the fleshly lusts, intellectual pride, and spiritual presumption which these errorists were promoting within the body of believers (16-19).

C. Date and Destination

Date: A passage in Eusebius' *Ecclesiastical History*[8] tells of the two grandsons of Jude who were summoned to Rome to be cross-examined by the emperor Domitian (A.D. 81-96) about their Davidic descent and current activities. If Jude, the brother of Jesus, authored this Epistle, then he must have done so before the reign of Domitian.

Since there is no sure way of dating Jude's document, this writer sides with Guthrie in leaving it an open question as to when—within the period between A.D. 65 to 80—the Epistle was composed and circulated.[9]

Destination: Neither internal nor external evidences assure us of the place of composition or the original destination of Jude's Epistle. His personal greeting, however, and his vivid description of "the false brethren" who had crept into the Church, suggest a firsthand contact with them, perhaps while on some preaching mission (I Cor. 9:5).

Some[10] view the letter as having been written to a "special community" of Gentile Christians, whereas others think Jude's use of the Old Testament and materials found in Jewish apocalypses as good evidence that his audience "probably consisted of

[6]*Ibid.*

[7]John A. T. Robinson, *Twelve New Testament Studies* (Naperville, Ill.: Alec R. Allenson, Inc., 1962), pp. 133-34.

[8]*The Ecclesiastical History of Eusebius Pamphilus*, translated by Rev. C. F. Cruse (London: G. Bell and Sons, Ltd., 1917), cc. XIX—XX, pp. 91-93.

[9]*Op. cit.*, p. 233; cf. Reicke, *op. cit.*, p. 191.

[10]Robert Robertson, "The General Epistle of Jude," *The New Bible Commentary*, ed. F. Davidson, *et al.* (Grand Rapids: Wm. B. Eerdmans Publishing Co., 1953), p. 1161.

Jewish Christians."[11] The latter is the more likely view. Jude is classed among "The General [often called 'catholic'] Epistles" because it is not addressed to any specific congregation or individual, although Jude has a definite audience in view (see the "you," "yourselves," and "your" usage in the Epistle).

D. Relation to II Peter

So much in Jude (vv. 4-19) parallels II Peter (2:1—3:3) that it has provoked unceasing discussion as how best to explain this similarity between them.

Four, if not five, explanations have been forthcoming: (1) Both Epistles are from the same hand—with either Jude or II Peter or both being pseudonymous; (2) Each author—by divine inspiration—wrote independently of the other or of any common source; (3) Jude borrowed from II Peter; (4) The author of II Peter borrowed from Jude; or (5) Quite possibly, each was dependent upon a common source (no longer extant). Only the last three views have been given any serious consideration by scholars.

While Charles Bigg[12] argues for viewpoint number 3, J. B. Mayor[13] defends number 4. Guthrie[14] leaves this an unresolved literary problem with leanings toward viewpoint 3. But Reicke holds view 5, assuming "a common tradition which may well have been oral rather than written."[15] This latter solution has much in its favor, especially when viewed in the light of Jude 3-4 and 17.

A careful study of either Jude or II Peter requires a constant comparing of scripture with scripture between them.

E. Reception by the Early Church

Beker advances the following reasons why the Epistle of Jude was not universally accepted in the Early Church: its "negative character"; its use of apocryphal literature; and the difficulties connected with a clear identification of its author, its earliest recipients, and the specific heretics to which it referred.[16] Ac-

[11]Reicke, *op. cit.*, p. 191.

[12]*The Epistles of St. Peter and St. Jude* ("The International Critical Commentary"; New York: Charles Scribner's Sons, 1905), p. 316.

[13]"The General Epistle of Jude," *The Expositor's Greek Testament*, ed. W. R. Nicoll, V (Grand Rapids: Wm. B. Eerdmans Publishing Co., 1951), 211-25.

[14]*Op. cit.*, p. 246.

[15]*Op. cit.*, p. 190.

[16]*Op. cit.*, p. 1009.

cording to Guthrie it was mainly Jude's "use of apocryphal books"[17] that kept it in "the disputed class." But in spite of its brevity and apocryphal quotations, it progressively won a firm place in the canon.[18]

F. Characteristics

Even though most of Jude is paralleled in II Pet. 2:1—3:3, it has its own vivid, vigorous style. Jude's thoughts are spontaneous and practical, yet structured and with a touch of poetry in them (12-13). One of his most distinctive features "is his fondness for triplets."[19] However, "the Epistle is not the work of a literary artist, but of a passionate Christian prophet."[20]

While many call attention to Jude's "invective language," several have missed his stress upon love and mercy. Like his Lord and Master (4), he pronounces his "woe" from a love-filled heart (Matt. 23:13-39; Jude 3, 11, 17, 20-21, 23).

Jude is alone among NT writers in his citing from a Jewish apocryphal writing, the *Book of Enoch,* and another noncanonical work called the *Assumption of Moses.* While it cannot be proved that Jude quoted from these books, instead of going back to a common source for him and them, yet most scholars assume that he did quote them when speaking of Enoch's prophecy (14-15) and of Michael's dispute over the body of Moses (9).

Did Jude regard these books as inspired? Most conservative scholars do not believe that he did. But finding truth in these sources, Jude, led by the Spirit, used it just as Paul did when quoting a heathen poet (Acts 17:29), a Cretian prophet (Titus 1:12), and a Hebrew Targum on Exod. 7:11 (when naming Jannes and Jambres, II Tim. 3:8). Jude's citation of these nonbiblical sources neither endorses them nor tells us anything about his "view of Jewish pseudepigrapha generally."[21] Under the Spirit's guidance Jude had as much right as Paul to use nonbiblical sources to illustrate truth.

G. Theological Value and Relevance

From first to last Jude is Christocentric. He builds, as all the apostles did, upon the one Foundation, "our Lord Jesus Christ"

[17]*Op. cit.*, p. 227.

[18]Beker, *loc. cit.*

[19]Joseph B. Mayor, *The Epistle of St. Jude and the Second Epistle of St. Peter* (Grand Rapids: Baker Book House, 1965), p. lvi. These triplets can be found in vv. 2, 3-8, 11, 16, 19, 20, and 21 (a double triplet), 22 and 23, and 25—ASV.

[20]Guthrie, *op. cit.*, p. 248.

[21]*Ibid.*, p. 240.

(1, 4, 17, 21, 25). Climaxing his Epistle on the note of "the only God our Saviour" (25, ASV), he makes it amply clear that he is a Christian theist—God is One in nature, yet threefold in personality—Father (1), Jesus Christ (1, 4), and Holy Ghost (20). Jude clearly implies that "the only God" is both Creator and Redeemer, Lawgiver and Judge of the whole universe. He is the God of grace and glory (4, 24), of mercy and majesty (2, 25), of love and judgment (2, 6, 15, 21), of peace and power (2, 25), of salvation and destruction (3, 5), of time and eternity (4, 25).

The Christian life depends upon grace expressing itself in godliness—the very opposite of what the errorists were doing (4, 15-16, 18). Basic to Jude's whole theology is the inescapable relationship between belief and behavior, between error and evil, between sound faith and good works.

"Last things" are also highlighted—the Lord's return (14), the judgment day (6, 15), eternal fire for the wicked (7), and eternal life for the righteous (21). He keeps a needed balance between the love and the wrath of God, between divine sovereignty and human freedom with *real* responsibility.

How relevant is Jude? In this generation with its defiance and denials of God (and Christ) and with its "new morality" (which is *the old immorality* of Sodom revived), nothing could be more relevant to our times. "As long as men need stern rebukes for their practices," writes Guthrie, "the Epistle of Jude will remain relevant."[22] Once more it ought to become "the fiery cross to rouse the churches" to vigorous action against today's blatant apostasy.

[22]*Ibid.*, p. 249.

Outline

I. The Greeting, 1-2
   A. The Bonds Acknowledged, 1
   B. The Believers Addressed, 1
   C. The Blessings Asked, 2

II. The Appeal, 3-4
   A. The Critical Situation, 3
   B. The Contending Saints, 3
   C. The Corrupting Sinners, 4

III. The Apostasies, 5-16
   A. Past Judgments on Corporate Apostasy, 5-7
   B. Perversions of Contemporary Apostates, 8
   C. The Pattern of Michael the Archangel, 9
   D. Practices of Contemporary Apostates, 10
   E. Past Judgments upon Individual Apostates, 11
   F. Predicted Judgments on Contemporary Apostates, 12-16

IV. The Admonitions, 17-23
   A. Remember the Predictions, 17-19
   B. Keep Yourselves in God's Love, 20-21
   C. Seek Others in Godly Fear, 22-23

V. The Benediction, 24-25
   A. A Song of Praise from the Godly, 24
   B. God Our Saviour, 25

Section I *The Greeting*

Jude 1-2

In Jude's greeting to his readers two chief characteristics of a New Testament letter stand out: The author introduces himself and then invokes blessing upon those whom he addresses.

A. The Bonds Acknowledged, 1

Rightfully Jude might have referred to his close physical kinship to Jesus, but chose rather to identify himself as a **servant of Jesus Christ.** The Greek word for **servant** (*doulos*), meaning "bondservant" or "slave," should not call to our minds that ignominious status we moderns attribute to slaves. *Doulos* here implies a willing subjection to one's master. Jude professes perfect submission to his heavenly Master and Lord (1, 4). He majors on the lordship **of Jesus Christ,** which visibly threads its way throughout the document. This particular letter was occasioned by those rejecting, even denying, the sovereignty of Jesus Christ over their lives (4).

Jude, like his brother James, does not speak simply of **Jesus** or of **Christ** but always of Him as Lord (cf. Jas. 1:1; 2:1).[1] The title "Lord" (4) is Jude's confession of faith in the deific nature and authority of One in whom he had not at first believed (John 7:3-5). Jude's early unbelief conditioned him to understand better those "denying" the lordship of Jesus.

Bypassing any reference to his blood ties with Jesus, Jude proceeds to call himself the **brother of James,** whom many, including this writer, believe to have been "James the Lord's brother" (Gal. 1:19). James had become well-known because of his prominence in the Jerusalem church. Jude's modest mention of himself as James's brother—and therefore a brother of Jesus as well—would give the note of authority necessary for such a stern letter as this one.

Jude's character shines through these references to himself in v. 1. "Few things," declares William Barclay, "tell more about

[1]Seven times Jude specifically mentioned the "Lord" (4, 5, 9, 14, 17, 21, 25—using the amended text in ASV, RSV, *et al.*).

a man than the way in which a man speaks of himself."[2] Like the Apostle Andrew, Jude was willing to be remembered "by his relationship to his far more famous brother."[3]

B. The Believers Addressed, 1

Jude's letter, like all NT Epistles, was addressed to professed believers. He writes **to them that are sanctified . . . preserved . . . called.** The better Greek MSS. have "beloved" (*egapemenois*) instead of **sanctified** (*egiasmenois*), and many translations also follow a different word order here. The ASV is probably correct: "to them that are called, beloved in God the Father, and kept for Jesus Christ."

The **called** are those who, hearing God's gracious invitation to salvation, respond in obedient faith. "Many are called," but only the "few" accepting the terms of the call "are chosen" (Matt. 20:16; 22:14). And those who "endure unto the end" (Matt. 24:13) are characterized by John as the "called, and chosen, and faithful" (Rev. 17:14; cf. I Pet. 1:5). No concept is more basic in the whole NT than the concept of God's callings for and of men.[4]

Those answering the call to salvation become the **sanctified**, or "beloved in God" (ASV). Is this Jude's love for those in God the Father, or is it the Father's love for Christians? Mayor approvingly quotes Hort's view that it refers to the Father's love for those "who have been kept safe in Jesus from the temptations to which others have succumbed."[5]

Those **preserved in Jesus Christ** underscores the spiritual qualities of Jude's first readers. **Preserved** (*teteremenois*), appearing here in the perfect tense, indicates that the keeping had been taking place up to the time Jude composed his Epistle. But Jude indicates this keeping process will not go on automatically. For his final admonition includes, "Keep yourselves in the love of God" (21).

C. The Blessings Asked, 2

Since Jude's first readers were "in God the Father, and kept for Jesus Christ" (1, ASV), they were already enjoying a meas-

[2]*Op. cit.*, p. 205. [3]*Ibid.*

[4]William Barclay, *A New Testament Wordbook* (New York: Harper & Brothers, n.d.), p. 61.

[5]EGT, V, 253.

ure of God's **mercy . . . peace, and love.** Knowing that spiritual growth is a necessary part of Christian life, Jude appropriately expresses his "heartfelt wish" for an unbounded increase in them of God's gifts of grace. This spiritual advance would equip them for the crucial struggle facing them.

Divine **mercy** (*eleos,* "the unmerited goodness of God") is ever the basis upon which God deals with His children. A heavenly **peace** (*eirene,* harmonious relationships) always accompanies **mercy** accepted. **Love** (*agape*) is "a gracious and holy affection, which the soul, upon the apprehension of God's love in Christ, returneth back to God again by his own grace";[6] it is not found among other NT writers in their opening greetings. **Love,** as well as **mercy** and **peace,** proceeds from God. Then "we love, because he first loved us" (I John 4:19, ASV).

In these first two verses we encounter Jude's fondness for triplets in both thought and word:

Jude, Jesus Christ, James
servant, "Master and Lord," **brother**
called, "beloved," **preserved**
mercy, peace, love

[6]Thomas Manton, *An Exposition on the Epistle of Jude* (London: The Banner of Truth Trust, 1958 [reprint]), p. 72.

Section II *The Appeal*

Jude 3-4

Although Jude is about to expose certain "ungodly men" who have stealthily infiltrated the Church and are now sabotaging her faith and morals, he does it under the canopy and consciousness of divine love (*agape*). Twice already he has mentioned God's love; here in v. 3 he speaks personally.

A. The Critical Situation, 3

The atmosphere of divine judgment overhanging much of this Epistle obscures for most readers the heartfelt attitude of its human author. Jude's use of **beloved** (3)—a term appearing over sixty times in the NT—was more than a transitional word between "The Greeting" (1-2) and "The Appeal" (3-4) of his Epistle. For him **beloved** (*agapetoi*) carried both personal and theological overtones. "It sums up," according to Cranfield, "the central motif of the Christian life, indicating at the same time the love of the speaker or writer for his brethren and, behind that and more important, the love of God in Christ for all."[1]

Jude's giving **all diligence to write** discloses his earnestness and zeal in behalf of the Lord's truth and His people's advances in that truth (cf. Heb. 6:11; II Pet. 1:5).

It was needful, that is, "it became urgently necessary to write at once" (NEB) to them. Jude felt divinely compelled to change his plans immediately and write this particular letter.

Having turned from writing an exposition on **the common salvation,** Jude felt compelled to **exhort** the saints to brace themselves for their critical situation. His whole aim, wrote Bengel, was to issue "an earnest appeal" for "double duty"—"*to fight* earnestly in behalf of the faith, against enemies; and to build one's self up in the faith: ver. 20."[2]

[1]*I & II Peter and Jude* ("Torch Bible Commentaries"; London: SCM Press, Ltd., 1960), p. 69.

[2]John Albert Bengel, *Gnomon of the New Testament,* translated by William Fletcher, 2nd ed., V (Edinburgh: T. & T. Clark, 1860), 163.

B. The Contending Saints, 3

The saints (*tois hagiois*), "the holy ones," was Jude's name for the true Church (cf. Acts 9:13, 32, 41; I Cor. 1:2). Mayor thinks Jude uses "the holy ones" here as "an appeal to the brethren to stand fast against the teaching and practice of the Libertines"[3]—those "unholy ones" who were demoralizing the Church.

Is **the faith** (*te pistei*) for which **the saints** must **contend** to be understood objectively or subjectively—or in a combined objective-subjective sense? With strong scholarly support Alford holds that **the faith** here means "the sum of that which Christians believe: faith *which is believed,* not faith *by which we believe.*"[4] But Robertson adds a needed emphasis, insisting that the objective aspect of **the faith** must include "the moral life which is the expression of it. . . . *The faith,* Christian religion as a whole, is committed to Christians to be defended not only by sound doctrine but also by the life they live."[5]

The faith which was once delivered—"which was once for all delivered" (ASV, RSV)—leaves no room for "innovations" such as the "ungodly men" (4) were introducing. The key word is "once for all" (*hapax*), which is here "used of what is so done as to be of perpetual validity and never need repetition."[6] Bengel insists that the particle *hapax* expresses "great urgency," since "no other faith will be given."[7]

Paul likewise stressed this unchanging quality of Christian faith (Gal. 1:8-9, 11-12; II Tim. 1:13; 2:2). "The principles of Christian truth and life," wrote W. H. Bennett, "were not a passing fashion, but permanent and irrevocable. . . . always binding, but the Holy Spirit guides each generation into an application and understanding of them suitable to its own needs."[8]

Earnestly contend—one word in the Greek, *epagonizesthai,* and only here in the NT—is a strong term, indicating a fight or

[3]EGT, V, 255.

[4]*The New Testament for English Readers* (Chicago: Moody Press, n.d.), p. 1770.

[5]*Op. cit.*, p. 1162.

[6]Joseph H. Thayer, *A Greek-English Lexicon of the New Testament* (New York: American Book Co., 1889), p. 54.

[7]*Op. cit.*, p. 163.

[8]*The General Epistles* ("The New Century Bible"; Edinburgh: T. C. & E. C. Jack, 1901), p. 331.

contest. Dr. Mombert understood the word to mean "to fight standing upon a thing which is assaulted, and which the adversary desires to take away"—but so fighting as to protect it and retain it.[9]

Jude is issuing "a call to arms." **The saints** must "put up a real fight for the faith" (Phillips). But they must do it, Wesley reminds us, "humbly, meekly, and lovingly; otherwise your contention will only hurt your cause, if not destroy your soul."[10] And Paul's words put a ban on all "carnal weapons" in this spiritual battle for **the faith** (II Cor. 10:3-5).

C. The Corrupting Sinners, 4

The influence within the Church of **certain . . . ungodly men** created the necessity for this particular Epistle. They **crept in unawares**—one word in the Greek, from *pareisduein,* meaning "to creep in stealthily."[11] This word, according to Barclay, "always indicates a secret, stealthy, and subtle insinuation of something evil into a society or a situation."[12]

These **certain men**—probably still a minority—were already under that **condemnation** (*krima;* sentence) which was **of old ordained** for the **ungodly.** Williams' translation says, "Their doom was written down long ago."[13] **Ordained** (*prographo*) means to write or describe beforehand (cf. Rom. 15:4; Eph. 3:3). Jude doubtless is referring to the OT scriptures, upon which he draws in vv. 5-15.

Here **ordained** does not mean, as Robertson correctly indicates, "that these men were 'foreordained' or 'elected' to condemnation, but that the condemnation which such men would bring on themselves had been ordained and even written down long before."[14]

[9]Quoted by N. M. Williams, "Commentary on the Epistle of Jude," *An American Commentary on the New Testament,* ed. Alvah Hovey (Philadelphia: American Baptist Publication Society, 1888), p. 8.

[10]*Explanatory Notes upon the New Testament* (London: The Epworth Press, 1958 [reprint]), p. 927.

[11]W. E. Vine, *An Expository Dictionary of New Testament Words* (London: Oliphants Ltd., 1957), pp. 255-56.

[12]*The Letters of John and Jude,* p. 211.

[13]*The New Testament in the Language of the People* (Chicago: Moody Press, 1960), p. 541.

[14]*Op. cit.,* NBC, p. 1162.

The **condemnation** hanging over these **ungodly men** resulted from their turning the grace of **our God into lasciviousness.** This was a severe indictment, but fully justified. **Lasciviousness** (*aselgeia*) denotes indecency, lack of restraint, excess, even rowdiness, and "drunken debauchery"[15] (cf. II Pet. 2:1-3).

These **ungodly** (*asebeia*)[16] **men** had so corrupted the concept of **the grace of . . . God** as to make it a cover for "blatant immorality." Following the Gnostic line of thinking, they believed their bodies to be essentially evil, and so it did not matter much what a person did with his appetites, desires, and passions. Especially so, if God's grace is extensive enough to cancel, cleanse, and cover all sin! Why be concerned about sin anyway, since grace is greater than all our sin? In short, God's costly grace "was being perverted into a justification for sin."[17]

Jude not only condemns these men for their *deceptiveness* of method and *distortion* of the gospel of grace, but also for their *denial* of **the only Lord God, and our Lord Jesus Christ.** In the best MSS. the word **God** is lacking in v. 4, giving Wesley and others the basis for the phrase, "our only Master and Lord, Jesus Christ." (II Pet. 2:1 extends the thought: "denying the Lord that bought them.") Early Christians regarded Jesus as absolute Ruler and Disposer of Life.[18]

In v. 4 (plus II Pet. 2:1) can be found "A Briefing on Apostasy": (1) The Deceptiveness of Apostates—enter stealthily; (2) The Distortions Among Apostates—turning grace into a cover for continued sinning; (3) The Denials by Apostates—rejecting the absolute lordship and atoning merits of Christ; (4) The Doom of Apostates—under "condemnation."

[15]Bennett, *op. cit.*, p. 243.

[16]**Ungodly** is a key word in Jude. While it appears four times in Romans, three times in Timothy and Titus, once in I Peter, and three times in II Peter, it occurs six times in Jude. It is the very opposite of "godly" or "godliness," which means "due reverence towards God, expressing itself in worship and in a devout and obedient life" (Bennett, *op. cit.*, p. 260).

[17]Barclay, *The Letters of John and Jude,* pp. 211-12.

[18]Adolf Deissmann, *Light from the Ancient East,* translated by Lionel R. M. Strachan, New and Completely Revised Edition (New York: Harper & Brothers, n.d.), pp. 350-55.

Section III *The Apostasies*

Jude 5-16

The word **remembrance** (5; cf. 17) indicates that Jude's reader-audience was familiar with the OT, perhaps with some of the Apocrypha, and with the words, if not the writings, of the Lord's apostles.

A. Past Judgments on Corporate Apostasy, 5-7

1. *Unbelieving Israel* (5)

These "ungodly men" should have learned from sacred history that their sins would bring upon them divine displeasure as surely as judgment fell upon unbelieving Israel, the unfaithful angels (6), and the immoral cities of Sodom and Gomorrah (7; cf. II Pet. 2:4-6).

The phrase **though ye once knew this** has been variously translated, depending both upon the meaning here of **once** (*hapax*) and its proper place in the word order. Moffatt and Mayor, following the Sinaitic MS., regard *hapax* as belonging with what the Lord did for Israel—"the Lord once brought the People safe out of Egypt."[1] Others retain *hapax* as related to what Jude's readers know—"though you were once for all fully informed" (RSV). Perhaps Phillips and the NEB have the best solution to the problem by regarding *hapax* in this context as simply meaning "ye already know," even though the same word in 3 is correctly translated "once for all."

The identity of **the Lord,** who **saved the people out of the land of Egypt** and then **afterward destroyed them that believed not** perplexes many scholars. Some MSS. have **the Lord** (*kurios*), which can apply either to the Father or the Son, while others have "Jesus" (*Iesous*) as the Deliverer. Wolff claims the weight of MS. evidence favors "Jesus" as the original reading, even though many scholars disagree. Wolff points to I Cor. 10:4 ("Christ") for Pauline support for Jude's usage of "Jesus" here. Jerome

[1]James Moffatt, *The General Epistles* ("The Moffatt New Testament Commentary"; New York: Harper and Brothers Publishers, n.d.), p. 231.

accepted the name "Jesus," holding however that "Joshua" was intended, even as in Heb. 4:8 (cf. KJV, RSV).[2] But nowhere else is Joshua regarded as the deliverer of Israel from Egypt.

The Lord . . . afterward destroyed them that believed not is Jude's way of saying that these "ungodly men" within "the new Israel" (the Church) will likewise be destroyed because of unbelief.

2. *Unfaithful Angels* (6)

Moving back beyond Israel's dreadful failure to the disastrous fall of certain **angels,** Jude gives a second instance of defection. Theirs was an apostasy from **their first estate** of holiness into an unredeemable state of wickedness.

The angels' **habitation** could mean their "proper dwelling" (RSV), "proper sphere" (Phillips), or "proper home" (Williams). They voluntarily **left their own** proper realm—that was their sin! But how they behaved outside their "proper sphere" has been debated from pre-Christian times to the present.

Many associate Jude's allusion with Gen. 6:1-4, understanding the latter passage to teach that the angels (called there "sons of God") came down to earth and, cohabiting with women, produced a half-human, half-demonic race of beings, called "giants" in Gen. 6:4. The *Book of Enoch* and other Jewish folklore have dramatized this "story of the fallen angels," and not a few scholars hold that both Jude 6 and II Pet. 2:4 refer to such an interpretation of Gen. 6:1-4. For this writer, Jesus sufficiently refutes the idea that angels could possibly commit fornication with humans (Matt. 22:30).

The Lord **hath reserved**—"hath kept," ASV—**the angels . . . in everlasting chains** (bonds) **under darkness unto the judgment of the great day.** Having refused to keep themselves within their divinely appointed sphere (of holiness and light), the angels were bound and confined in hell (*tartarus*) according to II Pet. 2:4.

The judgment of the great day points to the great white throne judgment (Rev. 20:11). Jude's eschatology is not the least of his theological interests.

[2]*A Commentary on the Epistle of Jude* (Grand Rapids: Zondervan Publishing House, 1960), p. 63.

3. *Immoral Cities* (7)

Repeatedly in Scripture the destruction of **Sodom and Gomorrha** is singled out as an example of God's wrath against sin (cf. Deut. 29:23; Isa. 1:9; Jer. 49:18; Amos 4:11; Luke 17:29; II Pet. 2:6). For Bible writers **Sodom** was synonymous with shamelessness in sin (Isa. 3:9; Lam. 4:6), especially sexual debauchery.[3] Sodomites gave **themselves over to . . . strange flesh**—perhaps with beasts as well as with those of the same sex (cf. Rom. 1:27).

Sodom and Gomorrha . . . are set forth for an example (specimen), **suffering the vengeance of eternal fire.** While those cities suffered a punishment which fell upon them about 2000 B.C., they have remained across the centuries a type of punishment by eternal fire which shall be the future lot of all the ungodly.

In brief, Jude unfolds "The Fate of Apostates" as that is progressively realized: (1) The unbelieving Israelites *were* buried in the wilderness, 5; (2) The unfaithful angels *are* bound in hellish darkness, 6 (cf. II Pet. 2:4); (3) The immoral cities were burned with fire—a type of *eternal* fire, 7.

B. Perversions of Contemporary Apostates, 8

Likewise also—"yet in like manner," RSV—in spite of divine warning through the examples of past apostasies of angels and men, Israel and the Gentiles (5-7), these apostates in the Church continue on in their unbelief, rebellion, and lusts.

These filthy (not in the Gk.) **dreamers** think they shall escape the judgment of God which fell upon sinners in the past. **Dreamers** (*enupniazomenoi*) is a present participle "predicatively attached to the subject [**these**] and thereby pertains to all three verbs"—**defile, despise,** and **speak evil.**[4] "In all that they do these libertinistic heretics act like dreamers, unreal images and pictures fill their minds."[5] How like the false prophets in the OT (Deut. 13:1-5)!

These dreamers of false dreams **defile the flesh** by giving way to bodily instincts and counting on the grace of God to take

[3]Ezekiel includes pride, plenty, prosperity, and callousness toward the poor and needy as part of Sodom's iniquity (16:49).

[4]R. C. H. Lenski, *The Interpretation of the Epistles of St. Peter, St. John and St. Jude* (Columbus, Ohio: The Wartburg Press, 1945), p. 625.

[5]*Ibid.*

care of any and every sin. To them "sin is nothing other than the means whereby grace is given its opportunity to operate."[6]

These . . . dreamers . . . despise dominion. They "reject authority" (RSV), showing an "utter contempt" for it (Phillips). Calvin held that Jude had civil magistrates in mind when referring to **dominion** and **dignities,**[7] while Bennett argued that ecclesiastical rulers are the more likely ones in Jude's thought.[8] Plumptre probably stands closest to the truth when regarding **dominion** (*kurioteta,* lit. "lordship") as "including all forms of authority"—divine and human—and **dignities** (*doxas,* lit. "glories") as indicating "all angels whether good or evil."[9] (Cf. II Pet. 2:10.)

These dreamers . . . speak evil—literally, "blaspheme." They repudiate "legitimate lordship," says Whedon, "and all glories and sanctities of earth and heaven they flaunt and blaspheme with terms and phrases borrowed from their own obscene vocabulary."[10]

C. The Pattern of Michael the Archangel, 9

Michael the archangel is one of two angels named in the whole of Scripture. The other is Gabriel (Dan. 8:16; 9:21; Luke 1:19, 26). **Michael**—literally, "Who is like God?"—is portrayed by Daniel as the Jews' guardian angel—"the great prince which standeth for the children of thy people" (12:1). In the Revelation he reappears as "the warrior angel" who fights against the devil and "his angels" (12:7-9).

Jude draws on Michael's "debate with the devil" (NEB) over **the body of Moses** as a timely rebuke to the ungodly with their sneering and blasphemous reactions to "dominion" and "dignities" (8). **Michael . . . durst not bring against** the devil—out of his respect for the devil's original angelic dignity—**a railing**

[6]Barclay, *The Letters of John and Jude,* p. 220.

[7]*Commentaries on the Catholic Epistles,* translated and edited by Rev. John Owen (Grand Rapids: Wm. B. Eerdmans Publishing Co., 1948), p. 438.

[8]*Op. cit.,* p. 334.

[9]*The General Epistles of St. Peter and St. Jude,* "The Cambridge Bible for Schools and Colleges," ed. J. J. S. Perowne (Cambridge: University Press, 1893), p. 181.

[10]*Commentary on the New Testament* (New York: Phillips & Hunt, 1880), V, 299.

accusation. He "did not dare to condemn him with mockery" (Phillips).

Refusing to make himself judge, Michael resisted the devil—as did Jesus in the wilderness—by quoting the Scriptures, saying, **The Lord rebuke thee** (cf. Zech. 3:1-2, II Pet. 2:11).

Jude's main thrust is, thinks Barclay, that "if the greatest of the good angels refused to speak evil of the greatest of the evil angels, even in circumstances like that, then surely no human being may speak evil of any angel."[11] The same would apply in human relations.

In v. 9 we have "The Pattern Court Case: Michael Versus the Devil": (1) Michael *resisted* the devil—as all Christians must do, Jas. 4:7; (2) He *refrained* from insulting words against his opponent; (3) He *relied* on the Lord's work and word—it is the Lord's work to judge, not men's or angels', and the divine Word is still sufficient to refute Satan, whether it is used by Christians, an archangel, or the Son of God.

D. Practices of Contemporary Apostates, 10

But these contemporary apostates feel themselves competent and at liberty to **speak evil of** (*blasphemousin,* "pour abuse upon," NEB), **those things which they know not.** The context clearly shows they know not the realms of the angels (8-9) and of the Spirit of God (19). Yet they "are ready to mock at anything that is beyond their immediate knowledge" (Phillips; cf. II Pet. 2:12).

But what they know naturally—i.e., their natural desires and instincts such **as brute beasts** have—they do not control and use rationally. They do not even use "animal sense" in following their appetites. Instead, **in those things** which they have in common with the animals **they corrupt themselves.** In fact, they sink lower than the beasts (Rom. 1:26-27).

Here is "The Gospel of the Full-fledged Sensualist": (1) He *mocks* at that beyond his knowledge; (2) He *is mastered* by his animal-like instincts; (3) He *mutilates* his human possibilities for true godliness.

E. Past Judgments upon Individual Apostates, 11

Woe unto them! Here Jude imitates Jesus in pronouncing a "woe" upon these corrupters of "the faith" (Matt. 23:13 ff.).

[11]*The Letters of John and Jude,* p. 221.

No other apostle did. II Peter, showing a like reaction to apostasy, uses "cursed children" (2:14).

"They corrupt themselves" (10) just as **Cain, Balaam,** and **Core** (Korah) did before them. They are progressing in evil, moving toward its climax (cf. Ps. 1:1). **They have gone** in the way of disobedience, and **ran greedily** (lit., "were poured out"—a "vigorous metaphor for excessive indulgence").[12] They sought after **reward** in the way of wrong, and shall end up as others who have **perished** in their sins. Each verb is an aorist, indicating completed action, "owing to the writer's placing himself in thought at the moment when these men reap the consequences of their sins: their punishment is so certain, that he regards it as having come."[13]

Here Jude lines up "A Trio of Religious Rebels": (1) Cain—the worshiper who presented (sacrificed) too little; (2) Balaam—the prophet who prayed too often (about the same thing); (3) Core—The minister who professed too much (claiming equal holiness and authority with Moses and Aaron).

F. Predicted Judgments on Contemporary Apostates, 12-16

1. *The Perverts Described* (12-13)

Having drawn parallels between these false brethren and their OT forerunners, Jude now uses a series of vivid metaphors to characterize them further.

These are spots (12; *spilades*). The word can also mean "hidden rocks" (ASV), "involving unsuspected peril of shipwreck of faith and character."[14] **Your feasts of charity** were called love feasts (*agapais*). They were common meals "eaten by early Christians in connection with their church services, for the purposes of fostering and expressing brotherly love."[15]

Having joined themselves to the love feasts, these heretics made them occasions of promoting gluttony and immorality, even

[12]A. T. Robertson, *Word Pictures in the New Testament* (Nashville: Sunday School Board of the Southern Baptist Convention, 1933), VI, 191.

[13]Charles John Ellicott (ed.), *The Epistles of Peter, John, and Jude* ("The 'Layman's Handy Commentary' Series"; Grand Rapids: Zondervan Publishing House, 1957), p. 278.

[14]Bennett, *op. cit.*, p. 336.

[15]W. F. Arndt and F. W. Gingrich, *A Greek-English Lexicon of the New Testament and Other Early Christian Literature* (Chicago: The University of Chicago Press, 1957), p. 6.

as the church at Corinth fell into cliquishness and drunken revelry (I Cor. 11:17-22)

The phrase **feeding themselves without fear** has been better rendered in the ASV as "shepherds that without fear feed themselves." Possibly Jude was thinking of the "false shepherds" in the OT who were **feeding themselves** but neglecting the flock (Ezek. 34:2, 8, 10).

They are **clouds . . . without water,** promising much but producing nothing. They are impressive in their claims but empty of the life-quickening power of a good shower. They are **carried about of winds,** being unstable and unpredictable (Heb. 13:9; II Pet. 2:17).

These errorists are **trees whose fruit withereth, without fruit, twice dead.** They are "in sin, first by nature, and afterwards by apostasy."[16] They shall therefore be **plucked up by the roots.** They have no fruit because they have no roots planted in the "grace of God" (cf. Matt. 7:20).

They are **raging waves of the sea** (13). This "picture of angry waves washing up all sorts of muck and refuse onto the shore (cf. Isa. 57:20) suggests vividly the shamelessness with which the false brethren by their words and actions bring to light their inner corruption."[17]

They are **wandering stars.** Moffatt calls them "erratic comets or shooting meteors," who have "deserted their proper orbit and broken away from the regulations of the Lord."[18] Out of their proper orbit, they are burning themselves out in sin, and heading for **the blackness of darkness for ever.**

2. *Punishment Declared* (14-15)

Notes of doom are sounded in 12-13, but here a judgment scene comes clearly into view.

a. Jude's pronouncement (14-15). The apostle is convinced that these contemporary apostates fulfill an ancient prophecy. He approvingly quotes the earliest known prophetic voice on judgment—Enoch's—and the most recent, even "the apostles of our Lord Jesus Christ" (17; cf. II Pet. 2:1-22).

b. Enoch's prophecy (14-15). Not only were these modern apostates typified by ancient examples of apostasy (5-11), but

[16]Wesley, *op. cit.*, p. 929. [17]Cranfield, *op. cit.*, p. 164.

[18]*Op. cit.*, p. 239.

Enoch . . . also prophesied of these men (14). Enoch, **the seventh from Adam** (Gen. 5:4-24)—not the first from Cain (Gen. 4:17-18)—is nowhere else in Scripture referred to as a prophet or "holy seer." The prophecy referred to here by Jude is found in the *Book of Enoch* 60:8; 93:3. This is in the apocryphal writing, familiar to the writers and Jewish readers of NT literature. (See Introduction, "Characteristics.")

Behold, the Lord cometh. "The first coming of Christ was revealed to Adam; His second, glorious coming, to Enoch."[19] While Adam foresaw Christ as the Saviour, Enoch foresaw the Saviour as the Judge and Avenger. **Ten thousands** (lit., "myriads") **of his saints** (holy ones) doubtless refers to the holy angels accompanying the Lord upon His return (cf. Deut. 33:2; Zech. 14:5; Matt. 25:31; II Thess. 1:7).

Enoch's words stressed the total depravity of the **ungodly** (15), i.e., their un-Godlikeness, in thought, word, and deed. Divine judgment will be executed in the light of all three aspects of men's sins.

To **convince** (*exelegai;* or *elegxai* in the better MSS.) is best translated "convict" (ASV, RSV) and means "to show to be guilty." If men do not feel their guilt here and now, they will at the Judgment!

c. The Lord's presence and power (14-15). **Ungodly sinners have spoken against him**—i.e., against the Lord—**hard speeches** ("defiant words," NEB). From the days of Cain and Lamech (Gen. 4:23-24) to those of Malachi (3:13-14), and then on to those of Peter (II Pet. 2:1) and Jude (4, 14-15), the spirit of Antichrist has been asserting itself in the world.

Jude sees the Lord's coming in judgment as the silencing of man's defiance and denials of Christ. What could be more relevant for our world, with its "God is dead" attitude and its international militant atheism, than Enoch's words on the Lord's return? Little is heard today about "Sinners in the Hands of an Angry God" (J. Edwards). The tide is completely reversed; it is now "God in the Hands of Angry Sinners!" (L. Ravenhill).

3. *The Persons Doomed* (16)

Jude leaves no doubt as to whom his vivid metaphors in 12-13 really apply, and upon whom divine judgment is certain to fall.

[19]Wesley, *op. cit.*, p. 929.

These "ungodly" ones are: (1) **murmurers** against men—"grumblers with the spirit of smouldering discontent"; (2) **complainers** (lit., "fate-blamers") against God, having become chronic malcontents; (3) those who, with respect to themselves, **walk after**, i.e., have become "slaves to their own carnal lusts";[20] (4) boasters or braggarts, whose mouths speak **great swelling words**—the essence of arrogance (cf. II Pet. 2:18); (5) flatterers who have **men's persons in admiration** (lit., "admiring the faces"). Mayor comments, "As the fear of God drives out the fear of man, so defiance of God tends to put man in His place, as the chief source of good or evil to his fellows";[21] (6) graspers of gain, ever taking **advantage** of "him whom he flatters." Bennett well characterizes them: "When it was safe to do so, they blustered, and bullied, and played the superior person, but they cringed to rich men, and flattered them for the sake of dinners and presents."[22]

[20]Mayor, *The Epistle of St. Jude and the Second Epistle of St. Peter*, p. 76.

[21]Mayor, EGT, V, 272.

[22]*Op. cit.*, p. 340.

Section IV *The Admonitions*

Jude 17-23

Having characterized the false brethren (4-16), Jude now counsels the true brethren (17-23), outlining how they ought to behave themselves (cf. I Tim. 3:15).

A. Remember the Predictions, 17-19

1. *The Author's Warning* (17)

Like Ezekiel, Jude feels himself a watchman on the walls of Zion. Dangerous subversives are at work within the house of God, so Jude urges his readers to **remember.** In effect he is saying, "Do not be taken off guard by what is happening. Be realistic!"[1] The words **but . . . ye** are in the emphatic position in both 17 and 20. Jude holds his reader-audience in sharp contrast from the ungodly "mockers."

2. *The Apostles' Words* (17-18*a*)

Is Jude referring to the oral or the written **words . . . of the apostles of our Lord** (17)? Scholars differ here. The best answer seems to be that we cannot be sure. It suffices to know that Jude's reader-audience had heard or read the apostles' words and needed only to recall them.

Paul (I Tim. 4:1-2; II Tim. 3:1-13) and Peter (II Pet. 2:1—3:4), following the pattern of **our Lord Jesus Christ** (Matt. 24:3-42), warned about **the last time** (18). This expression means the ending of the present world-order, which is to be climaxed by the Second Coming, and accompanied by the Messiah's judging work.

The last time, the years immediately before the Second Coming, will be marked by scoffing (II Pet. 3:3) at "the faith once for all delivered unto the saints." The "faith" will doubtless be "boycotted as if it were heresy, and the sole surviving

[1]E. G. Homrighausen, "The Epistle of Jude" (Exposition), *The Interpreter's Bible,* ed. G. A. Buttrick, *et al.,* XII (New York: Abingdon Press, 1957), 337.

heresy at that."[2] If these **mockers** have "turned the grace of God into licentiousness," writes Mayor, "they would naturally mock at . . . those who took a strict . . . view of the divine commandments: if they made light of authority and treated spiritual things with irreverence, if they foamed out their own shame and uttered proud and impious words, if they denied God and Christ, they would naturally laugh at the idea of a judgment to come."[3]

3. *The Apostates' Walk* (18*b*-19)

These mockers **walk after their own ungodly lusts** (18), letting their perverted desires dictate for them what is right and wrong. They are moral and spiritual anarchists! They **separate themselves** (19) from "the living fellowship of Christians." They "create factions" and "split communities" (Phillips).

They are **sensual** (*psuchikoi*—i.e., "natural"; cf. I Cor. 2:14; 15:44, 46). Ellicott prefers the translation "sensuous"—meaning "ruled by human reasoning, and human affections, and does not arise above the world of sense."[4] They have **not the Spirit.** As "separatists" in spirit and "sensualists" in mind and body, these ungodly men are without the Spirit of God (and of Christ), and therefore are none of His (Rom. 8:9).

B. Keep Yourselves in God's Love, 20-21

Keep (*teresate*—an aorist imperative, stressing urgency) **yourselves** (21), Jude admonishes, for both angels and men have apostatized (5-19). "The burden of Jude is that his readers continue to fight the good fight of faith."[5] Jude stresses both the divine (1, 24) and the human side (21) in Christian perseverance, just as Paul did in Phil. 2:12-13.

Spurgeon placed over the doorway to his London Pastor's College these words: "Holding, I am held." "A precious truth!" comments Shank. "But neither the first clause, nor the latter, can stand alone. They are complementary. Together, they comprehend the meaning of our Saviour's words, 'Remain in me, and I in you.' "[6]

[2]Carl F. H. Henry, "The Decline of Theology," *Christianity Today*, X (1966), 428.

[3]EGT, V, 273.

[4]*Op. cit.*, p. 283.

[5]Robert Shank, *Life in the Son* (2nd ed.; Springfield, Mo.: Westcott Publishers, 1961), p. 237.

[6]*Ibid.*, p. 282.

By **the love of God** Jude means first God's love for us and then His love through us for himself and for others. Believers are kept in His love by three spiritual disciplines: **building up, praying,** and **looking.** Each term is a present participle, indicating continuous activity. But "not independent and self-righteous activity"; it is voluntary dependence on and cooperation with God for His gracious activity in and through us (Phil. 2:12-13).

But ye (20), in contrast to the "mockers" (18) who are tearing down the faith, major on **building up yourselves.** As Bengel shows, "He who defends himself first, is able then, and not till then, to preserve others."[7] This **building up** of one's faith is inseparably linked with the Word of God—"the faith once for all delivered unto the saints" (3, ASV)—and with prayer (20). See Rom. 10:17; I Pet. 2:2; II Pet. 3:18.

Jude calls the historic Christian faith **most holy** (*hagiotate* —"than which nothing can be more holy"[8]), because, as Mayor says, "it comes to us from God, and reveals God to us, and because it is by its means that man is made righteous, and enabled to overcome the world (I John 5:4-5)."[9]

Praying in the Holy Ghost means, according to Ellicott, "that we pray in His strength and wisdom; He moves our hearts and directs our petitions."[10]

In NT thought the Holy Spirit is active in all true prayer, but there are lower and higher levels of His operation. He is "The World's Best Teacher of Prayer": (1) All true prayer—from the penitent to the glorified—is *by* the Holy Spirit, Eph. 2:18; I Cor. 12:3; (2) All praying people should *pray for* the Holy Spirit's fulness, Luke 11:13; Acts 4:31; 8:14-17; (3) Only Spirit-filled believers can *pray in* the Holy Spirit, 20; Rom. 8:26-27; Eph. 5:18; 6:18.

Looking for the mercy of our Lord Jesus Christ unto eternal life (21) is another necessity. "If the faithful are to be preserved in the Christian life, they must continually watch for their coming Lord."[11] Those who watch for Him, while keeping the faith (II Tim. 4:8) and themselves **in the love of God** (21), will certainly "love his appearing" (II Tim. 4:8). To them His coming will mean **mercy,** not "condemnation" (4); it will usher them into **eternal life,** not into "eternal fire" (7).

[7]*Op. cit.*, p. 169. [8]*Ibid.*

[9]*The Epistle of St. Jude and the Second Epistle of St. Peter,* p. 49.

[10]*Op. cit.*, p. 284. [11]Cranfield, *op. cit.*, p. 168.

While Jude has stressed a proper human responsibility in the Christian life, "yet," writes Adam Clarke, "this *building, praying,* and *keeping,* cannot merit heaven: for, after all their diligence, earnestness, self-denial, watching, obedience, &c., they must look for the **mercy** *of the Lord Jesus Christ, to bring them to* **eternal life.**"[12]

An overview of Jude compels one to agree with Weiss, who said, "Everything which comes from God is primarily designated in our Epistle as holy."[13]

"A New Testament Holiness Ministry" might well sum up Jude's message: (1) Deity is holy, 20; (2) Unfallen angels are holy, 14, NEB; (3) Biblically revealed faith is most holy, 3, 20; (4) Genuine Christian believers are holy, 3.

C. Seek Others in Godly Fear, 22-23

Here Jude shifts attention from watching over our own souls to seeking the souls of "the false brethren" and "those whom they have led astray."[14]

The text of 22-23 "has been preserved in several different forms," comments Bo Reicke, "and it is impossible to ascertain which is the original."[15] While the KJV considers only two classes of sinners in these verses, the ASV indicates three classes. Wesley's translation and comments here—approved by Clarke—seem highly satisfactory: (1) "Some, *that are wavering* in judgment, staggered by others' or by their own evil reasoning, endeavour more deeply to *convince* of the whole truth as it is in Jesus. (2) *Some snatch,* with a swift and strong hand, out of the fire of sin and temptation. (3) *On others* show *compassion* in a milder and gentler way; though still *with* a jealous *fear,* lest yourselves be infected with the disease you endeavour to cure."[16]

In effect Jude is saying that their defense of *vital evangelicalism* must not diminish their *vigorous evangelism.* The last part of v. 23 has been rendered: "Hate every trace of their sin while being merciful to them as sinners" (LL).

[12]*The New Testament of Our Lord and Saviour Jesus Christ* (New York: Abingdon press, n.d.), II, 956.

[13]*Biblical Theology of the New Testament,* translated by Rev. James E. Duguid (Edinburgh: T. & T. Clark, 1883), II, 239, fn.

[14]Cranfield, *op. cit.,* p. 169. [15]*Op. cit.,* p. 215.

[16]Wesley, *op. cit.,* p. 931; cf. Clarke, *op. cit.,* p. 956.

Section V *The Benediction*

Jude 24-25

"Here is the fullest doxology in the New Testament," says A. E. Harris, "a fitting close to so stern and sacred a writing."[1] If Jude is known or noticed at all by the masses of churchgoers, it is because of the frequent use of 24-25 in the liturgies and worship manuals.

A. A Song of Praise from the Godly, 24

Although fully aware of the "surrounding perils in his day," Jude has "no panic in his heart."[2] His faith is firmly rooted in **him** who **is able** to preserve in grace here and to present in glory hereafter every one who follows the admonitions of 17-23. Having urgently warned his readers of their present perils, Jude now directs their minds to the One who can protect them from the errors and evils about which he has been speaking.

God **is able to keep you from falling** (*aptaistous,* lit. "from stumbling or slipping"). Having kept us during our probation here, He is able **to present** us **faultless before the presence of his glory,** even at the judgment throne! The word **faultless** (*amomous,* blameless) is a technical term used of a sacrificial animal without "spot" or "blemish"; cf. Lev. 1:3, 10; 3:1; Eph. 1:4; 5:27; Col. 1:22; I Pet. 1:19. This final salvation will bring **exceeding joy**—literally, "a wild joy, a leaping for joy"—to those who are preserved "unto his heavenly kingdom" (II Tim. 4:18). Heaven will resound with songs of victory and triumph—"Let us be glad and rejoice, and give honour to him" (Rev. 19:7).

B. God Our Saviour, 25

Jude climaxes his letter on the note of **the only wise God our Saviour.** The word **wise** is not in the best MSS. and it is hardly needed here. **Only** (*mono*) rules out all other pretenders to Deity. Biblical religion is monotheistic, but Jude's **only . . . God**

[1]Arthur Emerson Harris, *Bible Books Outlined,* Student's Revised Edition (Philadelphia: The John C. Winston Co., 1933), p. 112.

[2]*Ibid.*

subsists in three Persons—"God the Father" (1, 21), "our Lord Jesus Christ" (1, 17, 21), and "the Holy Ghost" (20). (Cf. Deut. 6:4; Isa. 45:5; John 17:3.)

With others, Jude ascribes saviourhood to God the Father (Luke 1:47; I Tim. 1:1; 2:3; 4:10; Titus 1:3; 2:10; 3:4) as well as to Jesus Christ. But the Father saves men *through* Jesus Christ. Christians live, writes Barclay, "with the great and comforting certainty that at the back of everything there is a God whose name is Saviour."[3]

The phrase "through Jesus Christ our Lord," after **Saviour,** while omitted by some late MSS., should be read in the text (cf. ASV, RSV). Also "before all time" following **power** is omitted by some, but is in the best MSS. (cf. ASV, RSV). This, with **now and for ever,** gives "as complete a statement of eternity as can be made in human language."[4] With these phrases included v. 25 reads, "To the only God, our Savior through Jesus Christ our Lord, be glory, majesty, dominion, and authority, before all time and now and forever. Amen" (RSV).

Jude's fourfold ascription of praise to the one and only God of all eternity cannot be excelled. **Glory** is "the sum of all the divine attributes in their radiant shining forth."[5] **Majesty** (only here and in Heb. 1:3; 8:1) includes "everything that constitutes what is really great and magnificent."[6] **Dominion** speaks of His strength to carry out His purposes. **Power** speaks of His right to rule, and of His sovereign authority. **Glory** and **majesty** belong especially to His unique selfhood, while **dominion** and **power** pertain to His divine sovereignty.

Jude's conclusion is "grand and soul-stirring. It lifts the thoughts," writes Reicke, "from earthly conflicts with which the author has been compelled to busy himself, up to the heavenly realms, where God is enthroned amidst eternal might and honor."[7] From this "luminous cosmic perspective" we must ever view the Christian's calling, conflict, and ultimate conquest.

[3]*The Letters of John and Jude,* p. 245.

[4]A. T. Robertson, *op. cit.,* p. 196.

[5]Lenski, *op. cit.,* p. 650.

[6]Calvin, *op. cit.,* p. 449, fn.

[7]*Op. cit.,* p. 217.

Bibliography

I. COMMENTARIES

ALFORD, HENRY. *The New Testament for English Readers.* Chicago: Moody Press, n.d.

BARCLAY, WILLIAM. *The Letters of John and Jude.* "The Daily Study Bible." Philadelphia: The Westminster Press, 1960.

BARNETT, ALBERT E. "The Epistle of Jude" (Exegesis). *The Interpreter's Bible.* Edited by G. A. BUTTRICK, Vol. XII. New York: Abingdon Press, 1957.

BENNETT, W. H. *The General Epistles.* "The New Century Bible"; Edinburgh: T. C. & E. C. Jack, 1901.

BIGG, CHARLES. *The Epistles of St. Peter and St. Jude.* "The International Critical Commentary." Edited by C. A. BRIGGS, S. R. DRIVER, and ALFRED PLUMMER. New York: Charles Scribner's Sons, 1905.

CALVIN, JOHN. *Commentaries on the Catholic Epistles.* Edited by JOHN OWEN. Grand Rapids: Wm. B. Eerdmans Publishing Co., 1948.

CLARKE, ADAM. *The New Testament of Our Lord and Saviour Jesus,* Vol. II. Nashville: Abingdon Press, n.d.

CRANFIELD, C. E. B. *I & II Peter and Jude.* "Torch Bible Commentaries." London: SCM Ltd., 1960.

HOMRIGHAUSEN, E. G. "The Epistle of Jude" (Exposition). *The Interpreter's Bible.* Edited by G. A. BUTTRICK, Vol. XII. New York: Abingdon Press, 1957.

LENSKI, R. C. H. *The Interpretation of the Epistles of St. Peter, St. John and St. Jude.* Columbus, Ohio: Wartburg Press, 1945.

MANTON, THOMAS. *An Exposition of the Epistle of Jude.* London: The Banner of Truth Trust, 1958 (reprint).

MAYOR, J. B. *The Epistle of St. Jude and The Second Epistle of St. Peter.* Grand Rapids: Baker Book House, 1965 (reprint).

———. "The General Epistle of Jude." *The Expositor's Greek Testament.* Edited by W. R. NICOLL, Vol. V. Grand Rapids: Wm. B. Eerdmans Publishing Co., 1951.

MOFFATT, JAMES. *The General Epistles.* "The Moffatt New Testament Commentary." New York: Harper and Brothers Publishers, n.d.

PLUMPTRE, E. H. *The General Epistles of St. Peter & St. Jude.* "The Cambridge Bible for Schools and Colleges." Edited by J. J. S. PEROWNE. Cambridge: University Press, 1893.

REICKE, BO. *The Epistles of James, Peter, and Jude.* "The Anchor Bible." Edited by W. F. ALBRIGHT and D. N. FREEDMAN. Garden City, N.Y.: Doubleday & Company, Inc., 1964.

ROBERTSON, A. T. *Word Pictures in the New Testament.* Vol. VI. Nashville: Sunday School Board of the Southern Baptist Convention, 1933.

ROBERTSON, ROBERT. "The General Epistle of Jude." *The New Bible Commentary.* Edited by F. DAVIDSON. Grand Rapids: Wm. B. Eerdmans Publishing Co., 1953.

WESLEY, JOHN. *Explanatory Notes upon the New Testament.* London: The Epworth Press, 1958 (reprint).

WOLFF, RICHARD. *A Commentary on the Epistle of Jude.* Grand Rapids: Zondervan Publishing House, 1960.

II. OTHER BOOKS

ARNDT, W. F., and GINGRICH, F. W. *A Greek-English Lexicon of the New Testament and Other Early Christian Literature.* Chicago: University of Chicago Press, 1957.

BARCLAY, WILLIAM. *A New Testament Word Book.* New York: Harper & Bros., n.d.

CHARLES, R. H. *The Apocrypha and Pseudepigrapha of the Old Testament.* Oxford: Clarendon Press, 1913.

GRANT, ROBERT M. *A Historical Introduction to the New Testament.* New York: Harper & Row, 1963.

GUTHRIE, DONALD. *New Testament Introduction: Hebrews to Revelation.* Chicago: Inter-Varsity Press, 1962.

HARRISON, EVERETT F. *Introduction to the New Testament.* Grand Rapids: Wm. B. Eerdmans Publishing Co., 1964.

HAYES, D. A. *The New Testament Epistles.* "Biblical Introduction Series." New York: The Methodist Book Concern, 1921.

PAMPHILUS, EUSEBIUS. *The Ecclesiastical History of Eusebius Pamphilus.* Translated by C. F. CRUSE, London: G. Bell and Sons, Ltd., 1917.

ROSE, DELBERT R. "Epistles of John and Jude" (Leader's Guide). *Aldersgate Biblical Series.* Edited by DONALD M. JOY. Winona Lake, Ind.: Light and Life Press, 1964.

SHANK, ROBERT. *Life in the Son.* Second Edition. Springfield, Mo.: Westcott Publishers, 1961.

STEVENS, G. B. *The Theology of the New Testament.* "International Theological Library." New York: Charles Scribner's Sons, 1905.

VINE, W. E. *An Expository Dictionary of New Testament Words.* London: Oliphants Ltd., 1957.

WEISS, BERNHARD. *Biblical Theology of the New Testament.* "Clark's Foreign Theological Library." Translated by J. E. DUGUID, 2 vols. Edinburgh: T. & T. Clark, 1833.

ZAHN, THEODOR. *Introduction to the New Testament.* Translated by JOHN TROUT, *et al.*, Vol. II. Grand Rapids: Kregel Publications, 1953 (reprint).

III. ARTICLES

BEKER, J. C. "Letter of Jude." *The Interpreter's Dictionary of the Bible.* Edited by GEORGE A. BUTTRICK, *et al.*, Vol. II. New York: Abingdon Press, 1962.

MOOREHEAD, W. G. "The Epistle of Jude." *The International Standard Bible Encyclopedia.* Edited by JAMES ORR, Vol. III. Chicago: The Howard-Severance Co., 1930.

The Book of
THE REVELATION

Ralph Earle

Introduction

Someone has said of the Book of Revelation: "It is at one and the same time the most revered, the most misunderstood, and the most neglected of New Testament writings."[1] It has been called "the most abused writing in the Christian Scriptures."[2] Barclay observes: "The *Revelation* is notoriously the most difficult book in the New Testament."[3]

The truthfulness of this statement is highlighted by the fact that Calvin refrained from writing a commentary on this book. Adam Clarke, when he came to the Book of Revelation, almost decided not to write on it. He finally settled on the unhappy compromise of quoting at length from another writer. Clarke's own feelings are expressed in these words:

> I am satisfied that no *certain* mode of interpreting the prophecies of this book has yet been found out, and I will not add another monument to the littleness or folly of the human mind by endeavouring to strike out a new course. I repeat it, I do not understand the book; and I am satisfied that not one who has written on the subject knows anything more of it than myself. . . . I had resolved, for a considerable time, not to meddle with this book, because I foresaw that I could produce nothing satisfactory on it. . . . I changed my resolution and have added short notes, principally philological, where I thought I understood the meaning.[4]

John Wesley calls attention to the evident value of the opening and closing chapters of Revelation, and adds: "But the intermediate parts I did not study at all for many years, as utterly despairing of understanding them, after the fruitless attempts of so many wise and good men: and perhaps I should have lived and died in this sentiment, had I not seen the works of the great Bengelius."[5] He thereupon decided to furnish an

[1]Charles M. Laymon, *The Book of Revelation* (New York: Abingdon Press, 1960), p. 7.

[2]John Wick Bowman, *The Drama of the Book of Revelation* (Philadelphia: Westminster Press, 1955), p. 7.

[3]*The Revelation of John* (2nd ed.; "The Daily Study Bible"; Philadelphia: Westminster Press, 1960), I, ix.

[4]*The New Testament of Our Lord and Saviour Jesus Christ* (New York: Abingdon-Cokesbury Press, n.d.), II, 965-66.

[5]*Explanatory Notes upon the New Testament* (London: Epworth Press, 1941 [reprint]), p. 932.

abridgment of Bengel's notes. But that great German commentator had fallen into the trap of setting dates (e.g., June 18, 1836, for the destruction of the beast). Spurgeon warns: "When so princely an expositor maunders in this fashion it should act as a caution to less able men."[6]

A. Authorship

At both the beginning and the end the book claims to be written by a man named John (1:1, 4, 9; 22:8). But who was this John? That question has caused much discussion.

1. *External Evidence*

In his monumental, three-volume work, *New Testament Introduction* (1961, 1962, 1965), Guthrie shows that the Book of Revelation was widely cited by the church Fathers as having been written by the Apostle John. He says: "In the second and early third centuries, the following writers clearly witness to their belief in apostolic authorship: Justin, Irenaeus, Clement, Origen, Tertullian and Hippolytus."[7] Guthrie asserts that "there are few books in the New Testament with stronger early attestation."[8]

The earliest witness is Justin Martyr (*ca.* A.D. 150). In his *Dialogue with Trypho the Jew* (LXXXI) he says: "Moreover, a man among us named John, one of Christ's Apostles, received a revelation and foretold that the followers of Christ would dwell in Jerusalem for a thousand years."[9]

2. *Internal Evidence*

The situation becomes somewhat more complicated when we turn to the testimony of the book itself. The outstanding problem is that of the difference in language and style between the Gospel and Epistles of John on the one hand and Revelation on the other. This was noted at length by Dionysius, a famous bishop of Alexandria (died A.D. 264). He writes:

> We may, also, notice how the phraseology of the gospel and the epistle differs from the apocalypse. For the former are written not

[6]*Commenting and Commentaries* (rev. ed.; Grand Rapids: Kregel Publications, 1954), p. 198.

[7]*New Testament Introduction: Hebrews to Revelation* (Chicago: Inter-Varsity Press, 1962), pp. 254-55.

[8]*Ibid.*, p. 253.

[9]*Saint Justin Martyr*, trans. Thomas B. Falls, "The Fathers of the Church," ed. L. Schopp (New York: Christian Heritage, 1948), p. 278.

> only irreprehensibly, as it regards the Greek language, but are most elegant in diction in the arguments and the whole structure of the style . . . That the latter, however, saw a revelation, and received knowledge and prophecy, I do not deny. But I perceive that his dialect and language is not very accurate Greek; but that he uses barbarous idioms.[10]

For this and other reasons Dionysius felt that Revelation was not written by the same John who wrote the Gospel and I John. But he was careful to state his conviction that it was the work "of some holy and inspired man."[11]

The style of Revelation is described by Wikenhauser in these terms: "The author writes in Greek, but thinks in Hebrew; he often translates Hebrew expressions literally into Greek. Grammatical and stylistic irregularity is the rule with him."[12] Guthrie says of the writer of Revelation: "He places nominatives in opposition [apposition?] to other cases, irregularly uses participles, constructs broken sentences, adds unnecessary pronouns, mixes up genders, numbers and cases and introduces several unusual constructions."[13]

How are we to explain this difference in language? Westcott holds to an early date for Revelation and thinks that John's later close contact with Greek-speaking people would make it possible for him to use the good Greek found in the Gospel.[14] But, as we shall see later, it seems preferable to date the two books at about the same time.

Zahn suggests a more valid explanation. He says that the linguistic phenomena of Revelation are due in part "to the dependence of the visions themselves and their literary form upon the model of the prophetic writings of the O.T."[15] This argument seems to be supported by the fact that no other book of the New Testament makes such copious use of the Old Testament. In his New Testament translation Beck furnishes at the end of each book a list of Old Testament references which are either quoted from or clearly alluded to in that book. At the end of Revelation

[10]Eusebius, *Ecclesiastical History,* trans. C. F. Cruse (Grand Rapids: Baker Book House, 1955 [reprint]), p. 301.

[11]*Ibid.*, p. 298.

[12]*New Testament Introduction,* trans. J. Cunningham (New York: Herder & Herder, 1958), p. 551.

[13]*Op. cit.*, p. 260.

[14]*The Gospel According to St. John* (Grand Rapids: Wm. B. Eerdmans Publishing Co., 1950 [reprint]), p. lxxxvi.

[15]*Introduction to the New Testament,* trans. from the 3rd German ed. (Grand Rapids: Kregel Publications, 1953 [reprint]), III, 432.

he has nearly three hundred references from the prophetic books of the Old Testament—including nearly seventy from Daniel, which is not classified by the Jews with "the Prophets." This shows that the writer of Revelation was saturated with the spirit and teachings of the Hebrew prophets.

The author's especially heavy use of Daniel—more than of any other Old Testament book—brings in another factor. The language of Revelation is definitely apocalyptic. In keeping with the emphasis on *cataclysms* and *catastrophes*—two good Greek words—it is altogether natural that apocalyptic language should be abrupt and broken in style.

Daniel is the great apocalypse of the Old Testament—along with Ezekiel, which is also referred to very frequently in Revelation. In the intertestamental period many Jewish apocalypses appeared. Much has been made in recent years of the relationship of Revelation to these Jewish apocalypses, as well as to the Christian apocalypses of the first centuries of the Church. Numbers of books have been written in this field.[16] But it must always be remembered that the Book of Revelation is more than an apocalypse; it is also a prophecy. Bowman has well said:

> If we must find a prototype for the Apocalypse, it would be nearer the truth . . . to relate it both in form and content to the prophetic writing of the Old Testament than to any of the apocalyptic literature either Jewish or Christian which appeared between 175 B.C. and A.D. 100. Unlike that literature, John speaks of his book as "prophecy" in six passages as against his one reference to it as an "apocalypse" in its title.[17]

There is still another possibility that should be considered. John probably wrote his Gospel and Epistles in Ephesus, where he would have the services of excellent Greek amanuenses (secretaries). But if he wrote the Book of Revelation on the isle of Patmos, as seems likely, he would have had to write it himself. The unpolished Greek style would then be his.

Actually, the differences in language between Revelation and the Gospel and Epistles of John have been greatly exaggerated. Guthrie notes that "in spite of linguistic and grammatical differences the Apocalypse has a closer affinity to the Greek of the other Johannine books than to any other New Testament books."[18]

What has too often been overlooked is the fact of many striking affinities between Revelation and the Gospel of John.

[16]E. g., D. S. Russell, *The Method and Message of Jewish Apocalyptic: 200 B.C.—A.D. 100* (London: SCM Press, 1964).

[17]"The Revelation of John," *Interpretation,* IX (Oct., 1955), 438.

[18]*Op. cit.,* p. 262.

Guthrie calls attention to an important point: "Both books use the word 'Logos' of Christ, an expression used nowhere in the New Testament apart from the Johannine literature (Jn. 1.1; Rev. xix.13)."[19] Another comparison is: "There is a noticeable love of antithesis in both books."[20] Westcott had already called attention to this in his commentary on John's Gospel, where he wrote: "Both present a view of a supreme conflict between the powers of good and evil."[21] He adds: "In the Gospel the opposing forces are regarded under abstract and absolute forms, as light and darkness, love and hatred; in the Apocalypse under concrete and definite forms, God, Christ, and the Church warring with the devil, the false prophet and the beast."[22] These and other affinities tend to support common authorship.

It is sometimes assumed that all leading New Testament scholars today completely reject the idea that Revelation was written by John the son of Zebedee. But this is not true. Stauffer writes: "In view of all this we have sufficient ground to ascribe these five writings to a common author of remarkable individuality and great significance, and to identify him as the apostle John."[23] Alan Richardson says concerning the Gospel: "The evidence, such as it is, does not exclude the possibility that the tradition which connects the Fourth Gospel with the name of John the son of Zebedee may be right after all."[24] What of Revelation? He says: "To-day it can be seriously maintained that the author of Revelation is none other than the Evangelist himself, adopting the conventional style and imagery of current Jewish apocalyptic literature as the vehicle of the communication of his 'prophecy' to a persecuted church."[25]

B. Date

Two main dates for the writing of Revelation have been suggested. One is about A.D. 65, when the Christians were being persecuted by Nero. The other is about A.D. 95, during the persecutions by Domitian.

The great Cambridge triumvirate—Lightfoot, Westcott, and Hort—all held to the Neronic date for Revelation. But, as Swete

[19] *Ibid.*, p. 259.

[20] *Ibid.*

[21] *Op. cit.*, p. lxxxiv.

[22] *Ibid.*, pp. lxxxiv—lxxxv.

[23] *New Testament Theology*, trans. from the German by John Marsh (London: SCM Press, 1955), p. 41.

[24] *The Gospel According to Saint John* ("Torch Bible Commentaries"; London: SCM Press, 1959), p. 14.

[25] *Ibid.*, p. 12.

notes, "Early Christian tradition is almost unanimous in assigning the Apocalypse to the last years of Domitian."[26]

Irenaeus is the earliest important witness. As quoted by Eusebius, he says in the fifth book of *Against Heresies:* "If, however, it were necessary to proclaim his name [i.e., Antichrist] openly at the present time, it would have been declared by him who saw the revelation, for it is not long since it was seen, but almost in our own generation, at the close of Domitian's reign."[27] The majority of later Fathers follow Irenaeus in holding to this traditional date.

There are a number of supporting arguments for the later date. One is that the Book of Revelation seems clearly to reflect the presence of emperor worship in the province of Asia. While there is evidence of the unofficial deification and worship of earlier emperors, "there was no official attempt to enforce the cult until the latter part of the reign of Domitian."[28]

Another argument is the severity of the persecution reflected in Revelation (1:9; 2:12; 3:10; 6:9). Concerning Domitian, Guthrie writes: "This emperor put to death his relative Flavius Clemens and banished his wife on a charge of sacrilege (*atheotes*), which strongly suggests that it was on the basis of their Christianity, since the wife, Domitilla, is known from inscriptions to have been a Christian."[29] The picture given in Revelation seems to fit the reign of Domitian.

A third argument sometimes cited is that of the Nero *redivivus* myth. After the death of that maniacal emperor in A.D. 68 there arose a legend that he was still alive and that he would return at the head of a Parthian host to invade the Roman Empire. Swete comments: "The legend, indeed, was not without a counterpart of historical fact. When the Apocalypse was written, Nero had in truth returned in the person of Domitian."[30]

It is thought by some that this legend about Nero is referred to in Rev. 13:3; 17:8. McDowell asserts: "Of course, the author of Revelation did not believe this myth, but it seems fairly certain that he has employed it in connection with his symbolism."[31]

[26]*The Apocalypse of St. John* (Grand Rapids: Wm. B. Eerdmans Publishing Co., 1951 [reprint]), p. xcix.

[27]*Ecclesiastical History,* p. 102 (III. 18).

[28]Martin Kiddle, *The Revelation of St. John* ("Moffatt New Testament Commentary"; New York: Harper & Brothers, n.d.), p. xxxix.

[29]*Op. cit.,* p. 272. [30]*Op. cit.,* p. lxxxiv.

[31]*The Meaning and Message of the Book of Revelation* (Nashville: Broadman Press, 1951), p. 4.

A date in the reign of Nero (*ca.* A.D. 65) cannot be ruled out. But in view of the above arguments, and especially in the light of the strong tradition of the Early Church, it seems best to hold to a date in the latter part of Domitian's rule (*ca.* A.D. 95).

C. Destination

The book is addressed to "the seven churches which are in Asia" (1:4); that is, the province of Asia at the west end of Asia Minor (see map 1). The seven churches are named in 1:11.

D. Purpose

The primary purpose was to comfort and encourage the Christians in their present and coming persecutions by assuring them of the final triumph of Christ and His followers. Also it was necessary to warn the churches against failure in either doctrine or experience.

E. Structure

That the Book of Revelation is highly dramatic could hardly be questioned by any thoughtful reader. How far does this phenomenon affect the structure of the book?

Bowman has made this the dominant factor. After noting that the letter or epistolary form applies particularly to the opening salutation in 1:4-6 (1:1-3 being the title of the book) and the closing benediction (22:21), he treats the intervening material as a literary drama. Between the Prologue (1:7-8) and the Epilogue (22:6-20) he finds seven acts, each with seven scenes.[32] The entire scheme is worked out with great ingenuity—too much so for some reviewers! But the picture as a whole is a very impressive one and makes Bowman's volume exciting reading.

McDowell begins the drama with chapter four and suggests two acts, with seven scenes each.[33] Kepler finds "seven acts and ten scenes."[34]

Even though these outlines differ some in detail, they all underscore the fact that *seven* is the dominant number in Revelation. There are seven letters, seven seals, seven trumpets, and seven bowls. It would appear that the seals, trumpets, and bowls do not represent successive series of judgments, but should be

[32] *Drama*, pp. 7, 11.
[33] *Op. cit.*, pp. 19-22.
[34] *The Book of Revelation* (New York: Oxford University Press, 1957), p. 35.

interpreted in terms of repetition and review. Erdman sums up the structure of the book in this way:

> In fact, contrast and repetition and climax are evident features in the literary structure of the book. However, the most conspicuous feature is that of symmetry. Each of the letters to the seven churches follows the same exact literary scheme. All seven form a section descriptive of the Church in its present imperfection and peril. With these chapters the book opens, and, with poetic balance, it closes with the picture of the New Jerusalem, in the two chapters containing the vision of the Church, perfect and glorious.
>
> In the five central sections there is the same harmonious and artistic order. Two sections, those of the seals and the trumpets, depict revolution and catastrophe, out of which naturally emerge the great antagonists whose conflict forms the central point of the dramatic action, while the two sections of bowls and dooms paint vividly the destruction of Christ's enemies and prepare for the closing picture of his perfected Church in the splendor of the "new earth."[35]

F. Interpretation

There are three main schools of interpretation of Revelation which are significant today. The first, called the *preterist* view, holds that all of Revelation refers to the period of the Roman Empire. Imperial persecution of the Christians would be followed by the final overthrow of imperial power. The second, known as the *historicist* view, sees the book as predicting the succession of significant events throughout the Church age. This is more accurately labeled the "continuous-historical" method of interpretation. The third, the *futurist* view, holds that everything beginning with chapter four is yet to be fulfilled. At various points in the exposition we shall notice the application of these three views to the interpretation of specific passages. So far as we know, this is the first published commentary to do this.

Too often the proponents of these various schools of thought have been intolerant of one another's points of view. The simple fact, which no thoughtful person would deny, is that all three of these views may be held by men who are equally devout, Spirit-filled, and loyal to the Word of God. What is needed here is sympathetic mutual understanding in the Spirit of Christ.

Niles has wisely called attention to the fact that "the essential message which John is seeking to deliver is such that even major differences of interpretation do not affect it."[36] This

[35]*The Revelation of John* (Philadelphia: Westminster Press, 1936), p. 27.

[36]*As Seeing the Invisible* (New York: Harper & Brothers, 1961), p. 10.

message is that truth will ultimately triumph, in spite of all the forces of evil.

The proper attitude for every reader of Revelation is well expressed by Richardson: "We should approach the book with that humility of spirit which is willing at times to frankly say, 'I do not know.' "[37] He also says: "We should be concerned about the message and the value of the book for our generation. We should let this word of God for the first century become for us the word of God for the twentieth century."[38]

In this atomic age, when events streak across the stage of history at orbiting speed and crisis follows crisis, the Book of Revelation takes on new relevance. One is reminded of words written many years ago about this book, but illuminated now by two world wars: "The book must be read by the lurid glare of burning cities—Jerusalem and Rome—and, it might be added, by the light of martyr-fires."[39] Today with the spread of Communism, Christians face the threat of martyrdom more seriously than at any time in centuries.

What is the lesson that Revelation has to teach us? Richardson puts it this way:

> The Coming of the Lord is the dominant note of the book. "Surely I come quickly" is the word of Christ to His suffering saints. That coming is a progressive and repeated coming. At many times and in many ways Christ comes. He comes when in faith we first turn to Him; He comes in the crises of life when we call upon Him; He comes in the hour of death to receive us unto Himself . . . In the end, in the fullness of time, He shall come visibly in glory to close the scenes of our earthly history, and to usher in the final judgment.[40]

[37]*The Revelation of Jesus Christ* (Richmond, Va.: John Knox Press, 1964), p. 12.

[38]*Ibid.*

[39]George B. Stevens, *The Theology of the New Testament* (New York: Charles Scribner's Sons, 1899), p. 525.

[40]*Op. cit.*, p. 28.

Outline

I. The Past, 1:1-20
   A. The Superscription, 1:1-3
   B. The Salutation, 1:4-8
   C. The Son of Man, 1:9-20

II. The Present, 2:1—3:22
   A. The Letter to Ephesus, 2:1-7
   B. The Letter to Smyrna, 2:8-11
   C. The Letter to Pergamum, 2:12-17
   D. The Letter to Thyatira, 2:18-29
   E. The Letter to Sardis, 3:1-6
   F. The Letter to Philadelphia, 3:7-13
   G. The Letter to Laodicea, 3:14-22

III. The Future, 4:1—22:21
   A. The Throne and the Lamb, 4:1—5:14
   B. The Seven Seals, 6:1—8:1
   C. The Seven Trumpets, 8:2—11:19
   D. The Sevenfold Vision, 12:1—14:20
   E. The Seven Bowls, 15:1—16:21
   F. The Seven Last Scenes, 17:1—20:15
   G. The New Jerusalem, 21:1—22:21

Section I *The Past*

Revelation 1:1-20

The first chapter of Revelation forms an introduction to the book. It consists of a brief paragraph giving the title and purpose of the writing (1-3), followed by the salutation (4-8) and the vision of Christ (9-20).

A. The Superscription, 1:1-3

1. *The Source of the Revelation* (1:1)

The first three words of the Book of Revelation are *Apocalypsis Iesiou Christou.* This is obviously the title of the book. That is evidently why there is no definite article. But English idiom requires inserting it. So we translate the title: **The Revelation of Jesus Christ.**

This book is often called "The Apocalypse." That is because the Greek word for **Revelation** is *apocalypsis.* This comes from the verb *apocalypto,* "uncover." In the Septuagint and New Testament it is used in the special sense of a divine revelation. A good example from the Greek Old Testament is Amos 3:7—"Surely the Lord God will do nothing, but he revealeth his secret unto his servants the prophets." In the New Testament, Paul uses the noun thirteen times. For instance, he speaks of "the revelation of the mystery" (Rom. 16:25). He received his gospel "by the revelation of Jesus Christ" (Gal. 1:12). The term is also used of the Second Coming in I Cor. 1:7 ("coming") and II Thess. 1:7, as well as in I Pet. 1:7, 13; 4:13. Vincent writes: *"The Revelation* here is *the unveiling of the divine mysteries."*[1]

But what is the meaning of the phrase **of Jesus Christ?** It has been taken by some scholars as objective genitive; that is, Jesus Christ is being revealed. Some support for this view is found in the fact that we have a vision of Christ in this first

[1]*Word Studies in the New Testament* (Grand Rapids: Wm. B. Eerdmans Publishing Co., 1946 [reprint]), II, 407. Cf. T. F. Torrance, *The Apocalypse Today* (Grand Rapids: Wm. B. Eerdmans Publishing Co., 1959), p. 11—"Apocalypse or Revelation is the unveiling of history already invaded and conquered by the Lamb of God."

chapter. But this does not properly describe the contents of the book as a whole.

In the second place, it may be treated as the genitive of possession; that is, the revelation belongs to Jesus Christ. This is supported by the clause **which God gave unto him.** But this was for the purpose of His transmitting it to John.

A third view is that this is a subjective genitive; that is, Jesus Christ gives the revelation. This seems to be preferable. Lenski says: "The genitive is subjective: Jesus Christ made this Revelation."[2] Phillips highlights the point by translating the clause: "This is a Revelation from Jesus Christ." It is best, however, to leave out the verb, as the Greek does, and make this the title of the book.

The source of the revelation was God—**which God gave unto him.** Swete comments: "The Father is the ultimate Revealer . . . the Son is the medium through Whom the revelation passes to men."[3] This is in line with the teaching of the Gospel of John (3:35; 5:20-26; 7:16; 8:28; etc.).

The purpose for which God gave this revelation to Jesus was that the latter might **shew unto his servants things which must shortly come to pass.** The word for **servants** is *doulois,* which properly means "bond servants" or "slaves." But Simcox sounds a note of warning against interpreting this term in the modern Western sense. He says: "In the East (Luke xv. 17) servants bought with a price stood above, not below hirelings."[4] In Acts and the Epistles the term is frequently applied to Christians.

The word **must** (*dei*) is exceedingly significant. Charles writes: "The *dei* denotes not the merely hasty consummation of things, but the absolutely sure fulfilment of the divine purpose."[5]

Another important term is **shortly** (*en tachei*). Charles comments: "That this fulfilment would come 'soon' . . . has always been the expectation of all living prophecy and apocalyptic."[6] A. T. Robertson helpfully observes: "It is a relative term to be

[2]*The Interpretation of St. John's Revelation* (Columbus, Ohio: Wartburg Press, 1943), p. 26.

[3]*Op. cit.,* p. 2.

[4]W. H. Simcox, *The Revelation,* rev. G. A. Simcox ("Cambridge Greek Testament"; Cambridge: University Press, 1893), p. 40.

[5]*A Critical and Exegetical Commentary on the Revelation of St. John* ("International Critical Commentary"; Edinburgh: T. & T. Clark, 1920), I, 6.

[6]*Ibid.*

judged in the light of II Pet. 3:8 according to God's clock, not ours."[7] The same phrase occurs in Luke 18:8. Simcox says: "These last passages suggest that the object of these words is to assure us of God's practical readiness to fulfil His promises, rather than to define any limit of time for their actual fulfilment."[8] In God's timetable these events are scheduled definitely, but that timetable is not ours to read (cf. Acts 1:7). Yet everything will be fulfilled shortly—"soon," or "before long." Moffatt comments: "This is the hinge and staple of the book . . . . The keynote of the Apocalypse is the cheering assurance that upon God's part there is no reluctance or delay; His people have not long to wait now."[9] Newell makes this further helpful suggestion: " 'Shortly,' moreover, not only means imminency, but also *rapidity of execution* where action once begins."[10]

The next clause is also important to note: **And he sent and signified it by his angel unto his servant John.** The verb translated **signified** is *semaino.* It comes from *sema* (*semeion*), "a sign." So it means "to give a sign, signify, indicate,"[11] or "make known, report, communicate."[12] Lange says of it here: "*Esemanen* is a modification of *deixai* [**shew**], indicative of the signs employed, the symbolical representation."[13] Bengel notes: "the LXX use *semainein* to express a great sign of a great thing: Ezek. xxxiii. 3."[14] The verb is found only here in Revelation. Vincent writes: "The word is appropriate to the symbolic character of the revelation, and so in John xii. 33, where Christ predicts the mode of His death in a figure."[15]

It is on the basis of this etymological derivation that many Bible teachers have chosen to pronounce **signify** here as "sign-

[7]*Word Pictures in the New Testament* (New York: Harper & Brothers, 1933), VI, 283.

[8]*Op. cit.*, p. 40.

[9]"The Revelation of St. John the Divine," *Expositor's Greek Testament* (Grand Rapids: Wm. B. Eerdmans Publishing Co., n.d.), V, 335.

[10]*The Book of Revelation* (Chicago: Grace Publications, 1935), p. 5.

[11]G. Abbott-Smith, *A Manual Greek Lexicon of the New Testament* (2d ed.; Edinburgh: T. & T. Clark, 1923), p. 405.

[12]W. F. Arndt and F. W. Gingrich, *A Greek-English Lexicon of the New Testament* (Chicago: University of Chicago Press, 1957), p. 755.

[13]"Revelation," *Commentary on the Holy Scriptures,* ed. J. P. Lange (Grand Rapids: Zondervan Publishing House, n.d.), p. 89.

[14]*Gnomon of the New Testament,* trans. W. Fletcher (Edinburgh: T. & T. Clark, 1860), V, 185.

[15]*Word Studies,* II, 408.

ify"; that is, the material in this book is given in signs and symbols. Some recent commentators have objected to this. J. B. Smith, for instance, says: "The usage of the word elsewhere (John 12:33; 18:32; 21:19; Acts 11:28; 25:27) does not warrant such a meaning. In each case the sense is to signify by word and not by symbol."[16] It would seem, however, that the idea has some merit, though it should not be overstressed. In the Liddell-Scott-Jones *Lexicon* the first meaning given is: "show by a sign, indicate, point out."[17] It is also stated that when the verb is used "absolutely" (i.e., without an object) it means "give signs." That is the way the term is used here. After noting the original meaning of the word, McDowell observes: "The author implies that the message he has received is being given to his readers under signs or symbols. Attention to this fact should save us from crass literalism in interpreting the message of the book."[18]

The revelation was signified **by his angel.** Probably the best thing is to take this singular form *generically.* It would thus apply "to all the individual angels who in the different visions have the office of significative declaration."[19] Such angels (or angel) are mentioned in 17:1, 7, 15; 19:9; 21:9; 22:1, 6. The literal meaning of **angel** (*angelos*) is "messenger." Throughout both the Old and New Testaments we find God using angels as messengers to communicate His revelation to men.

In this case the revelation was sent to **his servant John.** Duesterdieck comments: "The seer designates himself as the servant of Jesus Christ in respect to his prophetic service. The addition of his own name contains, according to the old prophetic custom, an attestation of the prophecy."[20]

2. *The Content of the Revelation* (1:2)

John **bare record of the word of God, and of the testimony of Jesus Christ, and of all things that he saw.** This translation obscures the fact that the Greek words for **bare record** and

[16]*A Revelation of Jesus Christ* (Scottdale, Pa.: Herald Press, 1961), pp. 34-35.

[17]H. G. Liddell and R. Scott, *A Greek-English Lexicon* (new edition rev. H. S. Jones; Oxford: Clarendon Press, 1940), p. 1592.

[18]*Op. cit.*, p. 24.

[19]Friedrich Duesterdieck, *A Critical and Exegetical Handbook to the Revelation of John,* trans. H. E. Jacobs ("Meyer's Commentary on the New Testament"; New York: Funk & Wagnalls, 1886), p. 97.

[20]*Ibid.*

testimony are from the same root. *The Twentieth Century New Testament* preserves this connection by rendering the verse: "Who testified to God's Message and to the testimony about Jesus Christ, omitting nothing of what he saw."

The common Greek root is *martyr.* Rist notes that the combination here "may involve a play on words which is not reproducible in an English translation, for the word translated testimony may also mean 'martyrdom,' while bore witness is from a verb that may mean 'to become a martyr.' There is a close connection, for those who bore witness and gave testimony were candidates for martyrdom in the days of persecution."[21] That is why the Greek word *martyros,* "witness," finally came to mean "martyr."

Bare record is in the aorist tense. This is a good example of the epistolary aorist. John is bearing witness as he writes, but from the standpoint of his readers it would be past time. So the epistolary aorist is best translated as a progressive present in English.

Of the word of God, and of the testimony of Jesus are defined by Charles as meaning "the revelation given by God and borne witness to by Christ (subjective genitive)."[22] Similarly Swete gives this identification: "The revelation imparted by God and attested by Christ."[23]

And of all things that he saw is literally "as many things as he saw." There is no **and** in the best Greek text, so most commentators take this clause as being in apposition with **the word of God** and **the testimony of Jesus.** Swete says, "This word and witness reached John in a vision."[24] Goodspeed renders the passage: "Who testifies to what he saw—to the message of God and the testimony of Jesus Christ."

3. *The Blessedness of the Recipients* (1:3)

John pronounces a threefold benediction, on three groups. The first is **he that readeth.** The context indicates clearly that the reference is to one who reads the book to others—**they that hear.** This justifies the RSV rendering, "he who reads aloud." It is "not the private student . . . but . . . the person who reads

[21]"The Revelation" (Exegesis), *The Interpreter's Bible,* XII (New York: Abingdon Press, 1957), p. 367.

[22]*Op. cit.,* I, 7. [23]*Op. cit.,* p. 3. [24]*Ibid.*

aloud in the congregation."[25] This was at first a lay reader, but later a member of the clergy.

In referring to what he was writing as **the words of this prophecy,** John deliberately placed the Book of Revelation on the same level with the prophetic books of the Old Testament. He does the same thing again in 22: 7, 10, 18.

But the hearer must also be a doer—**and keep those things which are written therein.** The Greek verb *tereo* "is constantly used of 'keeping' the Law, the Commandments, etc., throughout the N. T.; but it is commoner in *all* St. John's writings than in any other."[26]

This is the first of seven beatitudes in the Book of Revelation (cf. 14:13; 16:15; 19:9; 20:6; 22:7, 14). A study of these seven "blesseds" would make a profitable study for both clergy and laity.

The final clause is: **for the time is at hand.** The word for **time** is not *chronos*—time in the sense of duration. Rather it is *kairos*—"time as it brings forth its several births."[27] Arndt and Gingrich define the word as meaning *"the right, proper, favorable time . . . definite, fixed time* . . . one of the chief eschatological terms, *ho kairos, the time of crisis, the last times."*[28] Lange translates it here "the decision time." Weymouth has: "For the time of its fulfilment is now close at hand."

Once again John emphasizes the imminence of what is going to take place (cf. "shortly," v. 1). Niles observes: "A quality of apocalypse as well as of prophecy is a fore-shortening of vision which sets out as imminent that which is certain."[29] Of Christ he says: "He is coming and will come. Indeed, it is in this fusion of the continuous present with the certain future that the distinctiveness of biblical eschatology lies."[30]

R. H. Charles has called attention to the fact that in these first three verses of Revelation we have three elements, each consisting of three parts. With regard to (1) the source of the Revelation, it was from God, through Christ, and communicated by John to his readers. (2) The contents of the revelation are specified as the word of God, the truth attested by Christ, gath-

[25]*Ibid.* [26]Simcox, *op. cit.,* p. 41.

[27]R. C. Trench, *Synonyms of the New Testament* (Grand Rapids: Wm. B. Eerdmans Publishing Co., 1947 [reprint]), p. 210.

[28]*Op. cit.,* pp. 395-96. [29]*Op. cit.,* p. 33.

[30]*Ibid.,* p. 34.

ered up in what John saw. (3) The benediction was threefold—on the public reader, the hearers, and especially the doers.[31]

B. The Salutation, 1:4-8

The first three verses form a superscription to the book, almost in the nature of an extended title such as one finds on the title pages of books written two or three hundred years ago. But this paragraph constitutes a salutation, indicating the epistolary character of Revelation. Charles says: "Indeed the whole Book from i. 4 to its close is in fact an Epistle."[32]

1. *The Greeting* (1:4-5*a*)

Contrary to the present custom of putting the sender's name only at the end of a letter, all the letters of this period followed the sensible custom of giving the writer's name first. Thus the reader would know at once who was addressing him.

So the main body of the Book of Revelation begins with **John.** This was probably John the son of Zebedee, the apostle who wrote the Fourth Gospel and the three Epistles which bear his name (see Introduction, "Authorship"). As the venerable patriarch of the Church he would not need to identify himself further.

The book is addressed **to the seven churches which are in Asia.** In the New Testament the term **Asia** does not mean the continent but the Roman province of Asia, situated at the west end of Asia Minor (see map 1). It had been formed about 130 B.C., with the addition of Phrygia in 116 B.C.

Why seven churches? There were Christian churches in several other cities of Asia, as Colossae and Hierapolis (Col. 1:2; 4:13), Troas (Acts 20:5), and two (Magnesia and Tralles) to which Ignatius wrote about A.D. 115. It has been suggested that Troas was omitted because of its distance from the seven. Also Hierapolis and Colossae were very near Laodicea, and Magnesia and Tralles to Ephesus, so that they were disregarded.

But a better explanation is that seven was the number of perfection. The writer of Revelation uses it as the main framework for his book. Here it signifies sacredness and completeness. Erdman writes: "The seven churches addressed were, therefore, representative of the whole Church in all the world and in all ages. Thus John is addressing the entire book to the Church

[31]*Op. cit.*, I, 1. [32]*Ibid.*, I, 8.

Universal."[33] The Muratorian Canon (end of the second century) already stated: "And John also in the Apocalypse, though he writes to seven churches, yet speaks to all."[34]

Grace be unto you, and peace is the same formula that is found at the beginning of Paul's Epistles and the two by Peter. (In I and II Timothy, as well as II John, the word "mercy" is added.) These highly significant words are discussed in the comments at the beginning of several of Paul's Epistles. Plummer notes that the combination of these two terms "unites Greek and Hebrew elements, and gives both a Christian fulness of meaning."[35]

Grace and **peace** come first **from him which is, and which was, and which is to come.** This refers primarily to the Father as the Eternal One. Lenski comments that " 'the One who Is' means, 'Who Is timelessly from eternity to eternity' . . . 'and the One who Was' means 'Who Was before time and the world began' . . . 'and the One who is coming' when time shall be no more, when he shall come for the final judgment."[36] He adds: " 'The Coming One' is highly Messianic."[37]

Simcox follows Alford in holding that the entire expression here is "a paraphrase of the 'Ineffable name' revealed to Moses" in Exod. 3:14 (i.e., Jehovah or Yahweh) and also perhaps "a paraphrase of the explanation of the Name given to him, 'I am That I am.' "[38] The Palestinian Targum of Deut. 27:39 has, "Behold now, I am He who Am and Was and Will Be." This identification seems reasonable, although one should allow Lenski's view that the Messiah is meant.

The third phrase here is not **which is to come,** but, literally, "He who is coming." Swete suggests that the latter was perhaps preferred "because it adumbrates at the outset the general purpose of the book, which is to exhibit the comings of God in human history."[39]

[33]*Op. cit.,* p. 35.

[34]Samuel M. Jackson (ed.), *The New Schaff-Herzog Encyclopedia of Religious Knowledge* (Grand Rapids: Baker Book House, 1950 [reprint]), VIII, 56.

[35]"Revelation" (Exposition), *Pulpit Commentary,* XXII (Grand Rapids: Wm. B. Eerdmans Publishing Co., 1950 [reprint]), 3.

[36]*Op. cit.,* p. 39. [37]*Ibid.*

[38]*Op. cit.,* p. 42.

[39]*Op. cit.,* p. 5. Cf. Kepler (*op. cit.,* p. 47): "The expression 'who is to come' instead of 'who shall be' emphasizes the message of the book; it anticipates the return of Christ."

The Greek grammar here is irregular. Literally it reads: "from he . . ." Moffatt calls this "a quaint and deliberate violation of grammar . . . in order to preserve the immutability and absoluteness of the divine name from declension."[40] Similarly Charles writes: "We have here a title of God conceived in terms of time. The Seer has deliberately violated the rules of grammar in order to preserve the divine name inviolate from the change which it would necessarily have undergone if declined."[41]

In the second place, grace and peace come from **the seven Spirits which are before the throne.** Though a number of recent commentators would interpret this as referring to angelic beings, it seems best to adopt the more common view that this is a symbolic designation for the Holy Spirit. Alford says: "The seven spirits betoken the completeness and universality of [the] working of God's Holy Spirit, as the seven churches typify and indicate the whole church."[42] Swete agrees with this.[43] Plummer thinks the expression means, "The Holy Spirit, sevenfold in His operations," and adds: "The number seven once more symbolizes universality, plenitude, and perfection; that unity amidst variety which marks the work of the Spirit and the sphere of the Church."[44] This interpretation is strongly supported by 5:6, which is related to Zech. 4:10.

The sevenfold Spirit is **before his throne.** Lenski concludes his discussion of this verse by saying: "Thus we must combine all these expressions; this 'seven' points to the Spirit's commission to proceed from the throne and to make God and man one."[45]

In the third place grace and peace come from **Jesus Christ** (5). He is described under three figures. He is first **the faithful witness.**[46] **Faithful** means "trustworthy." Duesterdieck would not limit this witnessing to Christ's earthly ministry. Rather, He is "the very one through whom each and every divine revelation occurs, who communicates predictions not only to the prophets

[40]EGT, V, 337. [41]*Op. cit.*, p. 10.

[42]*The Greek Testament*, rev. E. F. Harrison (Chicago: Moody Press, 1958), IV, 549.

[43]*Op. cit.*, p. 6. [44]*Op. cit.*, p. 3.

[45]*Op. cit.*, p. 43.

[46]The words are in the nominative case, instead of the genitive. Charles thinks this "is best explained as a Hebraism. Since the Hebrew noun in the indirect cases is not inflected, the Seer acts at times as if the Greek were similarly uninflected, and simply places, as in the present instance, the nominative in apposition to the genitive."

in general, as at present to the writer of the Apocalypse, but also testifies to the truth by reproving, admonishing, and comforting the churches."[47]

The Greek word for **witness** later came to mean "martyr," so that our word martyr is derived from it (gen., *martyros*). Moffatt comments: "Jesus [is] not merely the reliable witness to God but the loyal martyr: an aspect of his career which naturally came to the front in 'the killing times' "[48] (cf. 2:10). Only here and in 3:14 is Jesus called a **witness.**

He is also **the first begotten of the dead.** The term **first begotten** is better rendered "the Firstborn." This was a Messianic title.[49] Jesus is now **the prince** (ruler) **of the kings of the earth.** Charles finds the dominant idea of "firstborn" here to be sovereignty. He would translate these three clauses: "the true witness of God, the *sovereign* of the dead, the ruler of the living."[50] Swete says: "The Resurrection carried with it a potential lordship over all humanity . . . The Lord won by His Death what the Tempter had offered Him as the reward of sin . . . He rose and ascended to receive universal empire."[51] He also notes that the threefold title—**witness,** Firstborn, Ruler—"answers to the threefold purpose of the Apocalypse, which is at once a Divine testimony, a revelation of the Risen Lord, and a forecast of the issues of history."[52]

These two verses portray the Trinity—Father, Son, and Holy Spirit. "The Book of Revelation will be found to be trinitarian throughout."[53]

2. *The Doxology* (1:5b-6)

John's contemplation of Christ as the risen, ruling Lord of all caused him to break forth in a spontaneous outburst of praise. This is a common feature in Paul's Epistles as well. Devout souls have always responded in praise for the goodness and greatness of our Lord.

Unto him that loved us (5) should begin a new verse. Also

[47]*Op. cit.,* p. 103. [48]EGT, V, 338.

[49]Charles, *op. cit.,* p. 14.

[50]*Ibid.* [51]*Op. cit.,* p. 7. [52]*Ibid.*

[53]Julian Price Love, "The Revelation to John," *The Layman's Bible Commentary,* ed. Balmer H. Kelly (Richmond, Va.: John Knox Press, 1960), XXV, 54.

the verb is in the present (durative) participle and should be translated "to the One who loves us."

Instead of **washed,** the oldest and best Greek manuscripts have "loosed." The two forms are similar in spelling and practically the same in pronunciation (*lousanti . . . lusanti*) and so would very easily be confused, especially if the scribe was copying by dictation. The correct translation of these two clauses is: "To him who loves us and has freed us from our sins by his blood" (RSV). The first clause emphasizes the abiding love of the Redeemer; the second, His finished act of redemption. His blood was the price He paid to free us from the slavery of sin. This is the uniform teaching of the New Testament.

What is the result of this redemption? He **hath made us kings and priests unto God and his Father** (6). The Greek reads: "And He made us a kingdom, priests to His God and Father." **Priests** is in apposition to *kingdom.* This evidently reflects Exod. 19:6—"And ye shall be unto me a kingdom of priests." It is also parallel to the phrase found in I Pet. 2:9—"a royal priesthood." Charles comments: "Our text then means that Christ has made us a kingdom, each member of which is a priest unto God."[54] This is not only a great privilege but a grave responsibility. Erdman writes: "Since we are priests we should be offering continually the sacrifices of praise and of self-denial and of loving ministry, pouring out our lives in intercession and in sympathetic service of our fellow men."[55]

The doxology ends in almost typically Pauline style: **To him be glory and dominion for ever and ever. Amen.** This is the first of three doxologies to Christ in the book (cf. 5:13; 7:10). One occurs also in II Pet. 3:18. Those in Paul's Epistles refer mostly to God the Father. Moffatt observes: "The adoration of Christ, which vibrates in this doxology . . . is one of the most impressive features of the book."[56] Plummer calls attention to an interesting fact. He says: "St. John's doxologies increase in volume as he progresses—twofold here, threefold in ch. iv. 11, fourfold in ch. v. 13, sevenfold in ch. vii. 12."[57]

It has been suggested that I Chron. 29:11—"Thine, O Lord, is the greatness, and the power, and the glory, and the victory, and the majesty"—is the source of most later doxologies. Since

[54]*Op. cit.,* p. 16.
[55]*Op. cit.,* p. 36.
[56]EGT, V, 339.
[57]*Op. cit.,* p. 4.

Jesus is called "Lord" in the New Testament, He becomes, with the Father, the object of this adoration.

The expression **for ever and ever** is literally "to the ages of the ages"; that is, "for timeless ages" (Phillips). It occurs twelve times more in Revelation.[58]

Apparently the habit of putting **Amen** at the end of prayer or praise began very early. Swete notes: "*Amen* is well supported at the end of nearly all the N. T. doxologies."[59] The word means "So be it!" or "Truly!"

3. *The Prophecy* (1:7)

This verse is "a reminiscence and adaptation" of Dan. 7:13 and Zech. 12:10-14.[60] **Behold, he cometh with clouds** is from the passage in Daniel—"And, behold, one like the Son of man came with the clouds of heaven." This coming with clouds is mentioned at six other places in the New Testament (Matt. 24:30; 26:64; Mark 13:26; 14:62; Luke 21:27; Rev. 14:14). The language here also reflects Mark 14:62—"And ye shall see the Son of man . . . coming in the clouds of heaven."

The rest of this verse is taken largely from Zech. 12:10. When Christ comes in judgment, **every eye shall see him.** Included will be **they also which pierced him.** The reference is rather clearly to the piercing of the side of Jesus on the Cross (John 19:34). This same passage from Zechariah is quoted in that connection (John 19:37). The fact that this piercing is mentioned only in John's Gospel, and that the wording here and in John 19:37 agrees strikingly[61] affords considerable support to the common authorship of the Fourth Gospel and Revelation.

But this prediction of judgment should not be restricted to the Jewish nation. Plummer writes: "The reference here is to all those who 'crucify the Son of God afresh,' not merely to the Jews."[62] John adds: **And all kindreds** (tribes) **of the earth shall wail because of him.** This is "a free adaptation of the Hebrew in Zech. xii. 12."[63]

[58]See 1:18; 4:9-10; 5:13; 7:12; 10:6; 11:15; 14:11; 15:3, 7; 19:3; 20:10; 22:5.

[59]*Op. cit.*, p. 9.

[60]EGT, V, 339.

[61]Plummer (*op. cit.*, p. 4) notes: "Here and in John xix. 37 the writer, in quoting Zech. xii. 10, deserts the LXX and follows the Masoretic Hebrew text. The LXX softens down 'pierced' into 'insulted' . . . Here and in John xix. 37 the writer, in translating from the Hebrew, uses the uncommon Greek word *ekkentan*." (Cf. Charles, *op. cit.*, I, 18.)

[62]*Ibid.*

[63]Charles, *op. cit.*, I, 18.

The combination of these passages from Daniel and Zechariah had already been made in the Olivet Discourse (Matt. 24:30). Simcox declares: "This verse, as indeed may be said of the whole book, is founded chiefly on our Lord's own prophecy recorded in St. Matt. xxiv, and secondly on the Old Testament prophecies which He there refers to and sums up."[64]

Simcox adds this helpful observation on the relation to the OT passage: "But while the *words* here are taken from Zechariah, the *thought* is rather that of Matt. xxvi. 64: 'they which pierced Him' are thought of, not as looking to Him by faith, and mourning for Him in penitence, but as seeing Him Whom they had not believed in, and mourning in despair."[65]

In the Greek, **Even so, Amen** is *nai, amen.* Charles observes: "We have here the Greek and Hebrew forms of affirmation side by side."[66] Most briefly they should be translated: "Yea, Amen." The same combination is found in II Cor. 1:20. In 3:14, Jesus is designated "the Amen." Charles comments: "Here Christ is represented as the personalized divine Amen, the guarantor in person of the truth declared by Him."[67]

4. *The Proclamation* (1:8)

This verse seems to stand by itself, unrelated to what precedes or follows. John has been speaking, but now a new speaker makes a divine declaration.

But who is this speaker? Swete writes: "The solemn opening of the book reaches its climax here with words ascribed to the Eternal and Almighty Father."[68] Many recent commentators concur in this.

But Plummer disagrees. He says of the phrases used here: "To attribute them to the Father robs the words of their special appropriateness in this context, where they form a prelude to 'the Revelation of Jesus Christ' as God and as the Almighty 'Ruler of the kings of the earth.' "[69] He feels that John is here emphasizing the deity of Jesus, and he finds a progression in this: **Alpha and Omega** (1:8), "the first and the last" (1:17; 2:8), "Alpha and Omega, the beginning and the end" (21:6), "Alpha and Omega, the beginning and the end, the first and the last" (22:13).

[64]*Op. cit.*, p. 45.
[65]*Ibid.*
[66]*Op. cit.*, I, 19.
[67]*Ibid.*
[68]*Op. cit.*, p. 10.
[69]*Op. cit.*, p. 4.

J. B. Smith calls attention to the fact that the early Church fathers applied this verse to Christ. He quotes fully from Hippolytus and Origen, and documents the quotations.[70] This seems the best view.

Alpha and Omega are the first and last letters of the Greek alphabet. Probably these are used "as in Rabbinical proverbs the first and last letters of the *Hebrew* alphabet were, as symbols of 'the beginning and the end.' "[71] However, the explanatory words, **the beginning and the ending,** are not genuine here, though they are in 22:13. Of **Alpha and Omega,** Swete writes: "The phrase is seen to express not eternity only, but infinitude, the boundless life which embraces all while it transcends all."[72]

The Lord is "the Lord God" in the best Greek text. **Almighty** (*pantokrator*) occurs only once elsewhere in the New Testament (II Cor. 6:18), but is found nine times in Revelation.

Of John's purpose in writing vv. 7 and 8, Lenski says: "In dramatic form he states *the summary theme* of the whole book, of all the revelations he has seen (v. 7) and in v. 8 appends *Christ's own signature.*"[73]

C. The Son of Man, 1:9-20

1. *The Setting of the Vision* (1:9-11)

Before John could receive a preview of what was to take place in the future, he must view Christ himself. The setting of the vision was the apostle on the isle of Patmos (see map 1) **in the Spirit on the Lord's day** (10). The subject of the vision was the Son of Man, standing in the midst of His Church.

The author introduces himself as **I John** (9). A. R. Fausset calls attention to the parallels in Dan. 7:28; 9:2; 10:2 and comments: "[This is] one of many resemblances between the Old and the New Testament apocalyptic seers. No other Scripture writer uses the phrase."[74]

John describes himself as **your brother,** or fellow Christian, **and companion in tribulation, and in the kingdom and patience**

[70]*Op. cit.*, p. 46.
[71]Simcox, *op. cit.*, p. 45.
[72]*Op. cit.*, p. 11.
[73]*Op. cit.*, p. 48.

[74]"The Revelation," Robert Jamieson, A. R. Fausset, and David Brown, *A Commentary Critical, Experimental and Practical on the Old and New Testaments* (Grand Rapids: Wm. B. Eerdmans Publishing Co., 1948 [reprint]), VI, 657.

of Jesus Christ. This is more accurately translated: "fellow-partaker [*synkoinonos*] in the tribulation and kingdom and perseverance which are in Jesus" (NASB). The word **patience** is too passive a term for the Greek *hypomone,* which means "endurance" or "steadfastness."

On the phrase **in tribulation** Bengel makes the cogent observation: "This book has most relish for the faithful in tribulation."[75] The Book of Revelation was written in days of great distress for the Christians, and it becomes most meaningful in times like those.

John was on the island of **Patmos.** This was a small island about ten miles long from north to south, and not more than six miles wide, situated about thirty-seven miles southwest of Miletus (see map 1). It is composed of rocky, volcanic hills.

The apostle was there **for the word of God, and for the testimony of Jesus Christ.** That does not mean that he had gone to the island to preach the gospel. A correct paraphrase would be: "because I had preached God's word and borne my testimony to Jesus" (NEB). The small islands of the Aegean Sea were used by the Romans as places of banishment for political prisoners. A comparison with 6:9 and 20:4 will show that in the Book of Revelation **word of God** and **testimony** (or witness) are used in connection with the persecution of Christians. Speaking of the oppression by Domitian (A.D. 95), Eusebius writes: "In this persecution, it is handed down by tradition, that the apostle and evangelist John, who was yet living, in consequence of his testimony to the divine word, was condemned to dwell on the island of Patmos."[76] He also says: "But after Domitian had reigned fifteen years, and Nerva succeeded to the government, the Roman senate decreed, that . . . those who had been unjustly expelled, should return to their homes, and have their goods restored . . . It was then also, that the apostle John returned from banishment, and took up his abode at Ephesus, according to an ancient tradition of the church."[77]

It would appear that times of tribulation often set the stage for God's revelation to man. Plummer observes: "It was in exile that Jacob saw God at Bethel; in exile that Moses saw God at the burning bush; in exile that Elijah heard the 'still small voice;' in exile that Ezekiel saw 'the likeness of the glory of the

[75]*Op. cit.,* V, 199.

[76]*Op. cit.,* III. 18. 1 (p. 101).

[77]*Ibid.,* III. 20. 8-9 (p. 103).

Lord' by the river Chebar; in exile that Daniel saw 'the Ancient of days.' "[78]

John declares that when he received the vision he was **in the Spirit** (10). What does this mean? Translators have rendered it variously as: "in a trance" (20th Cent. NT), "inspired by the Spirit" (Weymouth), "rapt in the Spirit" (Moffatt), "Spirit-possessed" (Berk.), "in the Spirit's power" (C. B. Williams), "caught up by the Spirit" (NEB). Commentators differ as widely. Lange explains the phrase as meaning: "transported out of the ordinary every-day consciousness, and placed in the condition of prophetic ecstasy."[79] Simcox has: "Was caught up into a state of spiritual rapture."[80] Charles says that *egenomen en pneumati* (literally, "I became in spirit") "denotes nothing more than that the Seer fell into a trance."[81] Lenski writes: "The phrase means 'in spirit,' and we should not capitalize the word as though the Holy Spirit were referred to. This is John's *pneuma.*"[82] He favors the idea of a miraculous ecstasy, "a state that is wrought directly by God himself."[83] We prefer Swete's interpretation that the entire phrase "denotes the exaltation of the prophet under inspiration"[84] (of the Spirit).

This lofty spiritual experience came to John **on the Lord's day.** Some have taken this as meaning "the day of the Lord," a prophetic phrase common in both the Old and New Testaments. They think that the seer was transported in spirit to the time of the Second Coming.

But the Greek form of the expression here rules out that interpretation. **Lord's** is an adjective, not the usual genitive phrase "of the Lord." It occurs only once elsewhere in the New Testament (I Cor. 11:20—"the Lord's supper"). It means "belonging to the Lord," or "consecrated to the Lord."

The adjective is found a number of times in the inscriptions and the papyri of Egypt and Asia Minor, where it means "imperial."[85] The earliest known example of the use of this word is in an inscription dated the sixth of July, A.D. 68. Here are found the expressions "the imperial finances" and "the imperial treas-

[78]*Op. cit.*, p. 5.
[79]*Op. cit.*, p. 103.
[80]*Op. cit.*, p. 46.
[81]*Op. cit.*, I, 22.
[82]*Op. cit.*, p. 58.
[83]*Ibid.*
[84]*Op. cit.*, p. 13.
[85]Adolf Deissmann, *Bible Studies*, trans. A. Grieve (Edinburgh: T. & T. Clark, 1901), p. 217.

ury." Deissmann also notes that from 30 B.C. to the time of Trajan (A.D. 98-117) a certain day of every month was kept as *hemera Sebaste* in memory of the birthday of Augustus, and suggests that "the distinctive title 'Lord's day' [*kyriake hemera*] may have been connected with conscious feelings of protest against the cult of the Emperor with its 'Augustus day.' "[86] It would appear that the Christians adopted the name **Lord's day** in commemoration of Jesus' resurrection on the first day of the week. In modern Greek, Sunday is called *kyriake.* Of this passage in Revelation, Charles says: "Here 'Lord's Day' has become a technical designation of Sunday."[87]

The setting is not difficult to reconstruct. In exile on Patmos, John was deprived of the privilege of meeting with the saints on Sunday. Looking across the open sea, he was doubtless thinking of the Christians at Ephesus gathered together for worship. He may well have been meditating on the Resurrection. Moffatt suggests: "With his mind absorbed in the thought of the exalted Jesus and stored with O. T. messianic conceptions from Daniel and Ezekiel, the prophet had the following ecstasy in which the thoughts of Jesus and of the church already present to his mind are fused into one vision."[88]

T. F. Torrance puts together the statements in vv. 9 and 10—**I John . . . was in the isle that is called Patmos** and **I was in the Spirit on the Lord's day.** He then makes this observation: "In these two autobiographical sentences we are given right at the start the double situation out of which this book takes its rise. On the one hand, there is the hard cruel destiny of time, but on the other hand, there is the Spirit of Almighty God."[89]

Thus prepared in heart and mind for the revelation, John heard behind him a great voice (cf. Ezek. 3:12). The sound came as loudly and clearly as the blowing of a trumpet.

Saying (11) is equivalent to quotation marks. The speaker was evidently Jesus (cf. vv. 12-13). The words **I am Alpha and Omega, the first and the last: and** are not in the earliest Greek MSS. The same is true of **which are in Asia** (cf. vv. 4, 8). John is commanded to write in a book what he sees. The Greek word is *biblion,* origin of our word "Bible." It refers to a papyrus roll

[86]*Light from the Ancient East,* trans. L. R. M. Strachan (rev. ed.; New York: George H. Doran, 1927), p. 359.

[87]*Op. cit.,* I, 23. [88]EGT, V, 342.

[89]*Op. cit.,* p. 10.

or scroll, as distinguished from the more expensive parchment which was made from animal skins (cf. II Tim. 4:13). The scroll of Revelation would have been about fifteen feet in length.[90]

The written roll was to be sent to the seven churches (cf. 4). These are now designated by name. The distances between these cities is given as follows by Charles: "Smyrna lay 40 miles north of Ephesus, Pergamum 40 north of Smyrna, Thyatira 45 S.E. of Pergamum, Sardis 30 nearly due S. of Thyatira, Philadelphia 30 E.S.E. of Sardis, and Laodicea 40 S.E. of Philadelphia."[91] Bowman writes: "A glance at the map of the Roman province of Asia [see map 1] shows the *seven churches* to be arranged in the form of the seven-branched candlestick of the Herodian Temple—Nos. 1 and 7, 2 and 6, 3 and 5 forming pairs on opposite sides with No. 4 at the top."[92]

Sir William Ramsay, the greatest modern authority on the ancient history of Asia Minor, rightly insists that there must have been a reason for the selection of these particular seven churches. The first reason was the system of roads. He notes that "all the Seven Cities stand on the great circular road that bound together the most populous, wealthy, and influential part of the Province, the west-central region."[93] He finally comes to the conclusion: "The hypothesis inevitably suggests itself that the Seven groups of churches, into which the Province had been divided before the Apocalypse was composed, were seven postal districts, each having as its centre or point of origin one of the Seven Cities."[94] This is only a theory, but an interesting one.

2. *The Subject of the Vision* (1:12-20)

John turned "to see whose voice it was that spoke" (NEB) to him. **And being turned** (12)—better, "having turned" (ASV) —he **saw seven golden candlesticks**—rather, "lampstands." This is different from the seven-branched lampstand of Zech. 4:2. **In the midst** of the golden lampstands was **one like unto the Son of man** (13). Because the Greek does not have the definite article

[90]Frederick G. Kenyon, *Handbook to the Textual Criticism of the New Testament* (2d ed.; Grand Rapids: Wm. B. Eerdmans Publishing Co., 1951 [reprint]), p. 34.

[91]*Op. cit.*, I, 25; cf. comments on 2:12.

[92]*Op. cit.*, p. 23.

[93]*The Letters to the Seven Churches of Asia* (New York: A. C. Armstrong & Son, 1904), p. 183.

[94]*Ibid.*, p. 191.

before **Son,** many modern translators render it literally, "a son of man." Plummer favors this, and comments: "The glorified Messiah still wears that human form by which the beloved disciple had known Him before the Ascension."[95] Swete remarks: "The glorified Christ is human, but transfigured."[96] Similarly Lange writes that **like** (*homoios*) "is also in part expressive of the apostolic view that the *human* personality of Christ, in its glorification, is clothed with the splendor of *divine* majesty."[97]

The most satisfactory treatment of the phrase **one like unto the Son of man** seems to be that given by Simcox. He says: "The absence of the article here proves not that our Lord is not intended, but that the title is taken not from His own use of it but direct from the Greek of Daniel vii. 13, where also both words are without the article . . . the words themselves mean no more than 'I saw a human figure,' but their associations would make it plain to all readers of the Book of Daniel that it was a superhuman Being in human form; and to a Christian of St. John's day as of our own, Who that Being was."[98]

The **seven candlesticks** (lampstands) are later identified as symbolizing "the seven churches" (v. 20). So here the picture is that of Christ standing in the midst of His Church.

This is a most comforting thought. But there is also a challenge here. If the churches are lamps, they are supposed to illuminate the darkness of this world. Moffatt writes: "The function of the churches is to embody and express the light of the divine presence upon earth . . . their duty is to keep the light burning and bright, otherwise the reason for their existence disappears (ii. 5)."[99]

Now comes the detailed description of the glorified **Son of man.** The first item is: **clothed with a garment to the foot.** With the exception of **clothed with** (perfect passive participle) all the clause is one word in Greek, *podere.* It is actually an adjective, found only here and meaning "reaching to the feet." The word is used in Exodus (LXX) for priestly garments. Moffatt says that this term, "a long robe reaching to the feet, was an oriental mark of dignity."[100] The next clause, **and girt about the**

[95]*Op. cit.,* p. 6. [96]*Op. cit.,* p. 15.

[97]*Op. cit.,* p. 104.

[98]*Op. cit.,* p. 47. Charles thinks that the phrase here, "like a son of man," is "the exact equivalent" of "the Son of man" in the Gospels and Acts 7:56 (*op. cit.,* I, 27).

[99]EGT, V, 343. [100]*Ibid.,* p. 344.

paps with a golden girdle, is better rendered "and with a girdle of gold across his breast" (Weymouth). This was "another mark of lofty position, usually reserved for Jewish priests, though the Iranians frequently appealed to their deities as 'high-girt.' "[101] Putting these two clauses together we have a picture of both priestly and royal dignity. For no one else is this combination so appropriate as for our Lord.

The third item is: **His head and his hairs were white like wool, as white as snow** (14). Swete notes: "Ancient expositors find in the hair white as snow a symbol of the eternal preexistence of the Son."[102] Plummer writes: "This snowy whiteness is partly the brightness of heavenly glory, partly the majesty of the hoary head."[103] But several commentators call attention to the fact that white hair is a sign of decay when connected with age. So Lenski concludes: "We think this passage with the symbol of the hair that is white as snow and wool intends to represent Jesus as being crowned with holiness."[104] There is a close parallel in Dan. 7:9 (LXX).

The fourth point in the description of the glorified Christ is that **his eyes were as a flame of fire** (*phlox pyros*). This is quite evidently an allusion to Dan. 10:6—"and his eyes as lamps of fire"—a common metaphor in both Latin and Greek literature. J. B. Smith suggests that this feature symbolizes "omniscience and scrutiny."[105] Swete adds: "The penetrating glance . . . which flashed with quick intelligence, and when need arose with righteous wrath, was noticed by those who were with our Lord in the days of His Flesh . . . and finds its counterpart, as the Seer now learns, in the Risen and Ascended Life."[106]

The fifth item is: **And his feet like unto fine brass, as if they burned in a furnace** (15). Again there is a parallel in Dan. 10:6—"and his arms and his feet like in colour to polished brass" (cf. Ezek. 1:4, 7, 27; 8:2). The Greek word for **fine brass** is uncertain as to its etymological meaning. But the sense seems to be that given in our English versions. The symbolism suggested by Swete is: "Feet of brass represent strength and stability."[107] **Burned** is better rendered "glowing" or "refined." In the Scriptures **brass** seems to typify judgment.

[101]*Ibid.*
[102]*Op. cit.*, p. 16.
[103]*Op. cit.*, p. 7.
[104]*Op. cit.*, p. 65.
[105]*Op. cit.*, p. 53.
[106]*Op. cit.*, p. 17.
[107]*Ibid.*

A sixth feature is: **And his voice as the sound of many waters.** In Dan. 10:6 it is: "The voice of his words like the voice of a multitude." But John's ears were filled with the roar of the surf, as the Aegean Sea beat on the shores of rocky Patmos. So he uses this imagery to describe the voice. In doing so, however, he was echoing Ezek. 43:2—"And his voice was like a noise of many waters."

The Son of Man **had in his right hand seven stars** (16). The meaning of these is given in v. 20. **And out of his mouth went a sharp twoedged sword.** This was originally "a great, long, heavy sword, almost as tall as a man, that is wielded with both hands, a weapon of the Thracians."[108] But in the Septuagint it seems to be used synonymously with the more common word for an ordinary sword. Lenski adds: "For our 'two-edged' the Greek says 'two-mouthed,' the two edges biting, devouring like two mouths. 'Sharp' is added. It was whetted to a keen edge so as to bite deeply."[109]

The language of this clause seems to reflect Isa. 11:4, "He shall smite the earth with the rod of his mouth"; and Isa. 49:2—"And he hath made my mouth like a sharp sword." Charles comments: "The sword that proceeds from the mouth of the Son of Man is simply a symbol of his judicial authority."[110] Literal portrayals of this in religious art and prophetic diagrams appear ludicrous and border on the sacrilegious. They should warn us against visual representations of the symbolical figures used in Revelation.

The last item in the description is: **And his countenance was as the sun shineth in his strength.** This is an obvious echo of the Transfiguration (Matt. 17:2).

After noting the various borrowings from Daniel, Kiddle makes this comment: "But though so much of John's picture is derivative, it conveys a conception of the Messiah which is unique, for Christ is endowed with a splendour and authority which hitherto had been ascribed solely to God."[111] This is one of the unmistakable emphases of the New Testament.

The effect of the vision was overpowering: **I fell at his feet as dead** (17). Daniel experienced much the same reaction to his vision (Dan. 10:8-9). Similar words are used in Josh. 5:14 and Ezek. 1:28; 3:23; 43:3. Erdman comments: "Every vision of

[108]Lenski, *op. cit.*, p. 69.
[109]*Ibid.*
[110]*Op. cit.*, I, 30.
[111]*Op. cit.*, p. 16.

divine purity and majesty and power inspires awe and reverence and holy fear."[112]

Yet this stern-looking Christ of judgment was also the compassionate Christ. For **he laid his right hand upon** John (cf. Dan. 10:10; Matt. 17:7) and said, **Fear not** (cf. Dan. 10:12). **I am the first and the last** is applied to God in Isa. 44:6. But here it clearly refers to Christ, and stresses His deity, as also in 2:8 and 22:13.

I am he that liveth (18) is literally "and the Living One" (*kai ho zon*)—a divine title, applied to God in both the Old and New Testaments. Should it be taken with what precedes or with what follows, **and was dead** (*kai egenomen necros*)? Charles votes for the latter. He puts the two items together in one poetic line: "And He that liveth and was dead." Then he says: "Most recent commentators connect the *kai ho zon* with the preceding words. But in every instance, whether in Isaiah or in the Apocalypse, the phrase 'I am the first and the last' is complete in itself, and the phrase *kai ho zon* would simply impair the fulness of the claim made in these words. On the other hand, when taken with *kai egenomen necros* they are full of significance in the contrast between the ever abiding eternal life which He possesses and the condition of physical death to which He submitted for the sake of man."[113]

The One who was dead can now say: **Behold, I am alive for evermore.** In other words, He is the Eternal One. **Amen** is not found here in the best Greek MSS. and should be omitted.

One more statement is made: **And have the keys of hell and of death.** In the best MSS. **death** comes before **hell.** Also it seems best to transliterate *hades,* rather than to translate it **hell** (cf. NASB—"And I have the keys of death and of Hades").

Since there has been a great deal of discussion about this term, it would be well to look a little further into its meaning. In Greek thought Hades was first the name of the god of the underworld. Then it came to be used for the underworld itself, as the place of departed spirits. In the Septuagint it is the rendering of the Hebrew word *Sheol,* the realm of the dead.

Josephus, the Jewish historian of the first century, reveals the confused thinking of the Judaism of Jesus' day on this subject. He declares that the Pharisees placed the souls of both the righteous and ungodly in Hades.[114] But, though a Pharisee him-

[112]*Op. cit.,* p. 41.

[113]*Op. cit.,* I, 31.

[114]*Ant.* XVIII. 1. 3.

self, he writes that the souls of the obedient "obtain a most holy place in heaven . . . while the souls of those whose hands have acted madly against themselves are received by the darkest place in Hades."[115]

It would appear that Gehenna in Jesus' teaching (cf. Matt. 5:22) is to be identified with the "lake of fire" of Rev. 19:20; 20:10, 14-15. But Death and Hades are cast into the lake of fire (20:14). So obviously the place of everlasting punishment is Gehenna, not Hades. Jeremias writes: "Throughout the NT Hades serves only an interim purpose. It receives souls after death, and delivers them up again at the resurrection (Rev. 20: 13)."[116] Charles says of this term in Revelation: "Hades is the intermediate abode of only the wicked or non-righteous in our author."[117]

The keys signify authority. Jesus possesses full authority over the domains of Death and Hades.

R. H. Charles makes a fitting observation about 18: "This verse sets forth the threefold conception of Christ in John: the ever abiding life He had independently of the world; His humiliation even unto physical death, and His rising to a life not only everlasting in itself but to universal authority over life and death."[118]

Charles Simeon notes that in vv. 17-18 Jesus makes the threefold claim of being: (1) The eternal God; (2) The living Saviour; (3) The universal Sovereign.

John had already been ordered to write in a scroll "what thou seest" (11). Now the command is repeated and made more explicit: **Write**[119] **the things which thou hast seen, and the things which are, and the things which shall be hereafter** (19).

Erdman objects strongly to the "popular view" that this verse gives us a threefold outline of the Book of Revelation.[120] But we prefer to follow Charles when he writes: "These words summarize roughly the contents of the Book. The *ha eides* [**the things which thou hast seen**] is the vision of the Son of Man just

[115]*War* III. 8. 5.

[116]"Hades," *Theological Dictionary of the New Testament,* ed. Gerhard Kittel, I (Grand Rapids: Wm. B. Eerdmans Publishing Co., 1964), 148.

[117]*Op. cit.,* I, 32. [118]*Ibid.,* p. 31.

[119]The best Greek MSS. add "therefore"—in the light of Jesus' authority over Death and Hades, and the glorious vision of His deity and majesty.

[120]*Op. cit.,* p. 42.

vouchsafed to the Seer; *ha eisin* [**the things which are**] refers directly to the present condition of the Church as shown in chaps. ii—iii, and indirectly to that world in general; *ha mellei ginesthai meta tauta* [**the things which shall be hereafter**] to the visions from chap. iv. onwards, which, with the exception of a few sections referring to the past and present, deal with the future."[121] This is the outline adopted in this commentary.

The first chapter finishes with an explanation of **the mystery**
(20) **of the seven stars . . . and the seven golden lampstands.** Of this significant term Erdman writes: "A 'mystery' is, in New Testament usage, truth or reality divinely revealed."[122] Swete says it is "the inner meaning of a symbolical vision."[123]

John is informed that **the seven stars** represent **the angels of the seven churches.** Since the Greek word *angelos* means "messenger" and is clearly used for human messengers in Luke 7:24; 9:52; and Jas. 2:25, many have held that the reference here is to messengers who would be sent with the letters to the seven churches—perhaps delegates who had come from those places to visit John—or more simply to the "pastors" of the churches. To this it is objected that in the sixty or more times that *angelos* is used in this book apart from connection with the churches it always refers to superhuman beings. Swete concludes: "There is therefore a strong presumption that the *angeloi ton ecclesion* are 'angels' in the sense which the word bears elsewhere throughout the book."[124] Charles concurs firmly.[125] He also objects to identifying them as the "guardian angels" of the churches. He finally reaches this conclusion: "Hence the only remaining interpretation is that which takes these angels to be heavenly doubles or counterparts of the Seven Churches, which thus come to be identified with the Churches themselves."[126] Probably more acceptable is Erdman's view that the "angel" is "the prevailing spirit" of the church, "a personification of the character and temper and conduct of the church."[127]

It would seem that a better stated view is that of Alfred Plummer. He writes: "The identification of the angel of each Church with the Church itself is shown in a marked way by the fact that, although each epistle is addressed to the angel, yet the constantly recurring refrain is, 'Hear what the Spirit saith *to the*

[121]*Op. cit.*, I, p. 33.
[122]*Op. cit.*, p. 42.
[123]*Op. cit.*, p. 21.
[124]*Ibid.*, p. 22.
[125]*Op. cit.*, I, 34-35.
[126]*Ibid.*, I. 34.
[127]*Op. cit.*, p. 43.

Churches,' not 'to the *angels* of the Churches.' The angel and the Church are the same under different aspects: the one in its spiritual character personified; the other in the congregation of believers who collectively possess this character."[128]

But one wonders whether this interpretation makes adequate room for the distinction between the stars and the lampstands. The present writer is loath to give up the popular view that the angels are the pastors of the churches—an immensely comforting thought: they are held in Christ's own hands.

[128]*Op. cit.*, p. 8.

Section II *The Present*

Revelation 2:1—3:22

In c. 1 we find "the things which thou hast seen" (1:19)—the past. In cc. 2 and 3 are recorded "the things which are"—the present. It is best to take this section as describing current conditions in the seven churches of Asia.

Many writers have found here seven successive periods of church history. J. B. Smith gives a good summary of this interpretation. *Ephesus* pictures "the early decline of vital Christianity at the close of the first century," the loss of its first love. *Smyrna* depicts the period of persecution, in the second and third centuries. *Pergamos* portrays "the union of church and state under Constantine" (fourth century) with its consequent ecclesiastical and moral corruption. *Thyatira* describes "the domination of the Roman hierarchy," from the fifth to the fifteenth centuries. *Sardis* points to "the days of the Reformation," in the sixteenth century, when "a few names" had "not defiled their garments" (3:4). *Philadelphia* speaks of "a period of orthodoxy and evangelism by such leaders as Wesley and Whitefield [eighteenth century], at which time all the nations of the world presented 'open doors' for the reception of the Gospel." *Laodicea* shows "the end-time apostasy in language precisely the same as that employed concerning the last days by Jesus and the apostles Paul, James, Peter, John, and Jude."[1] This apostasy began with the German destructive criticism of the Bible in the nineteenth century and has reached the alarming stage represented by the "death of God" position claimed by theologians in 1965.

Unquestionably there is a remarkable coincidence between these seven letters and the sequence of periods suggested. But it is probably best to hold that all the letters taken together constitute a general picture of conditions not only in the seven churches of Asia at the end of the first century, but also throughout Christendom during the entire Church age. This is not to deny that certain characteristics described in these messages were more dominant in one period than in another.

[1]*Op. cit.*, pp. 61-62.

The letters agree rather closely in a balanced structure. Smith has a seven-part division for each: (1) the Annunciation; (2) the Presentation; (3) the Declaration; (4) the Approbation; (5) the Reprobation; (6) the Exhortation; (7) the Remuneration. We have adopted a somewhat similar outline.

Two of the churches, Smyrna and Philadelphia, have no word of disapproval said concerning them. At the opposite end is Laodicea, with no word of approval. Kiddle notes: "Two of the churches, the first and the last, are threatened with complete extinction, since each lacks qualities essential to the profession of the Christian faith. Unqualified praise is given to the second and sixth churches. The three central churches are complimented and castigated in varying degrees, for in each of them there exists a mixture of good and bad elements; the faithful are promised rewards and the faithless are threatened with the severest punishments."[2] Thus there seems to be a purposeful design worked out in presenting these seven churches as representative of conditions existing in all the churches.

A. The Letter to Ephesus, 2:1-7

1. *Address* (2:1*a*)

The first letter is written to the **angel** (see comments on 1:20) **of the church** at **Ephesus.** This was the leading city of the Roman province of Asia, at the west end of Asia Minor (see map 1). At the time when John wrote, it was a great seaport, situated near the mouth of the Cayster River. Caravans on Roman roads from north, east, and south converged here, to load their cargoes on ships sailing west for Corinth or far-off Italy. Ephesus was a seething metropolis. It was the gateway of Asia. The Roman proconsul was required to land here when he entered on his office as governor of Asia. At the same time it was the highway to Rome. In the early second century, when Christians were being shipped to Rome to be fed to the lions, Ignatius called Ephesus the Highway of Martyrs.[3]

Politically, Ephesus was a free city. That meant that it enjoyed a considerable measure of self-government. Here also the famous annual games were held.

Religiously Ephesus was the center of the worship of Artemis (see comments on Acts 19:24-27, BBC, VII, 482-83). Her temple

[2] *Op. cit.*, p. 6.

[3] Barclay, *op. cit.*, I, 70-71.

was one of the seven wonders of the ancient world. Ephesus was called "The Light of Asia." Yet it was a pagan city, filled with the darkness of heathen superstition. Swete writes: "The city was a hotbed of cults and superstitions, a meeting-place of East and West, where Greeks, Romans and Asiatics jostled one another in the streets."[4]

Because of its strategic importance, Paul had spent longer here (nearly three years, Acts 20:31) than at any other place on his three missionary journeys. He won many converts, both Jews and Gentiles (Acts 19:10), and built a strong church. In the A.D. sixties Timothy was stationed here (I Tim. 1:3). Early Church tradition affirms that John spent the last years of his life at this third great center of Christianity (after Jerusalem and Antioch).

Today this once mighty metropolis is a heap of ruins. The Cayster River has filled the harbor with silt, so that it is only a marsh of reeds. The sea is six miles away.

There are three logical reasons for John's writing first to the church at Ephesus. (*a*) It was the leading church in Asia and situated in the leading city of that province. (*b*) It was the nearest city to Patmos, about sixty miles away. It was the first city that would be reached by the messenger who carried these letters. (*c*) It was John's home church. On this Sunday morning the aged apostle was doubtless thinking about the needs and problems of that church, as well as of the other six churches which may well have been under his jurisdiction.

2. *Author* (2:1*b*)

The divine Author of these seven letters is Jesus Christ. At the beginning of each epistle, after the address, He is described in a unique way that fits the message of that letter. Each time the Author is introduced with the words: **These things saith.** Then follows the description of the glorified Lord. Swete says of this introductory formula: "It is followed in each case by a description of the Speaker, in which He is characterised by one or more of the features of the vision of ch. i . . . or by one or more of His titles . . . the features or titles selected appear to correspond with the circumstances of the church which is addressed."[5] But he also notes: "To the Church in Ephesus, the mother of the

[4] *Op. cit.*, p. 23. [5] *Ibid.*, p. 24.

Churches of Asia, the Lord writes under titles which express His relation to the Churches generally."[6]

In this verse it is: **He that holdeth the seven stars in his right hand, who walketh in the midst of the seven golden candlesticks.** This carries us back to the description of Christ in 1:12-20. Though the **candlesticks** (lampstands) are clearly identified by Jesus as symbolizing the churches, the interpretation of the **stars** as "angels" is variously explained (see comments on 1:20). We must confess to a strong sympathy with the view expressed by Richardson. After identifying "angels" as meaning messengers and seven as signifying "all," he says: "All the true ministers of all the churches are held in the hand of Christ . . . As Christ moves in the midst of the churches He holds the ministers in His hand."[7] If this interpretation can be accepted, it furnishes great consolation for the burdened pastor.

3. *Commendation* (2:2-3, 6)

God is never unmindful of what we do for Him. Jesus says to the church at Ephesus, **I know** (2). It is always a comfort to realize that our Lord knows us correctly.

The church at Ephesus is commended first for its **works.** This is found again in 2:19; 3:1, 8, 15. **Labour** (*kopos*) is a strong term. Barclay says that it describes "labour to the point of sweat; labour to the point of exhaustion; the kind of toil which takes everything of mind and sinew that a man can put into it."[8]

Patience is hardly an adequate translation for the Greek word here, which means "steadfast endurance" (see comments on 1:9). Barclay comments: "*Hupomone* is not the grim patience which resignedly accepts things, and which bows its head when troubles flow over it. *Hupomone* is the courageous gallantry which accepts suffering and hardship and loss and turns them into grace and glory."[9]

Smith makes an interesting observation about these three terms as used here. He writes: "Faith, hope, and love are sadly missing. Contrast this church with the Thessalonians: Ephesus had works, but not work of faith; labor, but not labor of love; patience, but not patience of hope" (I Thess. 1:3).[10] He then

[6]*Ibid.*
[7]*Op. cit.*, p. 42.
[8]*Op. cit.*, I, 75.
[9]*Ibid.*, I, 75-76.
[10]*Op. cit.*, pp. 63-64.

makes this significant statement: "It is not too much to say that a church may have all the virtues mentioned and yet be devoid of spiritual life."[11] One might well add: And so also may an individual.

The church at Ephesus was not only hardworking, but also careful in matters of discipline: it could **not bear them which are evil.** Unlike Corinth, it would not tolerate sin within its circle. It had **tried them which say they are apostles, and are not, and hast found them liars.** The close connection of these clauses suggests that the evil ones are to be identified with the fake apostles. Who these were is explained thus by Swete: "The false teachers claimed to be *apostoloi* in the wider sense, itinerant teachers with a mission which placed them on a higher level than the local elders" (cf. I Cor. 12:28; Eph. 4:11).[12]

These itinerant **apostles** posed a real problem in the Early Church. Evidently it was required that they should carry "letters of commendation" from some established church (II Cor. 3:1). In his First Epistle, John warns: "Try [test] the spirits whether they are of God: because many false prophets are gone out into the world" (I John 4:1). The *Didache,* written about the middle of the second century, tells how these itinerants are to be tested: "And every apostle who cometh to you, let him be received as the Lord; but he shall not remain more than one day; if, however, there be need, then the next day; but if he remain three days, he is a false prophet."[13] In other words, he is not to "sponge" on the hospitality of the church.

In the best Greek text **hast patience** (3) comes before **hast borne,** and the latter is connected with **for my name's sake;** that is, "You have patiently borne on account of My name." **Hast laboured, and hast not fainted** is in the Greek simply: "and you have not grown weary." The Ephesian Christians were tireless workers.

On the description of the church at Ephesus, Ramsay writes: "The best commentary on this is found in the letter of Ignatius to the Ephesians . . . The characteristics which he praises in the Ephesian Church are the same as those which St. John mentions . . . 'I ought to be trained for the contest by you in faith, in admonition, in endurance, in long suffering.' 3: 'for ye all live according to truth and no heresy hath a home among you,' 6."[14]

[11]*Ibid.*, p. 64.
[12]*Op. cit.*, p. 25.
[13]*Didache*, xi.
[14]*Op. cit.*, p. 241.

The church at Ephesus is also commended because it hates the deeds of the **Nicolaitanes** (6). Who these people were is not known with certainty. (They are mentioned again in 15.) Irenaeus (about A.D. 180) says that they were founded by Nicolaus of Antioch, mentioned in Acts 6:5. But Clement of Alexandria questions this. After discussing the various theories, Swete concludes: "On the whole it seems best to fall back upon the supposition that a party bearing this name existed in Asia when the Apocalypse was written, whether it owed its origin to Nicolaus of Antioch, which is not improbable . . . or to some other false teacher of that name."[15]

On the clause **which I also hate,** Swete makes this pertinent observation: "Hatred of evil deeds . . . is a true counterpart of the love of good, and both are divine."[16]

4. *Condemnation* (2:4)

The great Head of the Church found only one thing wrong with the congregation at Ephesus. Although it was orthodox, persevering, and zealous, it lacked love. Without this all else was in vain.

The KJV rendering minimizes the seriousness of the charge by inserting in italics the word **somewhat.** This distorts the statement. The Greek says: "But I have against thee *that* thou hast forsaken thy first love." This was no insignificant **somewhat.** The next verse shows that it was total tragedy, calling for a drastic remedy.

It is often said that the Ephesian church had "lost" its first love. But that is not what the text says. It reads: **Thou hast left thy first love.** The verb is *aphiemi,* which means "let go, send away, leave, give up, abandon." All this suggests willful neglect. That is why repentance was called for. Sins of omission can be just as fatal in their consequences as sins of commission.

What was their **first love** which the Ephesian church had left? Almost all commentators agree that **first** is to be taken chronologically: this was the love of the early church at Ephesus, especially during the days of Paul's ministry there (cf. Acts 19:20; 20:37). The attempts of some to interpret it qualitatively as meaning "first-class love" do not seem to find adequate sup-

[15]*Op. cit.,* p. 28. [16]*Ibid.*

port in the Greek word used here. It is true that it can mean "chief." But the thought is that of priority rather than quality.

Love is interpreted by most as meaning "brotherly love." The Greek Fathers of the Early Church felt that the reference was to a lack of care for the poorer brethren. Others connect this passage with Jer. 2:2, where God charges Israel with having forgotten "the love of thine espousals." That is, the Ephesians had left their love for Christ. The best suggestion is the inclusive position of Charles R. Erdman: "This love was love for Christ and love for fellow Christians. The two are inseparable."[17]

The question inevitably comes up: Did the zeal of the Ephesian church in its defense of orthodoxy contribute to its loss of love? This is very possible. In defending the truth and disciplining wayward members it is easy to develop a harsh, critical spirit that is destructive of love. And often when the warmth of divine love is gone, people become more zealous in contending for orthodox doctrines and standards. This is a danger against which all must guard.

5. *Exhortation* (2:5)

The first step back to God is: **Remember** (5). Recall the former days of spiritual blessing. This church had **fallen,** not merely stumbled. It was down. So was the prodigal son, in a grosser way. But he remembered (Luke 15:17) and went back.

How could this church come up again? The answer is: **Repent.** This means "change your mind" (see comments on Matt. 3:2, BBC, VI, 42-43). Then **do the first works;** that is, believe and obey. Heb. 6:1 speaks of "the foundation of repentance . . . and of faith toward God." That is evidently the combination here. Swete points out that **remember, repent,** and **do** "answer to three stages in the history of conversion."[18]

If the Ephesian church refused or failed to **repent, and do the first works,** Jesus warned, **I will come unto thee quickly, and will remove thy candlestick out of his place, except thou repent.** That is, the church at Ephesus would no longer exist as a Christian congregation. This finally happened at a later date, but the warning was evidently heeded at the time. Some twenty years later Ignatius wrote to the Ephesians: "I gave a godly welcome to your church which has so endeared itself to us by

[17]*Op. cit.,* p. 46.

[18]*Op. cit.,* p. 27.

reason of your upright nature, marked as it is by faith in Jesus Christ our Saviour, and by love of him."[19]

The church would be given a reasonable opportunity to repent. Swete notes that the Greek word for **remove** may be taken as indicating "deliberation and judicial calmness; there would be no sudden uprooting as in anger, but a movement which would end in the loss of the place that the Church had been called to fill; unless there came a change for the better, the first of the seven lamps of Asia must disappear."[20]

6. *Invitation* (2:7*a*)

The exhortation, **He that hath an ear, let him hear what the Spirit saith unto the churches,** occurs in each of the seven letters. In the first three it precedes the promise to the conqueror. In the last four it follows it. See also 13:9.

This is an echo of Jesus' words in the Gospels, where "He that hath an ear, let him hear" is found several times (Matt. 11:15; 13:9, 43; Mark 4:9, 23; Luke 8:8; 14:35).

7. *Remuneration* (2:7*b*)

With each letter there is a promise to the one who overcomes, or is victorious. The verb occurs frequently in the Book of Revelation, the main theme of which is the Church, through Christ, overcoming all evil. Swete says the term indicates " 'the conqueror,' the victorious member of the Church, as such, apart from all consideration of circumstances."[21]

The promise here to the overcomer is that he will be granted the right **to eat of the tree of life.** Adam failed when tested, and lost this right. Now it is promised to those who will be faithful under temptation. Swete comments: "To eat of the Tree is to enjoy all that the life of the world to come has in store for redeemed humanity."[22]

The word **paradise** obviously carries us back to Eden, where the tree of life is first mentioned as being "in the midst of the garden" (Gen. 2:9). Now it is said to be **in the midst of the paradise of God.** On the meaning of this term Swete observes: "In the N.T. 'Paradise' is either the state of the blessed dead

[19]Cyril C. Richardson (ed.), *Early Christian Fathers,* "Library of Christian Classics" (Philadelphia: Westminster Press, 1953), I, 88.

[20]*Op. cit.,* p. 27.

[21]*Ibid.,* p. 29.

[22]*Ibid.,* p. 30.

(Lk. xxiii. 43), or a supra-mundane sphere identified with the third heaven into which men pass in an ecstasy (2 Cor. xii. 2 f.); or, as here, the final joy of the saints in the presence of God and of Christ."[23]

In the message to Ephesus we see: (1) The inadequacy of works, 2-3; (2) The necessity of love, 4; (3) The nature of repentance, 5.

B. The Letter to Smyrna, 2:8-11

1. *Address* (2:8*a*)

Smyrna rivaled Ephesus for the honor of being called "the chief of Asia" and the "metropolis." So it logically comes second in the list here. The city, called "the Beauty of Asia," was situated at the head of a well-protected gulf, with an excellent harbor (see map 1). It was next to Ephesus in the volume of its export trade. It is still a large city, the only one of the seven which is now prosperous. Today "Smyrna figs" are sold around the world.

The church there was apparently founded when Paul was preaching at Ephesus (Acts 19:10). It continued to be a strong ecclesiastical center for several centuries. Modern Izmir has a population of about 300,000.

2. *Author* (2:8*b*)

Christ is here identified as **the first and the last.** We have met this already in 1:17. He is further described as the One **which was dead, and is alive**—literally, "who became dead and lived." This also looks back to 1:18—"And I became dead, and behold I am living forever" (lit.). The reference clearly is to Christ's crucifixion and resurrection.

But these words had peculiar relevance in a letter to Smyrna. For that city had become dead and now lived. Strabo says that the Lydians destroyed the place and that for four hundred years there was no city, but only some scattered villages. As Ramsay notes, "All Smyrnaean readers would at once appreciate the striking analogy to the early history of their own city."[24]

3. *Commendation* (2:9)

Once again Christ says, **I know.** These words carry both comfort and warning.

[23]*Ibid.*

[24]*Op. cit.,* p. 269.

Works is not in the best Greek text. Two things are mentioned: **tribulation** and **poverty.** Apparently their tribulation produced their poverty (cf. 10). Heb. 10:34 says: "For ye had compassion of me in my bonds, and took joyfully the spoiling of your goods, knowing in yourselves that ye have in heaven a better and an enduring substance." In a similar situation at Smyrna it would seem that Jewish and pagan mobs were pillaging the property of the Christians.

The Greek word for **tribulation** (*thlipsis*) is a strong one, meaning "pressed" or "squeezed." Our English word comes from the Latin *tribulum,* which means a flail, used in threshing grain. Thus we have two pictures. The Greek word suggests the figure of a winepress, in which the juice was squeezed out of the grapes. The Latin word conveys the picture of grain being beaten with a club, to break the kernels out of the husks. Together these suggest the nature of tribulation. It is a matter of pressure and blows.

Though outwardly the church at Smyrna was marked by **poverty,** actually it was **rich.** Materially poor, spiritually rich—that combination is noted more than once in the New Testament.

Jesus also knew **the blasphemy of them which say they are Jews, and are not.** Paul wrote to the Romans: "For he is not a Jew, which is one outwardly . . . but he is a Jew, which is one inwardly" (Rom. 2:28-29). These persecutors at Smyrna were Jews by race and religion, but they were not true sons of Abraham. That the Jews did persecute the Christians is abundantly evidenced in the Book of Acts, as well as in the second-century writings of Justin Martyr and Tertullian. Especially did the Jews hate the converts from Judaism to Christianity.[25] In opposing the gospel they often resorted to **blasphemy** (cf. Acts 13:45). The Greek word *blasphemia* meant "slander" when directed toward men, but **blasphemy** when toward God. Here it was probably both.

The story of the martyrdom of Polycarp at Smyrna is especially relevant. The Jews even surpassed the pagans in their hate and zeal. They accused Polycarp of hostility to the state religion. These enemies cried out "with ungovernable wrath and with a loud shout: 'This is the teacher of Asia, the father of the Christians, the puller down of our gods, who teacheth numbers not to sacrifice nor to worship.'" Although it was the Sabbath day, they collected wood for burning Polycarp alive.[26]

[25]Ignatius, *To the Smyrnaeans* 1:2. [26]*Ibid.* 12:2 and 13:1.

In the light of this hostile attitude it is not surprising that the Jews are called **the synagogue of Satan.** Because of the opposition of the Jews, the Christians avoided the use of the word *synagogue* and chose instead *ecclesia* (Gk., assembly) for their congregations. The only place in the New Testament where *synagoge* is used for a Christian assembly is in Jas. 2:2. This may have been written before Jewish persecution of Christians became general.

It is an interesting coincidence that the expression **synagogue of Satan** occurs only here and in the letter to Philadelphia. These are the only two letters with no words of condemnation. So in the message to this church we pass directly from commendation to exhortation.

4. *Exhortation* (2:10)

The church at Smyrna is admonished: **Fear none of those things which thou shalt suffer.** Worse things awaited this congregation: **The devil shall cast some of you into prison, that ye may be tried.** This shows that the Jews would work with the heathen authorities in the persecution. Both would be instigated by **the devil.** It was ultimately he who would cast the Christians into prison. **Tried** means "tested." The Greek verb was used of testing metals in the fire, to make sure they had no alloy or dross. So the souls of the believers would be tested in the furnace of affliction.

The **tribulation** (persecution) would last **ten days.** This expression indicates a short period of time (cf. Dan. 1:12, 14). Swete comments: "The number ten is probably chosen because, while it is sufficient to suggest continued suffering, it points to an approaching end."[27] God would see to it that they did not suffer above what they were able to bear. If they were **faithful unto death**—probably here a hint of martyrdom—they would receive **a crown of life.** The Greek word for **crown** is not *diadema,* signifying a royal diadem, but *stephanos,* the victor's crown. Appropriately Stephen (Gk., *Stephanos*), the first Christian martyr, had this name. Probably the phrase **crown of life** means that the crown is eternal life (epexegetical genitive).[28]

[27]*Op. cit.,* p. 32.

[28]So Swete, *op. cit.,* p. 33. Contra, Charles, *op. cit.,* I, 59.

5. *Invitation* (2:11*a*)

Here again we find the invitation-exhortation: **He that hath an ear, let him hear what the Spirit saith unto the churches.** The message of warning was needed not only by the believers at Smyrna, but by the Christians everywhere.

6. *Remuneration* (2:11*b*)

The promise to the overcomer here, as in the case of all seven letters, is appropriate to the message for the particular church. Even if these faithful ones at Smyrna should suffer physical death for the sake of Christ, they would never be hurt by **the second death**—that is, spiritual death. This striking expression occurs again in 20:6, 14 and 21:8, where it is identified as the lake of fire, the place of eternal punishment. The phrase is found also in the Jewish Targums (Aramaic paraphrases of the Heb. OT). **Shall not be hurt** is in the Greek a double negative: "shall by no means."

It has been suggested (*Pulpit Bible*) that this letter conveys "Words of Cheer from a Reigning Saviour to a Suffering Church": (1) A living Saviour over all, 8; (2) A living Saviour knowing all, 9*a*; (3) A living Saviour estimating all, **thou art rich;** (4) A living Saviour foreseeing all, 10; (5) A living Saviour limiting all, **ten days;** (6) A living Saviour cheering them all, 10*a*; (7) A living Saviour promising life at the end of all, 10*b*.

C. The Letter to Pergamum, 2:12-17

1. *Address* (2:12*a*)

Smyrna was some thirty-five miles up the shore from Ephesus. The continuing route is described thus by Swete: "After leaving Smyrna the road from Ephesus followed the coast for about 40 miles and then struck N.E. up the valley of the Caicus, for a further distance of 15 miles, when it reached Pergamum [see map 1]."[29] **Pergamos** is the form of this name in Xenophon, but Strabo and most other ancient writers have "Pergamum." The latter is the correct form to use.

The physical situation of Pergamum was striking. Ramsay writes: "Beyond all other sites in Asia Minor it gives the traveller the impression of a royal city, the home of authority; the rocky

[29]*Op. cit.*, p. 34.

hill on which it stands is so huge, and dominates the broad plain of the Caicus so proudly and boldly."[30] Charles says: "The earliest city was built on a hill, 1000 feet high, which became the site of the Acropolis and many of the chief buildings of the later city."[31]

Early in the third century B.C. the kingdom of Pergamum was founded. In 133 B.C. its ruling king, Attalus III, bequeathed his kingdom to the Romans. They formed it into the Province of Asia. Ramsay says: "Pergamum was the official capital of the Province for two centuries and a half: so that its history as the seat of supreme authority over a large country lasts about four centuries, and had not yet come to an end when the Seven Letters were written."[32]

2. *Author* (2:12*b*)

This time Christ is described as **he which hath the sharp sword with two edges** (cf. 1:16). The reason for this reference to the sword is clearly seen in 16. It is to be the instrument of judgment against the heretics in the church at Pergamum.

There is also another reason for this identification of the Author. Ramsay notes: "In Roman estimation the sword was the symbol of the highest order of official authority with which the Proconsul of Asia was invested. The 'right of the sword' . . . was roughly equivalent to what we call the power of life and death."[33]

3. *Commendation* (2:13)

Again (cf. 9) **thy works** is not in the best Greek text, which reads: "I know where you are dwelling." It was **where Satan's seat** is. The Greek word for **seat** is *thronos,* "throne."

Why is Pergamum called the place of "Satan's throne"? The answer is that it was the center of emperor worship for Asia. Ramsay writes: "The first, and for a considerable time the only, Provincial temple of the Imperial cult in Asia was built at Pergamum in honour of Rome and Augustus (29 B.C. probably).

[30]*Op. cit.,* p. 281. [31]*Op. cit.,* I, 60.

[32]*Op. cit.,* p. 283. There is some difference of opinion as to whether Pergamum or Ephesus was actually the seat of Roman government in Asia at this time (see the quotation from F. F. Bruce in BBC, VII, 470). Pellett says: "By the time of Augustus [27 B.C.—A.D. 14] the capital was changed to Ephesus" (IDB, I, 258).

[33]*Op. cit.,* pp. 292-93.

A second temple was built there in honor of Trajan, and a third in honour of Severus. Thus Pergamum was the first city to have the distinction of Temple-Warden both once and twice in the State religion; and even its third Wardenship was also a few years earlier than that of Ephesus."[34] So here Satan represents "the official authority and power which stands in opposition to the Church."[35]

R. H. Charles summarizes the situation well. He says: "Behind the city in the 1st cent. A.D. arose a huge conical hill, 1000 feet high, covered with heathen temples and altars, which in contrast to 'the mountain of God,' referred to in Isa. xiv. 13; Ezek. xxviii. 14, 16, and called 'the throne of God' in I Enoch xxv. 3, appeared to the Seer as the throne of Satan, since it was the home of many idolatrous cults, but above all of the imperial cult, which menaced with annihilation the very existence of the Church. For refusal to take part in this cult constituted high treason to the State."[36]

The second item in the commendation of the church at Pergamum is, **And thou holdest fast my name, and hast not denied my faith.** When the Roman authorities demanded that Christians say, "Lord Caesar," they replied, "Lord Jesus" (cf. I Cor. 12:3). They were steadfast **even in those days wherein Antipas was my faithful martyr**—literally "my witness (*martys*), my faithful one." In the second century *martys* (genitive, *martyros*) took on the technical meaning of "martyr." Whether it should be so translated here is disputed. But at any rate this witness was slain. In spite of legends, nothing certain is known of Antipas outside this passage.

Who was slain among you does not necessarily indicate that Antipas was a member of the church at Pergamum. Ramsay says that "many martyrs were tried and condemned there who were not Pergamenians. Prisoners were carried from all parts of the Province to Pergamum for trial and sentence before the authority who possessed the right of the sword . . . the power of life and death, viz., the Roman Proconsul of Asia."[37]

4. *Condemnation* (2:14-15)

The Head of the Church has a few things against the congregation at Pergamum. The first is: **Thou hast there them that**

[34]*Ibid.*, p. 283.
[35]*Ibid.*, p. 293.
[36]*Op. cit.*, I, 61.
[37]*Op. cit.*, pp. 297-98.

hold the doctrine of Balaam (14). As throughout the New Testament, **doctrine** (*didache*) should be translated "teaching."

Balaam is described as the one **who taught Balac to cast a stumblingblock before the children of Israel, to eat things sacrificed unto idols, and to commit fornication.** This statement fills in a slight gap in the Old Testament account. There we are told that Balaam was called by Balak, king of Moab, to curse the Israelites, whom he feared (Num. 22:1—24:25). When God did not permit the prophet to curse His people, apparently Balaam suggested an indirect way of bringing the divine curse on Israel. This is indicated in Num. 31:16, when Moses said of the women of Moab: "Behold, these caused the children of Israel, through the counsel of Balaam, to commit trespass against the Lord in the matter of Peor, and there was a plague among the congregation of the Lord." The "matter of Peor" was a combination of idolatry and immorality (Num. 25:1-9), as also in Revelation. What the account here makes more explicit is the fact that Balaam advised Balak to have his women seduce the Israelitish men into these two sins. The scheme worked all too well. Balaam is mentioned also in II Pet. 2:15 and Jude 11.

The Greek word for **stumblingblock** (*scandalon;* cf. scandal) was first used for the bait-stick of a trap or snare, and then for the snare or trap itself. This fits the picture here perfectly. Balak set a trap for the Israelites and they were caught in it. Swete comments: "The women of Moab were deliberately thrown in the way of unsuspecting Israel, in the hope of bringing about the downfall of the latter."[38] Lenski translates the expression here "to throw a trap before the sons of Israel."[39]

Apparently there were some members in the church at Pergamum who advised conformity to pagan customs in order to avoid persecution. They advocated eating in the heathen temples and participating in the idol worship which involved **fornication** with the temple "virgins." They may have been among those who said that what one does with his body does not affect his soul. The matter of eating meat **sacrificed unto idols** had already become a problem at Corinth, where Paul had to deal with it (I Corinthians 8). It was a vital issue in the first century.

As at Ephesus,[40] there were at Pergamum some **Nicolaitanes**

[38] *Op. cit.*, p. 37. [39] *Op. cit.*, p. 106.

[40] R. H. Charles thinks that **also** means "as well as the Ephesian Church" (*op. cit.*, I, 64).

(15). For their **doctrine** (teaching) see the comments on 6. Smith thinks that **Nicolaitanes** means "laity-conquerors" and that the description of Pergamum prefigures the rise of the papal hierarchy in the Roman Catholic church.[41]

5. *Exhortation* (2:16)

The Christians at Pergamum, as also those at Ephesus, are commanded to **repent** (see comments on 5). Repentance was the only thing that could avert severe judgment—**or else I will come unto thee quickly, and will fight against them with the sword of my mouth.** Swete writes: "The glorified Christ is in this book a Warrior, who fights with the sharp sword of the word" (cf. 1:16; 19:13-16).[42]

The situation at Pergamum was worse than that at Ephesus. To the church at Ephesus, Jesus said: "Thou hatest the deeds of the Nicolaitanes" (6). To Pergamum He wrote: "Thou hast those that hold the doctrines of the Nicolaitanes, which I hate." The changes from "hatest" to "hast" and from "deeds" to "doctrines" are probably both significant. Now the Nicolaitans were inside the church and their destructive teachings were being accepted by some. If the church does not **repent** at once (aorist tense), Christ **will come** (lit., "I am coming," prophetic present) **quickly** in judgment. There was no time to lose. **Will fight** (future tense) literally means "will wage war." These Nicolaitans were the enemies of Christ and Christianity. Both Lenski[43] and Charles[44] hold that the Balaamites and the Nicolaitans were the same group.

6. *Invitation* (2:17*a*)

Joseph Seiss gives a good threefold treatment of **He that hath an ear, let him hear what the Spirit saith unto the churches.** (1) "A solemn rebuke to those who call themselves Christians, and yet seldom if ever look into their Bibles to read and study them"; (2) "Everything touching our salvation depends on the giving of an attentive ear to the divine word and the diligent use of our privileges, to hear, mark, learn, and inwardly digest what it contains"; (3) "Every one has capacity to give attention, and so it is laid upon every one to employ that capacity."[45]

[41]*Op. cit.*, pp. 64, 73.
[42]*Op. cit.*, p. 38.
[43]*Op. cit.*, pp. 107-8.
[44]*Op. cit.*, I, 64.
[45]*Letters to the Seven Churches* (Grand Rapids: Baker Book House, 1956 [reprint]), pp. 55-57.

7. *Remuneration* (2:17b)

Some of the professing believers at Pergamum were evidently feasting themselves in the pagan temples. But to the faithful conquerors Christ promises that they shall **eat of the hidden manna.** The reference seems to be to the golden pot of manna placed in the ark in the ancient Tabernacle (Exod. 16:33; Heb. 9:4). There was a tradition among the Jews that the ark was hidden by Jeremiah in a cave at Mount Sinai, where it would not be discovered "until God gathers his people together again and shows his mercy" (II Maccabees 2:7).[46]

Charles thinks that the reference is more particularly to a heavenly manna described by the rabbis as being ground in the third heaven for the righteous. He says: "According to 2 Baruch xxix. 8 the treasury of manna was to descend from heaven during the Messianic Kingdom, and the blessed were to eat of it."[47] He also writes: "The 'hidden manna' probably signifies the direct spiritual gifts that the Church triumphant will receive in transcendent measure from intimate communion with Christ."[48] But may this **hidden manna** not also signify "intimate communion with Christ" in the present, feeding our souls on the Bread of Life?

The overcomer is additionally promised **a white stone.** What does this expression mean? Charles lists no less than five interpretations that have been offered: "1. The white stone used by jurors to signify acquittal . . . 2. The *psephos* which entitled him that received it to free entertainment . . . [at] royal assemblies . . . Hence here a ticket of admission to the heavenly feast. 3. The precious stones which according to Rabbinical tradition fell along with the manna . . . 4. The precious stones on the breastplate of the high priest bearing the names of the Twelve Tribes. 5. The white stone was regarded as a mark of felicity."[49]

In keeping with most scholarly commentators, Charles does not think that any of these explanations is satisfactory: "Either the *psephos* is not white or it has no inscription upon it."[50] He would look for the background in the popular superstitions of that time.

[46]*The Oxford Annotated Apocrypha,* ed. Bruce Metzger (New York: Oxford University Press, 1965), p. 265.

[47]*Op. cit.,* I, 65.

[48]*Ibid.,* p. 66.

[49]*Ibid.*

[50]*Ibid.*

Involved in the problem is the significance of the **new name** inscribed on the stone. Swete makes the helpful suggestion that the reference may be to "the engraved stones which were employed for magical purposes and bore mystic names."[51] Acts 19:19 indicates that sorcery was prevalent at Ephesus. Swete adds: "The Divine magic which inscribes on the human character and life the Name of God and of Christ is placed in contrast with the poor imitations that enthralled pagan society."[52] In 3:12, Jesus says of the overcomer at Philadelphia: "And I will write upon him the name of my God."

Ramsay thinks that the **stone** signifies the imperishableness of the name. He writes: "The name that was written on the white stone was at once the name of the victorious Christian and the name of God . . . Pergamum and Philadelphia are the two Churches which are praised because they 'held fast my name,' and 'did not deny it'; and they are rewarded with the New Name, at once the name of God and their own, an eternal possession, known to bearers only . . . they shall not merely be 'Christians,' the people of Christ; they shall be the people of His new personality as He is hereafter revealed in glory, bearing that New Name of His glorious revelation."[53]

The Greek word for **new** is not *neos,* which means "recent" in origin, but *kainos,* which signifies "fresh" in quality. "The Christian 'name,' i.e., the character of inner life which the Gospel inspires, possesses the property of eternal youth, never losing its power or its joy."[54]

D. The Letter to Thyatira, 2:18-29

1. *Address* (2:18*a*)

About forty miles southeast of Pergamum lay **Thyatira.** It was a city of Lydia near the border of Mysia (see map 1). Built by Seleucus I, founder of the Seleucid dynasty, it was peopled by veterans of Alexander the Great's campaigns in Asia. About 190 B.C. it had been taken over by the Romans. Though a thriving center of trade, it was much inferior to Ephesus, Smyrna, and Pergamum. Charles notes: "The longest letter is addressed to the least important of the Seven Cities."[55] There were evidently Jews

[51] *Op. cit.,* p. 40.
[52] *Ibid.*
[53] *Op. cit.,* pp. 307-8.
[54] Swete, *op. cit.,* p. 41.
[55] *Op. cit.,* I, 67.

there, for Acts 16:14 mentions "Lydia, a seller of purple, of the city of Thyatira, which worshipped God." It would appear that she was a proselyte to Judaism.

The church at Thyatira was apparently small. It is said to have disappeared by the end of the second century.

2. *Author* (2:18*b*)

The Author of this letter identifies himself as **the Son of God,** a phrase found only here in the Book of Revelation. Jesus claimed this title while on earth (Matt. 11:27; Luke 10:22) and commended Peter for confessing it (Matt. 16:16-17). It was for this claim that Jesus was condemned by the Sanhedrin (Matt. 26:63; John 19:7).

Christ is described as the One **who hath his eyes like unto a flame of fire, and his feet are like fine brass.** Here is an echo of 1:14-15. The appropriateness of the twofold characterization is expressed thus by Swete: "This mention of the eyes that flash with righteous indignation and the feet that can stamp down the enemies of the truth prepares the reader for the severe tone of the utterance which follows."[56] Erdman puts it even more succinctly: "Thus he is able to penetrate into the secrets of all hearts, and he has power to punish and subdue."[57] Those flaming eyes see through all sham and hypocrisy. In the Scriptures brass is often symbolical of judgment.

3. *Commendation* (2:19)

The wording of this verse in KJV is obviously incorrect, for it gives a list beginning and ending with **thy works**—a meaningless repetition. Furthermore, the best Greek text has **faith** before **service.** The RSV gives the correct translation: "I know your works, your love and faith and service and patient endurance, and that your latter works exceed the first."[58] *The New English Bible* has, "And of late you have done even better than at first."

Christ had commended the Ephesian church for its **works.** But the church at Thyatira was one step ahead. It is complimented for its **charity.** The Greek word is *agape* and should

[56]*Op. cit.*, pp. 41-42. [57]*Op. cit.*, p. 53.

[58]Of the **and** before **charity,** Charles (*op. cit.*, I, 69) says: "The *kai* here introduces an explanatory description of the *erga*" (**works**). That is, their **works** consisted of love, faith, service, and patient endurance.

always be translated "love." **Charity** represents the *caritas* of the Latin Vulgate, the official Bible of the Roman Catholic church. Today **charity** means a spirit of toleration or giving to needy causes. *Agape* is a much richer term than this. People of the world may be philanthropic and tolerant. But *agape* is divine love implanted in the human heart and flowing out in selfless, sacrificial service to others.

The Greek word *pistis* may mean either **faith** or "faithfulness" (NEB). It is not certain which is intended here. Perhaps the best way is to allow both meanings (cf. Phillips, "loyalty").

Service is *diakonia.* Beyer says that this word means "any 'discharge of service' in genuine love."[59] Lenski defines it as "voluntary service for the benefit and the help of those needing it and freely rendered."[60]

Patience (*hypomone*) means more than a passive putting up with hardships or trials. It is rather a positive steadfastness or endurance ("perseverance," NASB).

In view of the lengthy condemnation that follows, it is surprising that such an enthusiastic commendation is given to this church. Swete comments: "It is noteworthy that in these addresses praise is more liberally given, if it can be given with justice, when blame is to follow; more is said of the good deeds of the Ephesians and Thyatirans than of those of the Smyrnaeans and Philadelphians, with whom no fault is found."[61] This is in keeping with sound psychology, which advises saying everything favorable that is possible before calling attention to the other person's faults.

4. *Condemnation* (2:20-23)

The first part of 20 should be translated, "But I have this against you, that you tolerate the woman Jezebel" (RSV, NASB).[62] Toleration of evil was the besetting sin of the church at Thyatira. **Jezebel** is probably a symbolical name—"This 'Jezebel of a woman.' "[63] The reference is obviously to the wife of Ahab, who seduced the Israelites to worship Baal (I Kings 16:

[59]"Diakonia," *Theological Dictionary of the New Testament,* ed. G. Kittel, II (Grand Rapids: Wm. B. Eerdmans Publishing Co., 1964), 87.

[60]*Op. cit.,* p. 114.

[61]*Op. cit.,* p. 42.

[62]**A few things** has practically no support in the Greek text. Erasmus apparently derived it from the Latin Vulgate.

[63]Moffatt, *op. cit.,* p. 360.

31). Mention is also made of her "whoredoms" and "witchcrafts" (II Kings 9:22). Because some MSS. and early versions have "thy woman Jezebel" (i.e., "thy wife Jezebel"), Grotius (seventeenth century) suggested that the wife of the bishop at Thyatira is intended. But this notion is now almost universally rejected. Duesterdieck says that "a particular woman is meant; not the wife of a bishop, nor a woman who is actually called Jezebel, but some woman who under the pretence of being a prophetess had approved the doctrines of the Nicolaitans and for that reason was designated a new Jezebel."[64] This probably represents the majority opinion today.

It was not uncommon to have a **prophetess** in the Early Church (cf. Acts 21:9). In the Old Testament several women are given this title (e.g., Miriam, Deborah, Huldah). The only other place in the New Testament where *prophetis* (fem.) occurs is in Luke 2:36 (Anna).

The false **prophetess** at Thyatira was being permitted **to teach and to seduce my servants to commit fornication, and to eat things sacrificed unto idols.** These two things are attributed to the Balaamites (and Nicolaitans?) at Pergamum (14; see comments there).

Thyatira was noted for its numerous trade guilds. This posed a special problem. Charles writes: "Now, since membership in trade guilds . . . did not *essentially* involve anything beyond joining in the common meal, which was dedicated no doubt to some pagan deity but was exactly in this respect meaningless for the enlightened Christian, to avail oneself of such membership was held in certain latitudinarian circles to be quite justifiable."[65] For business or social reasons it seemed almost imperative to belong to some guild. But it is thought that these guild meetings often ended in drunken orgies. Hence the reference to **fornication.** The prophetess was advocating a loose attitude morally and religiously.

Apparently a definite warning had been given to this Jezebel, but she had refused to **repent** (21), i.e., change her mind and ways. Therefore the Lord must deal with her severely. Because of her **fornication** He would **cast her into a bed** (22). This expression is only one of many instances that show John's tendency, though writing in Greek, to think in Hebrew forms. (Cf. fn. 12 in Introduction.) Concerning the phrase Charles writes: "Now, if

[64] *Op. cit.*, p. 150.

[65] *Op. cit.*, I, 69.

we retranslate it literally into Hebrew, we discover that we have here a Hebrew idiom . . . 'to take to one's bed,' 'to become ill' (Ex. xxi. 18): hence 'to cast upon a bed' means 'to cast upon a bed of illness.' "[66]

And them that commit adultery with her into great tribulation is probably to be taken as parallel to the previous clause, in accordance with Hebrew parallelism. **Adultery** probably means spiritual adultery. But mercy's door is still left open—**except they repent of their deeds.** Genuine repentance always turns judgment aside.

Continued refusal to repent would result in more severe punishment: **And I will kill her children with death** (23). Probably **her children** means "her spiritual progeny, as distinguished from those who have been misled for a time."[67] **Kill . . . with death** is a typical Hebraism. It means "strike dead" (RSV, NEB).

This would be a warning to **all the churches.** They would **know that I am he which searcheth the reins and hearts** (cf. Jer. 11:20; 17:10). **Reins** (Gk. word only here in NT) is literally "the kidneys"; that is, "the movements of the will and affections."[68] **Hearts** in Hebrew psychology referred especially to the thoughts. The all-seeing gaze of Omniscience penetrates to the depths of man's intellect, emotions, and will.

Divine judgment is always just. **Every one** would receive **according to your works** (cf. Rom. 2:6).

5. *Exhortation* (2:24-25)

There is a word of comfort for **the rest in Thyatira** (24)—perhaps the majority of church members—who had not accepted Jezebel's **doctrine** (teaching), and who had **not known the depths of Satan.** With the Gnostics of the second century "the deep things" was a favorite phrase. They claimed an esoteric knowledge which was not known to the uninitiated.

Two interpretations have been given for **the depths of Satan.** One is that the Nicolaitans taunted the rest of the Christians as not knowing the deep things of God; but these were really the deep things of Satan. The other is that the followers of Jezebel actually gloried in knowing **the depths of Satan.** "These false teachers held that the spiritual man should know the deep things

[66]*Ibid.*, I, 71.

[67]Swete, *op. cit.*, p. 44.

[68]*Ibid.*, p. 45.

of Satan, that he should take part in the heathen life of the community, two of the most prominent characteristics of which were its sacrificial feasts and immoral practices."[69] Many Gnostics of later times asserted that, since all matter is evil and only spirit is good, it does not matter what one does with his body; his soul is still pure. Both of the interpretations above may have applied to doctrines of the immoral teachers at Thyatira.

As they speak means "as they call them." Paul spoke of the deep mysteries of divine truth (cf. Rom. 11:33; Eph. 3:18). These false teachers were distorting this idea.

To those who remained loyal to the faith, Christ declared, **I will put upon you none other burden.** Probably this looks forward to 25—**But that which ye have already, hold fast till I come.** Charles interprets this: "Once and for all take a firm hold (*kratesate*) on these duties incumbent on you, and shun absolutely the sacrificial feasts of the heathen and the moral evils that attend them."[70] He thinks that **none other burden** is a reference to the apostolic decrees of Acts 15:28. But many commentators question this. It seems doubtful that these would still be mentioned at this late date.

6. *Remuneration* (2:26-28)

To the recurring phrase, **he that overcometh** (26), there is added here: **and keepeth my works unto the end.** Swete remarks: "At Thyatira the battle was to be won by resolute adherence to the 'works of Christ,' i.e., to the purity of the Christian life, as opposed to the 'works of Jezebel.' "[71]

The promised reward is: **To him will I give power** (*exousia*, authority) **over the nations.** The glorified Christ will share His authority with His faithful followers. The language of this clause and what follows in the next verse is taken from Ps. 2:8-9, which was interpreted Messianically by the Jews in the first century B.C., as seen in the *Psalms of Solomon* (an apocryphal work).

The word **rule** (27) literally means to "shepherd." Hence the **rod of iron** is thought to be the shepherd's crook, tipped with iron to make a suitable weapon against enemies or wild animals. The wicked are compared to **the vessels of a potter** which will **be broken to shivers.** While these words may have

[69]Charles, *op. cit.*, I, 73-74. [70]*Ibid.*, I, 74.
[71]*Op. cit.*, p. 46.

some application to the Church's influence in the world today, it is obvious that their final fulfillment looks forward to the return of Christ. **Even as I received of my Father** is an echo of Ps. 2:7 and Acts 2:33.

In the statement, **I will give him the morning star** (28), there is an anticipation of 22:16—"I am the root and the offspring of David, and the bright and morning star." The greatest reward that any victorious Christian can receive is Christ himself. His presence will be heaven in its highest glory.

7. *Invitation* (2:29)

In the previous three letters this invitation preceded the promise to the overcomer. In this and the next three letters it follows the promise.

Someone has suggested (*Pulpit Commentary*) that this letter reveals "The Wrath of the Lamb": (1) Its reality, 18; (2) Its severity, 22-23; (3) Its forbearance, 21; (4) Its justice, 20; (5) Its discrimination, 24-25.

E. The Letter to Sardis, 3:1-6

1. *Address* (3:1*a*)

Continuing southeast from Thyatira, the messenger would travel about thirty miles to **Sardis,** the ancient capital of Lydia (see map 1). It was famous for its woolen manufactures and claimed to have been the first city to discover the art of dyeing wool.

Sardis reached its height of prosperity under the fabulously wealthy Croesus (*ca.* 560 B.C.). Conquered by Cyrus, it was obscure under Persian rule. In the Roman period there was some measure of restoration. But Charles says that even then "no city in Asia presented a more deplorable contrast of past splendour and present unresting decline."[72] For this reason Ramsay calls it "the city of death." He writes: "Thus, when the Seven Letters were written, Sardis was a city of the past, which had no future before it."[73] There is now a small village there, called Sart.

The main cult in Sardis was the worship of Cybele (or Artemis), which was degenerate. Charles says: "Its inhabitants had

[72]*Op. cit.*, I, 78.

[73]*Op. cit.*, p. 368.

long been notorious for luxury and licentiousness."[74] This made it difficult to maintain the Christian standards of purity.

2. *Author* (3:1b)

Here Christ is identified as **he that hath the seven Spirits of God, and the seven stars** (cf. 2:1). By **the seven Spirits of God** is evidently meant the Holy Spirit in His perfection and in His working through the seven churches, which represent the universal Church of Jesus Christ (see comments on 1:4). **The seven stars** represent the messengers (pastors) of the seven churches (cf. 1:20).

3. *Condemnation* (3:1c, 2b)

The expression **I know** occurs at the beginning of each of the seven letters (2:2, 9, 13, 19; 3:1, 8, 15). Nothing is hidden to the all-seeing eye of the omniscient Christ. Because He knows perfectly, He is able to judge fairly.

It would be difficult to imagine a more sweeping condemnation: **Thou hast a name that thou livest, and art dead.** Not only was this stricken city dead, but the church was also dead. It had lost its spiritual life. Smith comments: "Sardis apparently was reputed as being a 'live church'—there was much activity, but He who does not look on the outward appearance but on the heart declares, *Thou . . . art dead.*"[75]

Erdman carries this thought a step further: "Probably its services are well attended and properly conducted. It may have committees and anniversaries and rallies. It may number among its members prominent social leaders. Yet it is dead."[76]

The church had **works,** but these **works** were not **perfect before God** (2). Erdman comments: "It accomplished nothing in the spiritual realm: souls are not being saved; saints are not being strengthened; help is not being rendered to those in need; its services are formal, lifeless, meaningless: 'I have found no works of thine perfected before my God.' "[77]

The word for **perfect** literally means "filled," or "fulfilled." Swete makes the sage observation: " 'Works' are 'fulfilled' only when they are animated by the Spirit of life."[78] Precisely this is what makes the difference between a dead church and one that

[74]*Op. cit.,* I, 78.
[75]*Op. cit.,* p. 82.
[76]*Op. cit.,* p. 56.
[77]*Ibid.*
[78]*Op. cit.,* p. 50.

is alive. The one lacks the Holy Spirit; the other is filled and empowered by the Spirit. No amount of activity or efficient organization can take the place of the energizing dynamic of the Holy Spirit.

4. *Exhortation* (3:2*a*, 3)

Be watchful (2) is literally, "Keep on becoming in a state of continually watching." **Watchful** is the present participle of the verb *gregoreo,* which means "be awake" or "watch." Jesus used it twice in the Olivet Discourse (Mark 13:35, 37), calling for constant vigilance in preparation for His second coming.

The church at Sardis was warned to **strengthen the things which remain, that are ready to die.** In the midst of this dead church there were some elements of life. But even these are **ready to die**—literally, "were about [imperfect] to die." Swete comments: "The imperfect looks back from the standpoint of the reader to the time when the vision was seen, and at the same time with a delicate optimism it expresses the conviction of the writer that the worst would soon be past."[79] That is, the Christians at Sardis could say: "These things were about to die; but we won't let them."

Ramsay points out at length the significance of the command to the church at Sardis to **be watchful.** Twice the city had been captured by the enemy because of a lack of vigilance on the part of its people. The first was when the wealthy Croesus was king. Ramsay describes the situation thus:

> Carelessness and failure to keep proper watch, arising from over-confidence in the apparent strength of the fortress, had been the cause of this disaster, which ruined the dynasty and brought to an end the Lydian Empire and the dominance of Sardis. The walls and gates were all as strong as art and nature combined could make them. The hill on which the upper city stood was steep and lofty. The one approach to the upper city was too carefully fortified to offer any chance to an assailant. But there was one weak point: in one place it was possible for an active enemy to make his way up the perpendicular sides of the lofty hill, if the defenders stood idle and permitted him to climb unhindered.[80]

This was in 549 B.C. But in 218 B.C. it happened again. Ramsay writes:

> More than three centuries later another case of exactly the same kind occurred. Archaeus and Antiochus the Great were fighting

[79]*Ibid.*, p. 49.

[80]*Op. cit.*, p. 377.

> for the command of Lydia and the whole Seleucid Empire. Antiochus besieged his rival in Sardis, and the city again was captured by a surprise of the same nature: a Cretan mercenary led the way, climbing up the hill and stealing unobserved within the fortifications. The lesson of old days had not been learned; experience had been forgotten; men were too slack and careless; and when the moment of need came, Sardis was unprepared.[81]

The significance of this lesson for Christians is obvious. One needs to have only one weak point in his character, one unguarded spot in his spiritual life, to fall victim to Satan's cunning strategy. It is still true that "eternal vigilance is the price of safety."

The church at Sardis is further admonished: **Remember therefore how thou hast received and heard, and hold fast, and repent** (3). There is a frequent change of tense in the Greek which is difficult to represent in a simple English translation. Literally it would be: "Keep on remembering [present] therefore how you [singular] have been receiving [and still possess; perfect] and heard [aorist], and keep on holding fast [present], and repent [right now; aorist]." Lenski notes: "Prompt, true repentance is the one remedy for the death that has set in or has almost set in."[82] Such repentance always comes by remembering the Word of God which we have received and heard.

Swete points out well the force of the tenses in this verse: "The aor. [**heard**] looks back to the moment when faith came by hearing (Rom. x. 17) . . . ; the perf. [**hast received**] calls attention to the abiding responsibility of the trust then received . . . 'keep that which thou hast received, and promptly turn from thy past neglect.' "[83]

Verses 2-3 suggest "Five Steps to a Revival": (1) **Be watchful;** (2) **Strengthen the things which remain;** (3) **Remember;** (4) **Hold fast;** (5) **Repent.**

A further warning is sounded: **If therefore thou shalt not watch, I will come on thee as a thief, and thou shalt not know what hour I will come upon thee.** This is a clear echo of Matt. 24:42-44. Over and over we are warned that Christ will come at an unexpected moment.

5. *Commendation* (3:4)

Even in the dead church at Sardis there was a faithful remnant—**a few names.** Deissmann says that the Greek word for

[81]*Ibid.*, pp. 377-78.
[82]*Op. cit.*, p. 130.
[83]*Op. cit.*, p. 50.

"name" (*onoma*) occurs here "with the meaning of *person*."[84] It is used this way in the Septuagint of Num. 1:2, 20; 3:40, 43, where it probably carries the added thought of "persons reckoned by name." Some scholars feel that here it means "a few persons whose names were on the church register."[85]

The faithful ones **have not defiled their garments.** Moffatt comments: "The language reflects that of the votive inscriptions in Asia Minor, where soiled clothes disqualified the worshipper and dishonoured the god. Moral purity qualifies for spiritual communion."[86] To come into God's presence with our thoughts and feelings soiled by selfishness is to dishonor Him. The **garments** of our personalities must be kept pure if we would have fellowship with God.

To those who have maintained their purity the promise is made: **They shall walk with me in white.** The last word is plural in Greek, indicating "white clothes." Because they had kept their garments clean they would forever be clothed in **white,** symbolical of the divine holiness or the righteousness of Christ. Those who have remained pure are worthy of this honor.

6. *Remuneration* (3:5)

The promise to the overcomer at Sardis fits in with what has just been said: **The same shall be clothed in white raiment.** In the best Greek text **the same** is "thus"; that is, as just mentioned in the previous verse. **Raiment** is the same word in Greek as "garments" in 4. Charles says: "These garments are the spiritual bodies in which the faithful are to be clothed in the resurrection life."[87] He finds support for this in II Cor. 5:1, 4 and in the intertestamental literature. Swete would give the expression a wider connotation: "In Scripture white apparel denotes (*a*) festivity . . . (*b*) victory . . . (*c*) purity . . . (*d*) the heavenly state."[88] He adds: "All these associations meet here: the promise is that of a life free from pollution, bright with celestial gladness, crowned with final victory."[89] This seems a more adequate explanation.

The one who **overcometh,** who remains true to the close of life, is promised: **I will not blot out his name out of the book of**

[84]*Bible Studies,* p. 196.
[85]Lenski, *op. cit.,* p. 131.
[86]*Op. cit.,* p. 364.
[87]*Op. cit.,* I, 82.
[88]*Op. cit.,* pp. 51-52.
[89]*Ibid.,* p. 52.

life. This is what is meant by Jesus' words in Matt. 10:22—"He that endureth to the end shall be saved"; that is, eternally. Not only will his name remain securely on the heavenly register, but **I will confess his name before my Father, and before his angels.** Christ will not be ashamed to acknowledge His own. The language here is reminiscent of Matt. 10:32—"Whosoever therefore shall confess me before men, him will I confess also before my Father which is in heaven."

7. *Invitation* (3:6)

This recurring phrase emphasizes the responsibility to **hear** These letters were to be read aloud in **the churches.**

F. The Letter to Philadelphia, 3:7-13

1. *Address* (3:7*a*)

This city was a little less than thirty miles southeast from Sardis (see map 1). It was named after its founder, Attalus II (Philadelphus), who reigned 159-138 B.C. Often shaken by earthquakes, it was destroyed in A.D. 17, along with Sardis and ten other cities in the Lydian Valley. The result was that fear kept a large population from living within its walls. Apparently both the city and the church were small at this time.

The chief worship was that of Dionysos (later called Bacchus). But the letter indicates that the main opposition came from Jews rather than pagans.

When the Turks conquered Asia Minor in the Middle Ages, **Philadelphia** held out far longer than other cities. Ramsay says: "It displayed all the noble qualities of endurance, truth and steadfastness, which are attributed to it in the letter of St. John."[90] Today there is a sizable town there, with a railroad station.

2. *Author* (3:7*b*)

Christ characterizes himself as **he that is holy**—literally, "the Holy," a name for Deity. He is also **he that is true,** "the True." The Greek word for **true** (*alethinos*) means *"true,* in the sense of real, ideal, genuine."[91] Bultmann says: "In relation to divine things it has the sense of that which truly is, or of that which is

[90]*Op. cit.*, p. 400.

[91]Abbott-Smith, *op. cit.*, p. 20.

eternal."[92] Commenting on this twofold title of Jesus, Swete writes: "The Head of the Church is characterized at once by absolute sanctity . . . and by absolute truth; He is all that He claims to be, fulfilling the ideals which He holds forth and the hopes which He inspires."[93] Charles feels that in Revelation the classical Greek meaning of *alethinos* as "genuine" does not hold (as it does in John's Gospel). Rather it is the Hebrew emphasis on God's faithfulness. He says: "Hence *alethinos* implies that God or Christ, as true, will fulfil His word."[94]

Jesus further describes himself as **he that hath the key of David, he that openeth, and no man shutteth; and shutteth, and no man openeth.** These words are quoted from Isa. 22:22. There the Lord says of Eliakim, Hezekiah's faithful servant: "And the key of the house of David will I lay upon his shoulder; so he shall open, and none shall shut; and he shall shut, and none shall open." The **key** is the symbol of authority. Charles notes that the expression **the key of David** "has apparently a Messianic significance . . . The words teach that to Christ belongs complete authority in respect to admission to or exclusion from the city of David, the new Jerusalem."[95] But already in 1:18, Jesus had declared that He had the keys of death and of Hades. So He exercises authority in heaven, on earth, and even in the realm of death.

3. *Commendation* (3:8-10)

To the church at Philadelphia, Christ said: **Behold, I have set before thee an open door** (8)—literally, "a door which has been opened and remains open." The figure of an open door was a familiar one to the Christians of the first century. The pioneer missionaries, Paul and Barnabas, reported at Antioch that God had "opened the door of faith unto the Gentiles" (Acts 14:27). Concerning his work at Ephesus, Paul wrote: "For a great door and effectual is opened unto me" (I Cor. 16:9). A little later he says: "When I came to Troas to preach Christ's gospel . . . a door was opened unto me of the Lord" (II Cor. 2:12). He asked the Colossians to pray "that God would open unto us a door of utterance" at Rome (Col. 4:3). These passages from

[92]Kittel (ed.), *Theological Dictionary,* I, 250.

[93]*Op. cit.,* p. 53.

[94]*Op. cit.,* I, 86.

[95]*Ibid.*

Paul's Epistles seem to indicate what is meant here by an **open door.** It signifies a good opportunity for missionary work.

Ramsay calls Philadelphia "the missionary church." He says of the city:

> The intention of its founder was to make it a centre of the Graeco-Asiatic civilization and a means of spreading the Greek language and manners in the eastern part of Lydia and in Phrygia. It was a missionary city from the beginning . . . It was a successful teacher. Before A.D. 19 the Lydian tongue had ceased to be spoken in Lydia, and Greek was the only language of the country.[96]

But now the church at Philadelphia was called to a far more important kind of missionary work, that of spreading the gospel of Jesus Christ. For this task it had a most fitting situation. The road from the splendid harbor at Smyrna went through Philadelphia. Furthermore, "The Imperial Post Road from Rome to the Provinces farther east" passed through Troas, Pergamum, Thyatira, Sardis, and Philadelphia. "Along this great route the new influence was steadily moving eastwards from Philadelphia in the strong current of communication that set from Rome across Phrygia towards the distant East. . . . Philadelphia, therefore, was the keeper of the gateway to the plateau; but the door had now been permanently opened before the Church, and the work of Philadelphia had been to go forth through the door and carry the gospel to the cities of the Phrygian land."[97]

The church at Philadelphia thus becomes a symbol of the great world missionary enterprise, the next stage in the history of Christianity after the Protestant Reformation. In the first 150 years after the beginning of modern missions under William Carey in 1792 probably more real missionary work was done than in the previous 1,500 years.

Of this open door Jesus said: **No man can shut it.** The "key of David" (7) had unlocked the door, and no human or demonic force could close it. Never before in the 1900 years of Christian history has the challenge of the **open door** of world missions been greater than right now.

It seems surprising to read: **For thou hast a little strength.** Evidently the church at Philadelphia was rather small, and perhaps its members were drawn largely from the poorer classes. The statement, **And hast kept my word, and hast not denied my name,** should be translated, "And yet you kept My word and did

[96]*Op. cit.*, pp. 391-92. [97]*Ibid.*, p. 405.

not deny My name." Apparently the congregation had passed through a time of trial but had held true.

The phrase **the synagogue of Satan** (9) has already appeared in 2:9, in the letter to Smyrna. In these two cities the opposition to the church came mainly from the Jews. But they are not real Jews, because they do not follow in the footsteps of Father Abraham nor keep the spirit of the law of Moses (see comments on 2:9).

Of these false Jews the Lord says: **I will make them to come and worship before thy feet,**[98] **and to know that I have loved thee.** This seems to indicate that some Jews would be converted to Christianity. This interpretation is strengthened by the first clause of the verse, **I will make them of the synagogue of Satan.** In the Greek it reads: "I am giving *out of* the synagogue of Satan [not **I will make**]." Some would be saved.

Indirect confirmation of this is found in the letter of Ignatius to the Christians at Philadelphia (*ca.* A.D. 120), in which he warns them against listening to the Judaizers. Apparently Jews became influential in the congregation at Philadelphia.

Christ commended the church because it had **kept the word of my patience** (10), or "endurance." Erdman says that this phrase seems to mean: "The preaching of that steadfast endurance with which amid present hardships Christ is to be served."[99] But it is **my patience.** Trench is right when he comments: "Much better, however, to take the whole Gospel as *'the word of Christ's patience,'* everywhere teaching, as it does, the need of a patient waiting for Christ, till He, the waited-for so long, shall at length appear."[100] Lenski goes further and suggests that the phrase should be translated "the Word which deals with the Lord's endurance."[101] Perhaps these two thoughts should be combined: it is Christ's patient endurance as an example to us for remaining steadfast.

Because the church at Philadelphia had **kept** this word of Christ, He in turn **will keep thee from the hour of temptation, which shall come upon all the world** (inhabited earth), **to try them that dwell upon the earth.** The Greek noun for **temptation** is *peirasmos,* and the Greek verb for **try** is *peirazo.* The obvious

[98]Cf. the language in Isa. 45:14. [99]*Op. cit.,* p. 59.

[100]*Commentary on the Epistles to the Seven Churches* (London: Macmillan Co., 1883), p. 178.

[101]*Op. cit.,* p. 144.

connection in Greek should be represented in English. The verb means "test, try, prove." A correct translation would be "trial ... try" (RSV) or "testing ... test" (NASB).

The worldwide reach of this hour of testing shows that the primary reference is to the so-called Great Tribulation period at the time of the Second Coming. But there is perhaps a secondary application to the Roman persecutions of Christianity, which extended throughout the then known earth—the Roman Empire.

There has been considerable dispute as to whether **keep thee from the hour of temptation** means exemption from the trying time or being **kept** in it. The word **from** in Greek is not *apo*, "away from," but *ek*, which means "out of." In the light of this Carpenter writes: "The promise does not mean the being kept away from, but the being kept out from the tribulation"—as one's head is "kept above the waters."[102] Swete writes: "To the Philadelphian Church the promise was an assurance of safe-keeping in any trial that might supervene."[103] It is also a promise to us that our Lord will see us safely through any period of testing.

4. *Exhortation* (3:11)

In the letter to Philadelphia, as in that to Smyrna, there is no word of condemnation. So we pass immediately to the exhortation.

It begins with the mingled promise and warning: **I come quickly.**[104] Exception has been taken to the use of the word **quickly** here (cf. 22:20). The primary meaning is that the Lord will *not delay* His coming beyond the appointed time. But since we do not know when that is, we must be constantly ready. Then, too, with the Lord a thousand years is as one day (II Pet. 3:8). So two thousand years would still be **quickly.**

The close connection of this verse with the previous one would suggest that Christ's coming will deliver His own out of the hour of trial. Some have suggested that, just as the Israelites had to share the first three plagues (blood, frogs, lice) with the Egyptians (Exod. 8:22), so the Church may pass through the

[102]"The Revelation of St. John," *Commentary on the Whole Bible*, ed. C. J. Ellicott (Grand Rapids: Zondervan Publishing House, n.d.), VIII, 548.

[103]*Op. cit.*, p. 56.

[104]**Behold** has practically no support in the Greek MSS. It apparently comes from the Latin.

first part of the Great Tribulation before being caught up by Christ.

The church at Philadelphia is admonished: **Hold that fast which thou hast.** Swete wisely observes: "The promise of safe-keeping (v. 10) brings with it the responsibility of continual effort."[105] **Crown** means the victor's wreath (see comments on 2:10). The warning is against failing in the race of life and thus forfeiting the victor's crown. One must see **that no man take thy crown.** This is achieved by running successfully to the end.

5. *Remuneration* (3:12)

The overcomer will be made a **pillar in the temple of my God.** Swete comments: "There is a double fitness in this metaphor; while a pillar gives stability to the building which rests upon it, it is itself firmly and permanently fixed; and this side of the conception often comes into view . . . and is paramount here."[106]

Because he is thus fixed, **he shall go no more out.** When the period of probation is ended and the overcomer has become a pillar in God's eternal temple, there will be no further possibility of falling. The character of the glorified saints will be fixed forever.

Upon the overcomer Christ said He would write three names: **the name of my God . . . the name of the city of my God . . . my new name.** The name of God, signifying His ownership, was placed upon the Israelites; for immediately following the beautiful high-priestly blessing (Num. 6:24-26), there is added: "And they shall put my name upon the children of Israel; and I will bless them" (Num. 6:27). The **new Jerusalem** is further described in cc. 21—22. Here there is just a passing reference to it.

What is **my new name?** Trench says that it is "that mysterious and, in the necessity of things, uncommunicated and, for the present time, incommunicable name, which, in that same sublimest of all visions, is referred to: 'He had a name written, that no man knew, but He himself' (xix. 12) . . . But the mystery of this new name, which no man by searching could find out, which in this present condition no man is so much as capable of receiving, shall be imparted to the saints and citizens of the New Jerusalem. They shall know, even as they are known (I Cor.

[105]*Op. cit.*, p. 56. [106]*Ibid.*, p. 57.

xiii. 12)."[107] Swete suggests that the **new name** of Christ is "a symbol for the fuller glories of His Person and Character which await revelation at His Coming."[108]

Three thoughts thus stand out prominently in this "Promise to the Overcomer": (1) Complete consecration to God—**the name of my God;** (2) Inalienable citizenship in the celestial city—**the name of the city of my God;** (3) Fuller knowledge of Christ at the Second Coming—**my new name.**[109]

6. *Invitation* (3:13)

Let him hear means "let him heed." It is what we mean when we say, "Now *listen* to me."

G. The Letter to Laodicea, 3:14-22

1. *Address* (3:14*a*)

The KJV rendering here, **the church of the Laodiceans,** has caused considerable comment and interpretation. But the reading has practically no support in the Greek MSS. The correct reading is "the church in Laodicea." It is parallel in form to the addresses to the other churches.

Laodicea was forty miles southeast of Philadelphia. It was situated on the Lycus River, six miles south of Hierapolis and ten miles west of Colossae (see map 1). Founded by Antiochus II (261-246 B.C.), it was named in honor of his wife, Laodice. Since it was located at the junction of three important roads, it became a great commercial and administrative city. The fact that it was a banking center made it so wealthy that it was able to rebuild itself after the destructive earthquake of A.D. 60 without the help of an imperial subsidy. It was also known for its manufacture of clothes and carpets from a soft, glossy black wool. A flourishing medical school was located here.

The church at Laodicea was already in existence when Paul was in prison at Rome. He wrote a letter to it (cf. Col. 4:16) which has apparently been lost.

The city was overthrown by the Turks. Today the site is marked by a mass of ruins, still unexcavated.

[107]*Commentary,* pp. 186-87. [108]*Op. cit.,* p. 58.

[109]Adapted from Erdman, *op. cit.,* p. 60.

2. *Author* (3:14*b*)

Jesus here identifies himself as **the Amen.** This may be an echo of Isa. 65:16, where the Hebrew has "the God of Amen." The word was taken over from Hebrew into Greek and finally into English and other modern tongues. Today among Christians of all lands and languages one hears the same "Amen!"

Probably there is a closer connection with Jesus' frequent use of the term as reported in the Gospels. There it occurs fifty-one times in the Synoptics and fifty times in John's Gospel. It is translated "verily" (always doubled in John) in the phrase "Verily I say unto you."

The author further describes himself as **the faithful and true witness** (see comments on 1:5; 3:7). This is probably synonymous with **the Amen,** which is placed here "because this is the last of the seven Epistles, that it may confirm the whole."[110]

The third item in the description is: **the beginning of the creation of God.** Heretical teachers have seized on this as proof that Christ is not eternal. But in Colossians where He is designated "the firstborn of every creature" (1:15) it is immediately stated: "For by him were all things created . . . and he is before all things" (1:16-17). Furthermore, in his Gospel, John says of the Logos: "All things were made by him; and without him was not any thing made that was made" (John 1:3). The phrase here must be interpreted in the light of these other passages. It means "the origin (or 'primary source') of the creation of God."[111]

3. *Condemnation* (3:15-17)

In the case of the church at Laodicea there are no words of commendation. It is a striking fact that nothing here is said about the Nicolaitans or any other heretical groups. Apparently the church was orthodox. But it was a dead orthodoxy. The thing that was wrong with the Laodicean church was not head trouble but *heart* trouble. This was far more serious.

To this church the Lord said: **Thou art neither cold nor hot: I would thou wert cold or hot** (15). The Greek word for **cold** (*psychros*) is used only in 15-16 and in Matt. 10:42—"a cup of cold water." **Hot** is *zestos* (only in 15-16 in NT). It means "boiling hot," so that **cold** probably here means "icy cold."[112] The

[110]Simcox, *op. cit.*, p. 69.

[111]Charles, *op. cit.*, I, 94.

[112]Swete, *op. cit.*, p. 60.

church was neither coldly indifferent nor "fervent in spirit" (Rom. 12:11).

The reaction of the Head of the Church is expressed in strong terms: **So then because thou art lukewarm, and neither cold nor hot, I will spue thee out of my mouth** (16). Some foods taste good only when they are cold, others only when they are hot. Some things are acceptable both ways. Most people like iced tea or coffee and hot tea or coffee; but who wants a lukewarm drink? The Greek words for **lukewarm** and **spue** are found only here in the New Testament. The latter, *emeo,* means "to vomit."

The worst thing about this church's condition was its self-complacency: **Thou sayest, I am rich, and increased with goods, and have need of nothing** (17). The church apparently reflected the temper of the community (see comments on 14). **Increased with goods** is literally, "I have gotten riches" (same root as **rich** in previous clause); in other words, "I have gained my wealth by my own exertions." The first clause expresses self-satisfaction; the second, pride.

There could be no sadder example of senseless pride than that which is exhibited in the declaration, **and have need of nothing.** What a contrast is the realistic humility expressed in the words of the hymn "I Need Thee Every Hour"! That is the true Christian spirit of dependence.

Christ's evaluation of this church was quite different from its self-evaluation. He said: **and knowest not that thou art wretched, and miserable, and poor, and blind, and naked.** The Greek is considerably more vivid: "And thou dost not know that *thou* (emphatic in Gk.—thou who hast been boasting) art *the* wretched one, and pitiable and poor and blind and naked." **Wretched** is found only here and in Rom. 7:24—"O wretched man that I am! who shall deliver me from the body of this death?" **Miserable** occurs only here and in I Cor. 15:19—"If in this life only we have hope in Christ, we are of all men most miserable."

Swete summarizes the rest of the verse thus: "The next three adjectives state the grounds for commiseration; a blind beggar . . . barely clad (cf. Jo. xxi. 7) was not more deserving of pity than this rich and self-satisfied church."[113] **Poor . . . blind . . . naked** are to be taken metaphorically of the spiritual condi-

[113]*Ibid.*, p. 61.

tion of the church. Yet there may be an indirect allusion to the boasted assets of the city in which it was located. The church was **poor** in a wealthy banking center, **blind** in a community that had an excellent medical school, and **naked** in a place famous for its manufacture of the highest quality woolen garments. It is possible for the Church today to flourish outwardly in the midst of material prosperity, and yet to be poor, blind, and naked spiritually.

4. *Exhortation* (3:18-20)

To this self-satisfied church, that had "need of nothing," Jesus said: **I counsel thee to buy of me gold tried in the fire, that thou mayest be rich** (18). The term **buy** is an echo of Isa. 55:1—"Come ye, buy, and eat; yea, come, buy wine and milk without money and without price." That is the only way that any of us can buy from God. **Of me** (lit., "from me") is emphatic. These needed things can be acquired only from Christ.

Tried in the fire is literally "having been fired out of fire," that is, purified by fire. The same verb form occurs in the Septuagint of Ps. 18:30—"The word of the Lord is tried." In Prov. 30:5 it is translated "pure"—"The Word of the Lord is pure." So here it means that this gold is pure and unalloyed.

Furthermore, the church needed **white raiment, that thou mayest be clothed, and that the shame of thy nakedness do not appear.** The pure-white clothing was in contrast to the black wool for which Laodicea was famous.

In the third place, Jesus counseled the church to **anoint thine eyes with eyesalve, that thou mayest see.** Of this medicine Charles says: "In our text it is the famous Phrygian powder used by the medical school at Laodicea."[114]

The obvious point should not be missed that the three parts of 18 correspond to the last three adjectives of 17: "poor," "naked," "blind." The Laodicean church thought it needed nothing. Actually it was destitute of the barest necessities of spiritual life.

In this verse we see "What the Gospel Is": (1) Divine riches for our spiritual poverty; (2) The white robe of righteousness for our sinfulness; (3) Spiritual sight for our blindness.

The exhortation continues: **As many as I love, I rebuke and chasten: be zealous therefore, and repent** (19). Chastening

[114]*Op. cit.*, I, 98.

is a sign of God's loving care as Heavenly Father (cf. Heb. 12: 5-11). It is interesting that the verb **love** here is not the usual *agapao,* but *phileo,* which introduces a tender, emotional touch—to the church that deserved it least! **Rebuke** is "convict." **Chasten** is literally "train a child." All this shows the gentle compassion of Christ in dealing with this church as with a wayward child that needed a Father's love and discipline. Swete remarks: "Perhaps the deplorable condition of the Laodicean Church was due to lack of chastisement; there is no word of any trials hitherto undergone by this Church."[115]

This church lacked zest (see comments on "hot," 15). What it needed was zeal. So the Lord said: **Be zealous** (present imperative, be constantly zealous). **Repent** is aorist, calling for immediate action in a crucial decision.

It may seem strange that **Be zealous** precedes **repent.** Plumptre observes: "The root-evil of the Laodicean Church and its representative was their lukewarm indifference, the absence of any zeal, of any earnestness. And the first step, therefore, to higher things was to pass into a state in which those elements of life should no longer be conspicuous by their absence."[116]

To this call to repentance "Christ adds the most tender message found in any of his letters":[117] **Behold, I stand at the door, and knock: if any man hear my voice, and open the door, I will come in to him, and will sup with him, and he with me** (20). This is one of the greatest gospel texts in the New Testament and should be quoted frequently in both public evangelism and personal work. For that reason it should be memorized by every soul-winning Christian.

The simplicity of the gospel is expressed beautifully in this passage. Christ stands at the door of each sinner's heart, knocking for admittance. He will not batter down the door and force an entrance, for He has created us with free wills and will not violate these. But if the sinner opens the door, which only he can do, the Saviour has promised to come in. Holman Hunt's great painting, "The Light of the World," is evangelism made visual.

The idea of **sup** is that of fellowship, and specifically that of unhurried fellowship around the table at the evening meal, when

[115]*Op. cit.,* p. 63.

[116]*A Popular Exposition of the Epistles to the Seven Churches of Asia* (London: Hodder and Stoughton, 1891), p. 209.

[117]Erdman, *op. cit.,* p. 63.

the rush of the day is over. The thought is beautifully expressed by NEB—"and sit down to supper with him." It also looks forward to feasting eternally with Christ.

The fellowship is twofold. G. Campbell Morgan describes it thus: "I will first be his Guest, 'I will sup with him.' He shall be My guest, 'and he with Me.' I will sit at the table which his love provides, and satisfy My heart. He shall sit at the table which My love will provide, and satisfy his heart."[118]

5. *Remuneration* (3:21)

The closing promise is: **To him that overcometh will I grant to sit with me in my throne, even as I also overcame, and am set down with my Father in his throne.** This is an echo and extension of the promise which Jesus made to His twelve apostles in Matt. 19:28 and Luke 22:29-30. Through all the many temptations and tests of His life on earth, Jesus overcame and received His reward. For those who follow Him fully and faithfully to the end a like reward is waiting. This promise obviously looks forward to the next life.

6. *Invitation* (3:22)

Once more the listener to these letters is admonished to **hear what the Spirit saith unto the churches.** All seven messages are filled with salutary warning and exhortation for Christians today. We do well to take heed.

[118]*The Letters of Our Lord* (London: Pickering & Inglis, n.d.), p. 104.

Section III *The Future*

Revelation 4:1—22:21

At this point in the Book of Revelation there comes a startling change of both scene and subject. R. H. Charles writes: "The dramatic contrast could not be greater. Hitherto the scene of the Seer's visions had been earth; now it is heaven. . . . In ii—iii we have had a vivid description of the Christian Churches of Asia Minor. . . . But the moment we leave the restlessness, the troubles, the imperfectness, and apprehensions pervading ii—iii, we pass at once in iv into an atmosphere of perfect assurance and peace. . . . An infinite harmony of righteousness and power prevails."[1]

The scene shifts from earth to heaven. The subject changes from Christ's concern as Head of the Church for conditions prevailing in that Church to God's sovereign authority over His universe.

We have already noted that 1:19 suggests a threefold division of the Book of Revelation: (1) The Past—"the things which thou hast seen," c. 1; (2) The Present—"the things which are," cc. 2—3; (3) The Future—"the things which shall be hereafter," cc. 4—22. We now come to this third section.

About the interpretation of the first two divisions there is little difference of opinion. John saw a vision of the glorified Jesus standing in the midst of His Church (c. 1). That is clear. In cc. 2—3 are the letters to the seven churches of Asia. Most commentators agree that these letters describe actual conditions in actual churches in the first century—though they may well give a bird's-eye view of the general conditions to be found throughout Christendom in this age.

But when we come to the third section of Revelation the situation is quite different. Leaving out the "lunatic fringe" of numberless aberrations, we discover three main schools of interpretation. The first, called the *preterist,* finds the fulfillment of chapters 4—22 in the events of the imperial period. The great enemy of the Church, the beast, is the Roman Empire. The second, called the *historicist,* seeks the fulfillment in the succeed-

[1]*Op. cit.,* I, 102-3.

ing happenings of the entire Church age and the climactic events that follow. Here it is usually held that the beast is the Roman Catholic church or, more specifically, the papacy. The third, called the *futurist,* holds that the Book of Revelation from 4:1 on is yet to be fulfilled at the end of this age. It is still future from the standpoint of the reader today. The beast is identified as the Antichrist. We shall note all three of these interpretations in connection with key passages.

This third section of Revelation seems to consist of seven visions: (1) The Throne and the Lamb, 4:1—5:14; (2) The Seven Seals, 6:1—8:1; (3) The Seven Trumpets, 8:2—11:19; (4) The Sevenfold Vision, 12:1—14:20; (5) The Seven Bowls, 15:1—16:21; (6) The Seven Last Scenes, 17:1—20:15; (7) The New Jerusalem, 21:1—22:21.

A. The Throne and the Lamb, 4:1—5:14

1. *The Worship of God as Creator* (4:1-11)

The first vision is twofold. It shows the worship of God as Creator (c. 4) and the worship of Christ as Redeemer (c. 5). This worship John sees going on in heaven.

a. The throne of God (4:1-6*a*). John saw **a door . . . opened in heaven** (1). The KJV translation, **was opened,** distorts the meaning. The Greek clearly states that John saw a door which had been opened and still remained open (perfect passive participle). As Simcox says, "He saw the door standing open, he did not see it opened."[2] It was a door of revelation that opened a view into heaven.

Barclay notes that in these early chapters of the book we find "Three Important Doors in Life": (1) The door of opportunity, 3:8; (2) The door of the human heart, 3:20; (3) The door of revelation, 4:1.

The first voice which I heard is evidently the voice of Christ, referred to in 1:10. There, as here, it is described as sounding like **a trumpet,** powerful and penetrating. This voice said, **Come up hither, and I will shew thee things which must be hereafter.** John was to be given a preview of the future.

Immediately the seer was **in the spirit** (2). For the meaning of this phrase see the comments on 1:10. Here it apparently

[2]*Op. cit.,* p. 73.

means that John was transported spiritually (not bodily) into heaven.

There he saw **a throne** and One sitting on it. **Was set** is better translated "stood." The one seated on the throne looked **like a jasper and a sardine stone,** with an encircling halo like **an emerald** (3). Swete makes this helpful observation: "The description rigorously shuns anthropomorphic details. The Seer's eye is arrested by the flashing of gemlike colours, but he sees no form."[3]

The identification of these three stones is somewhat disputed. It is not certain whether the **jasper** was red or green. The **sardine stone,** or "sardius," was red. The **rainbow** (Gk., *iris*[4]) looked like **an emerald,** which is green. Phillips renders the passage: "His appearance blazed like diamond and topaz, and all around the throne shone a halo like an emerald rainbow."

On twenty-four seats around the throne were **four and twenty elders sitting** (4). Why twenty-four? Some have suggested that they represent the twenty-four courses of the priests (I Chronicles 24). Victorinus, the earliest Latin commentator on Revelation, says that the elders represent the twelve patriarchs and twelve apostles. Based on this, Swete finds "the double representation suggesting the two elements which coexisted in the new Israel, the Jewish and Gentile believers who were one in Christ. Thus the 24 elders are the Church in its totality."[5] Better still, they may be taken as representing all the people of God, both Old Testament saints and Christians.

These elders were **clothed in white raiment; and they had on their heads crowns of gold.** They were *cleansed* and *crowned.* The word for **crowns** signifies the victors' crowns (cf. 2:10).

Out of the throne came **lightnings and thunderings and voices** (5). These three elements are mentioned in connection with the giving of the law (Exod. 19:16). Barclay comments: "Here John is using the imagery which is regularly connected with the presence of God."[6]

The **seven lamps of fire burning before the throne** are identified as **the seven Spirits of God.** The reference is evidently to the Holy Spirit (see comments on 1:4).

[3]*Op. cit.,* p. 67.

[4]The Septuagint uses another word (*toxon*) for rainbow in Gen. 9:13. So Swete (p. 68) says that "it is precarious to press a reference to the rainbow of the covenant" here.

[5]*Op. cit.,* p. 69.

[6]*Op. cit.,* I, 195.

Before the throne there was a sea of glass (6). The Greek text says "as a sea of glass." That is, it looked like that. To emphasize its transparency, there is added, **like unto crystal.** For the significance of the glass-like sea Swete says: "It suggests the vast distance which, even in the case of one who stood at the door of heaven, intervened between himself and the Throne of God."[7]

b. The four living creatures (4:6b-8). These are **in the midst of the throne, and round about the throne** (6). This strange combination is thus explained by Moffatt: "and in the middle (of each side) of the throne and (consequently) round about the throne."[8]

Beasts (*zoa*) should be translated "living creatures." The rendering here is particularly unfortunate since "beasts" is the correct translation of *theria* in cc. 11—13. Of these two Greek words Trench writes: "Both play important parts in this book; both belong to its higher symbolism; while at the same time they move in spheres as far removed from one another as heaven is from hell. The *zoa* or 'living creatures,' which stand before the throne, and in which dwells the fulness of all creaturely life . . . constitute a part of the *heavenly* symbolism; the *theria,* the first beast and the second . . . these form part of the *hellish* symbolism."[9]

The four living creatures are described as **full of eyes before and behind.** This suggests that they knew all that was going on; that is, maintained ceaseless vigilance.

There has been a great deal of discussion as to the meaning of these four living creatures. Lenski writes: "The *zoa* have been called the Sphinx of Revelation. One writer offers twenty-one efforts at solution."[10] But this is making the situation needlessly difficult. Swete suggests this simple explanation: "The *zoa* represent Creation and the Divine immanence in Nature."[11] Somewhat more adequate is the interpretation of Donald Richardson: "Four is the cosmic number: and the four living creatures of verses 6-8 are the symbol of all creation redeemed, transformed, perfected, and brought under obedience to God's will and manifesting His glory."[12] Some would take the twenty-four elders as representing the redeemed saints of all time and the four living creatures as representing angelic beings.

[7]*Op. cit.,* p. 70.
[8]*Op. cit.,* p. 380.
[9]*Synonyms,* p. 310.
[10]*Op. cit.,* p. 179.
[11]*Op. cit.,* p. 71.
[12]*Op. cit.,* p. 50

The four living creatures are described as: **like a lion . . . like a calf . . . had a face as a man . . . like a flying eagle** (7). These are the same as the faces of the "four living creatures" of Ezek. 1:5-10 and similar to the faces of the "cherubim" of Ezek. 10:14. Following out his idea of the living creatures as representing all creation, Swete writes: "The four forms suggest [respectively] what is noblest, strongest, wisest, and swiftest in animate Nature."[13] Some would say that Matthew represents Christ as a **lion** (King), Mark as a **calf,** or ox (Servant), Luke as a **man** (Son of Man), and John as a **flying eagle** (Son of God). The parallels, though interesting, should not be pressed unduly.

Each of the four living creatures had **six wings about him; and they were full of eyes within** (8). A better translation is: "And the four living creatures, each one of them having six wings, are full of eyes around and within" (NASB). Donald Richardson suggests that the wings "symbolize the perfection of their equipment for the service of God."[14] For the significance of the **eyes** see the comments on 6.

Of the four living creatures it is said: **They rest not day and night.** Swete writes: "This ceaseless activity of Nature under the Hand of God is a ceaseless tribute of praise."[15] They cry: **Holy, holy, holy.** This is an echo of the seraphs' cry in Isa. 6:3. **Lord God Almighty** replaces Isaiah's "Lord of hosts." For the meaning of **which was, and is, and is to come** see the comments on 1:8.

In verse 8 we find "A Song of Praise to God": (1) For His holiness; (2) For His omnipotence; (3) For His everlastingness (Barclay).

c. *The universal praise* (4:9-11). The four living creatures give **glory and honour and thanks** to God (9). Swete says: "While *time* (honour) and *doxa* (glory) have regard to the divine perfections, *eucharistia* (thanks) refers to the divine gifts in creation and redemption."[16] **Who liveth for ever and ever** is found again in 4:10; 10:6; 15:7. God is supremely "the living One."

In their unceasing worship the four living creatures are joined by the twenty-four **elders,** who **fall down before him that sat on the throne** (10). They had been sitting in His presence (4). But now they are impelled to prostrate themselves in wor-

[13]*Op. cit.,* p. 71.
[14]*Op. cit.,* p. 50.
[15]*Op. cit.,* p. 72.
[16]*Ibid.,* p. 73.

ship before the Eternal One, casting their victors' **crowns** at His feet. This was "equivalent to an acknowledgment that their victory and their glory were from God, and were theirs only of His grace."[17]

As they did so they acclaimed Him **worthy . . . to receive glory and honour and power** (11). These were due Him as the great Creator of **all things.** For His **pleasure** (*thelema,* will) **they are and were created.** The Greek says: "they were, and were created." Again Swete gives the best explanation: "The Divine Will had made the universe a fact in the scheme of things before the Divine Power gave material expression to the fact."[18]

2. *The Worship of Christ as Redeemer* (5:1-14)

In c. 4 we saw God seated on His eternal throne, receiving perpetual praise. In c. 5 we find Christ, the Lamb, revealed as divine Redeemer.

a. The sealed book (5:1-5). The Eternal One seated on His throne had in His right hand **a book** (1). The Greek word is *biblion*—lit., "made from papyrus pith"—from which comes "Bible." It means a "roll" or "scroll" (see comments on 1:11). This roll was **written within and on the backside.** Ordinarily writing appeared only on the inside, where the strips of papyrus pith ran horizontally. But occasionally use was made of the reverse side, where it would be difficult to write across the perpendicular strips. Sheets of papyrus (from which comes "paper") were made by gluing together horizontal strips of papyrus pith on top of vertical strips. This is the material on which most, if not all, the New Testament was originally written. Our oldest Greek manuscripts, from the third century, are of papyrus.

This scroll was **sealed with seven seals. Sealed** is the perfect passive participle of a strong compound verb, suggesting that it was "completely sealed," or "sealed tight." This is further reinforced by the mention of **seven seals,** the number of perfection or completion.

Some have found in the mention of the **seven seals** a reference to a legal custom of that day. Charles describes it thus: "A will, according to the Praetorian Testament, in Roman law bore the seven seals of the seven witnesses on the threads that

[17]*Ibid.*, p. 74.

[18]*Ibid.*, p. 75.

secured the tablets or parchment . . . Such a Testament could not be carried into execution till all the seven seals were loosed."[19]

What was the **book** which John saw? Many answers have been given to this question. Simcox summarizes a few of them. He writes: "The traditional view, so far as there is one, of this sealed book is, that it represents the Old Testament, or more generally the prophecies of Scripture, which are only made intelligible by their fulfilment in Christ."[20] Rejecting this, he continues: "Many post-Reformation commentators, both Romanist and Protestant, have supposed the book to be the Apocalypse itself."[21] He adds: "Most modern commentators therefore generalize, and suppose that it is the Book of God's counsels."[22] Simcox himself prefers interpreting it as the Book of Life (20: 12; 21:27).

The most commonly held view today relates this book to the "things which must be hereafter" (4:1); that is, Revelation 4—22. Charles writes: "The roll contains the divine decrees and the destinies of the world . . . In other words, the Book is a prophecy of the things that fall out before the end."[23] He adds: "That this Book is sealed with seven seals shows that the divine counsels and judgments it contains are a profound secret . . . which can only be revealed through the mediation of the Lamb."[24] Swete calls it simply "the Book of Destiny."[25] Erdman says: "It contains all the decrees of God, an outline of all events to the very end of the age. What these contents are, the following chapters will disclose."[26]

And I saw (2) becomes a recurrent phrase (cf. 5:1; 6:1; 7:1; 8:2; 9:1; 10:1), introducing new sights. **With a loud voice,** reaching throughout the universe, **a strong angel** (cf. 10:1; 18:21) proclaimed: **Who is worthy to open the book, and to loose the seals thereof?** The breaking of the seals would necessarily precede the opening of the book, but the opening is placed first because it is the main object sought.

At first the loudly sounded proclamation received no answer: **And no man in heaven, nor in earth, neither under the**

[19]*Op. cit.*, I, 137-38.
[20]*Op. cit.*, p. 78.
[21]*Ibid.*, p. 79.
[22]*Ibid.*
[23]*Op. cit.*, I, 138.
[24]*Ibid.*
[25]*Op. cit.*, p. 75.
[26]*Op. cit.*, p. 67.

earth, was able to open the book, neither to look thereon (3). **No man** (*oudeis*) should be translated "no one," for the scope of the verse clearly includes angelic as well as human beings.

This predicament troubled John greatly. He says: **And I wept much, because no man** (no one) **was found worthy** (fit) **to open and to read the book** (4).

But the agonizing problem was soon solved. One of the elders told John to stop weeping. There was good news: **The Lion of the tribe of Juda, the Root of David, hath prevailed to open the book** (5). The first of these titles for Christ takes us back to the time when Jacob blessed his twelve sons. He described Judah as "a lion's whelp," or cub (Gen. 49:9). But Jesus was supremely **the Lion** of this tribe. He was also **the Root of David** (cf. 22:16). This expression is an echo of Isa. 11:1, 10; also quoted in part in Rom. 15:12. It is a Messianic term. In the intertestamental period it had seemed that the house of David had died. In Christ it took root again.

Hath prevailed (*enikesen*) is from *nike,* "victory" (cf. Phillips—"has won the victory"). Charles comments: "*Enikesen* is to be taken here, as always in the LXX and the N.T., absolutely. It states that once and for all Christ has conquered . . . and the object of this conquest was to empower Him to open the book of destiny and carry the history of the world throughout its final stages. . . . The victory has been won through His death and resurrection."[27]

b. The slain Lamb (5:6-7). A Lion had been announced, but **a Lamb** (6) appeared. This is one of the paradoxes of Christ. The Jews expected their Messiah to be "the Lion of the tribe of Judah." What they failed to realize was that He must first be "the Lamb of God, which taketh away the sin of the world" (John 1:29).

Because of the mention of the **Lamb . . . slain** some have interpreted the "book" of this chapter as referring to redemption. Straus declares: "The *subject* of the sealed scroll is redemption."[28]

The Greek word for **Lamb** (*arnion*) is used for Christ twenty-seven times in Revelation. Literally it means "little

[27]*Op. cit.,* I, 140.

[28]*The Book of Revelation* (Neptune, N.J.: Loizeaux Brothers, 1964), p. 139.

lamb."[29] However, Jeremias notes that in New Testament times it no longer has the diminutive force.[30]

Though a lamb is usually thought of as symbolizing helplessness and weakness, this **Lamb had seven horns,** meaning perfect power, **and seven eyes,** indicating perfect knowledge. He is omnipotent and omniscient. The **seven eyes** are further identified as being **the seven Spirits of God sent forth into all the earth.**[31] This means the Holy Spirit (see comments on 1:4).

Verse 7 reads literally: "And He came and has taken out of the right hand of the One sitting upon the throne." Thus John describes with rapid realism the action as it takes place. But obviously **the book** has to be supplied as the object of took, and some late copyist inserted it.

c. The singing company (5:8-14). When the Lamb had taken the scroll, the four living creatures and the twenty-four elders (see comments on 4:4, 6) **fell down before** Him (8). **Every one of them**—perhaps just the elders[32]—had **harps.** The best Greek text is singular: "Each one having a zither" (or lyre). They also had **golden vials full of odours**—better, "golden bowls full of incense." The incense symbolizes **the prayers of saints.** Swete notes that the use of incense in some churches in modern times, perhaps based on this passage, has no support from the Church Fathers of the first three centuries.

They sung a new song (9). Christina Rossetti aptly said: "Heaven is revealed to earth as the homeland of music."[33] The expression **a new song** occurs a number of times in the Psalms (33:3; 40:3; 96:1; 98:1; 144:9; 149:1). It is also found in Isa. 42:10.

The hymn that follows is one of adoration to Christ, the Redeemer. He was **worthy** (cf. 2) **to take the book, and to open the seals thereof.** Why? **For** (because) **thou wast slain, and hast redeemed** (bought) **us to God by thy blood.** The idea that we are purchased by the blood of Christ from the slavery of sin bulks large in the New Testament. This is redemption, the central theme of the Bible. We are bought **to** (for) **God**; therefore

[29]A different word is used in John 1:29, 36; Acts 8:32; I Pet. 1:19.

[30]Kittel, *op. cit.*, I, 340.

[31]In the Greek **which** is masculine, referring to **eyes** (masc.) but not **horns** (neut.).

[32]So Swete, Charles, Lenski, and others.

[33]Quoted in Charles, *op. cit.*, I, 146.

we belong to Him. It is not stated *from* whom we are purchased; the emphasis is on *by* whom and *to* whom.

This redemption extends to all mankind, to those **out of every kindred, and tongue, and people, and nation**—"representatives of every nationality, without distinction of race or geographical or political distribution."[34]

By His gracious redemption Christ has **made us unto our God kings and priests** (10). This combination of the royal and priestly functions of the believer is found several times in the New Testament. It has already occurred at 1:6 and will be found again at 20:6. Peter uses the expression "a royal priesthood" (I Pet. 2:9). What an exalted privilege!

We shall reign on the earth seems to point forward to the millennial Kingdom. Many scholars (including Swete and Charles) feel that the best reading here is: "They are reigning." Even this could be taken as a prophetic present. There is a sense in which the saints reign with Christ now. But the larger fulfillment looks to the future.

Swete points out the significance of vv. 9-10: "The 'new song' vindicates for Jesus Christ the unique place which He has taken in the history of the world. By a supreme act of self-sacrifice He has purchased men of all races and nationalities for the service of God, founded a vast spiritual Empire, and converted human life into a priestly service and a royal dignity."[35]

Verses 9-10 show "The Death of Jesus Christ" as: (1) A sacrificial death—**by thy blood;** (2) An emancipating death—**hast redeemed us;** (3) A universally atoning death—**out of every kindred;** (4) An effective death—**hast made us.**

And I beheld (11) is the same in Greek as "and I saw" in 1 and 2. This time the seer also **heard the voice of many angels** surrounding **the throne.** Their number was **ten thousand times ten thousand** (Gk., *myriadas myriadon,* "ten thousands of ten thousands"), **and thousands of thousands** (*chiliades chiliadon*). The same two expressions, in reverse order, are found in Dan. 7:10. It is typical apocalyptic language, emphasizing the greatness and majesty of God.

The **loud voice** (12) suggests a shout rather than a song. The myriads of angels cried: **Worthy is the Lamb that was slain to receive power, and riches, and wisdom, and strength, and**

[34]Swete, *op. cit.*, p. 81. [35]*Ibid.*, p. 82.

honour, and glory, and blessing. This is almost duplicated in 7:12. A similar sevenfold ascription of honor is found in I Chron. 29:11-12. The listing of *seven* items suggests perfection of power and glory.

Every creature (13) participated in this adoration of God and the Lamb. Four habitations are mentioned—**in heaven, and on the earth, and under the earth, and . . . in the sea.** The last item is added to the usual "three-story universe" (cf. 3). All creation was engaged in praising Father and Son. Charles comments: "Thus the universe of created things, the inhabitants of heaven, earth, sea, and Hades, join in the grand finale of praise that rose to the throne of God."[36]

Four items of praise are mentioned here, as over against seven in v. 12. But in the Greek the article is repeated with each one of the four, thus singling out the several items for individual emphasis. **Blessing** is *eulogia.* When applied to God, as here, it means "praise." **Honour** (*time*) suggests preeminence. **Glory** (*doxa*) speaks of the "splendor" of God, a brightness which radiates from His presence. **Power** is not *dynamis,* but *kratos,* which means "strength" or "might."

The four living creatures said, **Amen** (14), confirming the preceding doxology. The twenty-four elders joined in worshiping the Eternal One on the throne.

Charles suggests that there are four ways in which **Amen** is used in the Book of Revelation: (1) "The initial amen in which the words of a previous speaker are referred to and adopted as one's own," as in 5:14; 7:12; 19:4; 22:20; (2) "the detached amen," as here; (3) "the final amen with no change of speaker," as in 1:6-7; (4) "the Amen," as a name applied to God in 3:14.

B. The Seven Seals, 6:1—8:1

We come now to three series of judgments: the Seven Seals (cc. 6—7), the Seven Trumpets (cc. 8—11), and the Seven Bowls (cc. 15—16). The continuous-historical (*historicist,* see Intro., "Interpretation") school of interpretation finds in these a portrayal of successive cycles of judgments during this age. Probably a better view would be to understand them as concentric cycles of judgment, describing much the same thing under different symbolical figures. As always, the number seven indi-

[36]*Op. cit.,* I, 150.

cates completion. It is of interest to note that the seventh seal opens up into the seven trumpets, and the seventh trumpet opens up into the seven bowls. Thus the three series are tied very closely together.

The seven seals have been called "History's Pageant of Suffering." One shudders to think of what judgments are to befall this sin-sick world.

1. *The First Seal: Conquest* (6:1-2)

When the Lamb opened the first seal of the scroll, John **heard, as it were the noise of thunder** (1). This was the loud voice of **one of the four beasts** ("living creatures"; see comments on 4:6).

The first four seals form a series. Each is introduced by a loud call from one of the four living creatures, followed by the appearance of a horse and rider. A definite suggestion is then given as to what this symbolizes.

Come and see should be just "Come!" The **and see** is not in the best Greek text, here or in 3, 5, and 7. Some scribes evidently understood this as a call to John to come and see what was going to take place. Fausset comments: "It is more probably the cry of the redeemed to the Redeemer, 'Come,' deliver the groaning creature from the bondage of corruption."[37] The correct sense is more likely that given by Simcox: "The whole meaning of the phrase is that each of the living creatures by turns summons one of the four Horsemen."[38]

The opening of the first seal disclosed **a white horse: and he that sat on him had a bow; and a crown was given unto him: and he went forth conquering, and to conquer** (2).

On first thought the meaning of this seems obvious: the rider on the white horse is Christ (cf. 19:11-16). This is the view of Lange. He writes: "The single triumph of Christ, as set forth here, has in xix. 14 extended through the Church Triumphant; it appears as an array of victorious hosts on white horses."[39] Fausset agrees with this. So does Lenski, who identifies the rider as the Word of God and adds: "Its carrier, the horse, is white, which is the color of holiness and of heaven."[40]

But the context seems to be against that interpretation. Swete says: "A vision of the victorious Christ would be inappropriate

[37]*Op. cit.*, p. 677.
[38]*Op. cit.*, p. 85.
[39]*Op. cit.*, p. 171.
[40]*Op. cit.*, p. 222.

at the opening of a series which symbolizes bloodshed, famine, and pestilence. Rather we have here a picture of triumphant militarism."[41] Similarly Love says: "Hence, since the war, famine, and death are destined outcomes from the conquering, the 'white' here must be the victory, not of purity, but of selfish, lustful conquest."[42] Erdman gives a bit different slant: "The first represents the periods of peace granted, in the providence of God, under the Roman Empire, and to be repeated at various times in the history of the world."[43] It was the Roman conquests that brought peace.

2. *The Second Seal: War* (6:3-4)

This time the horse was **red** (4). The significance of this is clearly indicated by what follows. It was given to the rider of the red horse **to take peace from the earth, and that they should kill one another: and there was given unto him a great sword**—symbolizing widespread destruction. Clearly the **red** represents massive bloodshed.

3. *The Third Seal: Famine* (6:5-6)

The third horse was **black** (5). The rider had in his hand **a pair of balances.** The symbolism of this is immediately explained: **A measure of wheat for a penny, and three measures of barley for a penny** (6). The **measure** was about a quart, which was "the average daily consumption of the workman."[44] A **penny** was a *denarius,* which was apparently a day's wages (Matt. 20:2). This meant that famine prices were so high that it would take all a man earned just to feed himself, if he ate wheat. On the other hand, he could buy three quarts of barley—the food of the poor people—and have enough for a small family.

To the proclamation of price an admonition is attached: **and see thou hurt not the oil and the wine.** This would be olive oil and fermented grape juice. Swete notes: "Wheat and barley, oil and wine, were the staple food both of Palestine and Asia Minor."[45]

The probable significance of this warning is explained by Charles. He writes: "Owing to the lack of cereals and the super-

[41] *Op. cit.,* p. 86.
[42] *Op. cit.,* p. 67.
[43] *Op. cit.,* p. 73.
[44] Swete, *op. cit.,* p. 88.
[45] *Ibid.*

abundance of wine, Domitian issued an edict . . . that no fresh vineyards should be planted in Italy, and that half the vineyards in the provinces should be cut down."[46] But Suetonius records the fact that the imperial decree caused such an uproar in the Asiatic cities that it had to be withdrawn. Instead, punishment was imposed on those who allowed their vineyards to go out of cultivation! Charles thinks that John is here registering a protest against this selfish attitude: "Accordingly, he predicts an evil time, when men will have oil and wine in abundance, but suffer from lack of bread."[47] At least we can say that Domitian's decree may well have been the occasion for the wording here.

4. *The Fourth Seal: Death* (6:7-8)

Now there appeared a horse that was **pale** (8). The Greek word is *chloros,* which means "a pale green." It is used in Homer's *Iliad* (vii. 464) for "pale fear." Swete comments: "The 'pale' horse is a symbol of Terror, and its rider a personification of Death . . . with whom follows—whether on the same or another horse or on foot the writer does not stop to say or even to think—his inseparable comrade, Hades."[48] For the meaning of **Hell** see the comments on 1:18.

But there was a limit to the depredations of the grim reaper, Death, and the avaricious garner, Hades. They could destroy only **the fourth part of the earth.** The time of final judgment had not yet arrived.

The two executioners **kill** by four methods: **sword . . . hunger . . . death** (the Gk. word evidently means "pestilence" here, as often in the LXX) . . . **beasts of the earth.** There is an obvious reference to Ezek. 14:21—"For thus saith the Lord God; How much more when I send my four sore judgments upon Jerusalem, the sword, and the famine, and the noisome beast, and the pestilence." The Greek terms are the same in both passages, with only the order of the last two reversed. Wild beasts multiply and become more ferocious in times of famine and pestilence.

The vision of the four horsemen in the opening of the first four seals finds a striking parallel in Zech. 6:1-3. There the prophet sees four chariots drawn by horses that were respectively red, black, white, and "grizzled and bay." Here the horses are

[46]*Op. cit.,* I, 167. [47]*Ibid.,* p. 168.

[48]*Op. cit.,* pp. 88-89.

white, red, black, and pale green. As Swete notes, "The Apocalyptist borrows only the symbol of the horses and their colours, and instead of yoking the horses to chariots he sets on each of them a rider in whom the interest of the vision is centered."[49]

What is the application of these first four seals? Representing the *preterist* view (see Intro., "Interpretation"), Swete finds here the militarism and lust for conquest of the Roman Empire of that day, repeated in history often since.

Typical of those who hold the *historicist* view, Barnes goes more into detail. The first seal represents a period of prosperity and conquest lasting for some ninety years after Revelation was written (i.e., until A.D. 180). Building heavily on Gibbon's *Decline and Fall of the Roman Empire,* Barnes sketches this period at great length.[50] The second seal represents the ninety-two years after the assassination of Commodus in A.D. 193, when no less than thirty-two emperors and twenty-seven pretenders kept the empire in a state of constant civil war. The third seal symbolizes a period of oppressive taxation and severe restrictions on the liberty of the people. The fourth seal Barnes applies to A.D. 248-68, when the sword, famine, and pestilence are estimated by Gibbon to have destroyed half the population of the empire.[51]

The *futurist* interpretation holds that these seals refer to terrible judgments on humanity at the close of this age. For instance, Kuyper says that "what is here dealt with immediately precedes the end of all things, the coming of the antichrist and the Return of the Lord."[52]

5. *The Fifth Seal: Martyrdom* (6:9-11)

The opening of the **fifth seal** revealed **under the altar the souls of them that were slain for the word of God, and for the testimony which they held** (9). There is here no living creature, no voice calling, "Come." The significance of this change is thus noted by Swete: "With the fifth seal the Church comes into sight, in its persecuted, suffering, state. . . . The loosing of the fifth seal interprets the age of persecution, and shews its relation to the

[49]*Ibid.*, pp. 85-86.

[50]*Notes on the New Testament: Revelation,* ed. Robert Frew (Grand Rapids: Baker Book House, 1949 [reprint]), pp. 142-46.

[51]*Ibid.*, p. 157.

[52]*The Revelation of St. John,* trans. John H. de Vries (Grand Rapids: Wm. B. Eerdmans Publishing Co., 1964 [reprint]), p. 72.

Divine plan of history."[53] It does not take any stretch of imagination to realize that this could apply equally well to the Roman persecution of Christians (preterist), to the many persecutions of true believers throughout the church age, especially by the Roman Catholic church (historicist), and also to the martyrs of the Great Tribulation at the close of this age (futurist). To be true in the light of any one theory would not preclude its truth under another. The sensible position seems to be to accept all these interpretations of this passage as valid and meaningful.

Under the altar is perhaps a reference to the fact that the blood of the sin offering was to be poured "at the bottom of the altar of the burnt offering" (Lev. 4:7). "The altar here in view is the counterpart of the Altar of Burnt Offering, and the victims which have been offered at it are the martyred members of the Church, who have followed their Head in the example of His sacrificial death."[54]

The language of the last part of the verse is closely parallel to that of 1:9 (see comments there), which is echoed again in 12:11, 17; 19:10; 20:4. The repetition of **for** (*dia,* on account of) suggests two causes of martyrdom. These faithful witnesses were put to death for their confession of one true God, as against the polytheism and emperor worship of that day, and for their testimony to Jesus as the only Lord and Saviour. The *Martyrdom of Polycarp* records that just before the venerable bishop was put to death in A.D. 156 he was urged by the Roman proconsul to save his life by doing two things: (1) "Swear by the genius of Caesar . . . say, Away with those that deny the gods"; (2) "Revile Christ." Polycarp's reply has been quoted often: "Eighty and six years have I served him, and he never did me wrong; and how can I now blaspheme my King that has saved me?"[55]

There are many warnings in the Word of God that martyrdom for the faith will again become common at the end of this age. One may well pray for the same courageous spirit that was shown by the early martyrs of the Church.

The souls under the altar **cried** (aorist, once only) **with a loud voice . . . How long, O Lord, holy and true, dost thou not judge and avenge our blood on them that dwell on the earth?** (10) **Lord** is not the common term *kyrios,* but *despotes* (cf. despot). This is a title for God in the Septuagint and twice in the

[53]*Op. cit.,* p. 89. [54]*Ibid.,* p. 90.

[55]Eusebius *Ecclesiastical History* iv. 15 (*op. cit.,* p. 146).

New Testament (Luke 2:10; Acts 4:24). It is also used for Christ twice (II Pet. 2:1; Jude 4). Here it is not clear whether the term is applied to God or to Christ. The combination **holy and true** is used of Christ in 3:7.

The cry for vengeance has caused some consternation among Christians today. But Swete notes that "the holiness and truth of the Supreme Master demand the punishment of a world responsible for their deaths. The words only assert the principle of Divine retribution, which forbids the exercise of personal revenge."[56]

To each of the martyrs was **given** (11) "a white robe" (*stole,* sing.) emblematic of purity and victory. This Greek word is found again in 7:9, 13-14. The term represents a long, flowing garment which was a sort of status symbol. These martyred victims were actually victors. They were told **that they should rest yet for a little season, until their fellowservants also and their brethren, that should be killed as they were, should be fulfilled.** Their waiting will be a **rest** and it will be of short duration. When God's purposes have been **fulfilled,** the end will come.

6. *The Sixth Seal: The End of the Age* (6:12-17)

The first sign of the end that is noted is **a great earthquake** (12). This is probably an echo of Hag. 2:6-7 (LXX), "For thus saith the Lord of hosts; Yet once, it is a little while, and I will shake the heavens, and the earth, and the sea, and the dry land; and I will shake all nations." The last clause suggests that the reference is not only to a physical earthquake but also to racial, political, and social revolutions. It should be noted that earthquake is *seismos,* and "will shake" is *seiso.*

Accompanying terrors are indicated: **The sun became black as sackcloth of hair, and the moon became as blood.** This is almost a quotation of Joel 2:31, "The sun shall be turned into darkness, and the moon into blood, before the great and the terrible day of the Lord come."

Further celestial phenomena are noted: **And the stars of heaven fell unto the earth, even as a fig tree casteth her untimely figs, when she is shaken of a mighty wind** (13). The language is that of Isa. 34:4, "And all the host of heaven shall be

[56]*Op. cit.,* p. 90.

dissolved . . . and all their host shall fall down, as the leaf falleth off from the vine, and as a falling fig from the fig tree."

The clause we have omitted from this Isaiah quotation is "and the heavens shall be rolled together as a scroll," which is paralleled by the next statement in Revelation: **And the heaven departed as a scroll when it is rolled together** (14). Added is the prediction: **and every mountain and island were moved out of their places.** There will always be a dispute as to whether this language should be taken literally or figuratively. But why not both? As in the case of II Pet. 3:10-12, the atomic age has opened our eyes to the fact that such extreme language, long hailed as the poetic extravaganza of an overwrought imagination, may be fulfilled with horrible literalness.

In this awful vision of the last days, John saw that men of all strata of society (seven classes are mentioned), from kings to slaves, **hid themselves in the dens and in the rocks of the mountains** (15). They cried **to the mountains and rocks** to **fall** on them (cf. Hos. 10:8) and **hide** them **from the face of him that sitteth on the throne, and from the wrath of the Lamb** (16). What an amazing paradox: **the wrath of the Lamb!** Someone has said that God's wrath is God's love dammed up by man's disobedience, until it has to be poured forth in righteous judgment.

The reason for seeking to hide is clear: **For the great day of his wrath is come; and who shall be able to stand?** (17) There have been many days of God's judgment on sin and sinful men. But **the great day of his wrath**—a combination of "the great day" (Joel 2:11, 31; Zeph. 1:14) and "the day of wrath" (Zeph. 1:15, 18; 2:3)—is still to come. It will far exceed anything that has yet taken place.

Interlude: The Sealing of God's Servants (7:1-17)

Chapter 7 forms a sort of parenthesis between the sixth and seventh seals. The opening of the seventh seal (8:1) reveals the seven trumpets. Thus these two series of sevens are interlinked.

Chapter 7 divides itself naturally into two parts, as indicated by **And after these things I saw** in vv. 1 and 9.[57] What John saw was the Church Militant on earth (1-8) and the Church Triumphant in heaven (9-17).

[57]The best Greek text has, "After this I saw" (1), and, "After these things I saw" (9). The verb is exactly the same in both places.

a. The sealing of the 144,000 (7:1-8). John saw **four angels standing on the four corners of the earth, holding the four winds of the earth, that the wind should not blow on the earth, nor on the sea, nor on any tree** (1). The judgments of God were to be held back for a moment. Each of **the four angels** stood at one of **the four corners of the earth**—meaning the four directions of the compass—**holding** (holding fast, detaining) **the four winds of the earth,** symbolical of the judgments that were about to strike. No hurricane should sweep **earth** or **sea,** nor hit **any tree.**

John then **saw another angel ascending from the east** (2)—literally, "from rising of sun." He had **the seal of the living God.** The **seal** "is here the signet-ring . . . which the Oriental monarch uses to give validity to official documents or to mark his property."[58] Paul uses this figure several times (II Cor. 1:22; Eph. 1:13; 4:30). Perhaps the closest parallel in the New Testament is II Tim. 2:19, "Nevertheless the foundation of God standeth sure, having this seal, The Lord knoweth them that are his." The symbolism here in Revelation is probably related to that in Ezek. 9:3-4, where a man clothed in linen and carrying a writer's inkhorn is commanded to set a mark upon the foreheads of all the righteous ones in Jerusalem. Those who did not have this mark would be slain.

The four angels were warned: **Hurt not the earth, neither the sea, nor the trees, till we have sealed the servants of our God in their foreheads** (3). The use of **our God** underscores the fact that both saints and angels serve the same Lord.

The number sealed was 144,000 **of all the tribes of the children of Israel** (4). Just what do the 144,000 represent? That is a question which has had many answers. Some have held that the number indicates the elect remnant of Israel (cf. Rom. 11:5). Others think it means the Jewish Christians. The figure 144,000 is not to be taken literally, but symbolically. It stands for those who "were redeemed from among men, being the firstfruits unto God and to the Lamb" (14:4). The number (12 x 12 x 1,000) signifies a large and complete host. Probably the best view is that it represents "the whole number of the faithful."[59] This seems to be definitely favored by the further description of the 144,000 in 14:1-5.

In the listing of the twelve tribes (5-8) a problem appears: Why is Dan omitted? In several Old Testament lists (Num. 1:5-

[58] Swete, *op. cit.*, p. 96.

[59] *Ibid.*, p. 99.

15, 20-43; 13:4-15) the name of Levi is left out—"But the Levites after the tribe of their fathers were not numbered among them" (Num. 1:47). This was because they were set aside for special sacred service. To keep the number at twelve, the tribe of Joseph is divided into two tribes, Ephraim and Manasseh. These are named separately here, with **Joseph** (8) used for Ephraim. **Levi** (7) is included.

That still leaves the question as to why Dan is omitted. This tribe is missing in the genealogical tables of I Chron. 2:3—8:40. But so also is Zebulon, for some unknown reason.

It has been suggested that Dan is left out because this was the first tribe to go into idolatry (Judges 18). The early rabbinical writings emphasize the apostasy of Dan. *The Testaments of the Twelve Patriarchs* (a pseudepigraphic work) suggests an alliance between Dan and Belial.

Duesterdieck says: "The simplest reason for not naming Dan lies rather in the fact that it [the tribe of Dan] had died out long already before the time of John."[60] But so, apparently, had all the other ten northern tribes.

The earliest explanation, endorsed widely by the ancient Church Fathers, was first offered by Irenaeus (2nd cent.). He held that Dan was omitted because the Antichrist was to spring from this tribe (cf. Jer. 8:16). Charles insists that "this tradition of the origin of Antichrist is pre-Christian and Jewish."[61]

The order of the tribes as listed here has evoked considerable discussion. After mentioning Judah and Manasseh, Charles asserts: "The rest of the tribes are enumerated in a wholly unintelligible order."[62] Swete more reasonably writes: "The Apocalyptic order starts with the tribe from which Christ came . . . and then proceeds to the tribe of the firstborn son of Jacob, which heads most O.T. lists; next come the tribes located in the North, broken by the mention of Simeon and Levi, who in other lists usually follow Reuben or Judah; while Joseph and Benjamin bring up the rear."[63] He adds: "This arrangement seems to have been suggested partly by the birth order of the patriarchs and partly by the geographical situation of the tribes."[64] J. B. Smith gives a logical presentation by arranging the names in pairs, in-

[60]*Op. cit.*, p. 249.
[61]*Op. cit.*, I, 209.
[62]*Ibid.*, p. 207.
[63]*Op. cit.*, p. 98.
[64]*Ibid.*

stead of in triplets as found in the versification of our English Bibles.[65]

b. The multitude of the redeemed (7:9-17). John saw **a great multitude, which no man could number, of all nations, and kindreds, and people, and tongues** (9) standing before **the throne** in heaven. Sometimes one is tempted to feel that only a few people are serving the Lord. But the total redeemed of all time and all nations is a numberless host.

They wear **white robes**—symbolical of purity and victory—and carry **palms in their hands,** as did the joyful crowd at Jesus' triumphal entry into Jerusalem (John 12:13). Swete aptly remarks: "The scene of vii. 9 ff. anticipates the final condition of redeemed humanity. Like the Transfiguration before the Passion, it prepares the Seer to face the evil which is yet to come."[66]

The multitude of the redeemed cried out: **Salvation to our God which sitteth upon the throne, and unto the Lamb** (10). Here, as often in the New Testament, Christ is worshiped along with the Father. **All the angels,** the twenty-four **elders,** and **the four** living creatures joined in the adoration (11). The ascription of praise (12) is sevenfold, as in 5:12 (see the comments there). Each of the seven items carries the definite article in the Greek text, thus emphasizing them individually.

One of the elders (13) offered to explain the vision to John (cf. 5:5). He first asked a twofold question about those in white robes: **What are these . . . and whence come they?** John answered, **Sir, thou knowest** (14)—literally, "you have knowledge" (perfect tense). Then comes the explanation: **These are they which came out of great tribulation**—literally, "These are the ones who are coming out of the great tribulation." This wording has led to the name "The Great Tribulation," for a short period (three and one-half or seven years) at the close of this age. It has often been claimed that the reference here is to the so-called "tribulation saints," who are saved during the Great Tribulation. There is a sense in which all Christians must go "through much tribulation" (Acts 14:22). But at the close of this age there will be a period of intense trouble which could well be designated as the Great Tribulation (cf. Dan. 12:1). It remains an open question, however, whether the reference here should be restricted to the saints of this brief period.

The redeemed are described as having **washed their robes,**

[65]*Op. cit.*, p. 130. [66]*Op. cit.*, p. 100.

and made them white in the blood of the Lamb. The idea of clothes being literally washed white in blood is paradoxical. But this is not literal language. The whole story of salvation is a paradox, over which many sophisticated intellectuals have stumbled. The fact still remains that the only way of salvation is humbly to accept the atonement provided by the Son of God, who shed His blood for all sinners.

Only the Blood-washed can stand **before the throne of God** (15) and enjoy His presence forever. They **serve him day and night in his temple.** Heaven is a place of rest, but not of idleness. **Temple** is not *hieron,* used for the Temple area in Jerusalem, but *naos,* "sanctuary." In the earlier Tabernacle and later Temple only the priests and Levites could enter the sanctuary. But now all believers are priests and can serve in the sanctuary. Swete observes: "The 'temple' is here the Divine Presence, realized and enjoyed."[67] He makes this practical application for the present: "But the vision of ceaseless worship is realized only when life itself is regarded as a service. The consecration of all life to the service of God is the goal to which our present worship points."[68] On the last clause of v. 15 he comments: "Perpetual service will find its stimulus and its reward in the perpetual vision of Him Who is served."[69]

The Eternal One, who sits on the throne, **shall dwell among them.** The verb is *skenosei*—literally, shall "tent" or "tabernacle." Only John uses this word. Rev. 21:3 is similar to the statement here. In John 1:14 the term is used for the Incarnation: "And the Word was made flesh, and dwelt among us." The coming of Christ to earth prepared the way for all who would accept His salvation to enjoy God's presence forever in heaven. **Among them** is literally "upon them." So the clause may be translated, "And he that sitteth on the throne shall spread his tabernacle over them" (ASV).

The blessedness of the redeemed is further described thus: **They shall hunger no more, neither thirst any more; neither shall the sun light on them, nor any heat** (16). The language of this verse and much of the next is borrowed from Isa. 49:10, "They shall not hunger nor thirst; neither shall the heat nor sun smite them: for he that hath mercy on them shall lead them, even by the springs of water shall he guide them." And so we read

[67]*Ibid.*, p. 104. [68]*Ibid.*
[69]*Ibid.*

here: **For the Lamb which is in the midst of the throne shall feed them, and shall lead them unto living fountains of waters** (17)—literally, "to Life's water-springs." There is a reflection here not only of Isa. 40:11 and Ezek. 34:23, but also of the much-loved twenty-third psalm. Christ alone is the Water of Life (cf. John 4:14).

The chapter ends with the beautiful promise: **And God shall wipe away all tears from their eyes.** This is repeated in 21:4. Swete observes: "Indeed, the whole of the episode c. vii. 9-17 finds echoes in the last two chapters of the book, where the climax here anticipated is fully described."[70]

Chapters 6 and 7 present striking contrasts. Richardson notes: "The sixth chapter closes with the question, 'Who is able to stand?' Chapter seven gives the answer."[71] It is those who are saved and sealed by the blood of Christ. Of the combination found in c. 7 he says: "Victory and joy through struggle and tribulation is the message of the whole book."[72]

7. *The Seventh Seal: Silence* (8:1)

When the **seventh seal** was opened, **there was silence in heaven about the space of half an hour;** that is, for a short time. Apparently this was the silence of fearful apprehension, the sudden calm before the storm. McDowell suggests: "The hosts of heaven are transfixed and made speechless as they gaze raptly at the Lamb when he moves his hand to break the last seal of the scroll that was taken from the hand of God."[73] Richardson calls it "a silence of 'trembling suspense,' a dramatic pause; a silence of reverence, expectancy, and prayer."[74] Charles makes it a bit more specific: "The praises of the highest orders of angels in heaven are hushed that the prayers of *all* the suffering saints on earth may be heard before the throne. Their needs are of more concern to God than all the psalmody of heaven."[75]

C. The Seven Trumpets, 8:2—11:19

Introduction: The Seven Trumpeters (8:2-6)

The opening of the seventh seal reveals **seven angels** with **seven trumpets** (2). Thus the seventh seal becomes the seven

[70]*Ibid.*, p. 106.
[71]*Op. cit.*, p. 63.
[72]*Ibid.*, p. 66.
[73]*Op. cit.*, p. 102.
[74]*Op. cit.*, p. 68.
[75]*Op. cit.*, I, 224.

trumpets; the second series emerges out of the first. The prominence of the number seven in the Book of Revelation is highlighted here, as elsewhere.

The angels are described as **the seven angels which stood before God.** There is a striking parallel to this in an apocryphal book of the second century B.C. Tobit 12:15 reads: "I am Raphael, one of the seven holy angels who present the prayers of the saints and enter into the presence of the glory of the Holy One" (RSV). *The Book of Jubilees* (also 2nd cent. B.C.), which emphasizes the importance of the number seven in history, repeatedly refers to the "Angels of the Presence."

Trumpets are mentioned about one hundred times in the Old Testament in connection with the giving of the law at Sinai (Exod. 19:16), the calling of the congregation of Israel (Lev. 25:9), the conquest of Canaan (thirteen times in Joshua 6), and the sounding of a warning by the prophets (e.g., Isa. 58:1; Jer. 4:5; Ezek. 33:3; Hos. 8:1; Joel 2:1, 15; Amos 3:6; Zeph. 1:16; Zech. 9:14). This prophetic use provides the closest background for the employment of trumpets here to announce the plagues of judgment. This fits in also with their use as a signal for war.

And another angel came and stood at the altar (3). What follows seems to show that this was not the altar of burnt offering (as in 6:9), but the altar of incense.[76] It should be noted, however, that Charles insists, from his careful study of Jewish and Christian apocalypses, that there is only one altar in heaven, the altar of incense.[77]

This angel had **a golden censer.**[78] He was given **much incense** to **offer** with **the prayers of all saints** (see quotation from Tobit in comments on v. 2) **upon the golden altar which was before the throne**—as the ancient golden altar of incense was before the holy of holies in the Tabernacle. The picture is similar to that of the high priest ministering on the Day of Atonement, as described in Lev. 16:12-13, "And he shall take a censer full of burning coals of fire from off the altar before the Lord, and his hands full of sweet incense beaten small, and bring it within the veil: and he shall put the incense upon the fire before the Lord, that the cloud of the incense may cover the mercy seat that is upon the testimony."

[76]Swete, *op. cit.*, p. 108. [77]*Op. cit.*, I, 227-30.

[78]The Greek word for censer usually means "frankincense," but clearly here indicates a censer.

So here it is stated that **the smoke of the incense . . . with the prayers of the saints, ascended up before God out of the angel's hand** (4); that is, out of the censer which he held in his hand. The cloud of incense would represent the prayers before God. This idea is found in Ps. 141:2, "Let my prayer be set forth before thee as incense."

At first the censer was used for intercession (3-4). Now it is to be used for judgment. The angel **filled it with fire of the altar, and cast it into the earth** (5). Swete observes: "But now no incense is added, and no fragrant cloud goes up; the contents of the censer are poured upon the earth; the prayers of the saints return to the earth in wrath."[79] This may suggest that prayer would no longer avail (cf. Jer. 7:16). The period of probation was ended. The sentence against unrepentant sinners must now be executed. Judgment would replace mercy.

There was an immediate reaction to this casting of fire upon the earth: **And there were voices, and thunderings, and lightnings, and an earthquake.** The silence of v. 1 has been shattered. The stage is now set for the seven trumpet blasts of judgment. **And the seven angels which had the seven trumpets prepared themselves to sound** (6).

1. *The First Trumpet: Hail and Fire* (8:7)

When the **first angel sounded** his trumpet, **hail and fire mingled with blood . . . were cast upon the earth.** The first four trumpet-judgments consist of plagues on nature and are reminiscent of the ten plagues on Egypt. This one is an echo of the seventh plague, described in Exod. 9:24, "So there was hail, and fire mingled with hail."

The result of this judgment was that **the third part of trees was burnt up, and all green grass was burnt up.** So the destruction was only partial; this was not the final judgment. **Trees** means "the fruit-trees especially, the olive, the fig, and the vine, on which the inhabitants of Palestine and Asia Minor depended so largely."[80]

2. *The Second Trumpet: Burning Mountain* (8:8-9)

When the **second angel** blew his trumpet, **as it were a great mountain burning with fire was cast into the sea: and the**

[79]*Op. cit.*, p. 109.

[80]*Ibid.*, p. 111.

third part of the sea became blood (8). This reflects the first plague in Egypt, when water was turned into blood, causing the fish to die (Exod. 7:20-21). So here a **third part** of marine life **died** (9), and a **third part of the ships were destroyed.**

3. *The Third Trumpet: Blazing Star* (8:10-11)

At the third trumpet blast, **there fell a great star from heaven, burning as it were a lamp** (10). The result was that **the third part of the waters became wormwood; and many men died** (11). In the Old Testament **wormwood** is a symbol of suffering and divine chastisement (Jer. 9:15). It was sometimes mixed with water, to make it bitter and painful to drink. But here the water **became wormwood,** and so caused death. D. W. Richardson aptly observes: "The waters of the world become the very essence of bitterness to their own votaries."[81] He goes on to tell of a famous American cartoonist who committed suicide, leaving great wealth behind. But he also left a letter in which he said that he had gone from wife to wife and from country to country trying to escape himself. He ended his life because he was fed up with seeking to discover ways of getting through twenty-four hours of the day.

4. *The Fourth Trumpet: Darkness* (8:12-13)

When **the fourth angel sounded . . . the third part of the sun was smitten, and the third part of the moon, and the third part of the stars; so as the third part of them was darkened** (12). This is a reminder of the ninth plague in Egypt, that of darkness (Exod. 10:21-23).

Then John saw **and heard an angel** (13)—but the best Greek text says "one eagle." Swete comments: "The eagle is chosen not only for his strength of wing (xii. 14), but as the emblem of coming judgement (Mt. xxiv. 28)."[82] This lone eagle was **flying through the midst of heaven** (lit., "in the meridian," or "zenith"). He was crying out: **Woe, woe, to the inhabiters of the earth by reason of the other voices of the trumpet of the three angels, which are yet to sound!** The language of this verse suggests that in a very real sense the worst is yet to be. The remaining three trumpet-judgments will be far more severe than the preceding four. It is now to be **Woe, woe, woe!**

[81]*Op. cit.,* p. 70.

[82]*Op. cit.,* p. 113.

In the case of the seven seals the first four formed a distinctive group. They were successive visions of four horses (6:1-8). This is paralleled in the trumpets. The first four reveal catastrophes in nature, while the other three describe judgments of a different kind. Also in both cases the fifth and sixth stand by themselves, and there is an interlude before the seventh.

5. *The Fifth Trumpet: Locusts* (9:1-12)

The descriptions of the first four trumpet-judgments are brief. But those of the fifth and sixth are given at considerable length. That is probably because human beings are involved, not nature.

John **saw a star fall from heaven unto the earth** (1)—literally, "a star out of heaven having fallen to the earth." This was evidently a person, for it says: **And to him was given the key of the bottomless pit**—literally, "the shaft of the abyss" (*abyssos*). This may have been Satan, as suggested possibly by Jesus' words in Luke 10:18, "I beheld Satan as lightning fall [Gk., having fallen] from heaven." **To him was given** (by God) **the key of the** abyss; that is, the power to open or close its entrance.

Using this authority, **he opened** the shaft of the abyss (2). Out of it **there arose a smoke . . . as the smoke of a great furnace,** darkening the sky.

A startling thing then took place. **Out of the smoke** there came **locusts** (3). To them **was given power** (*exousia,* liberty or power to act), **as the scorpions of the earth have power** (*exousia*). A plague of locusts has always been one of the most dreaded catastrophes in the Mediterranean world. The first two chapters of Joel give a graphic portrayal of their work of destruction.

But that these are not literal locusts is shown by the fact that they were commanded not to hurt **grass, tree,** or **any green thing** (4). These are precisely the things that are always destroyed by a swarm of locusts. These locusts, however, were to hurt **those men which have not the seal of God in their foreheads** (cf. 7:3). Just as the Israelites were spared from the last seven plagues that came upon the Egyptians (Exod. 8:22), so the sealed saints will be exempted from these last severe woes. Is there here a hint that the Church will share in the sufferings at the beginning of the Great Tribulation?

These "locusts" would **not kill,** but the men would **be tormented five months** (5). The time is probably suggested by the fact that locusts are usually born in the spring and die at the end of the summer. Thus the life-span of the natural locust is about five months, from May through September.

The nature of the suffering inflicted is further defined in this way: **And their torment was as the torment of a scorpion, when he striketh a man.** Barclay gives the following vivid description of this creature:

> The scorpion was one of the scourges of Palestine. In shape it is like a small lobster. It has claws like a lobster, with which it clutches its prey. It has a long tail, which curves up over its back and over its head; at the end of the tail there is a curved claw; it is with this claw that the scorpion strikes, and this claw secretes poison as the blow is delivered. The scorpion can be up to six inches in length.[83]

As a result of the scorpion's sting men will **desire to die, and death shall flee from them** (6). Cornelius Gallus, a Latin writer, said: "Worse than any wound is to wish to die and yet not to be able to do so." Barclay adds: "Such will be the state of men that even death would be a relief and release."[84] But one does not escape oneself by dying.

The shape of the locusts is said to be **like unto horses prepared unto battle** (7). The same thought is expressed in Joel 2:4-5, and travelers have often commented on this similarity in appearance. But unlike literal locusts these had **on their heads . . . as it were crowns like gold,** the sign of the conqueror. Also **their faces were as the faces of men,** suggesting intelligence.

Furthermore, **they had hair as the hair of women** (8). In an Arabic proverb the antennae of locusts are said to be like a maiden's hair. Also, **their teeth were as the teeth of lions.** This is a quotation from Joel 1:6. Locusts not only eat the green grass and leaves but actually devour all the bark from trees. Their teeth have ferocious cutting power. The mention of **breastplates of iron** (9) is doubtless a reference to the scaly flanks and hard breasts of the locust.

A large swarm of locusts makes a heavy roaring sound, as many writers have testified. So here John says: **And the sound of their wings was as the sound of chariots of many horses running to battle.** This is an echo of Joel 2:5, "Like the noise of chariots on the tops of mountains shall they leap."

In v. 10 reference is made again to scorpions: "And they

[83]*Op. cit.,* II, 62. [84]*Ibid.*

have tails like scorpions, and stings; and in their tails is their power to hurt men for five months" (NASB). This is largely a repetition of v. 5.

The demonic hordes are described as having **a king,** who is "the angel of the abyss" (11, lit.). In **Hebrew** his **name** is **Abaddon, in Greek . . . Apollyon.** Both of these mean "Destroyer." As to his identity, Swete writes: "It is unnecessary to enquire whether by Abaddon, the Destroyer, the Seer means Death or Satan."[85]

The seriousness of the last three trumpet-judgments is again (cf. 8:13) emphasized: **One woe is past; and, behold, there come two woes more hereafter** (12). The bell seems to be tolling the death knell of life on earth.

6. *The Sixth Trumpet: Destroying Angels* (9:13-21)

When **the sixth angel sounded** his trumpet, John **heard a voice from the four horns of the golden altar which is before God** (13). This seems to be a reference to the prayers of the saints (cf. 6:10; 8:3-5).

The angel of the sixth trumpet is commanded: **Loose the four angels which are bound in the great river Euphrates** (14). These do not seem to be the same four angels as those in 7:1. For they were holding back the winds of judgment, while these are themselves **bound.**

The Euphrates marked the ideal eastern limit of the Promised Land (Gen. 15:18). Beyond it lay the great empires of Assyria and Babylonia. Assyria overthrew the northern kingdom of Israel, and Babylonia the southern kingdom of Judah. In olden times these were the dreaded foes of the Israelites. "Thus the idea presented by the angels of vengeance bound on the banks of the Euphrates is that the day of vengeance was held back only till God's time has come. When at length they are loosed, the flood will burst its barriers, and ruin will follow."[86] The Euphrates is mentioned again in connection with the sixth bowl (16:12). In the time of Domitian it was the Parthians, east of the Euphrates, who were the most dreaded enemies of Rome.

In response to the command, **the four angels were loosed, which were prepared for an hour, and a day, and a month, and a year** (15). This is literally, "for the hour and day and month

[85]*Op. cit.*, p. 120.

[86]*Ibid.*, p. 121.

and year." It is to be thought of as one period of time. The purpose of freeing the angels was **to slay the third part of men.** Here is death, not just torment as in the previous trumpet-judgment. Yet it is not final and complete: only a third of men are to be killed.

The number of the invading **army of the horsemen** (16) is given as 200,000,000. The **fire and smoke and brimstone** (17) is a reminder of the destruction of Sodom and Gomorrah (Gen. 19: 24, 28). These three plagues killed a **third part of men** (18). **For their power is in their mouth** (19) has already been explained in 17-18 as fire, smoke, and brimstone issuing from the horses' mouths. The **tails** of the horses are likened to **serpents** with **heads,** by means of which they **hurt** (inflicted injury). There may be here a reference to the Parthian custom of binding their horses' tails so that they looked like snakes.

One would have thought that all this would be a sufficient warning to those who remained alive. But such was not the case. **The rest of the men which were not killed by these plagues yet repented not of the works of their hands** (20). McDowell calls this section: "The Tragedy of Unrepenting Humanity."[87] Suffering does not always draw men to God; sometimes it drives them farther away from Him. That sad fact was illustrated widely in the Second World War. It resulted more in apostasy than revival.

These unrepentant men continued to **worship devils** (demons), **and idols.** The idols were made of various substances, but all were material—senseless, impotent images. Also the men refused to repent of their **murders . . . sorceries . . . fornication . . . thefts** (21). Idolatry and immorality, these twin sins of the heathen world, continued unabated in spite of divine judgment. Men have free wills, and God cannot compel them to repent.

Preterist interpreters (see Intro., "Interpretation") refer these trumpets to the turbulent times of the Roman Empire. *Futurists* identify them with the judgments of the Great Tribulation at the close of this age. Barnes, representing the *historicist* view, goes into much more detail. He refers the first trumpet to Alaric, king of the Goths (A.D. 410); the second to Attila, king of the Huns (447); the third to Genseric, king of the Vandals (455); and the fourth to Odoacer, king of the Herculi, who became king of Italy, thus overthrowing the Roman Empire in the West in 476. He then finds in 8:13 a shift from the West to the East. The locusts

[87]*Op. cit.*, p. 102.

(fifth trumpet) represent the Mohammedan conquerors, who swept over north Africa and western Asia. The sixth trumpet he refers to the rise of Turkish power, culminating in the capture of Constantinople in 1453, which brought to an end the Roman Empire in the East. This is a typical example of the historicist interpretation.

Between the sixth and seventh seals there was a lengthy interlude, covering all of c. 7. Now we find between the sixth and seventh trumpets an even more extended parenthesis (10:1—11:14). In both cases the seventh (seal or trumpet) opens up into a new series of revelations.

Interlude: Two Preparatory Visions (10:1—11:14)

As the interlude between the sixth and seventh seals (c. 7) consisted of two visions, so does this interlude between the sixth and seventh trumpets. Apparently two things had to be done in preparation for the sounding of the last trumpet.

a. The angel with the little book (10:1-11). John **saw another mighty angel come down** (lit., "coming down") **from heaven** (1). He was **clothed with a cloud**—the vehicle described in the Bible as used by heavenly beings in descending to earth and ascending again (cf. Ps. 104:3; Dan. 7:13; Acts 1:9; I Thess. 4:17). The angel had **a rainbow** (*iris*) **upon his head, and his face was as it were the sun.** This sounds like the description of the glorified Christ in 1:16; but it is generally agreed that **another mighty angel** would not refer to the Son of God. **His feet** (the Gk. word is better translated here as "legs") were **as pillars of fire.** He glowed with beauty and strength.

The angel **had in his hand a little book open** (2)—a small papyrus scroll. This is in contrast to the tightly sealed book of 5:1. Swete says of the one here: "The little open roll contained but a fragment of the great purpose which was in the Hand of God, a fragment ripe for revelation."[88]

The **mighty angel**—evidently mighty in size as well as in strength—**set his right foot upon the sea, and his left foot on the earth.** These two elements would represent the whole world. He thus dramatized the authority of heaven over all the earth.

Having taken this posture, the angel **cried** out **with a loud voice,** like the roar of **a lion** (3). This was in keeping with his colossal size. At his cry, **seven thunders uttered their voices.**

[88]*Op. cit.*, pp. 126-27.

This is an echo of the sevenfold "voice of the Lord" in Psalms 29.

John was **about to write** (4). But a voice from heaven commanded him: **Seal up those things which the seven thunders uttered, and write them not.** Paul had a similar experience (II Cor. 12:4). There has been much speculation as to what the seven thunders said. But Swete puts the case well when he writes: "What the utterances were, or why they were not to be revealed, it is idle to enquire."[89]

The mighty angel then **lifted up his hand to heaven** (5) and swore by the eternal Creator of all things **that there should be time no longer** (6). This is often misquoted as, "Time shall be no more," and applied to the beginning of eternity. But that is obviously incorrect. For in the Book of Revelation many more events take place in time before eternity is ushered in with the new heaven and earth (cc. 21—22). The correct meaning of the statement is: "There shall be no more delay!" (Phillips) The judgments of God on unrepentant humanity cannot be postponed any longer. They will soon fall, when **the seventh angel . . . shall begin to sound** (7). Then will be **the mystery of God.** This phrase is used by Paul in Col. 2:2, where it refers to Christ as the Saviour of all mankind, Jews and Gentiles alike—that is, all who will accept His salvation. Redemption will be **finished** (completed) at the second coming of Christ.

Then John was instructed to **take the little book** (8) from **the angel** who held it. When he asked for it, the angel answered: **Take it, and eat it up; and it shall make thy belly bitter, but it shall be in thy mouth sweet as honey** (9). The last clause reflects a truth expressed more than once in the Psalms: "The judgments of the Lord are . . . sweeter also than honey and the honeycomb" (Ps. 19:9-10); "How sweet are thy words unto my taste! yea, sweeter than honey to my mouth!" (Ps. 119:103)

When John ate the book, he found that the angel's prediction was fulfilled: **It was in my mouth sweet as honey: and as soon as I had eaten it, my belly was bitter** (10). It will be noted that the order here is the reverse of that in the previous verse. Charles gives a good explanation: "In 9 the importance of the results that followed the eating of the book is emphasized, and accordingly these are placed first; in this verse the events are given in the order of the Seer's experience."[90]

The incident recorded here looks back to a similar occasion

[89]*Ibid.*, p. 128.

[90]*Op. cit.*, I, 268.

in the life of Ezekiel. He was commanded to eat a "roll of a book" which was presented to him. He says that he ate it, "and it was in my mouth as honey for sweetness" (Ezek. 3:3). Nothing is said about its becoming bitter in his stomach. However, we are told that in the roll were written "lamentations, and mourning, and woe." Certainly the digestion of these ideas must have been unpleasant.

Also Jeremiah says: "Thy words were found, and I did eat them; and thy word was unto me the joy and rejoicing of mine heart." Yet he declares in the very next verse: "I sat alone because of thy hand: for thou hast filled me with indignation" (Jer. 15:16-17).

On this strange mixture Swete makes the helpful observation: "Every revelation of God's purposes, even though a mere fragment, a *biblaridion* [little roll], is 'bitter-sweet,' disclosing judgement as well as mercy. The Seer, if he would be admitted into a part of God's secret, must be prepared for very mixed sensations; the first joy of fuller knowledge would be followed by sorrows deeper and more bitter than those of ordinary men."[91] The same is true of the consecrated Christian today. To be close to Christ is to experience the exquisite sweetness of His presence. But there is also a price to pay, that of sharing His sorrows in the face of sin that destroys men for whom He died.

The commission, **Thou must prophesy again before many peoples, and nations, and tongues, and kings** (11), reminds us of similar binding orders given to Jeremiah (1:9-10). John the Revelator was in the royal succession of prophets who received divine revelations and were commanded to convey them to men.

John was to eat the roll before he prophesied. McDowell comments: "By the symbolism of the eating of the roll, he indicates the necessity of assimilating his message, of making his message a part of himself, as a prerequisite to its delivery."[92] This is what every preacher must do with the Word of God.

b. The two witnesses (11:1-14). John was given **a reed like unto a rod** (1). The **reed** was a cane plant that grew along the Jordan valley (cf. Matt. 11:7), often to the height of fifteen feet. This reed was **like unto a rod** ("staff," RSV) in strength and straightness, but longer. Ezekiel saw a man measuring the new temple with a reed about ten feet long (Ezek. 40:5). Zechariah also mentions a man measuring Jerusalem, but with a line (Zech.

[91]*Op. cit.*, p. 131.

[92]*Op. cit.*, p. 110.

2:1-2). In 21:15, John will see an angel measuring the new Jerusalem with a golden reed.

The seer was told to **rise, and measure the temple** (*naos,* sanctuary) **of God, and the altar, and them that worship therein.** The **temple** here evidently means the Church of Jesus Christ, as in Paul's Epistles (I Cor. 3:16; II Cor. 6:16; Eph. 2:21). Swete writes: "The measuring of the Sanctuary provides for its preservation from the general overthrow, and thus corresponds to the sealing of the 144,000, which preceded the seventh seal-opening as the measuring precedes the seventh trumpet-blast."[93] That the measuring corresponds to the sealing is suggested by the fact that John was to measure **them that worship therein.**

One restriction was made, however: **But the court which is without the temple leave out, and measure it not; for it is given unto the Gentiles** (2). This was the Court of the Gentiles in the Temple of Jesus' day, covering something like twenty acres. Only Jews could go beyond it to the inner courts. John was told that this outer court he was to **leave out**—literally, "cast out outside." It would be profaned along with the rest of the city. Swete comments: "If the *naos* [**temple,** sanctuary] represents the Church, the outer court is perhaps the rejected Synagogue; as in ii. 9, iii. 9, the tables are turned, and while the Church fills the court of Israelites and worships at the Altar of the Cross (Heb. xiii. 10), Israel after the flesh is cast out (Mt. viii. 12) . . . and delivered to the heathen."[94]

Of the Gentiles it is said, **And the holy city shall they tread under foot** (cf. Isa. 63:18; Dan. 8:13; Zech. 12:3; and especially Luke 22:22) **forty and two months;** that is, three and a half years. It is equivalent to **a thousand two hundred and threescore days** (3).

To what does this refer? Some *preterists* (see Intro., "Interpretation") find their answer in the three and a half years of the Jewish revolt, culminating in the destruction of Jerusalem by the Romans in A.D. 70. This put a final end to the offering of animal sacrifices in the Temple, which has never been rebuilt since that time. Other preterist interpreters, such as McDowell, think that the forty-two months simply represent "short, incomplete periods of time."[95] He does say, however: "The most likely explanation of the difficult symbolism of this section is that it

[93]*Op. cit.,* p. 133. [94]*Ibid.*

[95]*Op. cit.,* p. 113.

is to be understood against the background of the destruction of Jerusalem and the Temple."[96] Kepler says that three and a half years is "the conventional period in which evil forces reign, since Antiochus IV desecrated the Temple when the Olympian Zeus was worshiped there for three and one-half years, 168-165 B.C."[97] This was the worst crisis through which the Jews passed between the Babylonian captivity and the fall of Jerusalem in A.D. 70.

The *historicists* look at a later period. Barnes holds that c. 10 describes the Protestant Reformation (16th cent.). Using the so-called "year-day principle"—that each day in Revelation equals a year—he finds in the 1,260 days a reference to 1,260 years of papal supremacy, ending in 1517.

The *futurists* refer the time element to the three and a half years of the reign of the Antichrist, what is known as the Great Tribulation at the end of this age. The interpretation is based on Dan. 7:25, "And he shall speak great words against the Most High, and shall wear out the saints of the Most High . . . and they shall be given into his hand until a time and times and the dividing of time"; that is, three and a half years. This is usually connected with Daniel's seventieth week (a week means seven years), described in Dan. 9:27, "And he shall confirm the covenant with many for one week: and in the midst of the week he shall cause the sacrifice and the oblation to cease, and for the overspreading of abomination he shall make it desolate, even until the consummation, and that determined shall be poured upon the desolate." That is, the second half of the seventieth "week" will be the Great Tribulation. It should be noted that this interpretation inserts the whole Church age (beginning in A.D. 30) between the sixty-ninth and seventieth weeks of Daniel. According to the *futurist* view, the first two verses of c. 11 "portray the spiritual security of the Church during the era of Antichrist's sway."[98]

We come now to the identification of the **two witnesses** (3), who will prophesy for three and a half years, **clothed in sackcloth** (a sign of penitence and mourning). They have been identified as Moses and Elijah, Elijah and Elisha, or Enoch and Elijah. The reason for suggesting the last pair is that they are the only two individuals in the Old Testament who are said not to

[96]*Ibid.*, p. 112. [97]*Op. cit.*, p. 119.

[98]G. R. Beasley-Murray, "The Revelation," *The New Bible Commentary*, ed. F. Davidson (2nd ed.; London: Inter-Varsity Fellowship, 1954), p. 1182.

have died. The reasoning goes that they must come back to earth during the Great Tribulation and die (cf. 7), since all men must die sometime. But there is nothing in the passage here to indicate Enoch and Elijah, although Tertullian held this view in the second century. Swete would rule out all personal identifications. He writes: "Rather the witnesses represent the Church in her function of witness-bearing."[99]

The two witnesses are described symbolically as **the two olive trees, and the two candlesticks** (lampstands) **standing before the God of the earth** (4). The language is clearly derived from Zech. 4:2-3, where "two olive trees" are mentioned, although there are "seven lamps." The olive trees are evidently thought of as supplying the oil for the lamps (Zech. 4:12). So here the two witnesses shine brightly in testimony for their Lord. In Zech. 4:14 the "two anointed ones" are said to "stand by the Lord of the whole earth," as here.

The reference to destroying **their enemies** by **fire** (5) seems to point to Elijah (II Kings 1:10-12), as also the mention of **power to shut heaven, that it rain not in the days of their prophecy** (6; cf. I Kings 17:1). On the other hand, **have power over waters to turn them to blood, and to smite the earth with all plagues** is an even more striking allusion to Moses in Egypt. It was Moses and Elijah who were with Jesus on the Mount of the Transfiguration (Matt. 17:3), representing the law and the prophets. It would seem that if the two witnesses must be identified with individuals, Moses and Elijah would have the preference. Phillips interprets the last part of v. 5, "Indeed if any one should try to hurt them, this is the way in which he will certainly meet his death."

At the end of the three and a half years' ministry of the two witnesses, **the beast that ascendeth out of the bottomless pit** (the abyss, see comments on 20:1) **shall make war against them, and shall overcome them, and kill them** (7). **The beast** is identified by *preterists* (see Intro., "Interpretation") as being the imperial might of Rome. For instance, Swete writes: "The Seer anticipates a struggle between the Church and the whole power of the Roman Empire; he foresees that the troubles which began under Nero and Domitian will end in such a conflict as was actually brought about under Decius and in the last persecution under Diocletian"; he adds: "But his words cover in effect all the

[99]*Op. cit.*, p. 134.

martyrdoms and massacres of history in which brute force has seemed to triumph over truth and righteousness."[100]

Representing the *historicists,* Barnes identifies the two witnesses with the persecuted sects of the Middle Ages and the beast with the papacy. *Futurists* agree that the beast is the Antichrist, though they differ on the two witnesses.

The **dead bodies** (8) of the two prophets **lie in the street of the great city, which spiritually is called Sodom and Egypt, where also our Lord was crucified.** The last clause seems to identify this as Jerusalem. The rulers and people of Judah are called "ye rulers of Sodom" and "ye people of Gomorrah" (Isa. 1:10). It was in Jerusalem that the first Christian martyrs met their fate. There may also be a reference to Rome as the later center of persecution.

The dead bodies lie unburied—a tragic indignity in the eyes of Jews—for **three days and an half** (9). This was "as many days as the years of the witnesses' prophesying—a short triumph in point of fact, but long enough to bear the semblance of being complete and final."[101]

In his handling of the three and a half days Barnes shows the attention to minute detail which usually marks the historicist interpreters. According to his year-day principle, the three days and a half represent three and a half years. He dates this as being between May 5, 1514, when the Lateran council made the proclamation that all opposition to the papacy had ceased, and October 31, 1517, when Luther posted his ninety-five theses.[102] But this seems a bit fanciful.

After much gleeful celebrating by the people of the city—because the **two prophets** had **tormented** (10) the consciences of their hearers—**the Spirit of life from God** (11) entered into the two witnesses and **they stood to their feet. A voice from heaven** called to them . . . And **they ascended up to heaven in a cloud** (12), in plain sight of their enemies. At that time there was **a great earthquake, and the tenth part of the city fell** (13). **Seven thousand** men were slain in the earthquake, leaving the survivors thoroughly frightened, so that they **gave glory to the God of heaven.** John's first readers of Revelation, in Asia Minor, were all too familiar with destructive earthquakes. This figure would strike a note of terror in their hearts. **Earthquake** literal-

[100]*Ibid.*, p. 137.

[101]*Ibid.*, p. 138.

[102]*Op. cit.*, pp. 291-92.

ly means "a shaking." There have been many shocks and upheavals in the history of humanity, but the worst are yet to come at the close of this age.

In v. 14 we again have a pause: **The second woe is past; and, behold, the third woe cometh quickly.** This is similar to 9:12. These last three trumpet-judgments were far more severe than the first four. Now, after a lengthy interlude (10:1—11:14), the stage is set for the sounding of the seventh trumpet.

7. *The Seventh Trumpet: Consummation* (11:15-19)

When **the seventh angel sounded . . . there were great voices in heaven** (15). This is in marked contrast to the opening of the seventh seal, when "there was silence in heaven" (8:1). These **voices** may have been those of the four living creatures (cf. 6:1, 3, 5, 7), though they are not mentioned here.

John heard the most wonderful announcement ever made: **The kingdoms of this world are become the kingdoms of our Lord, and of his Christ; and he shall reign for ever and ever.** At this point the millennium is anticipated, though it does not actually arrive until c. 20.

Next John saw the twenty-four elders fall on their faces, worshiping God (16). From them came a hymn of thanksgiving to the **Lord God Almighty** (17). Once more He is described as the Eternal One, **which art, and wast, and art to come** (cf. 1:4, 8; 4:8). The **elders,** representing the redeemed of all time (see comments on 4:4), rejoice **because thou hast taken to thee thy great power, and hast reigned.** God's unlimited strength is about to be displayed in overcoming all enemies and setting up His kingdom.

The nations were angry (18) points back to the second psalm, which is quoted in Acts 4:25-26 in connection with Pilate's crucifixion of Christ. Here it is given a wider application. The world's hostility to the rule of God is coming into final focus.

The result is that **thy wrath is come, and the time of the dead, that they should be judged.** But it is also the time of giving **reward** (lit., "the wages") **unto thy servants the prophets, and to the saints, and them that fear thy name, small and great.** The least believer, if faithful, will get his reward. But God will **destroy them which destroy the earth.** All enemies of mankind will finally be done away with. The horrors of war will be ended forever.

The vision of the seventh trumpet closes with a surprising note: **And the temple** (sanctuary) **of God was opened in heaven, and there was seen in his temple the ark of his testament** ("covenant," 19). The ark, which was in the holy of holies of the ancient Tabernacle and Temple, disappeared in 586 B.C. when the Temple was destroyed. Probably it perished at the time. A later legend held that Jeremiah hid the ark in a cave (cf. II Maccabees 2:5). Regarding the significance of its mention here, Swete writes: "In Christ God has made a new covenant with men . . . and the appearance of the Ark of the Covenant through the opened doors of the heavenly temple, at the moment when the time has come for the faithful to receive their reward, indicates the restoration of perfect access to God through the Ascension of the Incarnate Christ."[103]

The manifestation of the divine presence was accompanied by **lightnings, and voices, and thunderings, and an earthquake, and great hail.** Appropriately Alford calls these "the solemn salvos, so to speak, of the artillery of heaven, with which each series of visions is concluded."[104]

John has brought us up to the time of final judgment and victory. But again he dips back to describe further scenes of tribulation.

D. The Sevenfold Vision, 12:1—14:20

It might be expected that the seven bowls (cc. 15—16) would follow immediately after the seven seals (cc. 6—7) and the seven trumpets (cc. 8—11). Instead we find this long interlude which reveals the real nature of the conflict between God and Satan. In one sense this is the core of the Book of Revelation, for it seems to summarize the entire Messianic period, from the birth of Christ until the full establishment of His kingdom.

1. *The Woman and the Dragon* (12:1-6)

John saw **in heaven** (in the sky) **a great wonder** (1); rather, "a great sign."[105] It was **a woman clothed with the sun, and the moon under her feet, and upon her head a crown of twelve**

[103]*Op. cit.*, p. 145. [104]*Op. cit.*, IV, 667.

[105]*Semeion* occurs seventy-seven times in the NT. In KJV it is correctly translated "sign" fifty times and incorrectly as "miracle" twenty-three times. **Wonder** is the rendering only here and in 12:3; 13:13. It may mean "token" (II Thess. 3:17).

stars. The stars represent the twelve tribes of Israel or the twelve apostles of the Early Church. She was about to give birth to a child and was already suffering in labor. Though clothed with glory, she **cried** with pain (2).

What is represented by the **woman?** Many answers have been given. The early Church Fathers held that the woman was the Church or, as some said, Mary the mother of Jesus. The woman's birth pangs symbolized the spiritual travail of the Church. R. H. Charles writes: "In its *present* context this woman represents the true Israel or the community of believers. This community embraces Jewish and Gentile Christians, all of whom are to undergo the last great tribulation"; he adds: "But since the woman is represented as the mother of the Messiah, the community which she symbolizes must embrace the true O.T. Israel."[106]

Seiss has usually been recognized as the standard expositor of the premillenarian point of view. He holds that the woman cannot represent either the Jewish or Christian Church exclusively, but both. He goes on to say: "There has really been but one Church on earth, existing through all times and under all economies. And so we have here, as the symbol of it, this one glorious woman, in whom all its highest excellencies and chief characteristics are summed up from the beginning even unto the great consummation."[107] This is probably the best view.

John saw **another wonder** ("sign," 3). It was **a great red dragon, having seven heads and ten horns, and seven crowns upon his heads.** We are not left in doubt as to the identity of the dragon, for it is specifically said to be Satan (9). **Red** is literally "fiery red," symbolizing the murderous work of the dragon. The **seven heads** and **seven crowns** speak of fullness of power and authority. **Horns** are also a symbol of power or strength. Of the **seven heads** Seiss writes: "Hence we have in these heads the symbol of the entire imperial government of this world from beginning to end, the universal secular dominion of the earth in all periods."[108] Concerning the **ten horns** he says: "The number of them is *ten,* the number of worldly completeness, especially in the line of worldly evil. All the tyrannies, oppressions, and hard in-

[106]*Op. cit.,* I, 315.

[107]*The Apocalypse* (10th ed.: New York: Charles C. Cook, 1909 [copyrighted 1865]), II, 277.

[108]*Ibid.,* p. 303.

flictions that have tortured mankind, from the beginning to the end of them, are ascribed to Satan."[109]

There may be some significance to the fact that, beginning with the late second century, the dragon came to be used, along with the eagle, as a Roman ensign.[110] Thus the Roman Empire thought of itself as having the characteristics of a dragon.

It is further stated of the dragon that **his tail drew the third part of the stars of heaven, and did cast them to the earth** (4). The language here is a reminder of Dan. 8:10, "And it waxed great, even to the host of heaven; and it cast down some of the host and of the stars to the ground, and stamped upon them."

Ancient interpreters took this passage in Revelation as referring to the fall of Satan, who took with him one-third of the angels of heaven (cf. Milton's *Paradise Lost*). This appears to find support in the statement that the dragon's "angels were cast out with him" (9). Most modern commentators take the reference in 4 only as emphasizing Satan's great power.

A period should be placed in the middle of verse 4. The new sentence reads: **And the dragon stood before the woman which was ready to be delivered, for to devour her child as soon as it was born.** The reference to Herod's attempt to kill the baby Jesus (Matt. 2:16-18) is too obvious to miss. But probably Christ's experiences in the Temptation (Matt. 4:1-11) and in Gethsemane (Luke 22:39-46) should also be included.

The account continues: **And she brought forth a man child, who was to rule all nations with a rod of iron** (5). The reference is clearly to the Messianic passage in Ps. 2:9, "Thou shalt break them [the nations] with a rod of iron." The **man child** is Christ. He was **caught up unto God, and to his throne.** This refers to the Ascension (Luke 24:51).

It is further stated that **the woman fled into the wilderness, where she hath a place prepared of God, that they should feed her there a thousand two hundred and threescore days** (6). There may be a minor reference here to the flight of Mary and Joseph to Egypt, taking the child Jesus to escape the wrath of Herod (Matt. 2:13-15). A more significant application would be to the flight of the Christians from Jerusalem to Pella, when threatened by the Roman armies (see comments on Matt. 24:16, BBC, VI, 217-18). But it may also have a more general reference to the Church's protection from persecution at many times in

[109] *Ibid.*, p. 305.

[110] Barnes, *op. cit.*, pp. 305-6.

its history, and particularly in the Great Tribulation at the close of this age. The last interpretation seems to be suggested by the mention again of 1,260 days.

2. *The Defeat of the Dragon* (12:7-17)

A war now ensued in heaven between **Michael and his angels** and **the dragon . . . and his angels** (7). Some commentators find here a reference to the ancient revolt of Lucifer, who became Satan. Others give it a general application to the seemingly endless conflict between the forces of good and evil.

Michael is described in Daniel as "one of the chief princes" (10:13) and "your prince" (10:21). Also Daniel is told: "And at that time shall Michael stand up, the great prince which standeth for the children of thy people: and there shall be a time of trouble, such as never was since there was a nation even to that same time: and at that time thy people shall be delivered, every one that shall be found written in the book" (12:1). This seems like a clear reference to the Great Tribulation at the close of this age. So the war between Michael and the dragon not only typifies the perennial struggle between God and Satan but also has special application to the final conflicts at the end of the present age.

But the dragon and his angels **prevailed not; neither was their place found any more in heaven** (8). **And the great dragon was cast out, that old serpent, called the Devil, and Satan, which deceiveth the whole world: he was cast out into the earth, and his angels were cast out with him** (9).

The mention of **serpent** carries us back to the Garden of Eden, where Satan under the guise of a serpent successfully tempted Eve to disobey God's command (Genesis 3). **The Devil** (*ho diabolos,* the Slanderer or False Accuser) is the term used in the Septuagint for **Satan** (Heb.), which is here taken over into Greek and also English. It means "the Adversary." But the use of *diabolos* (Gk.) in the Septuagint as the translation for *Satan* (Heb.) shows that the two terms were considered as synonymous. They are used interchangeably in the Gospels ("Satan" seventeen times; "devil" fifteen times).

When were Satan and his angels cast out of heaven to the earth? Milton in his *Paradise Lost* (Bk. I) portrays this as taking place in the dim past of pre-human history (cf. Jude 6). But in Job 1:6 he is pictured as still having access to God's presence. Jesus declared that He saw Satan as having fallen from heaven

(Luke 10:18). This evidently refers to the Christian mission as already toppling the enemy from his throne as "the prince of this world" (John 12:31). But the specific reference in this passage in Revelation seems to be to Satan's ejection from power at the close of this age.

Then John **heard a loud voice saying in heaven, Now is come salvation, and strength** (*dynamis,* power), **and the kingdom of our God, and the power** (*exousia,* authority) **of his Christ: for the accuser of our brethren is cast down, which accused them before our God day and night** (10)—that is, without interruption. Swete comments: "The downfall of Satan manifests afresh . . . the saving and sovereign power of God, and its active exercise by the exalted Christ."[111]

Next comes an oft-quoted statement: **And they overcame** (had the victory over) **him by** (Gk., because of) **the blood of the Lamb**—Christ's death on the Cross—**and by** (because of) **the word of their testimony** (11). Our victory depends on His victory at Gethsemane and Golgotha, but it also depends on our faithful "word of witness" for Christ.

Of the Christians at that day it is said: **And they loved not their lives** (*psyche,* soul) **unto the death.** This is an echo of an emphasis found several times in the teachings of Jesus (cf. Matt. 10:39; 16:25; Mark 8:35-36; Luke 9:24; 17:33; John 12:25). Paul expressed a similar sentiment (Acts 20:24). This attitude must characterize every consecrated Christian.

The inhabitants of heaven are bidden to **rejoice** (12). But in contrast it is: **Woe to the inhabiters of the earth and of the sea! for the devil is come down unto you, having great wrath, because he knoweth that he hath but a short time** (cf. 14). Satan was furious, knowing he was doomed, and was determined to do his worst in the brief time that remained to him. So **he persecuted** (the Gk. word also means "pursued") **the woman which brought forth the man child** (13; cf. 1-5). For the identification of **the woman** see comments on 2.

The woman is **given two wings of a great eagle, that she might fly into the wilderness, into her place, where she is nourished for a time, and times, and half a time** (14)—that is, for three and a half years. This is a repetition of the statement made in 6 (see comments there). Some would find here a reference to the preservation of the nation of Israel during the three

[111]*Op. cit.*, p. 155.

and a half years of the Great Tribulation. Others apply it to the protection of the Church. The thought of eagles' **wings** is an echo of Exod. 19:4 and Deut. 32:11.

So enraged was **the serpent** that he **cast out of his mouth water as a flood after the woman, that he might cause her to be carried away of the flood** (15). The figure of persecution or trouble as a flood is common in the Scriptures (cf. Ps. 18:4; 32:6; 124:4-5; Isa. 43:2; 59:19). The passage here in Revelation is applicable to the Roman persecutions of the early Christians, as well as to the final, fierce onslaughts of Satan at the end of the age.

But the woman was rescued: **The earth opened her mouth, and swallowed up the flood which the dragon cast out of his mouth** (16). Swete makes this general application: "Help would arise from unexpected quarters; the death of the persecuting Emperor, followed by a change of policy on the part of his successors, sudden revulsions of public feeling, or a fresh turn of events diverting public attention from the Church, would from time to time check or frustrate Satan's plans."[112] Just how literally this passage may be fulfilled in the Great Tribulation no one can say.

Bereft of his prey, the dragon "went off" (*apelthen*) **to make war with the remnant of her seed, which keep the commandments of God, and have the testimony of Jesus Christ** (17). To make these last two clauses refer respectively to Jewish and Gentile believers[113] seems oversubtle. All Christians are probably meant.

3. *The Beast Out of the Sea* (13:1-10)

John[114] **saw a beast** (*therion*, wild beast) **rise up out of the sea** (1). Swete writes: "The Sea is an apt symbol of the agitated surface of unregenerate humanity (cf. Isa. lvii. 20), and especially of the seething caldron of national and social life, out of which the great historical movements of the world arise."[115]

The connection of this chapter with the previous one (see note 114) is described by Charles in this way: "The dragon foiled

[112] *Ibid.*, p. 159. [113] Seiss, *op. cit.*, II, 382.

[114] **And I stood upon the sand of the sea** (1) is, in the oldest Greek MSS., "And he stood on the sand of the sea." This would place it with the previous chapter (cf. RSV).

[115] *Op. cit.*, p. 161.

in his attempt to destroy the Messiah and His Community proceeds to the shore of the sea and summons from it the Beast (i.e. the Roman Empire) in order to arm it with his own power."[116]

The beast had **seven heads and ten horns.** The same description is given of the scarlet beast in 17:3. The significance of these items is explained in 17:9-12 (see comments there). Upon the horns were **ten crowns.** The Greek word is *diadema* (royal crown).

The seer noted **upon his heads the name of blasphemy.** The first application of this, the *preterist* view (see Intro., "Interpretation"), would be to the blasphemous titles assumed by the Roman emperors of the first and second centuries. Abundant documentation for this has been found in the imperial letters discovered among the inscriptions at Ephesus. Several times "son of God" appears with an emperor's name, while others called themselves simply "God." On his coins Nero called himself "The Savior of the World." One can well imagine what a shock this was to the early Christians, who allowed these claims only to Christ. It is said that Domitian, who was reigning when John wrote the Book of Revelation, insisted on being called "our Lord and our God."[117] To the Christians this was double blasphemy.

Barnes, representing the *historicist* view, cites blasphemous claims made by the papacy.[118] *Futurists* interpret the passage as meaning that the Antichrist will arrogate to himself divine authority.

The beast which John **saw was like unto a leopard, and his feet were as the feet of a bear, and his mouth as the mouth of a lion** (2). The imagery is taken from Dan. 7:3-7. In Daniel's vision, four beasts came up from the sea. The first was like a lion, the second like a bear, the third like a leopard, and the fourth was "dreadful and terrible, and strong exceedingly."

The one beast of Revelation combines the features of the first three beasts of Daniel in reverse order. Like the fourth beast it has "ten horns." The four beasts of Daniel represent respectively the Babylonian, Medo-Persian, Greek, and Roman empires. It would seem, then, that the beast of Revelation first of all represents the Roman Empire, which had the characteristics of the previous three but was more "dreadful and terrible." There can be no doubt but that for John's first readers this was the

[116]*Op. cit.*, I, 344.

[117]Simcox, *op. cit.*, p. 132.

[118]See his *Notes* on II Thess. 2:3-4.

interpretation given to this passage. The persecuting emperors were motivated by Satan: **and the dragon gave him his power, and his seat** (*thronon,* throne), **and great authority.**

The first-century historical background of this passage shows up most strikingly in the next verse: **And I saw one of his heads as it were wounded to death; and his deadly wound was healed: and all the world wondered after the beast** (3). This seems to be a clear allusion to the so-called Nero *redivivus.* The story of this is given by Swete:

> In June 68 Nero, pursued by the emissaries of the Senate, inflicted upon himself a wound of which he died. His remains received a public funeral, and were afterwards lodged in the mausoleum of Augustus. Nevertheless there grew up in the eastern provinces of the Empire a rumour that he was still alive, and in hiding. Pretenders who claimed to be Nero arose in 69 and 79, and even as late as 88 or 89. . . . The legend of Nero's survival or resuscitation took root in the popular imagination, and Dion Chrysostom . . . at the end of the century sneers at it as one of the follies of the time. Meanwhile the idea of Nero's return had begun to take its place in the creations of Jewish and Christian fancy. . . . The legend has been used by St. John to represent the revival of Nero's persecuting policy by Domitian.[119]

This, of course, does not rule out an application to the Anti-Christ at the close of the age. But the first rule in interpreting any prophecy is to note its background in the history of its own day.

All the world **worshipped the dragon which** (Gk., "because he") **gave power** (Gk., "the authority") **unto the beast** (4). Using language such as is properly used of God (cf. Exod. 15:11), the people cried, **Who is like unto the beast?** adding: **who is able to make war with him?** Swete observes: "It was not moral greatness but brute force which commanded the homage of the provinces."[120]

The beast continued **speaking great things and blasphemies** (5). In relation to the Roman emperors Swete says: "The assumption of Divine Names in public documents and inscriptions was a standing and growing blasphemy."[121]

The statement that the beast continued in power for **forty and two months**—equivalent to 3½ years or 1,260 days—is difficult to fit into the period of the Roman Empire. Barnes, using the

[119] *Op. cit.,* p. 163.
[120] *Ibid.,* p. 165.
[121] *Ibid.*

year-day principle, applies this to 1,260 years of papal supremacy (see comments on 11:2-3). But the final fulfillment of the prediction will take place in the 3½ years of the Great Tribulation.

The language of the next two verses seems to reach beyond the past and present to the future. In the fullest sense only the Antichrist will speak in **blasphemy against God, to blaspheme his name, and his tabernacle, and them that dwell in heaven** (6). He particularly will have **power** (authority) **over all kindreds, and tongues, and nations** (7). Only of him could it truly be said: **And all that dwell upon the earth shall worship him, whose names are not written in the book of life of the Lamb slain from the foundation of the world** (8).

If any man have an ear, let him hear (9) is repeated from 2:7, 11, 17 (see comments there). It is an exhortation to take heed to the warning that follows.

Verse 10 contains an obscure epigrammatic statement: **He that leadeth into captivity shall go into captivity** ("If any one is to be taken captive, to captivity he goes," RSV): **he that killeth with the sword must be killed with the sword.** Swete suggests: "The whole is a warning against any attempt on the part of the Church to resist its persecutors. If a Christian is condemned to exile, as St John had been, he is to regard exile as his allotted portion, and to go readily; if he is sentenced to death, he is not to lift his hand against the tyrant; to do so will be to deserve his punishment."[122] Thus the Christians, under persecution, could show **the patience and the faith of the saints.** Cf. Weymouth, "Here is an opportunity for endurance, and for the exercise of faith, on the part of the saints."

4. *The Beast out of the Earth* (13:11-18)

John tells us that he saw **another beast coming up out of the earth** (11). This one **had two horns like a lamb.** Thus he was more gentle in appearance than the first beast. Carpenter makes this general application: "All who use their knowledge, their culture, their wisdom, to teach men that there is nothing worthy of worship save what they can see, and touch, and taste, are acting the part of the second wild beast."[123]

[122] *Ibid.*, p. 168.

[123] "The Revelation of St. John," *Commentary on the Whole Bible*, ed. C. J. Ellicott (Grand Rapids: Zondervan Publishing House, n.d.), VIII, 598.

But though it looked like a lamb, it roared **as a dragon.** Simcox says: "No doubt the obvious view is right, that he looks like Christ and is like Satan."[124] This second beast seems clearly to be identified with the false prophet (16:13; 19:20; 20:10).

He exerciseth all the power (authority) **of the first beast before him, and causeth** (makes) **the earth and them which dwell therein to worship the first beast** (12). He does **great wonders** (signs), making **fire come down from heaven on the earth in the sight of men** (13), as Elijah did (I Kings 18:38). And he **deceiveth them that dwell on the earth, by the means of those miracles** (signs) **which he had power to do** (lit., which were given him to do) **in the sight of the beast** (14). The Israelites were warned against accepting false prophets who would try to deceive them by performing miracles (Deut. 13:1-3). He instructed the earth-dwellers to **make an image to the beast.** Furthermore, **he had power** (lit., it was given him) **to give life** (Gk., spirit) **unto the image of the beast, that the image should both speak, and cause** those who **would not worship** it to be killed (15). One is reminded of the ancient demand for worshiping Nebuchadnezzar's golden image (Dan. 3:1-6).

Men of all classes and conditions are made to **receive a mark in their right hand, or in their foreheads** (16). This is what is popularly known as "the mark of the beast." All attempts to identify this with current symbols or names are only wild speculations which dishonor the Word of God.

Concerning the word **mark** (*charagma*), Simcox writes that it is "the brand put upon slaves to identify them; pagan devotees sometimes received such a brand, marking them as the property of their god."[125] Rist says that it was "the technical term for the imperial stamp on official documents."[126]

This "mark of the beast" is the opposite to what is described in 7:1. There "the servants of our God" are sealed in their foreheads, protecting them from the divine judgments about to be poured out on the earth.

In III Maccabees 2:29 it is stated that Ptolemy Philopator (217 B.C.) commanded the Jews of Alexandria to be branded with the ivy-leaf insignia of the god Dionysus. This forms a striking parallel.

No man could **buy or sell** unless he **had the mark, or the**

[124]*Op. cit.*, p. 135. [125]*Ibid.*, p. 136.

[126]*Op. cit.*, p. 465.

name of the beast, or the number of his name (17). Probably Swete is right in taking the last two phrases as being in apposition with **the mark.** Of the enigmatic relation of **name** and **number** he says: "Where the heathen provincial saw only the name of the reigning Emperor, the Christian detected a mystical number with its associations of vice and cruelty."[127] It must be remembered that in Hebrew, Greek, and Latin each letter of the alphabet has a numerical equivalent. So all names in these three languages represent exact numbers.

Then comes a cryptic saying: **Here is wisdom** (18). This and the following expression, **him that hath understanding** (lit., having a mind), are closely paralleled in 17:9, "And here is the mind which hath wisdom." There is perhaps an echo of Dan. 12:10, "And none of the wicked shall understand; but the wise shall understand." Another parallel is Eph. 1:17, "the spirit of wisdom and revelation." Those who had this Spirit would understand what John was saying.

The number of the beast . . . is the number of a man—that is, a human number, or one that "is reckoned simply by an ordinary human method,"[128] assigning numerical values to the letters of the name.

The number 666[129] has had numberless explanations. Disregarding the fantastic ones, we may say that probably the original reference was to Nero. In the Latin form *Neron* the letters total 666. Dropping the last letter, the value would be 616, which may be the reason some manuscripts have the smaller number (see note 129). A third way of computing the numerical equivalence of Nero is to write Neron Caesar with Hebrew letters—the Hebrew has only consonants, no vowels. The total value of the Hebrew letters is 666.

Irenaeus (2nd cent.) thought it might stand for "Teitan," and so represent titanic power. He also called attention to the fact that the number equals *Lateinos* in Greek letters and so might represent the Roman Empire ("they being Latins that now reign").

In modern times the number has been variously computed as representing Mohammed, Luther, Pope Benedict IX, Napoleon, Kaiser Wilhelm (during World War I), Hitler (during World

[127] *Op. cit.*, p. 174.

[128] Simcox, *op. cit.*, p. 137.

[129] Some Greek MSS. have 616. But 666 seems to be the correct reading. It is found in the third-century Papyrus 47.

War II), and Mussolini (in between). Saner students of the Bible refer it to the Antichrist, without trying to identify the coming archenemy of Christ with any living individual.

It might be well to sum up the main interpretations of the two beasts of this chapter. *Preterists* (see Intro., "Interpretation") say they represent respectively Roman civil power (the empire) and Roman religious power (the pagan priesthood supporting emperor worship, particularly in the province of Asia). *Historicists* find here the Roman Empire and the Roman Catholic church (or the papacy), the Catholic church seeking to exercise all the authority of the empire (cf. 12). *Futurists* identify the first beast as the Antichrist, and the second as the false prophet. All of these interpretations are significant. It would seem to be the part of wisdom not to insist that only one is valid and the rest are wrong. In a sense all of Revelation (except cc. 19—22) applies to the past, the present, and the future.

It has often been pointed out that the number 6 represents man as imperfect, incomplete, in contrast to Christ, who is represented by the number 7, signifying completion or perfection. The number 666 simply multiplies threefold this idea that man is imperfect.

In the light of this the worship of the beast, whose number is 666, takes on added significance. This age will end with the worship of man, instead of the worship of God.

Already this trend is gaining great impetus. By the beginning of the twentieth century humanistic theology, denying the deity of Jesus and eliminating the supernatural from the Bible, had swept from Germany and Britain into America. Two World Wars, which gave every evidence of being apocalyptic judgments, saw a reaction in the form of neoorthodoxy. But this has been largely replaced by neoliberalism. The final fruit of all this is the "God is dead" movement, which sprang into the open in 1965. Having dismissed God from His universe, man is now worshiping himself. The stage is set for the worship of the beast.

5. *The 144,000* (14:1-5)

These are identified by Charles as "the same as the 144,000 in vii. 4-8, i.e. the spiritual Israel, the entire Christian community, alike Jewish and Gentile, which were sealed to protect them from demonic woes, that are to follow speedily."[130] See also the com-

[130]*Op cit.*, II, 4.

ments on 7:4. Why are they mentioned again at this time? Swete says: "The vision of the two Beasts and their followers is fitly followed by a reassuring picture of the Lamb in the midst of His Church."[131] Before the last seven plagues are poured out on the earth we are told once more that Christ's own are safely sealed. In contrast to those who had received the mark of the beast in their foreheads, these have **his Father's name written in their foreheads** (1).

Many commentators hold that **stood on the mount Sion** means that Christ had come back to earth and was standing in Jerusalem. But the meaning here is probably better expressed by reference to Heb. 12:22, "But ye are come unto mount Sion, and unto the city of the living God, the heavenly Jerusalem." The Lamb's followers are safe with Him in the eternal Kingdom.

Again there came **a voice from heaven** (2). It was **as the voice of many waters,** emphasizing the volume of the sound; **as the voice of a great thunder,** suggesting its loudness; and **the voice of harpers harping with their harps,** indicating "that it was articulate and sweet."[132]

And they sung (Gk., sing)[133] **a new song before the throne, and before the four beasts** ("living creatures"; see comments on 4:6), **and the elders** (see comments on 4:4): **and no man could learn that song but the hundred and forty and four thousand, which were redeemed from the earth** (3). The picture seems to be that of a heavenly choir singing a new song of praise for those who have been redeemed by the Lamb. Only those who have had a spiritual experience of salvation can sing it.

The redeemed are further described as **not defiled with women; for they are virgins** (4). The word **virgins** (*parthenoi*) is masculine in form. Some have taken this literally, as favoring a celibate clergy. But in line with the symbolical language of Revelation it seems best to take it as describing spiritual purity, the state of being undefiled. There is also perhaps the hint of moral purity. Swete says: "That chastity should be chosen as the first distinctive virtue of the Christian brotherhood will not seem strange to those who reflect that pagan life was honeycombed with immorality of the grossest kind."[134]

These redeemed Christians **follow the Lamb whithersoever**

[131]*Op. cit.,* p. 176.

[132]Simcox, *op. cit.,* pp. 138-39.

[133]**As it were** is not in the best Greek text.

[134]*Op. cit.,* p. 179.

he goeth. The **Lamb** is here the Shepherd. The Gospels relate how Jesus called on men to **follow** Him. But this is more than a geographical term. To follow Christ is to *imitate* Him, to live as He lived. Following Jesus is both a glorious privilege and a solemnizing challenge.

The term **firstfruits** has occasioned considerable discussion. How can this be applied to the Tribulation saints? The preterists, such as Swete, find a logical reference to the Christians of the first century. It could even fit the idea of the 144,000 representing the redeemed of all ages (see comments on 7:4). But to use it for the believers at the end of this age would seem strange. However, Charles solves the difficulty by pointing out the fact that nearly three out of four times in the Septuagint the Greek word here (*aparche*) means "offering," "sacrifice," or "gift."[135] All the redeemed are an offering **unto God and to the Lamb.**

Lastly, it is said of the followers of the Lamb: **And in their mouth was found no guile: for they are without fault before the throne of God** (5). On the first of these clauses Swete comments: "After purity truthfulness was perhaps the most distinctive mark of the followers of Christ, when contrasted with their heathen neighbours; cf. Eph. iv. 20-25."[136]

Without fault (*amomos*) is used frequently in the Septuagint for the requirement that animals being sacrificed to the Lord must be without blemish. In view of the reference to "offering" in the previous verse, it would seem that *amomos* should be taken here in the sense of "unblemished," or "spotless" (RSV).

6. *The Three Angels* (14:6-13)

Three angels appeared in succession, each making an important proclamation. The stage is being set for the seven last plagues.

a. The angel with the gospel (14:6-7). The first angel was flying **in the midst of heaven** (6)—lit., "in the meridian" (see comments on 8:13). This was so that he could be seen and heard.

He had **the everlasting gospel to preach unto them that dwell on the earth.** Some have tried to distinguish three different gospels in the New Testament: "the gospel of the kingdom" (Matt. 4:23), which was for the Jews; "the gospel of Jesus Christ" (Mark 1:1), which is for all men; and "the everlasting gospel,"

[135] *Op. cit.*, II, 6. [136] *Op. cit.*, p. 180.

to be proclaimed at the end of this age. But this is a false trichotomy. There is only one gospel, the good news of salvation through Jesus Christ.

The first angel's message was: **Fear God, and give glory to him; for the hour of his judgment is come: and worship him that made heaven, and earth, and the sea, and the fountains of waters** (7). The last phrase is found in the Old Testament (cf. I Kings 18:5; II Kings 3:19). It refers to sources of water in springs or wells.

The day of God's judgment, His reckoning with man, has come. Therefore people should repent and worship Him.

b. The angel of doom (14:8). The second angel cried: **Babylon is fallen, is fallen, that great city** (lit., "It fell, it fell, Babylon the Great"), **because she made all nations drink of the wine of her fornication.** The early Fathers interpreted **Babylon** in Revelation as being a symbolical name for Rome. Of the correctness of this view there can be little doubt.

The language of this verse is reminiscent of Jer. 51:7-8: "Babylon hath been a golden cup in the Lord's hand, that made all the earth drunken: the nations have drunken of her wine; therefore the nations are mad. Babylon is suddenly fallen and destroyed." There is a blending of two ideas: "Babylon makes the nations drink of the cup of her fornication; and she is made, and they are made with her . . . to drink of the cup of God's wrath: v. 10; xvi. 19. In xviii. 6 as in Jer. 51:7, from which the image is taken, there is, as probably here, a combination of the two."[187]

c. The angel of judgment (14:9-13). The announcement of **the third angel** was: **If any man worship the beast and his image, and receive his mark in his forehead, or in his hand, the same shall drink of the wine of the wrath of God** (9-10). It had already been stated that if anyone would not worship the image of the beast he would be killed (13:15). Now comes the warning from heaven that if one *does* worship that image he will suffer a worse fate than death. He will **drink of the wine** of God's **wrath** (*thymos,* hot anger), **which is poured out without mixture** (lit., has been mixed unmixed) **into** (in) **the cup of his indignation** (*orge,* wrath). **Without mixture** means "undiluted" (Phillips), or "in full strength."

[187]Simcox, *op. cit.,* p. 140.

The fate of the image-worshiper is described graphically: **He shall be tormented with fire and brimstone** ("in sulphurous flames," NEB) **in the presence of the holy angels, and in the presence of the Lamb.** What an awful thing to suffer for disobedience in the presence of the Lamb who obediently suffered to save! The language of this passage looks back to Isa. 30:33 and Ezek. 38:22. But the most striking parallel is the destruction of Sodom and Gomorrah (Gen. 19:24).

Still echoing that account (Gen. 19:38), but speaking now in eternal terms, the record says: **And the smoke of their torment ascendeth up for ever and ever** (11). To worship Caesar or the Antichrist is to renounce Christ, and so to be guilty of apostasy. The penalty for this is eternal torment. There is no **rest** (cessation) for those who reject the call of the One who said, "Come unto me, all ye that labour and are heavy laden, and I will give you rest" (Matt. 11:28).

Again (cf. 13:10, 18) we have an enigmatic statement: **Here is the patience of the saints** (12). The Greek word for **patience** signifies "endurance" or "steadfastness." Swete comments: "The Caesar-cult supplied the Saints with a test of loyalty which strengthened and matured those who were worthy of the name."[138] These are the ones who **keep the commandments of God, and the faith of Jesus;** that is, their faith in Jesus.

Then John **heard a voice from heaven** (13) uttering words that are usually quoted at a funeral service: **Blessed are the dead which die in the Lord from henceforth: Yea, saith the Spirit, that** (in that) **they may rest from their labours; and their works do follow them** (lit., with them). There is a contrast between **labours** and **works.** The Christian's **labours** end at death, but his good **works** follow along with him into the next life.

7. *The Time of Harvest* (14:14-20)

Two harvest scenes are portrayed here. The first is that of the wheat, with the Son of Man as the Reaper. The second is that of the grapes, gathered by an angel.

a. The harvest of wheat (14:14-16). John saw **a white cloud** (14) and sitting on it One **like unto the Son of man.** This reflects the language of Dan. 7:13, "I saw in the night visions, and, behold, one like the Son of man came with the clouds of heaven."

[138]*Op. cit.*, p. 186.

Since the title **Son of man** is applied by Jesus to himself some eighty-one times in the Gospels, it seems justifiable to assume that He is the One who is meant here.[139]

He had **on his head a golden crown** (*stephanos,* victor's crown), **and in his hand a sharp sickle.** It was apparently the time for reaping the harvest.

Now **another angel** (cf. 9) **came out of the temple** (sanctuary), **crying with a loud voice to him that sat on the cloud, Thrust in thy sickle, and reap: for the time is come for thee to reap; for the harvest of the earth is ripe** (15)—lit., "was dried up"; that is, "fully ripe" (RSV), or possibly "over-ripe" (ERV, NEB). **Thrust in** is literally "send" (*pempson*). This is an echo of Joel 3:13, "Put ye in [LXX, 'send'] the sickle, for the harvest is ripe." Jesus said: "But when the fruit is brought forth, immediately he putteth in [Gk., he sends] the sickle, because the harvest is come" (Mark 4:29).

The One sitting **on the cloud thrust in** (*ebalen,* "cast" or "put") **his sickle on the earth; and the earth was reaped** (16). Barnes interprets this harvest as Christ coming "to gather his people to himself." On the last clause he comments: "So far as the righteous were concerned, the end had come; the church was redeemed; the work contemplated was accomplished, and the results of the work of the Saviour were like a glorious harvest."[140]

b. The harvest of grapes (14:17-20). Just as the vintage naturally followed the wheat harvest (cf. Deut. 16:9, 13), so it was in the prophetic vision here. **Another angel came out of the temple . . . he also having a sharp sickle** (17). Still **another angel** appeared **from the altar,** one who **had power over fire** (18). On this strange allusion Simcox comments: "It may . . . be that 'the Angel of Fire' is made to invoke the judgement on the wicked which will be executed by fire. But it is easiest to understand that this is the Angel 'who had power over *the* fire on the Altar'—perhaps therefore the Angel whom we have already heard of, viii. 3-5."[141]

This angel called to the angel with the sickle: **Thrust in** (send) **thy sharp sickle, and gather the clusters of the vine of the earth; for her grapes are fully ripe**—lit., "are at the prime." So **the angel thrust in** (19)—lit., "cast" (cf. 16)—**his sickle into**

[139]**The Son of man** is without the definite article in the Greek. So some have insisted the passage here means "like a human being."

[140]*Op. cit.,* p. 350. [141]*Op. cit.,* p. 144.

the earth, and gathered the vine of the earth, and cast it into the great winepress of the wrath of God.

The winepress was trodden (20) recalls the language of Isa. 63:2-6. The terrible judgment took place **without** (outside) **the city,** evidently Jerusalem. Joel prophesied: "I will also gather all nations, and will bring them down into the valley of Jehoshaphat" (Joel 3:2). This is just south of Jerusalem.

Blood came out of the winepress, even unto the horse bridles, by the space of a thousand and six hundred furlongs (Gk., *stadia*). This represents about 200 Roman, or 183 English, miles. The figure has caused much discussion. Some take it as referring roughly to the length of Palestine (actually about 140 miles). Others feel it is symbolical of completeness (1,600 = 4 x 4 x 100). Thus it would signify destruction everywhere (except in the city). It seems evident that the language should be taken figuratively, not literally.

What is the relation of the two harvests described in this section? It would appear that Swete's explanation is reasonable. He writes: "In the Prophets the harvest, whether wheat-harvest or vintage, represents the overthrow of the enemies of Israel, who are ripe for their fall . . . the Apocalypse . . . like the Gospels identifies the wheat with the true 'children of the kingdom' (cf. Mt. xiii. 30, 38) . . . the vintage, from its association with the 'wine of wrath' . . . represents the evil." He adds: "Thus, by a new treatment of the old metaphor of a Divine harvesting of men, the Apocalyptist gives full expression to the Lord's teaching as to the great separation between man and man which is reserved for the Parousia,"[142] the Second Coming. In the first harvest the righteous are gathered; in the second, the wicked.

E. The Seven Bowls, 15:1—16:21

Introduction (15:1-8)

Chapter 15 gives the setting for the pouring out of the plagues contained in the seven bowls. It consists of three visions: (1) the waiting angels; (2) the victorious saints; (3) the emerging angels. Chapter 16 gives a description of each of the seven plagues.

a. The waiting angels (15:1). This verse really forms a heading for the contents of cc. 15—16. John **saw another sign in**

[142] *Op. cit.,* p. 190.

heaven, great and marvellous, seven angels having the seven last plagues; for in them is filled up the wrath of God. There is an air of finality about this. The language shows that these plagues will be climactic. **Filled up** literally means "brought to an end," "completed," or "finished." **Wrath** is *thymos,* "hot anger." An end must be brought to the sin which so long had afflicted humanity.

b. The victorious saints (15:2-4). John **saw as it were a sea of glass mingled with fire** (2). Probably this is the same sea of glass as in 4:6. There it is described as "like unto crystal" in its transparency. Here it had a ruddy glow, as if **mingled with fire.** Swete suggests: "The red glow on the Sea spoke of the fire through which the Martyrs passed, and yet more of the wrath about to fall on the world which had condemned them."[143]

On this glassy sea, as on a solid pavement, were standing **them that had gotten the victory over the beast**—lit., "those (coming) victorious from the wild beast." Lenski comments: "The conquering ones have come as victors 'out of' the battle with the wild beast, his image, and the number of his name."[144] This number, of course, is 666 (13:18). These victors have **the harps of God;** that is, harps which God had given them, or which belonged to the service of God. Harps have already been mentioned in 5:8 and 14:2.

These harpists sing as well as play. **They sing the song of Moses the servant of God** (3). The context shows that the reference is not to Moses' final song in Deuteronomy 32. Rather it is to the hymn of praise sounded at the Red Sea when God delivered the Israelites from the pursuing Egyptians (Exodus 15). This hymn was likewise a song of deliverance from the threatening beast.

But they also sang **the song of the Lamb.** They are victors with Christ over all the power of the enemy. For those of the time when John wrote, this meant the persecuting emperor. For Christians of various periods there have been many applications. At the end of this age it will be victory over the Antichrist.

The hymn of adoration found in the rest of 3 and 4 is composed almost entirely of words and phrases from the Old Testament (e.g., Ps. 86:8-10; 111:2; 139:14; Amos 4:13). God is praised for His wonderful works. **King of saints** rests on very slim manuscript evidence. The choice lies between "King of the na-

[143] *Ibid.,* p. 194.

[144] *Op. cit.,* p. 456.

tions" (Phillips) and "King of the ages" (RSV).[145] The context might seem slightly in favor of "King of the nations," which is what the beast claimed to be. Ultimately **all nations shall come and worship before thee** (4). For God's **judgments** (*dikaiomata*, righteous acts) **are made manifest** ("have been made plain," Phillips).

c. *The emerging angels* (15:5-8). John writes: **And after that** (Gk., these things) **I looked** ("saw," same verb as in 1), and there was opened **the temple** (sanctuary) **of the tabernacle of the testimony in heaven** (5). Here the author of Revelation prefers the reference to the Tabernacle—called the "tent of witness" (Num. 9:15)—rather than to the later Temple. The writer of the Epistle to the Hebrews does the same thing. This is probably because its plan was given by divine revelation.

The seven angels . . . having the seven plagues came **out of the temple** (sanctuary). They were **clothed in pure and white linen,** with **golden girdles,** like the priests in the Temple.

One of the four beasts ("living creatures"; see comments on 4:6) **gave unto the seven angels seven golden vials full of the wrath of God** (7). The Greek word for **vials,** *phiale,* is found only in Revelation (5:8; 15:7; 16:1-17; 17:1; 21:9). It means "a shallow *bowl,* used for pouring libations, etc."[146] Since **vial** now means a small glass bottle, that term is misleading; NASB has "seven golden bowls."

This **God,** whose **wrath** will be poured out on the rebellious, is the One **who liveth for ever and ever.** The writer of Hebrews warns that it is "a fearful thing to fall into the hands of the living God" (Heb. 10:31).

At this juncture **the temple was filled with smoke from the glory of God, and from his power** (8). Swete notes: "Smoke is an O. T. symbol of the Divine Presence when the awful majesty of God is to be insisted upon."[147] No one (**man** is not in the Gk.) could enter the sanctuary until the **plagues . . . were fulfilled,** or "finished" (cf. Exod. 40:35; I Kings 8:10).

1. *The First Bowl: Ulcers* (16:1-2)

John **heard a great voice out of the temple** (sanctuary). Since we have just been told (15:8) that no one could enter the

[145]Supporting Greek MSS. for these two readings are almost equally balanced.

[146]Abbott-Smith, *op. cit.*, p. 469. [147]*Op. cit.*, p. 199.

sanctuary until the plagues were finished, presumably this was the voice of God. It commanded **the seven angels** to **pour out** their **vials** (bowls) of divine **wrath . . . upon the earth** (1). When the first angel emptied his bowl, **there fell** (Gk., came) **a noisome and grievous sore upon the men which had the mark of the beast, and upon them which worshipped his image** (2). This is similar to the sixth plague in Egypt (Exod. 9:10). **Noisome** means "noxious" or "harmful." For **noisome and grievous** the Greek has simply "bad and evil" (*kakon kai poneron*). Probably *poneron* here means "malignant." The Greek word for **sore** means "abscess" or "ulcer." A good translation of the whole phrase would be "loathsome and malignant ulcers" (Phillips).

2. *The Second Bowl: Death in the Sea* (16:3)

The second angel poured out his vial (bowl) **upon the sea,** which **became as the blood of a dead man**—like a murdered man lying in his own blood. The result was that **every living soul** (creature) **died in the sea.** This was like the first plague in Egypt (Exod. 7:20) and the second trumpet (8:8-9). But whereas in Egypt only the streams and ponds were affected, here it was the sea. And while only a third of life in the sea was destroyed by the second trumpet-judgment, now it is every living thing in the sea. All this suggests that these seven plagues poured out from the bowls are final and complete.

3. *The Third Bowl: Blood* (16:4-7)

The third angel poured out his bowl on **the rivers and fountains of waters; and they became blood** (4). This bears even closer relationship to the first Egyptian plague and is parallel to the third trumpet (8:11). But whereas the trumpet-judgment affected only a third part of the fresh-water supply, here it is all turned into blood.

Divine justice in this punishment is vindicated by **the angel of the waters** (5). He acknowledges that God had a right to use the waters for the punishment of sinful men. The best Greek text omits **and shalt be,** and instead of **O Lord** has "the Holy." The correct translation is: "Righteous art Thou, who art and who wast, O Holy One, because Thou didst judge these things" (NASB).

The reason for this justice is that **they** (indefinite) **have shed the blood of saints and prophets** (Christian leaders), **and thou hast given them blood to drink** (6). The last clause, **for they**

are worthy (*axioi*), forms a terrible contrast to the same expression in 3:4. The word *axios* literally means "befitting." The punishment fits the crime.

John **heard another out of the altar say** (7)—lit., "I heard the altar saying." Alford comments: "Certainly the simplest understanding of these words is, that they involve a personification of the altar. On the altar are the prayers of the saints, offered before God; beneath the altar are the souls of the martyrs crying for vengeance: when therefore the altar speaks, it is the concentrated testimony of these which speaks by it."[148] What the altar said was an echo of the song of Moses and the Lamb (15:3-4).

4. *The Fourth Bowl: Scorching Heat* (16:8-9)

The fourth angel poured out his bowl **upon the sun; and power was given unto him to scorch men with fire** (8). In the case of the fourth trumpet a third part of the sun was darkened. Here it seems that its heat was multiplied, so that men were scorched by it.

Not always does divine judgment produce repentance. In an agony of pain these men **blasphemed the name of God, which hath power over these plagues: and they repented not to give him glory** (9). It is a fearful thing to contemplate men in final, utter revolt against God. Yet there are many trends in our day that point in that direction. Suffering either melts people in repentance or hardens them in rebellion.

5. *The Fifth Bowl: Darkness* (16:10-11)

The fifth angel poured out his bowl **upon the seat** (*thronon*, throne) **of the beast; and his kingdom was full of darkness; and they gnawed** (chewed) **their tongues for pain** (10). Darkness was the ninth plague in Egypt (Exod. 10:21-23). This time the judgment struck right at the heart of the antichristian power—the throne of the beast. Again it is stated that people blasphemed **the God of heaven** (cf. Dan. 2:44) **because of their pains and their sores**—resulting from the previous plagues—**and repented not of their deeds** (11).

6. *The Sixth Bowl: Invasion* (16:12-16)

Earlier, when the sixth trumpet was sounded (9:13), four angels were loosed from the Euphrates River and millions of

[148]*Op. cit.*, IV, 698-99.

horsemen unleashed by them for destruction. Here we find a striking parallel. **The sixth angel poured out his** bowl on **the great river Euphrates; and the water thereof was dried up, that the way of the kings of the east might be prepared** (12). For John's day this would mean a threatened invasion of the Roman Empire by the Parthians. For the end of this age it apparently means a massive attack on Palestine by hosts from the east.

John **saw three unclean spirits like frogs** (13). There is probably a reference to the second plague in Egypt (Exod. 8:6). **Frogs** were also included among the unclean animals in the Mosaic law (Lev. 11:10).

These spirits came **out of the mouth of the dragon . . . the beast . . . the false prophet.** The Greek word for "spirit" is *pneuma,* the primary meaning of which is "breath." These demons are thought of as being breathed out of the mouths of Satan and his colleagues, just as Jesus "breathed" the Holy Spirit on His disciples (John 20:22).

The dragon has already been identified as "the Devil, and Satan" (12:9). **The beast** is clearly the one that came out of the sea (13:1), further called "the first beast" (13:9). From then on he is simply designated "the beast" (13:14-18; 14:9, 11; 15:2; 16:2, 10). **The false prophet** is unquestionably the second beast, which came out of the earth (13:11). He is associated with the first beast in 19:20 (cf. 13:14) and 20:10. These three comprise what is sometimes called "the trinity of evil," in contrast to the Holy Trinity of Father, Son, and Holy Spirit.

The unclean spirits are **spirits of devils** (*daimonion,* demons), **working miracles** (14)—lit., "doing signs." In Old Testament times the false prophets performed signs as supposed proofs of their divine calling (Deut. 13:1-3). Christ warned His disciples that such men would appear in the Church (Mark 13:22). A striking parallel to this passage is found in II Thess. 2:8-9: "And then shall that Wicked be revealed, whom the Lord shall consume with the spirit [breath] of his mouth . . . whose coming is after the working of Satan with all power and signs and lying wonders." Acts 13:6 mentions a Jewish "false prophet" named Bar-Jesus.

The three demons **go forth unto the kings**[149] **. . . of the whole world, to gather them to the battle of that great day of God Almighty.** That Satanic forces are responsible for many wars one

[149]**Of the earth and** is not in the best Greek text.

could hardly doubt. Swete observes: "There have been times when nations have been seized by a passion for war which the historian can but imperfectly explain. It is such an epoch that the Seer foresees, but one which, unlike any that has come before it, will involve the whole world in war."[150]

These words of Swete were written at the beginning of the twentieth century, before the two World Wars of the bloodiest century in human history. Modern means of communication and transportation have made it possible for the entire earth to be involved in the same war; in fact they have made it almost impossible for this *not* to happen. It does not take much prophetic insight to perceive that the stage is now being set for the great global conflict at the end of this age.

II Pet. 3:10 says: "But the day of the Lord will come as a thief in the night." And so here we read: **Behold, I come as a thief** (15). Christ is obviously speaking here (cf. 3:3). During His earthly ministry He had sounded this warning (Matt. 24:42-44). Paul had echoed it (I Thess. 5:2). Now it comes again, followed by: **Blessed is he that watcheth, and keepeth his garments, lest he walk naked, and they see his shame.** Unlike the Greeks, the Jews considered it to be a tragic disgrace to be caught **naked**; that is, not properly clothed. The spiritual application is obvious. We must be clothed with Christ's robe of righteousness if we would be ready for His coming (cf. Matt. 22:11).

It would appear that this verse is a parenthesis in the passage (cf. ASV). Jesus inserts a special note of warning to His own.

Now the narrative resumes. **And he** (rather "they,"[151] the three unclean demons) **gathered them** (the armies of the nations) **together into a place called in the Hebrew tongue Armageddon** (16; Har-Magedon, ASV).

This proper name has caused no end of comment. Charles writes: "No convincing interpretation has as yet been given of this phrase [*Har-Magedon*], which should probably be translated 'the mountains of Megiddo.' "[152] The form Armageddon (soft breathing in Gk.) means "the city of Megiddo." Megiddo—the

[150]*Op. cit.*, p. 208.

[151]While the verb (*synegagen*) is singular, yet the subject is *pneumata* (spirits, 13-14). In Greek a neuter plural noun ordinarily takes a singular verb.

[152]*Op. cit.*, II, 50.

mound can still be seen—stood at the entrance of a famous pass, overlooking the Plain of Esdraelon. It was on this plain that Deborah and Barak overthrew the hosts of Jabin, king of Canaan (Judg. 5:19-20). Pharaoh-necoh slew Josiah in "the valley of Megiddo" (II Chron. 35:22; cf. Zech. 12:11). Swete suggests: "Thus Megiddo fitly symbolizes the world-wide distress of the nations at the overthrow of their kings in the final war."[153]

7. *The Seventh Bowl: Destruction* (16:17-21)

The seventh angel poured out his vial (bowl) **into the air; and there came a great voice out of the temple** (sanctuary) **of heaven, from the throne, saying, It is done** (17)—lit., "It has come to pass." This was the final manifestation of divine wrath in punishing human rebellion.

The contents of the seventh bowl produced massive disturbances in nature: **There were voices, and thunders, and lightnings** (18). The order of the best Greek text is: "flashes of lightning and sounds and peals of thunder" (NASB). But the main phenomenon was **a great earthquake, such as was not since men were upon the earth, so mighty an earthquake, and so great.** The first century was noted for its many severe earthquakes, but this would be the worst one ever known to men.

The result of the earthquake was that **the great city was divided into three parts, and the cities of the nations fell** (19). Simcox thinks the great city is Jerusalem, citing Zech. 14:4-5 as a parallel.[154] It appears that Jerusalem is called "the great city" in 11:8. Other commentators (e.g., Swete, Charles, Lenski) identify the phrase with the **great Babylon** which is to drink of **the cup of the wine of the fierceness of his wrath,** and whose earth-shaking fall is described in the next two chapters. It seems impossible to decide dogmatically between these two views.

So great was the earthquake that **every island fled away, and the mountains were not found** (20). The same thing is asserted in connection with the sixth seal (6:14). It is impossible to tell how far this language should be taken literally, or how fully as figurative.

The last manifestation was in the form of **hail** (21). This is a reminder of the seventh plague in Egypt (Exod. 9:24). Each hailstone weighed about **a talent**—probably "about one hundred

[153]*Op. cit.*, p. 209. [154]*Op. cit.*, p. 156.

pounds" (NASB). But still men **blasphemed God,** instead of repenting.

The *preterist* (see Intro., "Interpretation") holds that these seven plagues would be poured out on the Roman Empire. The *futurist* makes the application to the Antichrist (the beast) and his followers at the end of this age.

Barnes, representing the *historicist* point of view, regards this chapter as a description of the "successive blows by which the Papacy [the Beast] will fall."[155] He interprets the first bowl as referring to the French Revolution; the second, to "a series of naval disasters that swept away the fleets of France, and that completely demolished the most formidable naval power that had ever been prepared by any nation under the Papal dominion"[156]; the third, to the invasion of Italy by Napoleon; the fourth, to the wars of Europe following the French Revolution; the fifth, to the direct attack on papal power by the French; the sixth, to the decline of Turkish power (Euphrates dried up). He thinks, however, that **Armageddon** (16) points forward to the future, so that the rest of the book is yet to be fulfilled.[157]

F. The Seven Last Scenes, 17:1—20:15

1. *The Scarlet Woman* (17:1-18)

Twice already Babylon has been mentioned and her doom predicted (14:8; 16:19). At last we are given a dress rehearsal of that terrifying event. The description covers two chapters (17—18).

The material of c. 17 divides itself naturally into two parts. There is first the vision (1-6) and then the interpretation (7-18).

a. The vision (17:1-6). **There came one of the seven angels** (1) that had the seven bowls and invited John to come and see **the judgment of the great whore** (harlot). This epithet is applied to Babylon four times in this chapter (1, 5, 15, 16), as well as in 19:2. It means "prostitute." **Many waters** means many people or nations (cf. 15).

The great harlot is further described as one **with whom the kings of the earth have committed fornication** (2). The last three words are an aorist form of the verb *porneuo,* derived from

[155]*Op. cit.,* p. 356. [156]*Ibid.,* p. 361.
[157]*Ibid.,* pp. 374-75.

porne (**whore**). The people of the earth had **been made drunk with the wine of her fornication** (*porneia*). The **kings** were probably vassal kings of the empire. Swete says: "The *porneia* of which these kings were guilty consisted in purchasing the favour of Rome by accepting her suzerainty and with it her vices and idolatries."[158]

John was then carried in spirit **into the wilderness** (3)—perhaps a clean, quiet spot from which he could view this scene. He saw **a woman sit** (Gk., sitting) **upon a scarlet coloured beast,** which was **full of names of blasphemy** (see notes on 13:1, 5). Swete observes: "The Empire reeked with the blasphemous worship of the Emperors."[159] The beast had **seven heads and ten horns.** This seems to identify it with the beast that came out of the sea (13:1). The significance of these items is explained in 17:9-17.

The woman was gorgeously **arrayed in purple and scarlet colour** (4). Tertullian and Cyprian, of north Africa (about A.D. 200), used this passage to warn Christians against an inordinate affection for sumptuous clothing. Later Protestant writers found here a reference to the expensive crimson robes of the Roman Catholic cardinals.

The woman was also **decked with gold and precious stones and pearls.** These were the typical paraphernalia used by prostitutes in plying their trade, as noted by Roman writers of that day. There was **a golden cup in her hand full of abominations**—"the cults and vices of Roman life"[160]—**and filthiness of her fornication** with the nations of the world.

As was the custom of Roman prostitutes, she bore **upon her forehead . . . a name.** Hers was: **MYSTERY, BABYLON THE GREAT, THE MOTHER OF HARLOTS AND ABOMINATIONS OF THE EARTH** (5). The term **mystery** indicates that there is a symbolism intended here. Swete comments: "The Woman on the Beast represents, is the symbol of, Babylon the Great, while Babylon itself is a mystical name for the city which is now the mistress of the world. Her gaily attired, jewelled, gilded person, and her cup of abominations, proclaim her to be the Mother-Harlot of the Earth."[161] It cannot be doubted that the primary identification of Babylon is with Rome. Among the Christians of

[158]*Op. cit.*, p. 213.
[159]*Ibid.*, p. 215.
[160]*Ibid.*, p. 216.
[161]*Ibid.*, p. 217.

that time **Babylon** was used as a mystical name for Rome, to avoid getting in trouble.

John saw **the woman drunken with the blood of the saints, and with the blood of the martyrs of Jesus** (6). The idea of being drunk with blood was a familiar one in Roman writers. The gladiatorial shows had accustomed the people to reveling in seeing bloodshed.

The seer had been invited to behold the judgment of the great prostitute. Instead he beheld her apparently in her full pride and power. So he **wondered with great admiration.** Obviously this last word does not fit. The Greek says: "wondered with great wonder," or "marveled greatly."

b. The interpretation (17:7-18). Noting the wonder on John's face, the angel asked, **Wherefore didst thou marvel? (7)** He then offered to explain **the mystery.**

Said he: **The beast that thou sawest was, and is not; and shall ascend out of the bottomless pit** (lit., and is about to go up out of the abyss), **and go into perdition** (8). The first reference was to Nero, who **was, and is not.** Evidently John thought of the Antichrist as being a sort of new Nero, who will come out of the abyss (see comments on 20:1). But he will finally go **into perdition. Wonder** will beset the inhabitants of the world, those **whose names were not written in the book of life from the foundation of the world** (cf. 13:8), **when they behold the beast that was, and is not, and yet is** (cf. 13:3).

Before proceeding to a definite explanation of details, the angel said: **And here is the mind which hath wisdom** (9; cf. 13:18). **The seven heads are seven mountains, on which the woman sitteth.** This is a clear reference to Rome, which was celebrated alike by poets and orators as the city set on seven hills.

But these seven heads also represent **seven kings: five are fallen, and one is, and the other is not yet come; and when he cometh, he must continue a short space** (10). **And the beast that was, and is not, even he is the eighth, and is of the seven, and goeth into perdition** (11).

It might seem that the identification of these kings would be a simple matter. But actually there has been considerable debate over it.

Alford takes the **five** that **are fallen** to be five empires that had been enemies to Israel: Egypt, Assyria, Babylon, Persia, Greece. The **one** that **is** he identifies as Rome. The one **not yet come** is the Byzantine Empire of Constantine. The **eighth** is "the ultimate antichristian power, prefigured by the little horn in Daniel, and expressly announced by St. Paul, 2 Thess. ii. 3 ff."[162]

But most *preterists* (see Intro., "Interpretation") interpret this passage as referring to successive Roman emperors, though they do not always see alike on the identifications. There is, however, general agreement on the **five** that have **fallen.** They are Augustus (27 B.C.—A.D. 14); Tiberius (14-37); Caligula (37-41); Claudius (41-54); Nero (54-68). Three minor emperors, who ruled very briefly, are omitted. This makes the sixth, who **is,** Vespasian (69-79); and the one who is **not yet come,** Titus (79-81), who continued only **a short space. The eighth** is then Domitian (81-96).

The problem with this is that it seems to place the writer in the time of Vespasian. In the Introduction we noted that the most likely time for writing the Book of Revelation was in the reign of Domitian. To take care of this some would arbitrarily make Domitian the one that **is,** and Trajan (98-117) the one who is **not yet come.** To do this one must leave out the two Flavian emperors, Vespasian and Titus. But Domitian was also a Flavian. Fortunately there is considerable agreement that **the eighth** king is the Antichrist. Many, however, identify **the eighth** as Nero, because he is called **the beast.**

A helpful new solution is offered by Rist. He suggests that the **five** be taken as those who were deified officially by the Roman Senate. These would be Caesar, Augustus, Claudius, Vespasian, and Titus. Domitian would then be the one who **is,** the ruling emperor. The one **not yet come** would be "the Neronic Antichrist."[163]

Barnes, as a *historicist,* takes **kings** as referring to successive forms of Roman government: kings, consuls, dictators, decemvirs, military tribunes, and emperors. He says: "Of these, five had passed away in the time when John wrote the Apocalypse; the sixth, the imperial, was then in power, and had been from the time of Augustus Caesar."[164] **The eighth** is "the Papal power."[165]

It would be very difficult to give a *futurist* interpretation to these details. All that one can say is that they refer to organizations or persons at the close of this age.

[162] *Op. cit.,* IV, 710-11.

[163] *Interpreter's Bible,* XII, 495.

[164] *Op. cit.,* pp. 389-90.

[165] *Ibid.,* p. 392.

The **ten horns** are identified as **ten kings, which have received no kingdom as yet; but receive power as kings one hour with the beast** (12). The figure is taken from Dan. 7:24. Swete gives a good *preterist* interpretation: "The 'ten kings' belong to a period which in St. John's time was still remote; they belong, as the sequel will shew, to the last days of the Roman Empire, and represent the forces which arising out of the Empire itself, like horns from a beast's head, and carrying on many of the worst traditions of the Empire, would turn their arms against Rome and bring about her downfall."[166]

The *historicist* application given by Barnes is to the short-lived governments that sprang into existence in Europe during and after the Germanic invasions of Italy.[167] The *futurists* envision a confederation of ten kings at the close of this age, all subservient to the Antichrist.

This last suggestion is borne out by the next statement: **These have one mind, and shall give their power and strength unto the beast** (13). This could, however, refer to vassal kings of the Roman Empire. Barnes, the *historicist,* solves his more difficult problem by making **the beast** represent the papacy, to which all give support.

These puppets of the beast **shall make war with the Lamb, and the Lamb shall overcome them** (14). The figure of the Lamb as a mighty Conqueror is one of the startling paradoxes of Revelation.

The Lamb is **Lord of lords, and King of kings.** Israel's first leader, Moses, declared: "For the Lord your God is God of gods, and Lord of lords" (Deut. 10:17). This is echoed in Ps. 136:2-3. In Dan. 2:47 He is called "God of gods" and "Lord of kings." Paul speaks of the Father as "King of kings, and Lord of lords" (I Tim. 6:15). But the striking fact is that in Revelation these titles are applied to the Son of God. The expression here occurs again in 19:16. Such titles had been claimed by Babylonian kings. But the special significance here is that Domitian, the reigning emperor, was called "Lord and our God." To the Christians this was sheer blasphemy. The Lamb, their Lord, alone was Lord of all.

The followers of the Lamb are **called, and chosen, and faithful.** This gives an excellent outline for "What Is a Christian?" He is (1) **Called** of God to salvation; (2) **Chosen** by God, as he

[166]*Op. cit.,* p. 222.

[167]*Op. cit.,* p. 393.

accepts the salvation offered in Christ; (3) **Faithful** in obedience to this call and choice.

The angel now proceeds to make another explanation. **The waters which thou sawest, where the whore sitteth, are peoples, and multitudes, and nations, and tongues** (15). "The waters on which the Harlot had been seen to dwell (v. 1) represented the teeming and mixed populations of the Empire."[168] The relationship of this to the verse that follows is thus pointed out by Swete: "The Harlot-city sat on the brink of a seething flood . . . the polyglot races of the Empire, her support and strength at present, but if they rose, as at some future time they might rise, the instrument of certain and swift destruction."[169]

And so we are told that the ten horns of the beast **shall hate the whore, and shall make her desolate and naked, and shall eat her flesh, and burn her with fire** (16). It is often true that passionate love turns suddenly into fierce hatred. This is true not only with individuals (cf. II Sam. 13:15) but also with nations. In our own day we have had the spectacle of Hitler turning violently on his ally, Russia. So the allies of Rome would suddenly turn against her and destroy her. Gibbon's massive work, *The Decline and Fall of the Roman Empire,* provides copious documentation for the language of this verse.

Why did this happen? Because **God hath put in their hearts to fulfil his will . . . until the words of God shall be fulfilled** (17). The word for **will** is *gnome,* which first meant "a means of knowing." But here it is used in the sense of "royal purpose" or "decree." Divine sovereignty will see to it that the purposes of divine love are carried out for the ultimate good of mankind.

Finally, **the woman** is identified as **that great city, which reigneth over the kings of the earth** (18). The reference to Rome, in terms of John's writing in his day, cannot be questioned.

2. *The Fall of Babylon* (18:1-24)

The seventeenth and eighteenth chapters of Revelation are tied closely together. Both have to do with "Babylon the great" (17:5; 18:2). In c. 17 Babylon is pictured as a prostitute, luxuriously garbed, but committing fornication with the kings of the earth (17:2). That same figure is carried over into this chapter (18:3). Throughout the chapter Babylon is referred to as "she." Her name might well be Madame Wickedness.

[168]Swete, *op. cit.,* p. 224. [169]*Ibid.*

a. Babylon's doom (18:1-8). **John saw another angel** (1), perhaps different from any previously mentioned, **come down** (Gk., coming down) **from** (*ek,* out of) **heaven, having great power** (*exousia,* authority); **and the earth was lightened** (lighted) **with his glory.** He possessed authority to execute the sentence he pronounced on Babylon. And coming fresh from the glory world, he diffused a radiance of heavenly light.

The angel **cried . . . with a strong voice**[170] **. . . Babylon the great is fallen, is fallen** (2). Exactly the same expression is found in 14:8 (see comments there), an echo of Isa. 21:9. The city has **become the habitation of devils** (demons), **and the hold** (prison) **of every foul** (unclean) **spirit, and a cage**—"prison," same word translated **hold—of every unclean and hateful** (hated) **bird.**

A similar doom was pronounced on the ancient Babylon (Isa. 13:21-22), and has been literally fulfilled. Babylon on the Euphrates is still in ruins, with only wild animals and birds for inhabitants. However, Rome is one of the great world capitals today. Apparently the reference is to the fall and desolation of the Roman Empire rather than to the city. There may also be an allusion to the fact that Rome's heathen temples were finally vacated by the conquest of Christianity.

That is the *preterist* view (see Intro., "Interpretation"). The *historicist* interpretation is given by Barnes: "The idea is that of utter desolation; and the meaning here is, that spiritual Babylon —Papal Rome (ch. xiv. 8)—will be reduced to a state of utter desolation resembling that of the real Babylon."[171]

Joseph Seiss presents a *futurist* interpretation. He devotes two long lectures (pp. 107-58) to seeking to prove that the **Babylon** of Revelation 17—18 is a literal Babylon to be rebuilt on the old site by the Euphrates River. He then has two lectures describing the fall of this restored city of Babylon in Mesopotamia.[172]

William Newell is a recent popular exponent of the *futurist* view. His work, *The Book of Revelation,* was first published in 1935 and was in its sixth printing in 1946. Under the heading "What Babylon Is," he writes: (1) "Babylon is *a literal city on the Euphrates River. . . . opposed to God's people Israel*";

[170]The adverb **mightily** is not in the Greek text. It was apparently added from the Latin Vulgate.

[171]*Op. cit.,* p. 396. [172]*Op. cit.,* III, 159-212.

(2) "Babylon, next, is the *same system* in another city—Rome, and *opposing the same idolatrous system to God's saints of the Church age*"; (3) "The final *form of Babylon is the literal city on the Euphrates, rebuilt* as Antichrist's capital of the last days, *opposing Israel as God's earthly people* who will have gathered back to their land (the Church of course, having been raptured)."[173]

As we see it, there are two, and possibly three, reasonable interpretations of **Babylon** in the Book of Revelation. For John's first readers the term unquestionably signified Rome. There can be no doubt that the *preterists* are right in asserting this. The *historicists* may also be right in applying the term to the papacy, which throughout the Church age has demanded worldwide subjection to its authority.

What of the *futurist* view? To us the idea that Babylon on the Euphrates will be literally rebuilt at the end of this age and become the leading center of world trade seems far-fetched. From a merely physical point of view it is almost unthinkable that an inland city should hold such a position today, though admittedly Rome did in ancient times.

A more reasonable view would seem to be that **Babylon** represents a federation of world power under a dictator at the end of this age. Just what form that federation will take is a secret known only to God. Speculation at this point is useless.

The first two clauses of verse 3 are an echo of 14:8 and 17:2. There is added here that **the merchants of the earth are waxed rich through the abundance of her delicacies.** Much of this chapter is devoted to describing the immense trade with Rome carried on by the merchants of that day. The Greek word for "merchant" is *emporos.* It first meant "a passenger on shipboard, one on a journey," and then "merchant."[174] Aside from Matt. 13:45 it is used only in this chapter. "Emporium," a place of trade, is from *emporion* (only in John 2:16). **Abundance** is literally "power" (*dynamis*). **Delicacies** is a strong word in Greek (only here in NT), meaning "insolent luxury." The last part of this verse may well be translated "through the might of her wanton luxury" (cf. Phillips—"from the extravagance of her dissipation"). There is abundant evidence of the luxurious, licentious living of the wealthy Romans in the first century.

Another voice from heaven (4) commanded: **Come out of her, my people, that ye be not partakers of her sins, and that ye**

[173]*Op. cit.*, p. 272.

[174]Abbott-Smith, *op. cit.*, p. 149.

receive not of her plagues. There is an echo here of similar warnings in the prophets (cf. Isa. 48:20; Jer. 50:8; 51:6). There is a sense in which every Christian is called out of Babylon (the spirit of the world) to follow Christ. In fact, the Greek word for "church," *ecclesia,* means an assembly of called-out ones.

This verse suggests "The Call to Come Out": (1) Who must come out—**my people;** (2) How we must come out—**be not partakers of her sins;** (3) Why we must come out—**that ye receive not of her plagues** (punishment).

Babylon's **sins** had **reached unto heaven** (5), so that **God** had **remembered her iniquities.** The verb **reached** literally means "glued." The picture is that of sins joined together until they were piled as high as the sky. For **remembered** cf. 16:19.

The angels of judgment are commanded: **Reward her even as she rewarded you** (6). There is a basic righteousness in the universe, flowing out of God's holy character, which demands that justice shall be administered to all. **Double unto her double** is a principle written into the Mosaic law (Exod. 22:4, 7, 9). Its purpose was to act as a deterrent to crime. If a man knew he had to restore only what he had stolen, he might take the chance; there would be nothing to lose. But if he knew he had to pay back double, he might well hesitate. The term **double** is also found in Isa. 40:2; Jer. 16:18.

Lived deliciously (7) is a verb (only here and 9) derived from the noun "delicacies" (3). It is better translated "lived luxuriously" or even "lived sensuously" (NASB). The first half of this verse might be translated: "The more she has given herself to pride and luxury the more you must give her torture and grief" (Goodspeed). The principle finds vivid application in the story of the rich man and Lazarus (Luke 16:19-31).

The destruction of Babylon would come suddenly: **in one day** (8). It would consist of **death, and mourning, and famine; and she shall be utterly burned with fire.**

b. Earth's lament (18:9-19). This passage bears many resemblances to Ezekiel's dirge over Tyre (Ezekiel 27), a city which was famous for its merchant marine. Here it is Babylon (Rome) which is the center of world commerce.

This section consists of three dirges chanted over the fallen city by: (1) the kings, 9-10; (2) the merchants, 11-17*a*; (3) the shipowners, 17*b*-19.

(1) *The kings* (18:9-10) It is said that these **kings of the earth . . . shall bewail her, and lament for her, when they shall**

see the smoke of her burning (9). The second clause of 9 has been translated, "who debauched and indulged themselves with her" (Phillips). The Greek word for **bewail** suggests any "loud expression of pain or sorrow, especially for the dead."[175] **Lament** is literally "beat their breasts with grief." The word for **smoke** is used only in Revelation (ten times), except in a quotation in Acts 2:19. It fits in well with these scenes of apocalyptic judgments.

Fearful of being caught in the city's torment, the kings stood **afar off** (10). They cried: **Alas, alas that great city Babylon, that mighty city! for in one hour is thy judgment come.** The Greek word for **judgment** is *crisis*. This was Babylon's hour, and it spelled disaster. Literally *crisis* means a separating, a selection, and so a decision.

(2) *The merchants* (18:11-17*a*). The reaction of **the merchants** is much the same. They **weep** (11)—same verb as "bewail" (9; see comment there)—**and mourn over her.** But the reason is selfish: **for no man buyeth their merchandise any more.** Rome was the chief market for produce in that day. Her people lived luxuriously and demanded the best of food and clothing from Asia and Africa.

A long list of **merchandise** (12) is given. It consisted of precious metals and stones, expensive textiles, choice woods, costly cosmetics, expensive foods, and a variety of livestock.

Silk is mentioned only here in the New Testament. The Macedonian conquerors had brought it back from the East. Josephus says that at Titus' triumphal procession in Rome he and Vespasian were dressed in silk robes and sat on **ivory** chairs.[176] **Thyine wood** was imported from north Africa and much prized for its striking veins and variety of color. Wealthy people had dining tables made of it, with ivory legs. One Roman writer said that the voluptuous rich could not enjoy their dinner unless their table rested on a leopard carved in ivory.

Cinnamon (13), thought to have come from south China, was an expensive cosmetic used at formal banquets. **Fine flour** was imported for use by the wealthy. **Wheat** came largely from Alexandria, Egypt (see comments on Acts 27:6, BBC, VII, 567).

Slaves is literally "bodies" (*somaton*). But the Greek word is used in the Septuagint for slaves. Deissmann says: "The Greek translators of the O.T. found the usage in Egypt: the Papyri of

[175]*Ibid.*, p. 247.

[176]*War* vii. 5.4.

the Ptolemaic period yield a large number of examples."[177] It is a terrible commentary on the lack of respect for the human personality that slaves should be called "bodies." **Souls** means persons, as in Ezek. 27:13 ("persons of men"), where the same Greek phrase (LXX) occurs as here. The slave trade was the worst feature of the merchandising of that period. A large percentage of the population of the Roman Empire was composed of slaves. It is thought that in the first century there were about three times as many slaves as free men. This would mean that at the middle of that century there would have been over twenty million slaves in Italy.[178] Here was one of the causes of the decline and fall of the Roman Empire.

A literal translation of 14 would be: "And the ripe fruit of the desire of thy soul has gone away from thee, and all the rich things and bright things have perished from thee." The word for **fruits** means autumn fruit, ready to be picked. **Dainty** probably refers to food, **goodly** to gay clothes and costly furniture. No more would these be enjoyed. The time of the Caesars was gone forever.

The merchants are pictured as **weeping and wailing** (15)—same two verbs as in 11, "weep and mourn." They had been made rich by Rome, but now their profitable trade was ended. They cry, **Alas** (16) for a city that once exhibited the greatest luxury of any metropolis, evidenced by expensive clothes and jewelry. **For in one hour** (cf. 10) **so great riches is come to nought** (17).[179]

(3) *The shipowners* (18:17*b*-19). **And every shipmaster, and all the company in ships**—lit., "and everyone who sails for (any) place"—**and sailors** (only here and Acts 28:27, 30), **and as many as trade by sea** (lit., "work the sea"; that is, make their living by it) **stood afar off** (17). As with the kings (cf. 10), apparently they were afraid to come near. They cried: **What city is like unto this great city!** (18) Rome had seemed supreme, invincible. But it was to be sacked more than once in the fifth century, as the empire came to an end. The mourning shipowners went so far as to **cast dust on their heads** (19) in a symbol of abject grief. As with the kings (10) and merchants (17*a*), they lamented Babylon's sudden destruction—**in one hour.**

[177]*Bible Studies*, p. 160.

[178]*Encyclopaedia Britannica* (1944), XX, 775.

[179]It is obvious that this clause belongs at the end of v. 16, not at the beginning of v. 17.

c. Heaven's rejoicing (18:20). In contrast to the wailing of kings, merchants, and shipowners on earth, **heaven** rejoices at the fall of Babylon. **Holy apostles and prophets** is in the best Greek text "the saints and the apostles and the prophets"—that is, all the Church. **God** had at last **avenged** His people **on her**—lit., "out of her," or at her expense.

d. Babylon's fall (18:21-24). **A mighty angel** (21) **took** what looked **like a great millstone, and cast it into the sea.** As he did so he proclaimed, **Thus with violence** (lit., "with a rush," as a stone hurtling through the air) **shall that great city Babylon be thrown down, and shall be found no more at all.** Swete notes: "The action symbolizes the complete submergence, the final disappearance of pagan Imperial Rome."[180]

Roman society had given itself over to music, with many kinds of instruments playing for the entertainment of the rich while they dined and drank. But all this would **be heard no more at all in thee** (22). The metropolis had been a busy place of work, but now **no craftsman** (*technites,* cf. technician), a workman in metal, stone, or textile fabric, **shall be found any more in thee.** Usually in the morning one could hear the women grinding their grain in each home with a small hand mill. But now **the sound of a millstone shall be heard no more at all in thee.** Never again would **the light of a candle** (23) shine in this metropolis, nor **the voice of the bridegroom and of the bride be heard.** All the normal life of a city would cease.

The relationship of the last two clauses of this verse is not clear. Both begin with **For** (*hoti*), which can mean either "that" or "because." Swete's suggestion is probably the best: "In the present instance it seems best to take the first *hoti* as controlling the whole sentence, and the second as explaining the first."[181] (The sentence should begin with the first **for.**) The sense, then, would be: "Traders who could make Rome their market rose to the first rank, became merchant princes (vv. 3, 15), while Rome on her part acquired a worldwide influence which she used for evil; through their traffic with her all nations had learnt to adopt her false standards of life and worship."[182]

The doom of Babylon was justified, for **in her was found the blood of prophets, and of saints, and of all that were slain upon the earth** (24). It may well be that this should be joined with

[180]*Op. cit.,* p. 239.
[181]*Ibid.,* pp. 240-41.
[182]*Ibid.,* p. 241.

the last two clauses of 23 as one sentence. For here we have a further reason for Babylon's fall. Nero had shed the blood of many Christians after the burning of Rome (A.D. 64). Domitian had intensified this persecution. In a sense, Rome was to blame for all the Christian martyrs throughout the empire (cf. the case of Jerusalem, Matt. 23:35).

3. *The Song of Triumph* (19:1-10)

This section is in startling contrast to what immediately precedes. Chapter 18 closes with a funeral dirge over Babylon and the announcement that no more music will be heard in her. Chapter 19 opens with a burst of song.

a. The four hallelujahs (19:1-6). One hallelujah was not enough. As if from a series of antiphonal choirs, four of them rang out in the heavenly spaces.

(1) *The first hallelujah* (19:1-2). John **heard a great voice of much people in heaven** (1). They were crying, **Alleluia.** In the New Testament this word is found only in this chapter (1, 3, 4, 6). It is the Greek transliteration of the Hebrew *hallelujah,* which means "Praise the Lord!" It is better to use the more familiar Hebrew form. The ending "jah" is short for Jehovah. The word is found at the beginning or end of fifteen of the psalms. The last five psalms have it at both the beginning and the end. In early Christian worship it was sung by the congregation.[183]

God was praised for His **salvation** (cf. 7:10), **and glory**[184] **. . . and power.** The reason for the praise is immediately stated: **For true and righteous are his judgments** (2). By executing justice on the great harlot, Babylon, God had brought **salvation** to His persecuted Church and **glory** to himself, at the same time demonstrating His **power.**

(2) *The second hallelujah* (19:3). Again the heavenly multitude cried, "Hallelujah!" They rejoiced that the great enemy of Christianity had been destroyed: **Her smoke rose up for ever and ever.**

(3) *The third hallelujah* (19:4-5). This time it was the twenty-four **elders** (4) and **the four beasts** (living creatures; see comments on 4:6), described in 4:4-11, who **worshipped God. Amen** (pronounced in the Gk. ah-main); **Alleluia** (Hallelujah!) are two

[183]Kittel, *op. cit.,* I, 264.

[184]**And honour** is not in the best Greek text.

words that are the same in every tongue. One can worship with Christians of a dozen different languages and always feel the warmth that comes from hearing them voice these two words.

From **the throne** (5) a voice cried: **Praise our God, all ye his servants, and ye that fear him, both small and great** (cf. Ps. 135:1, 20). Swete observes that **servants** "seems here to embrace Christians of all intellectual capacities and social grades, and of all stages of progress in the life of Christ . . . all are included in the summons to thanksgiving and are capable of bearing a part in it."[185]

(4) *The fourth hallelujah* (19:6). Again John **heard as it were the voice of a great multitude.** This is almost exactly the same in the Greek as the first part of v. 1 (cf. RSV). The same two Greek words are translated **of a great multitude** here and "of much people" there. But in this instance there is an added note: **and as the voice** (sound) **of many waters**—ocean surf, great waterfalls—**and as the voice** (sound) **of mighty thunderings.** All this underscores the tremendous volume of the sound.

The cry that came this time was: **Alleluia: for the Lord God omnipotent reigneth.** This is the confidence that holds every Christian steady in the confused and chaotic politics of earth. The first choir praised God for destroying the false world-power. This group rejoices in the fact that the kingdom of Heaven is now set up.

b. The marriage supper of the Lamb (19:7-10). Though still a part of the song, a new note is struck here: **The marriage of the Lamb is come, and his wife** (Gk., bride) **hath made herself ready** (7). Her readiness is further defined as being **arrayed in fine linen, clean and white: for the fine linen is the righteousness** (plural, "righteous deeds"; see comments on 15:4) **of** (the) **saints** (8). People usually speak of the "wedding garment" (Matt. 22:11-12) as being Christ's righteousness. But the **fine linen** is the manifestation (clothes) of that inwrought righteousness as it is worked out daily in godly living. Swete says that the expression here ("the righteous acts of the saints," NASB) "is the sum of the saintly acts of the members of Christ, wrought in them by His Spirit, which are regarded as making up the clothing of His mystical Body."[186]

By the angel (cf. 17:1) John was instructed to write: **Blessed are they which are called unto the marriage supper of the Lamb**

[185]*Op. cit.*, p. 244. [186]*Ibid.*, p. 247.

(9). The Old Testament portrays Israel as the bride of the Lord (Isa. 54:6; Hos. 2:19). Psalms 45, which many Jewish scholars interpreted as being Messianic, celebrates the wedding of the King.

Jesus took over all this imagery and applied it to himself. In Mark 2:19, He clearly indicates that He is the Bridegroom. John identified Jesus as the Bridegroom, while he himself was only a friend (John 3:29). Paul emphasized strongly the idea of the Church as the bride of Christ (II Cor. 11:2; Eph. 5:25-27). Now John the Revelator hears the announcement that at last the wedding festivities are to take place. The importance of this announcement and the certainty of its fulfillment are underscored by a further statement of the angel: **These are the true sayings of God.**

John wanted to **worship** (10) this heavenly being. But the angel quickly warned him not to do it. Said he: **I am thy fellowservant, and of thy brethren that have the testimony of Jesus;** that is, I am the fellow servant of all saints, for we all serve the same God. He admonished: **Worship God.** There was a tendency toward angel-worship in the churches of Asia Minor at a later time. John may have sensed this danger already and so recounted this incident as a warning against that heresy.

The last clause of this verse is a striking one: **For the testimony of Jesus**—that is, the testimony about Jesus—**is the spirit of prophecy.** This seems to mean that the test of a true spirit of prophecy is that the prophet witnesses to Jesus. Elsewhere John warns his readers to "try" (test) "the spirits whether they are of God" (I John 4:1).

4. *The Victorious Christ* (19:11-21)

The heavenly choir had proclaimed the reign of God (6). Now the Son of God is seen riding forth to triumph.

a. The Word of God (19:11-16). John **saw heaven opened,** and **a white horse** appeared. The rider was called **Faithful and True** (11). These terms are applied to Christ earlier in the book (cf. 1:5; 3:7, 14). **In righteousness he doth judge and make war.** There was much injustice in the courts of law, as persecuted Christians had learned to their sorrow. Also most wars were for selfish conquest, as often today. But everything that Christ does is done **in righteousness.**

His eyes were as a flame of fire (12; cf. 1:14; 2:18). Christ is the mighty Conqueror, before whom no enemy can stand. **On**

his head were many crowns. The Greek word is *diadema,* meaning a royal crown. The **many crowns** symbolized His powerful and worldwide authority as King of Kings. Also **he had a name written, that no man knew, but he himself.** Swete makes this helpful comment: "Notwithstanding the dogmatic helps which the Church offers, the mind fails to grasp the inmost significance of the Person of Christ, which eludes all efforts to bring it within the terms of human knowledge. Only the Son of God can understand the mystery of His own being."[187]

The Conqueror was **clothed with a vesture** (cloak) **dipped in blood** (13). The reference is clearly to Isa. 63:1-3, which the later Jews gave a Messianic meaning. This is not His own blood, but that of His enemies, as the Isaiah passage clearly shows.

The Rider on the white horse is called **The Word of God.** It is a striking fact that John is the only one who applies the significant Greek term *logos* **(Word)** to the Son of God. This he does in all of his three main writings (cf. John 1:1; I John 1:1). Here is one of the many points that link these three books together in a common authorship. Jesus is God's Word to man, the perfect Expression of His character and will. (The term *logos* means a thought and then the expression of that thought in a word.) The incarnate Christ was God's final Word to man (Heb. 1:1-2), the only perfect Revelation of the Father.

The Conqueror was **followed** by a heavenly host on **white horses** and **clothed in fine linen, white and clean** (14). This is a mark of purity (cf. 8). Here the reference seems to be to an angelic army.

Out of his mouth goeth a sharp sword (cf. 1:16), **that with it he should smite the nations** (15). The **sword** is His Word (cf. Eph. 6:17), that goes out of His mouth. He will **rule** the nations **with a rod of iron.** Christ's rule must be absolute. It must be so in our hearts, and it will one day be true over all the earth.

This Conqueror treads **the winepress** (cf. 14:19) **of the fierceness and wrath**—lit., the hot anger (*thymos*) of the wrath (*orge*)—**of Almighty God** (cf. 14:8, 10; 16:19). These are solemn words of warning.

The name that Jesus carries **on his vesture** (cloak) and **thigh**—the most exposed part of the body was here—is **KING OF KINGS, AND LORD OF LORDS** (16). These titles have already been applied to the Lamb (17:14; see comments there).

[187]*Ibid.*, p. 252.

b. The great supper of God (19:17-21). John **saw an angel standing in the sun** (17), where he could summon from the heights of the sky all the beasts of prey. He called them to **the supper of the great God**—rather, as the Greek clearly says, "the great supper of God."

The imagery of 18 is drawn from Ezek. 39:17-20. The victims of destruction range all the way from **kings** and **captains** to **bond** (slaves) and **small** men. Swete observes: "The great war between Christ and Antichrist, which is now about to enter upon its final stage, draws its recruits from every class, and in war there is no respect of persons."[188]

Then John saw **the beast, and the kings of the earth, and their armies, gathered together to make war against him that sat on the horse, and against his army** (19). This conflict is generally identified as the Battle of Armageddon, when the Antichrist and his forces will fight against Christ and His forces, and be defeated. It is placed at the close of the Great Tribulation.

Concerning this conflict Swete makes the following statement: "Those who take note of the tendencies of modern civilization will not find it impossible to conceive that a time may come when throughout Christendom the spirit of Antichrist will, with the support of the State, make a final stand against a Christianity which is loyal to the Person and teaching of Christ."[189]

Those words were written sixty years ago. But they are far more significant now. Never before in the history of Western nations has there been such a widespread spirit of revolt against all standards of decency and honesty. Never before have religious leaders advocated not only a "new theology" but a "new morality" which flouts God's laws and society's sense of right. The stage is being rapidly set for the end of the age.

The beast and **the false prophet** (20) are clearly identified by the language here as being the two beasts of c. 13. Their career now comes to a sudden end. After being captured, **these both were cast alive into a lake of fire burning with brimstone.** This lake is further identified in 20:14 (see comments there).

The followers of Antichrist **were slain** by the conquering Christ, and **all the fowls were filled with their flesh** (21). What a solemnizing end for the boasted pride and power of men who set themselves against God!

[188]*Ibid.*, p. 256. [189]*Ibid.*, p. 257.

5. *The Millennial Kingdom* (20:1-6)

John saw an angel come down (lit., coming down) **from** (out of) **heaven, having the key of the bottomless pit** (the abyss, here meaning place of punishment) **and a great chain in his hand** (1). Mention has already been made of "the abyss" (9:1-2, 11; 11:7; 17:8). The word occurs again in 3. Aside from these passages in Revelation the word is found (in NT) only in Luke 8:31 and Rom. 10:7. In the latter place it seems to signify the "realm of the dead," but in the remaining occurrences the "place of imprisonment for disobedient spirits."[190] The angel had **a great chain,** because he was going to manacle a great foe, none other than Satan himself.

Satan is here called **the dragon, that old serpent, which is the Devil, and Satan** (2). Exactly the same four names are used for him in 12:9 (see comments there).

The archenemy of God and man is **bound** for **a thousand years.** This significant expression is used six times in six verses (2-7).

The Greek word for **thousand** is *chilia.* So those who believe in a literal reign of Christ and His saints on earth for a thousand years are often called "chiliasts" (*ch* as in Christ).

The Latin word for **thousand years** is *millennium.*[191] With regard to the meaning of this term there are three main interpretations. *Premillennialists*[192] hold that Christ will come back *before* the millennium and will himself usher in His reign of a thousand years on earth. *Postmillennialists* believe that Christ will return *after* a millennium has been brought about by the Church. *Amillennialists* reject the idea of any literal reign of Christ on earth for a thousand years.

A typical example of this last view is found in Swete: "A thousand years, i.e. a long period of time, a great epoch in human history."[193] Lenski puts it a bit more precisely: "These 1,000 years thus extend from the incarnation and the enthronement of the Son (12:5) to Satan's final plunge into hell (20:10), which is the entire New Testament period."[194] Proponents of this view

[190] Jeremias, *"abyss,"* Kittel, *op. cit.,* I, 9.

[191] So a chiliast is also called a millenarian.

[192] It should perhaps be noted that during recent years there has been a great deal of controversy over the matter of a pre-tribulation rapture *vs.* a post-tribulation rapture. Both views are held by premillennialists.

[193] *Op. cit.,* p. 260.

[194] *Op. cit.,* p. 564.

emphasize the idea that *all* numbers in Revelation should be taken as symbolical rather than literal.

Satan is pictured as being sealed a prisoner in the abyss during the thousand years, so **that he should deceive the nations no more** (3). But **after that he must be loosed a little season;** that is, for a short time. More is said of this later (7-10).

Now comes a description of the millennial Kingdom. John saw **thrones, and they sat upon them** (4). The picture here is taken from Dan. 7:9, where the correct translation is: "Thrones were placed and one that was ancient of days took his seat" (RSV). **They** here evidently means Christ and His saints. **And judgment was given unto them** is an echo of Dan. 7:22, "Until the Ancient of days came, and judgment was given to the saints of the most high; and the time came that the saints possessed the kingdom." **Judgment** apparently means "the right of judging" (cf. I Cor. 6:2-3).[195]

The souls of the martyred saints (cf. 6:9) now appeared. **Beheaded** is "lit. 'struck with an axe,' the old Roman mode of execution by sentence of the supreme magistrate."[196] Swete remarks: "The Seer still has in his mind the martyrs of his own age, the victims of Nero and Domitian."[197]

And which is literally "and those who" (*kai hoitiness*). Swete writes: "*Kai hoitiness* introduces a second class of persons, 'confessors,' and others who were faithful in the age of persecution, with special reference to those who in St. John's day were resisting the Caesar-worship."[198] These had not necessarily been **beheaded.** They had refused to worship the beast or receive **his mark** (cf. 13:15-18; 14:9-11; 16:2; 19:20).

These all **lived and reigned with Christ a thousand years.** This is what is generally known as the millennial reign. **Christ** (Gk., *christos*) means "the Anointed One." This reflects Ps. 2:2.

On the last clause of this verse John Wesley comments: "And they lived—their souls and bodies being reunited. *And reigned with Christ*—not on earth, but in heaven. The 'reigning on earth' mentioned in Rev. xi. 15 is quite different from this."[199] Wesley also holds the rather curious view that "two distinct thousand years are mentioned throughout this whole passage . . . the thousand wherein Satan is bound (verses 2, 3, 7); the thousand wherein the saints shall reign (verses 4-6)."[200] The first

[195]Simcox, *op. cit.*, p. 182 [196]*Ibid.*
[197]*Op. cit.*, p. 262. [198]*Ibid.*
[199]*Op. cit.*, p. 1039. [200]*Ibid.*

precedes the second chronologically. Wesley adds: "During the former, the promises concerning the flourishing state of the Church (Rev. x. 7) shall be fulfilled; during the latter, while the saints reign with Christ in heaven, men on earth will be careless and secure."[201]

The account goes on to say that **the rest of the dead lived not again until the thousand years were finished. This is the first resurrection** (5). The verse is commonly taken as meaning that the resurrection of the righteous will take place before the millennium, whereas the resurrection of the wicked dead will occur after it (cf. 7, 13). This view has been, and still is, strongly opposed by many commentators who are both devout and scholarly. Since the time of Augustine, who was influenced against millenarianism by Jerome, Roman Catholic theologians have generally held that the first resurrection means a resurrection from the death of sin to a life of righteousness. Simcox opposes this spiritualizing interpretation. He holds that, since a literal resurrection is admittedly indicated in 12, so here "any view but the literal one seems exposed to insuperable exegetical difficulties."[202]

Those who have part in the first resurrection are **blessed and holy** (6). Wesley translates this "happy and holy" (see comments on **blessed** in BBC, VI, 66-67). This text might suggest "The Happiness of the Holy": (1) **On such the second death hath no power;** (2) **They shall be priests of God and of Christ;** (3) They **shall reign with him a thousand years.**

For the meaning of **second death** see the comments on 14 (below). The combination **of God and of Christ** implies strongly the coequal deity of Father and Son. The idea that believers are **priests** has already occurred in the book (cf. "kings and priests," 1:6; 5:10). Here also the priests **shall reign.** Priesthood and royalty—what a privilege for those who follow Christ!

6. *The Battle of Gog and Magog* (20:7-10)

This event is usually distinguished from the Battle of Armageddon, which occurs before the millennium (19:19-21). There the leader of the enemy host is the Antichrist; here it is Satan. We read: **And when the thousand years are expired, Satan shall be loosed out of his prison** (cf. 1-3), **and shall go out to deceive**

[201]*Ibid.* [202]*Op. cit.*, p. 237.

the nations which are in the four quarters of the earth, Gog and Magog, to gather them together to battle (7-8).

The terms **Gog** and **Magog** come from Ezekiel 38—39.[203] The prophet is commanded to set his face "against Gog, the land of Magog," declaring for the Lord, "I am against thee, O Gog, the chief prince of Meshech and Tubal" (Ezek. 38:2-3). This suggests that **Gog** is the ruler and **Magog** his territory. Josephus identifies the Magog of Ezekiel with the Scythians,[204] who erupted into Asia in 630 B.C., shortly before Ezekiel wrote his prophecy. Before the time of Christ, however, **Gog and Magog** represented different nations. Charles says: "By the second century B.C. this invasion of Palestine by the two peoples Gog and Magog was clearly expected."[205] The rabbinical writings make frequent reference to **Gog and Magog** as nations that will march against the Messiah. With regard to the use of these names in the Book of Revelation, Charles writes: "The terms 'Gog and Magog' comprehend all the faithless upon the earth."[206]

The expression **Gog and Magog** has often been taken as referring to Russia today. It is true that the ancient people of Magog were probably located, at least at one time, southeast of the Black Sea. But the identification with modern Russia rests on no sound basis. Some have identified *rosh*, the Hebrew word for "chief" in Ezek. 38:3, with Russia, and Meshech with Moscow. But this is extremely fanciful exegesis, without etymological foundation.

One simple, but significant, fact is too often overlooked. In the verse before us **Gog and Magog** is in apposition with **the nations which are in the four quarters of the earth.** Both expressions refer to the enemy armies gathered from everywhere for battle. Therefore to say that Gog or Magog means Russia is to deny the plain statement of Scripture.

This innumerable host (cf. 8) **went up on the breadth of the earth** (9). The same Greek word (*ge*) means **earth** and "land." Here it is probably the land of Israel, covered with the invading armies. This is suggested by the further statement that they **compassed the camp of the saints about, and the beloved city**

[203]In Ezekiel we have the Messianic reign in c. 37, the destruction of Gog and Magog in cc. 38—39, and the New Jerusalem in cc. 40—48 (cf. Rev. 20:4-6; 20:7-10; 21:1—22:21).

[204]*Ant.* i. 6. 1. [205]*Op. cit.*, II, 188.

[206]*Ibid.*, p. 189.

(Jerusalem). But **fire came down from God out of heaven and devoured them** (cf. Ezek. 39:6). When the time comes, God can make short work of destroying the enemies of good.

The climax was that **the devil that deceived them** (cf. 8) **was cast into the lake of fire and brimstone, where the beast and the false prophet are** (cf. 19:20), **and shall be tormented day and night for ever and ever** (10). The last phrase is literally, "to the ages of the ages," which is "as strong an expression for absolute endlessness as Biblical language affords."[207]

17. *The Great White Throne* (20:11-15)

The **throne** of judgment was **white** (11), symbolizing the absolute purity of the Judge. Does **him that sat on it** refer to the Father or the Son? Paul declares that "we must all appear before the judgment seat of Christ" (II Cor. 5:10), and, "We must all stand before the judgment seat of God" (Rom. 14:10, best Gk. text). It was John himself who recorded Jesus' words: "For the Father judgeth no man, but hath committed all judgment unto the Son" (John 5:22). But he also recorded the saying, "I and my Father are one" (John 10:30). Here the Judge is primarily thought of as God (cf. 12).

From His **face the earth and the heaven fled away.** Swete comments: "The non-eternity of the external order is taught in the O.T. . . . and the N.T. corroborates this doctrine."[208] However, he adds: "It is only the external order of the world which is to be changed and not its substance or material."[209] Of **earth** and **heaven** (the sky) it is said: **and there was found no place for them** (cf. 12:8; Dan. 2:35).

Then John writes: **And I saw the dead, small and great, stand before God; and the books were opened** (cf. Dan. 7:10)—the records of men's lives made manifest—**and another book was opened, which is the book of life** (cf. 3:5; 13:8)—"the roll of living citizens of the New Jerusalem."[210] Judgment was based on **the things which were written in the books, according to their works** (cf. Matt. 16:27; Rom. 2:6).

What is usually referred to as "the general resurrection" is described in these words: **And the sea gave up the dead which were in it; and death and hell** (*Hades,* the grave) **delivered up the dead which were in them** (13). The Greeks and Romans, as

[207]Simcox, *op. cit.,* p. 185.
[208]*Op. cit.,* p. 271.
[209]*Ibid.*
[210]*Ibid.,* p. 272.

well as the Jews, placed great emphasis on the proper burial of the body. It was therefore considered a great calamity to be lost or buried at sea. Hades was the name for the place of departed spirits (see comments on 1:18; 6:8). Swete observes: "Death and Hades are an inseparable pair . . . representing the two aspects of Death, the physical fact and its spiritual consequence."[211]

There is no escaping the Judgment. We read that **every man** was judged according to his works. Heb. 9:27 asserts: "It is appointed unto men once to die, but after this the judgment." In this life there is nothing more certain than death. Every man must die sometime. But just as certain as death is the judgment.

At long last **death** (cf. I Cor. 15:26) **and hell** (Hades) **were cast into the lake of fire** (14). This statement shows clearly that it is wrong to translate the Greek word *hades* by **hell.** For "hell" is the term usually employed for eternal torment. But here **the lake of fire** is the place of torment (cf. 10), and *hades* is cast into it. **The lake of fire** is further defined as **the second death** (cf. 2:11; 20:6; 21:8). This is eternal death—not annihilation, but separation forever from God and all good.

The final statement in John's record of time is this: **And whosoever was not found written in the book of life was cast into the lake of fire** (15). The significance of this solemn warning can hardly be missed. The entrance visa to heaven is indicated clearly: having one's name written in the book of life. This means acceptance of Jesus Christ as Saviour and Lord. To keep one's name there requires being an overcomer (3:5). Ultimately this is the only thing that really matters.

G. The New Jerusalem, 21:1—22:21

1. *A New Heaven and a New Earth* (21:1-8)

A startling change of theme takes place at this point. Beginning with the opening of the seven seals (c. 6) we have seen almost nothing but turmoil and tribulation, judgment and death. Now a new, eternal order is ushered in; the old is gone forever.

a. Old things passed away (21:1-4). John **saw a new heaven and a new earth** (1). We have already been told that "the earth and the heaven fled away; and there was found no place for them" (20:11). This is reiterated here: **For the first heaven and**

[211]*Ibid.*, p. 273.

the first earth were passed away. Heaven here does not mean the eternal abode of God, but rather the astronomical space which man is now busy exploring with telescope and spacecraft.

The concept of **a new heaven and a new earth** is found in the Old Testament. Isaiah prophesied in the name of the Lord: "For, behold, I create new heavens and a new earth: and the former shall not be remembered, nor come into mind" (Isa. 65: 17). Peter also refers to this (II Pet. 3:13).

The word for **new** is not *neos,* which describes something "which has recently come into existence," but *kainos,* which emphasizes "quality, the new, as set over against that which has seen service . . . marred through age."[212] Everything was to be "brand-new."

It may seem odd that there should be added the statement, **And there was no more sea.** But to the ancients, without compass or other modern aids to transportation, the ocean held great terror. For many it was a place of death (cf. 20:13). Specifically for John it spelled separation from home and his fellow Christians in Asia Minor. In the new order there would be neither death nor separation.

The account continues: **And I John saw the holy city, new Jerusalem, coming down from God out of heaven, prepared as a bride adorned for her husband** (2). The **new Jerusalem** takes the place of the old "Babylon" (cc. 17—18) as the great metropolis. This city had already been mentioned as one "which cometh down out of heaven from my God" (3:12).

To the ancient people of the East there was nothing more beautiful than **a bride adorned for her husband.** Previously John had been told that the Lamb's wife had made herself ready (19:7). Now he is to see her in all her glory. The actual description of her ornamental attire begins at 19:8. One of the features of the Book of Revelation is the mention by anticipation of what is later to be described in detail.

John heard an important announcement: **Behold, the tabernacle of God is with men, and he will dwell with them, and they shall be his people, and God himself shall be with them, and be their God** (3). This is a definite echo of Lev. 26:11-12; Jer. 31:33; Ezek. 37:27; Zech. 8:8. There is a significant change, however. In the Septuagint of every one of these Old Testament passages there occurs the word *laos,* "people." But here in Revelation

[212]Trench, *Synonyms,* p. 220.

people is *laoi* (plural). No longer was it just Israel, the people of God, but the redeemed peoples of all nations.

Tabernacle is *skene.* **Dwell** is *skenosei*—lit., "will tabernacle." In the wilderness the Tabernacle was always to be pitched in the center of the camp of Israel. The Shekinah in the holy of holies of the Tabernacle was the symbol of God's presence in the midst of His people. Now Christ is "the true tabernacle" (Heb. 8:2), or the "greater and more perfect tabernacle" (Heb. 9:11). He is Emmanuel, "God with us" (Matt. 1:23). The picture that John sees here is the final completion of that redemption purchased by Christ at such awful cost. The ultimate purpose of it all was that redeemed men might live forever in the presence of their Creator.

He is "the God of all comfort" (II Cor. 1:3). So here it is said: **And God shall wipe away all tears from their eyes; and there shall be no more death, neither sorrow, nor crying, neither shall there be any more pain: for the former** (Gk., the first) **things are passed away** (4). It has often been pointed out that many things which have their beginning in the first three chapters of Genesis have their ending in the last two chapters of Revelation. A very profitable exercise is to make a list of all things which are to be **no more,** and then see how many of these are found in Genesis 1—3.

b. All things new (21:5-8). The declaration came from the One who sat upon the throne: **Behold, I make all things new** (5). Swete remarks: "The Speaker is now, probably for the first time in the Book, God Himself."[213] He had already said through Isaiah: "Behold, I will do a new thing" (Isa. 43:19). But that applied only to the nation, this to the whole universe.

John is commanded to **write: for these words are true and faithful.** This is repeated in 22:6. It is almost like the "Verily, verily" of John's Gospel.

It is done (6) is literally, "They have come to pass." The same expression occurs in 16:17, but there the verb is singular, "It has come to pass." Apparently here the subject is the "all things" made new. In both cases the emphasis is on fulfilled prophecy. The **Alpha and Omega** is repeated from 1:8 (see comments there). The meaning of this is spelled out as: **the beginning and the end** (*telos,* goal). God is the Originator and

[213]*Op. cit.,* p. 279.

Goal of all life. Paul expressed the same idea in Rom. 11:36—"For of him, and through him, and to him, are all things."

A gracious promise is offered: **I will give unto him that is athirst of the fountain of the water of life freely.** Swete observes: "The Source and End of all life is the bountiful Giver of life in its highest perfection."[214] When God gives—and He is always giving—He does it freely.

He that overcometh (7) reminds us of the promise made to the overcomer in each of the letters to the seven churches (2:7, 11, 17, 26; 3:5, 12, 21). Here the promise embraces all the others: **shall inherit all things.** The best Greek text has "these things"; that is, the things of the new creation that John has been envisioning. All the blessings of the new heaven and earth belong to the one who overcomes. Initial salvation is not enough. It is he that endureth to the end who will be saved and enjoy the eternal blessings that salvation brings (Matt. 10:22).

The verb **inherit** occurs only here in Revelation. Dalman insists that a better translation is "take possession of," and notes that "to possess one's self of the future age" was a popular Jewish expression.[215] But Paul's emphasis that the Christian, as son, is an "heir of God" (Rom. 8:17; Gal. 4:7) supports the usual translation here. For the voice continues: **And I will be his God, and he shall be my son.**

This is followed by a considerable list of those who will **have their part in the lake which burneth with fire and brimstone: which is the second death** (8; cf. 20:14). It should be noted that the list is headed by **the fearful.** The Greek word (*deiloi*) means "cowardly." Swete says they are "members of the Church who, like soldiers turning their backs upon the enemy, fail under trial . . . the cowards . . . in Christ's army."[216] The second item is **unbelieving,** which may also be rendered "unfaithful." These two are listed right along with the vilest of sinners—a solemn warning.

2. *The New Jerusalem* (21:9—22:5)

The description of the New Jerusalem extends through the rest of this chapter and on into the next. It is a picture painted with vivid colors, and it has excited the imagination of many.

[214] *Ibid.*, p. 280.

[215] *The Words of Jesus,* trans. D. M. Kay (Edinburgh: T. & T. Clark, 1909), pp. 125-26.

[216] *Op. cit.*, p. 281.

a. The glorious bride (21:9-14). **And there came unto me one of the seven angels which had the seven vials** (bowls) . . . **and talked with me, saying, Come hither, I will shew thee** (9). All this is repeated verbatim (in the Gk.) from 17:1. There it was the great harlot which the angel showed John; here it is the pure bride of the Lamb. The sameness of the introductory formula only serves to accent the terrific contrast between the two visions.

John was taken **in the spirit**—rather, "in spirit" (cf. 1:10; 4:2; 17:3), not in body—**to a great and high mountain** (10); that is, he was lifted in spirit so that he could see this wonderful vision. There he saw **that great city, the holy Jerusalem, descending out of heaven from God** (cf. 2). The fact that this Jerusalem is identified as **the bride, the Lamb's wife** (9), keeps us from interpreting it too literally. What follows is a symbolical representation of the beauty and glory of the bride of Christ reflected in the imagery of her home—the eternal city of God.

The bride is described as **having the glory of God** (11). This reminds us of Paul's words in Eph. 5:27, "That he might present it to himself a glorious church." That is what the bride of Christ will be at the marriage supper of the Lamb (cf. 19:7, 9). **The glory of God** is His Shekinah presence in the midst of His people. All real glory that we have is derived from Him.

Now the attempt is made in material terms to depict something of the spiritual beauties of the bride. John says that **her light was like unto a stone most precious, even like a jasper stone, clear as crystal.** The combination of the last two phrases has caused some difficulty to commentators because the modern **jasper** is not transparent. Simcox writes: "Though jasper is the same word in Hebrew, Greek, Latin and modern languages, it appears to have changed its appearance. The most precious jasper was a quite transparent dark green chalcedony. Our opaque jasper, pure red, pure green and black, were all used for engraving."[217] The most we can say is that this is represented as a very costly jasper that shone brightly.

The city had a high **wall** with **twelve gates** (12), guarded by **twelve angels, and names written thereon** (i.e., on the gates), **which are the names of the twelve tribes of Israel.** There were **three gates** (13) on each of the four sides of the city. Most of this is taken rather closely from Ezekiel's description of the new Jerusalem (Ezek. 48:31-34). With regard to the **twelve tribes**

[217]*Op. cit.*, p. 74 (on 4:3).

Swete says: "The Seer's object in referring to the Tribes is simply to assert the continuity of the Christian Church with the Church of the O.T."[218]

The wall of the city had twelve foundations, and in them the names of the twelve apostles of the Lamb (14). Jesus said to His apostles: "Ye also shall sit upon twelve thrones judging the twelve tribes of Israel" (Matt. 19:28). Paul wrote that the Church is "built upon the foundation of the apostles and prophets" (Eph. 2:20). The symbolism of **twelve tribes of the children of Israel** (12) and **twelve apostles of the Lamb** (14) is carried through to the New Jerusalem.

b. *The dimensions of the city* (21:15-21). The man who talked with John had **a golden reed** (rod) **to measure the city, and the gates thereof, and the wall thereof** (15). **The city** was **foursquare**; in fact, **the length and the breadth and the height of it are equal** (16). It was in the form of a perfect cube, as was the holy of holies in the ancient Tabernacle. This was perhaps to suggest the perfection and holiness of the Church. The measurement was **twelve thousand furlongs** (*stadia*). This is generally computed as 1,500 miles. Some think this may be intended to represent the circumference of the city. But the more natural way would be to take it as applying to each measurement.

The wall was **an hundred and forty and four cubits** by a man's **measure, that is, of the angel** (17; "by human measurements, which the angel was using," (NEB). A **cubit** was a half-arm length, about 18 inches. So this figure would be about 216 feet. Since the height of the city has already been given, it would seem that this may refer to the thickness of the wall. The ancient city of Babylon was said by the Greek historian Herodotus (i. 178) to have had walls 300 feet high and 75 feet thick.

And the building of the wall of it was of jasper (18). The Greek for **building** is a rare word, *endomesis,* found only here (in NT). Since the verb *endomeo* means "build into," it would seem that the sense here is that the wall had jasper built into it. Lenski translates it, "the inlaying of her wall," and comments: "The inlaying made the whole wall glitter like a bracelet set with diamonds."[219]

It is also stated that **the city was pure gold, like unto clear glass**—"i.e., gold that glittered and shone with brilliance like

[218]*Op. cit.*, p. 286.

[219]*Op. cit.*, p. 639.

highly polished glass."[220] John may have been thinking of the Temple's gold dome as he had seen it shining brightly in the sunlight. Josephus wrote: "Now the outward face of the temple in its front . . . was covered all over with plates of gold of great weight, and, at the first rising of the sun, reflected back a very fiery splendour."[221]

Next comes a description of **the foundations of the wall** (19). They were **garnished** (*cosmeo,* from which comes "cosmetics"; so, "adorned") **with all manner of precious stones.** There follows a listing of the twelve stones which distinguished the twelve foundations (19-20). Eight of these are among the twelve stones in the breastplate of the high priest who ministered in the Tabernacle (Exod. 28:17-20).

R. H. Charles points out the fact that these twelve stones in Revelation are exactly the ones which on Egyptian and Arabian monuments are connected with the twelve signs of the zodiac—but in reverse order.[222] He suggests that John regards "the Holy City which he describes as having nothing to do with the ethnic speculations of his own and past ages regarding the city of the gods."[223] That is, the New Jerusalem is the true City of God.

Another striking feature of the city was that its **twelve gates were twelve pearls; every several gate was of one pearl** (21). Thus does the writer seek to describe in human language the magnificent beauty of the glorified Church. Also **the street** (lit., broad way) **of the city was pure gold, as it were transparent glass.** John is straining the powers of finite language to describe the indescribable. But he does not tarry long with this thought; he moves on to the wonder of God's continual presence in the city. To glory long in the idea of walking on streets of gold in the next life is to miss the real glory of living in the presence of God. Such an attitude shows a materialistic, not a spiritual, mind.

c. *The light of the city* (21:22-27). The New Jerusalem has **no temple** (22). It needs none, **for the Lord God Almighty and the Lamb are the temple of it.** The Temple was provided as a meeting place of God with man. But in the New Jerusalem, God is always present to those who are there, and so no temple is needed. His eternal presence makes the whole city a sanctuary.

Furthermore, **the city had no need of the sun, neither of the moon, to shine in it: for the glory of God did lighten it, and the**

[220]*Ibid.*

[221]*War* v. 5-6.

[222]*Op. cit.,* II, 167.

[223]*Ibid.,* p. 168.

Lamb is the light thereof (23). Except for the last clause, this verse is a close reflection of Isa. 60:19, "The sun shall be no more thy light by day; neither for brightness shall the moon give light unto thee: but the Lord shall be unto thee an everlasting light, and thy God thy glory." In the New Testament we have not only the statement, "God is light" (I John 1:5), but also Jesus' own words, "I am the light of the world" (John 8:12).

This bright light radiates all around. We read: **And the nations**[224] **. . . shall walk in the light of it** (24). This has been partially fulfilled throughout the Christian era, as the Church has been a light to the nations. Unfortunately in the history of the Church on earth there have been some dark shadows. Not so in the glorified Church, the New Jerusalem. There all is light. **And the kings of the earth do bring their glory and honour into it.** Verse 26 is practically a repetition of 24*b*. This prediction has had a partial fulfillment during the Church age.

The gates of this city **shall not be shut at all by day** (25; cf. Isa. 60:11). Since **there shall be no night there,** this means that the gates of the New Jerusalem are always open. So the doors to the Kingdom are wide open today to those who will enter.

But while the gates are always open, **there shall in no wise enter into it any thing that defileth, neither whatsoever worketh abomination, or maketh a lie: but they which are written in the Lamb's book of life** (27). In the Septuagint the Greek words for **abomination** and **lie** are both used for idols. There will be no idolatry, material or immaterial, in heaven. God alone will be loved and worshiped. Only those whose names are in the book of life can enter the New Jerusalem.

d. The river of life (22:1-5). John was shown **a**[225] **river of water of life, clear as crystal, proceeding out of the throne of God and of the Lamb** (1). The picture is drawn from Ezek. 47: 1-12. There waters flowed out from the Temple. Here they come from the throne.

On either side of the river, was there the tree of life (2). In Ezekiel's vision, "at the bank of the river were very many trees on the one side and on the other" (Ezek. 47:7). But here it is **the tree of life.** This phrase carries us back to the Garden of Eden (Gen. 2:9). There man sinned and was driven out of para-

[224]**Of them which are saved** is not in the best Greek text.

[225]**Pure** is not in the best Greek text.

dise, so that he no longer had access to the tree of life (Gen. 3:24). But in the New Jerusalem the redeemed find it growing in abundance.

This tree bore **twelve manner of fruits, and yielded her fruit every month: and the leaves of the tree were for the healing of the nations.** Ezekiel wrote of the trees on the river's bank that they would "bring forth new fruit according to his months . . . and the leaf thereof for medicine" (Ezek. 47:12).

In the New Jerusalem there will **be no more curse** (3). The Greek word is not the usual *anathema,* found half a dozen times in the New Testament, but *katathema,* which occurs only here. Behm says that it is "probably another and sharper form of *anathema.*"[226] It means an "accursed thing." Glasson says: "This perhaps looks back to Gen. 3:17-18. After the Fall . . . a curse was imposed; thorns and thistles began to grow. . . . Now the curse is taken away. Thus the last chapters of the Bible balance the first, and Paradise Lost gives place to Paradise Regained."[227]

No evil thing or person can enter the New Jerusalem, because **the throne of God and of the Lamb** is there. **And his servants shall serve** (or worship) **him** suggests that the next life will not be a time of idleness (cf. 7:15).

Furthermore, **they shall see his face** in perfect fellowship; **and his name shall be in their foreheads** (4). This is a sign of complete consecration to God and absolute ownership by Him.

Again (cf. 21:25) we are told that there will **be no night there** (5). Consequently **they need no candle,** not even **light of the sun** (cf. 21:23); **for the Lord God giveth them light**—all the light we have comes from Him—**and they shall reign for ever and ever.** This is not just for the thousand years of the millennial Kingdom (20:5). On entering c. 21 we moved from time into eternity. Here everything lasts forever.

3. *Epilogue* (22:6-21)

This closing section gives us the last words of the angel (6-11), of Jesus (12-16), of the Spirit and the bride (17), and of John (18-19); the last promise and prayer (20); and the last benediction (21).

[226]Kittel, *op. cit.*, I, 355.

[227]*The Revelation of John* ("The Cambridge Bible Commentary"; Cambridge: University Press, 1965), p. 121.

a. The last words of the angel (22:6-11). Before leaving, the angel gave his endorsement of what he had been showing and telling John: **These sayings are faithful and true** (6). This repeats 21:5. **These sayings** probably applies to the whole Book of Revelation. They are **faithful and true** because **the Lord God of the holy prophets sent his angel to shew unto his servants the things which must shortly be done.** The last part of this statement is taken verbatim in the Greek from 1:1. The Epilogue looks back to the Prologue.

Behold, I come quickly (7), is Christ's word through the angel. A special blessing is pronounced on the one who **keepeth the sayings of the prophecy of this book** (cf. 1:3). Swete notes that **this book** "points to the all but completed roll on the Seer's knee; throughout the Apocalypse he has represented himself as writing his impressions at the time (cf. x. 4) . . . and his task is now nearly ended."[228]

John not only **saw these things,** but **heard them** (8). So overcome was he with the vision of the New Jerusalem that again he fell at the feet of the angel **to worship** him, perhaps thinking he must be Christ (cf. 19:10). But, as before, he was admonished not to do this (9).

Then the angel commanded him: **Seal not** (do not conceal or withhold) **the sayings of the prophecy of this book: for the time is at hand** (10). Exactly the opposite order was given to Daniel. He was told: "Wherefore shut thou up the vision; for it shall be for many days" (Dan. 8:26). In Daniel's day the fulfillment was a long way off. But here the case is different: **for the time is at hand.** Honest exegesis would seem to demand an interpretation that permits an application to the period of the Early Church. That is why this commentary has taken the position that the predictions in Revelation 4—20 had a *partial* fulfillment in the time of the Roman Empire, that they have had a *continuing* fulfillment throughout the Church age, and that they will have a *complete* fulfillment in the future. This is the only view which seems to do justice to all the factors involved.

The period of probation is over. So the voice says: **He that is unjust** (lit., the one doing wrong), **let him be unjust still: and he which is filthy, let him be filthy still: and he that is righteous, let him be righteous still: and he that is holy, let him be holy still** (11). It will be noticed that these clauses are balanced, the **righ-**

[228]*Op. cit.*, p. 303.

teous against the **unjust** and the **holy** against the **filthy.** Also each of the four verbs beginning with **let him** is in the aorist imperative. This indicates a fixity of state, rather than a continuing process. Swete gives a good interpretation of this verse. He says: "It is not only true that the troubles of the last days will tend to fix the character of each individual according to the habits which he has already formed, but there will come a time when change will be impossible—when no further opportunity will be given for repentance on the one hand or for apostasy on the other."[229]

b. The last words of Jesus (22:12-16). **And, behold, I come quickly** (12; cf. 7). To this promise of His soon coming, Christ adds: **And my reward** (*misthos,* wages) **is with me, to give** (recompense) **every man according as his work shall be.** Every man will receive a just recompense for what he has done.

Verse 13 is a combination of the words found in 21:6 and 1:17; also 2:8. The same honor that is accorded God is claimed by Christ (see the comments on 1:17).

Verses 14 and 15 are not placed within quotation marks, as a part of the words of Jesus, in RSV, NEB, and NASB. But they are included by Phillips. For convenience we have placed them this way in our outline. They declare a blessing on those who **do his commandments** (14)—the best Greek text says, "who wash their robes"—for thereby they shall **have right to the tree of life, and may enter in through the gates into the city.**

Kept outside are **dogs** (15). This is a term used for unclean persons both in the Old Testament (Ps. 22:16) and the New (Matt. 7:6; Mark 7:27). Swete says that here **dogs** means "those who had been defiled by long contact with the foul vices which honeycombed pagan society."[230] The twentieth century has seen an alarming recurrence of the kind of pagan living that characterized the first century, so that these words take on new significance.

Along with **sorcerers, and whoremongers** (Gk., fornicators), **and murderers, and idolaters** is **whosoever loveth and maketh a lie**—better, "practices lying" (NASB). This shows the seriousness of deceit in the eyes of God.

Obviously it is Christ speaking now, as He says: **I Jesus have sent mine angel to testify unto you these things in the churches** (16). Throughout the book, since c. 3, it is angels who have done

[229]*Ibid.,* p. 305.

[230]*Ibid.,* p. 308.

practically all the talking. Now Jesus puts His personal endorsement on what they have said. It was He who sent them with the messages and visions for **the churches**—first of all, the seven churches of Asia, and then all the churches everywhere.

Jesus further declares: **I am the root** (cf. 5:5) **and the offspring of David**—both the Root and the Shoot of David's family—**and the bright and morning star.** This is a beautiful figure, and a familiar sight to those who rise before dawn and gaze at this striking harbinger of a new day. Christ is the Star of the Dawn, what James Stewart once called in a convocation at Edinburgh "the Star of the Eschaton." To every Christian, Christ is the Promise of a new day. Swete writes: "The Morning Star of the Church shines to-day as brightly as in the age of St. John; He does not fall or set."[231]

c. The last words of the Spirit and bride (22:17). **And the Spirit and the bride say, Come.** Most commentators take this as the prophetic Spirit in the Church responding to Christ's promise (12) with the cry, **Come.** All who hear are to join in that call for His coming. Fausset writes: " 'Come' is the prayer of the Spirit in the Church and in believers, in reply to Christ's 'I come quickly,' crying, Even so, 'Come' (vv. 7, 12); v. 20 confirms this."[232] In view of the reference in the previous verse to the "morning star," probably this interpretation should be adopted.

This requires an abrupt transition in the middle of the verse. For the invitation, **And let him that is athirst come,** is clearly an evangelistic invitation to come to Christ. This is even more evident in the next clause: **And whosoever will, let him take the water of life freely.** Only by so doing can one be ready for the coming of Christ.

d. The last words of John (22:18-19). Swete says of these two verses: "The Speaker is still surely Jesus, and not, as many commentators have supposed, St. John."[233] But Plummer writes: "Here is the solemn appendix or seal of the veracity of the book, somewhat similar to the prefatory words in ch. i. 1-3. This is the fulfilment of the duty laid on St. John in ch. i. 1, not an announcement of our Lord himself (cf. the wording of ch. i. 3)."[234]

[231]*Ibid.*, p. 310.

[232]"Revelation," *A Commentary . . . on the Old and New Testaments,* by Robert Jamieson, A. R. Fausset, David Brown (Grand Rapids: Wm. B. Eerdmans Publishing Co., 1948 [reprint]), VI, 730.

[233]*Op. cit.*, p. 311.

[234]*Op. cit.*, p. 548.

It would seem that the latter view is preferable, as indicated by the nonuse of quotation marks here in most recent translations.

At any rate a solemn warning is sounded here against anyone tampering with the teaching of this book. No one is to add to it or take away from it, on pain of the most serious penalties. These words, of course, apply to the original writing as divinely inspired. The injunction does not limit the work of patient Bible scholarship that compares existing manuscripts word by word in order to arrive at the most accurate text possible. It does forbid the attitude that would scorn the authority of God's Word and **add** to or **take away from** its teachings.

e. The last promise and prayer (22:20). **He which testifieth these things** is Jesus (cf. 16). He says: **Surely I come quickly**—the last promise of the Bible. The last prayer is, **Amen.**[235] **Come, Lord Jesus.** In days like these, this should increasingly be our prayer.

f. The last benediction (22:21). It is brief but adequate: **The grace of our Lord Jesus Christ be with you all.**[236] This is sufficient for every trusting soul.

[235]Even so is not in the best Greek text.

[236]Some ancient MSS. have "with all the saints" (cf. RSV).

Bibliography

I. COMMENTARIES

ALFORD, HENRY. *The Greek Testament.* Revised by E. F. HARRISON. Chicago: Moody Press, 1958.

BARCLAY, WILLIAM. *The Revelation of John.* 2nd ed. "The Daily Study Bible." Philadelphia: Westminster Press, 1960.

BARNES, ALBERT. *Notes on the New Testament: Revelation.* Edited by ROBERT FREW. Grand Rapids: Baker Book House, 1949 (reprint).

BEASLEY-MURRAY, G. R. "The Revelation." *The New Bible Commentary.* Edited by F. DAVIDSON. Second edition. London: Inter-Varsity Fellowship, 1954.

BENGEL, JOHN ALBERT. *Gnomon of the New Testament.* Translated by W. FLETCHER. Edinburgh: T. & T. Clark, 1860. Vol. V.

BLANEY, HARVEY J. S. "Revelation." *The Wesleyan Bible Commentary.* Vol. VI. Grand Rapids: Wm. B. Eerdmans Publishing Co., 1966.

BOWMAN, JOHN WICK. *The Drama of the Book of Revelation.* Philadelphia: Westminster Press, 1955.

CARPENTER, W. BOYD. "The Revelation of St. John." *Commentary on the Whole Bible.* Edited by CHARLES J. ELLICOTT. Grand Rapids: Zondervan Publishing House, n.d.

CHARLES, R. H. *A Critical and Exegetical Commentary on the Revelation of St. John.* "International Critical Commentary." Edinburgh: T. & T. Clark, 1920. 2 vols.

CLARKE, ADAM. *The New Testament of Our Lord and Saviour Jesus Christ.* New York: Abingdon-Cokesbury Press, n.d.

DUESTERDIECK, FRIEDRICH. *A Critical and Exegetical Handbook to the Revelation of John.* Translated by H. E. JACOBS. "Meyer's Commentary on the New Testament." New York: Funk & Wagnalls, 1886.

ERDMAN, CHARLES R. *The Revelation of John.* Philadelphia: Westminster Press, 1936.

FAUSSET, A. R. "Revelation." *A Commentary . . . on the Old and New Testaments.* By ROBERT JAMIESON, A. R. FAUSSET, DAVID BROWN, Vol. VI. Grand Rapids: Wm. B. Eerdmans Publishing Co., 1948 (reprint).

GLASSON, T. F. *The Revelation of John.* "The Cambridge Bible Commentary." Cambridge: University Press, 1965.

KEPLER, THOMAS. *The Book of Revelation.* New York: Oxford University Press, 1957.

KIDDLE, MARTIN. *The Revelation of St. John.* "Moffatt New Testament Commentary." New York: Harper & Brothers, n.d.

KUYPER, ABRAHAM. *The Revelation of St. John.* Translated from the Dutch by J. H. DEVRIES. Grand Rapids: Wm. B. Eerdmans Publishing Co., 1964 (reprint).

LANGE, JOHN PETER. "Revelation." *Commentary on the Holy Scriptures.* Edited by J. P. LANGE. Grand Rapids: Zondervan Publishing House, n.d.

LAYMON, CHARLES M. *The Book of Revelation.* New York: Abingdon Press, 1960.

LENSKI, R. C. H. *The Interpretation of St. John's Revelation.* Columbus, Ohio: Wartburg Press, 1943.

LOVE, JULIAN PRICE. "The Revelation to John." *The Layman's Bible Commentary.* Edited by BALMER H. KELLY, Vol. XXV. Richmond, Va.: John Knox Press, 1960.

McDOWELL, EDWARD A. *The Meaning and Message of the Book of Revelation.* Nashville: Broadman Press, 1951.

MOFFATT, JAMES. "The Revelation of St. John the Divine." *Expositor's Greek Testament.* Vol. V. Grand Rapids: Wm. B. Eerdmans Publishing Co., n.d.

NEWELL, WILLIAM R. *The Book of Revelation.* Chicago: Grace Publications, 1935.

NILES, D. T. *As Seeing the Invisible.* New York: Harper & Brothers, 1961.

PLUMMER, A. "Revelation" (Exposition). *The Pulpit Commentary.* Edited by H. D. M. SPENCE and JOSEPH S. EXELL. Grand Rapids: Wm. B. Eerdmans Publishing Co., 1950 (reprint). Vol. XXII.

RICHARDSON, DONALD W. *The Revelation of Jesus Christ.* Richmond, Va.: John Knox Press, 1964.

RIST, MARTIN. "The Revelation" (Exegesis). *The Interpreter's Bible.* Edited by GEORGE A. BUTTRICK, *et al.,* Vol. XII. New York: Abingdon Press, 1957.

SEISS, J. A. *The Apocalypse: A series of special lectures on the Revelation of Jesus Christ.* Tenth edition. New York: Charles C. Cook, 1909 (copyrighted 1865).

SIMCOX, W. H. *The Revelation.* Revised by G. A. SIMCOX. "Cambridge Greek Testament." Cambridge: University Press, 1893.

SMITH, J. B. *A Revelation of Jesus Christ.* Scottdale, Pa.: Herald Press, 1961.

STRAUSS, LEHMAN. *The Book of Revelation.* Neptune, N.J.: Loizeaux Brothers, 1964.

SWETE, HENRY B. *The Apocalypse of St. John.* Grand Rapids: Wm. B. Eerdmans Publishing Co., 1951 (reprint).

WESLEY, JOHN. *Explanatory Notes upon the New Testament.* London: Epworth Press, 1941 (reprint).

II. LETTERS TO SEVEN CHURCHES

BARCLAY, WILLIAM. *Letters to the Seven Churches.* London: SCM Press, 1957.

MARTIN, HUGH. *The Seven Letters.* Philadelphia: Westminster Press, 1956.

MORGAN, G. CAMPBELL. *The Letters of Our Lord.* London: Pickering & Inglis, n.d.

PLUMPTRE, E. H. *A Popular Exposition of the Epistles to the Seven Churches of Asia.* London: Hodder and Stoughton, 1891.

RAMSAY, W. M. *The Letters to the Seven Churches of Asia.* New York: A. C. Armstrong & Son, 1904.

SEISS, JOSEPH A. *Letters to the Seven Churches.* Grand Rapids: Baker Book House, 1956 (reprint).

TRENCH, R. C. *Commentary on the Epistles to the Seven Churches.* London: Macmillan Co., 1883.

III. OTHER BOOKS

ABBOTT-SMITH, G. *A Manual Greek Lexicon of the New Testament.* 2nd ed. Edinburgh: T. & T. Clark, 1923.

ARNDT, W. F., and GINGRICH, F. W. *A Greek-English Lexicon of the New Testament.* Chicago: University of Chicago Press, 1957.

DALMAN, GUSTAF. *The Words of Jesus.* Translated by D. M. KAY. Edinburgh: T. & T. Clark, 1909.

DEISSMANN, ADOLF. *Bible Studies.* Translated by ALEXANDER GRIEVE. Edinburgh: T. & T. Clark, 1901.

———. *Light from the Ancient East.* Translated by L. R. M. STRACHAN. Revised edition. New York: George H. Doran, 1927.

EUSEBIUS, PAMPHILUS. *Ecclesiastical History.* Translated by C. F. CRUSE. Grand Rapids: Baker Book House, 1955 (reprint).

GUTHRIE, DONALD. *New Testament Introduction: Hebrews to Revelation.* Chicago: Inter-Varsity Press, 1962.

KITTEL, GERHARD (ed.) *Theological Dictionary of the New Testament.* Vols. I-II. Grand Rapids: Wm. B. Eerdmans Publishing Co., 1964.

LIDDELL, H. G., and SCOTT, R. *A Greek-English Lexicon.* New edition revised by H. S. JONES. Oxford: Clarendon Press, 1940.

RICHARDSON, ALAN. *The Gospel According to St. John.* "Torch Bible Commentaries." London: SCM Press, 1959.

ROBERTSON, A. T. *Word Pictures in the New Testament.* Vol. VI. New York: Harper & Brothers, 1933.

RUSSELL, E. D. S. *The Method and Message of Jewish Apocalyptic: 200 B.C.—A.D. 100.* London: SCM Press, 1964.

STAUFFER, ETHELBERT. *New Testament Theology.* Translated by JOHN MARSH. London: SCM Press, 1955.

TORRANCE, THOMAS F. *The Apocalypse Today.* Grand Rapids: Wm. B. Eerdmans Publishing Co., 1959.

TRENCH, R. C. *Synonyms of the New Testament.* Grand Rapids: Wm. B. Eerdmans Publishing Co., 1947 (reprint).

VINCENT, MARVIN R. *Word Studies in the New Testament.* Grand Rapids: Wm. B. Eerdmans Publishing Co., 1946 (reprint).

WESTCOTT, B. F. *The Gospel According to St. John.* Grand Rapids: Wm. B. Eerdmans Publishing Co., 1950 (reprint).

WIKENHAUSER, ALFRED. *New Testament Introduction.* Translated by J. CUNNINGHAM. New York: Herder & Herder, 1958.

ZAHN, THEODOR. *Introduction to the New Testament.* Translated from the 3rd German edition. Grand Rapids: Kregel Publications, 1953 (reprint). 3 vols.

THE MEDITERRANEAN WORLD in the Time of Paul
SCALE OF MILES
EUROPE
Black Sea
Adriatic Sea
ITALY
Rome
Three Taverns
Appii Forum
Puteoli
Rhegium
SICILY
Syracuse
MELITA
MACEDONIA
Philippi
Amphipolis
Neapolis
Thessalonica
Berea
Apollonia
SAMOTHRACIA
Nicopolis
ACHAIA
Corinth
Cenchreae
Athens
Aegean Sea
Troas
Assos
Mitylene
CHIOS
SAMOS
PATMOS
Adramyttium
Pergamum
Thyatira
Sardis
Smyrna
Ephesus
Miletus
Philadelphia
Laodicea
Hierapolis
Colosse
ASIA
BITHYNIA
GALATIA
PONTUS
CAPPADOCIA
ARMENIA
PISIDIA
Antioch
Iconium
Lystra
Derbe
CILICIA
Tarsus
PAMPHYLIA
Attalia
Perga
LYCIA
Cnidus
Rhodes
RHODES
Patara
Myra
Seleucia
Antioch
SYRIA
Salamis
CYPRUS
Paphos
Phenice
CRETE
C. Salmone
CLAUDA
Lasea
Fair Havens
MEDITERRANEAN SEA
Sidon
Damascus
Tyre
Ptolemais
Caesarea
Samaria
Joppa
Jericho
Jerusalem
Gaza
Cyrene
LIBYA
Alexandria

Map 2

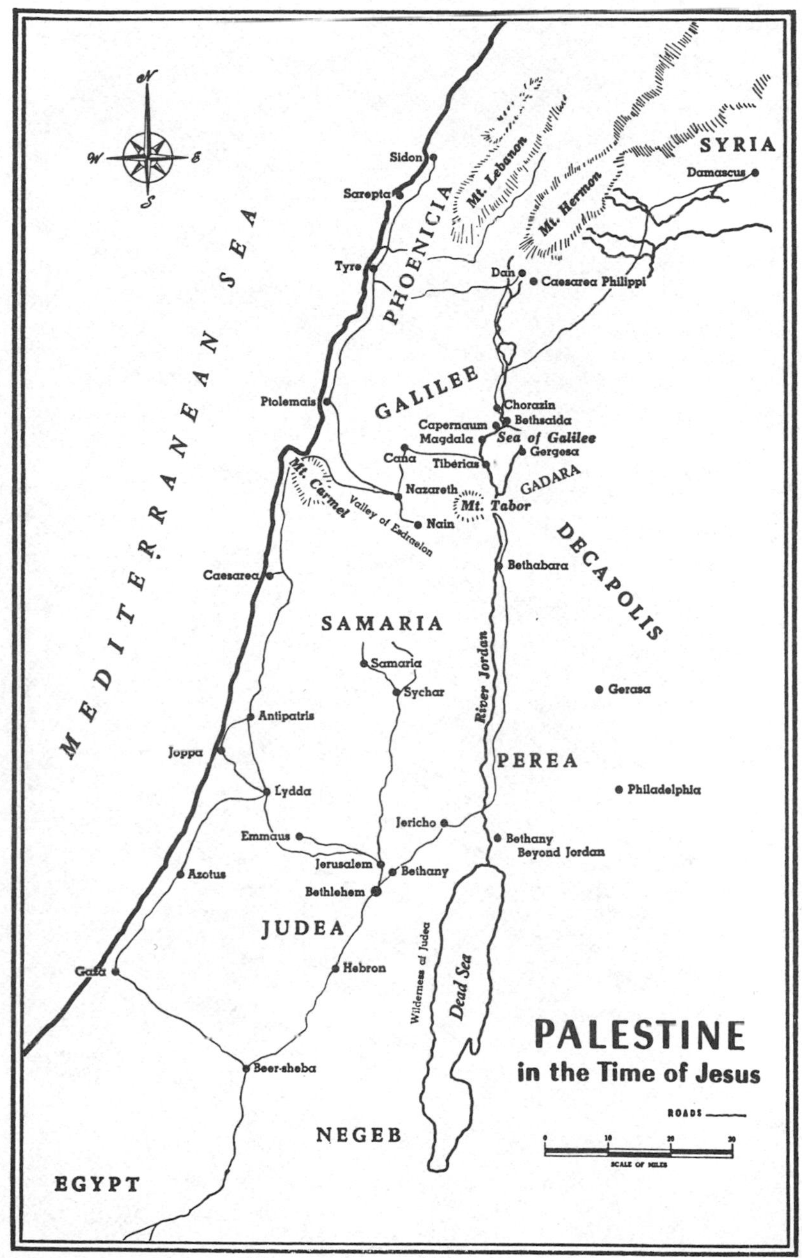
MEDITERRANEAN SEA
SYRIA
Damascus
Sidon
Sarepta
Mt. Lebanon
Mt. Hermon
PHOENICIA
Tyre
Dan
Caesarea Philippi
GALILEE
Ptolemais
Chorazin
Bethsaida
Capernaum
Magdala
Sea of Galilee
Gergesa
Cana
Tiberias
GADARA
Mt. Carmel
Nazareth
Mt. Tabor
Valley of Esdraelon
Nain
DECAPOLIS
Bethabara
Caesarea
SAMARIA
Samaria
Sychar
River Jordan
Gerasa
Antipatris
Joppa
PEREA
Lydda
Philadelphia
Jericho
Emmaus
Bethany
Beyond Jordan
Jerusalem
Bethany
Azotus
Bethlehem
JUDEA
Wilderness of Judea
Gaza
Hebron
Dead Sea
PALESTINE
in the Time of Jesus
ROADS
0
10
20
30
SCALE OF MILES
Beer-sheba
NEGEB
EGYPT

Chart A

PLAN OF THE TABERNACLE IN THE WILDERNESS

30 Cubits Long, 10 Cubits Wide, 10 Cubits High (45′ x 15′ x 15′)

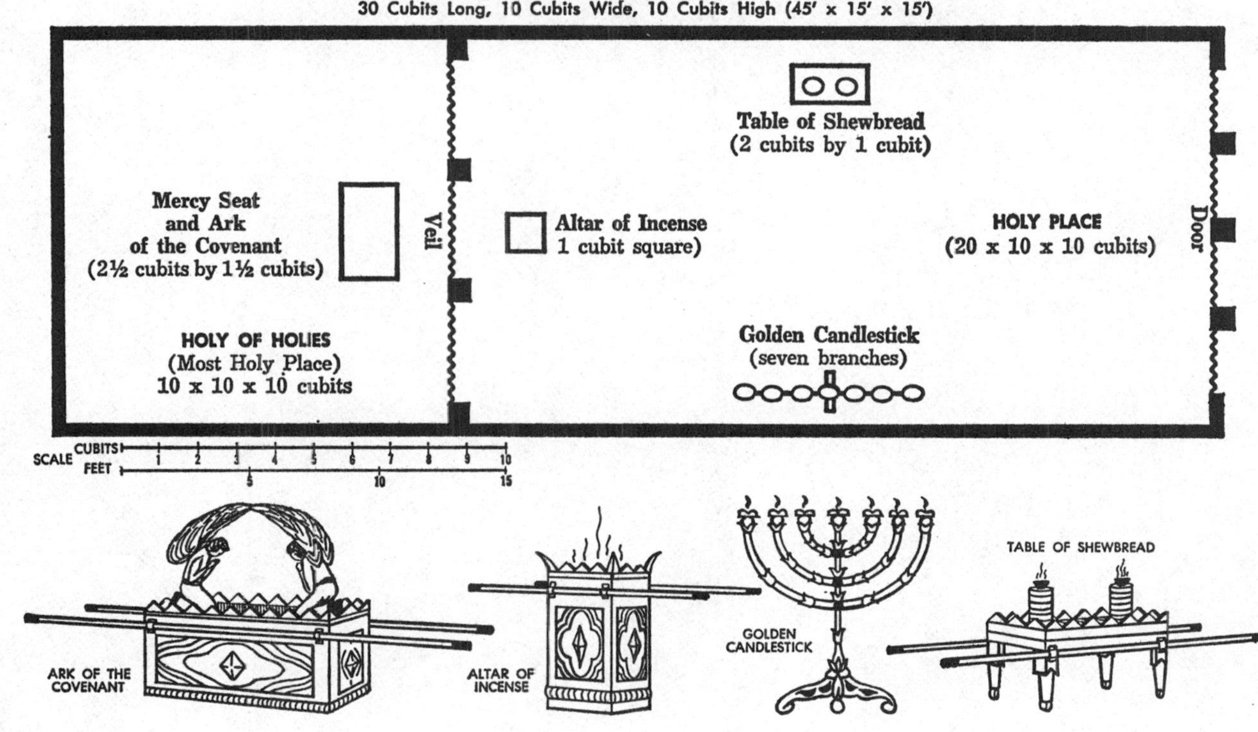